W9-AUF-307

ORCHESTRAL MUSIC

A Handbook

Third Edition

David Daniels

The Scarecrow Press, Inc.
Lanham, Md., & London
1996

SCARECROW PRESS, INC.

Published in the United States of America
by Scarecrow Press, Inc.
4720 Boston Way
Lanham, Maryland 20706

4 Pleydell Gardens, Folkestone
Kent CT20 2DN, England

Copyright © 1996 by David Daniels

First edition published by The Scarecrow Press, Inc., Metuchen, N.J.,
and London, 1972. ISBN 0–8108–0537–5.
Second edition published by The Scarecrow Press, Inc., Metuchen, N.J.,
and London, 1982. ISBN 0–8108–1484–6.

British Cataloguing-in-Publication Information Available

Library of Congress Cataloging-in-Publication Data

Daniels, David, 1933–
    Orchestral music : a handbook / David Daniels. —3rd ed.
        p.   cm.
    Includes bibliographical references and index.
    ISBN 0–8108–3228–3 (cloth : alk. paper)
    1. Orchestral music—Bibliography.   I. Title.
    ML128.O5D3   1996
    016.7842—dc20   96–34819

ISBN 0–8108–3228–3 (cloth : alk.paper)

⊖™ The paper used in this publication meets the minimum requirements of
American National Standard for Information Sciences—Permanence of
Paper for Printed Library Materials, ANSI Z39.48–1984.
Manufactured in the United States of America.

To certain members of a younger generation:

Ashley and Alex

Emma and Daniel

and any others who may be joining them

CONTENTS

PREFACE

The people who are reading this foreword are probably the same people who tolerated the first edition of *Orchestral Music*, made use of the second, and patiently awaited the long-delayed arrival of the third. Here it is—greatly improved but hugely imperfect, the product of your interest as much as my industry.

Ever since this book made its first tentative appearance in the orchestra world, I have been getting suggestions and advice and corrections. I have been buttonholed at conferences, parties and rehearsals; I have received phone calls and letters and faxes. And when I let it be known that a third edition was actually in the making, this trickle enlarged into a torrent. Conductors, orchestra managers, and librarians have all contributed, some with a few bits and pieces, others with pages and pages of information. I can't remember the names of all these helpful individuals, but I can assure them that I pursued doggedly every jot and tittle that I received, and incorporated most of them in one way or another.

New features. The third edition of *Orchestral Music* is the same old familiar book, with the following additions:

- An increase of about 1100 entries
- An increase of over 200 additional composers
- Durations of individual movements in many cases (but not all)
- Title index
- Significant anniversaries of composers' births and deaths
- List of useful resources

I have made many corrections, but of course all the new entries have flung the doors wide for the introduction of new errors. As before, I will be grateful to hear about them, if sorry to learn of their existence.

Selection of entries. I have been faithful to my original principle: no composition is included unless I have personally examined the score and verified the information that I print. This has led to some oddities: on the one hand the inclusion of fairly obscure works that caught my eye and piqued my interest; and on the other hand the omission of significant compositions that I was simply unable to track down. Many composers are doubtless not represented by their most important works, and to them, as well as to all users of this book, I apologize.

Nevertheless, as I observed once before, no canonization that I perform or withhold is going to make any difference in the long run. The repertoire grows in its own way, and there are plenty of composers, from John Adams to Ellen Taaffe Zwilich, who weren't even mentioned in earlier editions but whose omission from the present volume would be unthinkable.

Titles. The orientation of this book has always been toward American users. However, over the years I have been pleased and sobered to learn that it is in use more or less around the world. Therefore in this edition I have leaned much more heavily toward using the original language for distinctive titles (e.g. *Weihnachtsoratorium* rather than *Christmas Oratorio*). Wherever this change might trip up the English-language user, I have inserted cross-references from the English title. Also, the Title Index, new to the third edition, ought to help stymied Anglophones.

Generic titles, as before, are given in a format commonly used in libraries (e.g. Concerto, piano, no.3, op.37, C minor).

Editions of music. In the quarter-century since this book first appeared, the music world has become much more sophisticated about what constitutes a good edition. In the previous version of *Orchestral Music*, I waxed paternalistic, directing my readers to use this or that edition of Bruckner or of Mozart. Now I have become less dogmatic and more inclusive. I have attempted to provide the necessary information on alternative editions so that the conductor can make an informed decision.

Durations. Durations will of course vary from one performance to the next, even under the same conductor. The durations in this book should be considered reasonable approximations only. With the advent of CDs with their prominent display of inhumanly precise timings (to the nearest second!), it is much easier than it used to be to find reliable durations. This development has also made it possible for me to include in many cases the timings of up to ten individual movements in a little box under the overall duration. Like everything else in this book, that is information I want at my own fingertips for the planning of rehearsals, and so I assume it will be useful to others as well.

Instrumentation formula. The universal formula for woodwinds, brass, percussion and strings is used here. The symbols that indicate the presence of auxiliary instruments (*, +, and =) are explained in the list of abbreviations.

My main consideration is to show how many players of each instrument are required. Often there is a note in my listings to explain that, for example, two of the three flutists must play piccolo. I did not start that practice until my second edition, however, and there are probably still some holdovers from the first edition in which that information is lacking.

Percussion. In all cases I attempt to show the minimum number of players needed to cover all the notes, even if it means some shifting among the parts. (Some percussion sections may be able to get by with fewer players than I indicate.) My abbreviation *tmp+3*, for instance, means that one timpanist plus three other players are needed; in order for this number to work, the timpanist may well have to cover some parts other than timpani for a while. *2tmp* means two timpanists, and not two drums.

When bass drum and cymbals occur together, I have counted two players, although in much of the nineteenth century these would have been covered by one player with cymbal attached to the bass drum.

Sample entry with interpretation.

Concerto, violin, op.46   19'
  +3 *3 =3 3—basset horn—4 2 2 0—tmp+1—hp (opt)—str   9' 6' 4'
  Boosey   Kalmus

This hypothetical violin concerto calls for 3 flutes (including alto flute), 3 oboes (including English horn), 3 clarinets (including E-flat clarinet and bass clarinet), 3 bassoons, basset horn, 4 horns, 2 trumpets, 2 trombones, no tuba, timpanist plus 1 additional percussionist, and the usual string sections. A harp is optional. It is 19 minutes long, the movements being 9', 6' and 4' respectively. Score and parts are available from Boosey & Hawkes and from Kalmus.

Historical practices. In using this book it helps to have some knowledge of certain orchestral practices of earlier periods.

FLUTES AND RECORDERS. When a baroque composer used the term *flauto* or *flauto dolce*, he meant recorder. If he wanted a transverse flute, he took pains to call it *traversa* or *flauto traverso* or some such term.

WOODWIND DOUBLING. As late as the time of Mozart, players were likely to alternate on several instruments. This explains why an eighteenth-century work otherwise for 2 oboes, 2 horns and strings, suddenly uses 2 flutes and strings for a middle movement. The oboists switched to flute for that movement. Nowadays, of course, that is largely impractical.

BASSOONS. In eighteenth-century practice, a bassoon played the bass line of an orchestral work, whether specified in the score or not. The bassoon may have been optional in works for string orchestra, but if other winds were used, the bassoon was *de rigueur*. In such cases, some editions list the bassoon and some do not. I have merely followed the edition in hand, but conductors may wish to employ the bassoon, perhaps playing from a cello or bass part, whether it is called for or not.

Nineteenth-century French orchestras normally had 4 bassoons doubling two real parts. Occasionally they might split into four parts for a few bars. I have attempted to distinguish between the number of bassoons called for and the number of real parts involved, if different.

SARRUSOPHONE. The contrabass member of the sarrusophone family enjoyed a certain vogue in French works of the late nineteenth and early twentieth centuries. The instrument resembled the contrabassoon in certain ways. Its parts are normally played on contrabassoon today, and they are treated that way in this book.

TRUMPETS AND CORNETS. Nineteenth-century French and Russian composers often wrote for two trumpets and two cornets in their orchestral works. I have simply grouped them together here as four trumpets, partly because that at least tells the user the number of players required, and partly because the modern cornet unfortunately does not sound much different from a trumpet—surely not as different as trumpets and cornets would have sounded around the turn of the last century.

TROMBONES. In eighteenth-century choral music it was customary for trombones to double the altos, tenors, and basses of the chorus, and sometimes for a cornetto to double the sopranos. These instruments were often not mentioned in the score at all. It would be possible to add them when they are not indicated, and it would probably be defensible to omit them when they are, since in any case a modern chorus with large-bore trombones is not going to sound much like an eighteenth-century chorus (using boy sopranos and male altos) with the sackbutt-like trombones of the period.

TUBA. It is not until the mid-nineteenth century that the tuba entered the orchestra. Its predecessor was the ophicleide, a cup-mouthpiece instrument with keys like a saxophone rather than valves. The two existed side by side in the second half of the century, though progressive composers such as Berlioz and Wagner were quick to adopt the tuba. There is some interest in reviving the ophicleide for early nineteenth-century repertoire, but those parts are now most commonly played on tuba, and that is how they are recorded in this book.

Acknowledgements. In a project that has proceeded for over a quarter of a century, the number of persons to thank has grown very large. Let the brevity of their mention not be mistaken for any diminishing of its sincerity.

From the first edition: James Dixon, my teacher, mentor and friend of many years; Knox College and Oakland University, which funded the research; computer experts Charles J. Gibbs, William Ripperger, and Roger Harris; Harry Kownatsky of the Fleisher Collection; Walter S. Collins; and my wife Jimmie Sue Daniels.

From the second edition: William R. Eshelman of Scarecrow Press; Luck's Music Library; Lyle Nordstrom, of early music fame; conductor William Wilsen; researcher Helen Rowin; and my proofreading daughter Abigail Daniels (now Abigail Smith).

For the present version, many of these should be repeated. Luck's Music Library gave me (as it gives all conductors) complete run of their huge inventory. Helen Rowin of the Detroit Public Library once again did the research for the list of Jewish composers in Appendix G, and voluntarily went beyond her mandate to provide data on a number of other composers I had not managed to track down.

Michael Charry of Mannes College of Music one day expressed the wish for a list of composers' significant anniversaries and thus gave me the idea for Appendix F. Juan I. Cahis' article in the *Journal of the Conductors Guild* gave me a welcome new slant on the Bruckner symphonies (see Appendix I); Mr. Cahis also put me in touch with William Carragan, and both men were very helpful.

As mentioned before, many members of the profession made contributions to my work. All are appreciated, but a few whose generosity was extraordinary should be named: Clinton F. Nieweg, distinguished principal librarian of the Philadelphia Orchestra, sent me an enormous box of scores to peruse and return. James Kortz, librarian of the Saint Paul Chamber Orchestra, photocopied about a quarter of the pages from his copy of my second edition, including his pencilled corrections and additions. Stephen M. Kidd, conductor of the Great Lakes Symphony, dug up a large number of obscure durations for me. Robert Walls, the very knowledgeable head of Educational Music Service, talked with me at great length, giving me valuable insights into the way things work in the publishing business. He also took the time to send me a lengthy computer printout that I referred to frequently.

My wife, Jimmie Sue Daniels, dedicatee of the first two editions, proofread every single word—every single *digit*—of the huge database that forms the heart of this book. You have to have someone you trust completely to perform that critical but tedious chore. There will be errors found in this book, to be sure, but they will be my own errors, because she made sure that the database corresponds exactly to my research notes.

BIBLIOGRAPHY

Altmann, Wilhelm. *Orchester-Literatur-Katalog: Verzeichnis von seit 1850 erschienen Orchester-Werken.* 2. Auflage; 2 vols. Leipzig: F.E.C. Leuckart, 1926-36.

Aronowsky, Salomon. *Performing Times of Orchestral Works.* London: E. Benn, 1959.

Eaton, Quaintance. *Opera Production.* 2 vols. Minneapolis: University of Minnesota Press, 1961-74.

The Edwin A. Fleisher Collection of Orchestral Music in the Free Library of Philadelphia: A Cumulative Catalog, 1929-1977. Boston: G. K. Hall, 1979.

Farish, Margaret K. *Orchestral Music in Print.* Music-In-Print Series, v. 5, v.5s, v.5t, v.5x. Philadelphia: Musicdata, 1979-94.

Farish, Margaret K. *String Music in Print.* 2nd edition. New York: R. R. Bowker Co., 1973. 1984 Supplement, Philadelphia: Musicdata, 1984.

Koshgarian, Richard. *American Orchestral Music: A Performance Catalog.* Metuchen, N.J.: Scarecrow Press, 1992.

Müller-Reuter, Theodor. *Lexikon der deutschen Konzertliteratur: ein Ratgeber für Dirigenten, Konzertveranstalter, Musikschriftsteller und Musikfreunde.* 2 vols. Leipzig: G. F. Kahnt, 1909-21.

Saltonstall, Cecilia D. and Henry. *A New Catalog of Music for Small Orchestra.* Clifton, N.J.: European American Music Corporation, 1978.

Scott, William. *A Conductor's Repertory of Chamber Music: Compositions for Nine to Fifteen Solo Instruments.* Westport, CT: Greenwood Press, 1993.

Seibert, Donald C. *The Hyde Timings: A Collection of Timings Made at Concerts in New York City between 1894 and 1928.* New York: Juilliard School of Music, 1964.

Valentin, Erich. *Handbuch der Chormusik.* 2 vols. Regensburg: Gustav Bosse, 1953-58.

ABBREVIATIONS

A	alto voice		mvt	movement
afl	alto flute		Mz	mezzo-soprano voice
asx	alto saxophone			
			opt	optional
B	bass voice		ob	oboe
Bar	baritone voice		org	organ
bcl	bass clarinet			
bn	bassoon		perc	percussion
bsx	baritone saxophone		pf	pianoforte
btp	bass trumpet		pic	piccolo
cbn	contrabassoon		rec	recorder
cel	celesta			
cimb	cimbalom		S	soprano voice
cl	clarinet		scl	sopranino clarinet
cnt	continuo			(i.e. in E-flat or D)
			sd	snare drum
db	double bass, contrabass		str	strings
dbl	doubling, *or* doubles		ssx	soprano saxophone
			sx	saxophone
Eh	English horn		synth	synthesizer
elec	electric			
			T	tenor voice
fl	flute		tbn	trombone
			tmp	timpani
gtr	guitar		tp	trumpet
			tsx	tenor saxophone
harm	harmonium			
hn	horn		var	variable
hp	harp		va	viola
hpsd	harpsichord		vc	violoncello
			vib	vibraphone
mand	mandolin		vn	violin
max	maximum			
min	minimum		xyl	xylophone

---

*   auxiliary instruments: piccolo, English horn, bass clarinet, contrabassoon, respectively

\+   auxiliary instruments: alto flute, E-flat clarinet, respectively

\=   both auxiliary instruments: piccolo *and* alto flute, or bass clarinet *and* E-flat clarinet, respectively

/   doubling, *or* doubles

A

Abel, Karl Friedrich   1723 - 1787

Symphony, op.1, no.5, F major   10'
0 2 0 0—2 0 0 0—opt cnt—str
Oboes and horns may be omitted, or may be substituted for by
flutes and clarinets respectively.
Ed. Hilmar Hoeckner.
Vieweg

Symphony, op.1, no.6, G major   10'
0 2 0 0—2 0 0 0—opt cnt—str
Oboes and horns may be omitted, or may be substituted for by
flutes and clarinets respectively.
Ed. Hilmar Hoeckner.
Vieweg

Symphony, op.7, no.6, E-flat major   13'
0 0 2 1—2 0 0 0—str   4' 5' 4'
Formerly attributed to Mozart, and still published as Mozart's
Symphony no.3 by both Breitkopf and Kalmus.
Breitkopf   *Kalmus*   *Peters*

Symphony, op.14, no.2, E-flat major   15'
0 2 0 1—2 0 0 0—cnt—str
2fl may substitute for 2ob. Ed. Gwilym Beechey.
Oxford

Adam, Adolph-Charles   1803 - 1856

Giselle   126'
*2 2 2 2—4 4 3 1—tmp+3—hp—str   63' 63'
A reduced orchestration by Humphrey Searle is available from
Faber:
*1 *1 1 1—1 1 1 0—tmp+1—pf—str.
Kalmus

Si J'Étais Roi (If I were king): Overture   8'
*2 2 2 2—4 2 3 0—tmp+4—hp—str
In the Fritz Hoffmann version (Breitkopf & Kalmus), the
following instruments are designated "ad lib": pic, ob1&2, bn1&2,
hn3&4, tbn1&2, tmp, perc, hp. Thus the work would be playable
with: 1 0 2 0—2 2 1 0—str
Breitkopf   *Kalmus*   *Leduc*

ADAM

Adams, John   1947 -

The Chairman dances; foxtrot for orchestra   12'
*2 2 *2 2—4 2 2 1—tmp+3—hp, pf—str
Both flutists double on piccolo.
AMP

Chamber symphony   22'
*1 1 =2 *2—1 1 1 0—1perc—synth—str 1.0.1.1.1
Contents—Mongrel airs; Aria with walking bass; Roadrunner.
Boosey

Concerto, violin   32'
=2 *2 *2 2—2 1 0 0—tmp+1—2synth—str (min 6.6.5.5.2)
Both flutes double on piccolo.
Boosey

Fearful symmetries   27'
*2 *2 *3 1—4sx (sop, 2alto, bar)—2 3 3 0—tmp—pf, synth,
sampler—str 6.6.4.4.2
Both flutists double on piccolo.
Boosey

Grand pianola music   32'
3 amplified female voices (mostly non-text)   15' 8' 9'
*2 2 *2 2—2 2 2 1—3perc—2pf
Both flutists double on piccolo.
Schirmer, G.

Harmonielehre   40'
*4 *3 *4 *4—4 4 3 2—tmp+4—2hp, cel, pf—str   17' 12'
3 of the flutists double on piccolo; 2 of the clarinetists double on   11'
bass clarinet.
Schirmer, G.

Harmonium   35'
chorus
*4 3 *3 *3—4 4 3 1—tmp+4—hp, cel, pf/synth—str
3 of the flutists double on piccolo.
Schirmer, G.

Shaker loops   28'
str (or str septet: 3vn, va, 2vc, db)
Schirmer, G.

Short ride in a fast machine   4'
*4 *3 4 *4—4 4 3 1—tmp+3—2 synth (opt)—str
3rd & 4th cl optional.
Boosey

Tromba lontana   4'
2 solo trumpets
*4 2 2 0—4 0 0 0—3perc—hp, pf—str
Boosey

The wound-dresser 20'
solo baritone voice
*2 2 *2 2—2 1 0 0—tmp—synth (Yamaha SY77, Yamaha SY99, or
Korg Wavestation)—str (min 6.6.4.4.2)
Boosey

Adams, Leslie 1932 -
Ode to life 12'
*2 2 2 2—4 3 3 1—tmp+3—cel—str
ACA

Three Dunbar songs 20'
voice (mezzo-soprano or baritone)
*1 1 1 1—2 0 0 0—tmp+2—hp—str
ACA

Addinsell, Richard 1904 - 1977
Warsaw concerto 9'
solo piano
2 *1 2 2—4 3 3 0—tmp—str
Chappell

Adler, Samuel 1928 -
Concerto for orchestra 20'
*4 *3 =4 *3—4 3 4 1—tmp+4—hp, pf—str
Two of the flutists double on piccolo.
Boosey

Elegy for string orchestra 8'
str
Presser

Symphony no.5 (We are the echoes) 22'
mezzo-soprano solo
*3 *3 *3 *3—4 3 3 1—tmp+3—pf—str
Boosey

Adolphe, Bruce 1955 -
Three pieces for kids and chamber orchestra

1. Concertino 3'
solo flute & oboe
str
Kids (in the audience) sing.
ACA

2. Rainbow 4'
2 2 2 2—2 2 0 0—str
Kids (in the audience) sing.
ACA

3. TDT (Texture—dynamics—timbre)
1 2 2 2—2 0 0 0—str
Kids (in the audience) clap, "click," and stamp.
ACA

Albéniz, Isaac   1860 - 1909

Catalonia   7'
  *3 *3 *3 3—4 4 3 1—tmp+4—2 hp—str
  Originally for piano; orchestrated by the composer. Part I of an
  intended (but never-completed) three-part work.
  Durand   *Kalmus*

Concerto, piano, no.1, op.78, A minor (Concierto fantástico)   24'
  2 2 2 2—2 2 3 0—tmp—str
  UME

Iberia (arr. E. F. Arbós)   28'
  *3 *3 =4 *3—tsx—4 4 3 1—tmp+6—2hp, cel—str

| 7' 7' 5' |
| 4' 5' |

  Nos. 1-3 and 6-7 of the suite, originally for piano.
  Contents—Evocation; El puerto; Fête Dieu à Seville; Triana; El
  Albaicin.
  Eschig

Iberia (arr. Carlos Surinach)   50'
  *2 *2 2 2—4 2 3 1—tmp+2—hp—str

| 7' 7' 9' |
| 7' 5' 8' |
| 7' |

  Nos. 4-5 and 8-12 of the suite, originally for piano.
  Contents—Rondeña; Almería; El polo; Lavapies; Málaga; Jérez;
  Eritaña.
  AMP

Navarra   5'
  (arr. E. F. Arbós)
  *3 *3 *3 3—4 3 3 1—tmp+4—2hp—str
  Eschig

Rapsodia española, op.70   12'
  solo piano
  *3 *3 2 2—4 2 3 1—tmp+4—hp, cel—str
  UME

Albert, Stephen   1941 - 1992

Flower of the mountain   16'
  soprano solo
  *2 *2 2 2—2 2 0 0—tmp+2—hp—str
  Schirmer, G.

RiverRun   33'
  =3 *3 =4 *3—asx—4 3 3 1—tmp+3—2hp, pf—str

| 8' 9' 6' |
| 10' |

  Contents—Rain music; Leafy speafing; Beside the rivering
  waters; Rivers end.
  Schirmer, G.

Symphony no.2 25'
*3 *3 *3 *4—4 3 3 1—tmp+2—hp, pf—str
Orchestration completed by Sebastian Currier.
G.Schirmer

Albinoni, Tomaso 1671 - 1750

Concerto, op.5, no.4, G major 5'
cnt—str
Ed. Raffaele Cumar.
Ricordi

Concerto, op.5, no.7, D minor 10'
cnt—str
Ed. Ettore Bonelli.
Zanibon

Concerto, op.7, no.3, B-flat major 9'
solo oboe
cnt—str
Ed. Bernhard Paumgartner.
Boosey

Concerto, op.9, no.2, D minor 14'
solo oboe
cnt—str
Kneusslin   Suvini

Concerto, op.9, no.9, C major 11'
0 2 0 0—cnt—str
Musica Rara   Ricordi

Concerto, op.9, no.10, F major 11'
solo violin
cnt—str
Ed. Remo Giazotto.
Ricordi

Alfvén, Hugo 1872 - 1960

Midsommarvaka (Swedish Rhapsody no.1) 12'
*3 *3 =3 3—4 2 3 1—tmp+2—2hp—str
Hansen   Kalmus

Alwyn, William 1905 - 1985

Autumn legend 12'
solo English horn
str
Lengnick

Festival march 8'
*3 *3 *3 *3—4 3 3 1—tmp+2—hp—str
Possible with woodwinds: *3 2 2 2.
Lengnick

Lyra angelica 30'
  solo harp
  str   8' 7' 9' 6'
  Lengnick

Sinfonietta 26'
  str   8' 7' 11'
  Lengnick

Symphony no.1 41'
  *3 *3 2 2—4 3 3 1—tmp+3—hp, cel—str   11' 9'
  Lengnick   10' 11'

Symphony no.2 30'
  *3 *3 2 2—4 3 3 1—tmp+3—1 or 2hp—str   13' 17'
  Lengnick

Symphony no.5 (Hydriotaphia) 17'
  *3 *3 2 2—4 3 3 1—tmp+4—hp—str   3' 5' 3' 6'
  Lengnick

Amram, David   1930 -

Autobiography for strings 8'
  str
  Peters

Shakespearian concerto 22'
  0 1 0 0—2 0 0 0—str
  Peters

Triple concerto 25'
  3 solo quintets: woodwind (fl, ob, cl, bn, hn), brass (2tp, hn, tbn,
  tuba), and jazz (asx, bsx, pf, db, drums)
  *2 *2 *2 *2—2 2 2 0—tmp+5—cel—str
  Peters

Anderson, Leroy   1908 - 1975

Irish suite 20'
  *3 2 2 2—4 3 3 1—tmp+3—hp—str   3' 4' 3'
  Contents—The Irish washerwoman; The minstrel boy; The rakes   3' 4' 3'
  of Mallow; The wearing of the green; The last rose of summer;
  The girl I left behind me.
  Belwin

Anderson, T. J.   1928 -

Chamber symphony 14'
  *1 1 1 1—1 1 1 0—2perc—hp, cel—str
  CFE

Andriessen, Louis   1939 -

Dances   25'
  solo soprano
  1perc—hp, pf—str
  Donemus

Mausoleum   30'
  2 high baritones
  0 0 0 0—8 3 4 0—2perc—2hp, 2pf, bass gtr, cimbalom—str
  0.0.4.4.2
  Some instruments must be amplified.
  Donemus

De staat (The republic)   40'
  4 female voices
  0 *4 0 0—4 4 4 0—2hp, 2pf—2 elec gtr, elec bass gtr—4va
  Two of the oboists double on English horn.
  All instruments should be amplified for a perfect dynamic
  balance.
  Donemus

Antheil, George   1900 - 1959

Ballet mécanique   18'
  4pf, 2xyl, tmp, 8perc
  1953 edition.
  Schirmer, G.

Symphony no.4 (1942)   27'
  *3 *3 *3 *3—4 3 3 1—tmp+4—hp, pf—str
  Boosey

Symphony no.5 (The joyous)   21'
  *3 *3 *3 *3—4 3 3 1—tmp+5—pf—str
  Schirmer, G.

Symphony no.6 (After Delacroix)   24'
  *3 *3 *3 *3—4 3 3 1—tmp+4—pf—str
  Weintraub

Arensky, Anton   1861 - 1906

Variations on a theme by Tchaikovsky, op.35a   15'
  str
  Forberg   *Kalmus*

Argento, Dominick   1927 -

Casa Guidi   20'
  mezzo-soprano
  =3 *3 *3 2—4 3 3 1—tmp+2—hp, pf, opt mand—str
  Chamber orchestra version also available:
  *2 *2 *2 1—2 1 1 0—tmp+1—hp, pf, mand—str.
  Boosey

In praise of music; seven songs for orchestra 30'
=3 *3 *3 *3—4 3 3 1—tmp+3—hp, pf/cel—str
Boosey

Armer, Elinor   1939 -

The great instrument of the Geggerets 16'
narrator
*2 2 *2 *2—2 2 1 1—tmp+1—pf—str (10.8.6.6.3)
Part III of the series *Uses of music in uttermost parts.*
MMB

Arne, Thomas   1710 - 1778

Symphony no.1, C major 8'
0 2 0 1—2 0 0 0—cnt—str
Ed. Richard Platt.
Oxford

Symphony no.2, F major 9'
0 2 0 1—2 0 0 0—cnt—str
Ed. Richard Platt.
Oxford

Symphony no.3, E-flat major 8'
0 2 0 1—2 0 0 0—tmp—cnt—str
Ed. Richard Platt.
Oxford

Symphony no.4, C minor 11'
2 2 0 1—2 0 0 0—cnt—str
Ed. Richard Platt. Flute parts reconstructed by the editor.
Oxford

Arnold, Malcolm   1921 -

Concerto, clarinet, no.2, op.115 17'
*2 2 0 2—2 0 0 0—tmp—str
Faber   6' 8' 3'

Concerto, 2 violins & string orchestra, op.77 17'
str
Faber   6' 8' 3'

Four Cornish dances, op.91 8'
*3 2 2 2—4 3 3 1—tmp+2—hp—str
Faber   2' 2' 2' 2'

Symphony for strings 22'
str
Lengnick

Symphony no.3, op.63 33'
*3 2 2 2—4 3 3 1—tmp—str
Paterson   12' 14' 7'

Symphony no.6, op.95   27'
*3 2 2 2—4 3 3 1—tmp+3—str   9' 11' 7'
Faber

Tam O'Shanter overture, op.51   8'
*3 2 2 2—4 3 3 1—tmp+2—str
Paterson

Arriaga, Juan Crisóstomo   1806 - 1826
Los esclavos felices: Overture   8'
2 2 2 2—2 0 0 0—tmp—str
Heugel   Kalmus

Symphony, D major   25'
2 2 2 2—2 2 0 0—tmp—str
Kalmus   Luck

Aschaffenburg, Walter   1927 -
Three dances for orchestra, op.15   13'
*3 3 =4 *3—4 3 3 1—tmp+6—hp—str   3' 4' 6'
Presser

Asia, Daniel   1953 -
Symphony no.1   25'
*3 *3 *3 *3—4 3 3 1—tmp+3—hp, pf/cel—str
Merion

Auber, Daniel-François   1782 - 1871
Le Domino noir: Overture   8'
*2 2 2 2—4 2 3 0—tmp+3—str
Ricordi

Fra Diavolo: Overture   8'
*2 2 2 2—4 2 3 0—tmp+4—str
Breitkopf   Kalmus

Lestocq: Overture   8'
*2 2 2 2—4 2 1 0—tmp+3—str
Luck

Marco Spada: Overture   8'
*2 2 2 2—4 2 3 0—tmp+3—str
Luck

Masaniello (La Muette de Portici): Overture   8'
*3 2 2 2—4 2 3 1—tmp+4—str
Kalmus

Auric, Georges   1899 - 1983
La Chambre   18'
*2 1 2 1—2 2 1 1—tmp+2—pf—str
Ricordi

Phèdre; suite symphonique   20'
  *3 *3 *3 *3—4 4 3 1—tmp+4—2 hp, cel—str
  Salabert

B

Babadjanyan, Arno   1921 - 1983
Concerto, violoncello   17'
  *3 2 *3 2—4 1 0 0—tmp+1—pf/cel—str
  Russian

Babbitt, Milton   1916 -
Ars combinatoria   19'
  *2 *2 *2 *2—2 2 1 1—3perc—hp, cel, pf—str
  Peters

Composition for twelve instruments   7'
  1 1 1 1—1 1 0 0—hp, cel—vn, va, vc, db
  AMP

Concerto, piano   20'
  *2 *2 =3 *2—3 2 2 1—4perc—hp, cel—str
  Peters

Transfigured notes   19'
  str
  Peters

Bacewicz, Grażyna   1909 - 1969
Contradizione   16'
  *1 1 +1 1—1 1 0 0—2perc—hp, cel—2vn, va, vc, db
  Moeck

Bach, Carl Philipp Emanuel   1714 - 1788
Concerto, harpsichord, H.427 (W.23), D minor   23'
  cnt (in addition to solo hpsd)—str | 9' 7' 7' |
  Breitkopf

Magnificat, H.772 (W.215)   43'
  chorus   solos SATB | 3' 6' 4' |
  2 2 0 0—2 3 0 0—tmp—cnt—str | 8' 4' 6' |
  Eulenburg   *Kalmus* | 5' 2' 5' |

Symphony, H.657 (W.182/1), G major   12'
  cnt—str | 4' 4' 4' |
  Peters   *Schott*

Symphony, H.658 (W.182/2), B-flat major   12'
cnt—str   3' 4' 5'
Bärenreiter   *Breitkopf*   *Kalmus*   *Peters*

Symphony, H.659 (W.182/3), C major   11'
cnt—str   3' 3' 5'
Breitkopf   *Kalmus*   *Nagel*   *Peters*

Symphony, H.660 (W.182/4), A major   12'
cnt—str
Breitkopf   *Peters*   *Schott*

Symphony, H.661 (W.182/5), B minor   10'
cnt—str   4' 3' 3'
Breitkopf   *Kalmus*   *Nagel*   *Peters*

Symphony, H.662 (W.182/6), E major   8'
cnt—str   2' 3' 3'
Peters

Symphony, H.663 (W.183/1), D major   11'
2 2 0 2—2 2 0 0—tmp—str   6' 2' 3'
2nd bn, both tp, and tmp are optional.
Kalmus   *Peters*

Symphony, H.665 (W.183/3), F major   9'
2 2 0 1—2 0 0 0—cnt—str   4' 3' 2'
Kalmus   *Luck*   *Peters*

Bach, Jan   1937 -
The happy prince   38'
narrator
*1 *1 1 1—2 2 1 0—1 or 2perc—hp, pf/cel/hpsd—str 6.5.4.3.2
Highgate

Bach, Johann Christian   1735 - 1782
Concerto, harpsichord, op.7, no.5, E-flat major   17'
str (without va)
Ed. Christian Doebereiner.
Kalmus   *Peters*

Concerto, harpsichord, op.13, no.2, D major   14'
2 2 0 0—2 0 0 0—str
Kalmus   *Peters*

Concerto, harpsichord, op.13, no.4, B-flat major   20'
0 2 0 0—2 0 0 0—str
Kalmus   *Peters*

Concerto, harpsichord, E-flat major   27'
str
Ed. Ernst Praetorius.
Eulenburg   *Kalmus*

Sinfonia concertante, A major   18'
  solo violin and violoncello   `11' 7'`
  0 2 0 0—2 0 0 0—cnt—str
  Eulenburg   *Kalmus*

Sinfonia concertante, E-flat major   25'
  2 solo violins
  2 1 0 0—2 0 0 0—cnt—str
  Ed. Fritz Stein.
  Eulenburg   *Kalmus*

Sonatas, piano, op.5, nos.2-4
  see: Mozart, Wolfgang Amadeus, 1756-1791
      Concertos, piano, K.107 (21b) nos.1-3

Symphony, op.3, no.1, D major   10'
  0 2 0 0—2 0 0 0—cnt—str   `4' 4' 2'`
  Doblinger   *Eulenburg*

Symphony, op.3, no.2, C major   10'
  0 2 0 0—2 0 0 0—cnt—str   `3' 5' 2'`
  Ed. Erik G. S. Smith.
  Doblinger

Symphony, op.3, no.4, B-flat major   15'
  0 2 0 0—2 0 0 0—str   `5' 5' 5'`
  Doblinger   *Kalmus*   *Kneusslin*

Symphony, op.6, no.1, G major   9'
  0 2 0 0—2 0 0 0—cnt—str   `4' 3' 2'`
  Eulenburg

Symphony, op.6, no.6, G minor   13'
  0 2 0 0—2 0 0 0—cnt—str   `4' 6' 3'`
  Ed. Fritz Stein.
  Breitkopf

Symphony, op.9, no.2, E-flat major   12'
  0 2 0 0—2 0 0 0—cnt—str   `5' 3' 4'`
  Oboes may be replaced by flutes; horns are optional.
  Ed. Fritz Stein. J.C.Bach's op.9 was later republished as op.21.
  Eulenburg   *Kalmus*

Symphony, op.18, no.1, E-flat major   12'
  2 2 0 2—2 0 0 0—opt cnt—str   `5' 5' 2'`
  Double orchestra.
  Kalmus   *Peters*

Symphony, op.18, no.2, B-flat major   11'
  2 2 2 2—2 0 0 0—str   `3' 5' 3'`
  Ed. Fritz Stein. Overture to the opera *Lucio Silla.*
  Kalmus   *Peters*

Symphony, op.18, no.3, D major   14'
  2 2 0 1—2 0 0 0—str   `5' 6' 3'`
  Kalmus   *Peters*

Symphony, op.18, no.4, D major 12'
2 2 0 1—2 2 0 0—tmp—opt cnt—str 4' 5' 3'
Flutes are optional. Ed. Alfred Einstein.
Eulenburg

Symphony, op.18, no.5, E major 17'
2 2 0 1—2 0 0 0—cnt—str 7' 4' 6'
Double orchestra. Ed. Fritz Stein.
Breitkopf

Symphony, op.18, no.6, D major 14'
2 2 0 1—2 0 0 0—cnt—str 4' 4' 3' 3'
Ed. Fritz Stein.
Breitkopf

Symphony, op.21, no.1, B-flat major 15'
0 2 0 0—2 0 0 0—cnt—str
Ed. Fritz Stein.
Breitkopf

Symphony, op.21, no.2, E-flat major
see his: Symphony, op.9, no.2, E-flat major

Symphony, op.21, no.3, B-flat major 8'
0 2 0 0—2 0 0 0—cnt—str
Flutes may be substituted for oboes. Ed. Adam Carse
Augener

Symphony, D major 10'
2 2 *3 2—2 2 0 0—tmp—cnt—str
Overture to the opera *Temistocle.* The original called for 3
clarinette d'amore in D, which the editor has adapted
for 2cl and bcl. Ed. Fritz Stein.
Breitkopf

Bach, Johann Ludwig   1677 - 1741
Denn du wirst meine Seele
See: Bach, Johann Sebastian
        Cantata no.15

Bach, Johann Sebastian   1685 - 1750
Brandenburg concerto no.1, BWV 1046, F major 21'
solos: 3 oboes, 2 horns, violin (originally violino piccolo) 10' 6' 5'
0 0 0 1—cnt—str
Bärenreiter   *Breitkopf*   *Kalmus*   *Peters*

Brandenburg concerto no.2, BWV 1047, F major 13'
solos: recorder, oboe, trumpet, violin 5' 5' 3'
cnt—str
Bärenreiter   *Breitkopf*   *Kalmus*   *Peters*

Brandenburg concerto no.3, BWV 1048, G major 10'
cnt—3vn, 3va, 3vc, db 7' 3'
Bärenreiter   *Breitkopf*   *Kalmus*   *Peters*

Brandenburg concerto no.4, BWV 1049, G major   17'
   2 solo recorders, solo violin   7' 5' 5'
   cnt—str
   Bärenreiter   *Breitkopf*   *Kalmus*   *Peters*

Brandenburg concerto no.5, BWV 1050, D major   21'
   solos: harpsichord, flute, violin   10' 6' 5'
   str (without vn II)
   Bärenreiter   *Breitkopf*   *Kalmus*   *Peters*

Brandenburg concerto no.6, BWV 1051, B-flat major   18'
   2va, 2 viole da gamba, vc, db, cnt   7' 5' 6'
   Bärenreiter   *Breitkopf*   *Kalmus*   *Peters*

Cantata no.1 (Wie schön leuchtet der Morgenstern)   25'
   chorus   solos STB
   2 ob da caccia—2hn—cnt—str
   2 solo vn in one movement.
   Breitkopf   *Kalmus*

Cantata no.2 (Ach Gott, vom Himmel sieh darein)   18'
   chorus   solos ATB   4' 1' 4'
   0 2 0 0—cnt—str   2' 6' 1'
   4tbn doubling choral parts.
   Breitkopf

Cantata no.3 (Ach Gott, wie manches Herzeleid [I])   31'
   chorus   solos SATB
   2ob d'amore—hn, tbn—cnt—str
   Brass used only to strengthen the cantus firmus.
   Breitkopf

Cantata no.4 (Christ lag in Todesbanden)   20'
   chorus   (optional solos SATB)   1' 5' 3'
   cnt—str   2' 3' 3'
   Cornetto and 3tbn doubling choral parts.   2' 1'
   A critical edition of the score with historical and analytical
   essays is available from Norton.
   Breitkopf   *Kalmus*

Cantata no.5 (Wo soll ich fliehen hin)   21'
   chorus   solos SATB   4' 1' 6'
   0 2 0 0—0 1 0 0—cnt—str   2' 6' 1'
   Breitkopf   1'

Cantata no.6 (Bleib bei uns, denn es will Abend werden)   28'
   chorus   solos SATB
   0 2 0 0—ob da caccia—cnt—violoncello piccolo—str
   Bärenreiter   *Breitkopf*   *Kalmus*

Cantata no.7 (Christ unser Herr zum Jordan kam)   27'
   chorus   solos ATB
   2 ob d'amore—cnt—str
   Breitkopf   *Kalmus*

Cantata no.8 (Liebster Gott, wann werd' ich sterben)   16'
   chorus   solos SATB
   1 0 0 0—2ob d'amore—1 0 0 0—cnt—str   5' 3' 1'
   Horn is used only to strengthen the cantus firmus.   5' 1' 1'
   Breitkopf   *Kalmus*

Cantata no.9 (Es ist das Heil uns kommen her)   27'
   chorus   solos SATB
   1 0 0 0—ob d'amore—cnt—str
   Breitkopf   *Kalmus*

Cantata no.10 (Meine Seele erhebt den Herren)   24'
   chorus   solos SATB
   0 2 0 0—0 1 0 0—cnt—str
   Trumpet used only to strengthen the cantus firmus.
   Breitkopf   *Kalmus*

Cantata no.11 (Lobet Gott in seinen Reichen)   27'
   chorus   solos SATB   5' 1' 1'
   2 2 0 0—0 3 0 0—tmp—cnt—str   6' 1' 1'
   Also known as *Ascension oratorio* or *Himmelfahrts-Oratorium*.   2' 6' 4'
   Breitkopf   *Kalmus*

Cantata no.12 (Weinen, Klagen, Sorgen, Zagen)   27'
   chorus   solos ATB
   0 1 0 1—0 1 0 0—cnt—str
   Breitkopf   *Kalmus*

Cantata no.13 (Meine Seufzer, meine Tränen)   23'
   chorus   solos SATB
   2rec 1 0 0—cnt—str
   Oboe doubles ob da caccia.
   Breitkopf

Cantata no.14 (Wär Gott nicht mit uns diese Zeit)   17'
   chorus   solos STB
   0 2 0 0—1 0 0 0—cnt—str   6' 4' 1'
   Breitkopf   5' 1'

Cantata no.15 (Denn du wirst meine Seele)   15'
   solos SATB   chorus in final movement only
   0 0 0 0—0 3 0 0—tmp—cnt—str
   Actually composed by Johann Ludwig Bach.
   Breitkopf   *Kalmus*

Cantata no.16 (Herr Gott, dich loben wir)   21'
   chorus   solos ATB
   0 *2 0 0—1 0 0 0—cnt—str
   One movement calls for oboe da caccia (may be played by one of
   the oboists) *or* violetta (=viol; possible on viola).
   Breitkopf   *Kalmus*

Cantata no.17 (Wer Dank opfert, der preiset mich)   22'
chorus   solos SATB
2ob d'amore—cnt—str
Breitkopf   *Kalmus*

Cantata no.18 (Gleichwie der Regen und Schnee)   26'
chorus   solos STB
2rec 0 0 1—cnt—4va, vc (db)
An earlier Weimar version (in G minor rather than A minor) uses
no recorders.
Bärenreiter   *Breitkopf*   *Kalmus*

Cantata no.19 (Es erhub sich ein Streit)   22'
chorus   solos STB
0 *3 0 0—0 3 0 0—tmp—cnt—str
Two of the oboists double on oboe d'amore; one must double on
oboe da caccia. (Possible with only two oboists, omitting the
oboe da caccia.)
Breitkopf   *Kalmus*

Cantata no.20 (O Ewigkeit, du Donnerwort [I])   31'
chorus   solos ATB
0 3 0 0—0 1 0 0—cnt—str
Breitkopf   *Kalmus*

Cantata no.21 (Ich hatte viel Bekümmernis)   42'
chorus   solos SATB
0 1 0 1—0 3 4 0—tmp—cnt—str
Trombones only double choral parts. The timpani part was lost
and has been reconstructed.
Breitkopf   *Kalmus*

Cantata no.22 (Jesus nahm zu sich die Zwölfe)   20'
chorus   solos ATB
0 1 0 0—cnt—str
Breitkopf   *Kalmus*

Cantata no.23 (Du wahrer Gott und Davids Sohn)   18'
chorus   solos SAT
0 2 0 0—cnt—str
Cornetto and 3tbn doubling choral parts.
Breitkopf   *Kalmus*

Cantata no.24 (Ein ungefärbte Gemüte)   18'
chorus   solos SATB

5'	2'	3'
2'	4'	2'

0 2 0 0—0 1 0 0—cnt—str
Both oboes double ob d'amore.
Breitkopf   *Kalmus*

Cantata no.25 (Es ist nichts gesundes an meinem Leibe)   18'
chorus   solos STB
3rec 2 0 0—0 0 3 0—cornetto—cnt—str
Breitkopf

Cantata no.26 (Ach wie flüchtig, ach wie nichtig)   14'
chorus   solos SATB
1 3 0 0—1 0 0 0—cnt—str
Horn used only to strengthen cantus firmus.
Breitkopf   *Kalmus*

<table>
<tr><td>2'</td><td>5'</td><td>1'</td></tr>
<tr><td>4'</td><td>1'</td><td>1'</td></tr>
</table>

Cantata no.27 (Wer weiss, wie nahe mir mein Ende)   16'
chorus   solos SATB
0 2 0 0—1 0 0 0—org—str
1 oboe doubles on ob da caccia; horn used only to strengthen
cantus firmus.
Breitkopf   *Kalmus*

<table>
<tr><td>5'</td><td>1'</td><td>5'</td></tr>
<tr><td>1'</td><td>3'</td><td>1'</td></tr>
</table>

Cantata no.28 (Gottlob! nun geht das Jahr zu Ende)   16'
chorus   solos SATB
0 2 0 0—ob da caccia—cnt—str
Cornetto and 3tbn doubling choral parts.
Breitkopf   *Gray*   *Kalmus*

<table>
<tr><td>5'</td><td>5'</td><td>2'</td></tr>
<tr><td>1'</td><td>2'</td><td>1'</td></tr>
</table>

Cantata no.29 (Wir danken dir, Gott, wir danken dir)   22'
chorus   solos SATB
0 2 0 0—0 3 0 0—tmp—org—str
Breitkopf   *Kalmus*

<table>
<tr><td>3'</td><td>3'</td><td>5'</td></tr>
<tr><td>1'</td><td>5'</td><td>1'</td></tr>
<tr><td></td><td>2'</td><td>2'</td></tr>
</table>

Cantata no.30 (Freue dich, erlöste Schar)   43'
chorus   solos SATB
2 2 0 0—0 3 0 0—tmp—cnt—str
1 oboist doubles on oboe d'amore
Breitkopf   *C. Fischer*   *Kalmus*

Cantata no.31 (Der Himmel Lacht! die Erde jubiliert)   22'
chorus   solos STB
0 3 0 1—ob da caccia—0 3 0 0—tmp—cnt—str
Breitkopf   *Kalmus*

Cantata no.32 (Liebster Jesu, mein Verlangen)   27'
solos SB   chorus in final chorale only
0 1 0 0—cnt—str
Breitkopf   *Kalmus*

Cantata no.33 (Allein zu dir, Herr Jesu Christ)   20'
chorus   solos ATB
0 2 0 0—cnt—str
Breitkopf   *Kalmus*

<table>
<tr><td>5'</td><td>1'</td><td>8'</td></tr>
<tr><td>1'</td><td>4'</td><td>1'</td></tr>
</table>

Cantata no.34 (O ewiges Feuer, o Ursprung der Liebe)   21'
chorus   solos ATB
2 2 0 0—0 3 0 0—tmp—cnt—str
Bärenreiter   *Breitkopf*   *Kalmus*

Cantata no.35 (Geist und Seele wird verwirret)   26'
alto solo
0 2 0 0—ob da caccia—org—str
Breitkopf   *Kalmus*

<table>
<tr><td>5'</td><td>9'</td><td>2'</td></tr>
<tr><td>3'</td><td>3'</td><td>1'</td></tr>
<tr><td></td><td></td><td>3'</td></tr>
</table>

Cantata no.36 (Schwingt freudig euch empor)   29'
   chorus   solos SATB
   2ob d'amore—cnt—str
   Bärenreiter   *Breitkopf*   *Kalmus*

4'	3'	5'
1'	4'	2'
	9'	1'

Cantata no.37 (Wer da gläubet und getauft wird)   21'
   chorus   solos SATB
   2ob d'amore—cnt—str
   Breitkopf   *Kalmus*

Cantata no.38 (Aus tiefer Not schrei ich zu dir)   21'
   chorus   solos SATB
   0 2 0 0—0 0 4 0—cnt—str
   Trombones only double choral parts.
   Breitkopf   *Gray*   *Kalmus*

Cantata no.39 (Brich dem Hungrigen dein Brot)   21'
   chorus   solos SAB
   2rec 2 0 0—cnt—str
   Breitkopf   *Kalmus*

7'	2'	3'
3'	3'	2'
		1'

Cantata no.40 (Dazu ist erschienen der Sohn Gottes)   18'
   chorus   solos ATB
   0 2 0 0—2 0 0 0—cnt—str
   Breitkopf

5'	2'	1'
3'	1'	1'
	4'	1'

Cantata no.41 (Jesu, nun sei gepreiset)   33'
   chorus   solos SATB
   0 3 0 0—0 3 0 0—tmp—cnt—violoncello piccolo—str
   Breitkopf   *Kalmus*

Cantata no.42 (Am Abend aber desselbigen Sabbats)   29'
   solos SATB   chorus in final chorale only
   0 2 0 1—cnt—str
   Breitkopf   *Kalmus*

Cantata no.43 (Gott fähret auf mit Jauchzen)   28'
   chorus   solos SATB
   0 2 0 0—0 3 0 0—tmp—cnt—str
   Breitkopf

Cantata no.44 (Sie werden euch in den Bann tun [I])   21'
   chorus   solos SATB
   0 2 0 1—cnt—str
   Breitkopf   *Kalmus*

Cantata no.45 (Es ist dir gesagt, Mensch, was gut ist)   21'
   chorus   solos ATB
   2 2 0 0—cnt—str
   Bärenreiter   *Breitkopf*

7'	1'	4'
3'	4'	1'
		1'

Cantata no.46 (Schauet doch und sehet)   19'
   chorus   solos ATB
   2rec 0 0 0—2ob da caccia—0 1 0 0—cnt—str
   Breitkopf   *Kalmus*

| 7' | 2' | 3' |
| 1' | 4' | 2' |

Cantata no.47 (Wer sich selbst erhöhet)   23'
chorus   solos SB   7' 8' 2'
0 2 0 0—cnt—str   5' 1'
One movement calls for obligato organ *or* solo violin.
Breitkopf   *Kalmus*

Cantata no.48 (Ich elender Mensch)   16'
chorus   solos AT   4' 2' 1'
0 2 0 0—0 1 0 0—cnt—str   3' 1' 4'
Breitkopf   *Kalmus*   1'

Cantata no.49 (Ich geh und suche mit Verlangen)   27'
solos SB   7' 6' 2'
ob d'amore—org—violoncello piccolo—str   5' 2' 5'
Breitkopf   *Kalmus*

Cantata no.50 (Nun ist das Heil und die Kraft)   5'
double chorus
0 3 0 0—0 3 0 0—tmp—cnt—str
Breitkopf   *Kalmus*

Cantata no.51 (Jauchzet Gott in allen Landen!)   19'
soprano solo   5' 3' 5'
0 0 0 0—0 1 0 0—cnt—str   4' 2'
Breitkopf   *Kalmus*

Cantata no.52 (Falsche Welt, dir trau ich nicht)   15'
soprano solo   chorus in final chorale only   5' 1' 3'
0 3 0 1—2 0 0 0—cnt—str   1' 4' 1'
Breitkopf   *Kalmus*

Cantata no.53 (Schlage doch, gewünschte Stunde)   10'
alto solo
bells—cnt—str
Wrongly attributed to Bach; actual composer is Georg Melchior
Hoffmann.
Breitkopf   *Kalmus*

Cantata no.54 (Widerstehe doch der Sünde)   12'
alto solo   7' 2' 3'
cnt—str
Breitkopf   *Kalmus*

Cantata no.55 (Ich armer Mensch, ich Sündenknecht)   14'
tenor solo   chorus in final chorale only   5' 2' 4'
1 0 0 0—ob d'amore—cnt—str (without va)   2' 1'
Oboe d'amore part playable on oboe.
Breitkopf   *Kalmus*

Cantata no.56 (Ich will den Kreuzstab gerne tragen)   20'
bass solo   chorus in final chorale only   8' 2' 6'
0 2 0 0—ob da caccia—cnt—str   2' 2'
Breitkopf   *Kalmus*

Cantata no.57 (Selig ist der Mann)
solos SB   chorus in final chorale only
0 2 0 0—ob da caccia—cnt—str
Breitkopf   *Kalmus*

28'

5'	2'	7'
1'	6'	2'
4'	1'	

Cantata no.58 (Ach Gott, wie manches Herzeleid [II])
solos SB
0 2 0 0—ob da caccia—cnt—str
Breitkopf

17'

Cantata no.59 (Wer mich liebet [I])
solos SB   chorus in chorale only
0 0 0 0—0 2 0 0—tmp—cnt—str
Bärenreiter   *Breitkopf*   *Kalmus*

14'

Cantata no.60 (O Ewigkeit, du Donnerwort [II])
solos ATB   chorus in final chorale only
2ob d'amore—hn—cnt—str
Horn is used only to strengthen the cantus firmus.
Breitkopf

16'

| 5' | 2' | 3' |
| 5' | 1' | |

Cantata no.61 (Nun komm, der Heiden Heiland [I])
chorus   solos STB
0 0 0 1—cnt—str
Bärenreiter   *Breitkopf*   *Kalmus*

14'

| 3' | 1' | 4' |
| 1' | 4' | 1' |

Cantata no.62 (Nun komm, der Heiden Heiland [II])
chorus   solos SATB
0 2 0 0—1 0 0 0—cnt—str
Horn only used to strengthen the cantus firmus.
Bärenreiter   *Breitkopf*   *Kalmus*

21'

| 5' | 7' | 1' |
| 6' | 1' | 1' |

Cantata no.63 (Christen, äzet diesen Tag)
chorus   solos SATB
0 3 0 1—0 4 0 0—tmp—org—str
Bärenreiter   *Breitkopf*   *Kalmus*

28'

6'	3'	6'
1'	4'	1'
	7'	

Cantata no.64 (Sehet welch eine Liebe)
chorus   solos SAB
ob d'amore—cnt—str
Cornetto and 3tbn doubling choral parts.
Breitkopf   *Kalmus*

21'

3'	1'	1'
1'	6'	1'
	7'	1'

Cantata no.65 (Sie werden aus Saba alle kommen)
chorus   solos TB
2rec 0 0 0—2ob da caccia—2 0 0 0—cnt—str
Breitkopf   *Kalmus*

19'

Cantata no.66 (Erfreut euch, ihr Herzen)
chorus   solos ATB
0 2 0 1—0 1 0 0—cnt—str
Trumpet is optional.
Breitkopf

31'

Cantata no.67 (Halt im Gedächtnis Jesum Christ)   16'
chorus   solos ATB
1 0 0 0—2ob d'amore—1 0 0 0—cnt—str
Breitkopf   *Gray*   *Kalmus*

Cantata no.68 (Also hat Gott die Welt geliebt)   19'
chorus   solos SB   5' 4' 1'
0 2 0 0—ob da caccia—1 0 3 0—cornetto—cnt—violoncello   5' 4'
piccolo—str
Horn strengthens cantus firmus; cornetto and 3tbn double choral
parts.
Bärenreiter   *Breitkopf*   *Kalmus*

Cantata no.69 (Lobe den Herrn, meine Seele [I])   26'
chorus   solos SATB
0 3 0 1—0 3 0 0—tmp—cnt—str
One oboist doubles on oboe d'amore.
Breitkopf

Cantata no.70 (Wachet! betet! betet! wachet!)   28'
chorus   solos SATB
0 1 0 1—0 1 0 0—cnt—str
Breitkopf   *Kalmus*

Cantata no.71 (Gott ist mein König)   18'
chorus   solos SATB   2' 4' 2'
2rec 2 0 1—0 3 0 0—tmp—org—str   3' 1' 3'
The above instruments constitute a fourfold orchestra: 3'
3tp+tmp; 2rec+vc solo; 2ob+bn; str+org
Breitkopf   *Kalmus*

Cantata no.72 (Alles nur nach Gottes Willen)   20'
chorus   solos SAB
0 2 0 0—cnt—str
Breitkopf   *Kalmus*

Cantata no.73 (Herr, wie du willt, so schicks mit mir)   19'
chorus   solos STB
0 2 0 0—1 0 0 0—cnt—str
Organ may substitute for horn.
Breitkopf   *Kalmus*

Cantata no.74 (Wer mich liebet [II])   25'
chorus   solos SATB
0 2 0 0—ob da caccia—0 3 0 0—tmp—cnt—str
Breitkopf   *Kalmus*

Cantata no.75 (Die Elenden sollen essen)   40'
chorus   solos SATB
0 2 0 1—0 1 0 0—cnt—str
One oboist doubles on oboe d'amore (playable on oboe).
Breitkopf

Cantata no.76 (Die Himmel erzählen die Ehre Gottes)   38'
chorus   solos SATB
0 2 0 0—0 1 0 0—cnt—viola da gamba—str
One oboist doubles on oboe d'amore.
Breitkopf   *Kalmus*

Cantata no.77 (Du sollt Gott, deinen Herren, lieben)   17'
chorus   solos SATB

| 5' | 1' | 5' |
| 1' | 4' | 1' |

0 2 0 0—0 1 0 0—cnt—str
Breitkopf

Cantata no.78 (Jesu, der du meine Seele)   21'
chorus   solos SATB

5'	5'	2'
3'	2'	3'
		1'

1 2 0 0—1 0 0 0—cnt—str
Horn only used to strengthen the cantus firmus.
Bärenreiter   *Breitkopf*   *Kalmus*

Cantata no.79 (Gott der Herr ist Sonn und Schild)   18'
chorus   solos SAB
2 2 0 0—2 0 0 0—tmp—cnt—str
Breitkopf   *Kalmus*

Cantata no.80 (Ein feste Burg ist unser Gott)   25'
chorus   solos SATB

6'	4'	2'
3'	4'	1'
4'	1'	

0 2 0 0—ob da caccia—0 3 0 0—tmp—org—str
Breitkopf   *Kalmus*

Cantata no.81 (Jesus schläft, was soll ich hoffen?)   20'
solos ATB   chorus in final chorale only
2rec 0 0 0—2 ob d'amore—cnt—str
Breitkopf   *Kalmus*

Cantata no.82 (Ich habe genug)   24'
solo bass voice

| 8' | 2' | 9' |
| 1' | 4' | |

0 1 0 0—cnt—str
A later version exists that includes in addition solo soprano (or
mezzo-soprano), flute, and oboe da caccia (currently
unpublished).
Breitkopf   *Kalmus*

Cantata no.83 (Erfreute Zeit im neuen Bunde)   20'
solos ATB   chorus in final chorale only
0 2 0 0—2 0 0 0—cnt—str
Breitkopf

Cantata no.84 (Ich bin vergnügt mit meinem Glücke)   18'
soprano solo   chorus in final chorale only
0 1 0 0—cnt—str
Breitkopf   *Kalmus*

Cantata no.85 (Ich bin ein guter Hirt)   18'
solos SATB   chorus in final chorale only

| 4' | 4' | 5' |
| 1' | 3' | 1' |

0 2 0 0—cnt—violoncello piccolo—str
Breitkopf   *Kalmus*   *Ricordi*

Cantata no.86 (Wahrlich, wahrlich, ich sage euch)　　　　　19'
　　solos SATB　　chorus in final chorale only
　　2ob d'amore (playable on ob) —cnt—str
　　Breitkopf　　　*Kalmus*

Cantata no.87 (Bisher habt ihr nichts gebeten)　　　　　26'
　　solos ATB　　chorus in final chorale only
　　0 3 0 0—cnt—str
　　Two of the oboists double on oboe da caccia.
　　Breitkopf

Cantata no.88 (Siehe, ich will viel Fischer aussenden)　　　23'
　　solos SATB　　chorus in final chorale only
　　2ob d'amore, ob da caccia —2hn—cnt—str
　　Breitkopf

| 8' 1' 4' |
| 3' 3' 3' |
| 1' |

Cantata no.89 (Was soll ich aus dir machen, Ephraim?)　　12'
　　solos SAB　　chorus in final chorale only
　　0 2 0 0—1 0 0 0—cnt—str
　　Breitkopf　　　*Kalmus*

| 4' 1' 3' |
| 1' 2' 1' |

Cantata no.90 (Es reisset euch ein schrecklich Ende)　　　15'
　　solos ATB　　chorus in final chorale only
　　0 0 0 0—0 1 0 0—cnt—str
　　Breitkopf

Cantata no.91 (Gelobet seist du, Jesu Christ)　　　　　19'
　　chorus　　solos SATB
　　0 3 0 1—2 0 0 0—tmp—cnt—str
　　Bärenreiter　　*Breitkopf*　　*Kalmus*

Cantata no.92 (Ich hab in Gottes Herz und Sinn)　　　　37'
　　chorus　　solos SATB
　　2ob d'amore—cnt—str
　　Breitkopf

Cantata no.93 (Wer nur den lieben Gott lässt walten)　　24'
　　chorus　　solos SATB
　　0 2 0 0—cnt—str
　　Breitkopf　　　*Kalmus*

Cantata no.94 (Was frag ich nach der Welt)　　　　　28'
　　chorus　　solos SATB
　　1 2 0 0—cnt—str
　　One oboist doubles on oboe d'amore
　　Breitkopf　　　*Kalmus*

| 4' 2' 4' |
| 5' 3' 5' |
| 4' 1' |

Cantata no.95 (Christus, der ist mein Leben)　　　　　21'
　　chorus　　solos STB
　　0 2 0 0—1 0 0 0—cnt—str
　　Both oboists double on oboe d'amore.
　　Breitkopf　　　*Kalmus*

Cantata no.96 (Herr Christ, der einge Gottessohn) 20'
    chorus   solos SATB
    1 2 0 0—1 0 1 0—cnt—str
    Flutist doubles on sopranino recorder, or this part may be played
    by violino piccolo. Brass used only to strengthen the cantus
    firmus.
    Breitkopf

> 5' 2' 9'
> 1' 2' 1'

Cantata no.97 (In allen meinen Taten) 36'
    chorus   solos SATB
    0 2 0 1—cnt—str
    Breitkopf

Cantata no.98 (Was Gott tut, das ist wohlgetan [I]) 19'
    chorus   solos SATB
    0 2 0 0—ob da caccia—cnt—str
    2nd ob and ob da caccia only double inner chorus parts.
    Breitkopf   *Kalmus*

Cantata no.99 (Was Gott tut, das ist wohlgetan [II]) 17'
    chorus   solos SATB
    1 0 0 0—ob d'amore—1 0 0 0—cnt—str
    Horn only used to strengthen the cantus firmus.
    Breitkopf

> 5' 1' 6'
> 1' 3' 1'

Cantata no.100 (Was Gott tut, das ist wohlgetan [III]) 23'
    chorus   solos SATB
    1 0 0 0—ob d'amore—2 0 0 0—tmp—cnt—str
    Breitkopf

> 5' 4' 4'
> 4' 4' 2'

Cantata no.101 (Nimm von uns, Herr, du treuer Gott) 25'
    chorus   solos SATB
    1 2 0 0—ob da caccia—cnt—str
    Cornetto and 3tbn doubling choral parts.
    Breitkopf

> 7' 3' 3'
> 4' 2' 5'
>   1'

Cantata no.102 (Herr, deine Augen sehen) 23'
    chorus   solos ATB
    1 2 0 0—cnt—str
    Violino piccolo may substitute for flute.
    Breitkopf   *Kalmus*

> 8' 1' 5'
> 3' 3' 1'
>   2'

Cantata no.103 (Ihr werdet weinen und heulen) 19'
    chorus   solos AT
    sopranino rec, fl, 2ob d'amore—tp—cnt—str
    A solo violin may substitute for the flute.
    Breitkopf

Cantata no.104 (Du Hirte Israel, höre) 24'
    chorus   solos TB
    0 2 0 0—ob da caccia—cnt—str
    Breitkopf   *Kalmus*   *Ricordi*

Cantata no.105 (Herr, gehe nicht ins Gericht)   25'
 chorus   solos SATB
 0 2 0 0—1 0 0 0—cnt—str
 Breitkopf   *Kalmus*

Cantata no.106 (Gottes Zeit ist die allerbeste Zeit [Actus tragicus]) 19'
 chorus   solos SATB
 2rec—cnt—2 viole da gamba
 Breitkopf   *Kalmus*

Cantata no.107 (Was willst du dich betrüben)   23'
 chorus   solos STB
 2 0 0 0—2ob d'amore—1 0 0 0—cnt—str
 Horn used only to strengthen the cantus firmus.
 Breitkopf

Cantata no.108 (Es ist euch gut, dass ich hingehe)   20'
 chorus   solos ATB
 2ob d'amore—cnt—str
 Breitkopf   *Kalmus*

Cantata no.109 (Ich glaube, lieber Herr)   26'
 chorus   solos AT
 0 2 0 0—1 0 0 0—cnt—str
 Breitkopf   *Kalmus*

Cantata no.110 (Unser Mund sei voll Lachens)   27'
 chorus   solos SATB
 2 3 0 1—0 3 0 0—tmp—cnt—str
 1st oboe doubles on oboe d'amore; 3rd doubles on oboe da caccia
 Breitkopf   *Kalmus*

Cantata no.111 (Was mein Gott will, das g'scheh allzeit)   24'
 chorus   solos SATB
 0 2 0 0—cnt—str
 Breitkopf   *Kalmus*

Cantata no.112 (Der Herr ist mein getreuer Hirt)   14'
 chorus   solos SATB
 2ob d'amore—2hn—cnt—str
 Breitkopf

Cantata no.113 (Herr Jesu Christ, du höchstes Gut)   30'
 chorus   solos SATB
 1 0 0 0—2ob d'amore—cnt—str
 Breitkopf   *Kalmus*

Cantata no.114 (Ach, lieben Christen, seid getrost)   28'
 chorus   solos SATB
 1 2 0 0—1 0 0 0—cnt—str
 Horn used only to strengthen the cantus firmus.
 Breitkopf

The boxed duration values beside each entry:

Cantata no.105: 7' 1' 7' / 2' 6' 2'

Cantata no.106: 3' 8' 6' 2'

Cantata no.109: 7' 2' 6' / 1' 6' 4'

Cantata no.110: 9' 4' 1' / 4' 4' 4' / 1'

Cantata no.112: 3' 4' 2' / 4' 1'

Cantata no.115 (Mache dich, mein Geist, bereit)   21'
chorus   solos SATB
1 0 0 0—ob d'amore—1 0 0 0—cnt—violoncello piccolo—str
                         4' 9' 1'
                         5' 1' 1'
Horn used only to strengthen the cantus firmus.
Breitkopf   *Gray*   *Kalmus*

Cantata no.116 (Du Friedefürst, Herr Jesu Christ)   18'
chorus   solos SATB
2ob d'amore—hn—cnt—str
                         6' 4' 1'
                         5' 1' 1'
Horn used only to strengthen the cantus firmus.
Breitkopf

Cantata no.117 (Sei Lob und Ehr dem höchsten Gut)   22'
chorus   solos ATB
2 2 0 0—cnt—str
                         4' 1' 3'
                         1' 2' 3'
Both oboists double on oboe d'amore.   3' 1' 4'
Breitkopf   *Kalmus*

Cantata no.118 [1st setting] (O Jesu Christ, meins Lebens Licht)   7'
chorus
2hn, cornetto, 3tbn—(no str or cnt)
Breitkopf

Cantata no.118 [2nd setting] (O Jesu Christ, meins Lebens Licht)   7'
chorus
0 2 0 1—ob da caccia—2 0 0 0—cnt—str
Bassoon is optional.
Breitkopf

Cantata no.119 (Preise, Jerusalem, den Herrn)   29'
chorus   solos SATB
2rec 3 0 0—0 4 0 0—tmp—cnt—str
Two of the oboists double on oboe da caccia.
Breitkopf

Cantata no.120 (Gott, man lobet dich in der Stille)   28'
chorus   solos SATB
0 0 0 0—2ob d'amore—0 3 0 0—tmp—cnt—str
Breitkopf

Cantata no.121 (Christum wir sollen loben schon)   20'
chorus   solos SATB
ob d'amore—cnt—str
                         4' 5' 1'
                         8' 1' 1'
Cornetto and 3tbn doubling choral parts.
Breitkopf

Cantata no.122 (Das neugeborne Kindelein)   17'
chorus   solos SATB
3rec 2 0 0—ob da caccia—cnt—str
                         4' 6' 2'
                         3' 1' 1'
Breitkopf

Cantata no.123 (Liebster Immanuel, Herzog der Frommen)   24'
chorus   solos ATB
2 0 0 0—2ob d'amore—cnt—str
Breitkopf   *Kalmus*

Cantata no.124 (Meinen Jesum lass ich nicht)   19'
chorus   solos SATB
ob d'amore—hn—cnt—str
Horn used only to strengthen the cantus firmus.
Breitkopf   *Kalmus*

Cantata no.125 (Mit Fried und Freud ich fahr dahin)   29'
chorus   solos ATB
1 1 0 0—1 0 0 0—cnt—str
Oboist doubles on oboe d'amore; horn used only to strengthen the
cantus firmus.
Breitkopf

Cantata no.126 (Erhalt uns, Herr, bei deinem Wort)   21'
chorus   solos ATB
0 2 0 0—0 1 0 0—cnt—str
Breitkopf

Cantata no.127 (Herr Jesu Christ, wahr' Mensch und Gott)   21'
chorus   solos STB
2rec 2 0 0—0 1 0 0—cnt—str
Breitkopf   *Kalmus*

Cantata no.128 (Auf Christi Himmelfahrt allein)   21'
chorus   solos ATB
0 2 0 0—ob da caccia—2 1 0 0—cnt—str
The 2 oboists double on ob d'amore.
Breitkopf   *Kalmus*

Cantata no.129 (Gelobet sei der Herr, mein Gott)   19'
chorus   solos SAB   4' 4' 4'
1 2 0 0—0 3 0 0—tmp—cnt—str   5' 2'
One oboist doubles on oboe d'amore.
Breitkopf

Cantata no.130 (Herr Gott, dich loben alle wir)   17'
chorus   solos SATB
1 3 0 0—0 3 0 0—tmp—cnt—str
Breitkopf   *Kalmus*

Cantata no.131 (Aus der Tiefe rufe ich, Herr, zu dir)   27'
chorus   solos TB
0 1 0 1—cnt—str (2 va parts; only 1 vn part)
Breitkopf   *Kalmus*

Cantata no.132 (Bereitet die Wege, bereitet die Bahn!)   20'
solos SATB   chorus in final chorale only   8' 2' 3'
0 1 0 1—cnt—str   2' 4' 1'
Bärenreiter   *Breitkopf*   *Kalmus*

Cantata no.133 (Ich freue mich in dir)   20'
chorus   solos SATB   5' 5' 1'
2ob d'amore—cornetto—cnt—str   7' 1' 1'
Cornetto used only to strengthen the cantus firmus.
Breitkopf   *Kalmus*

Cantata no.134 (Ein Herz, das seinen Jesum lebend weiss)   29'
   chorus   solos AT
   0 2 0 0—cnt—str
   Bärenreiter   *Breitkopf*   *Kalmus*

Cantata no.135 (Ach Herr, mich armen Sünder)   15'
   chorus   solos ATB

6'	1'	3'
1'	3'	1'

   0 2 0 0—cnt—str
   Cornetto and trombone used only to strengthen the cantus firmus.
   Breitkopf

Cantata no.136 (Erforsche mich, Gott)   19'
   chorus   solos ATB

4'	4'	5'
1'	4'	1'

   2ob d'amore (1 doubling on ob)—hn—cnt—str
   Breitkopf

Cantata no.137 (Lobe den Herren)   15'
   chorus   solos SATB

4'	3'	4'
	3'	1'

   0 2 0 0—0 3 0 0—tmp—cnt—str
   Breitkopf   *Kalmus*

Cantata no.138 (Warum betrübst du dich, mein Herz?)   20'
   chorus   solos SATB
   2ob d'amore—cnt—str
   Breitkopf

Cantata no.139 (Wohl dem, der sich auf seinen Gott)   20'
   chorus   solos SATB

5'	6'	1'
6'	1'	1'

   2ob d'amore—cnt—str
   Breitkopf

Cantata no.140 (Wachet auf, ruft uns die Stimme)   29'
   chorus   solos STB

6'	1'	6'
4'	2'	8'
		2'

   0 2 0 1—ob da caccia—1 0 0 0—cnt—violino piccolo—str
   A critical edition of the score with historical and analytical
   essays is available from Norton.
   Boosey   *Breitkopf*   *Kalmus*

Cantata no.141 (Das ist je gewisslich wahr)   10'
   chorus   solos ATB
   0 2 0 0—cnt—str
   Wrongly attributed to Bach; actual composer is G. P. Telemann.
   Breitkopf

Cantata no.142 (Uns ist ein Kind geboren)   13'
   chorus   solos ATB

2'	2'	2'
1'	2'	1'
2'	1'	

   2rec 2 0 0—cnt—str
   Actual composer believed to be Johann Kuhnau.
   Breitkopf   *Galaxy*   *Kalmus*

Cantata no.143 (Lobe den Herrn, meine Seele [II])   14'
   chorus   solos STB

1'	2'	1'
4'	2'	2'
		2'

   0 0 0 1—3 0 0 0—tmp—cnt—str
   Breitkopf

Cantata no.144 (Nimm, was dein ist, und gehe hin)   16'
chorus   solos SAT
0 2 0 0—cnt—str
One oboist doubles on oboe d'amore.
Breitkopf   *Kalmus*

Cantata no.145 (Auf, mein Herz, des Herren Tag)   9'
chorus   solos STB   3' 1' 3'
1 0 0 0—2ob d'amore—0 1 0 0—cnt—str   1' 1'
Oboe d'amore parts are playable on oboe. The second movement
is actually by Telemann.
Breitkopf

Cantata no.146 (Wir müssen durch viel Trübsal)   40'
chorus   solos SATB
1 2 0 0—ob da caccia—org—str
Both oboists double on ob d'amore.
Breitkopf   *Kalmus*

Cantata no.147 (Herz und Mund und Tat und Leben)   28'
chorus   solos SATB   4' 2' 4'
0 2 0 1—0 1 0 0—cnt—str   2' 4' 2'
Both oboists double on oboe da caccia; one also doubles on oboe   3' 2' 3'
d'amore.   2'
The well-known *Jesu, joy of man's desiring*, for chorus, oboe,
strings and continuo, appears twice in this cantata: the sixth
movement (*Wohl mir, dass ich Jesum habe*), and the tenth and final
movement, with identical music but a different text (*Jesu bleibet
meine Freude*).
Breitkopf   *Kalmus*

Cantata no.148 (Bringet dem Herrn Ehre seines Namens)   19'
chorus   solos AT   4' 5' 2'
0 3 0 0—0 1 0 0—cnt—str   6' 1' 1'
3rd oboe part perhaps intended for oboe da caccia.
Breitkopf   *Kalmus*

Cantata no.149 (Man singet mit Freuden)   18'
chorus   solos SATB   4' 2' 1'
0 3 0 1—0 3 0 0—tmp—cnt—str   5' 1' 3'
Breitkopf   *Gray*   *Kalmus*   2'

Cantata no.150 (Nach dir, Herr, verlanget mich)   19'
chorus   solos SATB
0 0 0 1—cnt—str   (without va)
Breitkopf   *Kalmus*

Cantata no.151 (Süsser Trost, mein Jesus kömmt)   19'
solos SATB   chorus in final chorale only   10' 2' 5'
1 0 0 0—ob d'amore—cnt—str   1' 1'
Breitkopf   *Kalmus*

Cantata no.152 (Tritt auf die Glaubensbahn)   20'
   solos SB

   1rec 1 0 0—cnt—va d'amore, va da gamba
   Breitkopf   *Kalmus*

| 4' 3' 2' |
| 4' 2' 5' |

Cantata no.153 (Schau, lieber Gott, wie meine Feind)   18'
   solos ATB   chorus in three chorales only
   cnt—str
   Breitkopf

Cantata no.154 (Mein liebster Jesus ist verloren)   19'
   solos ATB   chorus in two chorales only
   2ob d'amore—cnt—str
   Breitkopf   *Kalmus*

Cantata no.155 (Mein Gott, wie lang, ach lange)   14'
   solos SATB   chorus in final chorale only
   0 0 0 1—cnt—str
   Breitkopf   *Kalmus*

Cantata no.156 (Ich steh mit einem Fuss im Grabe)   19'
   solos ATB   chorus only in final chorale and one soprano
   cantus firmus
   0 1 0 0—cnt—str
   Breitkopf   *Kalmus*

Cantata no.157 (Ich lasse dich nicht)   23'
   solos TB   chorus in final chorale only
   1 0 0 0—ob d'amore—cnt—str
   Breitkopf

Cantata no.158 (Der Friede sei mit dir)   14'
   bass solo   chorus only in final chorale and one soprano cantus
   firmus
   ob (used only to strengthen the cantus firmus)—cnt—vn
   Breitkopf   *Kalmus*

Cantata no.159 (Sehet, wir gehn hinauf gen Jerusalem)   16'
   solos ATB   chorus only in final chorale and one soprano
   cantus firmus
   0 1 0 1—cnt—str
   Breitkopf   *Kalmus*

Cantata no.160 (Ich weiss, dass mein Erlöser lebt)   15'
   tenor solo   vn, bn, cnt
   Wrongly attributed to Bach; actual composer is Telemann.
   Breitkopf   *Kalmus*

Cantata no.161 (Komm, du süsse Todesstunde)   22'
   chorus   solos AT
   2rec—org—str
   Breitkopf   *Kalmus*

Cantata no.162 (Ach, ich sehe, jetzt)   17'
   solos SATB   chorus in final chorale only
   0 0 0 1—1 0 0 0—cnt—str

| 4' 2' 3' |
| 2' 5' 1' |

Breitkopf

Cantata no.163 (Nur jedem das Seine)   18'
   solos SATB   chorus in final chorale only
   ob d'amore—cnt—str

| 5' 2' 4' |
| 3' 3' 1' |

Breitkopf

Cantata no.164 (Ihr, die ihr euch von Christo nennet)   19'
   solos SATB   chorus in final chorale only
   2 2 0 0—cnt—str
Breitkopf   *Kalmus*

Cantata no.165 (O heilges Geist- und Wasserbad)   18'
   solos SATB   chorus in final chorale only
   0 0 0 1—cnt—str
Breitkopf

Cantata no.166 (Wo gehest du hin?)   18'
   solos ATB   chorus in final chorale and one soprano cantus
   firmus only
   0 1 0 0—cnt—str
Bärenreiter   *Breitkopf*   *Kalmus*

Cantata no.167 (Ihr Menschen, rühmet Gottes Liebe)   17'
   solos SATB   chorus in final chorale only
   0 1 0 0—0 1 0 0—cnt—str

| 4' 2' 7' |
| 1' 3' |

   Oboist doubles on ob d'amore; trumpet used only to strengthen the
   cantus firmus.
Breitkopf

Cantata no.168 (Tue Rechnung! Donnerwort)   16'
   solos SATB   chorus in final chorale only
   2ob d'amore—cnt—str

| 4' 2' 4' |
| 2' 3' 1' |

Breitkopf   *Kalmus*

Cantata no.169 (Gott soll allein mein Herze haben)   29'
   solo alto   chorus in final chorale only
   2ob d'amore, ob da caccia—org—str
Breitkopf   *Kalmus*

Cantata no.170 (Vergnügte Ruh, beliebte Seelenlust)   24'
   alto solo
   ob d'amore—org—str

| 6' 2' 7' |
| 2' 7' |

   Flute may be used in one movement.
Breitkopf   *Kalmus*

Cantata no.171 (Gott, wie dein Name)   21'
   chorus   solos SATB
   0 2 0 0—0 3 0 0—tmp—cnt—str
Breitkopf

Cantata no.172 [1724 version—D major] (Erschallet, ihr Lieder)   25'
chorus   solos SATB
1 *1 0 1—0 3 0 0—tmp—cnt—str
As yet unpublished.

Cantata no.172 [1731 version—C major] (Erschallet, ihr Lieder)   16'
chorus   solos SATB
0 0 0 1—0 3 0 0—tmp—org—str
An oboe can substitute for organ in one movement.
Bärenreiter   *Breitkopf*   *Kalmus*

4'	1'	2'
5'	3'	1'

Cantata no.173 (Erhöhtes Fleisch und Blut)   20'
chorus   solos SATB
2 0 0 0—cnt—str
Breitkopf

1'	4'	2'
4'	1'	4'
2'	2'	

Cantata no.174 (Ich liebe den Höchsten)   21'
solos ATB   chorus in final chorale only
0 2 0 1—ob da caccia—2 0 0 0—cnt—str
The Sinfonia to this cantata is identical to the 1st movement of
Brandenburg Concerto No.3.
Breitkopf

6'	8'	2'
4'	1'	

Cantata no.175 (Er rufet seinen Schafen mit Namen)   16'
solos ATB   chorus in final chorale only
3rec 0 0 0—0 2 0 0—cnt—violoncello piccolo—str
Breitkopf

1'	4'	1'
3'	1'	4'
2'		

Cantata no.176 (Es ist ein trotzig und verzagt Ding)   14'
chorus   solos SAB
0 2 0 0—ob da caccia—cnt—str
Bärenreiter   *Breitkopf*   *Kalmus*

3'	1'	3'
2'	3'	2'

Cantata no.177 (Ich ruf zu dir, Herr Jesu Christ)   27'
chorus   solos SAT
0 2 0 1—cnt—str
One oboist doubles on oboe da caccia
Breitkopf

7'	7'	6'
5'	2'	

Cantata no.178 (Wo Gott, der Herr, nicht bei uns hält)   23'
chorus   solos ATB
0 2 0 0—1 0 0 0—cnt—str
Both oboists double on oboe d'amore. Horn used only to
strengthen the cantus firmus.
Breitkopf   *Kalmus*

5'	3'	4'
3'	2'	4'
2'		

Cantata no.179 (Siehe zu, dass deine Gottesfurcht)   17'
chorus   solos STB
0 2 0 0—cnt—str
Both oboists double on oboe da caccia.
Breitkopf

Cantata no.180 (Schmücke dich, o liebe Seele)   23'
   chorus   solos SATB   6' 6' 3'2'
   2rec 1 0 0—ob da caccia—cnt—violoncello piccolo—str   4' 1' 1'
   One recorder player doubles on flute.
   Breitkopf   *Gray*   *Kalmus*

Cantata no.181 (Leichtgesinnte Flattergeister)   15'
   chorus   solos SATB
   1 1 0 0—0 1 0 0—cnt—str
   Breitkopf

Cantata no.182 (Himmelskönig, sei willkommen)   30'
   chorus   solos ATB
   1rec—cnt—str
   Breitkopf   *Kalmus*

Cantata no.183 (Sie werden euch in den Bann tun [II])   14'
   solos SATB   chorus in final chorale only   1' 7' 1'
   2ob d'amore, 2ob da caccia—cnt—violoncello piccolo—str   4' 1'
   The oboe d'amore parts are playable on oboe.
   Breitkopf   *Kalmus*

Cantata no.184 (Erwünschtes Freudenlicht)   23'
   chorus   solos SAT   3' 9' 2'
   2 0 0 0—cnt—str   5' 1' 3'
   Breitkopf

Cantata no.185 (Barmherziges Herze der ewigen Liebe)   16'
   solos SATB   chorus in final chorale only   4' 3' 4'
   0 1 0 1—cnt—str   1' 3' 1'
   Trumpet may be used in two movements.
   Breitkopf   *Kalmus*

Cantata no.186 (Ärgre dich, o Seele, nicht)   38'
   chorus   solos SATB
   0 2 0 1—ob da caccia—cnt—str
   Breitkopf   *Kalmus*

Cantata no.187 (Es wartet alles auf dich)   23'
   chorus   solos SAB   7' 1' 4'
   0 2 0 0—cnt—str   3' 4' 2'
   Breitkopf   *Kalmus*   2'

Cantata no.188 (Ich habe meine Zuversicht)   20'
   solos SATB   chorus in final chorale only
   0 1 0 0—org—str
   The sinfonia of Cantata no.146 is believed to belong with this
   work also, in which case a 2nd oboe and an oboe da caccia are
   required, and the duration is 29'.
   Breitkopf

Cantata no.189 (Meine Seele rühmt und preist)   20'
solo tenor   rec, ob, vn, cnt
Wrongly attributed to Bach; the actual composer is Georg
Melchior Hoffmann.
Breitkopf   *Kalmus*

Cantata no.190 (Singet dem Herrn ein neues Lied!)   17'
chorus   solos ATB
0 3 0 1—0 3 0 0—tmp—cnt—str
One oboist doubles on oboe d'amore. Portions of the first two
movements were lost and have been reconstructed.
Breitkopf

Cantata no.191 (Gloria in excelsis Deo)   19'
chorus   solos ST
2 2 0 0—0 3 0 0—tmp—cnt—str
Breitkopf   *Schirmer, G.*   *Kalmus*

Cantata no.192 (Nun danket alle Gott)   15'
chorus   solos SB
2 2 0 0—cnt—str
The tenor part of the chorus is lost and has been reconstructed.
Breitkopf   *Kalmus*

Cantata no.193 (Ihr Tore [Pforten] zu Zion)   16'
chorus   solos SA
0 2 0 0—cnt—str
Certain missing parts have been reconstructed. The original
orchestra may have included 2 trumpets and timpani.
Breitkopf

Cantata no.194 (Höchsterwünschtes Freudenfest)   40'
chorus   solos STB
0 3 0 1—cnt—str
Breitkopf

Cantata no.195 (Dem Gerechten muss das Licht)   30'
chorus   solos SB
2 2 0 0—2 3 0 0—tmp—cnt—str
Both oboists double on oboe d'amore.
Breitkopf   *Kalmus*

Cantata no.196 (Der Herr Denket an uns)   17'
chorus   solos STB
cnt—str
Breitkopf   *Kalmus*

Cantata no.197 (Gott ist unsre Zuversicht)   40'
chorus   solos SAB
0 2 0 1—0 3 0 0—tmp—cnt—str
Both oboists double on oboe d'amore.
Breitkopf

Cantata no.198 (Lass, Fürstin, lass noch einen Strahl) 31'
  chorus   solos SATB
  2 0 0 0—2 ob d'amore—org, hpsd, 2 lutes—2va da gamba—str
  Breitkopf   *Kalmus*

| 5' 1' 4' |
| 1' 7' 1' |
| 2' 4' 2' |
| 4' |

Cantata no.199 (Mein Herze schwimmt im Blut) 26'
  soprano solo
  0 1 0 1—cnt—str
  Breitkopf   *Kalmus*

Cantata no.200 (Bekennen will ich seinen Namen) 5'
  alto solo
  cnt—str
  Only one aria surviving from an otherwise lost cantata. Peters
  lists two versions not as a cantata, but as an aria:
    Catalog no. 4209: Bekennen will ich seinen Namen (ed.
  Landshoff)
    Catalog no. 66032: With joyful heart I praise my Saviour
  Peters

Cantata no.201 (Der Streit zwischen Phoebus und Pan) 52'
  chorus   solos SATTBB
  2 2 0 0—0 3 0 0—tmp—cnt—str
  One oboist doubles on oboe d'amore.
  Breitkopf   *Kalmus*

Cantata no.202 (Weichet nur, betrübte Schatten) 22'
  soprano solo
  0 1 0 0—cnt—str
  Breitkopf   *Kalmus*   *Peters*

Cantata no.203 (Amore traditore) 15'
  bass solo   hpsd
  Of doubtful authenticity.
  Breitkopf

Cantata no.204 (Ich bin in mir vergnügt) 30'
  solo soprano
  1 2 0 0—cnt—str
  Breitkopf

| 2' 7' 2' |
| 4' 2' 6' |
| 3' 4' |

Cantata no.205 (Der zufriedengestellte Äolus) 43'
  chorus   solos SATB
  2 2 0 0—2 3 0 0—tmp—cnt—va d'amore, va da gamba—str
  One oboist doubles on oboe d'amore.
  Breitkopf   *Kalmus*

Cantata no.206 (Schleicht, spielende Wellen) 43'
  chorus   solos SATB
  3 2 0 0—0 3 0 0—tmp—cnt—str
  Both oboists double on oboe d'amore.
  Breitkopf   *Kalmus*

Cantata no.207 (Vereinigte Zwietracht der wechselnden Saiten)   32'
chorus   solos SATB
2 0 0 0—2ob d'amore, ob da caccia—0 3 0 0—tmp—cnt—str
Cantatas 207 and 207a are the same, except for text and
recitatives.
Kalmus

Cantata no.207a (Auf, schmetternde Töne)   31'
chorus   solos SATB
2 0 0 0—2ob d'amore, ob da caccia—0 3 0 0—tmp—cnt—str
Cantatas 207 and 207a are the same, except for text and
recitatives.
Breitkopf

Cantata no.208 (Was mir behagt)   38'
chorus   solos SSTB
2rec 2 0 1—ob da caccia—2 0 0 0—cnt—str
The well-known aria *Sheep may safely graze* for soprano, 2
recorders & continuo, is movement 9 of this cantata.
Bärenreiter   *Breitkopf*   *Kalmus*

Cantata no.209 (Non sa che sia dolore)   22'
soprano solo
1 0 0 0—cnt—str
Breitkopf   *Kalmus*

Cantata no.210 (O holder Tag, erwünschte Zeit)   32'
soprano solo
1 0 0 0—ob d'amore—cnt—str
Breitkopf

1'	7'	1'
6'	2'	4'
2'	3'	1'
	5'	

Cantata no.211 (Coffee cantata (Schweigt stille))   26'
solos STB   optional chorus (STB) in last movement
1 0 0 0—cnt—str
Breitkopf   *Kalmus*   *Ricordi*

1'	3'	1'
4'	1'	3'
1'	7'	1'
	4'	

Cantata no.212 (Peasant cantata [Mer hahn en neue Oberkeet])   30'
solos SB
1 0 0 0—1 0 0 0—cnt—str
Breitkopf   *Kalmus*   *Peters*

Cantata no.213 (Hercules auf dem Scheidewege)   45'
chorus   solos SATB
0 2 0 0—2 0 0 0—cnt—str
One oboist doubles on oboe d'amore.
Breitkopf

Cantata no.214 (Tönet, ihr Pauken! Erschallet, Trompeten!)   27'
chorus   solos SATB
2 2 0 0—0 3 0 0—tmp—cnt—str
One oboist doubles on oboe d'amore.
Breitkopf   *Kalmus*

Cantata no.215 (Preise dein Glücke, gesegnetes Sachsen)   37'
    double chorus   solos STB
    2 2 0 1—0 3 0 0—tmp—cnt—str
    Both oboists double on oboe d'amore.
    Broude, A.

Chorale-variations on "Vom Himmel hoch"
see under: Stravinsky, Igor

Christmas oratorio
see his: Weihnachtsoratorium

Concerto, flute, violin & harpsichord, BWV 1044, A minor   22'
    str   9' 6' 7'
    Breitkopf   *Kalmus*   *Peters*

Concerto, harpsichord, no.1, BWV 1052, D minor   24'
    str   8' 9' 7'
    Breitkopf   *Kalmus*   *Peters*

Concerto, harpsichord, no.2, BWV 1053, E major   19'
    str   8' 5' 6'
    Breitkopf   *Kalmus*   *Peters*

Concerto, harpsichord, no.3, BWV 1054, D major   16'
    str   7' 6' 3'
    Breitkopf   *Kalmus*   *Peters*

Concerto, harpsichord, no.4, BWV 1055, A major   14'
    str   5' 5' 4'
    Breitkopf   *Kalmus*   *Peters*

Concerto, harpsichord, no.5, BWV 1056, F minor   10'
    str   3' 3' 4'
    Breitkopf   *Kalmus*   *Peters*

Concerto, harpsichord, no.6, BWV 1057, F major   17'
    2rec—str   7' 5' 5'
    An arrangement by the composer of his Brandenburg concerto
    no.4.
    Breitkopf   *Peters*

Concerto, harpsichord, no.7, BWV 1058, G minor   14'
    str   4' 6' 4'
    Breitkopf   *Kalmus*   *Peters*

Concerto, 2 harpsichords, no.1, BWV 1060, C minor   14'
    str   5' 5' 4'
    Breitkopf   *Kalmus*   *Peters*

Concerto, 2 harpsichords, no.2, BWV 1061, C major   17'
    str   7' 4' 6'
    Breitkopf   *Kalmus*   *Peters*

Concerto, 2 harpsichords, no.3, BWV 1062, C minor   15'
    str   4' 6' 5'
    Breitkopf   *Kalmus*

Concerto, 3 harpsichords, no.1, BWV 1063, D minor   16'
str
Breitkopf   *Kalmus*   *Peters*   6' 5' 5'

Concerto, 3 harpsichords, no.2, BWV 1064, C major   18'
str
Breitkopf   *Kalmus*   *Peters*   7' 6' 5'

Concerto, 4 harpsichords, BWV 1065, A minor   10'
str
Breitkopf   *Kalmus*   *Peters*   4' 3' 3'

Concerto, violin, no.1, BWV 1041, A minor   15'
cnt—str
Breitkopf   *Kalmus*   *Peters*   4' 7' 4'

Concerto, violin, no.2, BWV 1042, E major   19'
cnt—str
Breitkopf   *Kalmus*   *Peters*   9' 7' 3'

Concerto, 2 violins, BWV 1043, D minor   17'
cnt—str
Breitkopf   *Kalmus*   *Peters*   4' 7' 6'

Concerto, violin & oboe, BWV 1060   17'
cnt—str   5' 8' 4'
A reconstruction of what is believed to have been the original
version of the Concerto no.1 for two harpsichords (BWV 1060).
The Bärenreiter edition is in C minor; the Breitkopf has been
transposed to D minor.
Bärenreiter   *Breitkopf*

Easter oratorio, BWV 249 (Oster-Oratorium)   52'
chorus   solos SATB
2rec 2 0 1—0 3 0 0—tmp—cnt—str
One recorder doubles on optional flute; one oboist doubles on
oboe d'amore.
Breitkopf   *Kalmus*   *Schott*

Jesu, joy of man's desiring (from Cantata no.147)   3'
2 2 2 2—4 3 3 1—str
Arr. Arthur Luck; chorus may substitute for brass.
Luck

Johannespassion, BWV 245 (St. John passion)   134'
chorus   solos SATBB   42' 92'
2 2 0 1—org, lute—2va d'amore, va da gamba—str
Both oboists double on oboe da caccia; one also doubles on oboe
d'amore.
Breitkopf   *Kalmus*   *Peters*

Komm, Gott, Schöpfer, heiliger Geist, BWV 631   5'
*4 *4 =6 *4—4 4 4 1—tmp+2—2hp—str
Orchestrated by Arnold Schoenberg.
Universal

Komm süsser Tod   4'
     3 *3 *1 *2—4 3 4 1—tmp—hp—str
     Arr. Leopold Stokowski.
     Broude Bros.

Magnificat, BWV 243   30'
     chorus   solos SSATB
     2 2 0 1—0 3 0 0—tmp—cnt—str
     Both oboists double on oboe d'amore.
     Bärenreiter   *Kalmus*   *Peters*

Mass, BWV 232, B minor   120'
     chorus   solos SSATB   22' 40'
     2 3 0 2—1 3 0 0—tmp—cnt—str   34' 16'
     Two of the oboists double on oboe d'amore.   8'
     Bärenreiter   *Breitkopf*   *Kalmus*   *Peters*

Mass, BWV 233, F major (Lutheran mass no.1)   29'
     chorus   solos SAB   5' 7' 4'
     0 2 0 2—2 0 0 0—cnt—str   5' 5' 3'
     One real bassoon part, but designated in the plural: *Fagotti.*
     Breitkopf   *Kalmus*   *Peters*

Mass, BWV 234, A major (Lutheran mass no.2)   37'
     chorus   solos SAB   9' 6' 7'
     2 0 0 0—cnt—str   7' 4' 4'
     Breitkopf   *Kalmus*   *Peters*

Mass, BWV 235, G minor (Lutheran mass no.3)   33'
     chorus   solos ATB   8' 4' 4'
     0 2 0 0—cnt—str   6' 5' 6'
     Breitkopf   *Kalmus*   *Peters*

Mass, BWV 236, G major (Lutheran mass no.4)   32'
     chorus   solos SATB   4' 5' 6'
     0 2 0 0—cnt—str   5' 7' 5'
     Breitkopf   *Gray*   *Kalmus*   *Peters*

Matthäuspassion, BWV 244 (St. Matthew passion)   131'
     double chorus   solos SATBB   semi-chorus of sopranos (boys)   61' 70'
     4 4 0 0—org—va da gamba—str
     Double orchestra. All four oboists double on oboe d'amore; two
     also double on oboe da caccia. Two flutists double on recorder in
     one movement; probably the 2 recorder parts were originally
     intended for 6 players or so, perhaps covered by some of the
     violinists not otherwise occupied in that particular movement.
     Bärenreiter   *Breitkopf*   *Kalmus*   *Peters*

Musikalisches Opfer, BWV 1079 (Musical offering)   47'
     1 *2 0 1—ob d'amore (or 3rd ob)—cnt—str   6' 6' 18'
     Ed. Landshoff.   10' 7'
     Kalmus   *Peters*

Musikalisches Opfer (Musical offering): Ricercare (arr. Anton   8'
Webern)
   1 *2 *2 1—1 1 1 0—tmp—hp—str
Universal

Passacaglia, BWV 582   13'
   =4 *4 *4 *4—8 4 4 2—tmp—str
   Arr. Leopold Stokowski. May be performed with winds:
   *3 *3 *3 *3—4 3 3 1.
   Broude Bros.

Prelude & fugue, BWV 552, E-flat major (St. Anne)   16'
   *4 *4 =6 *4—4 4 4 1—tmp+2—hp, cel—str
   Orchestrated by Arnold Schoenberg. Publisher offers also a
   reduced version by Erwin Stein with woodwinds 4 3 4 3.
   Universal

Saint John passion
   see his: Johannespassion

Saint Matthew passion
   see his: Matthäuspassion

Schmücke dich, o liebe Seele, BWV 654   2'
   *4 *4 =6 *4—4 4 4 1—tmp+2—hp, cel—str
   Orchestrated by Arnold Schoenberg.
   Universal

Sheep may safely graze (from Cantata no.208)   5'
   *3 *3 *3 *3—4 3 3 1—tmp—hp—str
   Arr. Lucien Cailliet. Eh, bcl, cbn, hp are optional.
   Boosey

Suite (Overture) no.1, BWV 1066, C major   21'
   0 2 0 1—cnt—str

		6' 2' 3'
Breitkopf	*Kalmus*	*Peters*	2' 3' 3'
			2'

Suite (Overture) no.2, BWV 1067, B minor   20'
   solo flute

		7' 2' 3'
cnt—str			2' 3' 1'
Breitkopf	*Kalmus*	*Peters*	2'

Suite (Overture) no.3, BWV 1068, D major   20'
   0 2 0 0—0 3 0 0—tmp—cnt—str

		7' 5' 4'
Breitkopf	*Kalmus*	*Peters*	1' 3'

Suite (Overture) no.4, BWV 1069, D major   19'
   0 3 0 1—0 3 0 0—tmp—cnt—str

		10' 3' 2'
Breitkopf	*Kalmus*	*Peters*	2' 2'

Toccata & fugue, BWV 565, D minor   9'
   4 *4 *4 *4—6 3 4 1—tmp—2hp, cel—str
   Arr. Leopold Stokowski. May be performed with winds:
   4 *3 *3 *3—4 3 3 1.
   Broude Bros.

Weihnachtsoratorium, BWV 248 (Christmas oratorio)   165'
  chorus   solos SATB
  2 4 0 1—2 3 0 0—tmp—cnt—str
  Two of the oboists double on oboe d'amore; the other two on
  oboe da caccia. A series of six cantatas.
  Bärenreiter   *Breitkopf*   *Kalmus*   *Peters*

```
28' 33'
26' 27'
26' 25'
```

Bach, Wilhelm Friedemann   1710 - 1784

Ehre sei Gott in der Höhe (Christmas cantata)
  chorus   solos STB
  0 0 0 0—2 0 0 0—cnt—str
  Vieweg

Sinfonia, D minor   9'
  2fl—str
  Ed. Bernhard Päuler.
  Eulenburg   *Kalmus*

Sinfonia, F major   12'
  cnt—str
  Breitkopf   *Luck*   *Schott*

```
4' 3' 3' 2'
```

Bacon, Ernst   1898 - 1990

The muffin man   4'
  *2 2 2 2—4 3 3 1—tmp+3—cel—str
  Schirmer, G.

Badings, Henk   1907 - 1987

Concerto, harp   21'
  2 2 *2 2—4 2 2 0—tmp+2—cel—str
  Donemus

Concerto, piano (1940)   27'
  *2 2 *3 2—4 3 3 1—tmp+3—cel—str
  Tuba is optional.
  Donemus

Baermann, Heinrich Joseph   1784 - 1847

Adagio, clarinet & strings, D-flat major   4'
  str
  Previously attributed to Richard Wagner and published under
  that composer's name by Kalmus.
  Breitkopf

Baker, David   1931 -

Le Chat qui pêche 28'
soliists: soprano voice and jazz quartet (alto/tenor saxophone;
acoustic/electric piano; acoustic/electric bass; drums)
*3 *3 *3 *3—4 3 3 1—tmp+3—hp—str
Contents—Soleil d'Altamira; L'Odeur du blues; Sons voiles;
Guadeloupe calypso; Le Miroir noir.
AMP

5' 6' 8'
4' 5'

Concerto, violoncello 17'
1 1 1 1—2 0 0 0—tmp+1—str (without vc)
AMP

6' 6' 5'

Kosbro 13'
*3 *3 *3 *3—4 3 3 1—tmp+4—pf—str
Schirmer, G.

Balakirev, Mily   1837 - 1910

Islamey (arr. Alfredo Casella) 9'
*4 *3 +3 *4—4 4 3 1—tmp+6—2hp—str
MCA   *Simrock*

Islamey (arr. Sergei Liapounow) 9'
*4 *2 +3 2—4 4 3 1—tmp+5—2hp—str
Russian

King Lear: Incidental music 35'
*3 *2 3 2—4 2 3 1—tmp—hp—str
Also band on stage: *6 4 4 4—4 2 3 1—4perc. Score has a version
(incorporating the music of the stage band into that of the main
orchestra) for the following forces: *3 *2 3 2—4 4 3
1—tmp+4—hp—str.
This work may be out of print, but materials are in the Fleisher
Collection. Original publisher was Zimmermann, Leipzig.

Overture on three Russian folk songs 8'
2 2 2 2—2 2 3 0—tmp—str
Optional bass drum and cymbals (2 additional players).
Russian   *Simrock*

Russia 15'
3 2 2 2—4 2 3 1—tmp+4—2hp—str
Kalmus

Symphony no.1, C major 45'
*3 *2 3 2—4 2 3 1—tmp+5—2hp (doubling a single part)—str
Kalmus

14' 8'
14' 9'

Symphony no.2, D minor 37'
*3 *2 3 2—4 2 3 1—tmp+5—hp—str
Kalmus

10' 9' 9'
9'

Thamar   20'
  3 *2 3 2—4 2 3 1—tmp+6—2hp—str
  Breitkopf   *Kalmus*

Balassa, Sándor   1935 -

Cantata Y, op.21   10'
  solo soprano
  3 2 3 2—3 2 3 0—tmp+5—cel, pf—str 12.12.8.6.4
  EMB

Bamert, Matthias   1942 -

Circus parade   12'
  narrator (may be the conductor)
  *2 2 *2 2—4 2 2 0—tmp+2—hp, pf—str
  EAM

Once upon an orchestra   50'
  narrator
  *3 *3 *3 *3—4 3 3 1—tmp+3—hp—str
  May be danced or mimed. Excerpts suitable for concert
  performance without narrator.
  EAM

Snapshots   15'
  *3 *3 *3 *3—4 3 3 1—tmp+3—hp, pf—str
  13 short movements with humorous titles.
  EAM

Barber, Samuel   1910 - 1981

Adagio for strings   8'
  str
  Schirmer, G.

Andromache's farewell, op.39   12'
  soprano solo
  *3 *3 *3 2—4 3 3 1—tmp+3—hp, cel—str
  Schirmer, G.

Capricorn concerto   15'
  solo flute, oboe, & trumpet   7' 3' 5'
  str
  Schirmer, G.

Commando march (orchestra version)   8'
  *3 *3 =4 *3—4 3 3 1—tmp+3—str
  Originally for band.
  Schirmer, G.

Concerto, piano, op.38   26'
  *3 *3 *3 2—4 3 3 0—tmp+2—hp—str   13' 7' 6'
  Schirmer, G.

Concerto, violin, op.14   25'
    2 2 2 2—2 2 0 0—tmp+1—pf—str
    Schirmer, G.   12' 9' 4'

Concerto, violoncello, op.22   27'
    2 *2 *2 2—2 3 0 0—tmp+1—str
    Schirmer, G.   12' 7' 8'

Die natali, op.37; chorale preludes for Christmas   16'
    *3 *3 *3 2—4 3 3 1—tmp+4—hp, cel—str
    Schirmer, G.

Die natali: Silent night   3'
    1 *2 *3 0—4 0 3 1—hp, cel—str
    Cued to be playable with winds: 1 1 2 1—2 0 1 0.
    Schirmer, G.

Essay no.1, op.12   8'
    2 2 2 2—4 3 3 1—tmp—pf—str
    Schirmer, G.

Essay no.2, op.17   10'
    *3 *3 *2 2—4 3 3 1—tmp+2—str
    Schirmer, G.

Essay no.3, op.47   14'
    *3 *3 =4 *3—4 3 3 1—euphonium—2tmp+5—2hp, pf—str
    Euphonium part is cued in other instruments.
    Schirmer, G.

Fadograph of a yestern scene, op.44   7'
    *3 *3 *3 2—4 3 3 1—tmp+1—1 or 2hp, cel, pf—str
    Schirmer, G.

Knoxville: summer of 1915, op.24   16'
    solo soprano
    *1 *1 1 1—2 1 0 0—1perc—hp—str
    Schirmer, G.

Medea, op.23 (ballet suite)   27'
    *2 *2 2 2—2 2 2 0—tmp+3—hp, pf—str
    Schirmer, G.   3' 5' 3'
                                                     3' 7' 3'
                                                         3'

Medea's meditation and dance of vengeance, op.23a   13'
    *3 *3 =4 *3—4 3 3 1—tmp+4—hp, pf—str
    Schirmer, G.

Music for a scene from Shelley, op.7   8'
    3 *3 *3 3—4 3 3 1—tmp+1—hp—str
    Schirmer, G.

Night flight, op.19a   8'
*3 *3 =4 2—4 3 3 1—1perc—pf—str
An "electric instrument", imitating a signal or radio beam, may
substitute for the E-flat clarinet. This work is a revised version
of a movement from the composer's Symphony no.2.
Schirmer, G.

Overture to The school for scandal   8'
*3 *3 *3 2—4 3 3 1—tmp+3—hp, cel—str
Schirmer, G.

Prayers of Kierkegaard, op.30   20'
chorus, solos ST
*3 *3 *3 2—4 3 3 1—tmp+4—hp, pf—str
Schirmer, G.

Souvenirs, op.28   18'
*2 *2 2 2—4 3 3 0—tmp+3—hp, cel—str
Schirmer, G.

Symphony no.1 in one movement, op.9   19'
*3 *3 *3 *3—4 3 3 1—tmp+1—hp—str
Schirmer, G.

Symphony no.2, op.19   26'
*3 *3 =4 *3—4 3 3 1—tmp+2—pf—str   10' 7' 9'
Schirmer, G.

Toccata festiva, op.36   14'
solo organ
*3 *3 *3 2—4 3 3 1—tmp+4—str
Alternate version: organ solo, trumpet, timpani, strings.
Schirmer, G.

Vanessa: Intermezzo   4'
*3 *3 *3 2—4 2 3 1—tmp+1—hp—str
Schirmer, G.

Vanessa: Under the willow tree (Country dance)   4'
optional mixed chorus
*3 *3 *3 2—4 2 3 0—tmp+3—hp—str
Schirmer, G.

Barbirolli, John   1899 - 1970

An Elizabethan suite   12'
4hn (in last movement only)—str
Arr. by Barbirolli from the following keyboard works: Byrd,
The Earle of Salisbury's pavane; Anon., *The Irishe ho hoane*;
Farnaby, *A toye*; Farnaby, *Giles Farnaby's dreame*; Bull, *The
King's hunt.*
Oxford

Barlow, Wayne   1912 -

Rhapsody for oboe (The winter's past)   5'
   solo oboe
   str
   C. Fischer

Bartók, Béla   1881 - 1945

Cantata profana   18'
   double chorus   solo tenor & baritone | 7' 8' 3' |
   *3 3 *3 *3—4 2 3 1—tmp+2—hp—str
   Boosey

Concerto for orchestra   36'
   *3 *3 *3 *3—4 3 3 1—tmp+1—2hp—str | 10' 6' 7' |
   A 2nd percussionist is required if alternate ending is used. | 4' 9' |
   Boosey

Concerto, piano, no.1   25'
   *2 *2 *2 2—4 2 3 0—tmp+3—str | 9' 9' 7' |
   Boosey

Concerto, piano, no.2   28'
   *3 2 2 *3—4 3 3 1—tmp+2—str | 10' 12' |
   Boosey | 6' |

Concerto, piano, no.3   23'
   *2 2 2 2—4 2 3 1—tmp+1—str | 7' 9' 7' |
   Revised edition from Boosey includes minor modifications of
   Bartok's that were not incorporated into the first published
   score, as well as modifications to the last 17 bars (which were
   orchestrated by Tibor Serly after Bartok's death).
   Boosey

Concerto, 2 pianos and percussion   25'
   *2 *2 2 *2—4 2 3 0—cel—str | 12' 6' 7' |
   This work is the orchestral version of the *Sonata for two pianos
   and percussion*; 2 percussion soloists are required.
   Boosey

Concerto, viola, op. posth.   21'
   *3 2 2 2—3 3 2 1—tmp+2—str | 11' 6' 4' |
   Completed by Tibor Serly. New edition by Peter Bartok, Nelson
   Dellamaggiore & Paul Neubauer in preparation.
   Boosey

Concerto, violin, no.1 (1907-8), op. posth.   21'
   *2 *3 *2 2—4 2 2 1—tmp+1—2hp—str | 9' 12' |
   Boosey

Concerto, violin, no.2 (1938)   36'
   *2 *2 *2 *2—4 2 3 0—tmp+2—hp, cel—str | 16' 9' |
   Boosey | 11' |

Dance suite   17'
   *2 *2 *2 *2—4 2 2 1—tmp+3—hp, cel, pf —str
   Brief passage requires pf 4-hands.
   Boosey

| 4' 2' 3' |
| 3' 1' 4' |

Dances of Transylvania   5'
   *2 2 *2 2—2 2 2 1—tmp—hp or pf—str
   A version for strings only is available from Kalmus.
   Boosey

| 2' 1' 2' |

Deux Portraits, op.5 (Two portraits)   12'
   *2 *2 *2 2—4 2 2 1—tmp+4—2hp—str
   First movement is for solo violin with orchestra accompaniment.
   Contents—Egy ideális (One ideal); Egy torz (One grotesque).
   Boosey

| 10' 2' |

Divertimento, (1939)   24'
   str
   Boosey

| 9' 8' 7' |

Four orchestral pieces, op.12   22'
   4 *3 =4 *4—4 4 4 1—tmp+2—2hp, cel, pf—str
   Boosey

| 7' 6' 4' 5' |

Hungarian peasant songs   9'
   *2 *2 *2 2—2 2 2 1—tmp—hp—str
   Boosey

Hungarian sketches   11'
   *2 2 *2 *2—2 2 2 1—tmp+2—hp—str
   Boosey

| 3' 2' 2' |
| 2' 2' |

Kossuth   21'
   *4 *4 =4 *4—8 4 3 1—bass tp, 2 tenor tubas
   —tmp+3—2hp—str 16.16.12.10.8
   Two of the flutists double on piccolo. Ed. D. Dille.
   EMB

Mikrokosmos suite   17'
   *3 *2 *2 *2—4 3 3 1—tmp+4—hp, cel—str
   Arr. Tibor Serly, with the cooperation and approval of Bartók.
   Boosey

The miraculous mandarin: Suite   20'
   *3 *3 =3 *3—4 3 3 1—tmp+4—hp, cel, pf, org—str
   Boosey

Music for strings, percussion and celesta   27'
   tmp+2—hp, cel, pf—double str orchestra
   Boosey

| 7' 7' 7' 6' |

Rhapsody, piano and orchestra, op.1   17'
   *3 2 *2 2—4 2 3 0—tmp+2—str
   Boosey

Rhapsody no.1 for violin and orchestra   10'
 *2 2 *2 2—2 2 1 1—cimbalom (or hp & pf)—str 5' 5'
 Boosey

Rhapsody no.2 for violin and orchestra   11'
 *2 *2 *2 2—2 2 1 1—tmp+1—hp, pf/cel—str 5' 6'
 Boosey

Rumanian folk dances   6'
 *2 0 2 2—2 0 0 0—str
 Version arr. for string orchestra by Arthur Willner available
 from Universal.
 Boosey

Scherzo, op.2   29'
 solo piano
 *4 *3 +4 *4—4 3 3 1—tmp+5—2hp—str
 One of the 4 clarinet parts is written for "clarinet in A-flat."
 Boosey

Suite no.1 for orchestra, op.3   35'
 *4 *3 =4 *4—4 3 3 1—tmp+3—2hp—str 7' 7' 8'
 Boosey   *Kalmus*   6' 7'

Suite no.2 for orchestra, op.4   34'
 *2 *2 =2 *2—3 2 0 0—tmp+2—2hp—str 9' 9' 8' 8'
 Boosey

Three village scenes   12'
 female voices (2 or 4 mezzo-sopranos & 2 or 4 altos) 4' 5' 3'
 *1 *1 +2 1—1 1 1 0—1perc—hp, pf—str quintet
 One clarinetist doubles on alto saxophone.
 Boosey

Two pictures, op.10 (Két kép)   17'
 *3 *3 *3 *3—4 4 3 1—tmp+1—2hp, cel—str 8' 9'
 Contents—Virágzás (In full flower); A falu tánca (Village dance)
 Boosey   *Kalmus*

The wooden prince: Suite   30'
 *4 *4 *4 *4—asx, tsx—4 6 3 1—tmp+5—2hp, cel (4-hands)—str
 2pic and 2Eh are required. There is also a *Little concert suite
 from The wooden prince,* 12' in duration.
 Boosey

Bassett, Leslie   1923 -

Concerto lirico   15'
 solo trombone
 *3 2 3 2—4 2 3 1—tmp+3—hp, pf/cel—str
 Peters

Echoes from an invisible world   17'
 *3 *3 *3 *3—4 4 3 1—tmp+3—hp, cel, pf—str
 Peters

From a source evolving 13'
   *3 *3 *3 *3—4 3 3 1—tmp+3—hp, pf—str
   Peters

Variations for orchestra 23'
   *2 *2 *2 *2—4 2 3 1—tmp+2—hp, cel, pf—str
   Peters

Bax, Arnold   1883 - 1953

In the faery hills 15'
   *3 *3 *4 2—4 3 3 1—tmp+2—2hp, cel—str
   Chappell

November woods 15'
   *4 *3 *4 *3—4 3 3 1—tmp—2hp, cel—str
   Chappell

Overture to a picaresque comedy 10'
   *3 *3 *4 *3—4 3 3 1—tmp+3—hp—str
   Chappell

Symphony no.7 47'
   *3 *3 *4 *3—4 3 3 1—tmp+4—hp—str
   Chappell   17' 16' 14'

Beach, Amy Marcy Cheney   1867 - 1944

Symphony no.2, op.32, E minor (Gaelic) 41'
   *3 2 *3 2—4 2 3 1—tmp+1—str
   Kalmus   11' 8' 13' 9'

Beaser, Robert   1954 -

Chorale variations for orchestra 20'
   *3 *3 =4 *3—4 4 3 1—tmp+4—hp, pf—str
   Helicon

Double chorus for orchestra 11'
   *3 *3 *3 *3—4 4 3 1—tmp+4—hp, pf—str
   Helicon

Becker, John J.   1886 - 1961

Concerto arabesque 13'
   solo piano
   1 1 1 *2—1 1 0 0—str
   ACA

Soundpiece no.1b 12'
   pf—str
   ACA

Soundpiece no.2b (Homage to Haydn) 13'
   str
   Presser

63799

Symphony no.3 (Symphonia brevis)   17'
   *3 *3 2 *4—4 4 3 1—tmp+6—pf—str
   Peters

Two pieces for orchestra
   These two works may be out of print, but orchestral materials
   are in the Fleisher Collection.

   1. Among the reeds and rushes   3'
   1 1 2 1—1 1 0 0—tmp—hp—str

   2. The mountains   3'
   *3 2 2 1—2 2 2 1—tmp+3—str

When the willow nods   15'
   1 1 1 1—1 1 0 0—tmp+1—pf—str
   This work may be out of print, but orchestral materials are in the
   Fleisher Collection.

Beethoven, Ludwig van   1770 - 1827

Ah, perfido, op.65   13'
   soprano scene and aria
   1 0 2 2—2 0 0 0—str
   Breitkopf   *Kalmus*

Cantata on the death of Emperor Joseph II   33'
   chorus   solos SSATB
   2 2 2 2—2 0 0 0—str
   Breitkopf   *Kalmus*   *Schirmer, G.*

Christus am Ölberg, op.85 (Christ on the Mount of Olives)   36'
   chorus   solos STB
   2 2 2 2—2 2 3 0—tmp—str
   Breitkopf   *Gray*   *Kalmus*

Concerto, piano, no.1, op.15, C major   36'
   1 2 2 2—2 2 0 0—tmp—str   17'10' 9'
   Breitkopf   *Henle*   *Kalmus*

Concerto, piano, no.2, op.19, B-flat major   28'
   1 2 0 2—2 0 0 0—str   14' 8' 6'
   Breitkopf   *Henle*   *Kalmus*

Concerto, piano, no.3, op.37, C minor   34'
   2 2 2 2—2 2 0 0—tmp—str   16' 9' 9'
   Breitkopf   *Henle*   *Kalmus*

Concerto, piano, no.4, op.58, G major   34'
   1 2 2 2—2 2 0 0—tmp—str   19' 5'
   Breitkopf   *Kalmus*   10'

Concerto, piano, no.5, op.73, E-flat major (Emperor)   38'
   2 2 2 2—2 2 0 0—tmp—str   20' 8'
   Breitkopf   *Kalmus*   10'

Concerto, piano, no.6, op.61, D major   42'
   1 2 2 2—2 2 0 0—tmp—str   23' 10'
   The composer has provided a piano version of the solo part of his   9'
   violin concerto, op.61. Use the orchestral parts for the violin
   concerto.

Concerto, violin, op.61, D major   42'
   1 2 2 2—2 2 0 0—tmp—str   23' 10'
   Breitkopf   *Henle*   *Kalmus*   9'

Concerto, violin, violoncello & piano, op.56, C major (Triple   33'
concerto)   17' 4'
   1 2 2 2—2 2 0 0—tmp—str   12'
   Breitkopf   *Henle*   *Kalmus*

Consecration of the house
   see his: Die Weihe des hauses

Contradances   12'
   1 2 2 2—2 0 0 0—1 perc—str (without va)
   Twelve dances.
   Kalmus   *Schott*

Coriolan overture, op.62   8'
   2 2 2 2—2 2 0 0—tmp—str
   Breitkopf   *Henle*   *Kalmus*

Deutsche tänze
   see his: German dances

Egmont (incidental music), op.84   40'
   soprano solo
   *2 2 2 2—4 2 0 0—tmp—str
   Overture and 9 movements, 2 of which are songs.
   Kalmus

Egmont: Overture   9'
   *2 2 2 2—4 2 0 0—tmp—str
   Breitkopf   *Kalmus*

Fantasia, piano, chorus & orchestra, op.80 (Choral fantasy)   19'
   chorus   solos SSATTB   solo piano
   2 2 2 2—2 2 0 0—tmp—str
   Breitkopf   *Gray*   *Kalmus*   *Schirmer, G.*

Fidelio: Overture, op.72b   6'
   2 2 2 2—4 2 2 0—tmp—str
   Breitkopf   *Kalmus*

German dances (Deutsche Tänze)   20'
   *3 2 2 2—2 2 0 0—tmp+3—posthorn or cornet—str (without va)
   Twelve dances.
   Breitkopf   *Kalmus*

Die Geschöpfe des Prometheus
   see his: Prometheus, op.43

Grosse Fuge, op.133   16'
  str
  Edited by Felix Weingartner for string orchestra. Originally for
  string quartet.
  Breitkopf   *Kalmus*

Jena symphony
  See under: Witt, Friedrich, 1770-1837

König Stephan, op.117 (King Stephen): Overture   8'
  2 2 2 *3—4 2 0 0—tmp—str
  Breitkopf   *Kalmus*

Leonore overture No.1   10'
  2 2 2 2—4 2 0 0—tmp—str
  Breitkopf   *Kalmus*

Leonore overture No.2   13'
  2 2 2 2—4 2 3 0—tmp—str
  Breitkopf   *Kalmus*

Leonore overture no.3   14'
  2 2 2 2—4 2 3 0—tmp—str
  Breitkopf   *Kalmus*

Mass, op.86, C major   43'
  chorus   solos SATB
  2 2 2 2—2 2 0 0—tmp—org—str
  Breitkopf   *Gray*   *Kalmus*   *Peters*

6'	9'	11'
	11'	6'

Meeresstille und glückliche Fahrt, op.112 (Calm sea and prosperous   10'
voyage)
  chorus
  2 2 2 2—4 2 0 0—tmp—str
  Breitkopf   *Kalmus*

Missa solemnis, op.123, D major   81'
  chorus   solos SATB
  2 2 2 *3—4 2 3 0—tmp—org—str
  Breitkopf   *Kalmus*   *Peters*   *Schirmer, G.*

10'	18'
20'	17'
	16'

Musik zu einem Ritterballet   13'
  *1 0 2 0—2 2 0 0—tmp—str
  8 movements.
  Breitkopf   *Kalmus*

Namensfeier overture, op.115   8'
  2 2 2 2—4 2 0 0—tmp—str
  Breitkopf   *Henle*   *Kalmus*

Prometheus, op.43 (Die Geschöpfe des Prometheus)   48'
  2 2 2 2—basset horn—2 2 0 0—tmp—hp—str
  Basset horn may be played by one of the clarinets.
  Kalmus

Prometheus (Die Geschöpfe des Prometheus): Overture 5'
2 2 2 2—2 2 0 0—tmp—str
Breitkopf   Kalmus

Romance no.1, op.40, G major 8'
violin solo
1 2 0 2—2 0 0 0—str
Breitkopf and Henle parts are published together with Romance
no.2.
Breitkopf   Henle   Kalmus

Romance no.2, op.50, F major 9'
violin solo
1 2 0 2—2 0 0 0—str
Breitkopf and Henle parts are published together with Romance
no.1.
Breitkopf   Henle   Kalmus

Die Ruinen von Athen, op.113 (The ruins of Athens): Overture 6'
2 2 2 2—4 2 0 0—tmp—str
Breitkopf   Kalmus

Die Ruinen von Athen, op.113: March and chorus (Schmückt die 6'
Altäre)
chorus
*2 2 2 2—2 2 3 0—tmp—str
Breitkopf   Kalmus

Die Ruinen von Athen, op.113: Turkish march 4'
*1 2 2 *3—2 2 0 0—3perc—str
Breitkopf   Kalmus

Septet, op.20, E-flat major 40'
0 0 1 1—1 0 0 0—vn, va, vc, db
Luck   Peters
| 9' | 9' | 3' |
| 7' | 3' | 9' |

Symphony no.1, op.21, C major 26'
2 2 2 2—2 2 0 0—tmp—str
Breitkopf   Henle   Kalmus
| 9' | 7' | 4' | 6' |

Symphony no.2, op.36, D major 32'
2 2 2 2—2 2 0 0—tmp—str
Breitkopf   Kalmus
| 10' | 11' |
| 4' | 7' |

Symphony no.3, op.55, E-flat major (Eroica) 47'
2 2 2 2—3 2 0 0—tmp—str
Breitkopf   Kalmus
| 15' | 15' |
| 5' | 12' |

Symphony no.4, op.60, B-flat major 34'
1 2 2 2—2 2 0 0—tmp—str
Breitkopf   Kalmus
| 13' | 10' |
| 4' | 7' |

Symphony no.5, op.67, C minor   31'
*3 2 2 *3—2 2 3 0—tmp—str   7' 10' 6'
A critical edition of the score with historical and analytical   8'
essays is available from Norton.
Breitkopf   Kalmus

Symphony no.6, op.68, F major (Pastorale)   39'
*3 2 2 2—2 2 2 0—tmp—str   9' 12' 5'
Contents—Erwachen heiterer Empfindungen bei der Ankunft auf   4' 9'
dem Lande (Awakening of cheerful feelings on arrival in the
country); Szene am Bach (Scene by the brook); Lustiges
Zusammensein der Landleute (Merry gathering of the
countryfolk); Gewitter, Sturm (Thunderstorm); Hirtengesang,
frohe und dankbare Gefühle nach dem Sturm (Shepherd's song,
glad and grateful feelings after the storm).
Breitkopf   Kalmus

Symphony no.7, op.92, A major   36'
2 2 2 2—2 2 0 0—tmp—str   12' 9' 8'
Breitkopf   Kalmus   7'

Symphony no.8, op.93, F major   26'
2 2 2 2—2 2 0 0—tmp—str   9' 5' 5' 7'
Breitkopf   Kalmus

Symphony no.9, op.125, D minor (Choral)   65'
chorus   solos SATB   15' 13'
*3 2 2 *3—4 2 3 0—tmp+3—str   13' 24'
Breitkopf   Kalmus

Die Weihe des Hauses, op.124 (Consecration of the house)   12'
2 2 2 2—4 2 3 0—tmp—str
Breitkopf   Henle   Kalmus

Wellingtons Sieg, op.91 (Wellington's victory)   16'
*3 2 2 2—4 6 3 0—tmp+3—str
Breitkopf   Henle   Kalmus

Zapfenstreich march   4'
*1 2 2 *3—2 2 0 0—4perc
Kalmus

Bellini, Vincenzo   1801 - 1835
Concerto, oboe, E-flat major
2 2 2 1—2 0 0 0—str
Leuckart

Norma: Overture   6'
*2 2 2 2—4 2 3 1—tmp+2—hp—str
Breitkopf   Kalmus   Luck   Ricordi

Il pirata: Overture   7'
    *2 2 2 2—4 2 3 1—tmp+3—str
    Lowest brass instrument in score (here listed as tuba) is
    "serpentone." Kalmus renders the part as a bass trombone (i.e. a
    4th trombone).
    Kalmus

Symphony, C minor   10'
    2 2 2 2—2 2 3 0—str
    Ed. Maffeo Zanon.
    Ricordi

Symphony, D major   8'
    2 2 2 2—2 2 3 0—tmp—str
    Ed. Maffeo Zanon.
    Ricordi

Benjamin, Arthur   1893 - 1960

Concertino, piano & orchestra   15'
    *2 2 2 2—2 2 0 0—tmp+4—asx—str
    Schott

Two Jamaican pieces   5'
    1 1 2 1—asx—2 1 0 0—tmp+2—str
    2nd cl, asx, and tmp are optional.
    Contents — Jamaican song; Jamaican rhumba.
    Boosey

Bennett, Richard Rodney   1936 -

Concerto, guitar & chamber ensemble   20'
    *1 *1 *1 0—1 1 0 0—tmp+1—cel—vn, va, vc
    Universal

Concerto for orchestra   23'
    *3 *3 *2 *3—4 3 3 1—tmp+3—hp, pf/cel—str
    Novello

Concerto, oboe   16'
    str
    Universal

Concerto, violin   22'
    *2 *2 *1 2—4 2 3 1—tmp+3—hp, pf/cel—str
    Novello

Serenade   14'
    *2 2 2 1—2 2 1 0—tmp+3—pf—str
    Novello

Sonnets to Orpheus   30'
    *2 *2 =2 *2—2 2 2 1—tmp+3—2hp, pf/cel—str (min 14.12.10.8.6)
    Novello

Zodiac   17'
   *3 *3 *3 *3—4 3 3 1—tmp+3—hp, pf/cel—str
   Novello

Bennett, Robert Russell   1894 - 1981

Suite of old American dances   16'
   *2 *2 *3 2—4 3 3 1—tmp+3—hp—str
   Chappell

Benson, Warren   1924 -

Chants and graces   8'
   *1 0 0 0—4perc—hp—str
   C. Fischer

A Delphic serenade   12'
   *2 2 2 2—4 3 3 1—tmp+3—hp—str
   C. Fischer

Five brief encounters   7'
   2 0 2 0—2 1 1 0—tmp—str
   C. Fischer

Berezowsky, Nicolai   1900 - 1953

Concerto, harp, op.31   22'
   *3 2 *3 2—4 2 3 1—tmp+2—str
   Elkan-Vogel

Berg, Alban   1885 - 1935

Altenberg Lieder, op.4   11'
  soprano solo | 3' 1' 2' |
   *3 *3 =4 *3—4 3 4 1—tmp+4—hp, cel, pf, harm—str | 1' 4' |
   Universal

Chamber concerto, op.8   41'
  solo violin   solo piano | 9' 15' |
   *2 *2 =3 *2—2 1 1 0 | 17' |
   1st mvt, piano & winds; 2nd mvt, violin & winds; 3rd mvt, tutti.
   1st or 2nd mvt may be performed separately.
   Universal

Concerto, violin   22'
   *2 *2 *4 *3—4 2 2 1—tmp+2—hp—str | 9' 13' |
   3rd clarinet doubles on alto saxophone.
   Universal

Lulu: Suite   32'
  coloratura soprano solo | 15' 3' 3' |
   *3 *3 *4 *3—asx—4 3 3 1—tmp+3—hp, pf—str | 3' 8' |
   Universal

Lyric suite

15'

str

6' 3' 6'

Originally for string quartet.
Universal

Sieben frühe Lieder (Seven early songs)

18'

high voice

4' 3' 2'

*2 *2 *3 *3—4 1 2 0—1perc—hp, opt cel—str

3' 2' 2'

Contents—Nacht (Night); Schilflied (Song amongst the reeds); Die
Nachtigall (The nightingale); Traumgekrönt (A crown of dreams);
Im Zimmer (Indoors); Liebesode (Lovers' ode); Sommertage
(Summer days).
Universal

2'

Three pieces for orchestra, op.6

19'

*4 *4 =5 *4—6 4 4 1—2tmp+5—2hp, cel—str

4' 6' 9'

Revised 1929.
Universal

Der Wein (concert aria)

15'

soprano solo
*2 *2 *3 *3—asx—4 2 2 1—tmp+2—hp, pf—str
Universal

Wozzeck: Three excerpts

20'

soprano solo
*4 *4 =5 *4—4 4 4 1—tmp+4—hp, cel—str
Playable with reduced winds.
Universal

Bergsma, William   1921 - 1994?

A carol on Twelfth Night

8'

*2 2 2 2—4 2 3 1—tmp+2—hp—str
Galaxy

Chameleon variations

13'

*3 2 *3 2—4 3 3 1—tmp+3—hp, pf—str
Galaxy

Documentary one; portrait of a city

18'

*2 *2 *2 2—4 2 3 1—tmp+2—str
4th movement may be performed separately under the title *Follow
the leader* (4').
Contents—1. Designers, builders; 2. Tintypes and lithographs; 3.
Lullaby in a railroad flat; 4. Rainy street, Follow the leader,
Kids at play.
Galaxy

Berio, Luciano   1925 -

Allelujah

10'

*4 2 =4 *3—asx, tsx—8 5 3 1—tmp+7—2hp, cel, pf—str
Suvini

Concertino, clarinet & violin   11'
    hp, cel—str
    Universal

Concerto, 2 pianos   25'
    *3 *3 =4 *4—asx, tsx—3 3 3 1—3perc—elec org, orchestral
    pf—str
    Universal

Nones   10'
    *3 2 2 *3—asx—4 4 3 1—tmp+5—hp, cel, pf, elec gtr—str
    Suvini

Rendering   25'
    2 2 2 2—2 2 3 0—tmp—cel—str
    Based on sketches by Franz Schubert for a 10th symphony
    (D.936a).
    Universal

Requies   13'
    *2 *2 =3 2—2 2 1 0—marimba—hp, cel—str 8.8.4.4.3
    Universal

Ritirata notturna di Madrid   10'
    *3 *3 *3 *3—4 4 3 1—tmp+3—hp—str
    Available in the United States from AMP.
    "Four original versions of the *Ritirata notturna di Madrid* of L.
    Boccherini, superimposed and transcribed for orchestra."
    Universal

Sinfonia   27'
    eight voices (SSAATTBB) | 7' 5' 12' |
    *4 *3 +4 *3—asx, tsx—4 4 3 1—tmp+2 | 3' |
    —hp, pf, elec org, elec hpsd (Baldwin)—str
    Universal

Still   12'
    3 *3 *4 *3—asx, tsx—4 4 3 1—3perc—hp, pf, elec org—str
    Universal

Tempi concertati   16'
    soloists: flute, violin, 2 pianos (one doubling on celeste)
    *1 *2 *3 1—1 1 1 0—4perc—2hp—2va, 2vc, db
    Not to be conducted in performance, though a conductor is
    necessary in rehearsal.
    Universal

Variazioni per orchestra da camera   12'
    *2 1 2 2—2 2 1 0—str 8.8.6.4.3
    Suvini

Berkeley, Lennox   1903 - 1989

Concerto, guitar, op.88   22'
    1 1 1 1—2 0 0 0—str
    Chester

Sinfonietta 13'
   2 2 2 2—2 0 0 0—tmp—str
   Chester

Symphony no.3 in one movement 14'
   *3 *3 2 *3—4 3 3 1—tmp+2—hp—str
   Chester

Windsor variations, for chamber orchestra 13'
   1 2 0 2—2 0 0 0—str
   Chester

Berlioz, Hector   1803 - 1869

Béatrice et Bénédict: Overture 8'
   *2 2 2 2—4 3 3 0—tmp—str
   Bote & Bock   *Breitkopf*   *Kalmus*

Benvenuto Cellini: Overture 11'
   *2 2 *2 4—4 6 3 1—3tmp+3—str
   4 real bassoon parts in only 3 bars of the total piece; otherwise 2
   real parts, each doubled.
   Breitkopf   *Kalmus*

Carnaval romain (Roman carnival) 8'
   *2 *2 2 2—4 4 3 0—tmp+4—str
   Breitkopf   *Kalmus*

Cléopâtre 22'
   soprano solo

| 3' 7' 5' |
| 3' 4' |

   *2 2 2 2—4 2 3 0—tmp—str
   Often listed as *La Mort de Cléopâtre*. Sometimes the two titles are
   incorrectly listed as separate works. Both flutes double on
   piccolo.
   Broude Bros.   *Luck*

Le Corsaire 8'
   2 2 2 4—4 4 3 1—tmp—str
   2 real bassoon parts, each doubled.
   Breitkopf   *Kalmus*

La Damnation de Faust, op.24 120'
   solos MzTBarB   chorus, optional children's chorus
   *3 *2 *3 4—4 4 3 2—2tmp+3—2hp—str
   Breitkopf   *Kalmus*   *Schirmer, G.*

La Damnation de Faust: Dance of the sylphs (Ballet des sylphs) 3'
   *3 0 2 0—tmp—2hp—str
   Breitkopf   *Kalmus*

La Damnation de Faust: Rakoczy march (Marche hongroise) 5'
   *3 2 2 4—4 4 3 1—tmp+4—str
   2 real bassoon parts, each doubled.
   Breitkopf   *Kalmus*

La Damnation de Faust: Will-o-the-wisps (Menuet de follets)   5'
    *3 2 *3 4—4 4 3 0—2tmp+2—str
    Two of the flutists double on piccolo.
    Breitkopf   *Kalmus*

L'Enfance du Christ, op.25 (Childhood of Christ)   93'
    solos S, 2T, Bar, 3B   chorus
    *2 *2 2 2—2 4 3 0—tmp—hp, org (or harm)—str
    Can be done with solos STBB.
    Breitkopf   *Gray*   *Kalmus*   *Schirmer, G.*

Les Franc-Juges, op.3 (Judges of the secret court)   13'
    *2 2 2 *3—4 3 3 2—tmp+1—str
    Kalmus

Harold in Italy, op.16   43'
    solo viola
    *2 *2 2 4—4 4 3 1—tmp+3—hp—str

| 15' 8' 7' |
| 13' |

    Breitkopf   *Kalmus*

Lelio, op.14b (The return to life)   53'
    speaker   invisible chorus & solos TTB
    *2 *2 2 2—4 4 3 1—2tmp+1—hp, pf 4-hands—str
    Continuation and ending of the *Symphonie fantastique*.
    Kalmus

Messe solennelle   62'
    solos STB   chorus
    2 2 2 2—4 2 3 1—tmp+2—optional hps—str
    The composer added a piccolo (i.e. a 3rd flutist) to the
    Resurrexit and then deleted it, though Bärenreiter includes the
    part as an option. Berlioz vacillated among serpent, buccin, and
    ophicleide for the lowest member of the brass family (listed above
    as tuba).
    Ed. Hugh Macdonald.
    Bärenreiter

Mort de Cléopâtre
    see his: Cléopâtre

Nuits d'été, op.7   31'
    solo voice (Mz or T or Bar, or several different voices
    alternating)

| 2' 7' 7' |
| 6' 5' 4' |

    2 1 2 2—3 0 0 0—hp—str
    Kalmus

Requiem, op.5 (Grande Messe des morts)   82'
    chorus   tenor solo
    4 *4 4 8—12 16 16 6—10tmp, 9perc—str

| 12' 12' |
| 3' 6' 5' |
| 11' 8' 3' |
| 10' 12' |

    2Eh required. Number of real parts for winds and percussion,
    exclusive of doublings: 4 *4 2 4—6 8 8 3—4tmp, 3perc.
    G. Schirmer publishes a reduced version.
    Breitkopf   *Kalmus*

Rêverie et Caprice, op.8   11'
    violin solo
    *2 2 2 2—2 0 0 0—str
    Breitkopf   *Kalmus*

Rob Roy   12'
    *2 *2 2 2—4 3 3 0—tmp—hp—str
    Breitkopf   *Kalmus*

Le Roi Lear (King Lear)   16'
    *2 2 2 2—4 2 3 1—tmp—str
    Breitkopf   *Kalmus*

Roman carnival
    see his: Carnaval romain

Roméo et Juliette, op.17   95'
    chorus   solos ATB   19' 40'
    *3 *2 2 4—4 4 3 1—2tmp+4—2hp—str   36'
    Breitkopf   *Kalmus*   *Schirmer, G.*

Roméo et Juliette: Love scene   19'
    2 *2 2 4—4 0 0 0—str
    Kalmus

Roméo et Juliette: Queen Mab scherzo   8'
    *3 *2 2 4—4 0 0 0—tmp+1—2hp—str
    Breitkopf   *Kalmus*

Roméo et Juliette: Romeo alone; Festivities at Capulet's   12'
    *3 2 2 4—4 4 3 0—2tmp+6—2hp—str
    Kalmus   *Luck*

Symphonie fantastique, op.14   49'
    *2 *2 +2 4—4 4 3 2—4tmp+2—4hp (doubling 2 real parts)—str   13' 6'
    Contents—Rêveries, Passions; Un Bal (A ball); Scène aux champs   15' 5'
    (Scene in the country); Marche au supplice (March to the   10'
    scaffold); Songe d'une nuit du sabbat (Dream of a witches'
    sabbath).
    A critical edition of the score with historical and analytical
    essays is available from Norton.
    Bärenreiter   *Breitkopf*   *Kalmus*

Symphonie funèbre et triomphale, op.15   32'
    optional chorus
    *2 2 =4 *3—6 6 4 2—tmp+5—optional str
    Contrabassoon, bass trombone, and timpani are also optional.
    Composer calls for doubling and tripling of all parts.
    Bärenreiter also offers a separate edition prepared for American
    wind bands by Jonathan Elkus.
    Bärenreiter   *Kalmus*

Te deum 52'
solo tenor   double chorus, optional children's chorus
*4 *4 *4 4—4 5 6 2—tmp+6—12hp (doubling 1 real part), org—str
Number of real parts for winds and percussion, exclusive of
doublings: *4 *2 *2 4—4 5 3 1—tmp+3.

8' 10' 9'
5' 8' 12'

Breitkopf   Kalmus   Schirmer, G.

Les Troyens: Overture 6'
2 2 *2 2—4 4 3 0—tmp—str
Kalmus   Luck

Les Troyens: Ballet 12'
*3 *2 2 2—4 4 3 0—tmp+1—str
Choudens   Kalmus

Les Troyens: Royal hunt and storm 7'
*3 2 2 2—4 4 3 1—2tmp+1—str
A 3rd timpanist is optional.
Choudens   Kalmus

Les Troyens: Trojan march 5'
2 2 2 2—4 4 3 1—tmp+2—2hp—str
Breitkopf   Choudens   Kalmus

Waverley 9'
*2 2 2 4—4 3 3 1—tmp—str
Kalmus

Bernstein, Leonard   1918 - 1990
The age of anxiety
see his: Symphony no.2

Arias and barcaroles (version for strings & percussion) 31'
solo Mz, Bar
2perc—str
Accompaniment originally for piano 4-hands; arr. for strings &
percussion by Bright Sheng.
Contents—Prelude; Love duet; Little Smary; The love of my life;
Greeting; At my wedding; Mr. & Mrs. Webb say goodnight;
Nachspiel.
Boosey

Candide: Overture 5'
*3 2 =4 *3—4 2 3 1—tmp+4—hp—str
Boosey

Chichester psalms 19'
chorus   solo boy or countertenor
0 0 0 0—0 3 3 0—tmp+7—2hp—str

4' 6' 9'

Publisher offers a reduction of the instrumental forces for harp,
organ, and percussion.
Boosey

Divertimento for orchestra   15'
   *3 *3 =4 *3—4 3 3 1—tmp+6—hp, pf—str
   Tubist doubles on baritone euphonium.
   Contents—Sennets and tuckets; Waltz; Mazurka; Samba; Turkey
   trot; Sphinxes; Blues; March: *The BSO forever.*
   Boosey

| 1' 2' 2' |
| 1' 2' 1' |
| 2' 4' |

Facsimile   21'
   *2 2 +2 2—4 3 2 1—tmp+1—pf—str
   Boosey

Fancy free: Suite   24'
   *2 2 2 2—4 3 3 1—tmp+1—pf—str
   Boosey

| 5' 3' 5' |
| 3' 3' 5' |

Halil   16'
   solo flute
   =2 0 0 0—tmp+6—hp—str
   Boosey

Jeremiah
   see his: Symphony no.1

Kaddish
   see his: Symphony no.3

Mass: Three meditations   17'
   solo violoncello
   tmp+7—hp, pf, org—str
   Boosey

| 5' 4' 8' |

On the town: Three dance episodes   11'
   *1 *1 =3 0—2 3 3 1—tmp+2—pf—str
   One clarinet doubles on alto saxophone.
   Contents—The great lover; Lonely town pas de deux; Times
   Square 1944.
   Boosey

| 2' 4' 5' |

On the waterfront: Symphonic suite   23'
   *3 2 =4 *3—asx—4 3 3 1—2tmp+3—hp, pf—str
   Boosey

Serenade   31'
   solo violin
   tmp+5—hp—str
   Boosey

| 7' 4' 2' |
| 8' 10' |

Slava! (A political overture)   5'
   *3 *3 =4 *3—ssx—4 3 3 1—tmp+5—pf, electric gtr—pre-recorded
   tape—str
   Boosey

Songfest   40'
  solo voices: S Mz A T Bar B
  *3 *3 =4 *3—4 3 3 1—tmp+6—hp, pf/cel, fender bass—str
  Pianist also doubles on electric keyboard.
  Boosey

> 3' 11' 9'
> 2' 11' 4'

Symphony no.1 (Jeremiah)   25'
  solo mezzo-soprano
  *3 *3 =3 *3—4 3 3 1—tmp+4—pf—str
  Warner

> 8' 7' 10'

Symphony no.2 (The age of anxiety)   35'
  solo piano
  *3 *3 *3 *3—4 3 3 1—tmp+5—hp, pianino—str
  Revised 1965.
  Boosey

> 2' 8' 6'
> 6' 5' 8'

Symphony no.3 (Kaddish)   39'
  speaker, soprano solo   mixed chorus, boy's chorus
  =4 *3 =4 *3—asx—4 4 3 1—tmp+7—hp, cel, pf—str
  Revised version, 1978.
  Boosey

> 3' 5' 6'
> 8'17'

West side story: Overture   5'
  *2 *2 =2 2—4 3 3 1—tmp+2—hp, pf, opt elec gtr—str
  Arr. Maurice Peress; original publisher G.Schirmer.
  Luck

West side story: Symphonic dances   22'
  *3 *3 =4 *3—asx—4 3 3 1—tmp+5—hp, cel, pf—str
  Newly engraved score and parts in 1995 rectify some errors.
  Boosey

Berwald, Franz   1796 - 1868

Estrella de Soria: Overture   8'
  2 2 2 2—4 2 3 0—tmp—str
  Concert-ending by Moses Pergament.
  Bärenreiter   *Gehrmans*

Symphony, C major (Sinfonie singulière)   29'
  2 2 2 2—4 2 3 0—tmp—str
  Sometimes listed as Symphony no.5.
  Bärenreiter   *Hansen*

> 11' 10'
> 8'

Symphony, D major (Sinfonie capricieuse)   24'
  2 2 2 2—4 2 3 0—tmp—str
  Bärenreiter

> 7' 7' 10'

Symphony, E-flat major (Sinfonie naïve)   27'
  2 2 2 2—4 2 3 0—tmp—str
  Published as Symphony no.3; sometimes referred to as Symphony
  no.6.
  Bärenreiter   *Gehrmans*   *Simrock*

> 9' 12' 6'

Symphony, G minor (Symphonie serieuse)   34'
   2 2 2 2—4 2 3 0—tmp—str   12' 8' 6'
   Sometimes listed as Symphony no.2.   8'
   Bärenreiter   *Gehrmans*

Biber, Heinrich von   1644 - 1704

Battalia   6'
   cnt—str
   Doblinger ed. by Nikolaus Harnoncourt; Kerby ed. by Joel
   Blahnik.
   Doblinger   *Kerby*

Birtwistle, Harrison   1934 -

Carmen arcadiae mechanicae perpetuum   12'
   *1 1 *1 *1—1 1 1 0—1perc—pf—str
   Universal

Endless parade   18'
   0 0 0 0—0 1 0 0—vib—str 7.7.4.4.2
   Universal

Machaut à ma manière   10'
   *2 *2 +2 *2—4 3 2 1—2perc—str (min 10.8.6.6.4)
   Both flutists double on piccolo.
   Universal

Nomos   15'
   ampflied solo group: flute, clarinet, horn, bassoon
   *4 *3 =3 *3—4 4 3 1—tmp+5—hp, cel—10va, 10vc, 8db
   Three of the flutists double on piccolo; two of the clarinetists
   double on E-flat clarinet.
   Universal

Verses for ensembles   28'
   =1 *1 =2 *1—1 2 2 0—3perc
   Universal

Bizet, Georges   1838 - 1875

L'Arlésienne: Suite no.1   17'
   2 *2 2 2—asx—4 4 3 0—tmp+1—hp (or pf)—str   6' 3' 3' 5'
   Alto saxophone cued in other instruments.
   Contents—Prélude; Minuet; Adagietto; Carillon.
   Breitkopf   *Choudens*   *Kalmus*

L'Arlésienne: Suite no.2   18'
   *2 *2 2 2—asx—4 4 3 0—tmp+3—hp (or pf)—str   5' 4' 4' 5'
   Alto saxophone cued in other instruments.
   Contents—Pastorale; Intermezzo; Menuet; Farandole.
   Breitkopf   *Choudens*   *Kalmus*

Carmen: Suite no.1   12'
  *2 *2 2 2—4 2 3 0—tmp+3—hp—str | 2' 4' 2' | 2' 2' |
  Contents—Prélude & Aragonaise; Intermezzo; Seguedille; Les
  Dragons d'Alcala; Les Toréadors.
  Breitkopf   *Choudens*   *Kalmus*

Carmen: Suite no.2   19'
  *2 *2 2 2—4 2 3 1—tmp+4—hp—str | 4' 2' 4' | 2' 3' 4' |
  Ed. Friedrich Hoffmann.
  Contents—Marche des contrabandiers; Habanera; Nocturne;
  Chanson du toréador; La Garde montante; Danse bohème.
  Breitkopf   *Choudens*   *Kalmus*

Carmen fantasie
  See under: Sarasate, Pablo de, 1844-1908

Jeux d'enfants, op.22: Petite Suite   12'
  *2 2 2 2—4 2 0 0—tmp+3—str | 2' 3' 1' | 4' 2' |
  Contents—Marche (Trompette et Tambour); Berceuse (La
  Poupée); Impromptu (La Toupie); Duo (Petit Mari, petite femme);
  Galop (Le Bal).
  Durand   *Kalmus*   *Ricordi*

Jolie Fille de Perth: Scènes bohémiennes   12'
  *2 *2 2 2—4 2 3 0—tmp+3—hp—str | 4' 2' 3' 3' |
  Contents—Prélude, Serenade, Marche, Danse bohémienne.
  Kalmus

Ouverture   14'
  *2 2 2 2—4 2 3 1—tmp—str
  Universal

Patrie   13'
  *2 2 2 2—4 4 3 1—tmp+3—hp—str
  Choudens   *Kalmus*

Les Pecheurs de perles (Pearlfishers): Overture   3'
  2 2 2 2—4 0 0 0—tmp—str
  Kalmus   *Luck*

Roma   33'
  2 *2 2 2—4 2 3 0—tmp—hp—str | 13' 5' 9' | 6' |
  Breitkopf   *Choudens*   *Kalmus*

Symphony no.1, C major   27'
  2 2 2 2—4 2 0 0—tmp—str | 8' 9' 4' 6' |
  Choudens   *Kalmus*   *Universal*

Blacher, Boris   1903 - 1975

Orchesterfantasie, op.51   20'
  solo string quartet
  *3 *3 *3 *3—4 3 3 1—tmp+4—hp—str
  Bote & Bock

Orchester-Ornament, op.44   14'
  *3 *3 3 3—4 3 3 1—tmp+4—str
  Bote & Bock

Orchestra-variations on a theme of Paganini   16'
  *3 *3 *3 *3—4 3 3 1—tmp—str
  Bote & Bock

Blackwood, Easley   1933 -

Symphony no.1, op.3   31'
  *4 *3 =4 *4—6 4 3 1—tmp+3—cel—str   9' 6' 5'
  Two of the flutists double on piccolo.   11'
  Elkan-Vogel

Symphony no.2, op.9   24'
  *3 *3 *3 *3—4 4 3 10—tmp+3—hp—str
  Schirmer, G.

Bliss, Arthur   1891 - 1975

Introduction and allegro   12'
  *3 *3 *3 *3—4 3 3 1—tmp+2—hp—str
  Boosey

Things to come: Concert suite   15'
  *2 *2 2 2—4 3 3 1—tmp+3—hp—str   4' 2' 2'
  Two of the flutists double on piccolo.   2' 1' 4'
  Novello

Bloch, Augustyn   1929 -

Enfiando per orchestra   11'
  3 3 3 3—4 3 3 1—tmp+3—org or pf—str (14.12.10.8.6)
  Possible with strings 12.8.6.4.2.
  Schott

Bloch, Ernest   1880 - 1959

America; an epic rhapsody in three parts   42'
  *3 *3 *3 *3—4 3 3 1—tmp+3—2hp, cel, optional org—str   16' 13'
  Brief unison choral passage at the end of the work, intended by   13'
  the composer to be sung by the audience.
  Contents—(1) ...1620; (2) ...1862-65; (3) 1926...
  Originally published by Birchard.
  Broude Bros.

Baal Shem (Three pictures of Chassidic life)   12'
  solo violin
  *2 2 2 2—4 3 0 0—tmp+1—hp, cel—str
  C. Fischer

Concertino   8'
   solo flute   solo viola (or clarinet)
   *3 2 2 2—4 3 3 1—tmp+3—str
   Winds and percussion play only last 14 bars; they may be omitted
   by using a special ending for strings.
   Schirmer, G.

Concerto, violin   36'
   *3 *3 *3 *3—4 3 3 1—tmp+2—hp, cel—str   18' 7'
   Boosey   11'

Concerto grosso no.1   25'
   solo piano   4' 7' 8' 6'
   str
   A new printing (1984) includes many corrections, as well as cuts
   suggested by the composer.
   Broude Bros.

Concerto grosso no.2   19'
   solo string quartet   6' 3' 4' 6'
   string orchestra
   Schirmer, G.

Evocations   18'
   *3 *2 2 2—4 2 3 1—tmp+5—hp, cel, pf—str   7' 5' 6'
   Schirmer, G.

Proclamation   6'
   solo trumpet
   2 2 2 2—4 2 0 0—tmp+1—str
   Broude Bros.

Sacred service (Avodath hakodesh)   52'
   chorus   solo baritone   12' 5' 9'
   *3 *3 *3 *3—4 3 3 1—tmp+3—2hp, cel—str   8' 18'
   Broude Bros.

Schelomo (Hebraic rhapsody)   20'
   solo violoncello
   *3 *3 *3 *3—4 3 3 1—tmp+2—2hp, cel—str
   Schirmer, G.

Suite hébraïque   12'
   solo viola (or violin)   6' 2' 4'
   2 2 2 2—4 3 0 0—tmp+2—hp—str
   Schirmer, G.

Suite modale   12'
   solo flute
   str
   Broude Bros.

Symphony for trombone and orchestra   17'
   solo trombone
   *3 *3 *3 *3—4 3 3 1—tmp+2—hp, cel—str
   Broude Bros.

Trois Poèmes juifs   24'
  *3 *3 2 *3—4 3 3 1—tmp+4—hp, cel—str
  Contents—Danse; Rite; Cortège funèbre.
  Schirmer, G.

Voice in the wilderness   25'
  violoncello obligato
  *3 *3 *3 *3—4 3 3 1—tmp+4—2hp, pf (dbl cel)—str
  Schirmer, G.

3'	4'	3'
5'	4'	6'

Blomdahl, Karl-Birger   1916 - 1968

Forma ferritonans   11'
  *3 3 2 *4—2 contrabass cl (1 doubling bcl)—4 4 5
  0—tmp+3—pf—str
  Two of the bassoons double on contrabassoon.
  Schott

Game for eight   25'
  *1 *1 *1 *1—1 1 2 0—tmp+7—hp, cel, pf—2vn, 2va, 2vc, 2db
  Clarinetist also doubles on alto saxophone.
  Schott

Sisyphos   20'
  *3 *3 *3 *3—4 4 3 1—tmp+6—hp, pf—str
  Schott

Symphony no.3 (Facets)   23'
  *3 *3 *3 *3—4 4 3 1—tmp+3—str
  Schott

Boccherini, Luigi   1743 - 1805

Concerto, flute, G.489, D major   20'
  str
  Wrongly attributed to Boccherini; actual composer is Franz
  Xaver Pokorny.
  Nagel

Concerto, violin, G.486, D major   24'
  2 2 0 0—2 0 0 0—str
  Ed. S. Dushkin. Authenticity very doubtful.
  Schott

Concerto, violoncello, G.474, E-flat major   18'
  0 2 0 0—2 0 0 0—str
  Ed. Franco Gallini.
  Suvini

Concerto, violoncello, G.477, C major   15'
  2hn opt—str
  Ed. Walter Lebermann.
  Schott

Concerto, violoncello, G.482, B-flat major   22'
0 0 0 0—2 0 0 0—str   9' 6' 7'
Ed. Richard Sturzenegger. This is the original version of the
well-known but unauthentic Grützmacher arrangement.
Eulenburg

Concerto, violoncello, G.482, B-flat major (Grützmacher version)   22'
0 2 0 0—2 0 0 0—str   9' 6' 7'
This frequently-played version of the concerto is more
Grützmacher than it is Boccherini, and heavily romanticized to
boot.
Breitkopf   *Kalmus*

Overture, op.43, G.521, D major   5'
0 2 0 1—2 0 0 0—str
Breitkopf edition calls for 2fl rather than 2ob. This work is
listed elsewhere as Symphony no.19 and (in the Almeida edition)
as Symphony no.28.
Breitkopf   *Zanibon*

Ritirata notturna di Madrid
see under: Berio, Luciano

Sinfonia concertante, strings, G.268, C major   9'
str
Ed. Pina Carmirelli. Originally a string quintet, op.10, no.4.
However, the composer himself indicated orchestral performance
as possible.
Zanibon

Symphonies
*The numbering system below is that of the Doblinger edition of
the complete Boccherini symphonies, ed. Antonio de Almeida.
Divergent numberings are given in the individual listings.*

Symphony no.1, G.490, D major   7'
0 2 0 1—2 0 0 0—cnt—str   3' 2' 2'
Ed. Antonio de Almeida.
Editor stipulates that continuo was not used, nor is one indicated
in score; however, a continuo part is included in the set of parts
for this particular symphony. This work was also the overture to
La confederazione dei Sabini con Roma, a cantata.
Doblinger

Symphony no.3, G.503, op.12, no.1,D major   22'
1 2 0 1—2 0 0 0—str
G. Schirmer edition (ed. Newell Jenkins) is published as op.16,
no.2.
Doblinger   *Schirmer, G.*

Symphony no.5, G.505, op.12, no.3, C major   17'
2 0 0 1—2 0 0 0—str   5' 4' 6' 2'
Ed. Antonio de Almeida
Doblinger

Symphony no.6, G.506, op.12, no.4, D minor (La casa del diavolo)   22'
   0 2 0 1—2 0 0 0—str   7' 6' 9'
   Listed elsewhere as Symphony no.4.
   Doblinger ed. Antonio de Almeida; Ricordi ed. Pina Carmirelli;
   Suvini ed. Gallini.
   Doblinger   *Ricordi*   *Suvini*

Symphony no.7, G.507, op.12, no.5, B-flat major
   2 0 0 0—2 0 0 0—str
   Ed. Antonio de Almeida
   Doblinger

Symphony no.8, G.508, op.12, no.6, A major   23'
   2 0 0 0—2 0 0 0—str
   Ed. Antonio de Almeida.
   Doblinger

Symphony no.9, G.493, op.21, no.1, B-flat major   11'
   2 0 0 1—2 0 0 0—str
   Ed. Antonio de Almeida.
   Doblinger

Symphony no.10, G.494, op.21, no.2, E-flat major   16'
   2 0 0 0—2 0 0 0—str
   Ed. Antonio de Almeida.
   Doblinger

Symphony no.11, G.495, op.21, no.3, C major   23'
   0 2 0 0—2 0 0 0—str   11' 6' 6'
   Ed. Antonio de Almeida.
   Doblinger

Symphony no.12, G.496, op.21, no.4, D major   8'
   0 2 0 0—2 0 0 0—str
   Ed. Antonio de Almeida.
   Doblinger

Symphony no.13, G.497, op.21, no.5, B-flat major   16'
   0 2 0 1—2 0 0 0—str   8' 5' 3'
   Ed. Antonio de Almeida.
   Doblinger

Symphony no.14, G.498, op.21, no.6, A major   13'
   0 2 0 0—2 0 0 0—str   4' 5' 4'
   Ed. Antonio de Almeida.
   Doblinger

Symphony no.15, G.509, op.35, no.1, D major   11'
   0 2 0 1—2 0 0 0—str   4' 4' 3'
   Ed. Antonio de Almeida.
   Doblinger

Symphony no.16, G.510, op.35, no.2, E-flat major   13'
   0 2 0 1—2 0 0 0—str   5' 5' 3'
   Ed. Antonio de Almeida.
   Doblinger

Symphony no.17, G.511, op.35, no.3, A major — **17'** — 6' 6' 5'
 0 2 0 1—2 0 0 0—str
  Doblinger ed. by Antonio de Almeida. Zanibon edition (ed. Ettore
  Bonelli) published as op.1, no.3. Listed elsewhere as Symphony
  no.9.
  Doblinger *Zanibon*

Symphony no.18, G.512, op.35, no.4, F major — **13'** — 4' 5' 4'
 0 2 0 1—2 0 0 0—str
  Doblinger ed. Antonio de Almeida. G. Schirmer version (ed.
  Newell Jenkins) is published as op.35, no.4. Ricordi version (ed.
  Guido Guerrini) also calls for one flute, and is published as
  Symphony no.4. This same work is elsewhere identified as
  Symphony no.10.
  Doblinger *Ricordi* *Schirmer, G.*

Symphony no.19, G.513, op.35, no.5, E-flat major — **11'** — 4' 4' 3'
 0 2 0 1—2 0 0 0—str
  Ed. Antonio de Almeida.
  Doblinger

Symphony no.20, G.514, op.35, no.6, B-flat major — **17'** — 5' 9' 3'
 0 2 0 1—2 0 0 0—str
  Doblinger ed. Antonio de Almeida. Zanibon edition (ed. Ettore
  Bonelli) published as op.1, no.6. Listed elsewhere as Symphony
  no.12.
  Doblinger *Zanibon*

Symphony no.21, G.515, op.37, no.1, C major — **17'** — 5' 5' 4' 3'
 1 2 0 2—2 0 0 0—str
  Ed. Antonio de Almeida.
  Doblinger

Symphony no.23, G.517, op.37, no.3, D minor — **18'** — 6' 3' 5' 4'
 1 2 0 2—2 0 0 0—str
  Doblinger edition ed. by Antonio de Almeida.
  Doblinger *Kalmus*

Symphony no.25, G.518, op.37, no.4, A major — **21'** — 7' 4' 6' 4'
 1 2 0 2—2 0 0 0—str
  Also listed elsewhere as Symphony no.16.
  Doblinger edition (ed. Antonio de Almeida) in preparation;
  Ricordi ed. by Riccardo Allorto; Universal ed. by Karl Geiringer.
  Doblinger *Ricordi* *Universal*

Symphony no.26, G.519, op.41, C minor — **17'**
 0 2 0 2—2 0 0 0—str
  Ed. Antonio de Almeida.
  Doblinger

Symphony no.27, G.520, op.42, D major — **20'** — 6' 7' 4' 3'
 1 2 0 2—2 0 0 0—str
  Doblinger ed. Antonio de Almeida; Suvini ed. Pietro Spada.
  Doblinger *Suvini*

Symphony no.28
see his: Overture, op.43, G.521, D major

Symphony "A", G.500, D major   9'
2hn opt—str   2' 3' 3' 1'
Ed. Walter Lebermann.
Authenticity has been disputed.
Schott

Boëllmann, Léon   1862 - 1897
Symphonic variations, op.23   13'
  solo violoncello
  2 2 2 2—4 2 3 1—tmp—hp—str
Durand   *C. Fischer*   *Kalmus*

Boieldieu, François   1775 - 1834
Le Calife de Bagdad (Caliph of Bagdad): Overture   8'
  *2 2 2 2—2 2 0 0—tmp+2—str
Breitkopf   *Heugel*   *Kalmus*

Concerto, harp, C major (In tre tempi)   20'
  2 2 0 2—2 0 0 0—str   9' 11'
Ricordi

La Dame blanche: Overture   9'
  *2 2 2 2—2 2 1 0—tmp—str
Breitkopf   *Kalmus*   *Luck*

Boismortier, Joseph Bodin de   1691 - 1755
Concerto, D major
  solo violoncello, or viola da gamba, or bassoon
  cnt—str (without va)
  Ed. Hugo Ruf.
Ricordi

Bolcom, William   1938 -
Commedia for (almost) 18th-century orchestra   10'
  *1 2 +1 2—2 0 0 0—opt tmp—pf—str 4.4.2.2.1
  Doublings of winds permissible; strings may be increased to
  10.10.9.7.4.
Marks

Concerto, violin   23'
  *2 *2 =2 *2—2 2 2 0—tmp+3—hp, pf/cel—str   10' 7' 6'
  May be done with chamber orchestra or full-sized orchestra; if
  the latter, horns should be doubled.
Marks

Concerto-serenade   17'
  solo violin
  str (minimum 4.3.3.2.1)
Marks

Fives   18'
    solo violin & piano
    3 str orchestras
    Merion

Orphée-sérénade   19'
    solo piano   3' 4' 2'
    *1 1 +1 1—1 0 0 0—2vn, va, vc, db   3' 4' 3'
    Chamber-size string sections may be used instead of individual
    players.
    Marks

Ragomania!—a classic festival-overture   10'
    *3 *3 *3 *3—4 3 3 1—tmp+3—pf, elec gtr, opt hp—str
    Guitar may be dispensed with if pianist has an electric piano in
    addition to an acoustic piano.
    Marks

Seattle Slew (dance suite) (Three dances in forequarter time)   24'
    *3 *3 *3 3—4 2 3 1—flugelhorn—tmp+3—hp, pf—str (minimum
    10.8.6.6.4)
    Marks

A summer divertimento   25'
    2 0 +1 1—0 1 0 0—1perc—pf, hpsd—3vn, 2va, 2vc, 2db
    Marks

Symphony no.1   16'
    2 1 1 1—4 2 1 0—tmp+2—pf—str   5' 5' 2' 4'
    Marks

Symphony no.3   35'
    =1 *2 =1 2—2 0 0 0—pf/cel/elec pf—str 6.4.4.3.1
    Formerly titled *Chamber symphony*, or *Symphony for chamber
    orchestra*.
    Contents—Alpha; Scherzo vitale; Chiaroscuro; Omega.

    Marks

Bond, Victoria   1945 -
Urban Bird   24'
    solo alto saxophone
    *2 *2 *2 2—4 4 3 1—tmp+2—str
    Presser

Borodin, Alexander   1833 - 1887
In the steppes of central Asia   9'
    2 *2 2 2—4 2 3 0—tmp—str
    Kalmus   *Ricordi*   *Russian*

La Mer   8'
  solo tenor
  2 2 2 2—4 2 3 1—tmp—str
  Transcribed by Rimsky-Korsakov.
  Kalmus

Nocturne (arr. N. Rimsky-Korsakov)   9'
  solo violin
  2 2 2 2—2 2 0 0—tmp—str
  From the composer's String quartet no.2.
  Kalmus

Nocturne (arr. Malcolm Sargent)   9'
  str
  From the composer's String quartet no.2.
  Boosey

Nocturne (arr. N. Tcherepnin)   9'
  3 2 3 2—4 3 3 1—tmp—hp—str
  From the composer's String quartet no.2.
  Universal

Petite Suite   23'
  *3 2 2 2—4 2 3 0—tmp+1—str | 5' 3' 4' |
  Arr. Glazunov. Two of the flutists double on piccolo. | 3' 2' 6' |
  Breitkopf   *Kalmus*   *Leduc*

Petite Suite: Scherzo & Nocturne   6'
  *3 2 2 2—4 2 3 0—tmp—str
  Arr. Glazunov.
  Luck

Prince Igor: Overture   10'
  *3 2 2 2—4 2 3 1—tmp—str
  Completed and orchestrated by Glazunov.
  Kalmus

Prince Igor: Polovtsian dances   14'
  optional chorus | 2' 12' |
  *3 *2 2 2—4 2 3 1—tmp+5—hp—str
  Nos. 8 & 17 from the opera.
  C. Fischer   *Kalmus*   *Schirmer, G.*

Prince Igor: Polovtsian march   5'
  optional chorus
  *3 2 2 2—4 2 3 1—tmp+4—str
  Optional backstage brass (4 2 0 1) and snare drum. Orchestrated
  by Rimsky-Korsakov.
  Belaieff   *Kalmus*

Symphony no.1, E-flat major   33'
  2 *2 2 2—4 2 3 0—tmp—str | 13' 7' 7' |
  Breitkopf   *Kalmus*   *Leduc*   *Universal* | 6' |

Symphony no.2, B minor   26'
    *3 *2 2 2—4 2 3 1—tmp+4—hp—str   8' 5' 6' 7'
    Breitkopf   *Kalmus*   *Leduc*   *Universal*

Symphony no.3, A minor   19'
    2 2 2 2—4 2 3 0—tmp—str   9' 10'
    Belaieff   *Kalmus*   *Leduc*

Bottesini, Giovanni   1821 - 1889

Concerto, double bass, no.2, B minor   17'
    1 2 0 2—2 0 0 0—tmp—str   7' 5' 5'
    Doblinger

Boudreau, Walter   1947 -

Versus
    1 1 1 1—2 1 1 0—3perc—pf
    A burlesque of a hockey game.
    CMC

Boulez, Pierre   1925 -

Le Marteau sans maître   35'
    solo mezzo-soprano
    alto flute—guitar—xylorimba, vibraphone—1 percussionist
    Universal

Le Soleil des eaux   10'
    chorus   solos STB
    *2 *2 *2 2—3 2 1 1—tmp+2—hp—str (12.10.8.8.6)
    Heugel

Bowles, Paul   1910 -

Concerto, 2 pianos, percussion & winds   17'
    0 *1 *1 0—0 1 0 0—2perc   5' 2' 6' 4'
    AME

Concerto, 2 pianos (full orchestra version)   17'
    *2 *2 *2 1—2 2 1 0—tmp+3—hp, cel—str   5' 2' 6' 4'
    AME

Boyce, William   1711 - 1779

Concerto grosso, B minor   9'
    solos: 2 violins, violoncello
    cnt—str
    Hinrichsen edition gives title as *Double concerto.*
    Eulenburg   *Hinrichsen*

Overture (Ode for his majesty's birthday [1769])   7'
    0 2 0 1—2 0 0 0—cnt—str
    Score only available in the collection *Musica Britannica,*
    v.13, p.1.
    Parts available from Galaxy.
    Galaxy

Overture (Ode for the new year [1758])   4'
0 2 0 1—0 2 0 0—tmp—cnt—str
Score only available in the collection *Musica Britannica*,
v.13, p.103.
Parts available from Galaxy.
Galaxy

Overture (Ode for the new year [1772])   4'
0 2 0 1—cnt—str
Score only available in the collection *Musica Britannica*,
v.13, p.55.
Parts available from Galaxy.
Galaxy

Overture (Peleus and Thetis)   7'
0 2 0 1—cnt—str
Score only available in the collection *Musica Britannica*,
v.13, p.131.
Parts available from Galaxy.
Galaxy

Symphony no.1, B-flat major   8'
2 2 0 1—cnt—str | 3' 3' 2' |
Doblinger edition (ed. Max Goberman) is to be preferred.
Doblinger   *Oxford*

Symphony no.2, A major   5'
0 2 0 1—cnt—str | 2' 1' 2' |
Doblinger edition (ed. Max Goberman) is to be preferred.
Doblinger   *Oxford*

Symphony no.3, C major   6'
0 2 0 1—cnt—str | 3' 1' 2' |
Doblinger edition (ed. Max Goberman) is to be preferred.
Doblinger   *Oxford*

Symphony no.4, F major   7'
0 2 0 2—2 0 0 0—cnt—str | 3' 2' 2' |
Doblinger edition (ed. Max Goberman) is to be preferred.
Doblinger   *Oxford*

Symphony no.5, D major   8'
0 2 0 1—0 2 0 0—tmp—cnt—str | 4' 2' 2' |
Doblinger edition (ed. Max Goberman) is to be preferred.
Doblinger   *Oxford*

Symphony no.6, F major   8'
0 2 0 1—cnt—str | 5' 3' |
Doblinger edition (ed. Max Goberman) is to be preferred.
Doblinger   *Oxford*

Symphony no.7, B-flat major   10'
2 2 0 1—cnt—str | 5' 3' 2' |
Doblinger edition (ed. Max Goberman) is to be preferred.
Doblinger   *Oxford*

Symphony no.8, D minor · 11'
2 2 0 1—cnt—str · 6' 2' 3'
Doblinger edition (ed. Max Goberman) is to be preferred.
Doblinger   *Oxford*

Brahms, Johannes 1833 - 1897

Akademische Festouvertüre, op.80 (Academic festival overture) · 10'
*3 2 2 *3—4 3 3 1—tmp+3—str
Breitkopf   *Kalmus*

Alto rhapsody, op.53 · 13'
alto solo   male chorus
2 2 2 2—2 0 0 0—str
Breitkopf   *C. Fischer*   *Kalmus*   *Peters*

Concerto, piano, no.1, op.15, D minor · 44'
2 2 2 2—4 2 0 0—tmp—str · 21' 11' 12'
Breitkopf   *Kalmus*

Concerto, piano, no.2, op.83, B-flat major · 44'
*2 2 2 2—4 2 0 0—tmp—str · 16' 9' 10' 9'
Breitkopf   *Kalmus*

Concerto, violin, op.77, D major · 38'
2 2 2 2—4 2 0 0—tmp—str · 21' 9' 8'
Breitkopf   *Kalmus*

Concerto, violin & violoncello, op.102, A minor (Double concerto) · 32'
2 2 2 2—4 2 0 0—tmp—str · 16' 8' 8'
Breitkopf   *Kalmus*

Ein deutsches Requiem, op.45 (German requiem) · 68'
chorus   soprano and baritone solos · 10' 14' 11' 6' 6' 11' 10'
*3 2 2 *3—4 2 3 1—tmp—org—2 or more hp dbl a single part—str
Contrabassoon and organ are optional.
Breitkopf   *Kalmus*   *Peters*

Haydn variations
see his: Variations on a theme of Joseph Haydn

Hungarian dances nos.1, 3, 10 (arr. Brahms) · 7'
*3 2 2 2—4 2 0 0—tmp+2—str · 3' 2' 2'
Breitkopf   *Kalmus*

Hungarian dances nos.2, 7 (arr. Andreas Hallén) · 5'
2 2 2 2—4 2 3 0—tmp+1—str · 3' 2'
Kalmus   *Simrock*

Hungarian dances nos.5, 6 (arr. A. Parlow) · 7'
*2 2 2 2—4 2 3 0—tmp—str · 3' 4'
Luck

Hungarian dances nos.5, 6, 7 (arr. M. Schmeling) · 9'
*3 2 2 2—4 2 3 0—tmp+3—str · 3' 4' 2'
Breitkopf   *Luck*

Hungarian dances nos.11-16 (arr. A. Parlow)   12'
*3 2 2 2—4 2 3 0—tmp—hp—str
Kalmus   *Simrock*
2' 2' 2'
2' 2' 2'

Hungarian dances nos.17-21 (arr. Dvořák)   10'
*2 2 2 2—4 2 3 0—tmp+3—str
Optional hp in no.21.
Kalmus   *Simrock*
2' 2' 2'
2' 2'

Liebeslieder waltzes, op.52   25'
str
Arr. Friedrich Hermann.
Kalmus   *Luck*   *Simrock*

Nänie, op.82   14'
chorus
2 2 2 2—2 0 3 0—tmp—hp (doubled if possible)—str
Breïtkopf   *Kalmus*   *Peters*

Rinaldo, op.50   45'
tenor solo   male chorus
*3 2 2 2—2 2 3 0—tmp—str
Luck   *Kalmus*   *Simrock*

Schicksalslied, op.54 (Song of destiny)   18'
chorus
2 2 2 2—2 2 3 0—tmp—str
Breitkopf   *Kalmus*   *Simrock*

Serenade no.1, op.11, D major   49'
2 2 2 2—4 2 0 0—tmp—str
Breitkopf   *Kalmus*
14' 7'
14' 4' 4'
6'

Serenade no.2, op.16, A major   29'
*3 2 2 2—2 0 0 0—str (without violins)
Breitkopf   *Kalmus*
8' 2' 8'
5' 6'

Symphony no.1, op.68, C minor   45'
2 2 2 *3—4 2 3 0—tmp—str
Breitkopf   *Henle*   *Kalmus*
13' 10'
5' 17'

Symphony no.2, op.73, D major   40'
2 2 2 2—4 2 3 1—tmp—str
Breitkopf   *Kalmus*
14' 10'
6' 10'

Symphony no.3, op.90, F major   33'
2 2 2 *3—4 2 3 0—tmp—str
Breitkopf   *Kalmus*
10' 8' 6'
9'

Symphony no.4, op.98, E minor   39'
*2 2 2 *3—4 2 3 0—tmp+1—str
Breitkopf   *Kalmus*
12' 11'
6' 10'

Tragische Ouvertüre, op.81 (Tragic overture) 13'
*3 2 2 2—4 2 3 1—tmp—str
Breitkopf   *Kalmus*

Variations on a theme of Joseph Haydn, op.56a (Haydn variations) 17'
*3 2 2 *3—4 2 0 0—tmp+1—str
A critical edition of the score with historical and analytical
essays is available from Norton.
Breitkopf   *Kalmus*

Brant, Henry   1913 -

Angels and devils 18'
solo flute, accompanied by a flute orchestra consisting of 3pic,
5fl, 2afl
MCA

Galaxy 2 5'
*1 0 1 0—2 1 1 0—tmp+1
MCA

Verticals ascending (after the Rodia Towers) 8'
*2 2 *3 2—opt asx—2 2 1 1—tmp+1—pf, opt elec org
One of the clarinetists doubles on alto clarinet. Alternate version
substitutes violins for organ and/or violas and violoncellos for
saxophone. Instruments divided into two widely separated
groups, each with its own conductor.
MCA

Brian, Havergal   1876 - 1972

Symphony no.22 (Symphonia brevis) 10'
*3 *3 *3 *3—4 3 3 1—tmp+7—hp—str 16.14.12.10.8

Brindle, Reginald Smith   1917 -
see: Smith Brindle, Reginald, 1917-

Britten, Benjamin   1913 - 1976

Canadian carnival, op.19 14'
*2 *2 2 2—4 3 3 1—tmp+2—hp—str
3rd tp optional.
Boosey

Cantata academica, carmen basiliense, op.62 21'
chorus   solos SATB
*2 2 2 2—4 2 3 1—tmp+4—1 or 2hp, pf (dbl opt cel)—str
Boosey

Cantata misericordium, op.69 20'
chorus   solos TB
tmp—hp, pf—solo string quartet—str orchestra
Boosey

Concerto, piano, no.1, op.13   **34'**
   *2 *2 2 2—4 2 3 1—tmp+2—hp—str
   Boosey

| 12' 4' |
| 18' |

Concerto, violin, no.1, op.15   **32'**
   *3 *2 2 2—4 3 3 1—tmp+2—hp—str
   Boosey

| 9' 23' |

Diversions on a theme, op.21   **23'**
   solo piano (left hand)
   *2 *2 +2 *3—asx—4 2 3 1—tmp+3—hp—str
   Saxophone, contrabassoon, and 1 percussionist are optional.
   Boosey

Gloriana: Symphonic suite   **26'**
   optional tenor solo
   *3 *3 *3 *3—4 3 3 1—tmp+4—hp—str
   Boosey

| 4' 5' 1' |
| 1' 2' 1' |
| 2' 2' 8' |

Gloriana: Courtly dances   **9'**
   2 2 2 2—4 2 3 1—tmp+2—str
   Boosey

| 1' 1' 2' |
| 1' 2' 2' |

Les Illuminations, op.18   **21'**
   high voice
   str
   Boosey

| 2' 2' 1' |
| 2' 2' 1' |
| 2' 4' 3' |
| 2' |

Matinées musicales, op.24 (after Rossini)   **13'**
   *2 2 2 2—2 2 3 0—tmp+2—hp (or pf), cel (or pf)—str
   Boosey

Nocturne, op.60   **25'**
   solo tenor
   1 *1 1 1—1 0 0 0—tmp—hp—str
   Boosey

Now sleeps the crimson petal   **5'**
   solo tenor, solo horn
   str
   Originally intended to be part of the composer's *Serenade for
   tenor, horn & strings*, q.v. Not to be performed in conjunction with
   the *Serenade*.
   Boosey

Paul Bunyan: Overture   **5'**
   *2 1 *3 1—2 2 2 1—tmp+3—opt hp, opt pf—str
   Orchestrated by Colin Matthews.
   Faber

Peter Grimes: Four sea interludes   **16'**
   *2 2 +2 *3—4 3 3 1—tmp+3—hp—str
   Boosey

| 3' 4' 4' 5' |

Peter Grimes: Passacaglia   7'
   *2 2 2 *3—4 3 3 1—tmp+3—hp, cel—str
   Boosey

Phaedra, op.93   15'
   mezzo-soprano solo
   tmp+2—hpsd—str
   Faber

The prince of the pagodas: Pas de six   11'
   *3 *3 +3 *3—4 3 3 1—tmp+2—hp, pf—str | 2' 3' 1' |
   Cued so that performance is possible with double woodwind. | 1' 2' 2' |
   Boosey

Saint Nicolas, op.42   50'
   tenor solo, 4 boy sopranos   chorus, semi-chorus of female voices
   tmp(+2perc opt)—pf 4-hands, org—str
   Boosey

Scottish ballade, op.26   13'
   2 solo pianos
   *2 2 2 *3—4 2 3 1—tmp+2—hp—str
   Contrabassoon is optional.
   Boosey

Serenade for tenor, horn & strings, op.31   25'
   solo tenor, solo horn | 2' 4' 3' |
   str | 5' 3' 2' |
   Boosey | 4' 2' |

Simple symphony, op.4   16'
   str | 3' 3' 7' 3' |
   Oxford

Sinfonia da requiem, op.20   21'
   =3 *3 =3 *3—asx—6 3 3 1—tmp+4—2hp, pf—str | 9' 5' 7' |
   The following instruments are optional:
   afl, asx, hn 5 & 6, 2nd hp, 4th perc.
   Boosey

Sinfonietta   15'
   1 1 1 1—1 0 0 0—str quintet (or small str orch) | 4' 11' |
   Boosey

Soirées musicales, op.9 (after Rossini)   10'
   *2 2 2 2—4 2 3 0—tmp+3—hp (or pf)—str | 1' 3' 2' |
   Playable with the following reduced instrumentation: | 2' 2' |
   1 1 1 0—0 1 1 0—2perc—hp (or pf)—str.
   Boosey

Spring symphony, op.44   45'
   chorus, boy chorus   solos SAT | 19' 12' |
   =3 *3 *3 *3—4 3 3 1—cow horn—tmp+4—2hp—str | 6' 8' |
   Boosey

Suite on English folk tunes, op.90 (A time there was...)   15'
  *2 *2 2 2—2 2 0 0—tmp+2—hp—str
  Faber

| 2' 3' 2' |
| 1' 7' |

The sword in the stone   10'
  1 0 1 1—0 1 1 0—1perc—hp
  Contents—Introduction and Boys' tunes; Merlyn's tune and Tree
  music; Merlyn's spell and Witch tune; Bird music; Lullaby; Water
  theme and End music.
  Faber

Symphony for violoncello & orchestra, op.68   35'
  *2 2 *2 *2—2 2 1 1—tmp+2—str
  Boosey

| 13' 4' |
| 10' 8' |

Variations on a theme of Frank Bridge   25'
  str
  Boosey

War requiem, op.66   78'
  chorus, boy choir   solos STB
  *4 *4 =4 *4—7 4 3 1—tmp+5—hp, pf, org—str
  A second conductor is intended for the separate chamber
  orchestra, the instrumentation of which is included above.
  Boosey

| 9' 26' |
| 10' 9' 3' |
| 21' |

Young Apollo, op.16   10'
  solo piano, solo string quartet
  str
  Faber

Young person's guide to the orchestra, op.34 (Variations and fugue   18'
on a theme of Purcell)
  optional speaker
  *3 2 2 2—4 2 3 1—tmp+7—hp—str
  7 percussionists required to play all the notes;
  composer-authorized omissions make performance possible with
  5 percussionists. Curiously, the published score specifies "at least
  3" percussionists; apparently some adaptation of the parts is
  expected, if not encouraged.
  Boosey

Brouwer, Leo   1939 -

Concerto de Toronto (Concerto no.4)   34'
  solo guitar
  *1 0 +2 0—1 1 0 0—2perc—pf—str
  EDY

| 10' 14' |
| 10' |

Concerto elegiaco (Concerto no.3)   22'
  solo guitar
  tmp+1—str
  Eschig

| 9' 4' 9' |

Retrats catalans 18'
   solo guitar
   *2 0 0 0—tmp+2—pf—str 4.3.2.2.1
   Eschig

Brown, Earle   1926 -

Available forms 1 var
   1 1 =3 1—1 1 1 0—tmp+1—hp, pf—str quintet (2vn, va, vc, db)
   AMP

Available forms 2 var
   =4 *3 =4 *3—6 3 4 2—bass tp—tmp+3—2hp, pf/cel, gtr—str
   (16.14.12.10.8)
   2 conductors are required.
   AMP

Brubeck, Howard   1916 -

Dialogues for jazz combo & orchestra 23'
   *2 *2 2 2—4 3 3 1—tmp+2—str
   The jazz combo may be varied in instrumentation. The length of
   the solo sections may be varied.
   Shawnee

Bruch, Max   1838 - 1920

Adagio appassionato, op.57 8'
   solo violin
   2 2 2 2—4 2 3 0—tmp—str
   C. Fischer   *Kalmus*   *Simrock*

Ave Maria, op.61 4'
   solo violoncello
   2 2 2 2—4 2 3 0—tmp—str
   This work may be out of print, but orchestra materials are in the
   Fleisher Collection.
   Simrock

Concerto, violin, no.1, op.26, G minor 24'
   2 2 2 2—4 2 0 0—tmp—str   9' 8' 7'
   Kalmus   *Peters*

Concerto, violin, no.2, D minor 27'
   2 2 2 2—4 2 3 0—tmp—str   9' 10' 8'
   C. Fischer   *Kalmus*

Concerto, violin, no.3, op.58, D minor 38'
   2 2 2 2—4 2 3 0—tmp—str   18' 11'
   Kalmus   9'

Kol nidrei, op.47 10'
   solo violoncello
   2 2 2 2—4 2 3 0—tmp—str
   C. Fischer   *Kalmus*

Loreley: Prelude   7'
   2 2 2 2—4 2 3 0—tmp—hp—str
   Adapted by George Dasch.
   Luck

Scottish fantasy, op.46   30'
   solo violin   9' 6' 6' 9'
   2 2 2 2—4 2 3 1—tmp+2—hp—str
   Kalmus   *Simrock*

Serenade, op.75, A minor   37'
   solo violin
   2 2 2 2—4 2 3 0—tmp—str
   Kalmus   *Simrock*

Swedish dances, op.63, nos.1-7 (series 1)   12'
   *2 *2 2 2—4 2 3 0—tmp+1—str
   Kalmus   *Lengnick*   *Luck*

Swedish dances, op.63, nos.8-15 (series 2)   11'
   2 *2 2 2—4 2 3 1—tmp+1—str
   Kalmus   *Lengnick*   *Luck*

Symphony no.1, op.28, E-flat major   29'
   2 2 2 2—4 2 3 0—tmp—str   10' 5' 6'
   Kalmus   8'

Symphony no.3, op.51, E major   36'
   2 2 2 2—4 3 3 1—tmp—str   12' 11'
   Breitkopf   *Kalmus*   7' 6'

Bruckner, Anton   1824 - 1896

Helgoland   14'
   male chorus
   2 2 2 2—4 3 3 1—tmp+1—str
   Bärenreiter   *MWV*   *Universal*

March in D minor   4'
   2 2 2 2—2 2 3 0—tmp—str
   Published with his *Three pieces for orchestra, q.v.* The Eulenburg
   version uses the collective title *Four orchestral pieces.*
   Doblinger   *Eulenburg*

Mass, C major (1841) (Windhaager Messe)
   chorus
   0 0 0 0—2 0 0 0—org—str
   Kalmus

Mass no.1, D minor   43'
   chorus   solos SATB
   2 2 2 2—2 2 3 0—tmp—str
   MWV

Mass no.2, E minor   37'
    chorus
    0 2 2 2—4 2 3 0
    Two versions are available from Bruckner Verlag:
    original version of 1866, and revised version of 1882
    MWV

Mass no.3, F minor (Great)   60'
    chorus   solos SATB
    2 2 2 2—2 2 3 0—tmp—str
    MWV

Missa solemnis, B-flat minor   31'
    chorus   solos SATB
    0 2 0 2—2 2 3 0—tmp—org—str
    MWV

Overture, G minor   12'
    *2 2 2 2—2 2 3 0—tmp—str
    Posthumous.
    MWV   *Universal*

Psalm 150   9'
    chorus
    2 2 2 2—4 3 3 1—tmp—str
    MWV

Requiem, D minor   37'
    chorus   solos SATB
    0 0 0 0—1 0 3 0—org—str
    MWV

Symphonies
    Regarding textual problems and editions of the Bruckner
    symphonies, as well as an explanation of the Cahis numbers, see
    Appendix I, p.565.

Symphony (Cahis 1), F minor (Studiensymphonie)   48'
    2 2 2 2—4 2 3 0—tmp—str | 18' | 13' |
    Ed. Leopold Nowak, 1973. | 6' | 11' |
    Sometimes referred to as *Symphony no.00.*
    MWV

Symphony (Cahis 3), D minor (Nullte)   46'
    2 2 2 2—4 2 3 0—tmp—str | 15' | 14' |
    Ed. Leopold Nowak, 1968. | 7' | 10' |
    Sometimes referred to as *Symphony no.0.*
    MWV

Symphony no.1 (Linz version 1866, Cahis 2), C minor   50'
    3 2 2 2—4 2 3 0—tmp—str | 13' | 14' |
    Slightly revised by the composer in 1877. Ed. Robert Haas, 1935; | 9' | 14' |
    Leopold Nowak, 1953.
    3rd flute in 2nd movement only.
    MWV   *Kalmus*

Symphony no.1 (Vienna version 1891, Cahis 17), C minor — 48'
3 2 2 2—4 2 3 0—tmp—str
13' 13'
9' 13'
Ed. Robert Haas, 1935; Günter Brosche, 1980.
3rd flute in 2nd movement only.
MWV   *Kalmus*

Symphony no.2 (1872 version, Cahis 4), C minor — 68'
2 2 2 2—4 2 3 0—tmp—str
20' 16'
11' 21'
Critical edition, ed. William Carragan, in preparation. The
Robert Haas edition of 1938, although labeled "original version,"
is actually a mixture of versions, and should not be used.
MWV

Symphony no.2 (1877 version, Cahis 8), C minor — 53'
2 2 2 2—4 2 3 0—tmp—str
18' 17'
3' 15'
Ed. Leopold Nowak, 1965. New edition in preparation.
MWV

Symphony no.3 (1873 version, Cahis 5), D minor — 65'
(Wagner-Symphonie)
2 2 2 2—4 3 3 0—tmp—str
24' 19'
6' 16'
Ed. Leopold Nowak, 1977.
MWV

Symphony no.3 (1877 version, Cahis 9), D minor — 61'
(Wagner-Symphonie)
2 2 2 2—4 3 3 0—tmp—str
21' 17'
7' 16'
Ed. Fritz Oeser, 1950; Leopold Nowak, 1981.
MWV

Symphony no.3 (1889 version, Cahis 15), D minor — 57'
(Wagner-Symphonie)
2 2 2 2—4 3 3 0—tmp—str
22' 16'
7' 12'
Ed. Leopold Nowak, 1959.
MWV

Symphony no.3: Adagio 2 (1876) — 18'
2 2 2 2—4 3 3 0—tmp—str
Ed. Leopold Nowak, 1980.
An intermediate version of the 2nd movement, later discarded
from the 1877 version of Symphony no.3 (Cahis 9).
MWV

Symphony no.4 (1874 version, Cahis 6) E-flat major (Romantic) — 70'
2 2 2 2—4 3 3 0—tmp—str
20' 20'
12' 18'
Ed. Leopold Nowak, 1975.
MWV

Symphony no.4 (1878 version, Cahis 10), E-flat major (Romantic):   17'
Finale 1878 (Volksfest)
    2 2 2 2—4 3 3 1—tmp—str
    Ed. Leopold Nowak, 1981.
    This finale to the 1878 version of Symphony no.4 (Cahis 10) was
    later replaced. To perform Cahis 10, use the first three movements
    of Cahis 11 (next entry) plus this finale.
    MWV

Symphony no.4 (1878/80 version, Cahis 11), E-flat major   70'
(Romantic)

21'	15'
11'	23'

    2 2 2 2—4 3 3 1—tmp—str
    Ed. Leopold Nowak, 1953. This edition includes a further
    revision of the finale, previously thought to be 1886, but which
    may be as early as 1881. This revision brings back in its final
    bars the horn motive from the first movement; it is the most
    frequently performed version of the symphony. (The Robert Haas
    edition of 1936, reprinted in 1944, does not include this return of
    the horn call.)
    MWV   *Kalmus*

Symphony no.4 (1888 version, Cahis Suppl.1/14+), E-flat major   65'
    Bruckner is said to have regarded this as his final, definitive

17'	18'
9'	21'

    version of this symphony. Not as yet available in a critical
    edition.

Symphony no.5 (Cahis 7), B-flat major   81'
    2 2 2 2—4 3 3 1—tmp—str

21'	21'
14'	25'

    Ed. Robert Haas, 1935; Leopold Nowak, 1951.
    Extra brass is often added at the end of the symphony.
    MWV   *Kalmus*

Symphony no.6 (Cahis 12), A major   54'
    2 2 2 2—4 3 3 1—tmp—str

16'	16'
9'	13'

    Ed. Robert Haas, 1935; Leopold Nowak, 1952.
    MWV

Symphony no.7 (Cahis 13), E major   64'
    2 2 2 2—4 3 3 1—4 Wagner tubas—tmp—str

20'	22'
10'	12'

    Ed. Robert Haas, 1944; Leopold Nowak, 1954.
    Although 4tp are listed on the first page of the finale, this is an
    error; there is no 4th tp part.
    MWV   *Kalmus*

Symphony no.8 (1887 version, Cahis 14), C minor   76'
    *3 3 3 *3—8 3 3 1—tmp+2—3 hp (playing a single real part)—str

14'	14'
27'	21'

    Horns 5-8 double on Wagner tubas.
    Ed. Leopold Nowak, 1972.
    MWV

Symphony no.8 (1890 version, Cahis 16), C minor   70'
    3 3 3 3—8 3 3 1—tmp+2—3 hp (playing a single real part)—str

15'	14'
21'	20'

    Horns 5-8 double on Wagner tubas.
    Ed. Leopold Nowak, 1955.
    MWV

Symphony no.9 (Cahis 18), D minor   63'
   3 3 3 3—8 3 3 1—tmp—str   25' 11'
   Horns 5-8 double on Wagner tubas.   27'
   Ed. Alfred Orel, 1934; Leopold Nowak, 1951.
   The finale of this symphony was left unfinished at the composer's
   death. See the following two entries.
   MWV   *Kalmus*

Symphony no.9 (Cahis 18), D minor: Finale (Carragan)   22'
   3 3 3 3—8 3 3 1—tmp—str
   Horns 5-8 double on Wagner tubas.
   Completion of the finale by William Carragan, based on the
   composer's sketches. For source of performance materials, see
   Appendix I, p.567.

Symphony no.9 (Cahis 18), D minor: Finale (Samale et. al.)   30'
   3 3 3 3—4 3 3 1—4 Wagner tubas—tmp—str
   Reconstruction of the autograph score from the surviving sources.
   Performance version by Nicola Samale, John A. Phillips &
   Giuseppe Mazzuca, in collaboration with Gunnar Cohrs. For
   source of performance materials, see Appendix I, p.567.

Te Deum   22'
   chorus   solos SATB
   2 2 2 2—4 3 3 1—tmp—opt org—str
   Peters

Three pieces for orchestra   9'
   2 2 2 2—2 2 1 0—tmp—str
   Published with his *March in D minor*, q.v. The Eulenberg edition
   gives the collective title *Four orchestral pieces*.
   Doblinger   *Eulenburg*

Buck, Dudley   1839 - 1909
Festival overture on the American national air (The star spangled   7'
banner)
   optional chorus
   *3 2 2 2—4 3 3 1—tmp+3—str
   Believed to be out of print, but orchestral materials (newly
   corrected) are in the Fleisher Collection.

Busoni, Ferruccio   1866 - 1924
Concertino, clarinet & chamber orchestra, op.48   9'
   0 2 0 2—2 0 0 0—1perc—str
   Breitkopf

Concerto, piano, op.39   64'
   *4 *3 *3 3—4 3 3 1—tmp+2—str   12' 8'
   Optional unseen male chorus of 48 voices in final movement. Two   23' 12'
   of the flutists double on piccolo.   9'
   Breitkopf   *Luck*

Divertimento, flute & chamber orchestra, op.52   8'
    0 2 2 2—2 2 0 0—tmp+1—str
    Breitkopf

Indianische Fantasie, op.44   28'
    solo piano
    2 *2 2 2—3 2 0 0—tmp+3—hp—str
    Breitkopf

Lustspiel overture, op.38   8'
    *3 2 2 2—4 2 0 0—tmp+2—str
    Breitkopf

Rondo arlecchinesco, op.46 (Harlekins Reigen)   12'
    tenor voice backstage
    *2 1 2 2—3 2 3 0—tmp+3—str
    Breitkopf

Turandot, op.41: Suite   37'
    *3 *3 *3 *3—4 4 3 1—tmp+4—hp—str

4'	3'	4'
7'	2'	5'
3'	9'	

    Optional women's chorus in one movement.
    Breitkopf

Butterworth, George   1885 - 1916
A Shropshire lad; rhapsody for orchestra   11'
    2 *3 *3 2—4 2 3 1—tmp—hp—str
    Kalmus

Buxtehude, Dietrich   ca.1637 - 1707
Four chorale preludes   20'
    *2 *2 2 2—3 3 3 1—str

7'	3'	4'	6'

    Arr. Gordon Binkerd.
    Contents—Gelobet seist du, Jesu Christ; Puer natus in Bethlehem;
    Nun komm der Heiden Heiland; Wie schön leuchtet der
    Morgenstern.
    AMP

Magnificat   14'
    chorus
    cnt—str
    Kalmus   *Presser*

Das neugebor'ne Kindelein
    chorus
    cnt—str
    Kalmus

C

Cadman, Charles Wakefield   1881 - 1946

American suite   10'
    str
    Luck

Oriental rhapsody from Omar Khayyam   9'
    *3 2 2 2—4 2 3 1—tmp+2—hp—str
    This work is out of print, but orchestral materials are in the
    Fleisher Collection.

Cage, John   1912 - 1992

Atlas eclipticalis   var
    3 3 3 3—5 3 3 3—3tmp+9—3hp—str (12.12.9.9.3)
    The instrumentation given is the maximum, but not all instruments
    need be used. The work may be played in whole or part by any
    ensemble, chamber or orchestral.
    Peters

Caltabiano, Ronald   1959 -

Concertini   20'
    *1 1 +1 1—2 1 1 0—1perc—str (min 10.8.7.5.4)
    Merion

Canning, Thomas   1911 -

Fantasy on a hymn by Justin Morgan   10'
    2 solo string quartets & string orchestra
    C. Fischer

Carpenter, John Alden   1876 - 1951

Adventures in a perambulator   28'
    *3 *3 *3 2—4 2 3 1—tmp+4—hp, cel, pf—str
    Schirmer, G.

3'	4'	4'
4'	5'	8'

Sea drift   17'
    2 *2 2 2—4 3 3 1—tmp+2—hp, cel, pf—str
    Schirmer, G.

Skyscrapers 28'
  optional chorus
  *3 *3 *3 *3—3sx (covering sop, alto, tenor, bar)—4 4 3 1
  —tmp+5—2pf, banjo—str
  One pianist doubles on cel. Duration with authorized concert
  cuts: 15'
  Schirmer, G.

Carter, Elliott   1908 -

Adagio tenebroso 20'
  *3 *3 =3 *3—4 3 3 1—tmp+4—pf—str
  Two of the flutists double on piccolo.
  Boosey

Concerto for orchestra 20'
  *3 *3 =3 *3—4 3 3 1—tmp+7—hp, pf—str (9.8.6.6.5)   5' 4' 6' 5'
  Two of the flutists double on piccolo. Minimum strings: 7.6.5.4.3.
  AMP

Concerto, oboe 20'
  =1 0 *1 0—1 0 1 0—2perc—str
  The solo oboe, 1 of the percussionists, and 4 of the violas form a
  concertino.
  Boosey

Concerto, piano 26'
  concertino: pf, fl, Eh, bcl, vn, va, vc, db
  *2 2 2 *3—4 3 3 1—2tmp—str
  Both ripieno flutes double on piccolo. Minimum strings
  14.12.10.8.6;
  max 20.18.14.14.10.
  AMP

Concerto, violin 26'
  *3 *3 =3 *3—4 3 3 1—2perc—str   9' 9' 8'
  Two of the flutists double on piccolo; 2 of the clarinetists double
  on bass clarinet.
  Boosey

Double concerto, harpsichord & piano 23'
  *1 1 +1 1—2 1 1 0—4perc—vn, va, vc, db.
  Two conductors are recommended.
  AMP

Elegy 5'
  str
  Peer

Holiday overture 10'
  *3 *3 *3 *3—4 3 3 1—tmp+4—pf—str
  AMP

The minotaur: Ballet suite 25'
  *2 *2 *2 2—4 2 2 0—tmp+3—pf—str
  AMP

A mirror on which to dwell 20'
   solo soprano
   =1 *1 =1 0—1perc—pf—vn, va, vc, db
   AMP

Partita 18'
   *3 *3 =3 *3—4 3 3 1—tmp+4—hp, pf—str
   Two of the flutists double on piccolo.
   Boosey

Pocahontas: Suite 20'
   *3 2 2 2—4 3 3 1—tmp+4—hp, pf—str
   Contents—Overture; John Smith and Rolfe lost in the Virginia
   forest; Princess Pocahontas and her ladies; Torture of John Smith;
   Pavane (Farewell of Pocahontas).
   AMP

Symphony no.1 (1942/54) 27'
   *2 2 +2 2—2 2 1 0—tmp—str   9' 11' 7'
   AMP

A symphony of three orchestras 17'
   *3 *3 =3 *3—5 3 3 1—tmp+3—pf—str
   Aggregate divided into 3 groups. All of the flutists double on
   piccolo; 2 of the clarinetists double on bass clarinet.
   AMP

Variations for orchestra 24'
   *2 2 2 2—4 2 3 1—tmp+3—hp—str
   AMP

Casella, Alfredo   1883 - 1947

Italia, op.11 19'
   *3 *3 =4 *4—4 4 3 1—tmp+6—2hp—str
   Universal

Paganiniana, op.65 18'
   *2 *2 *3 2—4 2 1 1—tmp+2—str   4' 4' 5' 5'
   Universal

Castelnuovo-Tedesco, Mario   1895 - 1968

Concerto, guitar, op.99, D major 19'
   1 1 2 1—1 0 0 0—tmp—str (2.2.2.2.1)   6' 7' 6'
   Schott

Chabrier, Emmanuel   1841 - 1894

Bourée fantasque 5'
   *3 *3 2 4—4 3 3 1—tmp+4—2hp—str
   Arr. Felix Mottl.
   Kalmus

España 8'
   *3 2 2 4—4 4 3 1—tmp+4—2hp—str
   Kalmus

Gwendolyn: Overture
*3 *3 *3 3—4 4 3 1—tmp+3—2hp—str
Kalmus
9'

Habanera
2 1 2 1—2 2 0 0—tmp+1—str
Kalmus
4'

Joyeuse Marche
*3 2 2 4—4 4 3 1—tmp+4—hp—str
Enoch   *Kalmus*
4'

Le Roi malgré lui (The king in spite of himself): Danse slav
*2 2 2 2—2 2 3 0—tmp+3—str
Two of the flutists double on piccolo.
Kalmus
5'

Le Roi malgré lui (The king in spite of himself): Fête polonaise
*2 2 2 2—2 2 3 0—tmp+3—str
Kalmus
10'

Suite pastorale
*2 1 2 2—2 2 3 0—tmp+3—opt hp—str
Kalmus
21'
5' 5' 6' 5'

Chadwick, George Whitefield   1854 - 1931

Aphrodite
*3 *3 *3 *3—4 4 3 1—tmp+4—hp, cel—str
Kalmus
20'

Euterpe
*3 2 2 2—4 2 3 1—tmp—hp—str
Kalmus   *Schirmer, G.*
8'

Melpomene; dramatic overture
*3 *2 2 2—4 2 3 1—tmp+1—str
Kalmus
12'

Rip van Winkle: Overture
*3 2 2 2—4 2 3 1—tmp+1—str
C. Fischer
10'

Sinfonietta, D major
*3 2 2 2—4 2 3 0—tmp+4—hp—str
Trombones are optional.
Kalmus   *Schirmer, G.*
19'
6' 3' 5' 5'

Symphonic sketches
*3 *2 *3 2—4 2 3 0—tmp+4—hp—str
Contents—Jubilee; Noël; Hobgoblin; A vagrom ballad.
Jubilee & Noël are available as a pair; the other movements are
available separately.
Schirmer, G.
30
8' 8' 6' 8'

Symphony no.2, B-flat major   37'
  2 2 2 2—4 2 3 0—tmp—str   13' 6' 9'
Score published by Da Capo Press. Parts arc out of print, but a   9'
set is in the Fleisher Collection.

Tam O'Shanter   18'
  *3 *3 =4 2—4 3 3 1—tmp+4—hp—str
Luck

Chaminade, Cécile   1857 - 1944

Callirhoe suite, op.37   14'
  *3 2 2 4—4 4 3 1—tmp+3—hp—str
Kalmus

Concertino, flute, op.107, D major   8'
  1 2 2 2—4 0 3 1—tmp—hp—str
Boosey   *Kalmus*

Charpentier, Gustave   1860 - 1956

Impressions d'Italie   32'
  *3 *3 *3 4—asx (dbl opt ssx)—4 4 3 1—tmp+4—2hp—str   7' 3' 4'
Heugel   *Kalmus*   6' 12'

Louise: Prelude to Act III & Air de Louise   10'
  2 *2 2 2—2 2 3 0—tmp+1—2hp, opt cel—str   6' 4'
Arr. Francis Casadesus. Set has special parts for 2 cornets to be
used in lieu of trumpets and horns. Piano-conductor score only.
Luck

Charpentier, Marc-Antoine   1634 - 1704

Noëls pour les instruments   18'
  2rec 0 0 1—cnt—str
Ed. H. Wiley Hitchcock.
Contents—Les Bourgeois de Châtre (1); Joseph est bien marié; Or
Nous Dites, Marie; Laissez Paître Vos Bêtes; Vous Qui Désirez
Sans Fin; À La Venue de Noël; Une Jeune Pucelle; Où S'En Vont
Ces Gais Bergers?; Le Bourgeois de Châtre (2).
Universal

Te deum   23'
  chorus   solos SSATB
  2 *3 0 1—0 1 0 0—tmp—cnt—str
Heugel   *Universal*

Chausson, Ernest   1855 - 1899

Poème de l'amour et de la mer, op.19   27'
  solo voice   11' 3'
  2 2 2 2—2 2 3 0—tmp—hp—str   13'
Available in 2 keys: G for high voice, and F for medium voice.
Kalmus   *Rouart*   *Salabert*

Poème, op.25   16'
  solo violin
  2 2 2 2—4 2 3 1—tmp—hp—str
  AMP   *Breitkopf*   *Kalmus*

Symphony, op.20, B-flat major   30'
  *3 *3 *3 3—4 4 3 1—tmp—2hp—str   11' 7'
  Kalmus   *Salabert*   12'

Chávez, Carlos   1899 - 1978

Concerto, 4 horns   23'
  0 *1 =4 3—tmp—str
  Kalmus

Concerto, piano   33'
  *3 *3 2 *3—4 2 3 1—tmp+3—hp, cel—str
  Schirmer, G.

La hija de Colquide (The daughter of Colchis)   24'
  *3 *3 =4 3—4 3 3 1—tmp+3—hp—str
  Belwin

Initium   18'
  *3 *3 *3 *3—4 3 3 1—tmp+3—hp—str
  Mills

Resonancias   15'
  *3 *3 *3 *3—4 2 3 1—tmp+3—str
  Belwin

Symphony no.1 (Sinfonia de Antigona)   11'
  =3 *2 =4 3—heckelphone—8 3 0 1—tmp+3—2hp—str
  Schirmer, G.

Symphony no.2 (Sinfonia india)   12'
  *4 3 =4 3—4 2 2 0—tmp+4—hp—str
  Numerous Indian instruments required for percussion section.
  Schirmer, G.

Symphony no.3   27'
  *3 *3 =4 *3—4 3 3 1—tmp+3—hp—str   6' 8' 5' 8'
  Boosey

Symphony no.4 (Sinfonia romantica)   22'
  *3 *3 2 *3—4 2 3 1—tmp+3—str   7' 7' 8'
  Boosey

Symphony no.5   21'
  str   6' 8' 7'
  Belwin

Toccata for percussion   14'
  6perc   5' 5' 4'
  Belwin

Xochipilli   6'
   *2 0 +1 0—0 0 1 0—6perc
   Belwin

Chen Yi   1953 -

Duo ye no.2   8'
   *3 *3 *3 *3—4 3 3 1—tmp+3—str 14.14.10.12.8
   Two of the flutists double on piccolo.
   A version for chamber orchestra also exists.
   Presser

Symphony no.2   18'
   3 *3 *3 *3—4 3 3 1—tmp+4—hp—str
   Presser

Cherubini, Luigi   1760 - 1842

Abenceragen: Overture   9'
   2 2 2 2—4 2 3 0—tmp—str
   Breitkopf   *Kalmus*

Ali Baba: Overture   7'
   *2 2 2 2—4 4 3 1—tmp+3—str
   Bärenreiter   *Breitkopf*   *Kalmus*

Anacreon: Overture   9'
   *2 2 2 2—4 2 3 0—tmp—str
   Breitkopf   *Kalmus*

Démophoon: Overture   10'
   2 2 2 2—2 2 3 0—tmp—str
   Ed. Pietro Spàda.
   Suvini

Les Deux Journées: Overture   8'
   2 2 2 2—4 0 1 0—tmp—str
   Also known as *Der Wasserträger*, or *The water carrier*.
   Breitkopf   *Kalmus*

Faniska: Overture   8'
   2 2 2 2—2 2 1 0—tmp—str
   Breitkopf   *Ricordi*

L'Hôtellerie portugaise (The Portuguese inn): Overture   8'
   2 2 2 2—2 2 1 0—tmp—str
   Breitkopf   *Kalmus*

Mass no.4, C major
   chorus   solos SSSSTTBB
   2 2 2 2—2 2 0 0—tmp—str
   Kalmus

Medea: Overture   9'
   2 2 2 2—4 0 0 0—tmp—str
   Bärenreiter   *Breitkopf*   *Kalmus*

Messa solenne, G major   50'
  chorus
  2 2 2 2—2 2 3 0—tmp—str
  Ed. Giovanni Carli Ballola.
  Boccaccini

Requiem, C minor   47'

				7' 2' 10'
chorus				16' 2' 3'
0 2 2 2—2 2 3 0—tmp—str				
Breitkopf	*Kalmus*	*Peters*	*Schirmer, G.*	7'

Requiem, D minor   52'

		10' 4'
male chorus		14' 7' 4'
*2 2 2 2—4 2 3 0—tmp—str		
Kalmus	*Peters*	4' 9'

Symphony, D major   24'
  1 2 2 2—2 2 0 0—tmp—str
  Ed. Adriano Lualdi.
  Suvini

Chin, Unsuk   1961 -

săntika Ekatāla   15'
  =3 *3 =3 *3—6 4 3 1—5perc—hp, cel, pf—str
  Boosey

Die Troerinnen (The Trojan women)   22'
  solos: 2 sopranos, mezzo-soprano   female chorus
  *3 3 3 3—4 3 3 0—tmp+1—hp, cel, pf—str
  New ed. 1986.
  Boosey

Chopin, Frédéric   1810 - 1849

Chopiniana (piano works orchestrated by Glazunov)
  see under: Glazunov, Alexander, 1865-1936

Concert-allegro (Allegro de concert), op.46   20'
  solo piano
  2 2 2 2—4 2 3 0—tmp—str
  Arr. J.L. Nicodé.
  C. Fischer   *Kalmus*   *PWM*

Concerto, piano, no.1, op.11, E minor   39'

			19' 10'
2 2 2 2—4 2 1 0—tmp—str			
Breitkopf	*Kalmus*	*PWM*	10'

Concerto, piano, no.2, op.21, F minor   32'

			15' 9' 8'
2 2 2 2—2 2 1 0—tmp—str			
Breitkopf	*Kalmus*	*PWM*	

Fantasy on Polish airs, op.13   16'
  solo piano   5' 4' 4' 3'
  2 2 2 2—2 2 0 0—tmp—str
  Breitkopf   *C. Fischer*   *Kalmus*   *PWM*

Grande Polonaise, op.22   10'
    solo piano
    2 2 2 2—2 0 1 0—tmp—str
    Preceded by an *Andante spianato* for unaccompanied piano (4'),
    for a total duration of 14'.
    Breitkopf   *Kalmus*   *PWM*

Krakowiak, op.14   14'
    solo piano
    2 2 2 2—2 2 0 0—tmp—str
    Breitkopf   *Kalmus*   *PWM*

Mazurka no.7, F-sharp minor   2'
    str
    Arr. Balakirev.
    Kalmus

Polonaise, op.40, no.1   4'
    *3 2 2 2—4 2 3 0—tmp+3—str
    Arr. Glazunov.
    Kalmus   *Luck*

Romanze   8'
    solo violin
    2 0 2 2—2 0 0 0—tmp—str
    Paraphrase by August Wilhelmj of the slow movement of Chopin's
    first piano concerto.
    Kalmus

Les Sylphides (arr. Glazunov)   20'
    2 2 2 2—4 2 0 0—tmp+3—hp—str
    Contents—Prelude, op.28 no.7; Nocturne, op.32 no.2; Valse, op.70
    no.1; Mazurka, op.33 no.2; Mazurka, op.67 no.3; Prelude, op.28
    no 7 (repeated); Valse, op.64 no.2; Grande Valse brillante, op.18.
    Kalmus

1'	5'	2'
2'	1'	1'
4'	4'	

Variations on "La ci darem la mano," op.2   18'
    solo piano
    2 2 2 2—2 0 0 0—tmp—str
    Kalmus   *PWM*

5'	2'	1'
1'	1'	1'
		7'

Chou Wen-chung   1923 -

All in the spring wind   8'
    *2 *2 *2 *2—2 2 2 1—tmp+3—hp, cel/pf—str
    Peters

And the fallen petals   10'
    *2 *2 *3 2—4 2 3 1—tmp+2—hp, cel—str
    Peters

Beijing in the mist   12'
    asx, bsx—tp, tbn—2perc—pf, elec gtr, elec bass, elec pf
    Peters

Landscapes   8'
*2 *2 0 0—2 0 2 0—tmp+1—hp—str
Peters

Pien; chamber concerto   14'
solo piano
+2 *1 1 1—1 2 2 0—4perc
Peters

Soliloquy of a bhiksuni   5'
solo trumpet
0 0 0 0—4 0 3 1—tmp+2
Peters

Yü ko   5'
+1 *1 *1 0—0 0 2 0—2perc—pf—vn
Peters

Cimarosa, Domenico   1749 - 1801

Concerto (concertante), 2 flutes, G major   17'
0 2 0 1—2 0 0 0—str   9' 4' 4'
Bote & Bock   *Southern*

Concerto, oboe, C minor   10'
str
Freely adapted by Arthur Benjamin from piano sonatas of
Cimarosa.
Boosey

Il maestro di cappella   22'
solo bass or baritone   3' 19'
1 2 0 2—2 0 0 0—tmp—hpsd or pf—str
Overture & scena ed. Maffeo Zanon.
Ricordi

Il maestro di cappella: Overture   4'
2 2 0 2—2 0 0 0—tmp—str
Ed. Alceo Toni.
Carisch

Il matrimonio segreto: Overture   8'
2 2 2 2—2 2 0 0—tmp—str
Carisch   *Kalmus*

Sinfonia, D major   8'
1 2 0 0—2 0 0 0—str
Zanibon

I traci amanti: Overture   7'
0 2 0 1—2 0 0 0—str
Zanibon

Clarke, Jeremiah   ca.1674 - 1707
The Prince of Denmark's march
See the following entry.
See also: Purcell, Henry, ca.1659-1695
                  Trumpet prelude   (*Trumpet voluntary*)

Suite, D major   10'
  solo trumpet | 1' 1' 1' |
  0 2 0 1—cnt—str | 1' 1' 1' |
  This suite includes the well-known *Prince of Denmark's march* as | 2' 1' 1' |
  one of its movements. The latter is often wrongly attributed to
  Henry Purcell, under the title *Trumpet voluntary* or *Trumpet
  prelude.*
  Contents—Prelude, The Duke of Gloster's March; Minuet;
  Sybelle; Rondeau, the Prince of Denmark's March; Serenade;
  Bourée; Ecossaise; Hornpipe; Gigue.
  Musica Rara

Clementi, Muzio   1752 - 1832
Symphony no.1, C major   26'
  2 2 2 2—2 2 3 0—tmp—str | 9' 6' 5' 6' |
  Ed. Pietro Spada.
  Suvini

Symphony no.2, D major   24'
  2 2 2 2—2 2 3 0—tmp—str | 9' 6' 4' 5' |
  Ed. Pietro Spada.
  Suvini

Symphony no.3, G major (Great national symphony)   27'
  2 2 2 2—2 2 3 0—tmp—str | 9' 8' 5' 5' |
  Ed. Pietro Spada.
  Suvini

Symphony no.4, D major   28'
  2 2 2 2—2 2 3 0—tmp—str | 10' 7' 6' 5' |
  Ed. Pietro Spada.
  Suvini

Coates, Eric   1886 - 1957
London suite   13'
  *2 *3 *3 2—4 3 3 0—tmp+4—hp—str | 4' 4' 5' |
  Contents—Covent Garden: Tarantelle; Westminster: Meditation;
  Knightsbridge: March
  Chappell   Luck

Coleridge-Taylor, Samuel   1875 - 1912
The bamboula (Rhapsodic dance no.1)   8'
  *3 2 2 2—4 2 3 1—tmp+3—str
  Boosey

Christmas overture   5'
2 1 2 2—2 2 3 0—tmp+2—hp—str
Boosey   *Luck*

Danse nègre, op.35, no.4   6'
*3 2 2 2—4 2 3 0—tmp+3—str
Luck

Hiawatha: Suite from the ballet music, op.82a   18'
*2 2 2 2—4 2 3 1—tmp+4—hp—str
Contents—The wooing; The marriage feast; Bird scene;
Conjuror's dance; The departure; Reunion.
Luck

Novellette, op.52, no.1, A major   5'
1perc—str
Kalmus

Novellette, op.52, no.2, C major   7'
1perc—str
Kalmus

Novellette, op.52, no.3, A minor (Valse)   5'
1perc—str
Kalmus

Novellette, op.52, no.4, D major   4'
1perc—str
Kalmus

Petite Suite de concert, op.77   16'
*3 2 2 2—4 2 3 0—tmp+3—str   4' 5' 4' 3'
Contents—Le Caprice de Nannette; Demande et Réponse; Un
Sonnet d'amour; Le Tarantelle fretillante.
Boosey

The song of Hiawatha, op.30

1. Hiawatha's wedding feast   31'
chorus   solo tenor
*3 2 2 2—4 2 3 1—tmp+3—hp—str
Gray   *Kalmus*   *Luck*

2. The death of Minnehaha   40'
chorus   solos SB
*3 2 2 2—4 2 3 1—tmp+2—hp—str
Gray   *Kalmus*   *Luck*

3. Hiawatha's departure   40'
chorus   solos STB
*3 2 2 2—4 2 3 1—tmp+2—hp, opt org—str
Gray   *Luck*

Colgrass, Michael   1932 -

As quiet as...   14'
   =3 *3 *3 3—4 3 3 1—tmp+3—2hp, pf/cel/hpsd (1 player)
   —str 12.10.8.8.4
   MCA

Déjà vu   18'
   solo percussion quartet
   =3 0 =3 *3—4 3 3 1—2hp, pf/cel—str
   C. Fischer

Letter from Mozart   16'
   =2 2 2 *2—2 2 2 1—4perc—hp, pf/cel, accordion—str
   Calls for 2 conductors; accordion part may be played by the
   keyboard player.
   C. Fischer

Rhapsodic fantasy   9'
   solo percussionist
   =2 1 1 1—1 1 1 0—tmp+3—hp, cel—str
   MCA

Converse, Frederick Shepherd   1871 - 1940

The mystic trumpeter   20'
   *3 *3 *3 *3—4 3 3 1—tmp+5—hp—str
   Schirmer, G.

Coolidge, Peggy Stuart   1913 - 1982

Pioneer dances   12'
   *3 2 2 2—4 3 3 1—tmp+4—hp—str
   Also available in versions for string orch. and for chamber orch.:
   1 1 2 1—1 2 1 0—tmp+3—hp—str.
   Peer

Copland, Aaron   1900 - 1990

Appalachian spring: Suite (original instrumentation)   23'
   1 0 1 1—pf—str 2.2.2.2.1
   Boosey

Appalachian spring: Suite (full orchestra version)   23'
   *2 2 2 2—2 2 2 0—tmp+2—hp, pf—str
   Boosey

Billy the Kid: Suite   21'
   *3 2 2 2—4 3 3 1—tmp+4—hp, pf—str
   Boosey

Billy the Kid: Prairie night & Celebration dance   5'
   *1 1 2 1—1 2 2 0—tmp+2—pf—str
   Boosey

Billy the Kid: Waltz (Billy and his sweetheart)   4'
  1 1 2 1—1 2 1 0—hp (or pf)—str
  This movement is not included in the suite.
  Boosey

Canticle of freedom   13'
  chorus
  *3 *3 2 2—4 3 3 1—tmp+4—hp—str
  Eh is optional. Rev. 1967.
  Boosey

Ceremonial fanfare   3'
  0 0 0 0—4 3 3 1
  Score available in the collection *Ceremonial music*, which
  includes the composer's *Fanfare for the common man, Jubilee
  variation, Preamble for a solemn occasion, Ceremonial fanfare,* and
  Inaugural fanfare. Parts are available separately.
  Boosey

Concerto, clarinet   18'
  hp, pf—str | 10' 8' |
  Boosey

Concerto, piano   16'
  *3 *3 =4 *3—asx—4 3 3 1—tmp+5—cel—str | 7' 9' |
  Boosey

Connotations   20'
  *4 *3 =4 *3—6 4 4 1—tmp+5—pf/cel—str
  Boosey

Dance symphony   20'
  *3 *3 =4 *3—4 5 3 1—tmp+4—2hp, pf/cel—str
  Boosey

Danzón cubano   7'
  *3 *3 *3 *3—4 3 3 1—tmp+5—pf—str
  Boosey

Down a country lane   3'
  2 1 2 1—2 1 1 0—str
  Boosey

Eight poems of Emily Dickinson   21'
  medium voice | 4' 2' 2' |
  *1 1 +2 1—1 1 1 0—hp—str 10.8.6.4.2 (min: 8.6.4.3.2) | 2' 2' 3' |
  Contents—Nature, the gentlest mother; There came a wind like a | 3' 3' |
  bugle; The world feels dusty; Heart, we will forget him; Dear
  March, come in; Sleep is supposed to be; Going to Heaven!; The
  chariot.
  Boosey

Fanfare for the common man   3'
  0 0 0 0—4 3 3 1—tmp+2
  Score available in the collection *Ceremonial music,* which
  includes the composer's *Fanfare for the common man, Jubilee*
  variation, Preamble for a solemn occasion, Ceremonial fanfare, and
  Inaugural fanfare. Parts are available separately.
  Boosey

Inaugural fanfare   4'
  *3 2 2 0—4 3 3 1—tmp+4
  1969, rev. 1975.
  Score available in the collection *Ceremonial music,* which
  includes the composer's *Fanfare for the common man, Jubilee*
  variation, Preamble for a solemn occasion, Ceremonial fanfare, and
  Inaugural fanfare. Parts are available separately.
  Boosey

Inscape   13'
  *3 *3 *3 2—4 3 3 1—tmp+4—hp, pf/cel—str
  Boosey

John Henry   4'
  *2 2 2 2—2 2 1 0—tmp+2—opt pf—str
  Possible with woodwinds 1 1 2 1.
  Boosey

Jubilee variation on a theme by Eugene Goosens   2'
  *3 *3 *3 *3—4 3 3 1—tmp+3—pf—str
  Score available in the collection *Ceremonial music,* which
  includes the composer's *Fanfare for the common man, Jubilee*
  variation, Preamble for a solemn occasion, Ceremonial fanfare, and
  Inaugural fanfare. Parts are available separately.
  Boosey

Lincoln portrait   14'
  speaker
  *2 *3 *3 *3—4 3 3 1—tmp+3—hp, cel—str
  Both flutists double on piccolo. Eh, bcl, cbn, 3rd tp, and cel are
  optional.
  Boosey

Music for a great city   24'
  =3 *3 *3 *3—4 3 3 0—tmp+5—hp, pf/cel—str   7' 7' 3' 7'
  Two of the flutists double on piccolo. The city of the title is
  London.
  Contents—Skyline; Night thoughts; Subway jam; Toward the
  bridge.
  Boosey

Music for movies   16'
  *1 1 1 1—1 2 1 0—1perc—pf (or hp)—str   5' 2' 3'
  Contents—New England countryside; Barley wagons; Sunday   3' 3'
  traffic; Grovers Corners; Threshing machines.
  Boosey

Music for the theatre   21'
  *1 *1 +1 1—0 2 1 0—1perc—pf—str
  Minimum number of strings: 2.2.2.2.1.   6' 3' 5'
  Boosey   3' 4'

Nonet for strings   18'
  3vn, 3va, 3vc
  Performance by larger ensembles of up to 48 strings authorized
  by the composer.
  Boosey

Old American songs: First set   14'
  medium voice or chorus
  *1 1 2 1—1 1 1 0—hp—str   4' 2' 3'
  Contents—The boatmen's dance; The dodger; Long time ago;   2' 3'
  Simple gifts; I bought me a cat.
  Boosey

Old American songs: Second set   13'
  medium voice or chorus
  *1 1 2 1—2 1 1 0—hp—str   3' 2' 4'
  Contents—The little horses; Zion's walls; The golden willow   2' 2'
  tree; At the river; Ching-a-ring chaw.
  Boosey

Orchestral variations   13'
  *2 *2 *2 2—4 2 3 1—tmp+3—hp—str
  Boosey

Our town   9'
  3 *3 *3 2—3 3 2 1—1perc—str
  3rd fl & 2nd ob are optional.
  Boosey

An outdoor overture   10'
  *3 2 2 2—4 2 3 0—tmp+3—pf, opt cel—str
  Boosey

Prairie journal   13'
  *2 2 2 1—2asx, tsx—2 3 2 1—tmp+1—hp, pf/cel—str
  Both asx double on cl; tsx doubles on bcl. Cues permit
  performance with winds: *2 2 2 2—4 2 2 1 (i.e. 3rd & 4th hn
  replace 2asx; 2nd bn replaces tsx). Original title: *Music for
  radio.*
  Boosey

Preamble for a solemn occasion   6'
  optional narrator
  *3 *3 *3 *3—4 3 3 1—tmp+2—hp—str
  Text is Preamble to the United Nations Charter.
  Score available in the collection *Ceremonial music,* which
  includes the composer's *Fanfare for the common man, Jubilee
  variation, Preamble for a solemn occasion, Ceremonial fanfare,* and
  Inaugural fanfare. Parts are available separately.
  Boosey

Quiet city   10'
    solo trumpet   solo English horn (or oboe)
    str
    Boosey

The red pony   25'
    *2 *2 =4 2—4 3 3 1—tmp+4—hp, pf/cel—str
    E-flat clarinet & 4th horn are optional.
    Boosey

| 5' 5' 5' |
| 3' 4' 3' |

Rodeo: Four dance episodes

    1. Buckaroo holiday   7'
    *3 *3 *3 2—4 3 3 1—tmp+3—hp, pf/cel—str
    Two of the flutists double on piccolo. Cued to be playable
    without Eh or bcl.
    Boosey

    2. Corral nocturne   4'
    1 1 2 1—2 2 1 0—hp, cel—str
    Boosey

    3. Saturday night waltz   4'
    1 1 *3 1—2 2 1 0—hp—str
    Bcl cued in other instruments.
    Boosey

    4. Hoe down   3'
    *3 *3 *3 2—4 3 3 1—tmp+3—pf—str
    Playable without Eh or bcl.
    Boosey

Rodeo: Hoe down   3'
    str
    Boosey

El salón México   11'
    *3 *3 =4 *3—4 3 3 1—tmp+4—pf—str
    Eh, scl, bcl, cbn, and 3rd tp are optional.
    Boosey

Statements   18'
    *3 *3 =3 *3—4 3 3 1—tmp+3—str
    Boosey

Symphonic ode   19'
    *4 *4 =4 *4—8 4 3 1—tmp+4—2hp, pf—str
    Two of the flutists double on piccolo; hn 5-8 are optional.
    1928-29; revised 1955.
    Boosey

Symphony for organ and orchestra (1924)   25'
    *3 *3 2 *3—4 3 3 1—tmp+4—1 or 2 hp, opt cel—str
    A revised version without solo organ was later published as
    Symphony no.1.
    Boosey

| 7' 7' 11' |

Symphony no.1   25'
   *3 *3 *3 *3—opt asx —8 5 3 1—tmp+5—2hp, pf/cel—str | 7' 7' 11' |
   A revision (without organ solo) of his *Symphony for organ and*
   orchestra.
   Boosey

Symphony no.1: Prelude (arr. for chamber orchestra)   5'
   1 1 1 1—1 1 0 0—hp or pf—str
   Arranged by the composer.
   Boosey

Symphony no.2   15'
   =3 *3 *3 *3—4 2 0 0—pf—str | 4' 5' 6' |
   English horn player doubles on optional heckelphone.
   Boosey

Symphony no.3   43'
   *4 *3 *3 *3—4 4 3 1—tmp+5—2hp, cel, pf—str | 11' 8' |
   Boosey | 10' 14' |

The tender land: Suite   19'
   *3 *2 *2 2—4 3 3 1—tmp+2—hp, opt pf/cel—str | 9' 5' 5' |
   Contents—Introduction and love music; Party scene; Finale: The
   promise of living.
   Boosey

Three Latin-American sketches   11'
   *1 1 1 1—0 1 0 0—1perc—1 or 2 pf—str (min 6.4.3.2.1) | 3' 4' 4' |
   Boosey

Two pieces   11'
   str (or str quartet)
   Boosey

Variations on a Shaker melody   4'
   *2 2 2 2—2 2 2 0—opt tmp, 1perc—pf, opt hp—str
   Adapted from the composer's *Appalachian spring.*
   Boosey

Corelli, Arcangelo   1653 - 1713

Concerti grossi, op.5
   see: Geminiani, Francesco, 1687-1762
        Concerto grosso in C major, after Corelli, op.5, no.3
        Concerto grosso no.12 , after Corelli, op.5, no.12 (La follia)

Concerto grosso, op.6, no.1, D major   12'
   2 solo violins, solo violoncello | 5' 3' 2' 2' |
   cnt—str
   Kalmus   *Peters*   *Ricordi*

Concerto grosso, op.6, no.2, F major   10'
   2 solo violins, solo violoncello | 4' 2' 4' |
   cnt—str
   Kalmus   *Peters*   *Ricordi*

Concerto grosso, op.6, no.3, C minor 10'
  2 solo violins, solo violoncello
  cnt—str
  Kalmus   *Peters*   *Ricordi*

> 4' 4' 2'

Concerto grosso, op.6, no.4, D major 9'
  2 solo violins, solo violoncello
  cnt—str
  Kalmus   *Peters*   *Ricordi*

> 3' 3' 3'

Concerto grosso, op.6, no.5, B-flat major 10'
  2 solo violins, solo violoncello
  cnt—str
  Kalmus   *Peters*   *Ricordi*

> 3' 2' 2' 3'

Concerto grosso, op.6, no.6, F major 12'
  2 solo violins, solo violoncello
  cnt—str
  Kalmus   *Peters*   *Ricordi*

> 2' 2' 3'
> 2' 3'

Concerto grosso, op.6, no.7, D major 8'
  2 solo violins, solo violoncello
  cnt—str
  Kalmus   *Peters*   *Ricordi*

> 2' 2' 2'
> 1' 1'

Concerto grosso, op.6, no.8, G minor (Christmas concerto) 13'
  2 solo violins, solo violoncello
  cnt—str
  Kalmus   *Peters*   *Ricordi*

> 3' 3' 1'
> 2' 4'

Concerto grosso, op.6, no.9, F major 9'
  2 solo violins, solo violoncello
  cnt—str
  Kalmus   *Peters*   *Ricordi*

> 1' 2' 2'
> 1' 3'

Concerto grosso, op.6, no.10, C major 12'
  2 solo violins, solo violoncello
  cnt—str
  Kalmus   *Peters*   *Ricordi*

> 2' 2' 1'
> 2' 3' 2'

Concerto grosso, op.6, no.11, B-flat major 8'
  2 solo violins, solo violoncello
  cnt—str
  Kalmus   *Peters*   *Ricordi*

> 2' 2' 2'
> 1' 1'

Concerto grosso, op.6, no.12, F major 10'
  2 solo violins, solo violoncello
  cnt—str
  Kalmus   *Peters*   *Ricordi*

> 2' 3' 1'
> 1' 3'

Suite for string orchestra 8'
  str
  A pastiche, assembled and arranged from various individual
  movements.
  Contents—Sarabanda; Giga; Badinerie.
  Luck

Corigliano, John   1938 -

Aria   6'
  solo oboe
  str orch (or str quartet)
  Adapted from his Oboe Concerto.
  Schirmer, G.

Campane di Ravello   4'
  *4 *4 *4 *4—4 4 3 1—tmp+5—hp, pf—str
  "A celebration piece for Sir Georg Solti." Based on *Happy birthday*.
  Schirmer, G.

Concerto, clarinet   30'
  *4 *4 *3 *4—6 4 3 1—2tmp+3—hp, pf—str
  Preferred number of string stands: 7.7.6.6.6 (less or more may be used). Special seating, including some players surrounding the audience.
  Schirmer, G.

Elegy for orchestra   8'
  *2 2 2 2—2 1 1 0—tmp+1—pf (or hp)—str
  Schirmer, G.

Fantasia on an ostinato   14'
  *3 3 3 *3—4 4 3 1—tmp+5—hp, pf—str
  Schirmer, G.

Promenade overture   8'
  *3 2 2 2—4 4 3 1—tmp+4—hp—str
  2 additional horns if possible. Starting with a bare stage, the players gradually enter.
  Schirmer, G.

Symphony no.1   41'
  *4 *4 =4 *4—6 5 4 2—2tmp+5—hp, pf—str   14' 9'
  3 of the flutists play piccolo; 1 clarinet optionally doubles on   14' 4'
  contrabass clarinet; 2 stands of violin II double on mandolin.
  Schirmer, G.

Three hallucinations   13'
  *3 3 =3 *3—4 3 3 1—2tmp+4—hp, pf/elec org,
  2nd small piano (deliberately mistuned)—str (min 12.10.8.8.6)
  Winds may be increased to *4 4 =4 *4—6 4 3 1, if the remainder of the ensemble is "large enough." Based on music for the film *Altered states*.
  Schirmer, G.

To music   5'
  *2 2 *2 2—4 3 3 1—tmp+1—str
  Some of the brass placed offstage around the audience. Adapted from the composer's *Fanfares to Music* for double brass quintet.
  Schirmer, G.

Tournaments   12'
    *3 *3 *3 *3—4 4 3 1—tmp+3—hp, pf—str
    Schirmer, G.

Voyage   7'
    str
    Originally for chorus.
    Schirmer, G.

Cornelius, Peter   1824 - 1874

Der Barbier von Bagdad: Overture (B minor)   8'
    *3 2 2 2—4 2 3 0—tmp+3—str
    An entirely different work from the following.
    Breitkopf   *Luck*

Der Barbier von Bagdad: Overture (D major; arr. Mottl)   7'
    *3 2 2 2—4 2 3 1—tmp+2—hp—str
    Arranged "after the original score" by Felix Mottl. An entirely
    different work from the preceding.
    Luck

Mass, D minor (CWV 91)   19'
    female chorus   solos SSA
    org—str
    Schott

Couperin, François   1668 - 1733

La Sultane: Overture and allegro   7'
    *3 *3 *3 2—3 3 3 1—tmp+1—hp—str
    Arr. Milhaud.
    Elkan-Vogel

Cowell, Henry   1897 - 1965

Ballad   4'
    str
    AMP

Carol for orchestra   9'
    2 2 2 2—2 2 0 0—hp (or pf)—str
    The composer's own version for "western orchestra" of his *Koto
    concerto*.
    AMP

Fiddler's jig   2'
    solo violin   str
    AMP

Hymn and fuguing tune no.2   7'
    str
    AMP

Hymn and fuguing tune no.3   7'
    *2 2 2 2—4 2 2 1—tmp+2—str
    3rd & 4th hn are optional.
    AMP

Hymn and fuguing tune no.16   6'
    2 2 2 2—4 3 3 1—str
    3rd & 4th hn are optional.
    Peters

Polyphonica for small orchestra   4'
    1 1 1 1—1 1 1 0—str
    AMP

Sinfonietta   15'
    1 1 1 1—1 1 1 0—str 2.2.1.1.1
    AMP

Synchrony   15'
    *3 3 +3 *3—4 3 3 1—tmp+4—str
    All three flutists double on piccolo; 2 of the clarinetists double on
    E-flat clarinet.
    Peters

Crawford (Seeger), Ruth   1901 - 1953
Music for small orchestra
    1 0 1 1—pf—4vn, 2vc

Creston, Paul   1906 - 1985
Dance overture   12'
    *4 *3 *3 *3—4 3 3 1—tmp+3—str
    Templeton

Invocation and dance, op.58   12'
    *4 *3 *3 *3—4 3 3 1—tmp+3—pf—str
    Possible with winds and percussion: 2 2 2 2—4 2 3 1—tmp+2.
    Schirmer, G.

Symphony no.2, op.35   26'
    *4 *3 *3 *3—4 3 3 1—tmp+4—pf—str   9' 9' 8'
    Schirmer, G.

Symphony no.3, op.48 (Three mysteries)   28'
    *4 *3 *3 *3—4 3 3 1—tmp—hp—str
    Shawnee

Two choric dances, op.17b   12'
    *3 2 2 2—4 2 3 1—tmp+1—pf—str
    Schirmer, G.

Crumb, George 1929 -

Echoes of time and the river 20'
*3 0 +3 0—3 3 3 0—6perc—hp, pf, pf/cel, mand—str (min
15.15.12.12.9)

| 5' | 5' | 5' | 5' |

A number of the wind and string players also play antique
cymbals. Players move in procession from place to place, on and
off stage, while playing. Many other special effects. All of the
flutists double on piccolo.
Belwin

Variazioni for large orchestra 25'
*3 *3 =4 *3—4 3 3 1—tmp+6—hp, cel, mand—str (min
14.14.12.12.10)
Two of the flutists double on piccolo.
Peters

Cunningham, Arthur 1928 -

Lullabye for a jazz baby 7'
*2 2 *3 1—2 2 2 0—3perc—hp—str
Presser

D

Dahl, Ingolf 1912 - 1970

Quodlibet on American folk tunes and folk dances 5'
3 2 *3 2—4 3 3 1—tmp+2—pf—str
Bcl, tuba & pf are optional.
Peters

Variations on a theme by C.P.E. Bach 12'
str
Broude, A.

Dallapiccola, Luigi 1904 - 1975

Canti di liberazione 30'
chorus

| 12' | 6' |
| 12' | |

*3 *3 =4 *3—asx, tsx—4 3 3 1—tmp+7 (incl 2 xyl)—2hp, cel—str
Contents—O frater, frater; Dominus quasi vir pugnator; Vocasti
et clamasti.
Suvini

Canti di prigionia 25'
   chorus
   8perc—2hp, 2pf

| 10' 5' |
| 10' |

   Contents—Preghiera di Maria Stuarda; Invocazione di Boezio;
   Congedo di Girolamo Savonarola.
   Carisch

Due pezzi per orchestra 11'
   2 *3 2 *2—4 3 2 1—tmp+4—2hp, cel, pf—str
   Contents—Sarabanda; Fanfara e fuga.
   Suvini

Piccola musica notturna 7'
   2 2 2 2—2 2 0 0—tmp+1—hp, cel—str
   A version for chamber orchestra also exists: 1 1 1 0—hp, cel—vn,
   va, vc.
   Schott

Variations for orchestra 15'
   *2 *2 2 2—4 2 3 1—tmp+3—hp, cel—str
   Suvini

Danielpour, Richard   1956 -

Concerto, violoncello 31'
   *3 *3 *3 *3—4 3 3 1—tmp+4—hp, pf/cel—str (min 14.12.10.8.6)
   AMP

First light (Concerto for orchestra in one movement) 13'
   2 *1 2 2—4 2 2 0—tmp+2—hp, pf (amplified)—str 10.10.8.6.4
   Original chamber version is also available:
   1 *1 1 1—2 1 1 0—tmp+2—hp, pf—str.
   AMP

Journey without distance (Symphony no.3) 29'
   solo soprano   mixed chorus or male chorus
   *3 *2 *3 *2—4 3 3 1—tmp+3—hp, amplified pf (2 players
   optional)—str
   AMP

Metamorphosis (Concerto for piano & orchestra) 28'
   solo piano
   *2 *2 *2 2—2 2 2 0—tmp+3—hp—str 10.10.8.7.5
   AMP

Daugherty, Michael   1954 -

Dead Elvis 10'
   solo bassoon
   0 0 1 0—0 1 1 0—1perc—vn, db
   Elvis Presley costuming for solo bassoon is optional. Note that
   instrumentation is identical to that of Stravinsky's *L'Histoire du
   soldat.*
   Peer

Flamingo   9'
   2 tambourine soloists
   *2 1 1 1—1 1 1 0—keyboard—str (sections or string quintet)
   Peer

Metropolis symphony   41'
   *3 *3 =3 *3—4 4 3 1—tmp+4—synth/pf—str
   Movements may be performed separately as listed below.
   Peer

| 9' 7' 7' |
| 7' 11' |

   1. Lex   9'
   solo violin (may be concertmaster)
   *3 *3 *3 *3—4 4 3 1—tmp+4—synth (or pf)—str
   Peer

   2. Krypton   7'
   *3 3 =3 *3—4 4 3 1—4perc—pf (or synth)—str
   Peer

   3. MXYZPTLK   7'
   2 solo flutes (2nd doubles on piccolo)
   0 2 2 2—2 1 1 0—2perc—synth—str
   Pronounced "Mix-yes-pittle-ick."
   Peer

   4. Oh Lois!   7'
   *2 2 2 2—4 3 3 0—tmp+2—synth (or keyboard)—str
   Peer

   5. Red cape tango   11'
   *3 *3 *3 *3—4 4 3 1—tmp+4—pf—str
   Peer

David, Ferdinand   1810 - 1873
Concertino no.4, trombone, op.4, E-flat major   13'
   2 2 2 2—4 2 3 0—tmp—str
   Kalmus

Davidovsky, Mario   1934 -
Inflexions   7'
   =2 0 *1 0—0 1 1 0—4perc—pf/cel—vn, va, vc, db
   Clarinet also doubles on alto saxophone.
   Marks

Davies, Peter Maxwell   1934 -
see: Maxwell Davies, Peter, 1934-

Davis, Anthony   1951 -
ESU variations   11'
   *4 4 4 *4—4 4 3 1—tmp+3—str
   Schirmer, G.

Notes from the underground   9'
   *2 2 2—2 2 2 1—tmp+4—pf—str
   Schirmer, G.

Wayang no.5   25'
   solo piano (must improvise)
   *2 1 *2 1—2 1 2 0—tmp+4—str
   The bass clarinet part is identified (wrongly?) in the score as for
   "contrabass clarinet in E-flat."
   Schirmer, G.

Dawson, William   1898 - 1990
Negro folk symphony   35'
   *3 *3 =4 *3—4 3 3 1—tmp+4—hp—str
   Contents—The bond of Africa; Hope in the night; O le' me shine,
   shine like a morning star.
   Shawnee

Debussy, Claude   1862 - 1918
La Boîte à joujoux (The toybox)   35'
   2 *3 2 2—2 2 0 0—tmp+4—hp, cel, pf—str

3'	11'	
10'	7'	2'
		2'

   Durand   *Kalmus*

Clair de lune   5'
   2 2 2 2—4 0 0 0—hp, cel—str
   Originally for piano; from *Suite bergamasque*. Arr. Arthur Luck.
   Luck

Le Coin des enfants (Children's corner)   17'
   *2 2 2 2—4 2 0 0—2perc—hp—str

3'	3'	3'
3'	2'	3'

   Originally for piano; orchestrated by André Caplet.
   Contents—Doctor Gradus ad Parnassum; Berceuse des éléphants
   (Jumbo's lullaby); Sérénade à la poupée (Serenade for the doll);
   La Neige danse (The snow is dancing); Le Petit Berger (The little
   shepherd); Golliwogg's cake-walk.
   Durand   *Kalmus*

La Damoiselle élue (The blessed damozel)   20'
   mezzo-soprano solo (or 2 Mz)   female chorus SSAA
   3 *3 *3 3—4 3 3 0—2hp—str
   Durand   *Kalmus*

Danse   6'
   2 2 2 2—2 2 0 0—tmp+3—hp—str
   Orchestrated by Maurice Ravel.
   Jobert

Danses sacrée et profane   9'
   solo harp
   str | 5' | 4' |
   Contents—Danse sacrée; Danse profane.
   Durand   *Kalmus*

L'Enfant prodigue   45'
    solos STBar   optional chorus
    *3 *3 2 2—4 2 3 1—tmp+2—2hp—str
    Durand   *C. Fischer*   *Kalmus*

Fantasie, piano & orchestra   26'
    3 *3 *3 3—4 3 3 0—tmp+1—2hp—str | 9' 17' |
    Jobert

Images

   1. Gigues   7'
    *4 *3 *4 *4—ob d'amore—4 4 3 0—tmp+1—2hp, cel—str
    Durand   *Kalmus*

   2. Ibéria   20'
    *4 *3 3 *4—4 3 3 1—tmp+4—2hp, cel—str | 7' 8' 5' |
    Contents—Par Les Rues et par les chemins (In the streets and
    byways); Les Parfums de la nuit (The fragrance of night); Le
    Matin d'un jour de fête (Morning of the festival day).
    Durand   *C. Fischer*   *Kalmus*

   3. Rondes de printemps   9'
    *3 *3 3 *4—4 0 0 0—tmp+3—2hp, cel—str
    Durand   *Kalmus*

L'Isle joyeuse   7'
    *3 *3 *4 *3—4 4 3 1—tmp+4—2hp, cel—str
    Orchestrated by Bernardino Molinari.
    Durand

Jeux; poème dansé   17'
    *4 *4 *4 *4—4 4 3 1—tmp+3—2hp, cel—str
    Kalmus edition by Clinton F. Nieweg.
    Durand   *Kalmus*

Marche écossaise sur un thème populaire   7'
    *3 *3 2 2—4 2 3 0—tmp+2—hp—str
    Orchestrated by the composer from a work for piano 4-hands.
    Jobert   *Kalmus*

Le Martyre de Saint Sébastien (The martyrdom of Saint Sebastian)   72'
    chorus   solos SAA | 19' 13' |
    *4 *3 *4 *4—6 4 3 1—tmp+1—3hp, cel, harm—str | 19' 15' |
    Incidental music to a play by d'Annunzio; orchestrated in part by | 6' |
    André Caplet. Most often performed in a format devised by D.E.
    Inghelbrecht, with the approval of Debussy and d'Annunzio,
    using a narrator. The music alone, without narration, lasts about
    an hour.
    Durand

Le Martyre de Saint Sébastien: Fragments symphoniques   22'
    *4 *3 *4 *4—6 4 3 1—tmp+1—3hp, cel—str | 4' 7' 6' 5' |
    Contents—La Cour des lys; Danse extatique et Final du premier
    acte; La Passion; Le Bon Pasteur.
    Durand   *Kalmus*

Le Martyre de Saint Sébastien: La Chambre magique   2'
   *4 *2 *4 *4—6 2 3 1—tmp+1—3hp, cel—str
   Durand

Le Martyre de Saint Sébastien: Two fanfares   3'
   0 0 0 0—6 4 3 1—tmp
   Elkan-Vogel

La Mer   23'
   *3 *3 2 *4—4 5 3 1—tmp+3—2hp—str   8' 7' 8'
   Kalmus edition by Clinton F. Nieweg & Nancy Bradburd.
   Durand   *Kalmus*

Nocturnes (original version)   25'
   *3 *3 2 3—4 3 3 1—tmp+2—2hp—str   8' 6' 11'
   16 women's voices in last movement.
   Ed. Robert Grossman & Clinton F. Nieweg.
   Kalmus

Nocturnes (revised version)   25'
   *3 *3 2 3—4 3 3 1—tmp+2—2hp—str   8' 6' 11'
   16 women's voices in last movement.
   Both the *Édition definitive*, 1930, based on changes the composer
   had entered into his personal score, and the *Nouvelle édition
   après corrections*, 1964, are published by Jobert.
   Jobert

Petite Suite   13'
   *2 *2 2 2—2 2 0 0—tmp+3—hp—str   3' 4' 3' 3'
   Orchestrated by Henri Büsser.
   Durand   *Kalmus*

Prélude à "L'Après-midi d'un faune" (Afternoon of a faun)   10'
   3 *3 2 2—4 0 0 0—1perc—2hp—str
   A critical edition of the score with historical and analytical
   essays, and including the composer's own metronome marks, is
   published by Norton. Kalmus edition by Clinton F. Nieweg.
   Jobert   *Kalmus*

Prélude à "L'Après-midi d'un faune" (arr.) (Afternoon of a faun)   10'
   1 1 1 0—1perc—pf, harm—2vn, va, vc, db
   Arr. "under the supervision of Arnold Schoenberg" for chamber
   ensemble.
   Belmont

Printemps   15'
   *2 *2 2 2—4 2 3 0—tmp+2—hp, pf 4-hands—str   9' 6'
   Orchestrated by Henri Büsser. Kalmus edition by Clinton F.
   Nieweg.
   Durand   *C. Fischer*   *Kalmus*

Rhapsody, alto saxophone & orchestra   10'
   3 *3 2 2—4 2 3 1—tmp+2—hp—str
   Originally for saxophone & piano. Orchestration sketched by
   Debussy, completed by Jean Roger-Ducasse (1919).
   Durand   *C. Fischer*   *Kalmus*

Rhapsody, clarinet & orchestra   8'
  3 *3 2 3—4 2 0 0—2perc—2hp—str
Durand   *C. Fischer*   *Kalmus*

Sarabande   6'
  2 *2 2 2—2 1 0 0—1perc—hp—str
Orchestrated by Maurice Ravel.
Jobert

Six Épigraphes antiques   15'
  *3 *3 *3 *3—4 3 3 0—tmp+1—2hp, cel—str
Eh can double on ob d'amore, optionally. Orchestrated by Ernest
Ansermet.
Contents—Pour Invoquer Pan, dieu du vent d'été; Pour Un
Tombeau sans nom; Pour Que La Nuit soit propice; Pour La
Danseuse aux crotales; Pour L'Egyptienne; Pour Remercier La
Pluie au matin.
Durand

Delibes, Léo   1836 - 1891

Coppelia   92'
  *2 2 2 4—4 4 3 1—tmp+4—hp—str   37' 55'
Orchestral reduction by Wm. McDermott available from
Mapleson: *2 *2 2 2—2 2 1 0—tmp, perc—hp—str .
Heugel   *Kalmus*

Coppelia: Suite no.1   25'
  *2 2 2 2—4 2 3 0—tmp+3—hp—str   6' 6' 3'
Contents—Slav folk-tune; Festive dance and Waltz of the hours;   6' 4'
Nocturne; Music of the automatons and Waltz; Czardas.
Kalmus

Coppelia: 4 petites suites   24'
    The following are sometimes grouped together as Ballet suite
no.2. *They are published separately. Some of the movements also
appear in* Suite no.1 *(see above).*

  1. Entr'acte & Waltz   4'
  *2 2 2 2—2 2 3 1—tmp—hp—str
Heugel   *Kalmus*

  2. Prelude & Mazurka   6'
  *2 2 2 2—4 4 3 1—tmp+4—hp—str
Heugel   *Kalmus*

  3. Ballade & Thème slave varié   9'
  *2 *2 2 4—4 4 3 1—tmp+3—hp—str
Heugel   *Kalmus*

  4. Valse de la poupée & Czardas   5'
  *2 2 2 2—4 4 3 1—tmp+3—str
Heugel   *Kalmus*

Sylvia: Suite   17'
  *2 2 2 2—4 4 3 1—tmp+3—hp—str   3' 6' 2' 6'
  Contents—Prélude; Intermezzo et Valse lente; Pizzicato; Cortège
  de Bacchus.
  Heugel   *Kalmus*

Delius, Frederick   1862 - 1934

Appalachia; variations on an old slave song with final chorus   34'
  chorus
  *3 *4 =4 *4—6 3 3 1—tmp+3—2hp—str
  Boosey   *Kalmus*

Brigg Fair   16'
  3 *3 *4 *4—6 3 3 1—tmp+3—hp—str
  Boosey   *Universal*

Concerto, piano, C minor   22'
  *3 *3 2 3—4 2 3 1—tmp+2—str
  Rev. 1906.
  Boosey

Concerto, violin   24'
  2 *2 2 2—4 2 3 1—tmp—hp—str
  Augener   *Schott*   *Stainer*

Concerto, violin & violoncello (Double concerto)   20'
  2 *2 2 2—4 2 3 1—tmp—hp—str   6' 7' 7'
  Augener

Concerto, violoncello   22'
  2 *2 2 2—4 2 3 1—tmp—hp—str   7' 5' 1'
  Boosey   2' 7'

Dance rhapsody no.1   12'
  *3 *2 *4 *4—bass oboe (=heckelphone?)—6 3 3
  1—tmp+2—2hp—str
  Universal

Dance rhapsody no.2   8'
  *3 *3 2 2—4 2 3 1—tmp+3—hp, cel—str
  Galaxy

Hassan: Intermezzo & Serenade   4'
  1 *2 1 1—2 1 0 0—tmp—hp—str
  Movements may be performed independently (*Serenade* is for hp,
  str, & solo vn only). Arr. Thomas Beecham.
  Boosey

Irmelin: Prelude   4'
  2 *2 *3 2—2 0 0 0—hp—str
  Boosey

Sea drift   30'
  chorus   baritone solo
  3 *4 *4 *4—6 3 3 1—tmp+1—2hp—str
  Boosey   *Kalmus*

Sleigh ride   5'
  *3 2 2 2—4 4 3 1—tmp+2—str
  Boosey

Two pieces for small orchestra

  1. On hearing the first cuckoo in spring   4'
  1 1 2 2—2 0 0 0—str
  Oxford

  2. Summer night on the river   5'
  2 1 2 2—2 0 0 0—str
  Oxford

The walk to the Paradise Garden   8'
  2 *2 2 2—4 2 3 0—tmp—hp—str
  Two differing versions are available from the publisher: one arr.
  Sir Thomas Beecham; the other ed. Keith Douglas.
  Boosey

Dello Joio, Norman   1913 -

Arietta   4'
  str
  Marks

Five images for orchestra   8'
  *3 2 *3 2—4 2 3 1—tmp+3—str | 2' 1' 1' |
  Intended primarily for youth audiences. Contents—Cortège; | 2' 2' |
  Promenade; Day dreams; The ballerina; The dancing sergeant.
  Marks

Lyric fantasies   17'
  solo viola
  str orchestra or str quintet
  AMP

Meditations on Ecclesiastes   22'
  str
  C. Fischer

The triumph of Saint Joan   29'
  *2 *2 2 2—4 2 3 1—tmp+1—str | 11' 8' |
  C. Fischer | 10' |

Variations, chaconne & finale   24'
  *3 *3 *3 *3—4 3 3 1—tmp+3—str | 11' 9' 4' |
  C. Fischer

Del Tredici, David   1937 -

An Alice symphony   41'
  solo soprano (amplified and with bull-horn)
  *2 2 +2 *2—ssx/asx, ssx/asx/tsx—4 2 2 1—tmp+5—mand, tenor
  banjo, accordion—str
  Both flutists double on piccolo.
  Contents—Speak roughly/Speak gently; The lobster quadrille;
  'Tis the voice of the sluggard; Who stole the tarts; Dream
  conclusion.
  This work may be excerpted in various ways. See the following
  three entries.
  Boosey

An Alice symphony: Illustrated Alice   17'
  solo soprano (amplified and with bull-horn)
  *2 2 2 *2—ssx/asx, ssx/asx/tsx—4 2 2 1—tmp+5—str
  Both flutists double on piccolo.
  Contents—Speak roughly/Speak gently; Who stole the tarts;
  Dream conclusion.
  Boosey

An Alice symphony: In Wonderland   24'
  solo soprano (amplified)
  *2 2 +2 *2—2ssx—4 2 2 1—tmp+4—mand, tenor banjo,
  accordion—str
  Both flutists double on piccolo.
  Contents—The lobster quadrille; 'Tis the voice of the sluggard;
  Dream conclusion.
  Boosey

An Alice symphony: The lobster quadrille   13'
  optional soprano solo (amplified)
  *2 2 +2 *2—2ssx—4 2 2 1—4perc—mand, tenor banjo,
  accordion—str
  Both flutists double on piccolo.
  Boosey

Child Alice   141'
  soprano solo (amplified)   63' 25'
  *3 *3 =4 *3—4 4 3 1—tmp+5—2hp, cel—str   21' 32'
  Two of the flutists double on piccolo.
  This full-evening entertainment based on Lewis Carroll's *Alice*
  in Wonderland may be excerpted individually and in various
  combinations. The composer has supplied concert-beginnings and
  concert-endings for this purpose. See individual listings below.
     Contents—Part I: In memory of a summer day; Part II: Quaint
  events, Happy voices, All in the golden afternoon.
  Boosey

Child Alice: In memory of a summer day   63'
   solo soprano (amplified)
   *3 *3 =4 *3—4 4 3 1—tmp+5—2hp, cel—str
   String players form an antiphonal whisper-chorus.
   Boosey

Child Alice: Quaint events   25'
   soprano solo (amplified)
   *3 *3 =4 *3—4 4 3 1—tmp+5—2hp, cel—str
   Spoken chorus (members of the orchestra); two of the flutists
   double on piccolo.
   Boosey

Child Alice: Happy voices; fuga for orchestra   21'
   *3 *3 =4 *3—4 4 3 1—tmp+5—2hp, cel—str
   Two of the flutists double on piccolo.
   Boosey

Child Alice: All in the golden afternoon   32'
   soprano solo (amplified)
   *3 *3 =4 *3—4 4 3 1—tmp+5—2hp, cel—str
   Spoken chorus (members of the orchestra); two of the flutists
   double on piccolo.
   Boosey

Final Alice   70'
   solo soprano (amplified and with bull-horn)
   *4 *4 =4 *4—2ssx—6 4 4 1—tmp+7—2hp, cel, mand, tenor banjo,
   accordion—str
   The composer indicates a possible cut which reduces the duration
   to 60', and lessens the complexity of the folk group amplification.
   Boosey

Pop-pourri   28'
   solo soprano (amplified)   chorus   opt counter-tenor or
   mezzo-soprano
   *2 *2 *2 *2—ssx, ssx/tsx—0 2 2 0—3perc—elect gtr, elect bass
   gtr—str
   One technician required. Both flutists double on piccolo. (Chorus
   may be omitted by cutting one movement.)
   Boosey

Syzygy   24'
   solo group: soprano (amplified), horn, tubular bells with
   extended range (2 players)
   =2 *2 *2 *2—0 2 0 0—2vn, 2va, vc, db
   Boosey

Vintage Alice; fantascene on a mad tea-party   28'
    solo soprano (amplified)
    *1 1 +1 1—2ssx—2 1 1 0—tmp+1—mand, tenor banjo,
    accordion—str
    May be done with solo strings rather than sections. If a large
    string complement is used, winds may be doubled.
    Boosey

Devienne, François   1759 - 1803
Concerto, bassoon, B-flat major
    see: Mozart, Wolfgang Amadeus, 1756-1791
        Concerto, bassoon, no.2, K.Anh.C14.03, B-flat major

Diamond, David   1915 -
Concerto, violin, no.3   23'
    =4 *3 =4 *3—4 3 3 1—tmp+3—hp, pf—str
    Peer

Music for Shakespeare's Romeo and Juliet   18'
    *2 *2 *2 2—2 2 1 0—tmp+1—hp—str   3' 4' 3'
    Contents—Overture; Romeo and Juliet: Balcony scene; Romeo and 2' 6'
    Friar Laurence; Juliet and her Nurse; The death of Romeo and
    Juliet.
    Boosey

Rounds for string orchestra   13'
    str   4' 3' 6'
    Elkan-Vogel

Symphony no.2   42'
    *3 *3 *3 *3—4 3 3 1—tmp+3—str   14' 6'
    Peer   14' 8'

Symphony no.5   17'
    *3 *3 =4 *3—4 4 3 1—2tmp+3—pf, org—str
    Peer

The world of Paul Klee   12'
    *3 *3 *3 2—4 3 3 0—tmp+3—hp, pf/cel—str
    Southern

Dittersdorf, Karl Ditters von   1739 - 1799
Concerto, double bass, E major   11'
    2 0 0 0—2 0 0 0—cnt—str
    Ed. Franz Tischer-Zeitz.
    Schott

Concerto, double bass, E-flat major   17'
    2 2 0 0—2 0 0 0—str
    Ed. Franz Ortner. Wind parts may be omitted.
    Schott

Concerto, harp, A major   22'
  0 2 0 0—2 0 0 0—str
  Arr. K.H. Pillney.
  Peters

Concerto, harpsichord, B-flat major   14'
  2 0 0 0—2 0 0 0—str (without va)
  Winds used only in slow movement.
  Kalmus   Peters

Sinfonia, C major (Die vier Weltalter)   12'
  1 2 0 2—2 2 0 0—tmp—str   3' 3' 3' 3'
  Doblinger

Sinfonia concertante, double bass & viola   16'
  0 2 0 0—2 0 0 0—str
  Ed. Wilhelm Altmann.
  Hofmeister

Dohnányi, Ernst von   1877 - 1960

Concerto, piano, no.1, op.5, E minor   45'
  *3 2 2 *3—4 2 3 0—tmp—str (min 12.12.8.8.6)   18' 10'
  Doblinger   Kalmus   17'

Ruralia hungarica, op.32b   25'
  *3 *3 =3 *3—4 3 3 1—tmp+4—hp, cel—str
  Boosey

Variations on a nursery song, op.25   22'
  solo piano
  *3 2 2 *3—4 3 3 1—2tmp+2—hp—str
  Simrock

Donizetti, Gaetano   1797 - 1848

Allegro in C major   6'
  str
  Peters

Ave Maria   4'
  chorus   soprano solo
  str
  Broude, A.   Peters

Concertino, clarinet, B-flat major   8'
  0 2 0 0—2 0 0 0—str
  Eulenburg   Peters

Concertino, English horn, G major   11'
  1 2 0 1—2 0 0 0—str
  Peters

Concertino, flute, C major   7'
  0 2 0 1—2 0 0 0—str
  Orchestrated by Wolfgang Hofmann after the composer's *Sonata*
  for flute and piano.
  Peters

Concertino, oboe, F major   7'
  2 0 0 1—2 0 0 0—str
  Orchestrated by Wolfgang Hofmann after the composer's *Sonata*
  for oboe and piano.
  Peters

Don Pasquale: Overture   6'
  *2 2 2 2—4 2 3 0—tmp+2—str
  Kalmus   *Luck*   *Ricordi*

La Fille du régiment (Daughter of the regiment): Overture   7'
  *2 2 2 2—4 2 3 0—tmp+2—str
  Breitkopf   *Kalmus*   *Ricordi*

Linda di Chamounix: Prelude   7'
  *3 2 2 2—4 2 3 1—tmp+1—str
  Kalmus

Roberto Devereux: Overture   8'
  *3 2 2 2—4 2 3 0—tmp+2—str
  Ricordi

Sinfonia for winds, G minor   5'
  1 2 2 2—2 0 0 0
  Ed. Douglas Townsend.
  Broude, A.

Dragonetti, Domenico   1763 - 1846
Grande allegro
  solo double bass
  str
  Doblinger

Pezzo di concerto   9'
  solo double bass
  1 2 0 1—2 0 0 0—str
  Ed. Rudolf Malaric.
  Doblinger

Druckman, Jacob   1928 - 1996
Aureole   12'
  +3 *3 *3 2—4 3 3 1—tmp+3—hp, pf—str
  Boosey

Brangle   22'
  =3 *3 *3 2—4 3 3 1—tmp+3—hp, pf—str
  Boosey

Dark upon the harp   22'
    mezzo-soprano solo
    0 0 0 0—1 2 1 1—2perc
    Contents—Psalm XXII; Psalm LVII; Psalm XVIII; Psalm XXX;
    Psalm CXXXIII; Psalm XVI.
    Presser

Lamia 24'
    soprano solo
    *3 2 *3 2—4 3 3 1—3perc—hp, pf, elec org—str
    Orchestra is divided into 2 groups, each with its own conductor.
    Boosey

Nor spell nor charm 15'
    +1 2 *2 2—2 0 0 0—pf/synth—str
    Boosey

Windows 21'
    *3 *3 *3 *3—4 3 3 1—3perc—hp, pf/elec org—str
    Both pf and elec org must have amplifier and reverberation unit.
    MCA

Dubois, Pierre Max   1930 -
Concerto, alto saxophone 17'
    str | 7' 6' 4' |
    Leduc

Dubois, Théodore   1837 - 1924
Les Sept Paroles du Christ (The seven last words of Christ) 46'
    chorus   solos STB
    *2 2 2 2—4 2 3 0—tmp+1—hp, opt org—str
    Kalmus

Dukas, Paul   1865 - 1935
L'Apprenti Sorcier (The sorcerer's apprentice) 12'
    *3 2 *3 *4—4 4 3 0—tmp+4—hp—str
    Kalmus edition by Clinton F. Nieweg
    Durand   *Kalmus*

La Pèri 19'
    *3 *3 *3 3—4 3 3 1—tmp+6—2hp, cel—str
    Durand   *Kalmus*

La Pèri: Fanfare 3'
    0 0 0 0—4 3 3 1
    Durand

Symphony in C major 40'
    *3 *2 2 2—4 3 3 1—tmp—str | 15' 14' |
    4bn may be used. | 11' |
    Salabert

Duruflé, Maurice   1902 - 1986

Requiem, op.9   38'
   chorus   solos Mz, Bar   8' 8' 3'
   *3 *3 *3 2—4 3 3 1—tmp+3—hp, cel, opt org—str   3' 4' 4'
   Reduced version of the instrumental accompaniment: 5' 3'
   0 0 0 0—0 3 0 0—tmp—hp, org—str.
   Durand

Dutilleux, Henri   1916 -

Symphony no.2   30'
   *3 *3 *3 *3—2 3 3 1—tmp+3—hp, cel, hpsd—str   8' 10'
   Divided into 2 orchestras, one large and one small (12 players).   12'
   Heugel

Dvořák, Antonín   1841 - 1904

Amid nature, op.91
   see his: In nature's realm

Carnival overture, op.92   10'
   *3 *3 2 2—4 2 3 1—tmp+3—hp—str
   Bärenreiter   *Kalmus*   *Supraphon*

Concerto, piano, op.33, G minor   34'
   2 2 2 2—2 2 0 0—tmp—str   15' 10'
   Bärenreiter   *Kalmus*   *Peters*   *Supraphon*   9'

Concerto, violin, op.53, A minor   32'
   2 2 2 2—4 2 0 0—tmp—str   10' 11'
   Bärenreiter   *Breitkopf*   *Kalmus*   *Supraphon*   11'

Concerto, violoncello, op.104, B minor   40'
   *2 2 2 2—3 2 3 1—tmp+1—str   16' 11'
   Bärenreiter   *Kalmus*   *Supraphon*   13'

Concerto, violoncello (no.2) op.posth., A major   30'
   2 2 2 2—4 2 0 0—tmp—str
   Originally for violoncello & piano. Bärenreiter edition
   orchestrated by Jarmil Burghauser. Breitkopf edition
   orchestrated by Günter Raphael.
   Bärenreiter   *Breitkopf*

Czech suite, op.39, D major   23'
   2 *3 2 2—2 2 0 0—tmp—str   4' 5' 4'
   Basset horn may substitute for English horn.   4' 6'
   Bärenreiter   *Kalmus*   *Supraphon*

Fest-Marsch, op.54a   5'
   2 2 2 2—4 2 3 1—tmp+1—opt hp—str
   Bärenreiter   *Bote & Bock*   *Kalmus*   *Supraphon*

Golden spinning wheel, op.109   22'
   *2 *3 2 *3—4 2 3 1—tmp+3—hp—str
   Bärenreiter   *Kalmus*   *Luck*   *Supraphon*

A hero's song, op.111   **23'**
   2 2 2 2—4 2 3 1—tmp+3—str
Bärenreiter   *Kalmus*   *Luck*   *Supraphon*

Husitská, op.67 (Hussite overture)   **14'**
   *3 *2 2 2—4 2 3 1—tmp+2—opt hp—str
Bärenreiter   *Kalmus*   *Luck*   *Supraphon*

In nature's realm, op.91   **12'**
   2 *3 *3 2—4 3 2 1—tmp+1—str
Bärenreiter   *Kalmus*   *Supraphon*

Legends, op.59: Nos.1-5   **25'**
   2 2 2 2—4 2 0 0—tmp—hp—str   5' 4' 4'
   Originally for pf duet.   7' 5'
Bärenreiter   *Kalmus*   *Simrock*

Legends, op.59: Nos.6-10   **21'**
   2 2 2 2—4 0 0 0—tmp—hp—str   5' 4' 5'
   Originally for pf duet.   3' 4'
Bärenreiter   *Kalmus*   *Simrock*

Mass, op.86, D major   **43'**
   chorus   opt soloists SATB   7' 9' 13'
   0 2 0 2—3 2 3 0—tmp—org—str   2' 7' 5'
Bärenreiter   *Gray*   *Kalmus*   *Supraphon*

Midday witch, op.108   **14'**
   *3 2 *3 2—4 2 3 1—tmp+3—str
   Also known as *The noon witch*.
Bärenreiter   *Luck*   *Supraphon*

Notturno, op.40, B major   **7'**
   str
Bote & Bock   *Kalmus*

Othello overture, op.93   **15'**
   *2 *3 2 2—4 2 3 1—tmp+2—hp—str
Bärenreiter   *Luck*   *Supraphon*

Requiem, op.89   **95'**
   chorus   solos SATB
   *3 *3 *3 *3—4 4 3 1—tmp—hp, org—str
Bärenreiter   *Kalmus*   *Supraphon*

Rhapsody, op.14, A minor   **19'**
   *3 *3 2 2—4 2 3 1—tmp+3—hp—str
Bärenreiter   *C. Fischer*   *Supraphon*

Romance, violin & orchestra, op.11, F minor   **8'**
   2 2 2 2—2 0 0 0—str
   Originally the slow movement of the String Quartet in F minor,
   op.9.
Bärenreiter   *Kalmus*   *Supraphon*

Scherzo capriccioso, op.66　　　　　　　　　　　　　　　12'
　*3 *3 *3 2—4 2 3 1—tmp+3—hp—str
　Bärenreiter　　　*Bote & Bock*　　*Kalmus*　　　*Supraphon*

Serenade, op.22, E major　　　　　　　　　　　　　　27'
　str
　Bärenreiter　　　*Bote & Bock*　　*Kalmus*　　　*Supraphon*　　4' 6' 6'
　　　　　　　　　　　　　　　　　　　　　　　　　　　5' 6'

Serenade, op.44, D minor　　　　　　　　　　　　　　　24'
　0 2 2 *3—3 0 0 0—vc, db
　　　　　　　　　　　　　　　　　　　　　　　　　　4' 6' 7' 7'
　Contrabassoon is optional.
　Bärenreiter　　　*Luck*　　　　*Simrock*　　　*Supraphon*

Slavonic dances, op.46, nos.1-4　　　　　　　　　　　19'
　*3 2 2 2—4 2 3 0—tmp+3—str
　　　　　　　　　　　　　　　　　　　　　　　　　4' 5' 4' 6'
　(3rd flutist appears in 3rd dance only.)
　Bärenreiter　　　*Breitkopf*　　*Kalmus*　　　*Simrock*

Slavonic dances, op.46, nos.5-8　　　　　　　　　　　16'
　*2 2 2 2—4 2 3 0—tmp+3—str
　　　　　　　　　　　　　　　　　　　　　　　　　3' 6' 4' 3'
　Bärenreiter　　　*Breitkopf*　　*Kalmus*　　　*Simrock*

Slavonic dances, op.72, nos.1-4 (9-12)　　　　　　　18'
　*2 2 2 2—4 2 3 0—tmp+3—str
　　　　　　　　　　　　　　　　　　　　　　　　　4' 6' 3' 5'
　Bärenreiter　　　*Kalmus*　　　*Simrock*

Slavonic dances, op.72, nos.5-8 (13-16)　　　　　　17'
　*2 2 2 2—4 2 3 0—tmp+3—str
　　　　　　　　　　　　　　　　　　　　　　　　　3' 4' 3' 7'
　Bärenreiter　　　*Kalmus*　　　*Simrock*

Slavonic rhapsody, op.45, no.1, D major　　　　　　10'
　*3 2 2 2—4 2 3 0—tmp+3—str
　Bärenreiter　　　*Kalmus*　　　*Simrock*

Slavonic rhapsody, op.45, no.2, G minor　　　　　　13'
　2 2 2 2—4 2 3 0—tmp+3—hp—str
　Bärenreiter　　　*Kalmus*　　　*Simrock*

Slavonic rhapsody, op.45, no.3, A-flat major　　　　14'
　*2 2 2 2—4 2 3 0—tmp+3—hp—str
　Bärenreiter　　　*Kalmus*　　　*Simrock*

Stabat mater, op.58　　　　　　　　　　　　　　　　81'
　chorus　　solos SATB
　　　　　　　　　　　　　　　　　　　　　　　　17' 10'
　2 *2 2 2—4 2 3 1—tmp—org or harm (in 1 mvt)—str　　7' 9' 6'
　Tuba only in one mvt (12 bars only).　　　　　　　7' 6' 6'
　Bärenreiter　　*Kalmus*　　*G.Schirmer*　　*Supraphon*　6' 7'

Suite, op.98b, A major　　　　　　　　　　　　　　19'
　*3 2 2 *3—4 2 3 1—tmp+3—str
　　　　　　　　　　　　　　　　　　　　　　　　5' 3' 4'
　Bärenreiter　　　*Simrock*　　　*Supraphon*　　　4' 3'

Symphonic variations, op.78　　　　　　　　　　　　21'
　*2 2 2 2—4 2 3 0—tmp—str
　Bärenreiter　　　*Kalmus*　　　*Supraphon*

Symphony no.1, op.3, C minor (Bells of Zlonice)   **40'**
*3 *3 2 2—4 2 3 0—tmp—str
Bärenreiter   *Kalmus*   *Supraphon*

> 11' 13'
> 6' 10'

Symphony no.2, op.4, B-flat major   **48'**
*3 2 2 2—4 2 3 0—tmp—str
Bärenreiter   *Kalmus*   *Supraphon*

> 12' 13'
> 13' 10'

Symphony no.3, op.10, E-flat major   **33'**
*3 *3 2 2—4 2 3 1—tmp+1—hp—str
Bärenreiter   *Kalmus*   *Simrock*   *Supraphon*

> 10' 14'
> 9'

Symphony no.4, op.13, D minor   **38'**
*2 2 2 2—4 2 3 0—tmp+3—hp—str
Bärenreiter   *Kalmus*   *Simrock*   *Supraphon*

> 10' 12'
> 6' 10'

Symphony no.5, op.76, F major   **36'**
2 2 *2 2—4 2 3 0—tmp+1—str
Formerly known as *Symphony no.3.*
Bärenreiter   *Kalmus*   *Supraphon*

> 9' 8' 7'
> 12'

Symphony no.6, op.60, D major   **41'**
*2 2 2 2—4 2 3 1—tmp—str
Formerly known as *Symphony no.1.*
Bärenreiter   *Kalmus*   *Supraphon*

> 13' 11'
> 7' 10'

Symphony no.7, op.70, D minor   **35'**
*2 2 2 2—4 2 3 0—tmp—str
Formerly known as *Symphony no.2.*
Bärenreiter   *Kalmus*   *Supraphon*

> 11' 9' 7'
> 8'

Symphony no.8, op.88, G major   **34'**
*2 *2 2 2—4 2 3 1—tmp—str
Formerly known as *Symphony no.4.*
Bärenreiter   *Kalmus*   *Supraphon*

> 9' 10' 6'
> 9'

Symphony no.9, op.95, E minor (From the New World)   **40'**
*2 *3 2 2—4 2 3 1—tmp+1—str
Playable with 2 oboists, one doubling English horn.
Formerly known as *Symphony no.5.*
Bärenreiter   *Breitkopf*   *Kalmus*   *Supraphon*

> 8' 12' 8'
> 12'

Te deum, op.103   **22'**
chorus   solos SB
2 *2 2 2—4 2 3 1—tmp+3—str
Bärenreiter   *Kalmus*   *Simrock*   *Supraphon*

Watersprite, op.107   **19'**
*3 *3 *2 2—4 2 3 2—tmp+4—str
2nd tuba is optional.
Bärenreiter   *Kalmus*   *Supraphon*

Wood dove, op.110   **19'**
*2 *3 *3 2—4 2 3 1—tmp+3—hp—str
Bärenreiter   *Simrock*   *Supraphon*

E

Effinger, Cecil   1914 -
Little symphony no.1, op.31   13'
  *2 1 2 1—2 1 0 0—str
  C. Fischer

Egk, Werner   1901 - 1983
Variationen über ein karibisches Thema (Variations on a   30'
Caribbean theme)
  2 2 2 2—4 3 3 0—tmp+3—hp, pf—str
  Schott

Einem, Gottfried von   1918 -
Ballade   14'
  *3 2 2 2—4 3 3 1—tmp—str
  Schirmer, G.

Capriccio, op.2   8'
  *3 2 2 2—4 3 3 1—tmp—str
  Bote & Bock

Meditations, op.18   21'
  *2 2 2 2—4 2 2 0—tmp—str
  Universal

Wiener Symphonie, op.49   32'
  *3 2 2 2—4 3 3 1—tmp—str   9' 6' 8' 9'
  Bote & Bock

Elgar, Edward   1857 - 1934
The apostles, op.49   130'
  solos SATBBB   chorus, semi-chorus of boys or women   75' 55'
  *3 *3 *3 *3—4 4 3 1—tmp+4—1 or 2hp, org—str
  Novello

Cockaigne, op.40   13'
  *2 2 2 *3—4 4 3 1—tmp+5—str
  optional: organ & 2 extra trombones
  Boosey   *Kalmus*

Concerto, violin, op.61, B minor   48'
  2 2 2 *3—4 2 3 1—tmp—str   18' 11'
  Contrabassoon and tuba are optional.   19'
  Kalmus   *Novello*

Concerto, violoncello, op.85, E minor   30'
2 2 2 2—4 2 3 1—tmp—str
| 7' 6' 6' |
| 11' |

Tuba is optional.
Novello

Dream-children, op.43   6'
2 2 2 2—4 0 0 0—tmp—hp—str
| 3' 3' |
Kalmus   *Novello*

The dream of Gerontius, op.38   100'
chorus, semi-chorus   solos ATB
*3 *3 *3 *3—4 3 3 1—tmp+4—1 or 2hp, org—str
Gray   *Kalmus*   *Novello*

Elegy, op.58   5'
str
Kalmus   *Luck*   *Novello*

Enigma variations, op.36   29'
*2 2 2 *3—4 3 3 1—tmp+3—opt org—str
Gray   *Kalmus*   *Novello*

Falstaff, op.68   30'
*3 *3 *3 *3—4 3 3 1—tmp+3 (or 4)—2hp—str
Kalmus   *Novello*

In the south, op.50   20'
*3 *3 *3 *3—4 3 3 1—tmp+3—hp—str
Kalmus   *Novello*

Introduction and allegro, op.47   14'
solo string quartet
str
Gray   *Kalmus*   *Novello*

The kingdom, op.51   104'
solos SATB   chorus
*3 *3 *3 *3—4 3 3 1—tmp+3—2hp, org—str
Kalmus   *Novello*

Pomp and circumstance, military marches, op.39

  No.1, D major   5'
*4 2 *3 *3—4 4 3 1—tmp+5—2hp, org—str
2nd pic ad lib.
Boosey   *Kalmus*

  No.2, A minor   3'
*3 2 *3 *3—4 4 3 1—tmp+5—str
Boosey   *Kalmus*

  No.3, C minor   5'
*3 *3 *3 *4—4 4 3 1—tmp+5—str
Boosey   *Kalmus*

No.4, G major   4'
*3 *3 *3 *3—4 3 3 1—tmp+3—hp—str
Boosey   *Kalmus*

No.5, C major   5'
*3 *3 *3 *3—4 3 3 1—tmp+4—str
Boosey

Salut d'amour (Love's greeting)   4'
1 2 2 2—2 0 0 0—str
Kalmus

Sea pictures   23'
alto solo   [5' 2' 6']
2 2 2 *3—4 2 3 1—tmp+2—hp, opt org—str   [4' 6']
Contents—Sea slumber song; In haven; Sabbath morning at sea;
Where corals lie; The swimmer.
Boosey   *Kalmus*

Serenade, op.20, E minor   12'
str   [3' 6' 3']
Breitkopf   *Kalmus*

Symphony no.1, op.55, A-flat major   50'
*3 *3 *3 *3—4 3 3 1—tmp+3—2hp—str   [19' 7']
Kalmus   *Novello*   [12' 12']

Symphony no.2, op.63, E-flat major   53'
*3 *3 =4 *3—4 3 3 1—tmp+4—2hp—str   [17' 14']
Kalmus   *Novello*   [8' 14']

Three Bavarian dances   12'
*2 2 2 2—4 2 3 1—tmp+5—str   [4' 3' 5']
Possible with perc: tmp+3. Nos. 1, 3 & 6 of the choral suite *From
the Bavarian highlands*.
Contents—The dance; Lullaby; The marksmen.
Kalmus   *Stainer*

Ellington, Edward Kennedy (Duke)   1899 - 1974

Black, brown and beige: Suite   18'
=3 2 *3 *3—asx—4 4 3 1—tmp+3—hp, jazz bass—str
Bass clarinet doubles on baritone saxophone.
Symphonic orchestration by Maurice Peress.
Contents—Black (A work song); Brown (Come Sunday); Beige
(Light).
Schirmer, G.

Grand slam jam   12'
jazz soloists, as many as possible—optional dance band
2 *3 *4 *3—4 4 3 1—tmp+2—hp—str
Arr. Luther Henderson, Jr.; ed. Maurice Peress.
Piece may be extended ad lib.
Schirmer, G.

Harlem   18'
    *3 *3 *3 2—2asx, 2tsx, bsx—4 4 3 1—tmp+3—hp—str
    Arr. Luther Henderson & Maurice Peress.
    Schirmer, G.

New world a-comin'   10'
    solo piano (must ad lib)
    *2 2 *3 2—4 4 3 1—tmp+3—hp—str
    Optional dance band. Arr. & ed. Maurice Peress.
    Schirmer, G.

Night creature   17'
    2 1 2 1—2asx, 2tsx, bsx—2 4 3 1—tmp+2—hp, pf, jazz bass—str
    Schirmer, G.

Things ain't what they used to be   var
    *2 2 *4 *3—5 4 4 1—vib, jazz drums—improvised pf
    (optional)—str
    Arranged & orchestrated by Calvin Jackson. Jazz solos in middle
    section may be of any length.
    G.Schirmer

Les Trois Rois noirs (The three black kings)   15'
    *3 *3 *3 *3—4 4 4 1—tmp+2—hp, pf, elec gtr—str
    Optional: 4th tp, 4th tbn, gtr. Trumpets double on flugelhorn.
    Contents—King of the magi; King Solomon; Martin Luther King.
    According to the publisher's catalog, there is also a "concerto
    grosso" version, arr. Luther Henderson, which includes jazz
    band (gtr, 5 reeds, trap set, jazz bass). There is also an arr. of the
    concerto grosso version for soloist and orchestra (ed. Maurice
    Peress).
    Schirmer, G.

Enesco, Georges   1881 - 1955

Rumanian rhapsody no.1, op.11, A major   11'
    *3 *3 2 2—4 4 3 1—tmp+3—2hp—str
    Kalmus   *Peer*

Rumanian rhapsody no.2, op.11, D major   11'
    3 *3 2 2—4 2 3 0—tmp+1—2hp—str
    Kalmus

Erb, Donald   1927 -

Concerto for solo percussionist & orchestra   10'
    *3 2 *3 *3—4 3 3 1—tmp—hp, pf/cel—str
    Merion

Symphony of overtures   16'
    *3 2 *3 *3—4 3 3 1—tmp+3—hp, pf—str   5' 4' 3' 4'
    Contents—The blacks; Endgame; The maids; Rhinoceros.
    Galaxy

Etler, Alvin   1913 - 1973
Elegy for small orchestra   5'
   1 1 2 2—2 0 0 0—str
   AMP

\

F

Falla, Manuel de   1876 - 1946
El amor brujo: Ballet suite   24'
   alto solo   4' 2' 2'
   *2 *1 2 1—2 2 0 0—tmp—pf—str   4' 3' 9'
   Eh is optional.
   Chester

El amor brujo: Ritual fire dance   5'
   *2 1 2 1—2 2 0 0—tmp—pf—str
   Chester

Concerto, harpsichord, D major   15'
   1 1 1 0—vn, vc   4' 6' 5'
   Eschig

Noches en los jardines de España (Nights in the gardens of Spain)   23'
   solo piano   10' 5' 8'
   *3 *3 2 2—4 2 3 1—tmp+2—hp, cel—str
   Contents—En el Generalife (In the gardens of the Generalife);
   Danza lejana (A dance is heard in the distance); En los jardines
   de la Sierra de Córdoba (In the gardens of the Sierra de Córdoba).
   Chester   *Eschig*

El sombrero de tres picos (Three-cornered hat)   30'
   *3 *3 2 2—4 3 3 1—tmp+5—hp, cel, pf—str
   Chester

El sombrero de tres picos (Three-cornered hat): Suite no.1   11'
   *2 *2 2 2—2 2 0 0—tmp+1—hp, pf—str
   Contents—Introduction - Afternoon; Dance of the miller's wife
   (Fandango); The corregidor; The grapes.
   Chester

El sombrero de tres picos (Three-cornered hat): Suite no.2   12'
   *3 *3 2 2—4 3 3 1—tmp+5—hp, pf/cel—str   3' 3' 6'
   Contents—The neighbors; Miller's dance; Final dance.
   Chester

La vida breve: Interlude & dance   8'
  *3 *3 *3 2—4 2 3 1—tmp+4—2hp, cel—str
  Eschig

La vida breve: Spanish dance no.1   4'
  *2 1 2 1—2 2 3 0—tmp+2—pf—str
  Condensed score only.
  Eschig

Farkas, Ferenc   1905 -

Prelude & fugue   9'
  *3 *3 *3 *3—4 2 3 0—tmp+1—str
  Belwin   *EMB*

Fasch, Johann Friedrich   1688 - 1758

Concerto, trumpet, D major   6'
  0 2 0 0—cnt—str | 2' 1' 3' |
  Sikorski

Fauré, Gabriel   1845 - 1924

Ballade, op.19   15'
  solo piano
  2 2 2 2—2 0 0 0—str
  Hamelle   *Kalmus*

Dolly, op.56   17'
  *2 2 2 2—4 2 3 0—tmp+3—hp—str
  Orchestrated by Henri Rabaud.
  Kalmus

Elegy, op.24   8'
  solo violoncello
  2 2 2 2—4 0 0 0—str
  C. Fischer   *Kalmus*

Fantasy, flute & chamber orchestra   6'
  0 2 2 2—2 0 0 0—str
  Clarinets are optional.
  Hamelle

Fantasy, piano & orchestra, op.111   18'
  2 2 2 2—4 1 0 0—tmp—hp—str
  Durand   *Kalmus*

Masques et Bergamasques, op.112   14'
  2 2 2 2—2 2 0 0—tmp—hp—str | 4' 3' 3' 4' |
  Durand   *Kalmus*

Pavane, op.50   7'
  optional chorus
  2 2 2 2—2 0 0 0—str
  Hamelle   *Kalmus*

Pelléas et Mélisande: Suite, op.80 — 18'
    2 2 2 2—4 2 0 0—tmp—hp—str   7' 2' 4' 5'
    Score lists "harpes," though there is only a single part.
    Contents—1. Prélude; 2. Entr'acte: Fileuse (The spinner); 3.
    Sicilienne; 4. La Mort de Mélisande (The death of Melisande).
    Hamelle   Kalmus

Pénélope: Prelude — 7'
    2 *3 *3 2—4 2 3 1—tmp—str
    Heugel

Requiem, op.48 (chamber version) — 39'
    chorus   solo soprano & baritone   solo violin   7' 9' 4'
    0 0 0 2—4 2 0 0—tmp—hp, org—str (without vn; min 0.0.5.4.1)   4' 6' 5'
    Of the instruments listed, the following are optional: 2bn, 3rd &   4'
    4th hn, 2tp, tmp.
    Ed. John Rutter.
    Hinshaw   Luck

Requiem, op.48 (full orchestra version) — 39'
    chorus   solo soprano & baritone   7' 9' 4'
    2 0 2 2—4 2 3 0—tmp—hp, org—str   4' 6' 5'
    Hamelle   Kalmus   Schirmer, G.   4'

Shylock, op.57 (incidental music) — 19'
    solo tenor   3' 3' 3'
    2 2 2 2—4 2 0 0—tmp+1—hp—str   3' 3' 4'
    Contents—Chanson; Entr'acte; Madrigale; Epithalame; Nocturne;
    Final.
    Kalmus

Shylock, op.57: Nocturne — 5'
    str
    Kalmus

Feldman, Morton   1926 - 1987

Atlantis — 8'
    *3 0 *2 *2—1 1 1 1—2perc—hp, pf—vc, db
    Graph notation.
    Alternate version: 1 0 *1 0—1 1 1 0—2perc—hp, pf—vc.
    Peters

Intersection no.1 for orchestra — 13'
    Woodwind, brass, strings (the precise number of players being
    indeterminate).
    Graph notation.
    Peters

Marginal intersection — 6'
    "Large orchestra," unspecified except that it includes piano,
    xylophone, vibraphone, amplified guitar, 2 oscillators, recording
    of riveting, and 6 percussionists, together with the usual
    woodwinds, brass, and strings. Graph notation.
    Peters

...Out of "Last pieces" — 9'
2 *3 *3 2—4 2 3 0—btp—8perc—hp, pf/cel, amplified gtr—str
(without vn or va)
Graph notation.
Peters

Structures for orchestra — 10'
+3 *3 *3 2—4 3 3 1—2perc—hp, cel—str
Conventional notation.
Peters

Fine, Irving   1914 - 1962

Diversions for orchestra — 8'
2 *2 2 2—4 3 3 1—tmp+2—pf or cel—str | 1' 2' 3' 2' |
Optional saxophones: 2 altos, tenor, baritone.
English horn is optional.
Broude Bros.

Serious song; a lament for string orchestra — 10'
str
Broude Bros.

Symphony (1962) — 24'
*3 *3 *3 *3—4 3 3 1—tmp+4—hp, pf/cel—str
Belwin

Finney, Ross Lee   1906 -

Hymn, fuguing tune & holiday — 10'
*3 *3 *3 *3—4 3 3 1—tmp+3—1 or 2hp, cel—str
C. Fischer

Landscapes remembered — 14'
=1 0 1 0—0 1 1 0—1perc—hp, pf—2vn, va, vc, db
Strings may be increased to 4.4.4.2.2.
Peters

Finzi, Gerald   1901 - 1956

Concerto, clarinet, op.31 — 30'
str | 8' 13' 9' |
Boosey

Dies natalis, op.8 — 25'
solo soprano (or tenor)
str
Boosey

The fall of the leaf, op.20 — 9'
*3 *3 2 *3—4 2 3 1—tmp+2—hp—str
Orchestration completed posthumously by Howard Ferguson.
Boosey

In terra pax; Christmas scene 15'
    chorus   solo soprano & baritone
    1perc—hp—str
    A version with winds also exists.
    Boosey

Introit, op.6 8'
    solo violin
    1 *2 2 1—2 0 0 0—str (max 10.8.6.6.4)
    Boosey   *Kalmus*

Nocturne, op.7 (New Year music) 9'
    *2 *3 *3 *3—4 3 3 1—tmp+1—hp—str
    optional: 2nd ob, bcl, cbn
    Boosey

Prelude 4'
    str
    Boosey

Romance, op.11 6'
    str
    Boosey

A Severn rhapsody, op.3 6'
    1 *1 *1 0—1 0 0 0—str
    Boosey   *Kalmus*

Flotow, Friedrich von   1812 - 1883
Alessandro Stradella: Overture 7'
    2 2 2 2—4 2 3 0—tmp+1—str
    Luck

Martha: Overture 9'
    *2 2 2 2—4 2 3 1—tmp+3—str
    Breitkopf   *Kalmus*

Floyd, Carlisle   1926 -
In celebration 10'
    2 *2 2 2—4 2 2 1—tmp+2—hp, cel—str
    Belwin

Foote, Arthur   1853 - 1937
Air & gavotte
    2 0 0 0—str
    Kalmus   *Luck*

Four character pieces after the Rubáiyát of Omar Khayyám 20'
    2 2 2 2—4 2 3 1—tmp+2—hp—str
    Kalmus

Irish folk song 4'
    str
    Luck

Serenade, op.25   17'
    str

| 2' 5' 3' |
| 4' 3' |

    May be out of print, but materials are in the Fleisher Collection.
    (Originally published by Arthur P. Schmidt, Leipzig, 1892.)

Suite, op.63, E major   15'
    str

| 4' 7' 4' |

    Kalmus

Fortner, Wolfgang   1907 - 1987

The creation   25'
    solo voice (medium)
    2 *2 *2 *1—0 2 2 0—tmp+5—hp, "cembalo"
    Schott

Foss, Lukas   1922 -

American fanfare   4'
    2 2 2 2—4 3 3 1—tmp+3—1 (or 2) hp, pf, opt elec org—str
    Woodwinds may be doubled.
    C. Fischer

Baroque variations   25'
    *3 *2 3 1—3 3 1 1—tmp+3—elec pf, elec gtr, elec org, hpsd, cel—str

| 8' 7' 10' |

    Optional recorder; 3rd cl doubles on ssx or E-flat cl.
    C. Fischer

Cello concert   23'
    solo violoncello
    0 0 0 0—2 1 2 0—4perc—hp, pf, org—str
    C. Fischer   *Schott*

Concerto, percussion   30'
    *1 1 1 1—1 2 2 1—3perc—pf, elec gtr, elec org—str (min: 3.2.2.2.1)
    Preferably clarinetist doubles on soprano saxophone.
    May be extended to 45' duration.
    Salabert

Elegy for Anne Frank   7'
    solo piano   optional narrator
    0 0 2 2—tp or hn (or both), tbn or tuba (or both)—1perc—str
    Clarinets & bassoons are optional.
    Pembroke

Exeunt   18'
    *2 2 2 2—4 2 3 1—tmp+3—hp, pf, elec gtr—str (min 8.6.6.6.4)
    Pembroke

Folksong for orchestra   15'
    *3 3 3 3—5 3 3 1—tmp+3—hp, pf—str
    Two of the flutists double on piccolo.
    Salabert

Geod   29'
+2 *1 *3 3—4 2 3 0—4perc—hp, pf, org—str (24vn, 8va, 8vc, 8db, with substitutions possible)
1 principal conductor and 4 sub-conductors. If possible, 4 microphones, 4 loudspeakers, and mixer. Also "11 or 12 instruments, several of these folk instruments of the country of performance."
C. Fischer

Night music for John Lennon   15'
solos: 2tp, hn, tbn, tuba (or 2nd tbn)
1 1 1 1—1 1 1 0—1perc—pf, elec gtr—str (min 5.4.4.3.1)
Pembroke

Ode for orchestra   10'
*3 *3 *3 *3—4 3 3 1—tmp+3—1 or 2hp, pf—str
Revised 1958.
C. Fischer

Quintets for orchestra   15'
2 *3 *3 2—3 3 3 1—tmp—elec org—str
Originally for brass quintet.
Pembroke

Salomon Rossi suite   10'
*1 *2 0 2—0 2 2 0—tmp—hp—str
Salabert

Song of anguish   19'
solo baritone (or bass)
*3 2 *3 *3—4 3 3 1—tmp+3—hp, cel/pf—str
C. Fischer

Song of songs   33'
soprano (or mezzo-soprano) solo
*3 *3 *3 *3—4 3 2 0—tmp+2—hp—str

6' 7' 13'
7'

3rd & 4th horns optional.
C. Fischer

Time cycle   21'
solo soprano
*2 0 *2 0—2 2 1 0—tmp+2—hp, cel/pf—str

4' 5' 6' 6'

Chamber version by the composer:
soprano—cl—1perc—pf/cel—vc.
Contents—We're late; When the bells justle; Sechzehnter Januar; O Mensch, gib Acht.
C. Fischer

Frackenpohl, Arthur   1924 -

Short overture   4'
1 1 2 2—2 2 2 1—tmp+3—str
Boosey

Françaix, Jean   1912 -

Concertino, piano   10'
  2 2 2 2—2 2 2 0—str
  Schott

Sei Preludi (Six preludes)   15'
  str 3.3.2.2.1
  Schott

Franck, César   1822 - 1890

Le Chasseur maudit (The accursed huntsman)   14'
  *3 2 2 4—4 4 3 1—tmp+3—str
  Kalmus   *Presser*   *Ricordi*

Les Djinns   13'
  solo piano
  2 2 2 4—4 2 3 1—tmp—str
  Kalmus

Eight short pieces, nos.1-4   10'
  1 1 1 1—1 1 0 0—tmp—str
  Kalmus

Eight short pieces, nos.5-8   9'
  *1 *1 1 1—1 1 0 0—tmp—str
  Kalmus

Les Éolides   11'
  2 2 2 2—4 2 0 0—tmp+1—hp—str
  Kalmus

Psalm 150   5'
  chorus
  2 2 2 2—4 2 3 0—tmp+1—hp, org—str
  Breitkopf   *Kalmus*   *Peters*   *Ricordi*

Psyché

  1. Sommeil de Psyché   8'
  2 *3 *3 4—4 4 3 1—tmp—str
  Kalmus

  2. Psyché enlevée par les Zéphirs   3'
  2 *3 *3 4—4 4 0 0—tmp—2hp—str
  Kalmus

  3. Les Jardins d'Eros   4'
  *3 *3 *3 4—4 4 3 1—tmp—str
  Kalmus

  4. Psyché et Eros   6'
  2 *3 *3 4—4 4 3 1—tmp—str
  Kalmus

Rédemption   75'
  chorus   solo soprano
  2 2 2 2—4 2 3 1—tmp+1—str
  Heugel   *Kalmus*

Rédemption: Morceau symphonique   13'
  2 2 2 2—4 2 3 1—tmp—str
  Heugel   *Kalmus*   *Ricordi*

Symphonic variations   15'
  solo piano
  2 2 2 2—4 2 0 0—tmp—str
  Ed. Clinton F. Nieweg.
  Kalmus

Symphony in D minor   37'
  2 *3 *3 2—4 4 3 1—tmp—hp—str   17' 10'
  Boosey   *Kalmus*   10'

Frederick II (The Great)   1712 - 1786
Concerto, flute, no.3, C major   14'
  cnt—str   5' 5' 4'
  Ed. Gustav Lenzewski.
  Vieweg

Concerto, flute, no.4, D major   15'
  cnt—str
  Ed. Gustav Lenzewski.
  Vieweg

Symphony no.1, G major   8'
  cnt—str
  Ed. Gustav Lenzewski.
  Vieweg

Symphony no.2, G major   8'
  cnt—str
  Ed. Gustav Lenzewski.
  Vieweg

Fučik, Julius   1872 - 1916
Der alte Brummbär, op.210 (The old grumbling bear)   5'
  solo bassoon (or saxophone)
  *2 2 2 0—3 2 3 0—2perc—str
  Luck

Fux, Johann Joseph   1660 - 1741
Overture, C major   12'
  opt cnt—str
  Ed. Paul Angerer.
  Doblinger

G

Gabrieli, Giovanni   1551 - 1612
Canzona   6'
   double string orchestra
   Ed. Franco Michele Napolitano.
   Kalmus   Zanibon

Canzona noni toni, a 12, for three brass choirs   6'
   brass 0663 or 3633 (tubas may be omitted)
   Ed. Robert Austin Boudreau.
   Peters

Sonata pian' e forte   7'
   0 0 0 0—1 2 4 1—baritone horn
   Possible with brass 4 1 3 0, or a variety of other combinations.
   One of the parts originally intended for viola.
   King

Sonata pian' e forte (ed. Fritz Stein)   7'
   brass 2 2 4 1 (tuba may be omitted)
   Peters

Gade, Niels   1817 - 1890
Efterklange af Ossian, op.1 (Echoes of Ossian; Nachklänge von   14'
Ossian)
   *2 2 2 2—4 2 2 1—tmp—hp—str
   Contrabassoon may substitute for tuba.
   Breitkopf

Symphony no.1, op.5, C minor   32'
   *3 2 2 2—4 2 3 1—tmp—str   9' 7' 9' 7'
   Contrabassoon may substitute for tuba.
   Kalmus

Galindo, Blas   1910 - 1993
Sones de mariachi   8'
   *3 *3 =4 3—4 3 3 1—tmp+3—hp—str
   EMM

Galuppi, Baldassare   1706 - 1785
Concerto, flute, D major   13'
   cnt—str
   Ed. Felix Schroeder.
   Breitkopf

Concerto, flute, G major
cnt—str
Ed. Johannes Brinckmann.
Peters

Concerto, 2 flutes, E minor 21'
cnt—str
Ed. Felix Schroeder.
Peters

Concerto, harpsichord, F major 14'
str
Ed. Edoardo Farina.
Zanibon

Concerto a quattro, no.1, G minor 9'
cnt—str
Ed. Horst Heussner.
Doblinger

Concerto a quattro, no.2, G major 4'
cnt—str
Ed. Horst Heussner.
Doblinger

Sinfonia, D major 7'
0 0 0 0—2 0 0 0—str
Ed. Ettore Bonelli.
Zanibon

Sinfonia, F major (Della serenata) 7'
0 0 0 0—2 0 0 0—str
Ed. Ettore Bonelli.
Zanibon

Garcia, José Mauricio Nunés   1767 - 1830
see: Nunés-Garcia, José Mauricio, 1767-1830

Gedike, Alexander   1877 - 1957
see: Goedicke, Alexander, 1877-1957

Geminiani, Francesco   1687 - 1762
Concerto grosso, C major, after Corelli, op.5, no.3 11'
solo concertino: 2vn, vc
cnt—str
Ed. Hugo Ruf.
Nagel

Concerto grosso no.5, G minor 9'
solos: 2vn, va, vc   3' 2' 2' 2'
cnt—str
Ed. Michelangelo Abbado.
Ricordi

Concerto grosso no.12, D minor, after Corelli, op.5, no.12 (La follia)   12'
    solo concertino: 2vn, va, vc
    cnt—str (without va)
    Ricordi   *Schott*

Concerto grosso, op.2, no.2, C minor   9'
    str
    Galaxy   *Luck*

Concerto grosso, op.2, no.3, D minor
    cnt—str
    Ed. Walter Upmeyer.
    Vieweg

Concerto grosso, op.3, no.1, D major   14'
    solo concertino: 2vn, va, vc
    cnt—str (without va)
    Kalmus   *Peters*

Concerto grosso, op.3, no.2, G minor   16'
    solo concertino: 2vn, va, vc
    cnt—str (without va)
    Kalmus   *Peters*   *Schirmer, G.*

Concerto grosso, op.3, no.3, E minor   9'
    solo concertino: 2vn, va, vc   3' 6'
    cnt—str (without va)
    Kalmus   *Peters*

Concerto grosso, op.3, no.4, D minor   13'
    solo concertino: 2vn, va, vc
    cnt—str (without va)
    Kalmus   *Peters*

Concerto grosso, op.3, no.5, B-flat major   9'
    solo concertino: 2vn, va, vc
    cnt—str (without va)
    Kalmus   *Peters*

Concerto grosso, op.3, no.6, E minor   10'
    solo concertino: 2vn, va, vc
    cnt—str (without va)
    Kalmus   *Peters*

Concerto grosso, op.7, no.1, D major   9'
    solo concertino: 2vn, va, vc
    cnt—str
    Bärenreiter   *Nagel*

Gerhard, Roberto   1896 - 1970

Albada, interludi i dansa   10'
    *2 *2 2 2—2 2 2 1—tmp+2—str
    Boosey

Alegrías: Suite — 13'
*2 *2 *2 1—2 1 1 0—tmp+1—hp, pf—str
Boosey

Cancionero de Pedrell — 19'
high voice
*1 *1 2 0—2perc—hp, pf—str (min: 2.2.1.1.1)
Contents—Sa ximbomba; La mal maridada; Laieta; Soledad;
Muera yo…; Farruquiño; Alalá; Corrandes.
Boosey

2'	2'	1'
3'	2'	3'
3'	3'	

Concerto for orchestra — 21'
*3 *3 *3 *3—4 4 3 1—2tmp+3—hp—str 16.14.12.10.8
All three flutists play piccolo.
Oxford

Concerto, piano — 24'
str
Boosey

Don Quixote: Dances — 16'
*2 2 *2 2—2 2 2 0—tmp+2—pf—str
Contents—Introduction; Dance of the muleteers; The golden age;
In the cave of Montesinos; Epilogue.
Boosey

Epithalamion — 17'
*4 *4 *4 *4—4 4 3 1—2tmp+6—hp, pf—str 16.14.12.10.8
Two of the flutists double on piccolo.
Oxford

Pedrelliana (en memoria) — 12'
*3 *2 2 2—4 2 2 1—tmp+3—hp—str
Boosey

Symphony no.1 — 39'
*2 *2 2 2—4 2 2 1—tmp+2—hp, pf—str
Boosey

11'	11'
	17'

German, Edward   1862 - 1936
Henry VIII: Three dances — 8'
2 2 2 2—2 2 3 0—tmp+2—str
Gray   *Kalmus*   *Novello*

2'	4'	2'

Gershwin, George   1898 - 1937
American in Paris — 16'
*3 *3 *3 2—asx, tsx, bsx—4 3 3 1—tmp+4—cel—str
Luck   *Warner*

Catfish Row (symphonic suite from Porgy and Bess)   23'
   *2 *2 *4 1—3 3 2 1—tmp+1—pf, banjo—str
   Excerpts from the opera, with vocal parts given to instruments
   where necessary.
   Contents—Catfish Row; Porgy sings; Fugue; Hurricane; Good
   mornin', Sistuh.
   Schirmer, G.   *Warner*

6' 5' 2'
3' 7'

Concerto, piano, F major   31'
   *3 *3 *3 2—4 3 3 1—tmp+3—str
   Luck   *Warner*

13' 11'
7'

Cuban overture   10'
   *3 *3 *3 *3—4 3 3 1—tmp+6—str
   Warner

"I got rhythm" variations   9'
   solo piano
   *2 *2 *4 2—(opt 2asx, tsx, bsx)—4 3 3 1—tmp+3—str
   Warner

Porgy and Bess: Symphonic picture   24'
   *3 *3 *3 2—2asx, tsx—4 3 3 1—tmp+3—2hp, banjo—str
   Symphonic version by Robert Russell Bennett. Bennett has also
   arranged a shorter and simpler *Selections from Porgy and Bess*
   (11'), which is available on rental from Luck's.
   Chappell

Promenade (Walking the dog, or The real McCoy)   3'
   *2 2 *3 2—4 3 2 1—tmp+2—hp, opt cel—str
   Often adapted as a novelty solo for clarinet or other instrument.
   Schirmer, G.

Rhapsody in blue (original jazz band version)   16'
   solo piano
   3 reed books (1. cl/ob/E-flat ssx; 2. ssx/asx/bsx; 3. ssx/tsx)
   —2hn, 2tp, 2tbn, tuba (doubling on string bass)—
   drum set/tmp—banjo, cel, pf—8vn
   Instrumentation by Ferde Grofé.
   Warner

Rhapsody in blue (full orchestra)   16'
   solo piano
   2 2 *3 2—2asx, tsx —3 3 3 1—tmp+3—banjo—str
   Orchestration by Ferde Grofé.
   A new edition by Alicia Zizzo (published by Warner under the
   title *Rhapsody in Blue addendum for piano and orchestra*) is said
   to restore some 50 bars deleted from Gershwin's original
   manuscript during the orchestration process.
   Luck   *Warner*

Second rhapsody for piano and orchestra   13'
   *3 *3 *3 2—4 3 3 1—tmp+4—hp—str
   Luck   *Warner*

Ghedike, Alexander   1877 - 1957
see: Goedicke, Alexander, 1877-1957

Giannini, Vittorio   1903 - 1966
Symphony no.2   22'
*3 2 2 2—4 3 3 1—tmp+1—str
Chappell

Gilbert, Henry F.   1868 - 1928
Dance in the Place Congo   20'
*3 2 *3 *3—4 3 3 1—tmp+4—hp—str
Gray

Gillis, Don   1912 - 1978
Short overture to an unwritten opera   4'
2 2 *3 2—3 3 3 1—tmp+2—hp—str
Boosey

Ginastera, Alberto   1916 - 1983
Concerto for strings, op.33   23'
str
Boosey

Concerto, harp, op.25   23'
*2 2 2 2—2 2 0 0—tmp+4—cel—str   8' 6' 9'
Boosey

Concerto, piano, no.1, op.28   27'
*3 *3 =4 *3—4 3 3 1—tmp+6—hp, cel—str   9' 6' 7' 5'
Barry

Estancia: Ballet suite   13'
*2 2 2 2—4 2 0 0—tmp+7—pf—str   3' 4' 2' 4'
Barry

Iubilum; symphonic celebration, op.51   11'
*3 *3 *3 *3—4 4 4 1—tmp+4—hp, cel—str
Boosey

Oberatura para el "Fausto" Criollo, op.9 (Overture to the Creole   9'
"Faust")
*2 2 2 2—4 3 3 1—tmp+5—hp, pf—str
Barry

Ollantay   14'
*3 *3 *3 2—4 3 3 1—tmp+7—hp, pf/cel—str   5' 3' 6'
Contents—Paisaje de Ollantaytambo; Los guerreros; La muerte de
Ollantay.
Barry

Pampeana no.3   18'
*3 *2 2 2—4 3 3 1—tmp+2—hp, pf/cel—str   6' 6' 6'
Barry

Panambí: Suite   12'
    *4 *4 =4 *4—4 4 3 1—tmp+7—2hp, cel, pf—str
    Barry

Popol vuh, op.44 (The creation of the Maya world)   23'
    *3 *3 =3 *3—4 4 4 1—tmp+4—2hp, pf/cel—str
    Two of the flutists double on piccolo; 1 percussionist doubles on
    2nd tmp.
    Boosey

Variaciones concertantes   21'
    *2 1 2 1—2 1 1 0—tmp—hp—str
    Solos for fl, ob, cl, bn, hn, tp, tbn, hp, vn, va, vc, db.
    Boosey

Glanville-Hicks, Peggy   1912 - 1990

Gymnopédie no.1   4'
    0 1 0 0—hp—str
    AMP

Glass, Philip   1937 -

Arioso no.2   6'
    str
    Elkan-Vogel

Glazunov, Alexander   1865 - 1936

Chant du ménestrel, op.71   3'
    solo violoncello
    *3 2 2 2—2 0 0 0—str
    Belaieff   *Kalmus*

Chopiniana   14'
    *3 2 2 2—4 2 3 0—tmp+4—str   4' 3' 3' 4'
    Chopin piano works orchestrated by Glazunov.
    Contents—Polonaise, op.40, no.1; Nocturne, op.15, no.1;
    Mazurka, op.50, no.3; Tarentelle, op.43.
    Belaieff   *Kalmus*

Concerto, alto saxophone, op.109   13'
    str
    Leduc

Concerto, violin, op.82, A minor   21'
    *3 2 2 2—4 2 3 0—tmp+3—hp—str   5' 10' 6'
    Belaieff   *Kalmus*

Cortége solennel [no.1], op.50   6'
    *3 2 3 2—4 3 3 1—tmp+4—hp—str
    Belaieff   *Kalmus*

Cortège solennel no.2, op.91   4'
  *3 2 3 2—4 3 3 1—tmp+4—str
  This work may be out of print, but orchestra materials are in the
  Fleisher Collection.
  Belaieff

Scènes de ballet, op.52   27'
  *3 *2 3 2—4 3 3 1—tmp+4—hp—str
  Belaieff   *Kalmus*

3'	2'	4'
1'	5'	3'
4'	5'	

The seasons: Autumn   11'
  *3 *2 2 2—4 2 3 1—tmp+5—hp, cel—str
  Contents—Bacchanal; Petit Adagio; Variation, Le Satyre.
  Belaieff   *Kalmus*

4'	4'	3'

The seasons: Three movements   4'
  *2 2 2 2—2 2 3 0—tmp+5—hp, cel—str
  Arr. Norman Richardson. Contents—Barcarolle; La Glace;
  Bacchanal.
  Boosey

2'	1'	1'

The seasons: Winter   9'
  *3 2 2 2—4 2 3 1—tmp+1—hp, cel—str
  Contents—Introduction; 4 variations (Frost, Ice, Hail, Snow).
  Belaieff   *Kalmus*

Stenka Razine, op.13   16'
  *3 2 2 2—4 2 3 1—tmp+3—hp—str
  Belaieff   *Kalmus*

Symphony no.4, op.48   31'
  *3 *2 3 2—4 2 3 1—tmp—str
  Belaieff   *Kalmus*

13'	5'
13'	

Valse de concert, no.1, op.47, D major   11'
  *3 *2 3 2—4 2 3 0—tmp+5—hp—str
  Belaieff   *Kalmus*

Valse de concert, no.2, op.51, F major   10'
  *3 2 2 2—4 2 3 0—tmp+3—hp—str
  Belaieff   *Kalmus*

Glière, Reinhold   1875 - 1956

Concerto, coloratura soprano & orchestra, op.82   14'
  2 2 2 2—3 0 0 0—tmp+1—hp—str
  Kalmus   *Schirmer, G.*

9'	5'

Concerto, harp, op.74, E-flat major   27'
  2 2 2 2—3 0 0 0—tmp+1—str
  Russian

11'	11'
5'	

Concerto, horn, op.91, B-flat major   26'
  3 2 2 2—3 2 3 1—tmp+4—hp—str
  Russian

The red poppy (Roter mohn): Suite   27'
   *3 *3 =3 *3—4 3 3 1—tmp+7—2hp, cel—str
   Contents—Victorious dance of the coolies; Scene and dance with
   the golden fingers; Coolie dance; The phoenix; Waltz; Dance of
   the Soviet sailors.
   Russian

| 4' | 9' | 2' |
| 6' | 2' | 4' |

The red poppy (Roter mohn): Russian sailors' dance   7'
   3 *3 *3 *3—4 3 3 1—tmp+5—str
   Kalmus   *Russian*

Symphony no.1, E-flat major, op.8   36'
   *3 2 2 2—4 2 3 1—tmp+2—str
   Kalmus

| 14' | 7' | 8' |
| | | 7' |

Symphony no.3 (Ilya Murometz)   76'
   *4 *4 *4 *4—8 4 4 1—tmp+4—2hp, cel—str
   Kalmus   *Russian*

| 22' | 22' |
| 7' | 25' |

Glinka, Mikhail   1804 - 1857

Jota aragonesa (Capriccio brillante) (Spanish overture no.1)   9'
   2 2 2 2—4 2 3 1—tmp+3—hp—str
   Kalmus   *Universal*

Kamarinskaya   7'
   2 2 2 2—2 2 1 0—tmp—str
   Belaieff   *Kalmus*

A life for the Tsar: Overture   10'
   2 2 2 2—4 2 3 0—tmp—str
   Kalmus

Russlan and Ludmilla: Overture   5'
   2 2 2 *3—4 2 3 0—tmp—str
   Belaieff   *Kalmus*   *Universal*

Summer night in Madrid (Spanish overture no.2)   10'
   2 2 2 2—4 2 1 0—tmp+5—str
   Kalmus   *Schirmer, G.*

Valse fantaisie   6'
   2 2 2 2—2 2 1 0—tmp+1—str
   Kalmus   *Schirmer, G.*   *Universal*

Gluck, Christoph Willibald   1714 - 1787

Alceste: Overture   10'
   2 2 2 *3—2 0 3 0—str
   Contrabassoon is optional. Concert-ending by Felix Weingartner.
   Bärenreiter publishes a version (presumably with the original
   ending) for: 2 2 0 2—2 0 3 0—str.
   Breitkopf   *Kalmus*

Ballet suite no.1   16'
   *3 *2 2 2—4 2 0 0—tmp+2—str   4' 6' 2' 4'
   Arr. Felix Mottl. Freely adapted from ballet music of various
   Gluck operas.
   Kalmus   *Peters*

Ballet suite no.2   15'
   *2 2 2 2—2 2 3 0—tmp+2—str
   Arr. Felix Mottl. Freely adapted from ballet music of various
   Gluck operas.
   Kalmus   *Peters*

Concerto, flute, G major   15'
   0 0 0 0—2 0 0 0—str
   Kalmus   *Peters*

Don Juan: Four movements   28'
   2 2 0 2—2 0 1 0—str
   Kalmus

Iphigenie in Aulis: Overture   10'
   2 2 2 3—4 3 0 0—tmp—str
   Concert-ending by Richard Wagner. Bärenreiter publishes
   a version (presumably with the original ending) for:
   2 2 0 2—2 2 0 0—str .
   Breitkopf   *Kalmus*

Orfeo ed Euridice: Dance of the blessed spirits   6'
   2 *1 0 0—2 0 0 0—str
   Arr. Felix Mottl.
   Kalmus

Orfeo ed Euridice: Dance of the furies   5'
   0 2 0 1—2 0 0 0—str
   Kalmus   *Luck*

Orfeo ed Euridice: Overture   5'
   0 2 0 1—2 2 0 0—tmp—str
   Kalmus   *Luck*

Overture, D major   5'
   cnt—str
   Kalmus   *Luck*

Sinfonia, D major   5'
   0 0 0 0—4 0 0 0—str   3' 1' 1'
   Supraphon

Sinfonia, F major   13'
   0 0 0 0—2 0 0 0—str
   Kalmus   *Luck*

Sinfonia, G major   8'
   cnt—str
   Kalmus

Goedicke, Alexander   1877 - 1957
Concert etude, trumpet & orchestra, op.49   6'
  1 1 1 1—1 0 0 0—tmp—opt hp—str
  2nd flute may substitute for oboe. Orchestrated by Gene Mullins.
  A version for solo trumpet with larger orchestra is available
  from Sikorski; a version for trumpet & strings is available from
  Kalmus (composer's name spelled "Gedike" in Kalmus
  catalog—probably more correctly).
  Brass Press

Gołabek, Jakub   1739 - 1789
Symphony in C major   14'
  2 2 0 0—2 0 0 0—str
  Probably originally for 2tp rather than 2hn; manuscript indicates
  "clarini."
  PWM

Symphony in D major (I)   14'
  0 2 0 1—2 0 0 0—str
  PWM

Symphony in D major (II)   18'
  0 2 0 0—2 0 0 0—str
  PWM

Goldmark, Karl   1830 - 1915
Concerto, violin, op.28, A minor   33'
  2 2 2 2—4 2 3 0—tmp—str
  Kalmus   Luck

14'	7'
	12'

Im Frühling, op.36 (Springtime)   10'
  *3 2 2 2—4 3 3 1—tmp—str
  Kalmus   Schott

Ländliche Hochzeit, op.26 (Rustic wedding symphony)   43'
  2 2 2 2—4 2 3 0—tmp+3—str
  Contents—1. Hochzeitsmarsch, Variationen; 2. Brautlied,

15'	4'	5'
10'	9'	

  Intermezzo; 3. Serenade, Scherzo; 4. Im Garten, Andante; 5. Tanz,
  Finale.
  Kalmus   Schott

Sakuntala: Overture   19'
  2 *3 2 2—4 2 3 1—tmp—hp—str
  Kalmus

Symphony no.2, op.35, E-flat major   30'
  2 2 2 2—4 2 3 1—tmp—str
  Original publisher: Schott.
  Kalmus

Goldschmidt, Berthold   1903 -

Concerto, violin   24'
  *2 *2 2 2—2 2 0 0—tmp+1—str
  Boosey

Concerto, violoncello   23'
  *2 *2 2 2—2 2 3 0—tmp+2—hp—str
  Boosey

Gomes, Antônio Carlos   1836 - 1896

Il Guarany: Overture   7'
  *4 2 2 2—4 4 3 1—tmp+3—hp—str
  Two of the flutists play piccolo. Arr. Ross Jungnickel.
  Luck

Goosens, Eugene   1893 - 1962

Concerto in one movement for oboe & orchestra, op.45   11'
  *2 0 *2 1—2 1 0 0—2perc—hp, cel—str
  Leduc

Górecki, Henryk   1933 -

Beatus vir, op.38   35'
  solo baritone   chorus
  4 4 4 *4—4 4 4 4—2perc—2hp, pf 4-hands—str
  2 additional tbn may substitute for 2 of the tubas; 2 of the bn
  double on cbn.
  Boosey

Old Polish music, op.24   27'
  0 0 0 0—5 4 4 0—str (min 8.8.8.8.8)
  Boosey

Symphony no.1 "1959", op.14   18'
  tmp+8—hp, pf, hpsd—str 16.16.14.12.10 | 5' 6' 3' 4' |
  Contents—Inwokacja; Antyfona; Choral; Lauda.
  Boosey

Symphony no.3 (Symphony of sorrowful songs) (Symfonia piesni   56'
zalosnych) | 27' 10' |
  solo soprano | 19' |
  *4 0 4 *4—4 0 4 0—hp, pf—str (16.14.12.10.8)
  Two of the flutists double on piccolo; 2 of the bassoonists play
  contrabassoon.
  Boosey

Three pieces in old style   10'
  str | 3' 2' 5' |
  Boosey   *PWM*

Gossec, François Joseph   1734 - 1829

Christmas suite (Première Suite de noëls)   10'
  optional chorus in last movement only
  0 2 0 0—2 0 0 0—cnt—str
  Horns are optional; flutes may substitute for oboes. Ed.
  Karlheinz Schultz-Hauser.
  Vieweg

Symphony op.6, no.6, B-flat major   20'
  str
  Ed. Fritz Zobeley.
  Breitkopf

Gottschalk, Louis Moreau   1829 - 1869

Grande Tarantelle, piano & orchestra, op.67   8'
  2 2 2 2—2 2 0 0—tmp+2—str
  Reconstructed and orchestrated by Hershy Kay.
  Boosey

La Nuit des tropiques (Symphony no.1) (Night in the tropics)   19'
  *3 2 +5 2—4 3 2 1—tmp+5—bsx, baritone horn—str | 13' 6' |
  Reconstructed by Gaylen Hatton.
  Boosey

Symphony no.2 (Romantique; Montevideo)   16'
  *3 2 2 2—2 2 2 1—tmp—str
  Belwin

Gould, Morton   1913 - 1996

Fall River legend: Ballet suite (1961 version)   21'
  *2 2 2 2—4 2 3 0—tmp+3—pf—str | 3' 3' 4' |
  Chappell | 5' 4' 2' |

Interplay   13'
  solo piano | 4' 2' 3' 4' |
  2 2 2 2—4 3 3 1—tmp+2—str
  Belwin

The jogger and the dinosaur; for rapper (narrator) & orchestra in 7   22'
scenes
  *2 1 2 1—2 2 2 1—tmp+2—str
  Tuba optional; 2nd narrator optional. Intended for performance
  with mimes or dancers. Alternate versions are possible without
  narrator: *Suite* (16'); *Dinosaurian Dances* (11').
  Schirmer, G.

Latin-American symphonette   17'
  *3 2 *4 2—2asx, tsx, bsx—4 3 3 1—tmp+4—hp, pf, gtr—str | 5' 4' 3' 5' |
  All saxophones double on clarinet; saxophones, guitar, and
  piano are optional, as are other (unspecified) instruments.
  Contents—Rhumba; Tango; Guaracha; Conga.
  Mills

Soundings   16'
  *3 *3 =3 *3—4 3 3 1—tmp+3—hp—str   10' 6'
  All 3 of the flutists double on piccolo.
  Contents—Threnodies; Paeans.
  Chappell

Spirituals for orchestra   20'
  *2 2 *3 2—4 3 3 1—tmp+4—hp, opt pf—str   5' 4' 5'
  Piccolo is optional.   3' 3'
  Belwin

Stringmusic   29'
  str   6' 4' 10'
  Contents—Prelude; Tango; Dirge; Ballad; Strum (perpetual   4' 5'
  motion).
  Schirmer, G.

Symphonette no.2   9'
  2 2 2 2—4 3 3 0—tmp+1—hp—str   3' 3' 3'
  (The well-known *Pavane* is the 2nd movement.)
  Belwin   *Kalmus*

Symphony of spirituals   27'
  *3 *3 =3 *3—4 3 3 1—tmp+3—hp, pf—str   8' 8' 4' 7'
  Contents—Hallelujah; Blues; Rag; Shout.
  G.Schirmer

Gounod, Charles   1818 - 1893
Faust: Ballet music   15'
  *2 2 *3 2—4 4 3 1—tmp+3—hp—str   2' 4' 2'
  Kalmus   1' 2' 2'
                                                                 2'

Faust: Waltz and chorus
  *2 2 2 2—4 2 3 0—tmp+3—str
  Kalmus   *Luck*

Marche funèbre d'une marionette (Funeral march of a marionette)   6'
  *2 2 2 2—2 2 3 1—tmp+3—str
  Tuba part originally for ophicleide.
  Bote & Bock   *Kalmus*   *Luck*

Messe solennelle (St. Cecilia)   41'
  chorus   solos STB
  *3 2 2 4—4 4 3 0—tmp+2—6hp (playing a single part), org—str
  Gray   *Kalmus*   *Leduc*

Petite Symphonie (Little symphony for wind instruments)   21'
  1 2 2 2—2 0 0 0   6' 6' 4' 5'
  Kalmus   *Luck*

Symphony no.1, D major   27'
  2 2 2 2—2 2 0 0—tmp—str   7' 5' 6' 9'
  Kalmus

Grainger, Percy   1882 - 1961

The immovable do (The cyphering C)   4'
    *4 *3 *3 *3—4 3 3 1—tmp+4—str
    May be performed with: *3 2 2 2—4 3 3 1—tmp+4—str;
    or by winds without strings; *or* by string orchestra; *or* by 9 solo
    strings.
    Schirmer, G.

In a nutshell   15'
    *3 *3 *3 *3—4 3 3 1—tmp+12—hp, cel, pf—str   `2' 2' 8' 3'`
    bcl, cbn & 4 of the percussionists are optional.
    Contents—Arrival platform humlet; Gay but wistful; Pastoral;
    The gum-suckers march.
    Kalmus

Irish tune from County Derry (Londonderry air)   3'
    2hn (opt)—str
    Kalmus   *Schott*

Molly on the shore   3'
    *3 2 2 2—4 2 3 1—tmp+4—cel—str
    "To *any* or *all* of the original 4 string parts (2 violins, viola &
    cello) can be added *any* or *all* of the [winds & percussion listed]."
    Kalmus   *Schott*

Shepherd's hey   3'
    *3 2 2 2—4 3 3 1—tmp+7—2hp, pf—str
    May be performed with: *2 2 2 2—4 2 3 1—tmp+3—hp—str.
    Another available version calls for: fl, cl, opt hn, concertina,
    3vn, 2va, 2vc, db.
    Kalmus   *Schott*

Granados, Enrique   1867 - 1916

Dante, op.21   15'
    alto solo
    3 *3 *3 *4—4 3 4 1—4 Wagner tubas—tmp+1—2hp—str
    Harps preferably doubled.
    Schirmer, G.

Goyescas: Intermezzo   4'
    3 *2 2 3—4 1 3 0—tmp+2—2hp—str
    From the opera *Goyescas*, rather than the piano work of the same
    name.
    Schirmer, G.

Tres danzas españolas   13'
    *3 *2 *3 2—4 2 3 1—tmp+3—hp—str
    Orchestrated by J. Lamote de Grignon.
    Contents—Oriental; Andaluza; Rondalla.
    UME

Grandjany, Marcel 1891 - 1975

Aria in classic style 4'
  solo harp
  str
  AMP

Graun, Johann Gottlieb 1703 - 1771

Concerto, violin & viola, C minor 23'
  cnt—str
  Breitkopf   *Kalmus*

Sinfonia, F major, M.95 8'
  2 0 0 0—2 0 0 0—str
  Ed. H. T. David.
  Kalmus

Graupner, Christoph 1683 - 1760

Concerto, bassoon, G major 8'
  cnt—str
  Kalmus   *Luck*

Concerto, oboe, F major 8'
  cnt—str
  Kalmus

Grétry, André 1741 - 1813

Concerto, flute, C major 14'
  0 0 0 0—2 0 0 0—str
  Kalmus   *Peters*

Zémire et Azor: Ballet suite 14'
  *2 2 2 2—2 0 0 0—2perc—str
  Ed. and arr. by Sir Thomas Beecham.
  Boosey

Grieg, Edvard 1843 - 1907

Bell ringing, op.54, no.6 (Klokkeklang) 3'
  2 2 2 2—4 2 3 1—tmp+1—hp—str
  Originally for piano.

Concerto, piano, op.16, A minor 30'
  2 2 2 2—4 2 3 0—tmp—str 13' 7'
  Kalmus   *Peters* 10'

Erotik, op.43, no.5 3'
  opt hp—str
  Arr. Max Spicker.
  Kalmus   *Luck*

Holberg suite, op.40 (Fra Holbergs tid)   21'
  str
  Kalmus   *Peters*

| 4' 4' 4' |
| 5' 4' |

In autumn, op.11 (I høst)   10'
  *3 2 2 2—4 2 3 1—tmp+3—str
  Kalmus   *Peters*

Landsighting, op.31 (Landkjenning)   7'
  male chorus   solo baritone
  2 2 2 2—4 2 3 1—tmp—opt org—str
  Peters

Lyric pieces, op.68, nos.4 & 5 (To lyriske stykker)   6'
  0 1 0 0—1 0 0 0—str
  Piano works arranged by the composer. Contents—Evening in the
  mountains (Aften på høfjeldet); At the cradle (Bådnlåt).
  Luck   *Peters*

Lyric suite, op.54 (Lyrisk suite)   17'
  *3 2 2 2—4 2 3 1—tmp+2—hp—str
  Contents—Shepherd's boy (Gjetergutt); Gangar; Notturno; March
  of the dwarfs (Trolltog).
  Kalmus   *Peters*

| 5' 4' 4' 4' |

Norwegian dances, op.35   17'
  *3 2 2 2—4 2 3 1—tmp+2—hp—str
  Orchestrated by Hans Sitt; originally for 2 pianos.
  Kalmus   *Peters*

| 6' 2' 4' 5' |

Old Norwegian melody with variations, op.51 (Gammelnorsk   22'
romanse med variasjoner)
  *3 2 2 2—4 2 3 1—tmp+4—hp—str
  Kalmus   *Peters*

Peer Gynt: Prelude (I bryllupsgården; Im Hochzeitshof)   10'
  *3 2 2 2—4 2 3 0—tmp—hp—str
  Kalmus

Peer Gynt: Suite no.1   15'
  *3 2 2 2—4 2 3 1—tmp+2—str
  Contents—Morning (Morgenstemning); Ase's death (Åses død);
  Anitra's dance (Anitras dans); In the hall of the mountain king (I
  dovregubbens hall).
  Kalmus   *Peters*

| 4' 4' 4' 3' |

Peer Gynt: Suite no.2   15'
  *3 2 2 2—4 2 3 1—tmp+4—hp—str
  Two of the flutists double on piccolo.
  Contents—Ingrid's lament (Bruderovet, & Ingrids klage); Arabian
  dance (Arabisk dans); Peer Gynt's homeward journey (Peer Gynts
  hjemfart); Solveig's song (Solveigs sang).
  Kalmus   *Peters*

| 3' 4' 4' 4' |

Sigurd Jorsalfar, op.56: Three orchestral pieces   18'
*2 2 2 2—4 3 3 1—tmp+3—hp—str   4' 5' 9'
Contents—Prelude; Intermezzo; Triumphal march
(Hyldningsmarsj).
Kalmus   *Peters*

Symphonic dances (Symfoniske danser), op.64   30'
*3 2 2 2—4 2 3 1—tmp—hp—str   7' 7' 5'
C. Fischer   *Kalmus*   11'

Symphony, C minor   38'
2 2 2 2—2 2 3 0—tmp—str

Two elegiac melodies, op.34 (To elegiske melodier)   9'
str   4' 5'
Contents—Heartwounds (Hjertesår); Last spring (Våren).
Kalmus   *Peters*

Two melodies, op.53 (To melodier)   8'
str   4' 4'
Contents—Norwegian (Norsk); The first meeting (Det første møte).
Kalmus   *Luck*   *Peters*

Two Norwegian airs, op.63 (Nordiske melodier)   11'
str   6' 5'
Contents—Popular song (I folketonestil); Cow keeper's tune and
Country dance (Kulokk og Stabbelåtten).
Kalmus   *Luck*

Wedding day at Troldhaugen, op.65, no.6 (Bryllupsdag på   6'
Troldhaugen)
2 2 2 2—4 2 3 1—2perc—str
This popular work, originally for piano, exists in several
arrangements with various instrumentations. The above version
(Luck's) arr. Theo. M. Tobani. Peters version (with harp but no
tuba) arr. Breuer; Kalmus version (smaller orchestra; a reprint of
a different Peters edition) arr. Huppertz; G.Schirmer version
(slightly larger orchestra) arr. Morton Gould. Luck's and Kalmus
versions have piano-conductor scores only.
Kalmus   *Luck*   *Peters*   *G.Schirmer*

Griffes, Charles Tomlinson   1884 - 1920

Bacchanale   5'
*3 *3 *3 *4—4 3 3 1—tmp+2—2hp, cel—str
Schirmer, G.

Clouds   5'
3 3 *3 3—4 0 0 0—1perc—2hp, cel—str
Schirmer, G.

The pleasure dome of Kubla Khan   13'
*3 *3 *3 3—4 3 3 1—tmp+2—2hp, cel, pf—str
Schirmer, G.

Poem for flute and orchestra   9'
   0 0 0 0—2 0 0 0—2perc—hp—str
   Schirmer, G.

The white peacock   6'
   *2 2 2 2—2 3 2 0—tmp—2hp, cel—str
   Schirmer, G.

Grofé, Ferde   1892 - 1972

American biographies: Henry Ford
   *3 *3 *3 2—4 3 3 1—tmp+3—hp, cel—str
   Robbins

Grand Canyon suite   33'
   *3 *3 *3 *3—4 3 3 1—tmp+3—hp, pf/cel—str   5' 6' 8'
   Contents—Sunrise; Painted Desert; On the trail; Sunset;   5' 9'
   Cloudburst
   Luck   *Presser*

Gruber, H[einz] K[arl]   1943 -

Concerto, violoncello   22'
   *1 1 1 1—1 1 1 0—1perc—pf—str
   Boosey

Frankenstein!!   28'
   baritone chansonnier
   *1 1 1 1—3 1 1 1—tmp+2—hp, cel—str
   Baritone and all players (except strings) double on an array of
   toy instruments, which are available with the rental material.
   An alternate version for 12 instruments & baritone is available.
   Boosey

Gruenberg, Louis   1884 - 1964

Concerto, violin, op.47   37'
   *3 *3 *3 *3—4 3 3 1—tmp+3—hp, pf/cel, harmonica—str
   This work may be out of print, but orchestral materials are in the
   Fleisher Collection.

The creation; a Negro sermon for voice and eight instruments, op.23   22'
   medium voice
   1 0 1 1—1 0 0 0—tmp+1—pf—va
   vc may substitute for bn.
   Gunmar

Gutche, Gene   1907 -

Holofernes overture, op.27, no.1   9'
   =3 *3 *3 *3—asx—4 4 3 1—tmp+8—str
   3rd & 4th tp, afl, & asx are optional. May be performed with 3
   percussionists.
   Highgate

Symphony no.5   22'
  str
  Highgate

H

Hadley, Henry   1871 - 1937

Salome, op.55   24'
  *3 *3 *3 *3—4 4 3 1—tmp+2—2hp—str
This work may be out of print, but materials are available in the
Fleisher Collection. The original publisher was Ries & Erler.

Symphony no.2, op.30, F minor (The four seasons (Die vier   36'
Jahreszeiten))   11' 7'
  *3 *2 2 2—4 2 3 1—tmp+2—str   10' 8'
Contents—Winter; Spring; Summer; Autumn.
This work may be out of print, but materials are available in the
Fleisher Collection. The original publisher was Arthur P.
Schmidt, Leipzig (1902).

Hahn, Reynaldo   1875 - 1947

Concerto, piano, E major   27'
  *2 *2 2 2—4 2 3 0—tmp+2—hp—str   13' 3'
  Heugel   11'

Hailstork, Adolphus   1941 -

Celebration (1975)   3'
  *2 3 3 2—4 3 3 1—tmp+5—str
  Wimbledon

Halévy, Jacques   1799 - 1862

La Juive: Overture   13'
  *3 2 2 2—4 4 3 1—tmp+3—str
Tuba part originally for ophicleide.
  Kalmus

Halffter, Ernesto   1905 - 1989

La muerte de Carmen (The death of Carmen): Habanera   9'
  *3 *3 *3 3—4 3 3 1—tmp+6—2hp—str
  Eschig

Hamilton, Iain   1922 -

Circus   17'
  2 solo trumpets
  2 2 2 2—4 0 3 1—tmp+1—hp, pf, gtr (amplified)—str
  Presser

Voyage, for horn & chamber orchestra   18'
  *1 1 +1 0—0 2 1 0—1perc—pf—str
  Solo strings may be used rather than sections.
  Presser

Handel, George Frideric   1685 - 1759

Alceste: Instrumental pieces   10'
  0 2 0 1—0 1 0 0—cnt—str
  Ed. H.T. David. Contents—Overture; Symphony; Grand Entrée.
  Kalmus

Alcina: Overture   5'
  0 2 0 0—cnt—str
  Oboes are optional. Published as "Festival music (Overture and
  dances from *Alcina*) for string orchestra."
  Hofmeister   *Kalmus*

Alexander's feast   85'
  chorus   solos STB   56' 29'
  2rec 2 0 3—2 2 0 0—tmp—cnt—str
  Bärenreiter   *Kalmus*

Alexander's feast: Overture   5'
  0 2 0 0—cnt—str
  Kalmus   *Luck*

L'Allegro, il penseroso ed il moderato   98'
  chorus   solos SATB   51' 47'
  2rec 2 0 2—2 2 0 0—tmp—cnt, carillon—str
  Bärenreiter   *Kalmus*

Belshazzar   147'
  chorus   solos SAATTBB   78' 36'
  0 2 0 0—0 2 0 0—tmp—cnt—str   33'
  Bärenreiter   *Peters*

Brockes' passion
  see his: Passion nach Barthold Heinrich Brockes

The choice of Hercules   55'
  chorus   solos SSAT
  2 2 0 1—2 2 0 0—cnt—str
  Bärenreiter   *Novello*

Concerto, harp, op.4, no.6, B-flat major   12'
  2rec—cnt—str   4' 6' 2'
  Solo part is for harp or organ.
  Bärenreiter   *Breitkopf*   *Peters*   *Schott*

Concerto, oboe, no.1, B-flat major   6'
  cnt—str
Also known as *Concerto grosso no.8.*
Breitkopf   *Kalmus*

Concerto, oboe, no.2, B-flat major   9'
  cnt—str (without va)
Also known as *Concerto grosso no.9.*
Breitkopf   *Kalmus*

Concerto, oboe, no.3, G minor   8'
  cnt—str
Also known as *Concerto grosso no.10.*
Breitkopf   *Kalmus*

Concerto, oboe, E-flat major   10'
  cnt—str
Ed. Fritz Stein, with added embellishments.
Peters

Concerto, organ, op.4, no.1, G minor   16'
  0 2 0 1—cnt—str   5' 6' 1' 4'
Bärenreiter   *Breitkopf*   *Kalmus*   *Schott*

Concerto, organ, op.4, no.2, B-flat major   10'
  0 2 0 1—cnt—str   1' 5' 4'
Bärenreiter   *Breitkopf*   *Kalmus*   *Schott*

Concerto, organ, op.4, no.3, G minor   13'
  solo vn & solo vc, in addition to solo organ
  0 2 0 1—cnt—str
Bärenreiter   *Breitkopf*   *Kalmus*   *Schott*

Concerto, organ, op.4, no.4, F major   16'
  0 2 0 1—cnt—str   4' 7' 2' 3'
Bärenreiter   *Breitkopf*   *Kalmus*   *Schott*

Concerto, organ, op.4, no.5, F major   7'
  0 2 0 1—cnt—str   2' 2' 1' 2'
Bärenreiter   *Breitkopf*   *Kalmus*   *Schott*

Concerto, organ, op.4, no.6, B-flat major   12'
  2rec—cnt—str   4' 6' 2'
Solo part for organ or harp.
Bärenreiter   *Breitkopf*   *Kalmus*   *Peters*

Concerto, organ, op.7, no.1, B-flat major   11'
  0 2 0 1—cnt—str   4' 3' 2' 2'
Breitkopf   *Kalmus*   *Schott*

Concerto, organ, op.7, no.2, A major   16'
  0 2 0 1—cnt—str   7' 3' 6'
Breitkopf   *Kalmus*   *Schott*

Concerto, organ, op.7, no.3, B-flat major   16'
  0 2 0 1—cnt—str   5' 3' 4' 4'
Breitkopf   *Kalmus*   *Schott*

Concerto, organ, op.7, no.4, D minor 16'
  0 2 0 2—cnt—str
Breitkopf   *Kalmus*   *Schott*

|6' 4' 3' 3'|

Concerto, organ, op.7, no.5, G minor 13'
  0 2 0 1—cnt—str
Breitkopf   *Kalmus*   *Schott*

|4' 5' 2' 2'|

Concerto, organ, op.7, no.6, B-flat major 10'
  0 2 0 1—cnt—str
Breitkopf   *Schott*

|3' 3' 4'|

Concerto, viola, B minor 12'
  2 0 0 2—str
An assortment of movements from various works of Handel,
compiled and arranged as a viola concerto by Henri Casadesus.
Eschig

|5' 4' 3'|

Concerto a due cori, no.1, B-flat major 14'
  0 4 0 2—cnt—str
Breitkopf title is *Concerto grosso no.27.*
Breitkopf   *Kalmus*

|1' 3' 2'|
|1' 2' 2'|
|3'|

Concerto a due cori, no.2, F major 16'
  0 4 0 2—4 0 0 0—cnt—str
Some authorities believe this and the *Concerto a due cori no.3* are
actually a single work. Breitkopf title is *Concerto grosso no.28.*
Breitkopf   *Kalmus*

|2' 2' 3'|
|2' 4' 3'|

Concerto a due cori, no.3, F major 13'
  0 4 0 2—4 0 0 0—str
Some authorities believe this and the *Concerto a due cori no.2* are
actually a single work. Breitkopf title is *Concerto grosso no.29.*
Breitkopf   *Kalmus*

|1' 3' 3'|
|1' 3' 2'|

Concerto grosso, no.7, C major (Alexanderfest) 13'
  solo concertino: 2 violins, violoncello
  0 2 0 0—2cnt—str
Bärenreiter   *Breitkopf*   *Kalmus*   *Peters*

Concerto grosso, nos.8-10
  see his: Concerto, oboe, nos.1-3

Concerto grosso, op.3, no.1, B-flat major 10'
  2rec 2 0 2—2cnt—str
Bärenreiter   *Breitkopf*   *Kalmus*   *Peters*

|3' 5' 2'|

Concerto grosso, op.3, no.2, B-flat major 12'
  solo concertino: 2 violins, violoncello
  0 2 0 1—2cnt—str
Bärenreiter   *Breitkopf*   *Kalmus*   *Peters*

|2' 3'|
|2'2'3'|

Concerto grosso, op.3, no.3, G major 8'
  solo concertino: violin, flute (or oboe)
  2cnt—str
Bärenreiter   *Breitkopf*   *Kalmus*   *Peters*

|3' 1' 4'|

Concerto grosso, op.3, no.4, F major — 11'
0 2 0 1—cnt—str — 4' 2' 2' 3'
Bärenreiter   *Breitkopf*   *Kalmus*   *Peters*

Concerto grosso, op.3, no.5, D minor — 10'
0 2 0 0—cnt—str — 2' 2' 1' 2' 3'
Bärenreiter   *Breitkopf*   *Kalmus*   *Peters*

Concerto grosso, op.3, no.6, D major — 7'
0 2 0 1—org—str — 3' 4'
Bärenreiter   *Breitkopf*   *Kalmus*   *Peters*

Concerto grosso, op.6, no.1, G major — 12'
solo concertino: 2 violins, violoncello
2cnt—str — 2' 2' 2' 3' 3'
Bärenreiter edition includes 2ob & 1bn.
Bärenreiter   *Breitkopf*   *Kalmus*   *Peters*

Concerto grosso, op.6, no.2, F major — 11'
solo concertino: 2 violins, violoncello
2cnt—str — 4' 2' 3' 2'
Bärenreiter edition includes 2ob & 1bn.
Bärenreiter   *Breitkopf*   *Kalmus*   *Peters*

Concerto grosso, op.6, no.3, E minor — 12'
solo concertino: 2 violins, violoncello
2cnt—str — 1' 2' 3' 5' 1'
Bärenreiter   *Breitkopf*   *Kalmus*   *Peters*

Concerto grosso, op.6, no.4, A minor — 11'
solo concertino: 2 violins, violoncello
2cnt—str — 3' 3' 2' 3'
Bärenreiter   *Breitkopf*   *Kalmus*   *Peters*

Concerto grosso, op.6, no.5, D major — 16'
solo concertino: 2 violins, violoncello
2cnt—str — 2' 2' 3' 2' 3' 4'
Bärenreiter edition includes 2ob & 1bn.
Bärenreiter   *Breitkopf*   *Kalmus*   *Peters*

Concerto grosso, op.6, no.6, G minor — 17'
solo concertino: 2 violins, violoncello
2cnt—str — 4' 2' 6' 3' 2'
Bärenreiter edition includes 2ob & 1bn.
Bärenreiter   *Breitkopf*   *Kalmus*   *Peters*

Concerto grosso, op.6, no.7, B-flat major — 14'
solo concertino: 2 violins, violoncello
2cnt—str — 1' 2' 3' 5' 3'
Concertino merely doubles ripieno in this work.
Bärenreiter   *Breitkopf*   *Kalmus*   *Peters*

Concerto grosso, op.6, no.8, C minor — 14'
solo concertino: 2 violins, violoncello
2cnt—str

| 4' 2' 2' |
| 1' 4' 1' |

Bärenreiter   *Breitkopf*   *Kalmus*   *Peters*

Concerto grosso, op.6, no.9, F major — 15'
solo concertino: 2 violins, violoncello
2cnt—str

| 1' 4' 4' |
| 2' 2' 2' |

Bärenreiter   *Breitkopf*   *Kalmus*   *Peters*

Concerto grosso, op.6, no.10, D minor — 14'
solo concertino: 2 violins, violoncello
2cnt—str

| 4' 3' 2' |
| 3' 2' |

Bärenreiter   *Breitkopf*   *Kalmus*   *Peters*

Concerto grosso, op.6, no.11, A major — 18'
solo concertino: 2 violins, violoncello
2cnt—str

| 5' 2' 1' |
| 4' 6' |

Bärenreiter   *Breitkopf*   *Kalmus*   *Peters*

Concerto grosso, op.6, no.12, B minor — 12'
solo concertino: 2 violins, violoncello
2cnt—str

| 2' 3' 4' |
| 1' 2' |

Bärenreiter   *Breitkopf*   *Kalmus*   *Peters*

Dettingen Te deum — 35'
chorus   solo bass voice
0 2 0 1—0 3 0 0—tmp—org, hpsd—str
This edition is full of added dynamics and other interpretive
markings.
Kalmus   *Peters*

Dixit dominus (Psalm 109) — 33'
chorus   solos SSATB
cnt—str

| 6' 3' 3' |
| 2' 2' 7' |
| 4' 6' |

Bärenreiter   *Kalmus*

Israel in Egypt — 100'
double chorus   solos SSATBB
0 2 0 2—0 2 3 0—tmp—org, hpsd—str
Bärenreiter edition includes 2fl.
Bärenreiter   *Kalmus*   *Peters*

Joshua — 105'
chorus   solos SSATB
2 2 0 1—2 3 0 0—tmp—cnt—str
Kalmus   *Peters*

Jubilate for the Peace of Utrecht — 19'
chorus   solos AAB
0 2 0 0—0 2 0 0—cnt—str

| 2' 2' 3' |
| 3' 3' 6' |

Kalmus

Judas Maccabaeus 100'
    chorus   solos SSATBB
    2 2 0 2—2 3 0 0—tmp—org, hpsd—str
    Kalmus   *Peters*

Judas Maccabaeus: Overture 7'
    0 2 0 1—cnt—str
    Kalmus   *Luck*

Largo
    see his: Xerxes: Largo

Messiah 120'
    chorus   solos SATB
    0 2 0 2—0 2 0 0—tmp—org, cnt—str
    Novello edition (ed. Watkins Shaw) offers the most extensive
    number of variant movements.
    Bärenreiter   *Novello*   *Peters*

Messiah (orchestrated by W. A. Mozart) 120'
    chorus   solos SATB
    2 2 2 2—2 2 3 0—tmp—org—str
    Peters

Messiah (orchestrated by Ebenezer Prout) 120'
    chorus   solos SATB
    2 2 2 2—2 2 3 0—tmp—org, pf—str
    Schirmer, G.

Occasional oratorio (Festoratorium) 144'
    double chorus   solos SSATB
    0 2 0 2—2 3 0 0—tmp—cnt—str
    Several of the movements were borrowed from the composer's
    Israel in Egypt. Some of these borrowed movements used 3
    trombones in the earlier setting, and parts for trombones are
    included by the editor with the *Occasional oratorio* materials,
    though apparently they were not intended by Handel.
    Breitkopf

Occasional oratorio: Overture 10'
    0 2 0 0—0 3 0 0—tmp—cnt—str
    Kalmus

Ode for St. Cecilia's Day 55'
    chorus   solos ST
    1 2 0 1—0 2 0 0—tmp—lute, cnt—str
    Bärenreiter

Orlando: Overture
    0 2 0 0—cnt—str
    Kalmus

Overture, D major 8'
    2 3 2 *3—4 3 0 0—tmp—str
    Arr. Franz Wüllner.
    Luck

Passion nach Barthold Heinrich Brockes   full
    chorus   solos: 6S, 4A, 3T, 5B   concert
    0 2 0 2—cnt—str
    Possible, by combining roles, with solos SATTBB.
    Bärenreiter

Il pastor fido (The faithful shepherd): Suite   25'
    2 2 2 2—4 2 0 0—tmp+1—str   5' 6' 2'
    Arr. Thomas Beecham.   2' 3' 4'
    Boosey   3'

Prelude & fugue, D minor   6'
    *3 *3 *3 2—4 3 3 1—tmp—pf—str
    Freely transcribed by Hans Kindler from the *Concerto grosso,
    op.3, no.5.*
    Belwin

Psalm 89 (My song shall be alway)   30'
    chorus   solos STB
    0 1 0 1—cnt—str (without va)
    Peters

Psalm 96 (O sing unto the Lord)   20'
    chorus   solos ST
    0 1 0 1—cnt—str (without va)
    Peters

Rodrigo: Overture   15'
    0 2 0 1—cnt—str
    Kalmus   *Peters*

Royal fireworks music   19'
    0 3 0 *3—3 3 0 0—tmp—cnt—str (opt)   9' 2' 3'
    Handel's original performance used 24ob, 12bn, unknown   2' 3'
    numbers of contrabassoons and serpents, 3hn, 3tp, and 3 sets of
    timpani. The strings were added later by the composer and may be
    considered optional. Another separate Peters edition (ed. Robert
    A. Boudreau) uses no strings and calls for one or more snare
    drums in addition to timpani.
    Contents—Overture; Bourrée; La Paix; La Réjouissance; Menuet I
    & II.
    Bärenreiter   *Breitkopf*   *Peters*

Royal fireworks music (ed. Baines & MacKerras)   21'
    *2 3 3 *3—3 5 3 0—tmp+3—str
    Ed. Anthony Baines & Charles MacKerras. Playable by a variety
    of instrumentations from a maximum (above) to a minimum of:
    0 3 0 2—2 2 0 0—tmp+1—[no str].
    Oxford

Royal fireworks music (arr. Hamilton Harty)   11'
    0 2 0 2—4 3 0 0—tmp+1—str
    Contents—Overture; Alla siciliana; Bourrée; Menuetto.
    Chappell

Samson   214'
   chorus   solos SATBB
   2 2 0 2—2 2 0 0—tmp—cnt—str
   Bärenreiter   *Kalmus*   *Peters*

> 78' 83'
> 53'

Samson: Overture   6'
   0 2 0 0—2 0 0 0—cnt—str
   Bärenreiter   *Kalmus*

Saul   180'
   chorus   solos: 2S, A , 5T, 4B
   2rec 2 0 2—0 2 3 0—tmp—hp, cnt, org, carillon—str
   Bärenreiter

> 14' 70'
> 48' 48'

Saul: Overture   14'
   0 2 0 1—cnt, org solo—str
   Bärenreiter   *Kalmus*

Solomon   151'
   chorus   solos SSSSATB
   2 2 0 2—2 2 0 0—tmp—cnt—str
   Bärenreiter   *Breitkopf*   *Gray*

> 4' 57'
> 52' 38'

Solomon: Overture   12'
   0 2 0 0—cnt—str
   Kalmus

Solomon: Entrance of the Queen of Sheba   3'
   0 2 0 0—cnt—str
   Kalmus   *Luck*

Te deum
   see his: Dettingen Te deum

Theodora: Overture   12'
   0 2 0 0—cnt—str
   Kalmus

Water music   50'
   1 2 0 1—2 2 0 0—cnt—str
   Flute doubles flageolet or sopranino recorder. This version is
   based on the old collected edition of Handel's works. More recent
   scholarship suggests that the division into three separate suites
   (as in the following entries) is preferable.
   Breitkopf   *Peters*

Water music: Suite no.1, F major   32'
   0 2 0 1—2 0 0 0—cnt—str
   Bärenreiter   *Eulenburg*

> 4' 2' 8'
> 4' 3' 3'
> 2' 2' 4'

Water music: Suite no.2, D major   12'
   0 2 0 1—2 2 0 0—cnt—str
   Bärenreiter   *Eulenburg*

> 3' 4' 1'
> 3' 1'

Water music: Suite no.3, G major   11'
   1 2 0 1—cnt—str
   Flute doubles on flageolet or sopranino recorder.
   Bärenreiter   *Eulenburg*

3'	3'	1'
2'	1'	1'

Water music suite (arr. Hamilton Harty)   16'
   *2 2 2 2—4 2 0 0—tmp—str
   Chappell

2'	5'	1'
1'	4'	3'

Xerxes: Largo   5'
   2 2 2 2—4 3 3 1—hp—str
   Arr. Arthur Luck.
   Luck

Zadok the priest (Coronation anthem no.1)   6'
   chorus   solos SSAATBB
   0 2 0 2—0 3 0 0—tmp—cnt—str
   Kalmus   *Schirmer, G.*

Hanson, Howard   1896 - 1981

Cherubic hymn   12'
   chorus
   *3 2 2 2—4 3 3 1—tmp+1—pf—str
   C. Fischer

Lament for Beowulf, op.25   19'
   chorus
   *3 2 2 *3—4 3 3 1—2tmp+2—hp—str
   C. Fischer

Lux aeterna, op.24   15'
   solo viola
   *3 2 2 *3—4 3 3 1—tmp+2—2hp, cel, pf—str
   C. Fischer

Merry Mount: Suite   15'
   *3 *3 *3 *3—4 3 3 1—tmp+6—2hp—str

3'	2'	4'	6'

   Contents—Overture; Children's dance; Love duet; Prelude to Act
   II and Maypole dances.
   Warner

Serenade, op.35   6'
   solo flute
   hp—str
   C. Fischer

Symphony no.1, op.21, E minor (Nordic)   27'
   *3 2 2 *3—4 3 3 1—tmp+1—hp—str

12'	6'	9'

   C. Fischer

Symphony no.2, op.30 (Romantic)   28'
   *3 *3 2 *3—4 3 3 1—tmp+2—hp—str

14'	7'	7'

   C. Fischer

Symphony no.3, op.33   **33'**
*3 *3 *3 *3—4 3 3 1—tmp—str
C. Fischer
10' 8' 6'
9'

Symphony no.4, op.34 (Requiem)   **27'**
*3 2 *2 *2—4 3 3 1—tmp+2—str
C. Fischer
10' 6' 3'
8'

Symphony no.5, op.43 (Sinfonia sacra)   **13'**
*3 2 2 2—4 3 3 1—tmp+2—hp—str
C. Fischer

Harbison, John   1938 -

Concerto, flute   **19'**
*2 2 2 *2—2 2 0 0—2perc—str
AMP

Merchant of Venice: Incidental music   **12'**
str orchestra (or str quintet)
AMP

The most often used chords (Concerto for chamber orchestra)   **18'**
2 2 2 2—2 2 0 0—tmp+1—hp, cel/pf—str
AMP

Music for 18 winds   **11'**
2 2 2 2—asx—4 2 2 1
AMP

Remembering Gatsby: Foxtrot for orchestra   **7'**
*3 *3 *3 *3—4 3 3 1—tmp+3—pf—str
3rd cl doubles on ssx as well as bcl.
AMP

Symphony no.1   **23'**
=3 *3 *3 *3—4 2 3 1—tmp+5—hp—str
AMP

Symphony no.2   **23'**
*3 *3 =4 *3—4 4 3 1—tmp+3—hp, pf/cel—str
Contents—Dawn; Daylight; Dusk; Dark.
AMP
5' 4' 6' 8'

Harris, Roy   1898 - 1979

Elegy for orchestra   **6'**
*3 *3 2 *3—4 3 3 1—tmp+1—hp, cel—str
AMP

Horn of plenty   **10'**
*3 *3 *3 3—4 4 3 1—baritone horn—tmp+3—str
AMP

Ode to consonance   **10'**
*2 *2 *3 2—2 3 2 1—baritone horn—tmp+1—hp—str
AMP

Symphony no.3   18'
  *3 *3 *3 2—4 3 3 2—tmp+2—str
  Schirmer, G.

Symphony no.5   26'
  *3 *3 *3 3—4 3 3 1—tmp+6—hp, pf—str
  Additional optional instruments: tsx, baritone tuba, E-flat cl.
  The composer specifies from 4 to 8 horns.
  Belwin

Symphony no.7   19'
  *4 *4 *4 *4—6 4 3 1—baritone horn—tmp+3—hp, pf—str
  5th & 6th horns and 4th trumpet are optional.
  AMP

Symphony no.9   27'
  *4 *4 *4 *4—6 4 4 1—baritone horn—tmp+3—hp, pf—str
  AMP

5'	11'
	11'

When Johnny comes marching home   8'
  *3 *3 *3 3—4 3 3 1—euphonium—2tmp+2—str
  Schirmer, G.

Harsányi, Tibor   1898 - 1954

L'Histoire du petite tailleur (The story of the little tailor)   30'
  narrator (optional)
  *1 0 1 1—0 1 0 0—1perc—pf—vn, vc
  25' without narration. Composed for marionettes, after a tale of
  Grimm.
  Eschig

Hartmann, Karl Amadeus   1905 - 1963

Symphony no.6   22'
  *3 *3 *3 *3—4 4 3 1—tmp+8—hp, cel, pf 4-hands, mand—str
  Schott

11'	11'

Hartway, James   1944 -

Cityscapes   20-25'
  jazz quartet: asx, pf, db, drums
  *3 2 *3 *3—6 4 4 1—tmp+3—str
  Contrabassoon optional. Duration varies depending on the
  extent of the jazz solos. Contents—Sunday morning; Weekdays;
  Saturday night.
  Luck

Country suite   15-20'
  jazz quartet: fl, pf, db, drums
  str
  Duration varies depending on the extent of the jazz solos.
  Luck

Freedom festival · · · 10'
optional speaking chorus
*3 *3 *3 *3—4 3 3 1—tmp+4—hp, pf—str
Players (or chorus members) whisper, speak, and shout cries for
freedom in 7 different languages at various points. Fragments of
12 different national anthems occur.
Luck

Haydn, Franz Joseph · · · 1732 - 1809

Concertino, harpsichord, Hob.XIV:11, C major · · · 10'
str
Ed. H.C. Robbins Landon.
Doblinger

3' 5' 2'

Concerto, flute, Hob.VIIf:D1, D major · · · 20'
opt cnt—str
Ed. Alexander Kowatscheff. Authenticity doubtful.
Leuckart

Concerto, 2 flutes, Hob.VIIh:1, C major · · · 13'
0 0 0 0—2 0 0 0—str
Ed. H.C. Robbins Landon. Originally for 2 lire organizzate.
Doblinger

4 ' 4' 5'

Concerto, flute & oboe, Hob.VIIh:2, G major · · · 12'
0 0 0 0—2 0 0 0—str
Ed. H.C. Robbins Landon. Originally for 2 lire organizzate.
Doblinger

5' 3' 4'

Concerto, flute & oboe, Hob.VIIh:3, G major · · · 13'
0 0 0 0—2 0 0 0—str
Ed. H.C. Robbins Landon. Originally for 2 lire organizzate.
Doblinger

5' 4' 4'

Concerto, flute & oboe, Hob.VIIh:4, F major · · · 14'
0 0 0 0—2 0 0 0—str
Ed. H.C. Robbins Landon. Originally for 2 lire organizzate.
Doblinger

5' 5' 4'

Concerto, flute & oboe, Hob.VIIh:5, F major · · · 12'
0 0 0 0—2 0 0 0—str
Ed. H.C. Robbins Landon. Originally for 2 lire organizzate.
Doblinger

5' 4' 3'

Concerto, harpsichord, Hob.XVIII:4, G major · · · 21'
0 2 0 0—2 0 0 0—str
Winds are optional. Ed. Bruno Hinze-Reinhold.
Nagel · · · *Peters*

9' 8' 4'

Concerto, harpsichord, Hob.XVIII:5, C major · · · 13'
str (without va)
Perhaps intended for piano rather than harpsichord. Ed. Horst
Heussner.
Nagel

Concerto, harpsichord, Hob.XVIII:7, F major   12'
   str (va optional)
   Ed. Klaas Weelink.
   KaWe

Concerto, harpsichord, Hob.XVIII:11, D major   18'
   0 2 0 0—2 0 0 0—str   7' 7' 4'
   Breitkopf   *Peters*

Concerto, harpsichord, Hob.XVIII:F1, F major   12'
   2 0 0 0—str
   Ed. Gustav Lenzewski. Probably incorrectly attributed to
   Haydn.
   Vieweg

Concerto, horn, no.1, Hob.VIId:3, D major   17'
   0 2 0 0—cnt—str   6' 7' 4'
   Boosey   *Bote & Bock*   *Kalmus*

Concerto, horn, no.2, Hob.VIId:4, D major   15'
   str
   Boosey   *Breitkopf*   *Kalmus*

Concerto, oboe, Hob.VIIg:C1, C major   23'
   0 2 0 0—2 2 0 0—tmp—str   11' 6' 6'
   Authenticity doubtful. Breitkopf ed. Alexander Wunderer;
   Oxford ed. Evelyn Rothwell; Peters ed. Rolf Julius Koch.
   Breitkopf   *Oxford*   *Peters*

Concerto, organ, Hob.XVIII:1, C major   20'
   0 2 0 0—str   8' 7' 5'
   Ed. Michael Schneider.
   Breitkopf

Concerto, organ, no.2, Hob.XVIII:8, C major   11'
   0 0 0 0—0 2 0 0—tmp—str   5' 3' 3'
   Trumpets & timpani are optional. Ed. H.C. Robbins Landon.
   Doblinger

Concerto, organ, F major   14'
   0 0 0 0—2 0 0 0—str   6' 5' 3'
   Ed. Belsky and Sramek. First published in 1962, and not listed in
   Hoboken.
   Breitkopf

Concerto, piano
   see his: Concerto, harpsichord

Concerto, trumpet, Hob.VIIe:1, E-flat major   13'
   2 2 0 2—2 2 0 0—tmp—str   6' 3' 4'
   Universal edition (1982) is by Edward Tarr & H.C.Robbins
   Landon.
   Boosey   *Breitkopf*   *C. Fischer*   *Kalmus*

Concerto, violin, Hob.VIIa:1, C major   19'
  cnt—str
  Breitkopf   *Eulenburg*   *Kalmus*   10' 5' 4'

Concerto, violin, Hob.VIIa:4, G major   21'
  cnt—str
  Breitkopf   *Doblinger*   *Kalmus*   9' 8' 4'

Concerto, violin, Hob.VIIa:B2, B-flat major   27'
  str
  Of very doubtful authenticity.
  Breitkopf

Concerto, violin & piano (or harpsichord), Hob.XVIII:6, F major   18'
  str
  Ed. Paul Bormann.   7' 7' 4'
  Boosey

Concerto, violoncello, Hob.VIIb:2, D major   25'
  0 2 0 0—2 0 0 0—str
  UCCP edition (ed. H.C. Robbins Landon, based on the newly   13' 6' 6'
  discovered autograph) incorporates baroque bowings in solo &
  orchestral parts.
  Peters   *Schott*   *UCCP*

Concerto, violoncello, Hob.VIIb:2, D major (arr. Gevaert)   25'
  Arr. F.A. Gevaert.
  2 2 2 2—2 0 0 0—str   13' 6' 6'
  Breitkopf

Concerto, violoncello, Hob.VIIb:5, C major   17'
  2 2 2 2—2 0 0 0—str
  Completed by David Popper after a sketch by Haydn.
  Kalmus

The creation
  see his: Die Schöpfung

Divertimento no.9, Hob.II:21, E-flat major
  0 0 0 0—2 0 0 0—str
  Score shows only str, but the material includes parts for 2hn. The
  work also exists as a string quartet (Hob.III:9).
  Möseler

Die Jahreszeiten (The seasons)   134'
  chorus   solos STB
  *2 2 2 *3—4 3 3 0—tmp+2—pf—str   31' 37'
  Breitkopf   *Gray*   *Kalmus*   *Peters*   34' 32'

Kindersymphonie, Hob.II:47, C major (Toy symphony or Sinfonia Berchtolsgadensis)　　　　　　10'

| 5' | 3' | 2' |

　　str (without va)
　　5 players for toys (trumpet, drum, cuckoo, nightingale, rattle, triangle, quail).
　　Though commonly attributed to Haydn and published in this edition under his name, the actual composer is believed to be Leopold Mozart.
　　Breitkopf　　　*Kalmus*

March for the Royal Society of Musicians　　　　4'
　　2 0 2 2—2 2 0 0—tmp—str
　　Ed. H.C. Robbins Landon. The second (orchestral) version of the *March for the Prince of Wales.*
　　Doblinger

Mass, Hob.XXII:1, F major (Missa brevis)　　　13'
　　chorus　　2 solo sopranos
　　org—str
　　Ed. Richard Moder. Also known as *Jugendmesse.* Additional instrumental parts were supplied later, supposedly at Haydn's suggestion: 1 0 2 2—0 2 0 0—tmp.
　　Doblinger

[Mass, Hob.XXII:2]
　　This work is for chorus *a cappella*—thus outside the scope of this book.

Mass, Hob.XXII:3, G major (Rorate coeli desuper)　　10'
　　chorus
　　str, org
　　Ed. H.C. Robbins Landon. Also known as *Missa brevis alla capella.*
　　Universal

Mass, Hob.XXII:4, E-flat major (Grosse Orgelsolo Messe)　　37'

| 5' | 9' | 10' |
| 2' | 5' | 6' |

　　chorus　　solos SATB
　　0 *2 0 1—2 0 0 0—org—str
　　Both oboists play English horn. Ed. Alois Strassl. Also known as *Missa in honorem beatissimae virginis Mariae.*
　　Doblinger

Mass, Hob.XXII:5, C major (St. Cecilia mass)　　70'

9'	31'
17'	2'	6'
		5'

　　chorus　　solos SATB
　　0 2 0 2—0 2 0 0—tmp—org—str
　　In the *Benedictus* the composer may have added 2hn later. Both this work and Hob.XXII:8 are also known as *Missa cellensis.*
　　Universal

Mass, Hob.XXII:6, G major (Missa Sancti Nicolai)   27'
    chorus   solos SATB
    0 2 0 1—0 2 0 0—org—str   3' 4' 6' / 8' 6'
    Faber ed. by H.C. Robbins Landon. Also sometimes referred to as
    Missa St. Josephi.
    Faber   Kalmus

Mass, Hob.XXII:7, B-flat major (Kleine Orgelmesse)   15'
    chorus   solo soprano   2' 1' 3' / 1' 5' 3'
    org—str
    Ed. H.C. Robbins Landon. Also known as *Missa brevis sancti
    Johannis de deo.*
    Bärenreiter

Mass, Hob.XXII:8, C major (Mariazeller Messe)   40'
    chorus   solos SATB
    0 2 0 1—0 2 0 0—tmp—org—str
    Both this work and Hob.XXII:5 are also known as *Missa
    cellensis.*
    Bärenreiter   Kalmus

Mass, Hob.XXII:9, C major (Missa in tempore belli, or Mass in time   45'
of war)
    chorus   solos SATB
    1 2 2 2—2 2 0 0—tmp—org—str
    Also known as *Paukenmesse.*
    Bärenreiter   Kalmus   Schirmer, G.

Mass, Hob.XXII:10, B-flat major (Heiligmesse)   45'
    chorus   solos SATB (or SSATBB)
    0 2 2 2—0 2 0 0—tmp—org—str
    Clarinets are used only in the *Incarnatus* and *Vitam.* Peters
    edition treats them as an alternative to the oboes (i.e. 2ob *or* 2 cl).
    Bärenreiter   Peters

Mass, Hob.XXII:11, D minor [original instrumentation]   42'
(Lord Nelson mass)   5' 11' / 10' 9' 7'
    chorus   solos SATB
    0 0 0 0—0 3 0 0—tmp—org—str
    3rd tp has no independent part; doubles 2nd tp in certain
    passages.
    Includes a *konzertierenden* organ part, because at the time the
    Esterhazy winds were gone. Haydn later suggested putting the
    concerted part of the organ back in the winds, resulting in the
    following two editions of this mass.
    Also known as: *Missa in angustiis, Nelsonmesse, L'Impérial,* and
    Coronation mass.
    Schott

Mass, Hob.XXII:11, D minor [2nd instrumentation] (Lord Nelson mass)   42'
    chorus   solos SATB   5' 11'
    1 2 0 2—0 3 0 0—tmp—org—str   10' 9' 7'
    3rd tp has no independent part; doubles 2nd tp in certain passages.
    Woodwinds added supposedly at Haydn's suggestion.
    Also known as: *Missa in angustiis, Nelsonmesse, L'Impérial,* and *Coronation mass.*
    Breitkopf   *Peters*

Mass, Hob.XXII:11, D minor [3rd instrumentation] (Lord Nelson mass)   42'
    chorus   solos SATB   5' 11'
    1 2 2 1—2 3 0 0—tmp—org—str   10' 9' 7'
    3rd tp has no independent part; doubles 2nd tp in certain passages.
    Optional clarinets and horns added supposedly at Haydn's suggestion. It is possible to play any of the earlier instrumentations from the Bärenreiter set of parts.
    Also known as: *Missa in angustiis, Nelsonmesse, L'Impérial,* and *Coronation mass.*
    Bärenreiter

Mass, Hob.XXII:12, B-flat major (Theresienmesse)   43'
    chorus   solos SATB   5' 12'
    0 0 2 1—0 2 0 0—tmp—org—str   11' 2' 6'
    An authentic copy has additional parts for 2ob and 2hn, though   7'
    these are not as yet available in any modern edition.
    Bärenreiter   *Gray*

Mass, Hob.XXII:13, B-flat major (Schöpfungsmesse)   46'
    chorus   solos SATB (or SSATTB)
    0 2 2 2—2 2 0 0—tmp—org—str
    Kalmus

Mass, Hob.XXII:14, B-flat major (Harmoniemesse)   48'
    chorus   solos SATB (or SSATTB)   9' 13'
    1 2 2 2—2 2 0 0—tmp—org—str   12' 3' 4'
    Bärenreiter   *Kalmus*   *Peters*   *Schirmer, G.*   7'

Die Schöpfung (The creation)   109'
    chorus   solos SSTBB (or STB)   40' 40'
    3 2 2 *3—2 2 3 0—tmp—hpsd—str   29'
    Breitkopf   *Kalmus*   *Peters*   *Schirmer, G.*

Die Schöpfung (ed. A. Peter Brown) (The creation)   109'
    chorus   solos STB (or SSTBB)

40' 40'

3 2 2 *3—2 2 3 0—tmp—fortepiano (or hpsd)—str

29'

Includes markings that permit reconstruction of Haydn's own
practice, including, for performances with the very largest forces,
the use of up to 3 "wind bands" and 2 brass groups. The aggregate
largest ensemble would be: 9 6 6 *7—6 4 5 0—2tmp—fortepiano
or hpsd—"with a string body comparable to modern dimensions."
Oxford

The seasons
    see his: Die Jahreszeiten

Die sieben letzten Worte [choral version] (Seven last words of   60'
Christ)
    chorus   solos SATB
2 2 2 *3—2 2 2 0—tmp—str
Bärenreiter   *Breitkopf*   *Kalmus*   *Peters*

Die sieben letzten Worte [orchestral version] (Seven last words of   67'
Christ)

5' 7' 9'

2 2 0 2—4 2 0 0—tmp—str

10' 8' 9'

Bärenreiter

7' 10' 2'

Sinfonia Berchtolsgadensis
    see his: Kindersymphonie

Sinfonia concertante, op.84, Hob.I:105, B-flat major   22'
    solos: oboe, bassoon, violin, violoncello

9' 6' 7'

1 2 0 2—2 2 0 0—tmp—str
Breitkopf

Stabat mater, Hob.XXbis   80'
    chorus   solos SATB
0 *2 0 1—org—str
Both oboists play English horn. Faber ed. by H.C. Robbins
Landon.
Faber   *Kalmus*

Symphonies
    *Although there are many editions of the various Haydn
symphonies, most fail to meet modern standards of scholarship.
The editions cited here (those of the Haydn-Mozart Presse, edited
by H.C. Robbins Landon) are by far the best.*

Symphony A, Hob.I:107, B-flat major   15'
0 2 0 1—2 0 0 0—cnt—str

6' 4' 5'

Doblinger

Symphony B Hob.I:108, B-flat major   15'
0 2 0 1—2 0 0 0—cnt—str

3' 4' 5' 3'

Doblinger

Symphony no.1, D major   11'
0 2 0 1—2 0 0 0—cnt—str

5' 4' 2'

Doblinger

Symphony no.2, C major   9'
  0 2 0 1—2 0 0 0—cnt—str   3' 3' 3'
  Doblinger

Symphony no.3, G major   16'
  0 2 0 1—2 0 0 0—cnt—str   5' 6' 3' 2'
  Doblinger

Symphony no.4, D major   13'
  0 2 0 1—2 0 0 0—cnt—str   4' 4' 5'
  Doblinger

Symphony no.5, A major   17'
  0 2 0 1—2 0 0 0—cnt—str   5' 6' 4' 2'
  Doblinger

Symphony no.6, D major (Le Matin)   24'
  1 2 0 1—2 0 0 0—cnt—str   6' 8' 5' 5'
  Doblinger

Symphony no.7, C major (Le Midi)   21'
  2 2 0 1—2 0 0 0—cnt—str   5' 7' 4'
                          2' 3'
  Doblinger

Symphony no.8, G major (Le Soir)   23'
  1 2 0 1—2 0 0 0—cnt—str   5' 8' 5' 5'
  Doblinger

Symphony no.9, C major   12'
  2 2 0 1—2 0 0 0—cnt—str   4' 5' 3'
  Doblinger

Symphony no.10, D major   13'
  0 2 0 1—2 0 0 0—cnt—str   5' 5' 3'
  Doblinger

Symphony no.11, E-flat major   18'
  0 2 0 1—2 0 0 0—cnt—str   8' 3' 4' 3'
  Doblinger

Symphony no.12, E major   16'
  0 2 0 1—2 0 0 0—cnt—str   3' 9' 4'
  Doblinger

Symphony no.13, D major   21'
  1 2 0 1—4 0 0 0—tmp—cnt—str   5' 6' 5' 5'
  Doblinger

Symphony no.14, A major   15'
  0 2 0 1—2 0 0 0—cnt—str   4' 4' 4' 3'
  Doblinger

Symphony no.15, D major   18'
  0 2 0 1—2 0 0 0—cnt—str   6' 5' 5' 2'
  Doblinger

Symphony no.16, B-flat major   12'
   0 2 0 1—2 0 0 0—cnt—str   4' 5' 3'
   Doblinger

Symphony no.17, F major   14'
   0 2 0 1—2 0 0 0—cnt—str   5' 6' 3'
   Doblinger

Symphony no.18, G major   16'
   0 2 0 1—2 0 0 0—cnt—str   7' 5' 4'
   Doblinger

Symphony no.19, D major   12'
   0 2 0 1—2 0 0 0—cnt—str   5' 4' 3'
   Doblinger

Symphony no.20, C major   15'
   0 2 0 1—2 2 0 0—tmp—cnt—str   3' 5' 4' 3'
   Doblinger

Symphony no.21, A major   15'
   0 2 0 1—2 0 0 0—cnt—str   5' 4' 3' 3'
   Doblinger

Symphony no.22, E-flat major (The philosopher)   16'
   0 *2 0 1—2 0 0 0—cnt—str   7' 3' 4' 2'
   Both oboists play English horn.
   Doblinger

Symphony no.23, G major   16'
   0 2 0 1—2 0 0 0—cnt—str   5' 6' 3' 2'
   Doblinger

Symphony no.24, D major   15'
   1 2 0 1—2 0 0 0—cnt—str   4' 4' 4' 3'
   Doblinger

Symphony no.25, C major   12'
   0 2 0 1—2 0 0 0—cnt—str   6' 3' 3'
   Doblinger

Symphony no.26, D minor (Lamentatione)   17'
   0 2 0 1—2 0 0 0—cnt—str   6' 6' 5'
   Doblinger

Symphony no.27, G major   11'
   0 2 0 1—2 0 0 0—cnt—str   4' 4' 3'
   Doblinger

Symphony no.28, A major   16'
   0 2 0 1—2 0 0 0—cnt—str
   Doblinger

Symphony no.29, E major   17'
   0 2 0 1—2 0 0 0—cnt—str   4' 5' 4' 4'
   Doblinger

Symphony no.30, C major (Alleluja)
  1 2 0 1—2 0 0 0—cnt—str
  Doblinger
12'
4' 4' 4'

Symphony no.31, D major (Horn signal)
  1 2 0 1—4 0 0 0—cnt—str
  Doblinger
25'
4' 6' 5'
10'

Symphony no.32, C major
  0 2 0 1—2 2 0 0—tmp—cnt—str
  Doblinger
20'

Symphony no.33, C major
  0 2 0 1—2 2 0 0—tmp—cnt—str
  Doblinger
18'
5' 7' 3' 3'

Symphony no.34, D minor
  0 2 0 1—2 0 0 0—cnt—str
  Doblinger
15'
6' 4' 3' 2'

Symphony no.35, B-flat major
  0 2 0 1—2 0 0 0—cnt—str
  Doblinger
20'
5' 7' 4' 4'

Symphony no.36, E-flat major
  0 2 0 1—2 0 0 0—cnt—str
  Doblinger
17'
5' 4' 4' 4'

Symphony no.37, C major
  0 2 0 1—2 0 0 0—cnt—str
An alternative version substitutes 2 trumpets and timpani for the
horns.
  Doblinger
13'
3' 3' 4' 3'

Symphony no.38, C major
  0 2 0 1—2 2 0 0—tmp—cnt—str
  Doblinger
13'
4' 3' 3' 3'

Symphony no.39, G minor
  0 2 0 1—4 0 0 0—cnt—str
  Doblinger
16'
5' 4' 3' 4'

Symphony no.40, F major
  0 2 0 1—2 0 0 0—cnt—str
  Doblinger
18'
5' 5' 5' 3'

Symphony no.41, C major
  1 2 0 1—2 2 0 0—tmp—str
  Doblinger
19'
6' 6' 4' 3'

Symphony no.42, D major
  0 2 0 2—2 0 0 0—str
  Doblinger
29'
10' 10'
5' 4'

Symphony no.43, E-flat major (Merkur; Mercury)
  0 2 0 1—2 0 0 0—str
  Doblinger
25'
7' 9' 4' 5'

Symphony no.44, E minor (Trauer-Symphonie)　　　　22'
　0 2 0 1—2 0 0 0—str
　　Doblinger　　　　　　　　　　　　　　　　7' 6' 6' 3'

Symphony no.45, F-sharp minor (Abschieds-Symphonie; Farewell　　25'
symphony)
　0 2 0 1—2 0 0 0—str　　　　　　　　　　6' 7' 4' 8'
　Musicians gradually leave the stage during finale.
　　Doblinger

Symphony no.46, B major　　　　　　　　　　19'
　0 2 0 1—2 0 0 0—str
　　Doblinger　　　　　　　　　　　　　　　6' 5' 4' 4'

Symphony no.47, G major　　　　　　　　　　22'
　0 2 0 1—2 0 0 0—str
　　Doblinger　　　　　　　　　　　　　　　6' 8' 3' 5'

Symphony no.48, C major (Maria Theresia)　　　　　27'
　0 2 0 1—2 2 0 0—tmp—str
　Trumpet & timpani parts by another hand, though probably　8' 10' 6'
　similar to Haydn's original parts which were lost.　　　　3'
　　Doblinger

Symphony no.49, F minor (La passione)　　　　　　24'
　0 2 0 1—2 0 0 0—cnt—str
　　Doblinger　　　　　　　　　　　　　　　10' 5' 6'
　　　　　　　　　　　　　　　　　　　　　　3'

Symphony no.50, C major　　　　　　　　　　18'
　0 2 0 1—2 2 0 0—tmp—str
　　Universal　　　　　　　　　　　　　　　4' 4' 6' 4'

Symphony no.51, B-flat major　　　　　　　　　23'
　0 2 0 1—2 0 0 0—str
　　Universal　　　　　　　　　　　　　　　7' 8' 4' 4'

Symphony no.52, C minor　　　　　　　　　　23'
　0 2 0 1—2 0 0 0—str
　　Universal　　　　　　　　　　　　　　　7' 7' 5' 4'

Symphony no.53, D major (L'imperiale)　　　　　　24'
　1 2 0 1—2 0 0 0—tmp—str
　Alternate finales, one of which calls for 2 bassoons.　　8' 7' 5' 4'
　　Universal

Symphony no.54, G major　　　　　　　　　　28'
　2 2 0 2—2 2 0 0—tmp—str
　　Universal　　　　　　　　　　　　　　　6' 11' 5'
　　　　　　　　　　　　　　　　　　　　　　6'

Symphony no.55, E-flat major (Der Schulmeister)　　22'
　0 2 0 2—2 0 0 0—str
　　Universal　　　　　　　　　　　　　　　5' 8' 5' 4'

Symphony no.56, C major　　　　　　　　　　25'
　0 2 0 1—2 2 0 0—tmp—str
　　Universal　　　　　　　　　　　　　　　6' 8' 7' 4'

Symphony no.57, D major   23'
  0 2 0 1—2 0 0 0—tmp—str   8' 6' 5' 4'
Universal

Symphony no.58, F major   18'
  0 2 0 1—2 0 0 0—cnt—str   5' 6' 3' 4'
Universal

Symphony no.59, A major (Feuersymphonie)   17'
  0 2 0 1—2 0 0 0—cnt—str   5' 5' 4' 3'
Universal

Symphony no.60, C major (Il distratto)   24'
  0 2 0 1—2 2 0 0—tmp—str   6' 4' 5'
Universal   3' 4' 2'

Symphony no.61, D major   22'
  1 2 0 2—2 0 0 0—tmp—str   7' 7' 5' 3'
Universal

Symphony no.62, D major   20'
  1 2 0 2—2 0 0 0—str   5' 5' 3' 7'
Universal

Symphony no.63, C major (La Roxelane)   20'
  1 2 0 1—2 0 0 0—str   6' 6' 4' 4'
Universal

Symphony no.64, A major (Tempora mutantur)   21'
  0 2 0 1—2 0 0 0—str   6' 9' 3' 3'
Universal

Symphony no.65, A major   17'
  0 2 0 1—2 0 0 0—str   5' 5' 3' 4'
Universal

Symphony no.66, B-flat major   23'
  0 2 0 2—2 0 0 0—str   9' 6' 4' 4'
Universal

Symphony no.67, F major   18'
  0 2 0 2—2 0 0 0—str   4' 6' 3' 5'
Universal

Symphony no.68, B-flat major   21'
  0 2 0 2—2 0 0 0—str   4' 4' 8' 5'
Universal

Symphony no.69, C major (Laudon)   16'
  0 2 0 2—2 2 0 0—tmp—str   4' 5' 3' 4'
Universal

Symphony no.70, D major   18'
  1 2 0 1—2 2 0 0—tmp—str   8' 4' 3' 3'
Universal

Symphony no.71, B-flat major
  1 2 0 1—2 0 0 0—str
Universal

23'

7' 6' 4' 6'

Symphony no.72, D major
  1 2 0 1—4 0 0 0—tmp—cnt—str
Universal

23'

5' 5' 4' 9'

Symphony no.73, D major (La Chasse)
  1 2 0 2—2 2 0 0—tmp—str
Universal

25'

10' 5' 5'
5'

Symphony no.74, E-flat major
  1 2 0 2—2 0 0 0—str
Universal

23'

7' 7' 4' 5'

Symphony no.75, D major
  1 2 0 1—2 2 0 0—tmp—str
Universal

20'

6' 8' 3' 3'

Symphony no.76, E-flat major
  1 2 0 2—2 0 0 0—str
Universal

24'

6' 8' 3' 7'

Symphony no.77, B-flat major
  1 2 0 2—2 0 0 0—str
Universal

18'

6' 5' 3' 4'

Symphony no.78, C minor
  1 2 0 2—2 0 0 0—str
Universal

20'

6' 6' 4' 4'

Symphony no.79, F major
  1 2 0 2—2 0 0 0—str
Universal

21'

6' 6' 4' 5'

Symphony no.80, D minor
  1 2 0 2—2 0 0 0—str
Universal

21'

5' 7' 4' 5'

Symphony no.81, G major
  1 2 0 2—2 0 0 0—str
Universal

26'

7' 8' 6' 5'

Symphony no.82, C major (L'Ours)
  1 2 0 2—2 2 0 0—tmp—str
  Trumpets are optional.
Universal

27'

8' 8' 5' 6'

Symphony no.83, G minor (La Poule)
  1 2 0 2—2 0 0 0—str
Universal

24'

8' 6' 5' 5'

Symphony no.84, E-flat major
  1 2 0 2—2 0 0 0—str
Universal

24'

7' 7' 4' 6'

Symphony no.85, B-flat major (La Reine)   20'
  1 2 0 2—2 0 0 0—str   8' 5' 4' 3'
Universal

Symphony no.86, D major   26'
  1 2 0 2—2 2 0 0—tmp—str   7' 7' 6' 6'
Universal

Symphony no.87, A major   23'
  1 2 0 2—2 0 0 0—str   7' 7' 5' 4'
Universal

Symphony no.88, G major   23'
  1 2 0 2—2 2 0 0—tmp—str   7' 8' 4' 4'
Universal

Symphony no.89, F major   22'
  1 2 0 2—2 0 0 0—str   7' 6' 4' 5'
Universal

Symphony no.90, C major   24'
  1 2 0 2—2 2 0 0—tmp—str   7' 7' 5' 5'
Universal

Symphony no.91, E-flat major   25'
  1 2 0 2—2 0 0 0—str   9' 7' 4' 5'
Universal

Symphony no.92, G major (Oxford)   28'
  1 2 0 2—2 2 0 0—tmp—str   8' 8' 6' 6'
Universal

Symphony no.93, D major   21'
  2 2 0 2—2 2 0 0—tmp—str   6' 6' 4' 5'
Universal

Symphony no.94, G major (Surprise)   23'
  2 2 0 2—2 2 0 0—tmp—str   7' 7' 5' 4'
  German title: *Paukenschlag.*
Universal

Symphony no.95, C minor   21'
  1 2 0 2—2 2 0 0—tmp—str   7' 6' 5' 3'
Universal

Symphony no.96, D major (The miracle)   20'
  2 2 0 2—2 2 0 0—tmp—str   5' 6' 6' 3'
Universal

Symphony no.97, C major   25'
  2 2 0 2—2 2 0 0—tmp—str   8' 5' 5' 7'
Universal

Symphony no.98, B-flat major   28'
  1 2 0 2—2 2 0 0—tmp—str   8' 5' 6' 9'
  Brief hpsd solo in 4th mvt.
Universal

Symphony no.99, E-flat major   25'
   2 2 2 2—2 2 0 0—tmp—str
   Universal   9' 8' 4' 4'

Symphony no.100, G major (Military)   24'
   2 2 2 2—2 2 0 0—tmp+3—str
   Universal   7' 5' 6' 6'

Symphony no.101, D major (The clock)   29'
   2 2 2 2—2 2 0 0—tmp—str
   Universal   9' 8' 7' 5'

Symphony no.102, B-flat major   24'
   2 2 0 2—2 2 0 0—tmp—str
   Universal   7' 6' 6' 5'

Symphony no.103, E-flat major (Paukenwirbel; Drum roll)   27'
   2 2 2 2—2 2 0 0—tmp—str
   A critical edition of the score with historical and analytical   8' 9' 4' 6'
   essays is available from Norton.
   Universal

Symphony no.104, D major (London)   29'
   2 2 2 2—2 2 0 0—tmp—str
   Universal   8' 9' 5' 7'

Te deum for the Empress Maria Therese, Hob.XXIIIc:2   12'
   chorus
   1 2 0 2—2 3 3 0—tmp—org—str
   Ed. H.C. Robbins Landon.
   Trombones only double chorus parts.
   Doblinger

Toy symphony
   see his: Kindersymphonie

Haydn, Michael   1737 - 1806

Andromeda ed Perseo, P.25: Overture   5'
   0 2 0 2—2 2 0 0—tmp—str
   Bärenreiter   *Doblinger*

Concertino, horn, D major   12'
   0 2 0 1—2 0 0 0—cnt—str
   Ed. Charles H. Sherman.
   Universal

Concerto, trumpet, no.2, C major   13'
   2 0 0 0—cnt—str
   Ed. Edward H. Tarr.   5' 8'
   Musica Rara

Concerto, violin, A major   25'
   0 2 0 1—2 0 0 0—str
   Ed. Charles H. Sherman.   10' 10'
   Doblinger   5'

Missa pro defunctis   45'
   chorus   solos SATB
   0 0 0 1—0 4 3 0—tmp—org—str
   Ed. Charles H. Sherman.
   Universal

Missa Sancti Hieronymi   45'
   chorus
   0 4 0 2—0 0 3 0—org—double basses
   Ed. Charles H. Sherman.
   Universal

Pastorello, P.91 (Christmas music, Salzburg, 1766)   10'
   0 0 0 0—0 4 0 0—tmp—cnt—str
   3rd & 4th trumpet parts may be played on trombones.
   Peters

Symphony, P.8, G major   5'
   str
   Ed. Charles H. Sherman.
   Doblinger

Symphony, P.16, G major   15'
   1 2 0 2—2 0 0 0—hpsd—str
   Ed. Charles Sherman.
   Previously known as Symphony no.37 by Mozart, whose
   contribution was only the adagio introduction.
   Breitkopf   *Doblinger*

Symphony, P.21, D major (1785)   19'
   1 2 0 2—2 0 0 0—str
   Ed. Pál Gombás.
   Doblinger

Symphony, P.26, E-flat major (1788)   8'
   0 2 0 2—2 0 0 0—str
   Ed. Antal Várhelyi.
   Doblinger

Symphony, P.29, D major (1788)   8'
   1 2 0 2—2 0 0 0—str
   Ed. Lászlo Kalmár.
   Doblinger

Symphony, P.33, A major   15'
   0 2 0 2—2 0 0 0—str
   Ed. Charles H. Sherman.
   Doblinger

Symphony, P.42, D major   18'
   0 2 0 1—2 0 0 0—str
   Ed. H.C. Robbins Landon.
   Doblinger

Veni, sancte spiritus
chorus
0 2 0 0—2 0 3 0—org—str (without va)
Trombones are optional. Ed. Harry Graf.
Peters

Hensel, Fanny Mendelssohn   1805 - 1847

Hiob   **8'**
chorus   solos SATB
2 2 2 2—2 2 0 0—tmp—str
Ed. Conrad Misch.
Furore

> 3' 2' 3'

Lobgesang   **12'**
chorus   SA solos
2 2 2 2—2 2 0 0—str
Ed. Conrad Misch.
Furore

> 2' 3' 1'
> 3' 3'

Henze, Hans Werner   1926 -

Antifone   **17'**
4 0 0 0—4sx (SATBar)—0 2 2 0—tmp+6—cel, pf—str (3.3.2.2.1)
The saxophones may be replaced by 4 B-flat clarinets.
Schott

Aria de la Folía española   **20'**
*1 *2 =1 2—2 0 0 0—1perc—cel, pf, mand—str
One of the oboists doubles on both Eh & ob d'amore.
Schott

Barcarola   **20'**
=3 *3 =3 *3—ssx, bsx—6 4 4 1—tmp+2—2hp, cel, pf—str
All three fl double on pic, 3rd also on afl; 2ob double on Eh, 3rd
also on heckelphone; all 3cl double on scl, 2nd also on bcl, 3rd
also on contrabass cl.
Schott

Los caprichos; fantasia per orchestra   **20'**
*3 *3 *3 *3—4 3 3 1—tmp+3—hp, cel, pf—str
Schott

Compases para preguntas ensimismadas (Music for viola and 22   **26'**
players)
solo viola
=1 *1 *1 1—rec—1 0 0 0—tmp+1
—hp, pf/cel, amplified hpsd—str 3.3.0.4.1
Schott

Concerto, piano, no.2   **45'**
*3 *3 =3 *3—4 2 2 1—tmp+7—hp—str
Two of the flutists double on piccolo.
Schott

Concerto, violin, no.2 29'
*3 *2 *3 2—2 2 1 0—4perc—hp, pf, prepared pf, gtr, mand—tape
(vns & voices)—solo bass baritone voice (partly on tape & partly
live)—4va, 3vc, 2db
All 3 fl double on pic. Voice parts may all be sung live. Gtr, mand,
& 1cl with contact microphones. Soloist occasionally plays a
violin with contact microphone. In one passage soloist may speak
some text ad lib.
Schott

Double concerto 30'
solo oboe & harp
str 4.4.4.4.2
Schott

Ode an den Westwind 22'
violoncello solo
*2 *2 *2 *2—2 2 1 1—tmp+8—hp, cel, pf—str 10.10.12.0.8
Schott

Quattro poemi 10'
*3 *3 *3 *3—4 2 2 1—str
Contents—Elogio; Egloga; Elegia; Ditirambo.
Schott

Requiem; neun geistliche Konzerte 78'
solo piano   trumpet concertante

| 5' 8' 8' |
| 12' 11' |
| 7' 10' 7' |
| 10' |

=2 *2 =2 *1—ssx/asx/bsx—2 2 2 0—tmp+3—hp, cel—4vn, 3va,
3vc, db
Both fl double on pic; bcl doubles on contrabass cl; 2tp double on
btp; 2nd tbn doubles on contrabass tbn.
Contents—Introitus; Dies irae; Ave verum corpus; Lux aeterna;
Rex tremendae; Agnus dei; Tuba mirum; Lacrimosa; Sanctus.
Schott

Symphony no.1 17'
=2 *2 *2 0—2 2 0 0—tmp—hp, cel, pf—str
Both flutists double on piccolo. Rev. 1991.
Schott

Symphony no.2 23'
*3 *3 *3 *3—4 4 3 1—tmp+3—hp, pf—str
Schott

Symphony no.3 25'
*3 *3 *3 *3—tsx—4 4 3 1—tmp+4—hp, cel, pf—str
Contents—Anrufung Apolls; Dithyrambe; Beschwörungstanz.
Schott

Symphony no.4 28'
*3 *3 *3 *3—4 3 2 1—tmp+3—hp, cel, pf—str
Schott

Symphony no.5   18'
　　=4 *4 0 0—4 4 4 0—tmp—2hp, 2pf—str
　　Two of the oboists double on English horn.
　　Schott

Symphony no.6   40'
　　=3 *3 =3 *2—tsx—4 3 3 0—tmp+4—hp, pf, elec org,
　　gtr/banjo—str 8.8.8.8.6
　　1vn, gtr & banjo have contact microphones. 3rd tbn doubles on
　　tenor tuba. Charango (with contact microphone) may substitute
　　for banjo.
　　Divided into two orchestras.
　　Schott

Symphony no.8   25'
　　=2 *2 *2 *2—4 2 2 1—tmp+3—hp, cel, pf—str
　　Both flutists double on piccolo.
　　Schott

Herbert, Victor   1859 - 1924
Concerto, violoncello, no.2, op.30, E minor   23'
　　2 2 2 2—4 2 3 0—tmp—str
　　Kalmus   *Luck*

Serenade, op.12   22'
　　str
　　Luck

Hérold, Louis Joseph F.   1791 - 1833
Zampa: Overture   8'
　　*2 2 2 2—4 2 3 1—tmp+3—str
　　Kalmus   *Luck*   *Ricordi*

Heseltine, Philip   1894 - 1930
　　see: Warlock, Peter, 1894-1930

Hindemith, Paul   1895 - 1963
Amor und Psyche
　　see his: Cupid and Psyche

Concert music for strings and brass, op.50   17'
　　0 0 0 0—4 4 3 1—str | 9' 8' |
　　Schott

Concert music for viola & large chamber orchestra, op.48   23'
　　*2 *2 *2 *3—3 2 1 1—4vc, 4db | 5' 8' 3' |
　　Schott | 4' 3' |

Concerto for orchestra, op.38   13'
　　*2 2 =3 *3—3 2 2 1—tmp+5—str | 3' 3' 4' 3' |
　　Schott

Concerto, horn (1949) 15'
  *1 2 2 2—tmp—str
  Schott

Concerto, organ, op.46, no.2 (Kammermusik no.7) 17'
  *2 1 *2 *3—1 1 1 0—str (without vn or va)
  Schott

Concerto, organ (1962) 25'
  *2 2 2 *3—2 2 3 1—tmp+2—cel—str
  Schott

Concerto, piano, op.36, no.1 (Kammermusik no.2) 20'
  1 1 *2 1—1 1 1 0—vn, va, vc, db
  Schott

Concerto, viola, op.36, no.4 (Kammermusik no.5) 17'
  *1 1 =3 *3—1 2 2 1—4vc, 4db
  Schott

Concerto, viola d'amore, op.46, no.1 16'
  1 1 *2 1—1 1 1 0—3vc, 2db
  Schott

Concerto, violin, op.36, no.3 (Kammermusik no.4) 23'
  *2 0 =3 *3—0 1 1 1—1perc—4va, 4vc, 4db
  Schott

Concerto, violin (1939) 29'
  *2 2 *3 2—4 2 3 1—tmp+3—str

9'	10'
	10'

  Schott

Concerto, violoncello, op.36, no.2 (Kammermusik no.3) 16'
  *1 1 +1 1—1 1 1 0—vn, vc, db
  Schott

Concerto for woodwinds, harp & orchestra (1949) 15'
  solos: flute, oboe, clarinet, bassoon, harp
  0 0 0 0—2 2 1 0—str
  Schott

Cupid and Psyche (Amor und Psyche): Overture 6'
  *2 2 2 2—2 2 2 0—tmp+1—str
  Schott

The four temperaments
  see his: Theme and variations

Die Harmonie der Welt: Symphony 35'
  *2 2 *3 *3—4 2 3 1—tmp+5—str

11'	10'
	14'

  Schott

Kammermusik no.1 mit Finale 1921, op.24, no.1 15'
  for 12 instruments
  *1 0 1 1—0 1 0 0—1perc—pf, accordion—2vn, va, vc, db
  Schott

Lustige Sinfonietta, op.4   22'
*2 *3 2 *3—2 2 0 0—tmp+2—str 8.6.6.6.4
Both flutists double on piccolo. Contents—Die Galgenbrüder;
Intermezzo (Zoologische Merkwürdikeiten); Palmström.
Schott

Mathis der Maler: Symphony   25'
*2 2 2 2—4 2 3 1—tmp+3—str   8' 4' 13'
Schott

Neues vom Tage: Overture   8'
*2 *2 =3 *3—asx—1 2 2 1—3perc—str
Schott

Nobilissima visione   21'
*2 2 2 2—4 2 3 1—tmp+4—str   7' 9' 5'
Schott

Philharmonic concerto   20'
*3 *3 *3 *3—4 3 3 1—tmp+3—str
Schott

Pittsburgh symphony   21'
*2 *3 *3 *3—4 2 3 1—tmp+4—str   6' 11' 4'
Schott

Der Schwanendreher   29'
solo viola   9' 10'
*2 1 2 2—3 1 1 0—tmp—hp—str (without vn or va)   10'
Schott

Sinfonietta in E   19'
*2 2 2 2—3 1 2 1—tmp+1—cel—str   5' 7' 2' 5'
Schott

Spielmusik, op.43, no.1   7'
2 2 0 0—str
Schott

Suite of French dances   8'
*2 *2 0 1—0 1 0 0—lute—str
Strings may consist of: 3va, 2vc; *or* 2vn, va, 2vc; *or* string
orchestra. Winds are optional.
After 16th-century dances.
Schott

Symphonia serena   29'
*3 *3 *3 *3—4 2 2 1—tmp+4—cel—str   8' 4' 9' 8'
Schott

Symphonic dances (1937)   32'
*2 2 2 2—4 2 3 1—tmp+3—str
Schott

Symphonic metamorphosis of themes by Carl Maria von Weber   21'
*3 *3 *3 *3—4 2 3 1—tmp+4—str   4' 8' 4' 5'
Schott

Symphony in E-flat   31'
  *3 *3 *3 *3—4 3 3 1—tmp+4—str
  Schott

| 5' 9' 7' |
| 10' |

Theme and variations (The four temperaments; Die vier   29'
Temperamente)
  solo piano

| 7' 7' 6' |
| 4' 5' |

  str
  Schott

Trauermusik (Music of mourning)   6'
  solo viola (or violin or violoncello)
  str
  Schott

Tuttifäntchen: Suite   20'
  *1 1 1 1—1 1 0 0—tmp+1—str
  The work from which the suite is drawn is a Christmas fairy tale
  in three scenes.
  Schott

Hoag, Charles Kelso   1931 -
An after-intermission overture for youth orchestra   3'
  2 2 2 2—4 3 3 1—tmp+1—pf—str
  Schirmer, G.

Hoddinott, Alun   1929 -
Concerto, horn, op.65   14'
  *2 2 2 2—3 2 3 0—tmp+2—hp—str
  Oxford

Sinfonietta 3, op.71   12'
  *3 2 2 *3—4 2 3 0—tmp+2—hp—str
  Oxford

Symphony no.5   25'
  *3 *3 *3 *3—4 3 3 1—tmp+4—hp—str
  Oxford

Hofer, Andreas   1629 - 1684
Te deum   9'
  double chorus
  2 cornetti (or 2ob or 2cl), bn, opt cbn—4tp, 3tbn, bass tp (or bn)
  —tmp—str, cnt.
  Forces are divided into 3 orchestras and 2 choruses.
  Ed. Charles H. Sherman.
  Universal

Hoffmann, Georg Melchior   ca.1685 - 1715
Meine Seele rühmt und preist
  see: Bach, Johann Sebastian
      Cantata no.189

Schlage doch, gewünschte Stunde
see: Bach, Johann Sebastian
            Cantata no.53

Höller, York   1944 -
Aura   20'
*4 *3 *3 *3—4 3 3 1—tmp+5—cel/pf/synth (2 players), hp
—str 14.12.10.8.6
Two of the flutists double on piccolo.
Boosey

Pensées   25'
solo piano (MIDI)
*3 *3 *3 *3—4 3 3 1—tmp+5—hp, synth, computer
—4-channel electronic tape—str 14.12.10.8.6
Boosey

Hollingsworth, Stanley   1924 -
Concerto, piano   14'
*2 2 2 2—2 1 0 0—tmp+2—str
Belwin

Concerto, violin (Lirico)   14'
2 2 2 2—2 1 0 0—str   5' 4' 5'

Divertimento   14'
*2 *2 *2 2—4 2 2 1—tmp+2—hp, cel, pf—str   1' 4' 3'
Contents—Entrance; Pas de deux; Merci Monsieur J.I.; Soliloquy;   3' 3'
Introduction & finale.
Belwin

Stabat mater   12'
chorus
2 2 2 2—2 2 1 0—tmp—hp, pf—str
Schirmer, G.

Three ladies beside the sea   12'
narrator
*2 1 1 1—0 1 0 0—tmp+1—hp, cel, pf—str
Belwin

Holloway, Robin   1943 -
Concerto, viola, op.56   24'
2 *2 1 1—2 1 1 0—cel—str
Boosey

Scenes from Schumann, op.13   22'
    =3 *2 *2 *2—2 2 1 0—1perc—hp, pf—str
    All 3 of the flutists double on piccolo. Minimum strings 8.6.4.4.2;
    max 12.12.10.8.6.
    Based on seven Schumann songs: Dedication (*Widmung*);
    Flowering lotus (*Die Lotosblume*); Dream vision (*Allnächtlich im
    Traume*); Enchanted forest (*Auf einer Burg*); Dream visitation
    (*Allnächtlich im Traume*); Moonlit night (*Mondnacht*);
    Spring-night-rounds (*Frühlingsnacht*).
    Boosey

Second concerto for orchestra, op.40   35'
    =3 *3 =3 *3—sx—4 3 3 1—tmp+4—hp, pf/cel—str (min
    16.14.12.10.8)
    All 3 of the flutists double on pic; sx apparently doubles on ssx &
    asx.
    Boosey

Holst, Gustav   1874 - 1934

Beni mora; oriental suite for orchestra   15'
    *3 *3 2 2—4 3 3 1—tmp+3—1 or 2hp—str
    Curwen

Brook Green suite   8'
    1 1 1 0—str | 2' 3' 3' |
    Woodwinds are optional.
    Curwen

Capriccio   6'
    *1 *2 *2 2—2 3 2 1—2perc—hp, cel, pf—str
    Ed. Imogen Holst.
    Faber

Christmas day   7'
    chorus   solos SATB
    *2 2 2 2—2 2 2 0—tmp+1—pf or org—str
    Piccolo, trombones, and one percussionist are optional.
    Carols introduced include: *Good Christian men rejoice; God rest
    you merry gentlemen; Come ye lofty, come ye lowly; The first
    nowell.*
    Novello

Concerto, 2 violins, op.49   16'
    2 2 2 2—2 2 0 0—tmp—str | 5' 5' 6' |
    Optional: 2nd fl, 2nd ob, 2nd hn, 2nd tp.
    Rev. Imogen Holst.
    Kalmus

Egdon Heath, op.47   15'
    2 *3 2 *3—4 3 3 1—str
    The following are optional: 2nd ob, cbn, hn 3 & 4, 3rd tp, tuba.
    Novello

First choral symphony, op.41   52'
    chorus   solo soprano
    *3 *3 *3 *3—4 3 3 1—tmp+2—hp, cel, org—str
    Minimum instrumentation (should be used if the chorus is small):
    *2 *2 2 2—2 2 3 0—tmp—hp—str.
    Novello

Hammersmith, op.52   15'
    *3 *3 *3 *3—4 3 3 1—tmp+2—str
    May be played with: *2 *2 2 1—2 2 3 1—tmp—str. Originally for
    military band. Contents—Prelude; Scherzo.
    Boosey

The lure   9'
    *3 *3 *3 *3—4 3 3 1—tmp+3—hp, cel—str
    Faber

Lyric movement for viola & small orchestra   10'
    solo viola
    1 1 1 1—str
    Ed. Colin Matthews.
    Oxford

The perfect fool: Ballet music   13'
    *3 *3 *3 *3—4 4 3 1—tmp+3—hp, cel—str
    Playable with: *3 *2 2 2—4 2 3 1—tmp+3—hp—str.
    Gray

The planets   51'
    hidden female chorus in last movement
    =4 *4 *4 *4—6 4 3 1—tenor tuba—2tmp+4—2hp, cel, org—str
    3rd ob doubles on bass ob; 2 flutists double on pic. Cued to make
    performance possible with the following minimum
    instrumentation: *3 *3 *3 2—4 3 3 1—2tmp+3—2hp, cel—str.
    New edition prepared by Imogen Holst & Colin Matthews.
    Schirmer, G.

6'	10'	4'
7'	11'	6'
		7'

St. Paul's suite   12'
    str
    Curwen

3'	2'	4'	3'

A Somerset rhapsody   10'
    2 2 2 2—4 2 3 1—tmp+3—str
    One of the oboists should use oboe d'amore if possible.
    Boosey

Honegger, Arthur   1892 - 1955

Chant de joie   7'
    *3 *3 *3 *3—4 3 3 1—2perc—hp, cel—str
    Salabert

Concertino, piano & orchestra   13'
    *2 *2 *2 2—2 2 1 0—str
    Salabert

Concerto da camera   18'
   solo flute & English horn   6' 8' 4'
   str
   Salabert

Le Dit des jeux du monde   50'
   *1 0 0 0—0 1 0 0—tmp+3—str
   Salabert

Jeanne d'Arc au bûcher (Joan of Arc at the stake)   80'
   chorus, childrens' chorus   solos SSSATB
   4 spoken roles (1 female, 3 male)
   *2 2 =3 *4—3asx—0 4 4 0—tmp+2—2pf, cel, ondes martenot—str
   Salabert

Mouvement symphonique no.3   10'
   *3 *3 2 *3—asx—4 3 3 1—2perc—str
   Salabert

Pacific 231 (Mouvement symphonique no.1)   7'
   *3 *3 *3 *3—4 3 3 1—4perc—str
   Salabert

Pastorale d'été   7'
   1 1 1 1—1 0 0 0—str
   Salabert

Prélude pour "La Tempête" de Shakespeare   8'
   *2 *2 *2 *2—4 2 3 1—4perc—str
   Salabert

Le Roi David (original version) (King David)   69'
   chorus   solos SAT   speaker   30' 13'
   *2 *1 *2 1—1 2 1 0—tmp+3—pf, cel, harm—db, opt vc   26'
   EAM

Le Roi David (version with large orchestra) (King David)   69'
   chorus   solos SAT   speaker   30' 13'
   *2 *2 *2 *2—4 2 3 1—tmp+3—hp, cel, org—str   26'
   EAM

Rugby (Mouvement symphonique no.2)   8'
   *3 *3 *3 *3—4 3 3 1—str
   Salabert

Symphony no.1   21'
   *3 *3 *3 *3—4 3 3 1—1perc—str   6' 8' 7'
   Salabert

Symphony no.2   25'
   opt tp—str   11' 9' 5'
   Salabert

Symphony no.3 (Symphonie liturgique)   30'
   *3 *3 *3 *3—4 3 3 1—tmp+4—pf—str   6' 12'
   Salabert   12'

Symphony no.4 (Deliciae Basilienses)   28'
    2 1 2 1—2 1 0 0—2perc—pf—str
    Salabert

12' 8' 8'

Symphony no.5 (Di tre re)   23'
    *3 *3 *3 3—4 3 3 1—tmp—str
    Timpani are optional.
    Salabert

8' 9' 6'

Horne, David   1970 -

Concerto, piano   21'
    =2 2 *2 *2—2 2 2 1—2perc—hp, cel—str
    Boosey

Hovhaness, Alan   1911 -

Artik   15'
    solo horn
    str
    Peters

And God created great whales   12'
    *3 2 2 2—4 3 3 1—tmp+4—2hp—tape of whale sounds—str
    Peters

Exile symphony (Symphony no.1)   20'
    2 2 2 2—4 3 3 1—tmp—hp—str
    Peters

7' 4' 9'

Floating world   12'
    3 *3 2 2—4 3 3 1—tmp+7—1 or 2hp, cel—str
    4 of the percussionists are optional.
    Peters

Fra Angelico   17'
    3 *3 *3 *3—4 3 3 1—tmp+6 (or 4)—2hp, cel—str 16.16.12.12.10
    (or 8)
    Peters

Magnificat, op.157   33'
    chorus   solos STB
    0 2 0 0—2 2 1 0—2perc—hp—str
    Peters

Meditation on Orpheus, op.155   13'
    3 *3 *3 *3—4 3 3 1—tmp+2—hp, cel—str
    Peters

Mysterious mountain (Symphony no.2)   16'
    3 *3 *3 *3—5 3 3 1—tmp—hp, cel—str
    AMP

Overture, op.76, no.1   5'
    solo trombone
    str
    Peters

Psalm and fugue, op.40a   11'
  str
  Peters

Symphony no.15 (Silver pilgrimage)   20'
  2 *2 2 2—4 3 3 1—tmp+2—hp—str
  Peters

Variations and fugue   13'
  3 *3 2 2—4 3 3 1—tmp+1—hp—str
  Peters

Hummel, Johann Nepomuk   1778 - 1837

Concerto, trumpet, E major (original key)   21'
  1 2 2 2—2 0 0 0—tmp—str   12' 5' 4'
  Ed. Edward Tarr. For the same work in a transposed version, see
  below.
  Universal

Concerto, trumpet, E-flat major (transposed version)   21'
  1 2 2 2—2 0 0 0—tmp—str   12' 5' 4'
  A version without clarinets is published by Billaudot; a version
  without clarinets or timpani is published by EMT.
  Kalmus   *King*

Humperdinck, Engelbert   1854 - 1921

Dornröschen (Sleeping Beauty): Suite   19'
  2 2 2 2—4 2 3 1—tmp+1—hp—str   8' 4' 3'
  This work is out of print, but orchestral materials are in the 2' 2'
  Fleisher Collection.
  Contents—Prelude; Ballade; Irrfahrten; Das Dornenschloss;
  Festklänge.

Hänsel und Gretel: Prelude   8'
  *3 2 2 2—4 2 3 1—tmp+2—str
  Kalmus   *Schott*

Hänsel und Gretel: Hexenritt (Witch's ride)   4'
  *3 2 2 2—4 2 3 1—tmp+4—str
  Kalmus

Hänsel und Gretel: Knusperwalzer (Crackle-waltz)   5'
  *2 2 2 2—4 2 3 0—tmp+2—str
  Trombones and 3rd & 4th horns are optional. Arr. Hans Steiner.
  Kalmus

Hänsel und Gretel: Three excerpts   13'
  *3 *2 2 2—4 2 3 1—tmp+1—hp—str   3' 3' 7'
  Contents—Lied des Sandmännchens (Sandman's song);
  Abendsegen (Evening prayer); Traumpantomime (Dream
  pantomime).
  Kalmus   *Luck*   *Schott*

Königskinder: Prelude   8'
*2 2 *3 *3—4 3 3 1—tmp+1—str
Kalmus does not list this work separately, but has the complete
opera and will provide excerpts, including, presumably, this
prelude.
Kalmus

Königskinder: Introduction to Act II   4'
*3 2 2 *3—4 2 3 1—tmp+2—str
Kalmus

Königskinder: Introduction to Act III   9'
*3 *3 *3 *3—4 3 3 1—tmp—hp—str
Kalmus

Eine Trauung in der Bastille   10'
2 *2 2 2—4 3 3 1—tmp+2—hp, opt org or harmonium—str
Introduction and interlude from the opera *Die Heirat wider
Willen*.
This work may be out of print. Materials are available in the
Fleisher Collection.

Husa, Karel   1921 -

Apotheosis of this earth   26'
chorus | 13' 7' 6' |
*4 *4 *4 *3—4 4 4 1—tmp+4—str
AMP

Concerto for orchestra   38'
*3 *3 *3 *3—5 4 3 1—tmp+4—2hp, pf—str
Flutes 2 & 3 double on piccolo; flute 1 doubles on bass flute; 5th
horn in last movement only.
AMP

Concerto, trumpet & wind orchestra   14'
*3 *3 2 *3—asx—4 3 3 1—tmp+4—3 or 4db
AMP

Fantasies for orchestra   20'
*2 1 1 0—0 3 0 0—2perc—pf—str ("symphonic or chamber")
Schott

Music for Prague 1968 (orchestral version)   24'
*3 *3 *3 *3—4 4 3 1—tmp+4—hp, pf—str | 7' 6' 4' 7' |
Originally for concert band.
AMP

Symphonic suite for orchestra   19'
*3 3 *3 *3—4 3 3 1—tmp+3—hp, pf—str
Contents—Celebration; Meditation; Vision
AMP

Symphony no.1   28'
*3 *3 *3 *3—4 3 3 1—tmp+3—1 or 2hp, pf—str
Schott

Two sonnets by Michelangelo   16'
  *3 *3 2 2—asx—4 3 3 1—tmp+2—hp—str
  AMP

I

Ibert, Jacques   1890 - 1962

Bacchanale   10'
  *3 *3 *3 *4—4 3 3 1—tmp+5—hp—str
  Leduc

Bostoniana   8'
  *3 *3 *3 *3—4 4 3 1—tmp+3—2hp—str
  Leduc

Le Chevalier errant   27'
  *3 *3 *3 *4—asx—6 4 3 1—tmp+5—2hp, cel, gtr—str
  Contents—Les Moulins; Danse des galériens; L'Age d'or; Les
  Comédiens et Finale.
  Leduc

Concertino da camera, alto saxophone & orchestra   13'
  1 1 1 1—1 1 0 0—str quintet or small str complement   5' 8'
  Leduc

Concerto, flute   18'
  2 2 2 2—2 1 0 0—tmp—str   5' 6' 7'
  Leduc

Divertissement   15'
  *1 0 1 *1—1 1 1 0—1perc—pf/cel—3vn, 2va, 2vc, db   1' 5' 2'
  Durand   3' 2' 2'

Escales (Ports of call)   14'
  *3 *3 2 3—4 3 3 1—tmp+7—2hp, cel—str   6' 3' 5'
  Two of the flutists double on piccolo.
  Leduc

Hommage á Mozart   5'
  2 2 2 2—2 2 0 0—tmp—str
  Leduc

Louisville concerto   12'
  *2 2 2 2—4 2 3 1—tmp+3—hp—str
  Leduc

Symphonie marine   14'
  0 1 0 1—asx—1 1 1 0—2perc—hp, pf/cel—str (min 3.2.2.2.1)
  Leduc

Imbrie, Andrew   1921 -

Concerto, violin   37'
 *3 *3 *3 *3—4 3 3 1—tmp+3—hp, cel—str
 Malcolm

Legend   14'
 *3 *3 *3 *3—4 3 3 1—tmp+3—hp, cel—str
 Malcolm

Symphony no.1   32'
 *3 *3 =3 *3—4 3 3 1—tmp+4—2hp, cel—str | 12' 8' 4' |
 Malcolm | 8' |

Symphony no.3   20'
 *3 *3 *3 *3—4 3 3 1—tmp+1—2hp, cel—str
 Shawnee

Indy, Vincent d'   1851 - 1931

Istar; variations symphoniques, op.42   17'
 *3 *3 *3 3—4 3 3 1—tmp+2—2hp—str
 Durand   *Kalmus*

Symphonie sur un chant montagnard français, op.25 (Symphony on   24'
a French mountain air) | 11' 6' 7' |
 solo piano
 *3 *2 *3 3—4 4 3 1—tmp+3—hp—str
 Hamelle   *Kalmus*

Ingelbrecht, Désiré-Émile   1880 - 1965

Rapsodie de printemps   10'
 *3 *3 *4 2—4 3 3 1—tmp+2—2hp, pf—str
 backstage: 10 children's voices, harm, solo va, triangle.
 Salabert

Ippolitov-Ivanov, Mikhail   1859 - 1935

Caucasian sketches   21'
 *3 *2 2 2—4 4 3 0—tmp+5—hp—str | 8' 4' 4' 5' |
 Contents—In the mountain pass; In the village; In the mosque;
 Procession of the Sardar.
 Kalmus   *Russian*

Turkish fragments, op.62   13'
 *3 *3 2 2—3 2 3 1—tmp+5—hp—str | 3' 5' 2' 3' |
 Contents—The caravan; During a rest; In the night; At the
 festival.
 Kalmus   *Russian*

Ishii, Maki   1936 -

Kyō-Sō   22'
 *3 3 *3 *3—6 4 3 1—tmp+5—hp, cel—str (min 16.14.10.8.6)
 Moeck

Ives, Charles   1874 - 1954

The Charles Ives Society since 1973 has been supporting the preparation along scholarly-critical lines of performing editions of Ives' music. These are brought out by various publishers, and should be sought out as they become available, since the previous editions have many errors.

Calcium light night
see his: The gong on the hook and ladder

Charlie Rutlage   3'
  optional medium voice
  *1 *1 +1 1—0 1 1 1—pf—str
  Realized by Kenneth Singleton, based on the original piano-vocal score with the composer's directions for instrumentation (Ives Society).
  AMP

Chromâtimelôdtune   6'
  0 1 1 1—1 1 1 1—2perc—pf—3vn, va, vc, db
  Reconstructed and completed by Gunther Schuller.
  MJQ

Country band march, for theater orchestra   4'
  *1 0 1 0—asx—0 1 2 0—3perc—pf—str (without va)
  Ed. James Sinclair (Ives Society).
  Merion

Firemen's Parade on Main Street
see his: The gong on the hook and ladder

General William Booth enters into heaven   5'
  medium voice (or chorus)
  1 1 1 1—1 1 1 0—1perc—pf—str
  Orchestrated by John J. Becker in collaboration with the composer.
  Merion

The gong on the hook and ladder   3'
  1 0 1 1—0 2 1 0—tmp+2—pf, opt gong—str
  Alternative titles: *Firemen's parade on Main Street, Calcium light,* or *Calcium light night.*
  Critical ed. 1979 by James Sinclair (Ives Society).
  Peer

Holidays symphony
  The movements may be performed separately.

  1. Washington's Birthday   9'
  *1 0 0 0—3 Jew's harps (or 2 cl)—1 0 0 0—bells (or pf)—str
  Optional: bn or tbn.
  Critical edition by James B. Sinclair, 1987 (Ives Society).
  AMP

2. Decoration Day   10'
*3 *3 +3 2—4 2 3 1—tmp+5—str
An *ossia* is provided for the E-flat clarinet.
Critical edition by James B. Sinclair, 1987 (Ives Society).
Peer

3. The Fourth of July   7'
*3 2 2 *3—4 4 3 1—tmp+6—pf—str
Critical edition by Wayne D. Shirley (Ives Society).
AMP

4. Thanksgiving and/or Forefathers' Day   15'
optional chorus
*3 2 2 *3—4 3 3 1—tmp+5—cel, pf—str
Piccolo, contrabassoon, and 4 of the percussionists are optional.
In several isolated passages, Ives suggests various additional
instruments: fl, cl, bn, cbn, hn, tp. An optional offstage band can
be covered by instrumentalists who leave the stage.
Critical edition by Jonathan Elkus, 1991 (Ives Society).
Peer

Hymn (Largo cantabile)   3'
   str
   Peer

Lincoln the great commoner   4'
   chorus
   2 2 2 2—0 2 2 1—tmp+1—pf—str
   Kalmus   *Presser*

Overture and march 1776 for theater orchestra   3'
   *2 1 1 0—0 2 1 0—3perc—pf—str
   Ed. James B. Sinclair (Ives Society).
   Merion

Ragtime dances   11'
   *1 1 1 1—asx /bsx—1 1 1 1—2perc—pf—str (max 6.6.4.4.2)   3' 2' 3' 3'
   Ed. James B. Sinclair (Ives Society).
   Peer

Symphony no.1, D minor   32'
   2 *3 2 *3—4 2 3 1—tmp—str   10' 6' 4'
   Contrabassoon is optional.   12'
   Peer

Symphony no.2   37'
   *3 2 2 *3—4 2 3 1—tmp+2—str   6' 11' 8'
   New printing in 1988 has some corrections, but errors still   2' 10'
   abound.
   Southern

Symphony no.3 (The camp meeting)   19'
   1 1 1 1—2 0 1 0—opt distant bells—str   7' 8' 4'
   Critical edition by Kenneth Singleton, 1989 (Ives Society).
   AMP

Symphony no.4 (1965 edition)   33'
  chorus   3' 13' 8'
  *3 2 3 3—4 6 4 1—tmp+9—2hp, 2pf (6 hands), cel, org—str   9'
  The following are optional: 1 saxophonist (dbl alto, tenor, &
  baritone); Theremin; quarter-tone piano. Use of an assistant
  conductor is also optional.
  AMP

Symphony no.4 (critical edition)   33'
  chorus   3' 13' 8'
  *4 2 2 2—4 6 4 1—tmp+9—hp, cel, 2pf (6-hands), org—str   9'
  Extra quarter-tone piano optional (no extra player needed).
  Ives Society critical edition; Gunther Schuller, general
  supervising editor. Editors of the individual movements are
  William Brooks, James B. Sinclair, Kenneth Singleton, and Wayne
  Shirley, respectively.
  AMP

Symphony no.4: Fugue (From Greenland's icy mountains)   8'
  1 0 1 0—1 0 0 0—tmp—opt org—str
  Trombone may substitute for horn. Ed. Leopold Stokowski.
  AMP

Three harvest home chorales   8'
  chorus
  0 0 0 0—0 4 3 1—org—db
  Contents—The harvest dawn is near; Lord of the harvest, Thee
  we hail; Come ye thankful people, come.
  Ives Society critical edition in preparation.
  Mercury

Three places in New England (chamber orchestra version)   18'
  *2 *2 1 1—4 4 3 1—tmp+2—pf, opt cel, opt org—str   8' 6' 4'
  This chamber version was actually intended for:
  1 *2 1 1—2 2 1 0—tmp—pf—str 4.3.2.2.1.
  The extra instruments were probably considered optional.
  Published 1935.
  Contents—The Saint-Gaudens in Boston Common; Putnam's
  Camp; From the Housatonic at Stockbridge.
  Mercury

Three places in New England (large orchestra version)   18'
  *3 *2 2 *3—4 2 3 1—tmp+4—1 or 2hp, pf/cel, opt org—str   8' 6' 4'
  Full orchestration restored and edited by James B. Sinclair, 1976
  (Ives Society).
  Contents—The Saint-Gaudens in Boston Common; Putnam's
  Camp; From the Housatonic at Stockbridge.
  Merion

Tone roads no.1   8'
  1 0 1 1—str
  Ives Society critical edition in preparation.
  Peer

Tone roads no.3   9'
   1 0 1 0—0 1 1 0—1perc—pf—str
   Ives Society critical edition in preparation.
   Peer

The unanswered question   6'
   4fl—tp (or Eh or ob or cl)—backstage str quartet or str orchestra
   Oboe may substitute for 3rd flute; clarinet may substitute for 4th
   flute. Critical ed. by Paul Echols & Noel Zahler, 1985 (Ives
   Society).
   Southern

Universe symphony   37'
   =4 *3 *4 *3—4 4 4 1—24perc—hp, 2pf (1 dbl cel)—16-track tape
   & 25 headphones—str
   Requires principal conductor plus 4 assistant conductors. Forces
   divided into 7 separate orchestras. Afl also doubles on 2nd pic;
   extra bn may substitute for tuba; extra tuba may substitute for
   4th tbn.
   Realized & completed by Larry Austin, from the composer's
   sketches.
   Contents—Past; Present; Future (all played without pause).
   Peer

Variations on America   8'
   *3 2 2 2—4 3 3 1—tmp+3—str
   Orchestrated by William Schuman; originally for organ.
   Merion

J

Jacob, Gordon   1895 - 1984

The barber of Seville goes to the devil; comedy overture   4'
   *2 1 2 1—2 2 2 0—tmp+2—hp (or pf)—str
   Oxford

Fantasia on the Alleluia hymn   8'
   2 2 2 2—4 2 3 1—tmp+2—str
   3rd & 4th horns are optional.
   Galaxy

Janáček, Leos   1854 - 1928

Adagio   6'
   *2 *2 2 2—2 2 2 0—tmp—str
   Universal

Glagolitic mass (M'sa glagolskaja) 40'
   chorus   solos SATB
   *4 *3 *3 *3—4 4 3 1—tmp+2—2hp, cel, org—str
   3 of the flutists double on piccolo.
Universal

> 3' 3' 6'
> 12' 6' 5'
> 3' 2'

Idyla 30'
   str
   Supraphon

> 4' 3' 4'
> 4' 7' 4'
> 4'

Jealousy 6'
   *2 *3 *3 2—4 2 3 1—tmp—hp—str
   Universal

Lachian dances 19'
   *2 *3 *3 2—4 2 3 0—tmp+1—hp, org—str
   Optional: Eh, bcl, org.
   Supraphon

> 6' 2' 2'
> 4' 2' 3'

Sinfonietta 23'
   *4 *2 =3 2—4 12 4 1—2 bass tp, 2 tenor tubas—tmp+1—hp—str
   Two reduced versions are available from the publisher: one by
   the composer, and one by Joseph Keilberth.
   Universal

> 2' 6' 5'
> 3' 7'

Sokal fanfare 4'
   (1st movement of the Sinfonietta)
   9tp, 2 tenor tubas (B-flat), 2 bass tp—tmp
   Baritone horns or trombones may substitute for the tenor tubas;
   trombones may substitute for the bass trumpets.
   Universal

Taras Bulba 23'
   *3 *3 +2 *3—4 3 3 1—tmp+2—hp, org—str
   Supraphon

> 9' 5' 9'

Janiewicz, Feliks   1762 - 1848
Divertimento
see under: Panufnik, Andrzej, 1914-1991

Järnefelt, Armas   1869 - 1958
Praeludium 3'
   1 1 2 1—2 2 0 0—tmp+2—str
   Breitkopf   *Kalmus*   *Luck*

Joachim, Joseph   1831 - 1907
Concerto, violin, op.11, D minor (Hungarian) 35'
   2 2 2 2—4 2 0 0—tmp—str
   Breitkopf   *Kalmus*

> 19' 9' 7'

Jolivet, André   1905 - 1974
Symphony no.1   25'
    *3 *3 *3 3—4 4 3 1—tmp—hp—str 14.12.10.10.8
    Heugel

Jones, Samuel   1935 -
Elegy   5'
    str
    C. Fischer

Fanfare and celebration   5'
    *4 *4 *4 *4—4 3 3 1—tmp+5—2hp—str
    Available in two versions: *Version A* (above) and *Version B*
    (woodwinds in 3s, but otherwise identical).
    C. Fischer

In retrospect   8'
    *2 *2 2 2—2 2 1 0—tmp—str
    C. Fischer

Let us now praise famous men   16'
    *3 *3 *3 *3—4 3 3 1—tmp+3—hp—str
    offstage fl choir: 3fl & afl, preferably doubled or tripled at the
    conductor's discretion.
    May be performed without the offstage flute choir by using flutes
    =4 in the orchestra. Two of the onstage flutists double on piccolo.
    C. Fischer

Symphony no.2 (Canticles of time)   23'
    double chorus in one movement
    *3 *2 *2 *3—4 3 3 1—tmp+5—hp—str
    C. Fischer

Symphony no.3 (Palo Duro Canyon)   23'
    *3 *3 *3 *3—4 3 3 1—tmp+5—hp, cel—tape of wind sounds—str
    A special percussion instrument, "bundle of sticks," supplied with
    the rental material.
    C. Fischer

The temptation of Jesus   73'
    mixed chorus, small chorus, children's chorus   solo bass
    *2 *2 *2 2—2 2 3 0—tmp+1—hp, (cel played by
    percussionist)—str
    C. Fischer

Joplin, Scott   1868 - 1917
    see also: Turok, Paul
                A Joplin overture

The entertainer   5'
    *1 0 1 0—0 1 1 1—1perc—pf—opt str (2vn, va, vc)
    Arr. D.S. Delisle; ed. Gunther Schuller.
    Belwin

Maple leaf rag   3'
 *1 0 1 0—0 1 1 1—1perc—pf—2vn, va, vc, opt db
 Arranger unknown; ed. Gunther Schuller.
 Belwin

Ragtime dance   4'
 1 0 1 0—0 1 1 1—1perc—pf—2vn, va, vc, db
 Ed. Gunther Schuller.
 Belwin

K

Kabalevsky, Dmitri   1904 - 1987

Colas Breugnon: Overture   5'
 *3 3 3 *3—4 3 3 1—tmp+5—hp—str
 Kalmus   *Russian*

Colas Breugnon: Suite   20'
 *3 *3 3 *3—4 3 3 1—tmp+5—hp—str
 Contents—Overture; Fête populaire; Fléau publique; Insurrection.
 Kalmus   *Russian*

The comedians, op.26; suite for small orchestra   13'
 *1 *1 2 1—2 2 1 1—tmp+4—pf—str | 1' 1' 1' |
 Contents—Prologue; Galop; March; Waltz; Pantomime; | 1' 2' 1' |
 Intermezzo; Little lyrical scene; Gavotte; Scherzo; Epilogue. | 1' 1' 2' |
 Kalmus   *Russian* | 2' |

The comedians: Galop   2'
 1 1 2 1—2 2 1 1—tmp+3—pf—str
 Kalmus

Concerto, piano, no.3, op.50, D major (Youth)   18'
 2 2 2 2—2 2 2 0—tmp+3—str
 Kalmus   *Russian*

Concerto, violin, op.48   16'
 1 1 2 1—2 1 1 0—tmp+4—str
 Kalmus   *Russian*

Concerto, violoncello, no.1, op.49, G minor   18'
 1 1 2 1—2 1 1 0—tmp+2—str | 6' 6' 6' |
 Russian

Overture pathétique, op.64   4'
 *3 *3 *3 *3—4 3 3 1—tmp+3—hp, pf—str
 Kalmus

Symphony no.1, op.18　　　　　　　　　　　　　　　　　21'
　*3 *3 *3 *3—4 3 3 1—tmp+4—str
　Kalmus　　　　　*Russian*　　　　　　　　　　　　 10' 11'

Symphony no.2, op.19　　　　　　　　　　　　　　　　　29'
　*3 *3 *3 *3—4 3 3 1—tmp+4—str
　Kalmus　　　　　*Russian*　　　　　　　　　　　　 9' 12' 8'

Symphony no.3, op.22 (Requiem)　　　　　　　　　　　　20'
　chorus
　*3 *3 *3 *3—4 3 3 1—tmp+4—pf—str
　Russian

Kalinnikov, Vassili　　　1866 - 1901

Chanson triste　　　　　　　　　　　　　　　　　　　2'
　str
　Luck

Symphony no.1, G minor　　　　　　　　　　　　　　　35'
　*3 *3 2 2—4 2 3 1—tmp+1—hp—str
　Kalmus　　　　　*Russian*　　　*Universal*　　　 11' 6' 7'
　　　　　　　　　　　　　　　　　　　　　　　　　　11'

Symphony no.2, A major　　　　　　　　　　　　　　　37'
　*3 *2 2 2—4 2 3 1—tmp—hp—str
　Kalmus　　　　　*Universal*　　　　　　　　　　 10' 8' 8'
　　　　　　　　　　　　　　　　　　　　　　　　　　11'

Karłowicz, Mieczysław　　　1876 - 1909

Lithuanian rhapsody, op.11　　　　　　　　　　　　　　19'
　*3 *3 *3 2—4 2 3 0—tmp+2—str
　PWM

Odwieczne piesni, op.10 (Eternal songs)　　　　　　　　24'
　*3 *3 *3 *3—4 3 3 1—tmp+2—str
　PWM　　　　　　　　　　　　　　　　　　　　　9' 10' 5'

Stanislaw i Anna Oswiecimowie, op.12　　　　　　　　　22'
　*4 *4 =4 *4—6 3 3 1—tmp+3—2hp—str
　PWM

Kay, Hershy　　　1919 - 1981

Cakewalk: Concert suite　　　　　　　　　　　　　　　24'
　*2 2 *2 2—4 2 3 1—tmp+3—hp, pf/cel—str
　Both tp double on cornet. After piano melodies of Louis Moreau　3' 6' 4'
　Gottschalk and early minstrel tunes.　　　　　　　　　　 7' 4'
　Boosey

Kay, Ulysses　　　1917 - 1995

Chariots　　　　　　　　　　　　　　　　　　　　　15'
　*3 *3 *3 *3—4 3 3 1—tmp+3—hp—str
　C. Fischer

Fantasy variations   15'
   *2 2 2 2—4 3 3 1—tmp+4—str
   MCA

Markings   18'
   *3 *3 *3 *3—4 3 3 1—tmp+4—str
   MCA

Of new horizons   8'
   *3 *3 *3 *3—4 3 3 1—tmp+4—hp, pf/cel—str
   Peters

Scherzi musicali for chamber orchestra   17'
   1 1 1 1—1 0 0 0—str
   MCA

Serenade for orchestra   18'
   *2 2 2 2—4 2 3 1—tmp—str
   AMP

Six dances for string orchestra   19'
   str
   MCA

Southern harmony   20'
   *3 *3 *3 *3—4 3 3 1—tmp+2—str
   Two of the flutists double on piccolo. Eh & cbn are optional.
   Quotes tunes from the shape-note collection *Southern Harmony.*
   C. Fischer

Suite for orchestra   17'
   *3 *3 *3 *3—4 3 3 1—tmp+3—pf—str
   Schirmer, G.

Suite for strings   14'
   str
   Peters

Theater set for orchestra   15'
   *3 *3 *3 2—4 3 3 1—tmp+3—hp—str
   MCA

Umbrian scene   15'
   2 2 2 2—4 3 3 1—tmp+4—hp—str
   MCA

Kechley, David   1947 -

Alexander and the wind-up mouse   17'
   narrator
   *2 2 *2 2—2 2 1 0—2perc—hp, pf/cel—str
   Based on a children's book by Leo Lionni.
   Pine Valley

Kelley, Edgar Stillman   1857 - 1944

The pit and the pendulum 16'
  *3 *3 *3 3—4 3 3 1—tmp+3—hp—str
  This work may be out of print, but materials are available in the
  Fleisher Collection.
  G.Schirmer

Kennan, Kent   1913 -

Night soliloquy 4'
  solo flute
  pf—str
  C. Fischer

Kernis, Aaron Jay   1960 -

Musica celestis 11'
  str
  An arrangement of the 2nd movement from his string quartet.
  Schirmer, G.

Symphony in waves 30'
  *1 *2 =1 *2—3 1 0 0—1perc—pf/cel—str (min. 6.6.4.4.2)
  Contents—Continuous wave; Scherzo; Still movement;
  Intermezzo; Finale.
  Schirmer, G.

Khachaturian, Aram   1903 - 1978

Concerto, piano 33'
  *2 2 *3 2—4 2 3 1—tmp+2—flexatone—str
  Kalmus   *Russian*

| 14' 11' |
| 8' |

Concerto, violin 35'
  *3 *3 2 2—4 3 3 1—tmp+3—hp—str
  Kalmus   *Russian*

| 14' 12' |
| 9' |

Concerto-rhapsody, violin & orchestra 23'
  *3 2 2 2—4 2 0 0—tmp+3—hp—str
  Russian

Concerto-rhapsody, violoncello & orchestra 23'
  2 2 2 2—4 2 0 0—tmp+4—hp—str
  Russian

Gayane
  Although this ballet has been excerpted in various ways, the
  following three suites are the only ones authorized by the
  composer. The "Three pieces" (wrongly published as Suite no.1)
  and the "Sabre dance" are available separately.

Gayane: Suite no.1   36'
*3 *3 *3 2—4 3 3 1—tmp+4—hp, cel—str
One of the clarinetists doubles on alto saxophone.
Contents—Introduction; Dance of the young maidens; Ayshe's
awakening and dance; Mountaineers' dance; Lullaby, Gayane
and Guiko; Gayane's adagio; Lesginka.
Kalmus   *Russian*

Gayane: Suite no.2   30'
*3 *3 *3 2—4 3 3 1—tmp+4—hp, pf—str
Contents—Dance of welcome; Lyric duet; Russian dance; Noune's
variation; Dance of an old man and carpet weavers; Armen's
variation; Fire.
Kalmus   *Russian*

Gayane: Suite no.3   23'
*3 *3 *3 2—asx—4 3 3 1—tmp+4—hp, pf—str   5' 2' 2'
Contents—Cotton picking; Dance of the young Kurds;   5' 5' 4'
Introduction and Dance of the old men; The carpet weavers;
Sabre dance; Hopak.
Kalmus   *Russian*

Gayane: Sabre dance   2'
*3 *3 *3 2—asx—4 3 3 1—tmp+3—hp, pf—str
Kalmus   *Russian*

Gayane: Three pieces   9'
*3 *3 *3 2—asx—4 3 3 1—tmp+3—hp, cel—str   2' 5' 2'
Originally published by Leeds as *Suite no.1*.
Contents—Sabre dance; Lullaby; Dance of the young rose
maidens.
Kalmus   *Russian*

Masquerade: Suite   18'
*2 2 2 2—4 2 3 1—tmp+3—str   4' 5' 3'
Contents—Waltz; Nocturne; Mazurka; Romance; Galop.   3' 3'
Kalmus   *Russian*

Spartacus: Suite no.1   26'
*3 *3 *3 2—4 4 3 1—tmp+5—hp, cel, pf—str   5' 7' 4'
Contents—Introduction and Dance of nymphs; Introduction,   4' 6'
Adagio of Aegina and Harmodius; Variation of Aegina and
Bacchanalia; Scene and dance with crotalums; Dance of
Gaditanae and Victory of Spartacus.
Kalmus   *Russian*

Spartacus: Suite no.2   21'
*3 *3 *3 2—4 3 3 1—tmp+4—hp, pf—str   9' 6' 5' 1'
Contents—Adagio of Spartacus and Phrygia; Entrance of
merchants, Dance of a Roman courtesan, General dance; Entrance
of Spartacus, Quarrel, Treachery of Harmodius; The dance of the
pirates.
Kalmus

Spartacus: Suite no.3   16'
    *3 *3 *3 2—4 3 3 1—tmp+5—hp, pf—str
    Contents—Market; Dance of a Greek slave; Dance of an Egyptian
    girl; Dance of Phrygia and the Parting scene; Sword dance of
    young Thracians.
    Kalmus

3'	2'	3'
5'	3'	

Symphony no.2   43'
    *3 *3 =4 2—4 3 3 1—tmp+4—hp, pf—str
    Kalmus   *Russian*

13'	9'
11'	10'

Khrennikov, Tikhon   1913 -

Concerto, violin, op.14   20'
    *3 2 *3 *3—4 3 0 0—tmp+4—hp, pf/cel—str
    Kalmus   *Russian*

| 9' | 6' | 5' |

Symphony no.1, op.4   18'
    *3 2 2 2—4 2 3 1—tmp+4—cel—str
    Kalmus   *Russian*

| 6' | 5' | 7' |

Kirchner, Leon   1919 -

Music for orchestra   13'
    *3 *3 *3 *3—4 3 3 1—tmp+5—pf/cel—str
    AMP

Toccata   14'
    0 1 1 1—1 1 1 0—4perc—cel—str
    AMP

Kirk, Theron   1919 -

An orchestra primer   13'
    narrator
    *2 2 2 2—4 3 3 1—tmp+2—str
    Possible with reduced winds: *1 1 2 1—3 2 1 0.
    Oxford

Kleinsinger, George   1914 - 1982

Tubby the tuba   13'
    solo tuba   narrator
    *2 2 *2 2—2 2 1 0—tmp+1—pf/cel—str
    Bcl part may be played on bn.
    Music Theatre

Knussen, Oliver   1952 -

Choral   10'
    *4 *4 +4 *4—contrabass cl, 2asx, tsx, bsx—4 3 4 2—3perc—1-4db
    4 extra horns may be substituted for saxophones. If possible, one
    additional Eh should be used to double the written Eh part in
    selected passages.
    Gunmar

Symphony no.2, op.7   16'
  high soprano solo   5' 3' 4' 4'
  2 2 2 2—2 0 0 0—4perc (opt)—str 6.6.4.4.2
  The 4 percussionists play bowed antique cymbals; these parts
  may also be prerecorded or omitted.
  Faber

Where the wild things are: Songs and a Sea-interlude   17'
  solo soprano
  *3 *2 +3 *2—4 0 3 0—4perc—hp, pf 4-hands—str 6.6.4.4.4
  Schirmer, G.

Kodály, Zoltán   1882 - 1967

Concerto for orchestra   21'
  *3 2 2 2—4 3 3 1—tmp+1—hp—str   4' 8' 5'
  Boosey   3' 1'

Galanta dances   15'
  2 2 2 2—4 2 0 0—tmp+2—str   5' 3' 1'
  Universal   3' 3'

Háry János: Suite   25'
  *3 2 +2 2—4 6 3 1—tmp+6—cel, pf, cimbalom (or hpsd)—str   4' 2' 6'
  One clarinet doubles on alto saxophone.   4' 5' 4'
  3 cornets plus 3tp in last mvt; otherwise 3tp throughout.
  Contents—Prelude (The fairy tale begins); Viennese musical
  clock; Song; The battle and defeat of Napoleon; Intermezzo;
  Entrance of the emperor and his court.
  Universal

Háry János: Intermezzo   5'
  3 2 2 2—4 3 0 0—tmp+4—cimbalom or pf—str
  3rd fl & 3rd tp are optional.
  Universal

Marosszek dances   13'
  *2 2 2 *2—4 2 0 0—tmp+3—str   2' 1' 2'
  Universal   3' 1' 1'
               1' 2'

Missa brevis   31'
  chorus   2' 3' 5'
  *3 2 2 2—4 3 3 1—tmp—opt org—str   6' 2' 4'
  Boosey   6' 3'

Psalmus hungaricus   23'
  chorus   solo tenor   opt boy choir
  3 2 2 2—4 3 3 0—tmp+1—hp, opt org—str
  Universal

Summer evening   16'
  1 *2 2 2—2 0 0 0—str
  Universal

Symphony   29'
  *3 2 2 2—4 3 3 1—tmp+1—str   [12' 9' 8']
  Boosey

Te deum   21'
  chorus   solos SATB
  2 2 2 2—4 3 3 1—tmp—opt org—str
  Universal

Theater overture   12'
  *3 2 2 2—4 3 3 1—tmp+4—pf—str
  Also known as the *Overture for Háry János*.
  Universal

Variations on a Hungarian folksong (The peacock)   25'
  *3 *2 2 2—4 3 3 0—tmp+1—hp—str
  Boosey

Koechlin, Charles   1867 - 1950

Les Bandar-log, op.176   15'
  *4 *3 =4 *3—ssx, tsx —4 4 4 1—bugle in B-flat—tmp+9—2hp, cel, pf—str
  Two of the flutists play piccolo.
  Symphonic poem after Kipling's *The jungle book*.
  Eschig

La Course de printemps, op.95   28'
  *4 *3 *3 *3—4 4 4 2—2tmp+3—2hp, cel, pf, org—str (min 14.12.10.8.8)
  All 4 flutes double on piccolo; 1 oboe doubles on oboe d'amore.
  Symphonic poem after Kipling's *The jungle book*.
  Eschig

Partita, op.205   16'
  *2 *2 2 2—1 1 0 0—tmp—optional ondes martenot—str   [2' 2' 4' 4' 4']
  Salabert

Kolb, Barbara   1939 -

Chromatic fantasy   13'
  narrator
  +1 1 0 0—ssx—0 1 0 0—vibraphone—elec gtr (or elec hpsd or elec pf)
  Amplification required.
  Text by Howard Stern.
  Boosey

Grisaille   15'
  *4 *3 =4 *3—4 3 3 1—5perc—str
  Boosey

Soundings   16'
    3 3 3 3—3 0 0 0—2perc—2hp—str 3.3.3.3.0
    Divided into 2 orchestras, requiring 2 conductors. Also possible
    in a chamber version for pre-recorded tape and 11 players (1
    conductor):
    1 1 1 1—1 0 0 0—1perc—hp—str quartet.
    Boosey

Voyants   21'
    solo piano
    *2 1 1 1—1 1 1 0—1perc—str (or str quintet)
    Boosey

Korngold, Erich Wolfgang   1897 - 1957

Concerto, violin, op.35, D major   24'
    *2 *2 *3 *2—4 2 1 0—tmp+2—hp, cel—str   9' 8' 7'
    Schott

Schauspiel-Ouvertüre, op.4   16'
    *3 2 *3 *3—4 3 3 1—tmp+3—hp—str
    Schott

Sinfonietta, op.5   43'
    *3 *2 *3 *3—4 3 3 1—tmp+2—2hp, cel, pianino—str 16.16.12.12.8   11' 9' 8'
    Kalmus   15'

Symphonic serenade, op.39   35'
    str 16.16.12.12.8   10' 4'
    Schott   14' 7'

Theme and variations, op.42   7'
    2 1 2 1—2 2 2 0—tmp+2—pf, opt hp—str
    May be performed with winds: 2 0 2 0—0 2 2 0.
    Belwin

Koussevitzky, Serge   1874 - 1951

Concerto, double bass, op.3, F-sharp minor   20'
    2 2 2 2—4 0 0 0—tmp—hp—str
    Boosey

Concerto, double bass, op.3, F-sharp minor (arr.)   20'
    2 2 *3 2—3 2 0 0—tmp—str
    Orchestrated by Wolfgang Meyer-Tormin.
    Forberg

Kraft, William   1923 -

Configurations; concerto for 4 percussionists & jazz orchestra   16'
    4 percussion soloists
    3 woodwind players with extensive doublings (pic/fl/cl/asx
    —fl/afl/cl/tsx—cl/bcl/bsx)—brass 2 3 3 1—pf, elec gtr, db
    MCA

Contextures: Riots — decade '60   17'
   *4 *4 =4 *4—4 4 4 1—tmp+6—hp, pf/cel—str 16.14.12.12.10   2' 4' 3'
   Offstage jazz quartet including ssx and (from the orchestra) tp,   3' 5'
   db, drums. 4th cl also doubles asx.
   MCA

Three miniatures for percussion and orchestra   14'
   solo percussion: tmp+3
   *3 2 *3 *3—4 3 3 1—str
   Belwin

Kraus, Joseph Martin   1756 - 1792
Symphony, C minor (1783)   23'
   0 2 0 2—4 0 0 0—str   10' 6' 7'
   Ed. Richard Engländer.
   Kalmus   *Nordiska*

Der Tod Jesu (The death of Jesus)   46'
   solos SAB   chorus
   0 0 0 0—2 2 0 0—tmp—cnt—str
   Ed. Bertil van Boer, Jr.
   A-R Editions

Krenek, Ernst   1900 - 1991
Eleven transparencies for orchestra   20'
   *2 2 2 2—4 2 2 1—tmp+2—hp—str
   Schott   *Universal*

Sinfonietta (The Brazilian)   15'
   str
   Universal

Symphonic elegy   12'
   str
   Elkan-Vogel

Symphony (Pallas Athena)   21'
   *2 2 *2 2—4 2 2 0—tmp+3—hp, cel/pf—str
   Schott   *Universal*

Kubik, Gail   1914 - 1984
Divertimento I for thirteen players   16'
   *1 *1 *1 1—1 1 1 0—tmp—pf/hpsd—vn, va, vc, db
   MCA

Gerald McBoing Boing   9'
   solo percussion   narrator
   1 1 1 1—1 1 0 0—pf—va, vc
   Southern

Symphony concertante   25'
   solos: trumpet, viola, piano
   *2 2 *2 *2—2 1 1 0—1perc—str
   Colombo

Kuhlau, Friedrich   1786 - 1832
Concertino, 2 horns, F minor
2 2 2 2—2 2 1 0—tmp—str
Hofmeister   Musica Rara

Concerto, piano, op.7, C major   30'
1 2 2 2—2 2 0 0—tmp—str
Samfundet

William Shakespeare, op.74: Overture   11'
*2 2 2 2—4 2 1 0—tmp+2—str
Dania

Kuhnau, Johann   1660 - 1722
Uns ist ein Kind geboren
see: Bach, Johann Sebastian
          Cantata no.142

Kurka, Robert   1921 - 1957
The good soldier Schweik: Suite   19'
*2 *2 *2 *2—3 2 1 0—tmp+1 | 3' 4' 3' |
Double bass may substitute for contrabassoon. | 2' 4' 3' |
Weintraub

L

Laderman, Ezra   1924 -
Concerto for orchestra   22'
*3 *3 *3 *3—4 3 3 1—tmp+5—hp, cel—str
Oxford

Magic prison   25'
2 narrators (one female, one male)
2 2 *3 2—4 3 3 0—tmp+2—hp, cel, org—str
Text selected by Archibald MacLeish from the poems and letters
of Emily Dickinson and the recollections of T.W. Higginson.
Oxford

Lalande, Michel-Richard de   1657 - 1726
Christmas symphony (Symphonie de Noël)
2 0 0 1—cnt—str
Fl parts may be played by ob, or both fl and ob may be used.
Ed. Felix Schroeder.
Vieweg

Lalo, Edouard   1823 - 1892

Concerto, piano, F minor   23'
  2 2 2 2—4 4 3 0—tmp—str
  Heugel   *Kalmus*

Concerto, violin, op.20, F minor   27'
  *3 2 2 2—2 2 3 0—tmp+1—str   15' 6' 6'
  Durand   *Kalmus*

Concerto, violoncello, D minor   26'
  2 2 2 2—4 2 3 0—tmp—str   13' 6' 7'
  Bote & Bock   *Kalmus*

Namouna: Ballet suite no.1   25'
  2 2 2 4—4 4 3 1—tmp+3—2hp—str   7' 3' 6'
  Kalmus   5' 4'

Namouna: Ballet suite no.2   15'
  *2 *2 2 4—4 4 3 1—tmp+3—2hp—str   3' 3' 4'
  Both oboists play English horn.   3' 2'
  Kalmus

Rapsodie norvégienne   10'
  *3 2 2 2—4 4 3 1—tmp+2—hp—str
  Also known as *Rapsodie pour orchestre.*
  Bote & Bock   *Kalmus*

Le Roi d'Ys: Overture   11'
  2 2 2 4—4 4 3 1—tmp+2—str
  Two real bassoon parts, each doubled.
  Heugel   *Kalmus*

Symphonie espagnole, op.21   33'
  solo violin   8' 4' 6'
  *3 2 2 2—4 2 3 0—tmp+2—hp—str   7' 8'
  Breitkopf   *Durand*   *Kalmus*

Lambert, Constant   1905 - 1951

Rio Grande   15'
  solo piano   chorus   solo alto
  0 0 0 0—0 4 3 1—tmp+4—str
  Oxford

La Montaine, John   1920 -

Birds of paradise, op.34   13'
  solo piano
  *3 *3 2 2—4 3 3 1—tmp+3—hp—str
  C. Fischer

Concerto, piano, op.9   25'
  *3 *3 *3 *3—4 3 3 0—tmp+2—str
  Galaxy

Songs of the rose of Sharon   15'
   solo soprano
   2 2 2 *3—4 2 3 1—tmp—hp—str
   Tuba and timpani are optional.
   Broude Bros.

A summer's day   5'
   1 1 1 0—1 1 0 0—tmp—hp—str
   Schirmer, G.

Lanner, Joseph   1801 - 1843

Die Werber Walzer, op.103   7'
   *2 1 +2 1—2 2 1 0—tmp+1—str
   Luck

Larsen, Libby   1950 -

Mary Cassatt; seven songs   29'
   solo mezzo-soprano   solo trombone
   *3 2 2 2—4 2 0 1—tmp+2—hp—str
   2 slide projectors with a dissolve unit to project 15 slides of
   Mary Cassatt's paintings.
   Oxford

Overture for the end of a century   6'
   *3 2 2 2—4 3 3 1—tmp+3—pf—str
   Oxford

Larsson, Lars-Erik   1908 - 1987

Concertino, horn, op.45, no.5   13'
   str
   Gehrmans

Lavista, Mario   1943 -

Clepsidra   10'
   *3 *3 *3 2—4 2 2 0—1perc—hp, cel—str
   Peer

Lazarof, Henri   1932 -

Concerto for orchestra   21'
   *4 *4 *4 *4—6 4 4 1—tmp+3—2hp, cel, pf—str
   Two of the flutists double on piccolo; 2 oboists double on English
   horn.
   Merion

Leclair, Jean Marie   1697 - 1764

Concerto, violin, op.7, no.4, F major   14'
   cnt—str | 5' 5' 4' |
   Ed. Claude Crussard.

Concerto, violin, op.7, no.5, A minor   15'
   cnt—str   6' 4' 5'
   Ed. Hugo Ruf.
   Nagel

Sonata, D major (transcribed for string orchestra)   10'
   str
   Kalmus

Lees, Benjamin   1924 -

Concerto for chamber orchestra   17'
   *2 *2 *2 *2—2 2 0 0—1perc (incl tmp)—str
   Both flutists double on piccolo.
   Boosey

Concerto, piano, no.2   22'
   *3 3 *3 *3—4 3 3 1—tmp+3—str
   Boosey

Concerto, string quartet & orchestra   22'
   solos: 2vn, va, vc   8' 8' 6'
   *2 *2 2 2—4 3 3 1—tmp+3—str
   Boosey

Concerto, violin   24'
   *3 *3 *3 *3—4 3 3 1—tmp+2—str   11' 8' 5'
   Boosey

Symphony no.2   21'
   *2 *2 2 2—4 3 3 1—tmp+3—hp—str
   Boosey

Symphony no.3   20'
   *3 *3 *3 *3—tsx—5 4 3 1—tmp+3—cel—str
   Boosey

Symphony no.5 (Kalmar Nyckel)   26'
   *3 3 *3 *3—4 3 3 1—tmp+4—hp, cel—str
   Two of the flutists double on piccolo.
   Boosey

The trumpet of the swan   17'
   narrator
   *2 *2 2 2—4 3 3 1—tmp+4—str
   Boosey

Lehár, Franz   1870 - 1948

The merry widow: Overture   9'
   *3 *3 *3 *3—4 2 3 1—tmp+4—hp, cel—str
   Glocken   *Luck*

Leo, Leonardo   1694 - 1744

Concerto, violoncello, D major   14'
  cnt—str (without va)
  Ed. Felix Schroeder.
  Eulenburg

Santa Elena al Calvario: Sinfonia   5'
  0 2 0 0—2 0 0 0—cnt—str
  Ed. Richard Engländer.
  Eulenburg

León, Tania   1943 -

Batá   7'
  *2 *2 *2 2—2 2 2 1—tmp+2—hp, pf/cel—str
  Peer

Para viola y orquesta   14'
  solo viola   3' 3' 8'
  =2 2 *2 *2—2 2 1 0—2perc—cel/hpsd—str
  Southern

Leoncavallo, Ruggero   1858 - 1919

I pagliacci: Intermezzo   4'
  *3 *2 *3 3—4 2 3 1—tmp—2hp (doubling a single part)—str
  Kalmus

Lewis, John   1920 -

The golden striker   5'
  solo piano, bass, drums
  0 0 0 0—4 4 2 1
  MJQ

Jazz ostinato   6'
  solo jazz quartet: vibraphone, piano, bass, drums
  *3 *3 *3 *3—4 4 3 1—tmp+2—hp, cel—str
  MJQ

Lewis, Robert Hall   1926 -

Three movements on scenes of Hieronymous Bosch   23'
  =4 *3 =3 *3—4 3 3 1—tmp+4—hp, cel, pf, cimbalom, mand—str
  Two of the flutists double on piccolo; a 2nd conductor may be
  needed briefly in one passage.
  Contents—Garden of earthly delights; The last judgement;
  Visions of the hereafter.
  Presser

Liadov, Anatol   1855 - 1914

Baba-Yaga, op.56   4'
  *3 *3 *3 *3—4 2 3 1—tmp+3—str
  Belaieff   *Kalmus*

Eight Russian folk songs, op.58   13'
   *3 *3 2 2—4 2 0 0—tmp+2—str

2' 1' 2'
1' 2' 2'
1' 2'

   Contents—Religious chant; Christmas carol; Plainte; Humorous
   song; Legend of the birds; Cradle song; Dancing school; Dancing
   chorus.
   Belaieff   *Kalmus*

The enchanted lake, op.62   6'
   3 2 3 2—4 0 0 0—tmp+1—hp, cel—str
   Belaieff   *Kalmus*

Kikimora, op.63   7'
   *3 *3 *3 2—4 2 0 0—tmp+1—cel—str
   Belaieff   *Kalmus*

Liebermann, Lowell   1961 -

The domain of Arnheim, op.33   16'
   2 2 2 2—2 2 1 0—tmp+1—hp, cel, pf—str
   Presser

Ligeti, György   1923 -

Apparitions   9'
   *3 0 +3 *3—6 4 3 1—4perc—hp, cel, pf, hpsd—str
   Universal

Atmosphères   9'
   *4 4 +4 *4—6 4 4 1—pf (2 players)—str 14.14.10.10.8
   If possible the 2 pianists should be percussionists.
   Universal

Lontano   11'
   =4 *4 *4 *4—4 3 3 1—str
   Two of the flutists double on piccolo; 1 clarinetist doubles on
   contrabass clarinet.
   Schott

Melodien   13'
   *1 1 1 1—2 1 1 1—1perc—pf/cel—str
   Oboist doubles on oboe d'amore.
   Schott

Ramifications   9'
   string orchestra or 12 solo strings
   Two groups, tuned a quarter-tone apart.
   Schott

Requiem   27'
   2 mixed choruses   solos S, Mz
   *3 *3 =3 *3—4 3 2 1—bass tp, contrabass tbn—3perc
   —hp, hpsd—str 12.12.10.8.6
   3rd cl doubles on contrabass clarinet; 2 of the flutists double on
   piccolo.
   Peters

Liszt, Franz   1811 - 1886

Battle of the Huns (Hunnenschlacht)   16'
  (Symphonic poem no.11)
  *3 2 2 2—4 3 3 1—tmp+1—org (opt)—str
  The organ part is cued in the winds.
  Breitkopf   *Kalmus*

Ce Qu'on Entend Sur La Montagne (Bergsymphonie)   38'
  (Symphonic poem no.1)
  *3 2 *3 2—4 3 3 1—tmp+3—hp—str
  Breitkopf   *Kalmus*

Christus   165'
  chorus   solos SATB | 60' 50' |
  *3 *3 2 2—4 3 3 1—tmp+2—hp, harm, org—str | 55' |
  In three parts: I. Christmas oratorio; II. After Epiphany; III.
  Passion and resurrection.
  Kalmus   *Peters*

Concerto, piano, op. posth., E-flat major (1839)
  *3 2 2 2—2 3 3 0—tmp+1—str
  Ed. Jay Rosenblatt.
  EMB

Concerto, piano, no.1, E-flat major   19'
  *3 2 2 2—2 2 3 0—tmp+2—str | 6' 7' 6' |
  Breitkopf   *Kalmus*

Concerto, piano, no.2, A major   21'
  *3 2 2 2—2 2 3 1—tmp+1—str | 7' 5' 7' 2' |
  Breitkopf   *Kalmus*

Concerto pathétique   14'
  solo piano
  *3 2 2 2—2 2 3 0—tmp+2—hp—str
  Originally for 2 pianos; arranged for solo piano with orchestral
  accompaniment by Eduard Reuss.
  Breitkopf   *Kalmus*

Dante symphony   52'
  chorus of women's or boys' voices | 23' 29' |
  *3 *3 *3 2—4 2 3 1—2tmp+3—2hp, harm—str
  Breitkopf   *Kalmus*

Episodes from Lenau's Faust
  see separate entries:
      Mephisto waltz no.1
      Nocturnal procession

A Faust symphony   65'
   male chorus   tenor solo
   *3 2 2 2—4 3 3 1—tmp+2—hp, org—str
   Contents—Faust; Gretchen; Mephistopheles.
   Voices enter only in the 3rd movement. An alternative ending
   without organ or voices is 5-7' shorter.
   Breitkopf   *Kalmus*

> 23' 19'
> 23'

Festklänge   18'
   (Symphonic poem no.7)
   2 2 2 2—4 3 3 1—tmp+2—str
   Breitkopf   *Kalmus*

From the cradle to the grave
   see his: Von der Wiege bis zum Grabe

Funeral triumph of Tasso (Le Triomphe funèbre du Tasso)   11'
   (Symphonic poem no.2a)
   *3 2 2 2—4 2 3 1—tmp+1—str
   Epilogue to *Tasso, lament and triumph* (see below).
   Breitkopf   *Kalmus*

Hamlet   10'
   (Symphonic poem no.10)
   *3 2 2 2—4 2 3 1—tmp—str
   Breitkopf   *Kalmus*

Héroïde funèbre   20'
   (Symphonic poem no.8)
   *3 *3 2 2—4 2 3 1—tmp+5—str
   Breitkopf   *Kalmus*

Huldigungs-Marsch   6'
   *3 2 2 2—4 2 3 1—tmp+1—str
   Bote & Bock   *Kalmus*

Hungaria   22'
   (Symphonic poem no.9)
   *3 *3 2 2—4 3 3 1—tmp+4—str
   Breitkopf   *Kalmus*

Hungarian fantasy, piano & orchestra   15'
   *3 2 2 2—2 2 3 0—tmp+3—str
   Kalmus   *Peters*

Hungarian rhapsodies
   *Of the nineteen Hungarian rhapsodies for solo piano, six were
orchestrated by the composer in collaboration with Franz Doppler,
and were renumbered in the process. Some were also transposed
into other keys for the orchestral versions. Later orchestrators did
not always follow Liszt's numbering or choice of keys (as in the
case of the well-known Müller-Berghaus version of No.2).*

Hungarian rhapsody no.1, F minor   11'
    (piano version no.14)
    *3 2 2 3—4 3 3 1—tmp+2—2hp (in unison)—str
    Orchestrated by the composer and Franz Doppler.
    Kalmus

Hungarian rhapsody no.2, D minor   11'
    (piano version no.2)
    *3 2 +3 2—4 2 3 1—tmp+2—str
    Orchestrated by the composer and Franz Doppler.
    Originally published as no.4 of the orchestral series; renumbered
    in the reprinting.
    Kalmus

Hungarian rhapsody no.2, C minor (arr. Müller-Berghaus)   11'
    (piano version no.2)
    *2 2 2 2—4 2 3 0—tmp+4—hp—str
    Orchestrated by Karl Müller-Berghaus.
    Kalmus

Hungarian rhapsody no.3, D major   7'
    (piano version no.6)
    *3 2 2 2—4 2 3 1—tmp+3—hp, cimbalom—str
    Orchestrated by the composer and Franz Doppler.
    Kalmus

Hungarian rhapsody no.4, D minor   11'
    (piano version no.12)
    *3 2 2 2—4 2 3 1—tmp+3—hp—str
    Orchestrated by the composer and Franz Doppler. Originally
    published as no.2 of the orchestral series; renumbered in the
    reprinting.
    Kalmus

Hungarian rhapsody no.5, E minor   8'
    (piano version no.5)
    2 2 2 2—4 0 3 0—tmp—hp—str
    Orchestrated by the composer and Franz Doppler.
    Kalmus

Hungarian rhapsody no.6, D major (Pesther Carneval)   10'
    (piano version no.9)
    *3 2 2 2—4 2 3 1—tmp+3—hp—str
    Orchestrated by the composer and Franz Doppler.
    Kalmus

Die Ideale   30'
    (Symphonic poem no.12)
    2 2 2 2—4 2 3 1—tmp+1—str
    Breitkopf   *Kalmus*

Légendes   18'
  *3 *3 2 2—4 2 3 1—tmp+1—hp—str   9' 9'
  Eh optional. Contents—San Francesco d'Assisi; San Francesco di
  Paola.
  EMB

Malédiction   13'
  solo piano
  str
  Breitkopf   Kalmus

Mazeppa   17'
  (Symphonic poem no.6)
  *3 *3 =3 3—4 3 3 1—tmp+3—str
  Breitkopf   Kalmus

Mephisto waltz no.1 (Der Tanz in der Dorfschenke)   11'
  *3 2 2 2—4 2 3 1—tmp+2—hp—str
  One of two *Episodes from Lenau's Faust.*
  Breitkopf   Kalmus

Mephisto waltz no.2   11'
  *3 2 2 2—4 2 3 1—tmp+2—hp—str
  Kalmus

Nocturnal procession (Der nächtliche Zug)   15'
  3 *3 2 2—4 2 3 1—tmp+1—hp—str
  Playable without Eh. One of two *Episodes from Lenau's Faust.*
  Kalmus

Orpheus   13'
  (Symphonic poem no.4)
  *3 *3 2 2—4 2 3 1—tmp—2hp—str
  Breitkopf   Kalmus

Les Préludes   16'
  (Symphonic poem no.3)
  *3 2 2 2—4 2 3 1—tmp+3—hp—str
  Breitkopf   Kalmus

Prometheus   12'
  (Symphonic poem no.5)
  *3 *3 2 2—4 2 3 1—tmp—str
  Breitkopf   Kalmus

Rákóczi march (Hungarian march)   6'
  *3 2 2 2—4 2 3 1—tmp+3—str
  Breitkopf   Broude, A.   Kalmus

Rhapsodie espagnole   14'
  solo piano
  *3 2 2 2—4 2 3 1—tmp+2—str
  Originally for piano; arranged as a concert piece for piano and
  orchestra by Ferruccio Busoni.
  Kalmus

Tasso, lament and triumph   19'
   (Symphonic poem no.2)
   *3 2 *3 2—4 4 3 1—tmp+4—hp—str
   Breitkopf   *Kalmus*

Totentanz, piano & orchestra   16'
   *3 2 2 2—2 2 3 1—tmp+3—str
   Breitkopf   *Kalmus*

Von der Wiege bis zum Grabe (From the cradle to the grave)   14'
   (Symphonic poem no.13)
   *3 *2 2 2—4 2 3 1—tmp+1—opt hp—str
   Bote & Bock   *Kalmus*   *Schirmer, G.*

Wanderer fantasy
   see under: Schubert, Franz, 1797-1828

Litolff, Henry Charles   1818 - 1891

Concerto symphonique, no.4, op.102, D minor   37'
   solo piano   13' 7' 6'
   *2 2 2 2—4 2 3 0—tmp+1—str   11'
   Kalmus

Robespierre: Overture   10'
   *2 2 2 2—4 2 3 0—tmp+3—str
   Kalmus   *Peters*

Lloyd, Jonathan   1948 -

Symphony no.2   25'
   =4 *3 *3 *3—4 3 3 1—tmp+2—hp, cel—str 16.14.12.10.8
   Optional: 4rec (descant, 2 trebles, bass) off-stage. Two of the
   flutists double on piccolo; 1 clarinet doubles on alto saxophone.
   Boosey

Locatelli, Pietro   1695 - 1764

Concerto grosso, op.1, no.6, C minor   12'
   cnt—str
   Ed. Arthur Egidi.
   Kalmus   *Vieweg*

Concerto grosso, op.1, no.8, F minor   20'
   solos: 2 violins, 2 violas, violoncello
   cnt—str
   Ed. Arnold Schering.
   Kahnt

Concerto grosso, op.1, no.9, D major   12'
   solos: 2 violins, violoncello
   str
   Ed. Ettore Bonelli.
   Kalmus   *Zanibon*

Concerto grosso, op.7, no.6, E-flat major (Il pianto d'Arianna)   17'
   solos: 2 violins, viola, violoncello
   str
   Ed. Remo Giazotto.
   Ricordi

| 5' 3' 3' |
| 2' 1' 3' |

Concerto grosso, op.7, no.12, F major   12'
   4 solo violins
   cnt—str
   Ed. Newell Jenkins.
   Peters

Trauer-Symphonie   15'
   cnt—str
   Kahnt   *Kalmus*

Loeffler, Charles Martin   1861 - 1935
La Mort de Tintagiles, op.6   25'
   solo viola d'amore
   *3 *3 =4 2—4 4 3 1—2tmp+3—hp—str
   Schirmer, G.

A pagan poem   22'
   *3 *3 *3 2—4 6 3 1—tmp+1—hp, pf—str
   Schirmer, G.

Lombardo, Mario   1931 -
Drakestail; a symphonic fairy tale for children   18'
   narrator
   *3 *3 *3 2—4 3 3 1—tmp+3—hp, cel—str
   Chappell

London, Edwin   1929 -
A hero of our time   17'
   *4 *3 =4 *3—4 4 3 1—tmp+4—hp, pf—str
   Peters

The imaginary invalid: Overture   4'
   1 0 *2 1—0 1 0 0—str
   This work may be out of print.
   EAM

In Heinrich's shoes   30'
   =1 *1 *2 0—2 1 2 0—tmp+2—str
   Bcl doubles on ssx. "An orchestral fantasy based on the *St. John's Passion* by Heinrich Schütz."
   Peters

Peter Quince at the clavier   30'
   solo tenor
   *3 2 *3 2—4 3 3 1—tmp+2—hp, cel/pf—str (min. 10.8.6.5.3)
   Peters

Lortzing, Albert   1801 - 1851
Zar und Zimmermann: Overture   7'
   *2 2 2 2—4 2 3 0—tmp+2—str
   Playable with winds: 1 0 2 0—2 2 1 0.
   Breitkopf   *Kalmus*

Luening, Otto   1900 -
Prelude to a hymn tune by William Billings   10'
   1 1 1 1—1 0 0 0—pf—str
   Peters

Rhapsodic variations   17'
   (composed with Vladimir Ussachevsky)
   *2 2 2 2—4 2 3 0—tmp+1—electronic tape—str
   Peters

Synthesis   9'
   *2 2 2 2—2 2 3 0—3perc—pf, electronic tape—str
   Peters

Luigini, Alexandre   1850 - 1906
Ballet égyptien   20'
   *3 2 2 2—4 2 3 1—tmp+4—2hp—str
   Kalmus

Lully, Jean Baptiste   1632 - 1687
Ballet music
   str (without va)
   Ed. Arthur Egidi.
   Vieweg

Ballet suite   15'
   2 2 2 2—4 2 0 0—tmp—str
   Arr. Felix Mottl from ballet music of five Lully operas.
   Contents—Introduction; Nocturno; Menuetto; Prelude, Les Vents,
   Marche.
   Kalmus   *Peters*

Roland: Chaconne
   2 1 0 1—cnt—str (vn I, vn II, vn III, va, vc/db)
   Ob, bn & cnt optional. Ed. H. Wiley Hitchcock.
   Peters

Roland: Suite   9'
   1 2 0 1—2 2 0 0—tmp—str
   Arr. William Lynen.
   Contents—Overture; Marsch; Air; Menuet; Gavotte; Gigue
   Kalmus

Le Triomphe de l'amour: Ballet suite   20'
  str
  Ed. Paul Angerer.
  Doblinger

Lutosławski, Witold   1913 - 1994

Concerto for orchestra   28'
  *3 *3 *3 *3—4 4 4 1—tmp+5—2hp, cel, pf—str   7' 6' 15'
  Chester   *PWM*

Little suite (Mala suita)   11'
  *2 2 2 2—4 3 3 1—tmp+1—str   3' 2' 3' 3'
  Chester   *PWM*

Overture for strings   5'
  str
  PWM

Postludium   4'
  *3 3 *3 *3—4 3 3 1—tmp+2—hp, cel, pf—str
  No.1 of the *Three postludes.*
  Chester

Preludes & fugue for 13 solo strings   34'
  7vn, 3va, 2vc, 1db
  Any of the preludes in any order can be played with or without
  the fugue, which can itself be shortened four possible ways.
  Chester   *Hansen*   *PWM*

Preludia taneczne (Dance preludes)   7'
  solo clarinet
  tmp+1—hp, pf—str 8.8.6.6.4
  PWM

Symphony no.2   30'
  *3 *3 *3 3—4 3 3 1—tmp+2—hp, cel, pf—str (16.14.12.9.6)
  All three flutists double on piccolo.
  Chester   *Hansen*   *PWM*

Three postludes for orchestra   18'
  *3 3 *3 *3—4 3 3 1—tmp+3—2hp, cel, pf—str   4' 5' 9'
  Chester   *PWM*

Venetian games   13'
  *2 1 *3 1—1 1 1 0—tmp+3—hp, pf 4-hands doubling cel—str
  2.2.3.3.2
  Moeck   *PWM*

Lysenko, Mykola   1842 - 1912

Taras Bulba: Overture   5'
  *3 *3 *3 *3—4 3 3 1—tmp+4—hp—str
  Revised by L. Revutsky.
  Russian   *G.Schirmer*

M

MacDowell, Edward   1861 - 1908

Concerto, piano, no.1, op.15, A minor   25'
   2 2 2 2—4 2 0 0—tmp—str   10' 7' 8'
   Breitkopf   *Kalmus*

Concerto, piano, no.2, op.23, D minor   26'
   2 2 2 2—4 2 3 0—tmp—str   13' 5' 8'
   Breitkopf   *Kalmus*

Hamlet & Ophelia, op.22   17'
   *3 2 2 2—4 2 3 0—tmp+1—str
   Contents—Hamlet (above instrumentation);
   Ophelia (2 2 2 2—4 2 0 0—tmp—str).
   Kalmus

Lamia, op.29 (Symphonic poem no.3)   18'
   *3 2 2 2—4 2 3 1—tmp+1—str
   Kalmus

Lancelot and Elaine, op.25 (Symphonic poem no.2)   20'
   *3 2 2 2—4 2 3 1—tmp+1—str
   Kalmus   *Schirmer, G.*

The Saracens: Two fragments after the Song of Roland, op.30   10'
   *3 2 2 2—4 2 3 1—tmp+2—str
   Contents—The Saracens; Lovely Aldâ.
   Breitkopf   *Kalmus*

Suite no.1, op.42   20'
   *3 2 2 2—4 2 3 1—tmp+2—str   6' 2' 3'
   Kalmus   4' 5'

Suite no.2, op.48 (Indian)   30'
   *3 2 2 2—4 2 4 1—tmp+2—str
   Breitkopf   *Kalmus*

Mackey, Steven   1956 -

Deal   20'
   solo electric guitar; solo drum set (optional)
   =1 *1 *1 1—1 1 1 0—1perc—hp, pf—pre-recorded tape—2vn, va,
   vc, db
   Amplification required.
   Boosey

Eating greens 23'
*3 *3 *3 *3—tsx/bsx—4 3 3 1—tmp+4—hp, pf/cel/harm
—pre-recorded tape—str
Two of the flutists double on piccolo; bass clarinetist doubles on
contrabass clarinet.
Boosey

TILT 13'
*3 *3 *3 *3—4 3 3 1—tmp+4—hp, pf—str
Two of the flutists double on pic; 2nd cl doubles on asx; bcl
doubles on contrabass cl.
Boosey

MacMillan, James 1959 -

The confession of Isobel Gowdie 20'
*2 *2 *2 *2—4 3 3 1—tmp+2—str
Boosey

Epiclesis
solo trumpet
*3 *3 *3 *3—6 3 3 1—tmp+4—str
Boosey

Veni, veni, Emmanuel 26'
solo percussion
*2 *2 *2 *2—2 2 2 0—tmp—str (min 8.6.4.4.2)
Boosey

Maderna, Bruno 1920 - 1973

Aura 20'
*4 *4 =5 *3—4 5 4 0—tmp+13—2hp, cel—str 12.12.12.10.8
All four flutists play piccolo; 2 of the clarinetists play bass
clarinet.
Ricordi

Serenata no.2 16'
*1 0 *2 0—1 1 0 0—vibr/xylo, pf/glock, hp—vn, va, db
Suvini

Mahler, Gustav 1860 - 1911

*Mahler frequently revised his works. Though much of his music
is available through reprint houses, these are often not the
definitive or final versions.*

Blumine
see his: Symphony no.1: *Blumine* movement

Kindertotenlieder 26'
solo voice (medium)
*3 *3 *3 *3—4 0 0 0—tmp+1—hp, cel—str 6' 5' 5'
3' 7'
A reduced orchestration by de Leeuw is published by Donemus.
Kalmus   *Peters*   *Universal*

Das klagende Lied   37'
   chorus   solos SAT | 18' 19' |
   *6 *5 =7 *3—8 6 3 1—2tmp+5—2hp—str
   The above instrumentation includes backstage winds and
   percussion as follows: *3 2 +4 0—4 2 0 0—tmp+2 . Two of the
   flutists double on piccolo; 2 of the clarinetists double on E-flat
   clarinet.
   A version revised by Pierre Boulez calls also for an optional boy
   alto soloist.
   Contents—Der Spielmann (The minstrel); Hochzeitsstück
   (Wedding piece). Originally these two parts were preceded by an
   opening movement, *Waldmärchen (Forest Legend)*, which the
   composer later withdrew; see separate entry for *Waldmärchen.*
   Universal

Das Lied von der Erde   63'
   alto (or baritone) & tenor solos | 9' 10' 3' |
   *4 *3 =4 *3—4 3 3 1—tmp+3—2hp, cel, mand—str | 7' 4' 30' |
   Universal

Lieder aus Des Knaben Wunderhorn (Youth's magic horn)   42'
   solo voice | 6' 4' 4' |
   *3 *3 +3 3—4 2 1 1—tmp+4—hp—str | 2' 3' 4' |
   Songs are available individually, each with a choice of high or | 3' 5' 7' |
   low key (the original keys are indicated by italics in the contents | 4' |
   list below). Instrumentation varies from song to song within the
   aggregate given above.
     Contents—Der Schildwache Nachtlied (C major, *B-flat major*);
   Verlorne Müh' (*A major*, G major); Trost im Unglück (*A major*, G
   major); Wer hat dies Liedlein erdacht? (*F major*, E-flat major);
   Das irdische Leben (*E-flat minor*, D minor); Des Antonius von
   Padua Fischpredigt (D minor, *C minor*); Rheinlegendchen (*A*
   major, G major); Lied des verfolgten im Turm (*D minor*, C minor);
   Wo die schönen Trompeten blasen (*D minor*, C minor); Lob des
   hohen Verstandes (*D major*, C major).
     Other songs from *Des Knaben Wunderhorn* appear as movements
   of Symphonies nos. 2, 3, and 4, and are also available separately,
   though only in the original keys.
     Five of these songs are available from Presser in arrangements
   by Philip West for voice and chamber orchestra.
   Universal

Lieder eines fahrenden Gesellen (Songs of a wayfarer)   16'
   solo voice (medium) | 4' 4' 3' 5' |
   *3 *2 *3 2—4 2 3 0—tmp+2—hp—str
   Contents—Wenn mein Schatz Hochzeit macht; Ging heut Morgen
   über's Feld; Ich hab' ein glühend Messer; Die zwei blauen Augen.
   Kalmus   *Weinberger*

Rückert Lieder
   see his: Sieben Lieder aus letzten Zeit

Sieben Lieder aus letzten Zeit (Seven last songs) 30'
    solo voice

7' 5' 2'
2' 5' 6'
3'

    *2 *3 *3 *3—4 3 3 1—tmp+3—hp, pf/cel—str
One oboist doubles on oboe d'amore.
Songs are available individually, each with a choice of high, medium, or low key (the original keys are indicated by italics in the contents list below). Instrumentation varies from song to song, within the aggregate given above.
  Contents—Revelge (*D minor*, C minor, B-flat minor); Der Tamboursg'sell (E minor, *D minor*, C minor); Blicke mir nicht in die Lieder (A-flat major, *F major*, E-flat major); Ich atmet' einen Linden Duft (F major, *D major*, C major); Ich bin der Welt abhanden gekommen (*F major*, E-flat major, D-flat major); Um Mitternacht (B-minor, *A minor*, G minor); Liebst du um Schönheit? (E-flat major, *C major*, B-flat major).
  This group of songs is often referred to as *Rückert Lieder*, after the poet.
  Four of these songs are available from Presser with orchestration arranged by Philip West for woodwind quintet, harp, and string quartet.
Universal

Symphony no.1, D major (Titan) 53'
    *4 *4 =4 *3—7 4 3 1—2tmp+3—hp—str

15' 8'
12' 18'

  A 5th trumpet and 4th trombone may be used in the last movement to strengthen the horns if necessary. A reduced version is available from Universal.
Universal

Symphony no.1: Blumine 8'
    2 2 2 2—4 1 0 0—tmp—hp—str
In its original form, the symphony included this piece as the second of five movements. The five-movement version was performed under Mahler's direction in 1889 and 1894, but this movement was deleted in the published version of 1899.
Presser

Symphony no.2, C minor (Resurrection) 80'
    chorus   solos SA

22' 11'
11' 4'
32'

    *4 *4 =5 *4—10 8 4 1—2tmp+4—2hp (preferably doubled), org—str
All 4 flutists double on piccolo; 2 of the oboists double on English horn; 2 of the clarinetists double on E-flat clarinet. Possible with 6tp. A reduced version is also available from the publisher.
Universal

Symphony no.3, D minor 99'
    alto solo   women's chorus, boys' chorus

33' 10'
18' 9' 4'
25'

    *4 *4 =5 *4—8 4 4 1—2tmp+5—2hp—str
One of the trumpets doubles on posthorn in B-flat.
Universal

Symphony no.4, G major   **54'**
  soprano solo
  *4 *3 =3 *3—4 3 0 0—tmp+4—hp—str
  Universal

> 17' 10'
> 18' 9'

Symphony no.5, C-sharp minor   **68'**
  *4 *3 =3 *3—6 4 3 1—tmp+4—hp—str
  Ed. Erwin Ratz. The earlier Peters edition, not by Ratz, should
  not be used.
  Peters

> 12' 15'
> 17' 9'
> 15'

Symphony no.5: Adagietto   **9'**
  str, hp
  Peters

Symphony no.6, A minor (Tragic)   **77'**
  *5 *5 =5 *5—8 6 4 1—tmp+5—2hp, cel—str
  Ed. Erwin Ratz.
  Kahnt

> 21' 12'
> 15' 29'

Symphony no.7, E minor   **77'**
  *5 *4 =5 *4—4 3 3 1—tenorhorn—tmp+5—2hp, gtr, mand—str
  Bote & Bock

> 22' 15'
> 9' 15'
> 16'

Symphony no.8, E-flat major (Symphony of a thousand)   **79'**
  double chorus, boys' chorus   solos SSSAATBB
  *6 *5 =6 *5—8 8 7 1—tmp+3—2hp, cel, pf, harm, org, mand—str
  A reduced version is available from the publisher.
  Universal

> 24' 55'

Symphony no.9, D major   **81'**
  *5 *4 =5 *4—4 3 3 1—tmp+3—1 or 2hp—str
  2nd hp, if used, merely doubles certain passages. Ed. Erwin Ratz.
  Rev. ed. in preparation by Internationale Gustav Mahler
  Gesellschaft.
  Universal

> 29' 18'
> 13' 21'

Symphony no.10
  *This work was left incomplete at the composer's death. In
  Mahler's manuscript, the first two movements are complete, or
  almost complete, in score sketch; the third movement has 30
  measures of score sketch, and the whole movement in short score;
  the fourth and fifth movements are in 4-stave short score, with
  sparse indications of instrumentation.*
  *The following entries give various attempts to complete the
  work, listed in chronological order. The Cooke, Wheeler,
  Carpenter and Mazzetti versions are discussed in Theodore
  Bloomfield's article "In Search of Mahler's Tenth," Musical
  Quarterly, vol.74 no.2, 1990.*

Symphony no.10 (Krenek): Movements I and III only   **25'**
  *3 3 3 3—4 4 3 1—tmp+1—hp—str
  Performing version by Ernst Krenek, 1924 (ed. Otto A. Jokl).
  AMP

Symphony no.10 (Ratz): 1st movement (Adagio) only   22'
  *3 3 3 3—4 4 3 1—hp—str
Ed. Erwin Ratz, 1964.
Universal

Symphony no.10 (Cooke)   72'
  *4 *4 =5 *4—4 4 4 1—2tmp+2—hp—str
  Two of the bassoons double on contrabassoon. Performing
  version by Deryck Cooke, 1964; 2nd version1972, rev.1976.
  Score is published by Faber; parts are available from AMP.
AMP   *Faber*

23'	12'
5'	12'
	20'

Symphony no.10 (Wheeler)   74'
  *4 *4 =5 *4—4 4 4 1—tmp+3—2 or more hp—str
  Two of the fl double on pic; 2ob double on Eh; 2cl double on scl;
  2bn double on cbn.
  Cuing permits performance with 3bn (one doubling on cbn), 3tbn,
  and 1hp.
  Performing version by Joe Wheeler, 1965.
AMP

23'	12'
5'	12'
	22'

Symphony no.10 (Carpenter)   80'
  *5 *4 =5 *4—4 4 3 1—tmp+4—2hp—str
  Two of the bassoonists double on contrabassoon.
  Completion by Clinton A. Carpenter, 1966, rev. 1988.
AMP

24'	13'
6'	13'
	24'

Symphony no.10 (Mazzetti)   75'
  *5 *4 =5 *4—4 4 4 1—2tmp+4—2hp—str
  Two of the bassoonists double on contrabassoon.
  Completion by Remo Mazzetti Jr., 1985, rev. 1986.
AMP

24'	12'
4'	11'
	24'

Waldmärchen (A forest legend)   28'
  solo SATBar   chorus
  *3 *3 *3 3—4 4 3 1—tmp+2—2-6hp—str
  2 real harp parts; composer asks that each be tripled in certain
  passages. Originally composed as Part I of *Das klagende Lied* and
  subsequently withdrawn. Score, but not parts, available from
  Kalmus.
Belwin

Malipiero, Gian Francesco   1882 - 1973

Concerto, violoncello   14'
  *3 2 2 2—4 0 0 0—2perc—str
Suvini

Sinfonia per Antigenida   17'
  *3 *3 2 2—4 2 3 1—3perc—hp, cel—str
Ricordi

4'	6'	3'	4'

Mamlok, Ursula   1928 -

Grasshoppers; six humoresques for orchestra   5'
    *3 2 2 *3—2 2 3 1—tmp+2—str
    Contents—Sunday walk; Night serenade; In the rain; Minuet; In
    the army; Hurrying home.
    ACA

Manfredini, Francesco   1684 - 1762

Christmas symphony, op.2, no.12, D major (Sinfonia pastorale per il
Santissimo Natale)
    cnt—str
    Ed. Felix Schroeder.
    Vieweg

Concerto grosso, op.3, no.9, D major   11'
    solo concertino: 2 violins, violoncello
    str
    Ed. Ettore Bonelli.
    Zanibon

Concerto grosso, op.3, no.10, G minor   12'
    solo concertino: 2 violins
    cnt—str
    Ed. Bernhard Paumgartner.
    Peters

Concerto grosso, op.3, no.12, C major (Christmas concerto)   10'
    solo concertino: 2 violins
    cnt—str
    Eulenburg   *Kahnt*   *Schott*

Marcello, Alessandro   ca.1684 - ca.1750

Concerto, oboe, C minor
    see under: Marcello, Benedetto, 1686-1739

Marcello, Benedetto   1686 - 1739

Concerto, oboe, C minor   10'
    str
    Ed. Ettore Bonelli. Actually by Alessandro Marcello.
    Zanibon

Concerto grosso, op.1, no.1, D major   10'
    solo concertino: 2 violins, violoncello
    cnt—str
    Ed. Ettore Bonelli.
    Zanibon

Concerto grosso, op.1, no.2, E minor 12'
   solo concertino: 2 violins, viola, violoncello
   cnt—str
   Ed. Ettore Bonelli.
   Zanibon

Concerto grosso, op.1, no.3, E major 10'
   solo concertino: 2 violins, viola, violoncello
   cnt—str
   Ed. Ettore Bonelli.
   Zanibon

Concerto grosso, op.1, no.4, F major 15'
   solo concertino: 2 violins, viola, violoncello
   cnt—str
   Ed. Ettore Bonelli.
   Zanibon

Concerto grosso, op.1, no.5, B minor 13'
   solo concertino: 2 violins, viola, violoncello
   cnt—str
   Ed. Ettore Bonelli.
   Zanibon

Concerto grosso, op.1, no.6, B-flat major 10'
   solo concertino: 2 violins, violoncello
   cnt—str
   Ed. Ettore Bonelli.
   Zanibon

Concerto grosso, op.1, no.7, F minor 10'
   solo concertino: 2 violins, violoncello
   cnt—str
   Ed. Ettore Bonelli.
   Zanibon

Concerto grosso, op.1, no.8, F major 9'
   solo concertino: 2 violins, violoncello
   cnt—str
   Ed. Ettore Bonelli.
   Zanibon

Concerto grosso, op.1, no.9, A major 10'
   solo concertino: 2 violins, violoncello
   cnt—str
   Ed. Ettore Bonelli.
   Zanibon

Concerto grosso, op.1, no.10, C major 12'
   solo concertino: 2 violins, violoncello
   cnt—str
   Ed. Ettore Bonelli.
   Zanibon

Introduction, aria & presto, A minor   9'
   str
   Ed. Ettore Bonelli.
   Zanibon

Martin, Frank   1890 - 1974

Ballade, saxophone & orchestra   13'
   solo alto saxophone
   tmp+1—pf—str
   Universal

Concerto, 7 winds   20'
   solos: fl, ob, cl, bn, hn, tp, tbn   6' 7' 7'
   tmp+3—str
   Universal

Etudes for string orchestra   20'
   str   4' 2' 3'
   Universal   4' 7'

Passacaille.   11'
   str
   Universal

Petite Symphonie concertante   23'
   hp, pf, hpsd—2 string orchestras   14' 5' 4'
   Universal

Les Quatre Éléments (The four elements)   20'
   *3 *3 =3 *3—asx—4 3 3 1—tmp+4—2hp, cel, pf—str
   Universal

Le Vin herbé   93'
   solo voices: 3S, 3A, 3T, 3B   32' 21'
   pf—2vn, 2va, 2vc, db   40'
   Universal

Martino, Donald   1931 -

Concerto, alto saxophone   24'
   *1 *2 1 *2—2 1 2 0—2perc—pf—str (min 6.4.3.3.2)
   Trumpet doubles on flugelhorn if possible.
   Dantalian

Concerto, piano   27'
   *3 *2 *3 *3—4 2 3 1—tmp+4—hp, cel/orchestral pf
   —str (min 14.12.10.10.8)
   Bcl doubles on contrabass cl; tuba doubles on euphonium; 2
   flutists double on piccolo.
   Ione

Concerto, violoncello   28'
  *3 *3 *3 *3—4 4 3 1—tmp+4—hp, pf/cel—str
  Two of the flutists double on piccolo; bcl doubles on contrabass
  cl. Strings: min 12.10.8.6.4; preferred 16.14.12.10.8.
  Dantalian

Divertisements for youth orchestra   7'
  2 2 2 2—2 2 2 0—2-3perc—pf—str
  Oboes, bassoons, horns & trombones are optional.
  Contents—The kick-off quadrille; Songs of solitaire; Miss
  Phoebe's waltz; Little Joe's lament.
  Dantalian

Mosaic for grand orchestra   16'
  =4 *4 *4 *4—4 4 4 1—tmp+5—2hp, cel/elec org, elec gtr
  —str 16.14.10.10.9
  Two of the flutists double on piccolo; one clarinetist doubles on
  contrabass clarinet in B-flat.
  Dantalian

Paradiso choruses   29'
  chorus (including opt children's voices)   solos 3S, 4Mz, 3T,
  2Bar
  *3 *3 *3 *4—4 4 4 1—tmp+4—hp, org, pf (preferably elec)
  —pre-recorded tape—str
  Two of the flutists double on piccolo.
  Dantalian

Ritorno   15'
  2 *3 *3 2—4 3 3 1—tmp+3—hp, cel/pf—str
  Dantalian

The white island   22'
  chorus
  *1 *1 1 1—1 1 2 0—2perc—cel, pf—str (min 6.4.3.3.2) or 5 solo str
  Also one contrabass cl doubling bcl, *or* cbn doubling bn2. Tp
  doubles on flugelhorn.
  Dantalian

Martinu, Bohuslav   1890 - 1959

Comedy on the bridge: Little suite   6'
  *1 1 1 1—2 1 1 0—3perc—pf—str
  Boosey

Concerto, oboe   15'
  2 0 2 1—2 1 0 0—pf—str   5' 6' 4'
  Eschig

Concerto, violin   27'
  2 2 2 2—4 3 3 1—tmp+2—str
  Boosey

Estampes   20'
  *2 *2 2 2—4 2 3 0—tmp+2—hp, pf—str
  Southern

Fantasia concertante, piano & orchestra   20'
  *3 2 2 2—4 2 3 0—tmp+3—str
  Universal

The frescos of Piero della Francesca   18'
  *4 *3 3 3—4 3 3 1—tmp+3—hp—str | 7' 6' 5' |
  Universal

Overture   8'
  2 2 2 2—4 2 0 0—tmp—str
  Eschig

Rhapsody-concerto   22'
  solo viola
  2 2 2 2—4 2 0 0—tmp+1—str
  Bärenreiter

Sinfonia concertante for 2 orchestras   16'
  1st orch: 0 3 0 1—2 0 0 0—str
  2nd orch: *2 0 2 1—2 2 3 1—tmp+2—str
  Schott

Symphony no.1   36'
  *3 *3 3 *3—4 3 3 1—tmp+3—hp, pf—str | 10' 8' 8' |
  Boosey | 10' |

Symphony no.2   24'
  *3 3 3 2—4 3 3 1—tmp+3—hp, pf—str | 6' 8' 5' 5' |
  Boosey

Symphony no.3   26'
  *3 *3 3 2—4 3 3 1—tmp+3—hp, pf—str | 9' 7' 10' |
  Boosey

Symphony no.4   33'
  *4 *4 3 2—4 3 3 1—tmp+3—pf—str | 7' 9' 9' 8' |
  Boosey

Symphony no.5   31'
  *3 3 3 3—4 3 3 1—tmp+3—pf—str | 9' 10' |
  Boosey | 12' |

Symphony no.6 (Fantaisies symphoniques)   28'
  *4 3 3 3—4 3 3 1—tmp+4—str | 9' 8' 11' |
  Boosey

Toccata e due canzoni   25'
  *1 2 1 1—0 1 0 0—tmp+1—pf—str | 9' 7' 9' |
  Boosey

Martirano, Salvatore   1927 -

Contrasto   9'
  *3 *3 *3 *3—4 3 3 1—tmp+3—hp, cel—str
  Schott

Mascagni, Pietro   1863 - 1945

L'amico Fritz: Intermezzo   4'
   *3 2 2 2—4 2 3 1—tmp+1—hp—str
   Luck

Cavalleria rusticana: Intermezzo   3'
   2 2 0 0—opt hp, org—str
   Organ may be replaced by 2cl, 2bn, hn.
   Kalmus

Cavalleria rusticana: Prelude & Siciliana   6'
   *3 2 2 2—4 2 3 1—tmp+2—opt hp—str
   Kalmus   *Luck*

Mason, Daniel Gregory   1873 - 1953

Chanticleer; festival overture, op.27   15'
   *3 *3 *3 *3—4 3 3 1—tmp+2—hp—str
   Presser

Massenet, Jules   1842 - 1912

Le Cid: Ballet music   17'
   *2 *2 2 2—4 4 3 1—tmp+3—2hp—str | 3' 2' 2' |
   Contents—Castillane; Andalouse; Aragonaise; Aubade; | 1' 3' 3' |
   Catalane; Madrilene; Navarraise. | 3' |
   Heugel   *Kalmus*

Concerto, piano   30'
   *3 2 2 2—4 2 3 0—tmp+3—cel—str | 14' 9' 7' |
   Heugel

Hérodiade: Prelude to Act III   2'
   0 1 2 2—4 0 0 1—tmp—hp—str
   Heugel

Manon: Minuet & Gavotte   5'
   *2 2 2 2—4 2 3 0—tmp+2—str | 3' 2' |
   Arr. Theo. M. Tobani; piano-conductor score only.
   Luck

Phèdre: Overture   9'
   *3 2 2 2—4 4 3 1—tmp—str
   Heugel   *Kalmus*

Scènes alsaciennes (Suite no.7)   21'
   *2 2 2 2—4 4 3 1—tmp+3—str | 7' 5' 5' 4' |
   Contents—Sunday morning; In the tavern; Under the linden trees;
   Sunday evening.
   Heugel   *Kalmus*

Scènes pittoresques (Suite no.4)   18'
   *2 2 2 2—4 4 3 0—tmp+4—str | 4' 3' 6' 5' |
   Contents—Marche; Air de ballet; Angelus; Fête bohême.
   Heugel   *Kalmus*

Suite no.1, op.13   23'
    *3 2 2 2—4 4 3 1—tmp+3—2hp—str   `6' 5' 6' 6'`
    Contents—Pastorale et Fugue; Variations; Nocturne; Marche et
    Strette.
    Durand

Thaïs: Méditation   5'
    solo violin
    2 *2 *3 *3—4 0 0 0—tmp—hp (single part marked "Harpes
    soli")—str
    Playable with: 0 0 2 2—1 0 0 0—hp—str.
    Instructions *au théâtre*: backstage ob, Eh & wordless chorus.
    Instructions *au concert*: 4 or 8 solo voices seated in orchestra.
    (The voices sing only for 15 bars and are often omitted; Kalmus
    version gives these notes to 2tp & 2tbn.)
    Kalmus   *Luck*

Maurice, Paule   1910 - 1967

Tableaux de Provence   12'
    solo alto saxophone   `2' 1' 1'`
    *2 *2 2 1—2 1 0 0—tmp+1—hp, cel—str   `4' 4'`
    English horn is optional.
    Contents—Farandoulo di chatouno (Farandoles des jeunes filles);
    Cansoun per ma Mio (Chanson pour ma mie); La Boumiano (La
    Bohémienne); Dis Alyscamps, l'amo souspire (Des Alyscamps,
    l'ame soupire); Lou Cabridan (Le Cabridan).
    Lemoine

Maxwell Davies, Peter   1934 -

Black Pentecost   54'
    solo mezzo-soprano & baritone   `18' 10'`
    +3 *3 *3 *3—4 3 2 0—tmp+5—cel—str   `8' 18'`
    Chester

Caroline Mathilde: Suite from Act I   25'
    =2 *2 *2 *2—2 2 2 0—tmp+2—hp—str
    Contents—A public square; Inside the castle; The queen's
    chamber; The royal chambers.
    Chester

Caroline Mathilde: Suite from Act II   30'
    female voices (a small chorus SA, or 2 soloists)
    =2 *2 *2 *2—2 2 2 0—tmp+2—hp—str
    Contents—A public square; The conspiracy; Court dance;
    Pas-de-deux; The arrest; The execution; Exile of Caroline
    Mathilde.
    Chester

Carolísima serenade   16'
    *1 1 *2 *1—1 1 1 0—1perc—str 1.1.1.1.1
    Schott

Chat Moss   6'
    2 1 1 1—0 2 0 0—tmp+2—str
    Intended for school orchestra.
    Chester

Concerto, trumpet   28'
    +3 *3 *3 *3—4 3 3 1—tmp+4—str
    Boosey

Concerto, violin   30'
    2 2 2 2—2 2 0 0—tmp—str
    Chester

Cross Lane Fair   14'
    solo: Northumbrian pipes & bodhran
    *2 2 2 *2—2 2 2 1—tmp+2—str
    Contents—Introduction; The fairground; Ghost train; Transition
    (the fairground); The bearded lady and the five-legged sheep;
    Transition (the fairground); The juggler; Transition (the
    fairground); Carousel.
    Chester

First fantasia on an In nomine of John Taverner   11'
    2 2 2 2—2 2 2 1—1perc—str
    Schott

Five Klee pictures   10'
    2 2 2 2—4 2 2 0—5perc—pf—str
    Boosey   1' 2' 2'
                                                                 2' 3'

Into the labyrinth   32'
    solo tenor
    2 2 2 2—2 2 0 0—str
    Chester

Jimmack the postie   9'
    =2 2 *2 2—2 2 2 0—tmp—str
    Chester

Ojai Festival overture   6'
    *2 *2 2 2—2 2 0 0—tmp—str
    Boosey

An Orkney wedding, with sunrise   13'
    solo bagpiper
    2 2 *2 2—4 2 2 1—tmp+4—str
    Piper marches through hall in traditional costume.
    Reduced version available: 2 2 *2 2—2 2 2 0—tmp+1—str.
    Boosey

Prolation   20'
    *3 *3 *3 *2—4 3 4 1—tmp+2—hp, cel—str
    Schott

St. Thomas Wake; foxtrot for orchestra on a pavan by John Bull   21'
*4 2 *4 *3—4 4 4 1—tmp+4—hp (with and without
amplification),
pf (out of tune)—str
The above total aggregate of musicians are divided into 2
ensembles: the main orchestra and a quasi-1930s dance band. The
distribution is as follows:
Main orchestra: *3 2 *3 *3—4 3 3 1—tmp+3—hp—str
Dance band: *1 0 1 0—0 1 1 0—1perc—pf—vn, vc, db
Boosey

Second fantasia on John Taverner's "In nomine"   40'
=2 *2 *2 *2—4 4 2 2—tmp+4—hp—str
Boosey

The shepherd's calendar   21'
chorus   treble soloist
1 1 5 1—6rec—0 1 1 0—11perc—handbells—str quartet
Treble soloist may be replaced by a soprano, or group of trebles
and/or sopranos, doubled by a flute if necessary.
Boosey

Sinfonia concertante   30'
1 1 1 1—1 0 0 0—tmp—str
Chester

Sinfonia for chamber orchestra   20'
1 1 1 1—1 0 0 0—str
Schott

Sinfonietta accademica   32'
*2 2 2 2—2 2 0 0—str
Chester

Sir Charles—his pavan   4'
=3 2 *3 *3—4 2 3 1—tmp+1—hp—str
Schott

A spell for green corn (The MacDonald dances)   20'
solo violin
*2 2 *2 *2—2 2 2 0—tmp+1—str
Tbn & 1perc are optional.
Chester

Stone litany; Runes from a house of the dead   20'
solo mezzo-soprano   4' 1' 3'
*2 0 =2 *2—2 2 2 1—tmp+5—hp, cel—str   2' 3' 7'
The text is Old Norse.
Boosey

Strathclyde concerto no.1   27'
solo oboe
*2 0 *2 0—2 0 0 0—tmp—str
Boosey

Strathclyde concerto no.2
  solo violoncello
  *2 2 *2 2—2 2 0 0—tmp—str
  Chester

32'

Strathclyde concerto no.3
  solo horn & trumpet
  +2 *2 *2 *2—tmp—str
  Boosey

29'

| 9' 6' 3' |
| 6' 5' |

Strathclyde concerto no.4
  clarinet solo
  *2 2 *1 *2—2 0 0 0—tmp—str
  Chester

30'

| 2' 9' 12' |
| 4' 3' |

Strathclyde concerto no.5
  solo violin & viola
  str
  Boosey

34'

| 15' 10' |
| 9' |

Strathclyde concerto no.6
  solo flute
  0 0 *2 1—2 2 0 0—tmp+1—str (without vn)
  Chester

25'

| 11' 7' 7' |

Strathclyde concerto no.7
  solo double bass
  +2 *2 *2 *2—2 0 0 0—str
  Boosey

21'

| 11' 10' |

Strathclyde concerto no.8
  solo bassoon
  =2 0 *2 *1—2 0 0 0—tmp—str
  Chester

25'

| 12' 6' 7' |

Strathclyde concerto no.9
  solos: pic, afl, Eh, scl, bcl, cbn
  str
  Chester

25'

Symphony [no.1]
  =3 *3 *3 *3—4 3 3 0—tmp+4—hp, cel—str
  Two of the flutists play piccolo.
  Boosey

55'

| 17' 10' |
| 15' 13' |

Symphony no.2
  =3 2 *3 *3—4 3 2 0—tmp+3—hp—str
  Boosey

55'

| 17' 16' |
| 9' 13' |

Symphony no.3
  =3 *3 *3 *3—4 3 3 1—tmp—str
  Boosey

58'

| 19' 9' 8' |
| 22' |

Symphony no.4
  =2 *2 *2 *2—2 2 0 0—tmp—str
  Boosey

42'

Symphony no.5   26'
  =3 *3 *3 *3—4 3 3 1—tmp+4—hp, cel—str
  Boosey

Threnody on a plainsong   3'
  0 2 0 2—2 2 0 0—tmp—str
  Chester

The turn of the tide
  children's chorus
  =2 2 *2 *2—2 2 3 1—tmp+4—hp, cel—str
  5 groups of young instrumentalists.
  Alternative scoring for chamber orchestra omits tbn, tuba, hp, cel.
  May be performed in a short version or a complete version.
  Chester

Veni sancte spiritus   20'
  solos SAB   chorus
  1 1 0 2—2 2 2 0—str
  Boosey

Worldes blis; motet for orchestra   37'
  *3 2 *3 *3—4 3 3 1—2tmp+5—2hp, org (or chamber org)—str
  Boosey

Mayuzumi, Toshirō   1929 -

Concertino, xylophone   13'
  2 2 2 2—asx—2 2 2 1—tmp+1—hp—str
  Peters

McBride, Robert   1911 -

Pumpkin-eater's little fugue   4'
  *2 2 2 2—4 2 3 1—tmp+2—str
  Optional: 2nd ob, 2nd bn, 3rd tbn.
  AMP

McCabe, John   1939 -

The lion, the witch and the wardrobe: Suite   15'
  1 1 2 1—1 2 1 0—tmp+2—pf—str
  Novello

McPhee, Colin   1900 - 1964

Tabuh-Tabuhan   19'
  *4 *3 *3 *3—4 3 3 1—6perc—hp, cel, 2pf—str   7' 6' 6'
  Two of the flutists double on piccolo.
  Contents—Ostinatos; Nocturne; Finale.
  AMP

Mecham, Kirke   1925 -

The jayhawk: Magic bird overture, op.43   8'
  *3 2 *3 2—4 3 3 1—tmp+2—opt pf—str
  Schirmer, G.

Melby, John   1941 -

Symphony no.1   41'
=3 *3 =4 *3—4 3 3 1—tmp+3—2hp—str
2nd cl doubles on contrabass cl; 4hn double on Wagner tubas;
3rd tp doubles on flugelhorn.
Merion

Mendelssohn, Fanny   1805 - 1847
see: Hensel, Fanny Mendelssohn, 1805-1847

Mendelssohn, Felix   1809 - 1847

Athalia: Overture   10'
2 2 2 2—2 2 3 0—tmp—hp—str
Breitkopf   Kalmus

Athalia: Kriegsmarsch der Priester (War march of the priests)   5'
2 2 2 2—2 2 3 1—tmp—str
Kalmus   Luck

Beautiful Melusina
see his: Märchen von der schönen Melusine

Calm sea and prosperous voyage
see his: Meeresstille und glückliche Fahrt

Capriccio brillant, op.22, B minor   12'
   solo piano
2 2 2 2—2 2 0 0—tmp—str
Breitkopf   Kalmus

Christus, op.97   21'
   chorus   solos STBB   8' 13'
2 2 2 2—2 2 3 0—tmp—org—str
Fragments of an unfinished oratorio, ed. Larry R. Todd.
Contents—Die Geburt Christi; Das Leiden Christi.
Breitkopf   Carus

Concerto, piano, no.1, op.25, G minor   21'
2 2 2 2—2 2 0 0—tmp—str   8' 7' 6'
Breitkopf   Kalmus

Concerto, piano, no.2, op.40, D minor   25'
2 2 2 2—2 2 0 0—tmp—str   11' 6' 8'
Breitkopf   Kalmus

Concerto, 2 pianos, A-flat major   30'
2 2 2 2—2 2 0 0—tmp—str   13' 8' 9'
Ed. Karl-Heinz Köhler.
Breitkopf   Kalmus

Concerto, 2 pianos, E major   28'
1 2 2 2—2 2 0 0—tmp—str   12' 8' 8'
Ed. Karl-Heinz Köhler.
Breitkopf   Kalmus

Concerto, violin, op.64, E minor   26'
   2 2 2 2—2 2 0 0—tmp—str   12' 8' 6'
   Breitkopf   *Kalmus*   *Peters*

Concerto, violin (posth.), D minor (1822)   22'
   str   9' 9' 4'
   Discovered and edited by Yehudi Menuhin for Peters; Breitkopf
   edition ed. R. Unger.
   Breitkopf   *Peters*

Elijah, op.70 (Elias)   131'
   chorus   solos SSATB (or more)   66' 65'
   2 2 2 2—4 2 3 1—tmp—org—str
   Breitkopf   *Kalmus*   *Peters*   *Schirmer, G.*

Die erste Walpurgisnacht, op.60   35'
   chorus   solos ATBB
   *3 2 2 2—2 2 3 0—tmp+2—str
   Breitkopf   *Kalmus*   *Peters*   *Schirmer, G.*

Fair Melusina
   see his: Märchen von der schönen Melusine

The Hebrides, op.26 (Fingal's Cave)   10'
   2 2 2 2—2 2 0 0—tmp—str
   Breitkopf   *Kalmus*

Heimkehr aus der Fremde, op.89 (Son and stranger)   7'
   2 2 2 2—2 2 0 0—str
   Breitkopf   *Kalmus*

Die Hochzeit des Camacho (Camacho's wedding): Overture   6'
   2 2 2 2—4 2 3 0—tmp—str
   Breitkopf

Hymne, op.96 (Lass', o Herr, mich Hülfe finden)   10'
   mezzo-soprano or alto solo   chorus
   2 2 2 2—2 2 0 0—tmp—str
   Breitkopf   *Kalmus*

Lauda Sion, op.73   28'
   chorus   solos SATB
   2 2 2 2—2 2 3 0—tmp—str
   Breitkopf   *Belwin*

Lobgesang, op.52 (Hymn of praise)   74'
   chorus   solos SST
   2 2 2 2—4 2 3 0—tmp—org—str
   A "symphony-cantata." The opening instrumental sections are
   separately published as *Symphony no.2.*
   Breitkopf   *Gray*   *Kalmus*   *Schirmer, G.*

Märchen von der schönen Melusine (Fair Melusina)   10'
   2 2 2 2—2 2 0 0—tmp—str
   Breitkopf   *Kalmus*

Meeresstille und glückliche Fahrt, op.27 (Calm sea and prosperous   12'
voyage)
   *3 2 2 *3—2 3 0 1—tmp—str
   Score calls for "contrafagotto e serpente," rendered above as
   contrabassoon and tuba.
   Breitkopf   *Kalmus*

Midsummernight's dream, op.21 & 61   62'
   women's chorus   2 solo sopranos
   2 2 2 2—2 3 3 1—tmp+2—str
   C. Fischer   *Gray*   *Kalmus*

Midsummernight's dream: Overture, op.21   12'
   2 2 2 2—2 2 0 1—tmp—str
   Breitkopf   *Kalmus*

Midsummernight's dream, op.61: Intermezzo   4'
   2 2 2 2—2 0 0 0—str
   Breitkopf   *Kalmus*

Midsummernight's dream, op.61: Nocturne   6'
   2 2 2 2—2 0 0 0—str
   Breitkopf   *Kalmus*

Midsummernight's dream, op.61: Scherzo   5'
   2 2 2 2—2 2 0 0—tmp—str
   Breitkopf   *Kalmus*

Midsummernight's dream, op.61: Wedding march   5'
   2 2 2 2—2 3 3 1—tmp+1—str
   Breitkopf   *Kalmus*

Octet, strings, E-flat major, op.20   33'
   4vn, 2va, 2vc
   Kalmus   13' 10'
                                    4' 6'

Overture for winds, op.24, C major   10'
   *2 2 +4 *3—2 basset horns—4 2 3 1—4perc
   2 of the clarinets are in F, the other 2 in C. An arrangement by
   Felix Greissle for contemporary band is published by G.
   Schirmer.
   Kalmus

Psalm 42, op.42 (Wie der Hirsch schreit; As pants the hart)   27'
   chorus   solo soprano   solo male quartet (TTBB)
   2 2 2 2—4 2 3 0—tmp—str
   4hn playing 2 real parts.
   Gray   *Kalmus*   *Schirmer, G.*

Psalm 95, op.46 (Kommt, lasst uns anbeten; O come let us sing)   27'
   chorus   solos SST
   2 2 2 2—2 2 3 0—tmp—str
   Breitkopf   *Broude, A.*   *EMS*   *Kalmus*

Psalm 98, op.91 (Singet dem Herrn ein neues Lied; Sing unto the   8'
Lord)
    double chorus
    2 2 2 2—2 2 3 0—tmp—hp, org—str
    Breitkopf   *EMS*   *Kalmus*

Psalm 114, op.51 (Da Israel aus Ägypten zog; When Israel out of   15'
Egypt came)
    chorus
    2 2 2 2—4 2 3 0—tmp—str
    Breitkopf   *Broude, A.*   *EMS*   *Kalmus*

Psalm 115, op.31 (Nicht unserm Namen, Herr; Not unto us, o Lord)   12'
    chorus   solos STBar
    2 2 2 2—2 0 0 0—str
    Also known as *Non nobis, domine.*
    Breitkopf   *EMS*   *Kalmus*

Rondo brillant, op.29   10'
    solo piano
    2 2 2 2—2 2 0 0—tmp—str
    Breitkopf   *C. Fischer*   *Kalmus*

Ruy Blas, op.95: Overture   7'
    2 2 2 2—4 2 3 0—tmp—str
    Breitkopf   *Kalmus*

St. Paul, op.36 (Paulus)   130'
    chorus   solos SATBB
    2 2 2 *3—4 2 3 1—tmp—org—str
    Score calls for "contrafagotto e serpente," rendered above as
    contrabassoon and tuba.
    Breitkopf   *Gray*   *Kalmus*   *Peters*

St. Paul: Overture   7'
    2 2 2 2—2 2 3 1—tmp—org—str
    Breitkopf   *Kalmus*

Sinfonia no.1, C major   10'
    str   3' 4' 3'
    Breitkopf   *Kalmus*

Sinfonia no.2, D major   9'
    str   3' 4' 2'
    Breitkopf   *Kalmus*

Sinfonia no.3, E minor   7'
    str   2' 3' 2'
    Breitkopf   *Kalmus*

Sinfonia no.4, C minor   8'
    str   3' 3' 2'
    Breitkopf   *Kalmus*

Sinfonia no.5, B-flat major   7'
    str   2' 2' 3'
    Breitkopf   *Kalmus*

Sinfonia no.6, E-flat major   11'
   str
   Breitkopf   *Kalmus*   3' 4' 4'

Sinfonia no.7, D minor   21'
   str
   Breitkopf   *Kalmus*   *Luck*   5' 5' 5' 6'

Sinfonia no.8, D major (string version)   31'
   str
   Breitkopf   *Deutscher*   *Kalmus*   10' 6' 5' 10'

Sinfonia no.8, D major (version with winds)   31'
   2 2 2 2—2 2 0 0—tmp—str
   Breitkopf   *Kalmus*   10' 6' 5' 10'

Sinfonia no.9, C major (Swiss)   32'
   str
   Breitkopf   *Deutscher*   *Kalmus*   11' 8' 3' 10'

Sinfonia no.10, B minor   11'
   str
   Breitkopf   *Kalmus*   *Luck*   2' 9'

Sinfonia no.11, F major   40'
   3perc (tmp+2) in one brief passage—str
   Breitkopf   *Deutscher*   *Kalmus*   12' 4' 8' 6' 10'

Sinfonia no.12, G minor   20'
   str
   Breitkopf   *Kalmus*   *Luck*   5' 7' 8'

Ein Sommernachtstraum
   see his: Midsummer night's Dream

Son and stranger
   see his: Heimkehr aus der Fremde, op.89

Symphony no.1, op.11, C minor   32'
   2 2 2 2—2 2 0 0—tmp—str
   Breitkopf   *Kalmus*   *Peters*   10' 7' 7' 8'

Symphony no.2 (from the Lobgesang, op.52)   27'
   2 2 2 2—4 2 3 0—tmp—str   12' 6' 9'
   This symphony consists of the opening instrumental sections of
   the symphony-cantata *Lobgesang*. Breitkopf previously offered
   also an edition of this symphony "with final chorus in the version
   shortened by Mendelssohn"; this requires chorus and solos SST
   in addition to the above instrumentation, but it may now be out of
   print. Total duration of that version: 37'
   Breitkopf   *Kalmus*

Symphony no.3, op.56, A minor (Scottish)   40'
   2 2 2 2—4 2 0 0—tmp—str   14' 5' 11' 10'
   Breitkopf   *Kalmus*

Symphony no.4, op.90, A major (Italian) — 27'
2 2 2 2—2 2 0 0—tmp—str — 8' 7' 6' 6'
Breitkopf   *Kalmus*

Symphony no.5, op.107, D major (Reformation) — 27'
2 2 2 *3—2 2 3 1—tmp—str — 10' 5' 4'
Score calls for "contrafagotto e serpente," rendered above as — 8'
contrabassoon and tuba.
Breitkopf   *Kalmus*

Trumpet overture, op.101 (Trompeten-Ouvertüre) — 8'
2 2 2 2—2 2 3 0—tmp—str
Kalmus

Tu es Petrus, op.111 — 10'
chorus
2 2 0 0—2 2 3 0—tmp—str

Verleih' uns Frieden (Dona nobis pacem) — 6'
chorus
2 0 2 2—str
Breitkopf   *Broude, A.*

Mennin, Peter   1923 - 1983
Canto — 8'
*3 *3 *3 2—4 3 3 1—tmp+3—str
C. Fischer

The Christmas story — 24'
chorus   solos ST
0 0 0 0—0 2 2 0—tmp—str
C. Fischer

Concertato (Moby Dick) — 11'
*3 *3 *3 2—4 3 3 1—tmp+3—str
C. Fischer

Symphony no.6 — 28'
*3 *3 *3 2—4 2 3 1—tmp+3—str — 8' 10'
C. Fischer — 10'

Symphony no.7 (Variation symphony) — 26'
*3 *3 *3 *3—4 3 3 1—tmp+3—str
C. Fischer

Menotti, Gian Carlo   1911 -
Concerto, piano — 33'
*3 2 +2 2—4 3 3 1—tmp+4—str — 14' 9'
Ricordi — 10'

Concerto, violin — 24'
*3 2 2 2—2 2 0 0—tmp+3—hp—str
Schirmer, G.

Sebastian: Suite
*1 *1 *2 1—2 2 2 0—tmp+2—hp, pf—str
Colombo

24'

2'	4'	2'
5'	3'	4'
		4'

Messiaen, Olivier 1908 - 1992

L'Ascension
3 *3 *3 3—4 3 3 1—tmp+2—str
Leduc

27'

6'	6'	5'
		10'

Chronochromie
*4 *3 =4 3—4 4 3 1—6perc—str
Leduc

30'

Couleurs de la cité céleste
solo piano
0 0 3 0—2 4 4 0—6perc
Leduc

18'

Hymne
3 *3 *3 3—4 3 3 0—tmp+2—str
Broude Bros.

12'

Les Offrandes oubliées
3 *3 *3 3—4 3 3 1—tmp+3—str
Durand

11'

Oiseaux exotiques
solo piano
*2 1 =4 1—2 1 0 0—7perc
Universal

14'

Trois Petites Liturgies de la présence divine
solo piano, solo ondes martenot   women's chorus
4perc—cel—str
If 18 voices, str 4.4.3.3.2; if 36 voices, str 8.8.6.6.4.
Durand

37'

10'	7'
	20'

Turangalîla-symphonie
solo piano, solo ondes martenot
*3 *3 *3 3—4 5 3 1—7perc—cel—str
Revised version 1990.
Durand

74'

7'	7' 5'
12'	5'
11'	4'
11'	5' 7'

Meyerbeer, Giacomo 1791 - 1864

Fackeltanz no.1 (Torch dance no.1)
*2 2 2 2—4 2 3 1—tmp+3—str
Bote & Bock   Kalmus

6'

Les Huguenots: Overture
*3 *3 2 2—4 4 3 1—tmp+1—str
C. Fischer   Kalmus

7'

Le Prophète: Ballet music — 16'
*3 2 2 4—4 4 3 1—tmp+3—str
Kalmus

Le Prophète: Coronation march — 4'
*3 2 2 4—4 4 3 1—tmp+3—str
Breitkopf   *Kalmus*

Miari, Giangiacomo   1929 -

Concerto, double bass — 12'
str
Zanibon

Miaskovsky, Nikolai   1881 - 1950

Sinfonietta, op.32, no.2 — 27'
str — 7' 13' 7'
Kalmus   *Russian*

Symphony no.21, op.51, F-sharp minor — 16'
*3 *3 *3 *3—4 3 3 1—tmp—str
Russian

Symphony no.22, op.54, B minor (Symphonic ballad) — 35'
*3 *3 *3 *3—4 3 3 1—tmp+3—str
Russian

Milhaud, Darius   1892 - 1974

Aubade — 18'
2 2 2 2—2 2 2 0—tmp+3—hp, cel—str
Heugel

Le Boeuf sur le toit, op.58 — 15'
*2 1 2 1—2 2 1 0—2perc—str
Eschig

Le Carnaval d'Aix; fantasy for piano & orchestra — 19'
*2 1 2 1—2 2 1 1—tmp+3—str
Heugel

Le Carnaval de Londres — 30'
*1 1 1 1—asx—0 1 1 0—2perc—hp—str
Salabert

Les Choëphores — 34'
chorus   solos SSA
*3 *3 *3 4—4 3 3 1—tmp+14—hp, cel—str
Three of the movements are scored for speaking chorus and
percussion only.
Heugel

Concertino de printemps, violin & orchestra — 9'
1 1 1 1—1 1 0 0—tmp+1—str
Salabert

Concertino d'hiver, trombone & strings   18'
   str
   AMP

Concerto, marimba & vibraphone, op.278   18'
   1 solo percussionist, alternating on marimba & vibraphone
   2 2 2 2—2 2 2 1—tmp+3—hp, cel—str
   May be performed with a piano soloist, rather than marimba and
   vibraphone, under the title *Suite concertante, piano & orchestra,
   op.278, q.v.*
   Enoch

Concerto, percussion & small orchestra   7'
   1 percussion soloist, using a large number of percussion
   instruments
   *2 0 2 0—0 1 1 0—str 2.2.2.2.1
   Universal

Concerto, piano, no.1   12'
   *2 2 =3 2—2 3 2 1—tmp+2—hp—str | 4' 4' 4' |
   Salabert

Concerto, piano, no.3   19'
   *2 2 2 2—2 2 2 1—tmp+2—str
   AMP

Concerto, violin, no.2   22'
   *2 *3 *3 2—2 2 2 1—tmp+1—str
   AMP

Concerto, violoncello, no.1   14'
   *2 *2 2 2—2 2 2 1—tmp+2—hp—str | 5' 6' 3' |
   Salabert

Concerto, violoncello, no.2   20'
   *2 2 2 2—2 2 2 1—tmp+2—hp—str
   AMP

Cortège funèbre   14'
   *2 1 2 1—0 2 2 1—2perc—hp—str
   Clarinets may be replaced by 2 alto saxophones.
   AMP

La Création du monde (The creation of the world)   16'
   2 1 2 1—asx—1 2 1 0—tmp+1—pf—2vn, vc, db | 4' 1' 3' |
   Eschig | 2' 4' 2' |

Les Funérailles de Phocion   8'
   *3 2 *3 *3—4 3 3 1—tmp+3—str
   Heugel

Murder of a great chief of state   4'
   2 2 2 2—4 3 3 1—tmp—str
   Eschig

Ouverture méditerranéene 5'
2 2 2 2—4 2 2 0—tmp+3—str
Heugel

Ouverture philharmonique 9'
*2 *2 *3 *3—4 3 3 1—tmp+3—hp—str
EMT

Saudades do Brazil 40'
*2 *2 2 2—2 2 2 0—tmp—str
Eschig

Scaramouche 9'
solo alto saxophone or clarinet | 3' 3' 3' |
*2 2 2 2—2 2 2 0—1perc—str
Salabert

Suite concertante, piano & orchestra, op.278 18'
2 2 2 2—2 2 2 1—tmp+3—hp, cel—str
May be performed using a marimba (and vibraphone) soloist
instead of piano, under the title *Concerto, marimba & vibraphone,
op.278*, q.v.
Enoch

Suite française 15'
*2 2 2 2—2 2 2 0—tmp+2—str | 2' 3' 2' |
Orchestrated by the composer from a work for concert band. | 5' 3' |
Contents—Normandie; Bretagne; Ile de France; Alsace-Lorraine;
Provence.
MCA

Suite provençale 16'
*2 *3 +2 2—4 3 3 1—tmp+3—str | 2' 2' 2' |
Salabert | 1' 2' 1' |
| 2' 4' |

Suite symphonique no.2 (Protée) 22'
*3 *3 *3 4—4 3 3 1—tmp+1—hp, cel—str
Drawn from incidental music to Claudel's *Protée*.
Durand

Symphonies for small orchestra

1. Le Printemps 4'
*2 1 1 0—hp—str quartet
Universal

2. Pastorale 4'
1 *1 0 1—vn, va, vc, db
Universal

3. Sérénade 3'
1 0 1 1—vn, va, vc, db
Universal

4. Dixtuor à cordes   6'
4vn, 2va, 2vc, 2db
Universal

5. Dixtuor d'instruments à vent   6'
*2 *2 *2 2—2 0 0 0
Universal

6. Sinfonie   6'
chorus *or* soloists SATB—ob, vc
Universal

Symphony no.1   29'
 *3 *3 *3 *3—4 3 3 1—tmp+3—hp—str | 8' 5' 9' 7' |
 Heugel

Symphony no.2   27'
 *3 *3 *3 *3—4 3 3 1—tmp+3—hp, cel—str | 6' 5' 8' |
 One clarinetist doubles on alto saxophone. | 3' 5' |
 Heugel

Symphony no.3   32'
 chorus | 5' 11' 4' |
 *3 *3 =4 *3—4 3 3 1—tmp+4—hp—str | 12' |
 Heugel

Symphony no.10   23'
 *3 *3 *3 *3—4 3 3 1—tmp+4—hp—str | 4' 9' 5' 5' |
 Heugel

Symphony no.11 (Romantique)   18'
 *3 *3 *3 *3—4 3 3 1—tmp+2—hp—str | 4' 9' 5' |
 Heugel

Symphony no.12 (Rurale)   17'
 *2 2 *3 2—2 2 3 1—tmp+5—hp—str
 Heugel

Moncayo (García), José Pablo   1912 - 1958
Huapango   7'
 *3 2 +3 2—4 3 3 1—tmp+3—hp—str
 EMM

Moniuszko, Stanisław   1819 - 1872
The countess (Hrabina): Overture   8'
 *2 2 2 2—4 2 3 1—tmp+4—str
 PWM

Halka: Mazur   4'
 *2 2 2 2—4 2 3 1—tmp+4—str
 PWM

Monn, Georg Matthias   1717 - 1750
Concerto, harpsichord (1746)
  see: Schoenberg, Arnold, 1874-1951
        Concerto, violoncello

Monroe, Ervin   1942 -
The amazing symphony orchestra   24'
  narrator   9' 8' 7'
  *3 *3 =3 *3—4 4 3 1—tmp+5—str
  30 excerpts from familiar orchestral works tied together with a
  narration describing the expressive powers of the orchestra.
  Playable with: *2 *2 2 2—4 2 3 1—tmp+3—str.
  Contents—Moods; Pictures; Dances
  Little Piper

Monteverdi, Claudio   1567 - 1643
Combattimento di Tancredi e Clorinda   20'
  solos SAT   3' 9' 3' 5'
  cnt—str
  Chester edition by G.F. Malipiero; Oxford edition by Denis
  Stevens.
  Chester   *Oxford*

Laudate dominum (Psalm 117)   4'
  chorus   solos SSTTB
  0 0 0 0—0 0 4 0—cnt—str (without va)
  Trombones are optional. Ed. Denis Arnold
  Eulenburg

Orfeo: Overture   5'
  *2 2 0 0—0 2 3 0—2hp (or lute & chittarone), org—str
  Arranger not identified.
  Kalmus

Orfeo: Sinfonie e ritornelli   9'
  str
  Arr. G.F. Malipiero.
  Kalmus   *Ricordi*

Orfeo: Toccata & ritornelli   4'
  *3 2 *3 2—4 3 4 0—1perc—hp—str
  4th tbn is optional; two of the flutists double on piccolo.
  Arr. Maurice Peress.
  Schirmer, G.

Vespro della beata vergine (ed. Walter Goehr, 1956)   106'
  chorus   solos SSATTBB   50'56'
  *2 0 0 *2—2rec (opt)—0 0 3 0—3 cornetti—org, positiv org, hpsd
  —va da gamba—str
  Universal

Vespro della beata vergine (ed. Jürgen Jürgens, 1977)   **106'**
   double chorus   solos SSATTBB   50'56'
   2rec/fl, 2bn—3cornetti (or tps & obs), 4tbn—org, hpsd, hp
   —chitarrone/lute—str
   A "practical Urtext" edition.
   Universal

Moore, Carman   1936 -

Gospel fuse   **23'**
   gospel quartet: S solo with accompanying trio SAA
   *3 *3 *4 *3—ssx—4 3 3 1—tmp+2—hp, pf, elec bass, elec org—str
   Pianist & organist do some improvisation.
   Peer

Moore, Douglas   1893 - 1969

Pageant of P.T. Barnum   **16'**
   *3 *3 *3 *3—4 3 3 1—tmp+6—hp, cel—str
   Contents—Boyhood at Bethel; Joice Heth, 161 year old Negress;
   General and Mrs. Tom Thumb; Jenny Lind; Circus parade.
   C. Fischer

Mosolov, Alexander   1900 - 1973

Iron foundry, op.19   **3'**
   *3 *3 *3 *3—4 3 3 1—tmp+5—str
   Kalmus   *Russian*

Moussorgsky, Modeste   1839 - 1881

see: Mussorgsky, Modest, 1839-1881

Mozart, Leopold   1719 - 1787

Concerto, trumpet, D major   **9'**
   0 0 0 0—2 0 0 0—cnt—str
   Kalmus   *Kneusslin*   *Schott*

Concerto, trumpet, G major   **14'**
   0 0 0 0—2 0 0 0—str   8' 6'
   Schott

Musikalische Schlittenfahrt (Musical sleigh-ride)   **25'**
   0 2 0 2—2 4 0 0—tmp+3—str
   Ed. Raimund Rüegge.
   Kunzelmann

Toy symphony
   see: Haydn, Franz Joseph
         Kindersymphonie

Mozart, Wolfgang Amadeus   1756 - 1791

In the works of this composer, the original K-number (from the first edition of the Köchel Verzeichnis) is primary; K-numbers with letters appended indicate the additions or renumberings of the 3rd and 6th editions (the 2nd, 4th, and 5th editions may be disregarded for scholarly purposes). In these listings, the original K-number is generally given first; the K-number from the 6th edition, if different, is second. If a third K-number is found, it is from the 3rd edition, and is included because some published editions (such as those of Bärenreiter) follow that numbering.

A questo seno—Or che il cielo, K.374   9'
  soprano recitative and rondo
  0 2 0 0—2 0 0 0—str
  Bärenreiter   *Breitkopf*

Abduction from the seraglio
  see his: Entführung aus dem Serail

Adagio, violin & orchestra, K.261, E major   5'
  2 0 0 0—2 0 0 0—str
  Written for the Concerto, violin, no.5, K.219.
  Breitkopf   *Kalmus*

Adagio & fugue, K.546, C minor   9'
  str
  Fugue originally for 2 pianos.
  Bärenreiter   *Breitkopf*   *Kalmus*

Ah, lo previdi—Ah, t'invola—Deh, non varcar, K.272   12'
  soprano recitative, aria, and cavatina
  0 2 0 0—2 0 0 0—str
  Bärenreiter   *Breitkopf*

Ah se in ciel, benigne stelle, K.538   7'
  soprano aria
  0 2 0 2—2 0 0 0—str
  Bärenreiter   *Breitkopf*   *Broude Bros.*   *Kalmus*

Alcandro, lo confesso—Non so d'onde viene, K.294   8'
  soprano recitative and aria
  2 0 2 2—2 0 0 0—str
  Bärenreiter   *Breitkopf*   *Kalmus*

Alcandro, lo confesso—Non so d'onde viene, K.512   9'
  bass recitative and aria
  1 2 0 2—2 0 0 0—str
  Bärenreiter   *Breitkopf*

Alma dei creatoris, K.277 (272a)   5'
  chorus   solos SAT
  0 0 0 1—0 0 3 0—org—str
  Kalmus   *Peters*

Alma grande e nobil core, K.578   4'
  soprano aria
  0 2 0 2—0 2 0 0—str
Bärenreiter   *Breitkopf*   *Kalmus*

Andante, flute & orchestra, K.315 (285e), C major   6'
  0 2 0 0—2 0 0 0—str
Bärenreiter   *Breitkopf*   *Kalmus*

Apollo et Hyacinthus, K.38: Prelude   3'
  0 2 0 0—2 0 0 0—str
Bärenreiter   *Kalmus*

Ave verum corpus, K.618   4'
  chorus
  org—str
Bärenreiter   *Breitkopf*   *Kalmus*

Un bacio di mano, K.541   2'
  bass arietta
  1 2 0 2—2 0 0 0—str
Bärenreiter   *Breitkopf*   *Kalmus*

Basta, vincesti—Ah non lasciarmi, K.486a (295a)   7'
  soprano recitative and aria
  2 0 0 2—2 0 0 0—str
Bärenreiter   *Breitkopf*

Bastien und Bastienne, K.50 (46b): Overture   2'
  0 2 0 0—2 0 0 0—str
Breitkopf   *Kalmus*

Bella mia fiamma—Resta, oh cara, K.528   10'
  soprano recitative and aria
  1 2 0 2—2 0 0 0—str
Bärenreiter   *Breitkopf*   *Kalmus*

Benedictus sit deus, K.117 (66a)   9'
  chorus   soprano solo
  2 0 0 0—2 2 0 0—tmp—org—str
Kalmus

Betulia liberata, K.118 (74c)   145'
  solos SSSATB   chorus
  2 2 0 2—4 2 0 0—str
Bärenreiter

Betulia liberata, K.118 (74c): Overture   5'
  0 2 0 2—4 2 0 0—str
Breitkopf   *Kalmus*

Cassation no.1, K.63, G major   24'
  0 2 0 0—2 0 0 0—str
Breitkopf   *Kalmus*

Cassation no.2, K.99 (63a), B-flat major   17'
  0 2 0 0—2 0 0 0—str
  Breitkopf   *Kalmus*

Ch'io mi scordi di te—Non temer, K.505   7'
  soprano scene and rondo
  0 0 2 2—2 0 0 0—obligato pf—str
  Bärenreiter   *Breitkopf*   *Kalmus*

Chi sà, chi sà, qual sia, K.582   3'
  soprano aria
  0 0 2 2—2 0 0 0—str
  Bärenreiter   *Breitkopf*   *Kalmus*

Church sonatas
  see his: Sonatas, organ & orchestra

Clarice cara mia sposa, K.256   2'
  tenor aria
  0 2 0 0—2 0 0 0—str
  Bärenreiter   *Kalmus*

La clemenza di Tito, K.621: Overture   5'
  2 2 2 2—2 2 0 0—tmp—str
  Bärenreiter   *Breitkopf*   *Kalmus*

Con ossequio, con rispetto, K.210   3'
  tenor aria
  0 2 0 0—2 0 0 0—str
  Bärenreiter   *Breitkopf*

Concerto, bassoon, K.191 (186e), B-flat major   20'
  0 2 0 0—2 0 0 0—str   8' 6' 6'
  Bärenreiter   *Breitkopf*   *Kalmus*

Concerto, bassoon, no.2, K.Anh.C14.03, B-flat major   19'
  0 2 0 0—2 2 0 0—tmp—str   7' 7' 5'
  Ed. Max Seiffert. Probably spurious; perhaps composed by
  François Devienne (1759-1803).
  Peters

Concerto, clarinet, K.622, A major   25'
  2 0 0 2—2 0 0 0—str   12' 7' 6'
  The Bärenreiter score shows also what is believed to be
  the original version for basset-clarinet.
  Bärenreiter   *Breitkopf*   *Kalmus*

Concerto, flute, no.1, K.313 (285c), G major   25'
  2 2 0 0—2 0 0 0—str   10' 9' 6'
  The 2 orchestral flutes are used in the second movement only,
  where the oboes are tacet. (Probably in Mozart's time the oboists
  doubled on flute.)
  Bärenreiter   *Breitkopf*   *Kalmus*

Concerto, flute, no.2, K.314 (285d), D major   **21'**
0 2 0 0—2 0 0 0—str   8' 7' 6'
A reworking by the composer of the oboe concerto in C major,
K.314 (285d).
Bärenreiter   Breitkopf   Kalmus

Concerto, flute & harp, K.299 (297c), C major   **30'**
0 2 0 0—2 0 0 0—str   11' 9' 10'
Bärenreiter   Breitkopf   Kalmus

Concerto, horn, no.1, K.412 (386b), D major   **9'**
0 2 0 2—str   5' 4'
Bärenreiter   Breitkopf   Kalmus

Concerto, horn, no.2, K.417, E-flat major   **16'**
0 2 0 0—2 0 0 0—str   8' 4' 4'
Bärenreiter   Breitkopf   Kalmus

Concerto, horn, no.3, K.447, E-flat major   **16'**
0 0 2 2—str   7' 5' 4'
Bärenreiter   Breitkopf   Kalmus

Concerto, horn, no.4, K.495, E-flat major   **16'**
0 2 0 0—2 0 0 0—str   9' 4' 3'
Bärenreiter   Breitkopf   Kalmus

Concerto, oboe, K.314 (285d), C major   **21'**
0 2 0 0—2 0 0 0—str   8' 7' 6'
The original version of the D major flute concerto, K.314 (285d).
Bärenreiter ed. Franz Giegling; Boosey ed. Bernhard
Paumgartner.
Bärenreiter   Boosey

Concerto, piano, no.1, K.37, F major   **17'**
0 2 0 0—2 0 0 0—str
Based on sonata movements by H.F. Raupach & L. Honauer.
Breitkopf

Concerto, piano, no.2, K.39, B-flat major   **15'**
0 2 0 0—2 0 0 0—str
Based on sonata movements by H.F. Raupach & J. Schobert.
Breitkopf

Concerto, piano, no.3, K.40, D major   **13'**
0 2 0 0—2 0 0 0—str
Based on sonata movements by L. Honauer, J.G. Eckard, & C.P.E.
Bach.
Breitkopf   Kalmus

Concerto, piano, no.4, K.41, G major   **15'**
2 0 0 0—2 0 0 0—str
Based on sonata movements by L. Honauer & H.F. Raupach.
Breitkopf

Concerto, piano, K.107 (21b) no.1, D major   13'
    str (without va)
    After Johann Christian Bach's piano sonata, op.5, no.2.

Concerto, piano, K.107 (21b) no.2, G major   10'
    str (without va)
    After Johann Christian Bach's piano sonata, op.5, no.3.

Concerto, piano, K.107 (21b) no.3, E-flat major   9'
    str (without va)
    After Johann Christian Bach's piano sonata, op.5, no.4.

Concerto, piano, no.5, K.175, D major   21'
    0 2 0 0—2 2 0 0—tmp—str   7' 9' 5'
    Breitkopf   *Kalmus*

Concerto, piano, no.6, K.238, B-flat major   12'
    2 2 0 0—2 0 0 0—str   6' 3' 3'
    The 2 flutes are used in the second movement only, where the
    oboes are tacet. (Probably in Mozart's time the oboists doubled
    on flute.)
    Bärenreiter   *Breitkopf*   *Kalmus*

Concerto, 3 pianos, no.7, K.242, F major (Lodron)   20'
    0 2 0 0—2 0 0 0—str   8' 7' 5'
    A version by the composer for 2 pianos is also available; use the
    same orchestral materials.
    Bärenreiter   *Breitkopf*   *Kalmus*

Concerto, piano, no.8, K.246, C major (Lützow)   20'
    0 2 0 0—2 0 0 0—str   7' 7' 6'
    Bärenreiter   *Breitkopf*   *Kalmus*

Concerto, piano, no.9, K.271, E-flat major (Jeunehomme)   32'
    0 2 0 0—2 0 0 0—str   11' 12'
    Bärenreiter   *Breitkopf*   *Kalmus*   9'

Concerto, 2 pianos, no.10, K.365 (316a), E-flat major   24'
    0 2 2 2—2 2 0 0—tmp—str   11' 7' 6'
    The parts for 2cl, 2tp, and tmp were added later, and may be
    considered optional.
    Bärenreiter   *Breitkopf*   *Kalmus*

Concerto, piano, no.11, K.413 (387a), F major   23'
    0 2 0 2—2 0 0 0—str   10' 8' 5'
    Peters edition lists the wind parts as optional.
    Bärenreiter   *Breitkopf*   *Kalmus*   *Peters*

Concerto, piano, no.12, K.414 (385p), A major   25'
    0 2 0 0—2 0 0 0—str   10' 9' 6'
    Peters edition lists the wind parts as optional.
    Bärenreiter   *Breitkopf*   *Kalmus*   *Peters*

Concerto, piano, no.13, K.415 (387b), C major   26'
  0 2 0 2—2 2 0 0—tmp—str   10' 8' 8'
  Peters edition lists the wind and timpani parts as optional.
Bärenreiter   *Breitkopf*   *Kalmus*   *Peters*

Concerto, piano, no.14, K.449, E-flat major   21'
  0 2 0 0—2 0 0 0—str   8' 7' 6'
  Peters edition lists the wind parts as optional.
Bärenreiter   *Breitkopf*   *Kalmus*   *Peters*

Concerto, piano, no.15, K.450, B-flat major   25'
  1 2 0 2—2 0 0 0—str   11' 6' 8'
Bärenreiter   *Breitkopf*   *Kalmus*

Concerto, piano, no.16, K.451, D major   25'
  1 2 0 2—2 2 0 0—tmp—str   10' 8' 7'
Bärenreiter   *Breitkopf*   *Kalmus*

Concerto, piano, no.17, K.453, G major   30'
  1 2 0 2—2 0 0 0—str   12' 10' 8'
Bärenreiter   *Breitkopf*   *Kalmus*

Concerto, piano, no.18, K.456, B-flat major (Paradis)   30'
  1 2 0 2—2 0 0 0—str   12' 11' 7'
Bärenreiter   *Breitkopf*   *Kalmus*

Concerto, piano, no.19, K.459, F major   28'
  1 2 0 2—2 0 0 0—str   13' 8' 7'
Bärenreiter   *Breitkopf*   *Kalmus*

Concerto, piano, no.20, K.466, D minor   30'
  1 2 0 2—2 2 0 0—tmp—str   13' 9' 8'
Bärenreiter   *Breitkopf*   *Kalmus*

Concerto, piano, no.21, K.467, C major   29'
  1 2 0 2—2 2 0 0—tmp—str   13' 9' 7'
Bärenreiter   *Breitkopf*   *Kalmus*

Concerto, piano, no.22, K.482, E-flat major   34'
  1 0 2 2—2 2 0 0—tmp—str   14' 8' 12'
Bärenreiter   *Breitkopf*   *Kalmus*

Concerto, piano, no.23, K.488, A major   26'
  1 0 2 2—2 0 0 0—str   11' 7' 8'
Bärenreiter   *Breitkopf*   *Kalmus*

Concerto, piano, no.24, K.491, C minor   31'
  1 2 2 2—2 2 0 0—tmp—str   14' 8' 9'
Bärenreiter   *Breitkopf*   *Kalmus*

Concerto, piano, no.25, K.503, C major   30'
  1 2 0 2—2 2 0 0—tmp—str   15' 7' 8'
  A reprint of the Bärenreiter score, together with historical and
  analytical essays, is published by Norton (ed. Joseph Kerman).
Bärenreiter   *Breitkopf*   *Kalmus*

Concerto, piano, no.26, K.537, D major (Coronation)   28'
  1 2 0 2—2 2 0 0—tmp—str   13' 6' 9'
Bärenreiter   *Breitkopf*   *Kalmus*

Concerto, piano, no.27, K.595, B-flat major   32'
  1 2 0 2—2 0 0 0—str   15' 8' 9'
Bärenreiter   *Breitkopf*   *Kalmus*

Concerto, piano, no.28, K.382, D major
  see his: Concert-rondo, piano & orchestra, K.382, D major

Concerto, 2 pianos, K.242, F major
  See note to no.7 in the series of piano concertos above.

Concerto, 2 pianos, K.365 (316a), E-flat major
  Listed as no.10 in the series of piano concertos above.

Concerto, 3 pianos, K.242, F major
  Listed as no.7 in the series of piano concertos above.

Concerto, violin, no.1, K.207, B-flat major   21'
  0 2 0 0—2 0 0 0—str   7' 8' 6'
Bärenreiter   *Breitkopf*   *Kalmus*

Concerto, violin, no.2, K.211, D major   21'
  0 2 0 0—2 0 0 0—str   8' 9' 4'
Bärenreiter   *Breitkopf*   *Kalmus*

Concerto, violin, no.3, K.216, G major (Strassburg)   24'
  2 2 0 0—2 0 0 0—str   9' 9' 6'
  The 2 flutes are used in the second movement only, where the
  oboes are tacet. (Probably in Mozart's time the oboists doubled
  on flute.)
Bärenreiter   *Breitkopf*   *Kalmus*   *Schott*

Concerto, violin, no.4, K.218, D major   26'
  0 2 0 0—2 0 0 0—str   10' 9' 7'
Bärenreiter   *Breitkopf*   *Kalmus*

Concerto, violin, no.5, K.219, A major (Turkish)   31'
  0 2 0 0—2 0 0 0—str   10' 12' 9'
  For an alternative slow movement, see his Adagio, violin &
  orchestra, K.261.
Bärenreiter   *Breitkopf*   *Kalmus*

Concerto, violin, no.6, K.268 (Anh.C 14.04), E-flat major   24'
  1 2 0 2—2 0 0 0—str   12' 7' 5'
  Authenticity doubtful.
Breitkopf   *Kalmus*

Concerto, violin, no.7, K.271a (271i), D major   29'
  0 2 0 0—2 0 0 0—str   10' 10' 9'
  Substantially by Mozart, though the earliest extant source (the
  autograph is lost) shows signs of alterations made in the early
  19th century.
Breitkopf   *Kalmus*

Concertone, 2 violins & orchestra, K.190 (186e), C major   28'
   0 2 0 0—2 2 0 0—str
     Bärenreiter   *Breitkopf*   *Kalmus* | 8' 11' 9' |

Concert-rondo, horn & orchestra, K.371, E-flat major   5'
   0 2 0 0—2 0 0 0—str
   Completed by Waldemar Spiess.
     Breitkopf   *Universal*

Concert-rondo, piano & orchestra, K.382, D major   8'
   1 2 0 0—2 2 0 0—tmp—str
   Composed as a new finale for Mozart's Concerto, piano, no.5,
   K.175. Sometimes listed as piano concerto no.28.
     Breitkopf   *Kalmus*

Contradances, K.267 (271c)   7'
   1 2 0 1—2 0 0 0—str (without va)
   4 dances.
     Breitkopf   *Kalmus*

Contradance, K.534 (Das Donnerwetter)   2'
   0 2 0 0—2 0 0 0—str (without va)

Contradance, K.535 (La Battaille)   2'
   *1 0 2 1—0 1 0 0—1perc—str (without va)
     Breitkopf

Contradance, K.587 (Der Sieg vom Helden Koburg)   2'
   1 1 0 1—0 2 0 0—str (without va)
     Breitkopf

Contradances, K.603   4'
   *1 2 0 2—2 2 0 0—tmp—str
   2 dances. | 2' 2' |
     Bärenreiter

Contradances, K.609   8'
   1 0 0 0—1perc—str (without va)
   5 dances.
     Breitkopf   *Kalmus*

Contradance, K.610, G major (Les Filles malicieuses)   2'
   2 0 0 0—2 0 0 0—str (without va)

Così dunque—Aspri rimorsi atroci, K.432 (421a)   5'
   bass recitative and aria
   2 2 0 2—2 0 0 0—str
     Bärenreiter   *Breitkopf*   *Kalmus*

Così fan tutte, K.588: Overture   5'
   2 2 2 2—2 2 0 0—tmp—str
     Breitkopf   *Kalmus*

Davidde penitente, K.469   47'
   chorus   solos SST
   1 2 1 2—2 2 3 0—tmp—str
   Most of the music adapted from the Mass, K.427 (417a).
   Bärenreiter   *Breitkopf*   *Kalmus*

Deutsche Tänze
   see his: German dances

Dite almeno in che mancai, K.479   5'
   solo quartet: soprano, tenor, 2 basses
   0 2 2 2—2 0 0 0—str
   Bärenreiter   *Breitkopf*

Divertimento [no.1] K.113, E-flat major   14'
   0 *4 2 2—2 0 0 0—str | 4' 5' 2' 3' |
   2 of the oboists play English horn.
   Alternative version: 0 0 2 0—2 0 0 0—str.
   Breitkopf   *Kalmus*

Divertimento [no.2] K.131, D major   31'
   1 1 0 1—4 0 0 0—str | 5' 6' 6' |
   Breitkopf   *Kalmus* | 3' 4' 7' |

Divertimenti, K.136, 137, 138 (125a, 125b, 125c)   34'
   str | 13' 9' |
   Each divertimento has three movements. | 12' |
   Bärenreiter   *Kalmus*   *Peters*

Divertimento, K.166 (159d), E-flat major   13'
   0 *4 2 2—2 0 0 0
   2 of the oboists play English horn.
   Breitkopf

Divertimento, K.186 (159b), B-flat major   12'
   0 *4 2 2—2 0 0 0
   2 of the oboists play English horn.
   Breitkopf

Divertimento, K.188 (240b), C major   10'
   2 0 0 0—0 5 0 0—tmp
   Breitkopf

Divertimento [no.7] K.205 (167a), D major   21'
   0 0 0 1—2 0 0 0—str (without vn II) | 5' 3' 6' |
   Breitkopf   *Kalmus* | 3' 4' |

Divertimento [no.10] K.247, F major (First Lodron)   31'
   0 0 0 0—2 0 0 0—str | 8' 4' 4' |
   Breitkopf   *Kalmus* | 6' 3' 6' |

Divertimento [no.11] K.251, D major   26'
   0 1 0 0—2 0 0 0—str | 5' 4' 4' |
   Breitkopf   *Kalmus* | 5' 6' 2' |

Divertimento [no.15] K.287 (271h), B-flat major (Second Lodron) 39'
  0 0 0 0—2 0 0 0—str
  Breitkopf   *Kalmus*

| 9' 8' 3' |
| 8' 4' 7' |

Divertimento [no.17] K.334 (320b), D major (Robinig von
Rottenfeld) 43'
  0 0 0 0—2 0 0 0—str
  Breitkopf   *Kalmus*

| 7' 8' 5' |
| 6' 8' 9' |

Dixit et Magnificat, K.193 (186g) 17'
  chorus   solos STB
  0 0 0 1—0 2 3 0—tmp—org—str
  Schirmer, G.

Don Giovanni, K.527: Overture 7'
  2 2 2 2—2 2 0 0—tmp—str
  In the opera, the overture elides with the first number, thus
  necessitating a special ending for concert performance. The
  Bärenreiter edition gives the composer's concert-ending;
  Breitkopf gives a concert-ending by Johann André. Either version
  may be had from Kalmus (specify which is desired).
  Bärenreiter   *Breitkopf*   *Kalmus*

Don Giovanni, K.527: Overture (arr. Busoni) 9'
  2 2 2 2—2 2 3 0—tmp—str
  Concert-ending by Busoni, using material from Act I and from
  the closing scene of the opera.
  Kalmus

Die Entführung aus dem Serail, K.384 (The abduction from the
seraglio): Overture 6'
  *1 2 2 2—2 2 0 0—tmp+3—str
  In the opera the overture elides with the first number,
  necessitating a concert ending. Breitkopf offers three versions,
  with concert endings by Mozart, Johann André, and Feruccio
  Busoni respectively; Kalmus offers the latter two versions only.
  Bärenreiter   *Breitkopf*   *Kalmus*

Die Entführung aus dem Serail: Marsch der Janitscharen (Janissary
march) 2'
  2 0 2 2—2 2 0 0—2perc
  Bärenreiter

Ergo interest—Quaere superna, K.143 (73a) 6'
  soprano recitative and aria
  str, org
  Breitkopf

Exsultate jubilate, K.165 (158a) 17'
  soprano solo
  0 2 0 0—2 0 0 0—org—str
  Bärenreiter   *Breitkopf*   *Kalmus*

| 5' 1' 8' 3' |

La finta giardiniera, K.196: Overture   5'
   0 2 0 0—2 0 0 0—str   3' 2'
   See also his: Symphony, K.196/121, D major.
   Bärenreiter   *Breitkopf*   *Kalmus*

La finta semplice, K.51 (46a): Overture   6'
   2 2 0 2—2 0 0 0—str   3' 2' 1'
   Drawn from the composer's Symphony no.7, K.45, D major.
   Bärenreiter

German dances, K.509   17'
   *3 2 2 2—2 2 0 0—tmp—str (without va)
   6 dances.
   Breitkopf   *Kalmus*

German dances, K.536   12'
   *3 2 0 2—2 2 0 0—tmp—str (without va)   2' 2' 2'
   6 dances.   2' 2' 2'
   Breitkopf

German dances, K.567   14'
   *1 2 2 2—2 2 0 0—tmp+1—str (without va)
   6 dances.
   Breitkopf   *Kalmus*   *Luck*

German dances, K.571   16'
   *2 2 2 2—2 2 0 0—tmp+2—str (without va)
   6 dances.
   Breitkopf   *Kalmus*

German dances, K.586   26'
   *3 2 2 2—2 2 0 0—tmp—str (without va)
   12 dances.
   Breitkopf   *Kalmus*

German dances, K.600   15'
   *2 2 2 2—2 2 0 0—tmp—str (without va)
   6 dances. Includes *Der Kanarienvogel.*
   Breitkopf   *Kalmus*

German dances, K.602   10'
   *2 2 2 2—2 2 0 0—tmp—lira [da braccio?]—str (without va)
   4 dances. Includes *Der Leiermann.*
   Breitkopf   *Kalmus*

German dances, K.605   6'
   *2 2 0 2—2 2 0 0—2 posthorns—tmp—str (without va)
   Posthorns probably played by horn players. Timpanist covers
   sleighbells (=pitched jingles).
   3 dances. Trio of no.3 is the famous *Schlittenfahrt* (Sleighride).
   Breitkopf   *Kalmus*

Gloria from the Twelfth mass, K.Anh.C 1.04   4'
chorus
0 2 0 2—2 2 0 0—tmp—str
Spurious; is probably by Wenzel Müller.
Kalmus   *Schirmer, G.*

Ich möchte wohl der Kaiser sein, K.539   3'
bass solo
*1 2 0 2—2 0 0 0—3perc—str
Bärenreiter

Idomeneo, K.366: Overture (original version)   5'
2 2 2 2—2 2 0 0—tmp—cnt—str
No continuo in Breitkopf or Kalmus edition.
Bärenreiter   *Breitkopf*   *Kalmus*

Idomeneo, K.366: Overture (with concert-ending)   5'
2 2 2 2—2 2 0 0—tmp—cnt—str
Concert-ending by Carl Reinecke.
Breitkopf   *Kalmus*

Idomeneo: Ballet music   15'
2 2 0 2—2 2 0 0—tmp—str
Bärenreiter   *Breitkopf*   *Kalmus*

The impresario, K.486
see his: Der Schauspieldirektor

Inter natos mulierum, K.72 (74f)   6'
chorus
str, org
Bärenreiter   *Breitkopf*

Io ti lascio, K.621a   4'
bass aria
str
Bärenreiter   *Kalmus*

Eine kleine Nachtmusik (Serenade, K.525)   16'
str   5' 5' 2' 4'
Bärenreiter   *Breitkopf*   *Kalmus*   *Peters*

Kommet her, ihr frechen Sünder, K.146 (317b)   5'
solo soprano
org—str
Breitkopf

Kyrie, K.341 (368a)   6'
chorus
2 2 2 2—4 2 0 0—tmp—org—str
Bärenreiter   *Luck*

Laut verkünde unsre Freude, K.623   14'
male chorus   solos TTB
1 2 0 0—2 0 0 0—str

Litaniae de venerabili altaris sacramento, K.125, B-flat major 42'
   chorus   solos SATB
   2 2 0 0—2 2 0 0—org—str
   Bärenreiter   *Gray*   *Kalmus*

Litaniae de venerabili altaris sacramento, K.243, E-flat major 34'
   chorus   solos SATB
   2 2 0 2—2 0 3 0—org—str
   Breitkopf   *Kalmus*

Litaniae lauretanae, K.109 (74e), B-flat major (Litaniae de beata 10'
virgine)
   chorus   solos SATB
   org—str
   Kalmus

Litaniae lauretanae, K.195 (186d), D major 27'
   chorus   solos SATB   6' 7' 3'
   0 2 0 0—2 0 0 0—org—str   5' 6'
   Breitkopf   *Kalmus*

Lucio Silla, K.135: Overture 9'
   0 2 0 0—2 2 0 0—tmp—str
   Bärenreiter   *Breitkopf*   *Kalmus*

Ma che vi fece—Sperai vicino il lido, K.368 9'
   soprano recitative and aria
   2 0 0 2—2 0 0 0—str
   Bärenreiter   *Breitkopf*

The magic flute, K.620
   see his: Die Zauberflöte

Mandina amabile, K.480 5'
   trio for soprano, tenor, & bass
   2 2 2 2—2 0 0 0—str
   Bärenreiter   *Breitkopf*   *Kalmus*

March, K.62, D major 4'
   0 2 0 0—2 2 0 0—tmp—str
   Believed to have been intended as an introduction to the
   Serenade, K.100 (62a).

March, K.189 (167b), D major 5'
   2 0 0 0—2 2 0 0—str (without va)
   Used as introduction to the Serenade, K.185 (167a).
   Kalmus

March, K.214, C major 4'
   0 2 0 0—2 2 0 0—str

March, K.215 (213b), D major 4'
   0 2 0 0—2 2 0 0—str
   Used as introduction to the Serenade, K.204 (213a).
   Breitkopf

March, K.237 (189c), D major   4'
   0 2 0 2—2 2 0 0—str (without va)
   Used as introduction to the Serenade, K.203 (189b).
   Breitkopf

March, K.249, D major   4'
   0 2 0 2—2 2 0 0—str
   Used as introduction to the Serenade, K.250 (248b), "Haffner."
   Breitkopf   *Kalmus*

Marches, K.335 (320a), D major   8'
   2 2 0 0—2 2 0 0—str   4' 4'
   Two marches used as the introduction and conclusion
   respectively of Serenade no.9, K.320. Oboes appear in the 1st
   march only; flutes only in the 2nd march.
   Breitkopf

Marches, K.408 (383e, 385a, 383F)   12'
   2 2 0 2—2 2 0 0—tmp—str   5' 3' 4'
   Contents—No.1, K.383e, C major; No.2, K.385a, D major; No.3,
   K.383F, C major.
   No.2, K.385a, was originally intended as the introduction to the
   serenade which became Symphony no.35 (Haffner).
   Breitkopf   *Kalmus*

The marriage of Figaro, K.492
   see his: Le nozze di Figaro

Masonic funeral music
   see his: Maurische Trauermusik

Mass
   see also: Missa brevis

Mass, K.66, C major (Dominicus)   41'
   chorus   solos SATB
   2 2 0 0—2 4 0 0—tmp—org—str
   Probably in Mozart's time 2 woodwind players alternated on
   flute and oboe.
   Bärenreiter   *Breitkopf*   *Kalmus*

Mass, K.139 (114a), C minor (Waisenhaus)   45'
   chorus   solos SATB
   0 2 0 0—0 4 3 0—tmp—org—str
   Breitkopf

Mass, K.167, C major (Trinity)   31'
   chorus
   0 2 0 0—0 2 2 0—tmp—org—str (without va)
   Trombone parts were originally for trumpet in C basso.
   Bärenreiter   *Breitkopf*   *Kalmus*

Mass, K.257, C major (Credo-Messe)   30'
   chorus   solos SATB
   0 2 0 0—0 2 3 0—tmp—org—str (without va)
   Breitkopf

Mass, K.258, C major (Spaur-Messe; Piccolomini)   17'
  chorus   solos SATB | 2' 3' 6' |
  0 0 0 0—0 2 0 0—tmp—org—str (without va) | 1' 2' 3' |
  Kalmus

Mass, K.262 (246a), C major (Longa)   30'
  chorus   solos SATB | 3' 6' 13' |
  0 2 0 0—2 2 0 0—org—str (without va) | 1' 3' 4' |
  Breitkopf

Mass, K.317, C major (Coronation)   24'
  chorus   solos SATB | 3' 4' 6' |
  0 2 0 1—2 2 3 0—tmp—org—str (without va) | 2' 3' 6' |
  Bärenreiter   Breitkopf   Kalmus

Mass, K.337, C major (Missa solemnis; Aulica)   22'
  chorus   solos SATB | 2' 4' 5' |
  0 2 0 2—0 2 3 0—tmp—org—str (without va) | 5' 6' |
  Bärenreiter   Kalmus

Mass, K.427 (417a), C minor (The great)
  This work was unfinished at its first performance in 1783.
  Various attempts to complete it are listed below in chronological
  order.

Mass, K.427 (417a), C minor (Schmitt)   75'
  chorus   solos S Mz T B
  2 2 2 2—2 2 4 0—tmp—org—str
  Ed. Alois Schmitt, 1901.
  Mozart's unfinished score does not constitute a liturgically
  complete mass; Schmitt's version renders it complete by
  substituting movements from other works of Mozart: K.139, 262,
  322, 333, 337, and K.Anh.21 (=K.Anh.A2=K.93c; this movement,
  wrongly attributed to Mozart, is actually by Ernst Eberlin).
  Schmitt adapted the opening *Kyrie* to form the final *Agnus dei*.
  Breitkopf   Kalmus

Mass, K.427 (417a), C minor (Robbins Landon)   60'
  chorus   solos SSTB
  1 2 0 2—2 2 3 0—tmp—org—str
  Ed. H.C. Robbins Landon, 1956.
  Individual movements have been reconstructed by the editor, but,
  unlike the Alois Schmitt edition, no movements have been added
  to make the work liturgically complete.
  Peters

Mass, K.427 (417a), C minor (Holl & Köhler)   55'
  chorus   solos SSATB
  1 2 0 2—2 2 3 0—tmp—org—str
  Ed. Monika Holl in collaboration with Karl-Heinz Köhler,
  1987. *Credo in unum deum, Et incarnatus est, Sanctus,* and
  Hosanna reconstructed and completed by Helmut Eder. No
  movements have been added to make the work liturgically
  complete.
  Bärenreiter

Die Maurerfreude, K.471 (Sehen, wie dem starren Forscherauge die Natur) — 7'
  tenor solo   male chorus
  0 2 1 0—2 0 0 0—str
  Breitkopf   *Kalmus*

Mauerische Trauermusik, K.477 (479a) (Masonic funeral music) — 6'
  0 2 1 *1—basset horn—2 0 0 0—str
  2 additional basset horns may be substituted for the 2 horns.
  Bärenreiter   *Breitkopf*   *Kalmus*

Mentre ti lascio, o figlia, K.513 — 8'
  bass aria
  1 0 2 2—2 0 0 0—str
  Bärenreiter   *Breitkopf*   *Kalmus*

Mia speranza—Ah, non sai, K.416 — 10'
  soprano scene and rondo
  0 2 0 2—2 0 0 0—str
  Bärenreiter   *Breitkopf*   *Kalmus*

Misera, dove son—Ah, non son io che parlo, K.369 — 7'
  soprano recitative and aria
  2 0 0 0—2 0 0 0—str
  Bärenreiter   *Breitkopf*   *Kalmus*

Misericordias domini, K.222 (205a) — 6'
  chorus
  org—str
  Bärenreiter   *Kalmus*

Misero, o sogno—Aura, che intorno spiri, K.431 (425b) — 10'
  tenor recitative and aria
  2 0 0 2—2 0 0 0—str
  Bärenreiter   *Breitkopf*   *Kalmus*

Missa brevis, K.49 (47d), G major — 18'
  chorus   solos SATB
  org—str
  Bärenreiter   *Breitkopf*   *Kalmus*

Missa brevis, K.65 (61a), D minor — 15'
  chorus   solos SATB
  0 0 0 0—0 0 3 0—org—str (without va)
  Breitkopf   *Kalmus*

Missa brevis, K.140 (Anh.C1.12), G major — 15'
  chorus   solos SATB
  org—str (without va)
  Breitkopf edition supplies parts for the *colla parte* trombones.
  Bärenreiter   *Breitkopf*

Missa brevis, K.192 (186f), F major — 25'
  chorus   solos SATB
  org—str (without va)
  Bärenreiter   *Breitkopf*   *Kalmus*   *Schirmer, G.*

Missa brevis, K.194 (186h), D major 22'
 chorus solos SATB
 org—str (without va)
 Bärenreiter *Breitkopf* *Kalmus*

Missa brevis, K.220 (196b), C major (Spatzenmesse) 20'
 chorus solos SATB
 0 0 0 0—0 2 0 0—tmp—org—str (without va)
 Breitkopf *Kalmus*

Missa brevis, K.259, C major (Orgelsolo) 14'
 chorus solos SATB
 0 0 0 0—0 2 0 0—tmp—org—str (without va)
 Breitkopf *Kalmus* *Peters*

Missa brevis, K.275 (272b), B-flat major 20'
 chorus solos SATB 2' 3' 5'
 org—str (without va) 1' 3' 6'
 Breitkopf *Kalmus* *Peters*

Mitridate, K.87 (74a): Overture 5'
 2 2 0 0—2 0 0 0—str
 Breitkopf

Ein musikalischer Spass, K.522 (A musical joke) 18'
 0 0 0 0—2 0 0 0—str 3' 5' 6' 4'
 Breitkopf *Kalmus* *Peters*

Nehmt meinen Dank, K.383 4'
 soprano solo
 1 1 0 1—str
 Bärenreiter *Breitkopf* *Kalmus*

No, no, che non sei capace, K.419 4'
 soprano aria
 0 2 0 0—2 2 0 0—tmp—str
 Bärenreiter *Breitkopf* *Kalmus*

Notturno, K.286 (269a)
 see his: Serenade no.8, K.286 (269a), D major

Le nozze di Figaro, K.492: Overture 4'
 2 2 2 2—2 2 0 0—tmp—str
 Bärenreiter *Breitkopf* *Kalmus*

Nun liebes Weibchen, ziehst mit mir, K.625 (592a) 2'
 duet for soprano and bass
 1 2 0 2—2 0 0 0—str
 Arrangement by Mozart of a duet with keyboard accompaniment;
 the original possibly by Mozart, but more likely not.
 Kalmus

Ombra felice—Io ti lascio, K.255 8'
 alto recitative and aria
 0 2 0 0—2 0 0 0—str
 Bärenreiter *Breitkopf* *Kalmus* *Kneusslin*

Overture, K.311a (Anh.C11.05), B-flat major (Paris)   10'
   2 2 2 2—2 2 0 0—tmp—str
   Authenticity doubtful.
   Peters

Per pietà, non ricercate, K.420   6'
   tenor aria
   0 0 2 2—2 0 0 0—str
   Bärenreiter   *Breitkopf*   *Kalmus*

Per questa bella mano, K.612   8'
   bass aria with obligato double bass
   1 2 0 2—2 0 0 0—str
   Bärenreiter   *Breitkopf*   *Doblinger*   *Kalmus*

Les Petits Riens, K.Anh.10 (299b)   22'
   2 2 2 2—2 2 0 0—tmp—str
   Previously believed to be spurious; now considered authentic.
   Bärenreiter   *Breitkopf*   *Kalmus*

Popoli di Tessagua—Io non chiedo, eterni dei, K.316 (300b)   11'
   soprano recitative and aria
   0 1 0 1—2 0 0 0—str
   Bärenreiter   *Breitkopf*

Il re pastore, K.208: Overture   4'
   0 2 0 0—2 2 0 0—str
   Breitkopf   *Kalmus*

Regina coeli, K.108 (74d), C major   15'
   chorus   solo soprano
   2 2 0 0—2 2 0 0—tmp—org—str
   May be out of print.
   Breitkopf

Regina coeli, K.127, B-flat major   15'
   chorus   solo soprano
   2 2 0 0—2 0 0 0—org—str
   Breitkopf

Regina coeli, K.276 (321b), C major   7'
   chorus   solos SATB
   0 2 0 0—0 2 0 0—tmp—org—str (without va)
   Breitkopf   *Kalmus*

Requiem, K.626 (completed by Franz Süssmayr)   55'
   chorus   solos SATB
   0 0 0 2—2 basset hn—0 2 3 0—tmp—org—str
   Basset horns may be replaced by clarinets.
   Completed by Mozart's pupil Franz Süssmayr.
   Bärenreiter   *Breitkopf*   *Kalmus*   *Peters*

Requiem, K.626 (instrumentation by Franz Beyer)　　　　　55'
　　chorus　　solos SATB
　　0 0 0 2—2 basset hn—0 2 3 0—tmp—org—str
　　More than a mere reorchestration. Beyer left the voice parts
　　unchanged from the traditional Süssmayr version, but attempted
　　to improve the rest of the texture and voice-leading. Though both
　　Eulenburg (1971) and Kunzelmann (1979) editions are by Beyer,
　　and are very similar, there are a few differences in detail.
　　Eulenburg　　　*Kunzelmann*

Requiem, K.626 (completed by Richard Maunder)　　　　　44'
　　chorus　　solos SATB
　　0 0 0 2—2 basset hn—0 2 3 0—tmp—org—str
　　Starts from Mozart's autograph, using none of Süssmayr's
　　contributions. Orchestration reworked throughout. *Lacrymosa*
　　has new continuation which leads to a completion of Mozart's
　　sketch for an *Amen* fugue. (Süssmayr's *Sanctus* and *Benedictus*
　　are included as appendices.)
　　Oxford

Rivolgete a lui lo sguardo, K.584　　　　　　　　　　　5'
　　bass aria
　　0 2 0 2—0 2 0 0—tmp—str
　　Breitkopf

Rondo, horn & orchestra, K.371, E-flat major
　　see his: Concert-rondo, horn & orchestra, K.371, E-flat major

Rondo, piano & orchestra, K.382, D major
　　see his: Concert-rondo, piano & orchestra, K.382, D major

Rondo, violin & orchestra, K.269 (261a), B-flat major　　　8'
　　0 2 0 0—2 0 0 0—str
　　Breitkopf　　　*Kalmus*

Rondo, violin & orchestra, K.373, C major　　　　　　　4'
　　0 2 0 0—2 0 0 0—str
　　Breitkopf　　　*Kalmus*

Sancta Maria, K.273　　　　　　　　　　　　　　　4'
　　chorus
　　org—str
　　Bärenreiter　　　*Kalmus*

Scande coeli limina, K.34 (Offertorium in festo St. Benedicti)　5'
　　chorus　　solo soprano
　　0 0 0 0—0 2 0 0—tmp—org—str (without va)
　　Breitkopf

Der Schauspieldirektor, K.486 (The impresario): Overture　　5'
　　2 2 2 2—2 2 0 0—tmp—str
　　Breitkopf　　　*Kalmus*

Se al labbro mio non credi, K.295
9'
  tenor aria
  2 2 0 2—2 0 0 0—str
  Bärenreiter   *Breitkopf*

Serenade no.1, K.100 (62a), D major
37'
  2 2 0 0—2 2 0 0—str
  The 2 flutes are used in a single movement only, where the oboes
  are tacet. (Probably in Mozart's time the oboists doubled on
  flute.) The March, K.62, is believed to have been intended as an
  introduction to this serenade.
  Breitkopf   *Kalmus*

Serenade no.2, K.101 (250a), F major
6'
  1 2 0 1—2 0 0 0—str (without va)
1' 2' 2' 1'
  Four contradances.
  Breitkopf   *Kalmus*

Serenade no.3, K.185 (167a), D major (Andretter)
37'
  2 2 0 0—2 2 0 0—str
6' 8' 3' 3' 6' 5' 6'
  The March, K189 (167b), is used as an introduction to this
  serenade.
  Breitkopf   *Kalmus*

Serenade no.4, K.203 (189b), D major
41'
  solo violin
  2 2 0 1—2 2 0 0—str
7' 6' 3' 6' 4' 5' 5' 5'
  Solo violin printed in ripieno part. The March, K.237 (189c), is
  used as an introduction to this serenade.
  Breitkopf   *Kalmus*

Serenade no.5, K.204 (213a), D major
39'
  2 2 0 1—2 2 0 0—str
6' 8' 6' 3' 6' 4' 6'
  The March, K.215 (213b), is used as an introduction to this
  serenade. Movements 1, 5, 6, & 7 are used as the Symphony, K.204
  (231a).
  Breitkopf   *Kalmus*

Serenade no.6, K.239, D major (Serenata notturna)
13'
  solo string quartet
  tmp—str
4' 4' 5'
  Bärenreiter   *Breitkopf*   *Kalmus*

Serenade no.7, K.250 (248b), D major (Haffner)
58'
  2 2 0 2—2 2 0 0—str
7' 12' 4' 8' 6' 8' 6' 7'
  The March, K.249, is used as an introduction to this serenade.
  Movements 1, 5, 6, 7 & 8 are used as the Symphony, K.250 (248b).
  The latter is *not*, however, the "Haffner" Symphony (K.385).
  Breitkopf   *Kalmus*

Serenade no.8, K.286 (269a), D major (Notturno)
19'
  4 orchestras, each consisting of 2hn & str
9' 3' 7'
  Breitkopf   *Kalmus*

Serenade no.9, K.320, D major (Posthorn)   40'
  *2 2 0 2—2 2 0 0—posthorn—tmp—str   8' 4' 8'
  Posthorn may be covered by one of the other brass players. The   6' 5' 5'
  two marches, K.335 (320a) *q.v.*, are used as introduction and   4'
  conclusion, respectively, to this serenade. Movements 1, 5 & 7 are
  used as Symphony, K.320.
  Breitkopf   *Kalmus*

Serenade no.10, K.361 (370a), B-flat major (Gran partita)   43'
  0 2 2 *3—2 basset hn—4hn   7' 9' 5'
  Double bass may substitute for contrabassoon.   5' 5' 9'
  Breitkopf   *Kalmus*   3'

Serenade no.11, K.375, E-flat major   24'
  0 2 2 2—2 0 0 0   8' 4' 6'
  An earlier version without oboes also exists.   3' 3'
  Breitkopf   *Kalmus*

Serenade no.12, K.388 (384a), C minor   21'
  0 2 2 2—2 0 0 0   6' 4' 4' 7'
  Kalmus

Serenade K.525, G major
  see his: (Eine) kleine Nachtmusik

Si mostra la sorte, K.209   3'
  tenor aria
  2 0 0 0—2 0 0 0—str
  Bärenreiter   *Breitkopf*

Sinfonia concertante, K.297b (Anh. C14.01), E-flat major   32'
  solos: oboe, clarinet, horn, bassoon   14' 9' 9'
  0 2 0 0—2 0 0 0—str
  The authenticity of this work is in question; it is believed to be an
  arrangement by another hand of a lost Mozart composition for
  flute, oboe, horn, and bassoon.
  Breitkopf   *Kalmus*

Sinfonia concertante, K.297b (Anh. I/9), E-flat major (Levin   30'
reconstruction)   10' 7'
  solos: flute, oboe, horn, bassoon   13'
  0 2 0 0—2 0 0 0—str
  A reconstruction by Robert D. Levin of the hypothetical original.
  The music of the solo quartet has been adapted to the changed
  instrumentation, and the orchestral tuttis and accompaniments
  have been recomposed. The score includes the solo quartet parts
  of the "standard version" (K.Anh. C14.01) for comparison.
  Bärenreiter

Sinfonia concertante, K.364 (320d), E-flat major   30'
  solo violin, solo viola   13' 11'
  0 2 0 0—2 0 0 0—str   6'
  Solo viola part originally notated in D major, with the intention
  that the instrument be tuned a half-step higher than normal.
  Bärenreiter   *Breitkopf*   *Kalmus*

Il sogno di Scipione, K.126
see his: Symphony, K.141a, D major

Sonatas, organ & orchestra
Under the title *Church sonatas*, Kalmus offers the following
collections:
Eight church sonatas (nos.1-8)
Five church sonatas (nos. 9, 10, 11, 13, 15)
Two church sonatas (nos. 12, 14)

Sonata, organ & orchestra, no.1, K.67 (41h), E-flat major   3'
    str (without va)
    Bärenreiter   *Mercury*

Sonata, organ & orchestra, no.2, K.68 (41i), B-flat major   2'
    str (without va)
    Bärenreiter   *Kalmus*   *Mercury*

Sonata, organ & orchestra, no.3, K.69 (41k), D major   2'
    str (without va)
    Bärenreiter   *Mercury*

Sonata, organ & orchestra, no.4, K.144 (124a), D major   2'
    str (without va)
    Bärenreiter   *Mercury*

Sonata, organ & orchestra, no.5, K.145 (124b), F major   2'
    str (without va)
    Bärenreiter   *Mercury*

Sonata, organ & orchestra, no.6, K.212, B-flat major   2'
    str (without va)
    Bärenreiter   *Mercury*

Sonata, organ & orchestra, no.7, K.224 (241a), F major   3'
    str (without va)
    Bärenreiter   *Mercury*

Sonata, organ & orchestra, no.8, K.225 (241b), A major   3'
    str (without va)
    Bärenreiter   *Mercury*

Sonata, organ & orchestra, no.9, K.244, F major   6'
    str (without va)
    Bärenreiter   *Kalmus*   *Mercury*

Sonata, organ & orchestra, no.10, K.245, D major   3'
    str (without va)
    Bärenreiter   *Kalmus*   *Mercury*

Sonata, organ & orchestra, no.11, K.274 (271d), G major   3'
    str (without va)
    Bärenreiter   *Mercury*

Sonata, organ & orchestra, no.12, K.278 (271e), C major   4'
    0 2 0 0—0 2 0 0—tmp—str (without va)
    Bärenreiter   *Kalmus*   *Mercury*

Sonata, organ & orchestra, no.13, K.328 (317c), C major   5'
   str (without va)
   Bärenreiter   *Kalmus*   *Mercury*

Sonata, organ & orchestra, no.14, K.329 (317a), C major   4'
   0 2 0 0—2 2 0 0—tmp—str (without va)
   Believed to have some connection with the Mass, K.317
   (Coronation).
   Bärenreiter   *Mercury*

Sonata, organ & orchestra, no.15, K.336 (336d), C major   5'
   str (without va)
   Bärenreiter   *Kalmus*   *Mercury*

Sonata, organ & orchestra, no.16, K.241, G major   2'
   str (without va)
   Bärenreiter   *Mercury*

Sonata, organ & orchestra, no.17, K.263, C major   3'
   0 0 0 0—0 2 0 0—str (without va)
   Bärenreiter   *Mercury*

Symphonies
   The published symphonies that are not a part of the established
   canon (nos.1-41) are inserted below in the order of the K-numbers.

Symphony no.1, K.16, E-flat major   13'
   0 2 0 0—2 0 0 0—str   6' 5' 2'
   Breitkopf   *Kalmus*

Symphony no.2, K.17 (Anh.C 11.02), B-flat major   12'
   0 2 0 0—2 0 0 0—str
   Authenticity doubtful; perhaps by Leopold Mozart.
   Breitkopf   *Kalmus*

Symphony no.3, K.18 (Anh.A 51), E-flat major   12'
   0 0 2 1—2 0 0 0—str
   Though published under Mozart's name, this is actually
   Symphony op.7, no.6, by Karl Friedrich Abel.
   Breitkopf   *Kalmus*

Symphony no.4, K.19, D major   7'
   0 2 0 0—2 0 0 0—str   2' 3' 2'
   Breitkopf   *Kalmus*

Symphony, K.Anh.223 (19a), F major   11'
   0 2 0 1—2 0 0 0—cnt—str   5' 4' 2'
   Bärenreiter

Symphony no.5, K.22, B-flat major   7'
   0 2 0 0—2 0 0 0—str   3' 3' 1'
   Breitkopf   *Kalmus*

Symphony no.6, K.43, F major   17'
   0 2 0 0—2 0 0 0—str   5' 6' 2' 4'
   Breitkopf   *Kalmus*

Symphony no.7, K.45, D major
0 2 0 0—2 2 0 0—tmp—str
This symphony was later revised for use as the overture to *La finta semplice*, K.51 (46a), *q.v.*
Bärenreiter   Kalmus

12'
3' 2' 4' 3'

Symphony no.8, K.48, D major
0 2 0 0—2 2 0 0—tmp—str
Kalmus

15'
4' 4' 4' 3'

Symphony no.9, K.73, C major
0 2 0 0—2 2 0 0—tmp—str
Bärenreiter   Breitkopf   Kalmus

12'
3' 4' 3' 2'

Symphony no.10, K.74, G major
0 2 0 0—2 0 0 0—str
Breitkopf   Kalmus

8'
3' 3' 2'

Symphony no.11, K.84 (73q), D major
0 2 0 0—2 0 0 0—str
Attribution uncertain.
Breitkopf   Kalmus

10'
4' 2' 4'

Symphony no.12, K.110 (75b), G major
0 2 0 0—2 0 0 0—str
Bärenreiter   Breitkopf   Kalmus

17'

Symphony, K.111/120 (111a), D major
2 2 0 0—2 2 0 0—tmp—str
Overture and no.1 from *Ascanio in Alba* with added finale.

6'

Symphony no.13, K.112, F major
0 2 0 0—2 0 0 0—str
Bärenreiter   Breitkopf   Kalmus

17'

Symphony no.14, K.114, A major
2 2 0 0—2 0 0 0—str
The 2 oboes are used in the second movement only, where the flutes are tacet. (Probably in Mozart's time the flutists doubled on oboe.)
Bärenreiter   Breitkopf   Kalmus

19'
7' 5' 3' 4'

Symphony no.15, K.124, G major
0 2 0 0—2 0 0 0—str
Bärenreiter   Breitkopf   Kalmus

16'
5' 5' 3' 3'

Symphony no.16, K.128, C major
0 2 0 0—2 0 0 0—str
Bärenreiter   Breitkopf   Kalmus

13'
4' 5' 4'

Symphony no.17, K.129, G major
0 2 0 0—2 0 0 0—str
Bärenreiter   Breitkopf   Kalmus

16'
6' 6' 4'

Symphony no.18, K.130, F major
2 0 0 0—4 0 0 0—str
Bärenreiter   Breitkopf   Kalmus

18'
5' 4' 2' 7'

Symphony no.19, K.132, E-flat major   17'

  0 2 0 0—4 0 0 0—str   5' 3' 5' 4'

  An alternative slow movement exists for this symphony.

  Bärenreiter   *Breitkopf*   *Kalmus*

Symphony no.20, K.133, D major   19'

  1 2 0 0—2 2 0 0—str   7' 4' 3' 5'

  Flute plays only in the second movement, during which the other winds are tacet. In Mozart's time one of the oboists would have doubled on flute. This work probably originally called for timpani.

  Bärenreiter   *Breitkopf*   *Kalmus*

Symphony no.21, K.134, A major   20'

  2 0 0 0—2 0 0 0—str   6' 5' 4' 5'

  Bärenreiter   *Breitkopf*   *Kalmus*

Symphony, K.141a, D major (Il sogno di Scipione)   8'

  2 2 0 0—2 2 0 0—tmp—str   3' 3' 2'

  The first two movements are the overture to *Il sogno di Scipione*, K.126. The finale, K.161/163, was added later.

  Bärenreiter   *Kalmus*

Symphony no.22, K.162, C major   10'

  0 2 0 0—2 2 0 0—str   4' 4' 2'

  This work probably originally called for timpani.

  Bärenreiter   *Breitkopf*   *Kalmus*

Symphony no.23, K.181 (162b), D major   9'

  0 2 0 0—2 2 0 0—str   5' 2' 2'

  This work probably originally called for timpani.

  Bärenreiter   *Breitkopf*   *Kalmus*

Symphony no.24, K.182 (173dA; 166c), B-flat major   9'

  2 2 0 0—2 0 0 0—str   4' 2' 3'

  Flutes play only in the second movement, during which the oboes are tacet. In Mozart's time the oboists would have doubled on flute.

  Bärenreiter   *Breitkopf*   *Kalmus*

Symphony no.25, K.183 (173dB), G minor   24'

  0 2 0 2—4 0 0 0—str   10' 5' 2'

  Bärenreiter   *Breitkopf*   *Kalmus*   7'

Symphony no.26, K.184 (161a; 166a), E-flat major   8'

  2 2 0 2—2 2 0 0—str   3' 3' 2'

  This work probably originally called for timpani.

  Bärenreiter   *Breitkopf*   *Kalmus*

Symphony, K.196/121, D major (La finta giardiniera)   8'

  0 2 0 0—2 0 0 0—str   3' 2' 3'

  The first two movements are the overture to *La finta giardiniera*, K.196. The finale, K.121 (207a) was added later.

  Bärenreiter   *Kalmus*

Symphony no.27, K.199 (161b; 162a), G major
2 0 0 0—2 0 0 0—str
Bärenreiter   *Breitkopf*   *Kalmus*

18'
6' 6' 6'

Symphony no.28, K.200 (189k; 173e), C major
0 2 0 0—2 2 0 0—str
This work originally called for timpani; an autograph copy of the timpani part once existed, but has been lost.
Bärenreiter   *Breitkopf*   *Kalmus*

23'
7' 6' 4' 6'

Symphony no.29, K.201 (186a), A major
0 2 0 0—2 0 0 0—str
Bärenreiter   *Breitkopf*   *Kalmus*   *Peters*

28'
10' 7' 4'
7'

Symphony no.30, K.202 (186b), D major
0 2 0 0—2 2 0 0—str
This work probably originally called for timpani.
Bärenreiter   *Breitkopf*   *Kalmus*

16'
5' 3' 4' 4'

Symphony, K.204 (213a), D major
2 2 0 1—2 2 0 0—str
Movements 1, 5, 6, & 7 of the Serenade K.204 (213a).
Bärenreiter

22'
6' 6' 4' 6'

Symphony, K.250 (248b), D major
2 2 0 2—2 2 0 0—tmp—str
Movements 1, 5, 6, 7 & 8 of the Serenade, K.250 (248b) (*Haffner*).
Bärenreiter

34'
7' 6' 8'
6' 7'

Symphony no.31, K.297 (300a), D major (Paris)
2 2 2 2—2 2 0 0—tmp—str
Mozart revised this work and substituted an entirely new (6/8) slow movement. Most editions give the revised version; Bärenreiter includes the original (3/4) slow movement as an alternative. The Bärenreiter score (but not the parts) also includes the original version of the 1st movement, the differences of which are interesting, but not particularly striking.
Bärenreiter   *Breitkopf*   *Kalmus*

17'
7' 6' 4'

Symphony no.32, K.318, G major
2 2 0 2—4 2 0 0—tmp—str
Bärenreiter   *Breitkopf*   *Kalmus*

9'
3' 4' 2'

Symphony no.33, K.319, B-flat major
0 2 0 2—2 0 0 0—str
Bärenreiter   *Breitkopf*   *Kalmus*

20'
7' 5' 3' 5'

Symphony, K.320, D major
0 2 0 2—2 2 0 0—tmp—str
Movements 1, 5 & 7 of the Serenade K.320 (*Posthorn*).
Bärenreiter

15'

Symphony no.34, K.338, C major   **21'**
0 2 0 2—2 2 0 0—tmp—str   7' 6' 8'
This work lacks a minuet; see the following entry, which includes a minuet.
Bärenreiter   *Breitkopf*   *Kalmus*

Symphony no.34, K.338, C major (with minuet K.409)   **25'**
2 2 0 2—2 2 0 0—tmp—str   7' 6' 4' 8'
Includes the minuet K.409 (383f), which some authorities believe was intended for this symphony. The minuet requires 2 flutes in addition to the instrumentation of K.338.
Alkor   *Bärenreiter*

Symphony no.35, K.385, D major (Haffner)   **18'**
2 2 2 2—2 2 0 0—tmp—str   5' 6' 3' 4'
Originally intended as a serenade, with the March, K.408/2 (385a) and another minuet, which has been lost. Not related to the "Haffner" Serenade, K.250 (248b).
Bärenreiter   *Breitkopf*   *Kalmus*

Symphony no.36, K.425, C major (Linz)   **26'**
0 2 0 2—2 2 0 0—tmp—str   9' 7' 4' 6'
Bärenreiter   *Breitkopf*   *Kalmus*

Symphony no.37, K.444 (425a), G major   **15'**
1 2 0 0—2 0 0 0—str
Only the adagio introduction is by Mozart; the remainder of this symphony is by Michael Haydn (P.16). Breitkopf and Doblinger publish this work under Michael Haydn's name.
Kalmus

Symphony no.38, K.504, D major (Prague)   **22'**
2 2 0 2—2 2 0 0—tmp—str   9' 8' 5'
Bärenreiter   *Breitkopf*   *Kalmus*   *Peters*

Symphony no.39, K.543, E-flat major   **29'**
1 0 2 2—2 2 0 0—tmp—str   10' 10'
    4' 5'
Bärenreiter   *Breitkopf*   *Kalmus*   *Peters*

Symphony no.40, K.550, G minor   **35'**
1 2 2 2—2 0 0 0—str   7' 14' 5'
    9'
A critical edition of the score with historical and analytical essays is available from Norton.
An earlier version of the work, without the clarinets, is also available from Bärenreiter.
Bärenreiter   *Breitkopf*   *Kalmus*   *Peters*

Symphony no.41, K.551, C major (Jupiter)   **29'**
1 2 0 2—2 2 0 0—tmp—str   9' 9' 4' 7'
Bärenreiter   *Breitkopf*   *Kalmus*   *Peters*

Tantum ergo, K.142 (Anh.C3.04; 186d), B-flat major   5'
   chorus   solo soprano
   0 0 0 0—0 2 0 0—org—str
   Actually by Friedrich Zachau, arranged by Mozart, and with a
   newly composed *Amen.*
   Bärenreiter   *Kalmus*

Tantum ergo, K.197 (Anh.186e), D major   4'
   chorus
   0 0 0 0—0 2 0 0—tmp—org—str
   Bärenreiter   *Kalmus*

Te deum laudamus, K.141 (66b)   11'
   chorus
   0 0 0 1—0 4 0 0—tmp—org—str (without va)
   Ed. Hellmut Federhofer. The Bärenreiter score, following the
   original performance material with Leopold Mozart's
   handwritten annotations, calls for 2 *clarini* (typical Mozart
   trumpet parts) and 2 *trombe* (somewhat lower than the *clarini*,
   though still in a trumpet range). The lost timpani part has been
   reconstructed by the editor.
   Parts for the Kalmus edition—clearly spurious—distribute the
   clarini and *trombe* music among pairs of oboes, bassoons and
   trumpets, although the score shows only the strings. Breitkopf
   and Peters catalogs list only chorus, organ and strings.
   Bärenreiter

Thamos, König in Ägypten, K.345 (336a): Zwischenaktmusiken   19'
   0 2 0 2—2 2 0 0—tmp—str | 7' 5' 3' 4' |
   Bärenreiter   *Kalmus*

Titus
   see his: La clemenza di Tito

Turkish march, from Piano sonata in A major, K.331 (300i)   4'
   *3 2 2 2—2 2 0 0—3perc—str
   Arr. Prosper Pascal.
   Luck

Vado, ma dove, o dei, K.583   4'
   soprano aria
   0 0 2 2—2 0 0 0—str
   Bärenreiter   *Breitkopf*   *Kalmus*

Veni sancte spiritus, K.47   4'
   chorus   solos SATB
   0 2 0 0—2 2 0 0—tmp—org—str
   Kalmus

Venite populi, K.260 (248a) (Offertorium de venerabili sacramento)   5'
   double chorus
   0 0 0 1—0 0 3 0—org—str (without violas)
   Bärenreiter

Vesperae de dominica, K.321   35'
  chorus   solos SATB
  0 0 0 1—0 2 3 0—tmp—org—str (without va)
  Bärenreiter   *Breitkopf*   *Kalmus*

| 5' 8' 5' |
| 5' 6' 6' |

Vesperae solennes de confessor, K.339   26'
  chorus   solos SATB
  0 0 0 1—0 2 3 0—tmp—org—str (without va)
  Bärenreiter   *Breitkopf*   *Kalmus*

| 4' 4' 4' |
| 4' 5' 5' |

Voi avete un cor fedele, K.217   6'
  soprano aria
  0 2 0 0—2 0 0 0—str
  Bärenreiter   *Breitkopf*

Vorrei spiegarvi, oh Dio, K.418   6'
  soprano aria
  0 2 0 2—2 0 0 0—str
  Bärenreiter   *Breitkopf*   *Kalmus*

Die Zauberflöte, K.620 (The magic flute): Overture   7'
  2 2 2 2—2 2 3 0—tmp—str
  Bärenreiter   *Breitkopf*   *Kalmus*   *Ricordi*

Müller, Wenzel   1767 - 1835
Gloria from the Twelfth mass
  see: Mozart, Wolfgang Amadeus, 1756-1791
         Gloria from the Twelfth mass, K.Anh.C 1.04

Musgrave, Thea   1928 -
Chamber concerto no.1   10'
  0 1 1 1—1 1 1 0—vn, va, vc
  Chester

Concerto for orchestra   20'
  *3 *3 *3 *3—4 3 3 1—tmp+3—hp—str
  Chester

Concerto, viola
  1 *2 *2 1—3 2 1 0—1perc—hp—str 14.14.9.8.6
  Novello

Night music, for chamber orchestra   18'
  *1 2 0 1—2 0 0 0—str
  Minimum strings 6.4.3.2.1; max 10.8.6.4.3.
  Chester

Peripeteia   15'
  *2 2 2 2—4 2 3 1—tmp+2—hp—str
  Novello

Rainbow   12'
  *2 2 2 2—4 3 3 1—tmp+3—hp, synth—str
  Novello

Mussorgsky, Modest 1839 - 1881

Boris Godunov: Polonaise 6'
*3 *3 3 3—4 4 3 1—tmp+4—str
Arr. Rimsky-Korsakov.
Breitkopf Kalmus

The fair at Sorochinsk: Introduction 5'
*3 *3 2 2—4 2 3 1—tmp+2—str
Arr. Liadov.
Breitkopf Kalmus

The fair at Sorochinsk: Gopak 3'
*3 2 2 2—4 2 3 1—tmp+2—str
Arr. Liadov.
Breitkopf Kalmus

Intermezzo in the classic style 7'
2 2 2 2—4 2 3 1—tmp+1—str
Arr. Rimsky-Korsakov.
Universal Russian

Khovantchina: Introduction 5'
2 2 2 2—4 0 0 0—tmp+1—hp—str
Arr. Rimsky-Korsakov.
Breitkopf Kalmus Universal

Khovantchina: Dance of the Persian maidens (Persian dances) 6'
*3 *2 2 2—4 2 3 1—tmp+3—hp—str
Arr. Rimsky-Korsakov.
Breitkopf Kalmus Russian

Khovantchina: Entr'acte (Act 4, Scene 2) 4'
3 2 2 2—4 2 3 1—tmp—str
Arr. Rimsky-Korsakov.
Luck

Solemn march in A-flat (Vzyatiye Karsa; The capture of Kars) 6'
*3 2 2 2—4 4 3 1—tmp+4—str
Arr. Rimsky-Korsakov.
Originally from the unfinished opera *Mlada*, with a new middle
section. Alternative titles: Feierlicher Marsch, Festive march,
March with trio alla turca, Triumphal march, Turkish march.
Kalmus Russian Universal

Night on bald mountain (original version) 12'
*3 2 2 2—4 4 3 1—tmp+4—str
Ed. Georgi Kirkor; rev. Clark McAlister.
Kalmus

Night on bald mountain (arr. Rimsky-Korsakov) 12'
*3 2 2 2—4 2 3 1—tmp+3—hp—str
Kalmus edition by Clinton F. Nieweg.
Kalmus Russian Universal

Pictures at an exhibition (arr. Goehr)   25'
  *2 *2 *2 2—4 2 3 0—tmp+3—hp, org, pf—str
  2nd cl doubles on asx. Cross-cued for smaller combinations.
  Boosey

Pictures at an exhibition (arr. Ravel)   30'
  *3 *3 *3 *3—asx—4 3 3 1—tmp+5—2hp, cel—str
  Two of the flutists double on piccolo.
  Contents—Promenade; Gnomus; Promenade; The old castle;
  Promenade; Tuileries; Bydlo; Promenade; Ballet of the chicks in
  their shells; Samuel Goldenberg and Schmuyle; Limoges;
  Catacombs; Cum mortuis in lingua mortua; The hut on fowl's legs;
  The great gate of Kiev.
  Boosey

Pictures at an exhibition (arr. Tushmalov)   20'
  *3 *3 *3 2—4 2 3 1—tmp+5—hp, pf—str
  Instrumentation by M. Tushmalov with collaboration by
  Rimsky-Korsakov.
  Contents—Promenade; The old castle; Ballet of the chicks; Two
  Jews; Limoges; Catacombs; Con mortuis; Baba Yaga; Great gate of
  Kiev.
  Kalmus

Scherzo, B-flat major   5'
  2 2 2 2—2 2 3 0—tmp—str
  Arr. Rimsky-Korsakov.
  Kalmus   *Russian*   *Universal*

Songs and dances of death   19'
  solo voice (medium)   5' 4' 5' 5'
  *2 2 *2 *2—4 2 3 1—tmp+2—hp—str
  Orchestrated by Shostakovich.
  Contents—Kolabelnaya (Lullaby); Serenada (Serenade); Trepak;
  Polkavodets (Commander in chief).
  Kalmus   *Russian*

N

Nelhybel, Vaclav   1919 - 1996

Music for orchestra   8'
  *4 2 *3 2—4 3 3 1—tmp+4—str
  Colombo

Nicolai, Otto   1810 - 1849

The merry wives of Windsor (Die lustigen Weiber von Windsor): Overture   8'
  2 2 2 2—4 2 3 0—tmp+2—str
  Bote & Bock   *Breitkopf*   *Kalmus*

Nielsen, Carl   1865 - 1931

Aladdin: 7 pieces, op.34   23'
  *2 2 2 2—4 2 3 1—tmp+4—str
  Contents—Oriental festive march; Aladdin's dream and Dance of the morning mist; Hindu Dance; Chinese dance; Marketplace in Ispahan; Prisoners' dance; Negro dance.
  Hansen   *Kalmus*

> 3' 3' 3'
> 3' 3' 4'
> 4'

Concerto, clarinet, op.57   24'
  0 0 0 2—2 0 0 0—1perc—str
  Kalmus   *Samfundet*

Concerto, flute (1926)   19'
  0 2 2 2—2 0 1 0—tmp—str
  Samfundet

> 12' 7'

Concerto, violin, op.33   34'
  *2 2 2 2—4 2 3 0—tmp—str
  Hansen   *Kalmus*

> 6' 12' 6'
> 10'

Helios overture, op.17   12'
  *3 2 2 2—4 3 3 1—tmp—str
  Hansen   *Kalmus*

Little suite, op.1   16'
  str
  Hansen   *Kalmus*

> 4' 5' 7'

Maskarade: Overture   5'
  *3 2 2 2—4 3 3 1—tmp+2—str
  Hansen   *Kalmus*

Maskarade: Hanedans (Dance of cocks)   5'
  *3 2 2 2—4 3 3 1—tmp—str
  Hansen   *Kalmus*

Saul and David: Prelude to Act II   6'
  3 2 2 2—4 3 3 1—tmp—str
  Hansen

Symphony no.1, op.7   27'
  *3 2 2 2—4 2 3 0—tmp—str
  Hansen   *Kalmus*

> 8' 6' 6' 7'

Symphony no.2, op.16 (The four temperaments)   32'
  3 2 2 2—4 3 3 1—tmp—str
  Hansen   *Kalmus*

> 8' 4' 12'
> 8'

Symphony no.3, op.27 (Sinfonia espansiva)   39'
   soprano and baritone voices (textless)   12' 10'
   *3 *3 3 *3—4 3 3 1—tmp—str   7' 10'
   A clarinet and trombone are cued to substitute for the voices.
   Hansen   *Kahnt*   *Kalmus*

Symphony no.4, op.29 (The inextinguishable)   36'
   *3 3 3 *3—4 3 3 1—2tmp—str   12' 5'
   In one movement.   10' 9'
   Hansen   *Kalmus*

Symphony no.5, op.50   34'
   *3 2 2 *2—4 3 3 1—tmp+3—cel—str   19' 15'
   Contrabassoon doubling is optional.
   A revised version by Erik Tuxen (1950) was not specifically
   authorized by the composer. The Hansen edition is apparently
   the original 1926 version; Kalmus offers both the original and
   the Tuxen revision, each with a useful preface by Clark
   McAlister.
   The Tuxen version has a contrabassoon part which, however,
   never appears in the score. The part appears to be a doubling of
   the 2nd bn in certain passages; perhaps intended to be optional.
   Hansen   *Kalmus*

Symphony no.6 (Sinfonia semplice)   31'
   *2 2 2 2—4 2 3 1—tmp+3—str   12' 4' 5'
   Although the score indicates 2 flutes plus piccolo, the composer   10'
   apparently intended 2 players, one doubling on piccolo.
   Hansen   *Kalmus*   *Samfundet*

Nono, Luigi   1924 - 1990
Canti di vita e d'amore   18'
   soprano and tenor solos
   3 3 3 3—4 4 4 0—tmp+5—str 8.8.8.6.6
   Schott

Il canto sospeso   28'
   chorus   solos SAT
   *4 2 *3 2—6 5 4 0—3tmp+3—2hp, cel—str
   Schott

Noskowski, Sigismund   1846 - 1909
The steppe   18'
   *3 2 2 2—4 2 3 1—tmp+1—hp—str
   PWM

Nunés-Garcia, José Mauricio   1767 - 1830
Requiem   40'
   chorus
   2 2 2 2—2 0 0 0—tmp—str
   Ed. Dominique-René de Lerma.
   Schirmer, G.

O

Offenbach, Jacques   1819 - 1880
La Belle Hélène: Overture   8'
  *2 2 2 2—4 2 3 0—tmp+4—hp—str
  Not the overture to the operetta, but a pastiche of various
  instrumental passages from it.
  Kalmus   *Luck*

Les Contes d'Hoffmann (Tales of Hoffmann): Intermezzo &   6'
Barcarolle   2' 4'
  2 2 2 2—4 2 3 0—tmp+3—hp—str
  Contents—Prelude & Entr'acte to Act II; Intermezzo from end of
  Act IV (includes an orchestral reprise of the Barcarolle).
  Bote & Bock   *Kalmus*   *Luck*

Orpheus in the underworld: Overture   10'
  *2 2 2 2—4 2 3 1—tmp+3—hp—str
  Not the actual overture to the operetta, but composed on tunes
  from it by Carl Binder.
  Kalmus

La Vie parisienne: Overture   5'
  *2 2 2 2—4 2 2 0—tmp+3—2asx, tsx—str
  Arr. Antal Dorati on themes of Offenbach.
  Kalmus

Orbón, Julián   1925 - 1991
Tres versiones sinfónicas   23'
  *4 2 *4 *4—4 4 3 1—tmp+6—hp, cel, pf—str   10' 10'
  Contents—Luis Milan; Perotin; Congo   3'
  Peer

Orff, Carl   1895 - 1982
Carmina burana   59'
  large chorus, small chorus, boy chorus   solos STB, short solos   27' 11'
  TTBBB   21'
  *3 *3 =3 *3—4 3 3 1—tmp+6—cel, 2pf—str
  Schott

Trionfo di Afrodite   45'
  chorus   solos SSTTB
  *3 *3 +3 *3—6 3 3 2—tmp+9—2hp, 3pf, 3gtr—str
  Schott

Overton, Hall   1920 - 1972

Symphony for strings   21'
    str
    Peters

Symphony no.2   14'
    *3 2 2 2—4 3 3 1—tmp+4—hp—str
    Peters

P

Pachelbel, Johann   1653 - 1706

Canon   5'
    opt cnt—str
    Arr. Helmut May. Originally for 3 solo violins and continuo.
    Schott

Paderewski, Ignace Jan   1860 - 1941

Concerto, piano, op.17, A minor   33'
    *3 *2 2 2—4 2 3 0—tmp—str   16' 8' 9'
    Bote & Bock   *Kalmus*

Symphony   59'
    *3 *3 *3 *3—3 contrabass sarrusophones—4 4 3 1—tmp+2—hp,   22' 14'
    org—str   23'
    Heugel

Paganini, Niccolò   1782 - 1840

Concerto, violin, no.1, op.6, D major   35'
    2 2 2 *2—2 2 3 0—tmp+2—str   20' 5'
    Originally in E-flat, with the soloist tuned a half-step sharp; now   10'
    normally performed in D.
    Breitkopf   *Kalmus*   *Luck*

Concerto, violin, no.1, op.6, D major (arr. Wilhelmj)   20'
    2 2 2 2—4 2 1 0—tmp—str
    A free transcription of the first movement of the concerto by
    August Wilhelmj.
    Kalmus   *Luck*

Concerto, violin, no.2, op.7, B minor (La Clochette)   31'
    1 2 2 1—2 2 3 0—str   15' 7' 9'
    C. Fischer   *Kalmus*

Moto perpetuo, op.11
> *The following are only a few of the many versions and arrangements of this popular work, some with violin solo and some without. The work was originally composed for solo violin and orchestra.*

Moto perpetuo, op.11   4'
solo violin
2 2 2 2—2 0 3 1—str
Luck

Moto perpetuo, op.11 (arr. Wilhelm Jerger)   4'
solo violin
*2 2 2 2—2 0 0 0—1perc—str
Universal

Moto perpetuo, op.11 (arr. Bernardino Molinari)   4'
2 2 2 2—2 0 3 1—str
First violins play original solo part in unison.
Ricordi

Paine, John Knowles   1839 - 1906

As you like it: Overture, op.28   8'
*3 2 2 2—4 2 3 0—tmp—str
Kalmus

Oedipus tyrannus: Prelude   8'
2 2 2 2—4 2 3 0—tmp—str
Kalmus

Poseidon and Amphitrite; an ocean fantasy   10'
*3 *3 2 2—4 2 3 1—tmp—hp—str
Kalmus

Shakespeare's Tempest   25'
*3 2 2 2—4 2 3 1—tmp—hp—str
Contents—1.The storm; 2. Calm and happy scene before Prospero's cell; 3. Prospero's tale; 4. The happy love of Ferdinand and Miranda, Episode with Caliban, Triumph of Prospero's "potent art."
Breitkopf   *Kalmus*

Symphony no.1, op.23, C minor   38'
2 2 2 2—4 2 3 0—tmp—str   11' 8'
AMP   *Kalmus*   10' 9'

Symphony no.2, op.34 (Im Frühling)   51'
2 2 2 2—4 2 3 0—tmp—str   16' 10'
This work may be out of print, but orchestra materials are in the   14' 11'
Fleisher Collection. The original publisher was Arthur Schmidt of Boston.

Paisiello, Giovanni   1740 - 1816

Nina (La pazza per amore): Overture   5'
  0 2 2 2—2 0 0 0—str
  Ed. Giuseppe Piccioli.
  Carisch

La scuffiara: Overture   6'
  2 2 0 2—2 2 0 0—str
  Ed. Giuseppe Piccioli.
  Carisch

Sinfonia, D major   7'
  0 2 0 0—2 0 0 0—str
  Ed. Bernhard Päuler.
  Peters

Sinfonia funebre   10'
  2 2 2 2—2 2 0 0—tmp—str
  Ed. Giuseppe Piccioli.
  Carisch

Sinfonia in tre tempi, D major   6'
  0 2 0 0—2 0 0 0—str
  Ed. Giuseppe Piccioli.
  Carisch

Panufnik, Andrzej   1914 - 1991

Autumn music   16'
  3 0 3 0—2perc—hp, cel, pf—str 0.0.6.6.4 (or 0.0.3.3.2)
  Rev. 1965.
  Boosey

Concertino for timpani, percussion & strings   16'
  solo timpani, solo percussionist | 3' 4' 2' |
  str | 4' 3' |
  Boosey

Concerto in modo antico   15'
  solo trumpet
  tmp—1 or 2hp, opt hpsd—str
  strings: max 8.8.12.8.6; min 3.3.4.3.2.
  Boosey

Concerto, bassoon   20'
  1 0 2 0—str (min 6.5.4.3.2) | 2' 4' 2' |
  Boosey | 10' 2' |

Concerto, piano   20'
  *3 2 *3 *3—4 3 3 1—2perc—str | 13' 7' |
  Recomposed 1972.
  Boosey

Divertimento 15'
  str
  Arranged from string trios by Felix Janiewicz (1762-1848).
  Rev.1955.
  Boosey

Harmony; a poem for chamber orchestra 17'
  2 2 2 2—str 8.6.4.3.0
  Minimum strings 6.4.4.3.0; max 12.10.8.6.0.
  Boosey

Heroic overture 6'
  *3 2 *3 *3—4 3 3 1—4perc—str
  Composer prefers extra horns & percussion.
  Boosey

Jagiellonian triptych 7'
  str (min 6.6.4.3.2)
  Contents—Preambulum; Cantio; Chorea polonica.
  Boosey

Lullaby 8'
  2hp—str 6.6.6.6.5
  Boosey

Nocturne 16'
  *3 2 *3 *3—4 3 3 1—tmp+4—pf—str
  Boosey

Old Polish suite 12'
  str
  Contents—Cenar; Interlude; Wyrwany; Chorale; Hayduk.
  Boosey

Symphony no.10 21'
  3 2 *3 *3—6 3 3 1—2perc—hp, pf amplified if possible—str
  Boosey

Parker, Horatio   1863 - 1919

Hora novissima 62'
  chorus   solos SATB
  2 2 2 2—4 2 3 1—tmp+2—hp, org—str | 33' 29' |
  Gray   *Kalmus*   *Luck*

Parry, Hubert   1848 - 1918

An English suite 21'
  str

4'	3'	4'
3'	2'	2'
		3'

  Kalmus

Ode on St. Cecilia's Day 45'
  chorus   solos SBar
  2 2 *3 *3—4 2 3 1—tmp—hp, org—str
  Kalmus

Suite in F (Lady Radnor's suite)   21'
   str
   Kalmus

Symphonic fantasy   55'
   2 *3 *3 *3—4 2 3 1—tmp—2hp—str
   Contents—Stress; Love; Play; Now.
   Curwen

Symphony no.3 in C (The English)   34'
   2 2 2 2—4 2 3 0—tmp—str   8' 10' 5'
   Trombones are optional.   11'
   Kalmus   *Novello*

Pärt, Arvo   1935 -

Credo   12'
   chorus   solo piano
   *4 2 *4 *4—4 4 3 1—tmp+10—str
   Two of the flutists double on piccolo; 2 of the clarinetists play
   bass clarinet; 2 of the bassoonists play contrabassoon.
   Universal

Festina Lente   6'
   optional hp—str
   Rev. 1990.
   Universal

Fratres   12'
   1perc—str
   Rev.1991.
   Universal

Silouans song (My soul yearns after the Lord...)   5'
   str
   Universal

Wenn Bach Bienen gezüchtet hätte...   10'
   *1 1 1 1—1 0 0 0—pf—str 4.4.4.4.2 (or 8.8.8.8.4)
   Universal

Partos, Ödön   1907 - 1977

Yiskor (In memoriam)   9'
   solo viola
   str
   Israeli

Pasatieri, Thomas   1945 -

Sieben Lehmannlieder   26'
  solo soprano
  *2 2 *2 *2—4 2 2 1—tmp+1—hp, cel—str
Poems by Lotte Lehmann.
Contents—Ich bin allein auf Bergesgipfeln; Wie lieb' ich diese
klare Stunde; So hörte ich wieder deiner Stimme; Wie schön ist
diese tiefe Schlummer; Kein Abenteuer lockte ihn; Die Welt
scheint ganz aus Glut gesponnen.
Presser

Paulus, Stephen   1949 -

Concertante   11'
  *3 3 3 3—4 3 3 1—tmp+3—pf—str
EAM

Concerto for orchestra   25'
  *3 *3 3 *3—4 4 3 1—tmp+3—hp, pf/cel—str
EAM

Peck, Russell   1945 -

The glory and the grandeur   12'
  3 solo percussion
  *3 2 *3 *3—4 3 3 1—tmp+1—1 or 2hp—str
Pecktacular

Peace overture   11'
  *3 *3 *3 *3—4 3 3 1—tmp+4—pf—str
Pecktacular

Playing with style   10'
  narrator (may be conductor)
  2 2 2 2—4 2 3 1—tmp+2—str
Also available for: 2 2 2 2—2 2 1 1—tmp(+1)—str.
Pecktacular

Signs of life   12'
  str (min 3.3.2.2.1)   6' 6'
Pecktacular

The thrill of the orchestra   13'
  narrator
  *3 *3 *3 *3—4 3 3 1—tmp+3—str
Cued to be playable with: 2 2 2 2—4 2 3 1—tmp+2—str. A
smaller version is also available for: 2 2 2 2—2 2 0 0—tmp—str
(plus optional trombone, tuba & percussion).
Pecktacular

Penderecki, Krzysztof   1933 -

Adagio (Symphony no.4)   33'
  *3 *3 =4 *3—5 6 4 1—tmp+3—str
Schott

Als Jakob erwachte...   8'
  *3 *3 3 *3—5 3 3 1—tmp+1—str 12.12.10.10.8
  Two of the flutists double on piccolo; all woodwind players
  double on ocarinas.
  Schott

Anaklasis   9'
  tmp+5—hp, cel, pf—str 10.10.8.8.6
  Moeck   *PWM*

Concerto, viola   18'
  *2 2 2 *2—2 2 2 0—tmp+3—cel—str
  Schott

Concerto, violin   39'
  *3 *3 =4 *3—contrabass cl—4 3 3 1—tmp+2—hp, cel—str
  Rev. 1988.
  Schott

De natura sonoris [no.1]   8'
  *4 *4 *3 *4—2asx—6 4 3 1—tmp+5—pf, harm—str
  Two of the flutists double on piccolo.
  Moeck   *PWM*

De natura sonoris no.2   10'
  0 0 0 0—4 0 4 1—tmp+6—pf, harm—str 12.12.8.8.6
  PWM   *Schott*

Emanations   8'
  Two str orchestras (min 10.10.8.6.5; max 20.20.16.16.12)
  One orchestra tuned a half-step higher than the other.
  Moeck   *PWM*

Flourescences   14'
  *4 4 4 4—6 4 3 2—tmp+5—pf—str 12.12.8.8.6
  Moeck   *PWM*

Passio et mors domini nostri Iesu Christi secundum Lucam (St. Luke   80'
  passion)
  mixed chorus, boy chorus   solos SBB, reciter
  =4 0 *1 *4—2asx—6 4 4 1—tmp+6—hp, pf, harm, org—str
  12.12.10.10.8
  Moeck   *PWM*

Sonata, violoncello & orchestra   10'
  0 0 0 *4—6 0 3 1—4perc—pf—str
  Belwin   *PWM*

Symphony no.1   29'
  *3 *3 =4 *3—5 3 4 1—2tmp+4—hp, cel, pf, harm—str 12.12.8.8.6
  Two of the flutists double on piccolo.
  Schott

Symphony no.2 (Weihnachtssinfonie; Christmas symphony)   36'
  *3 *3 =3 *3—5 3 3 1—2tmp+5—cel—str
  Schott

To the victims of Hiroshima (Threnody)   9'
   str 12.12.10.10.8
   Belwin   *PWM*

Pentland, Barbara   1912 -

Symphony for ten parts   10'
   1 1 0 0—1 1 0 0—tmp+1—vn, va, vc, db
   Berandol

Pergolesi, Giovanni Battista   1710 - 1736

Concertino, E-flat major   7'
   str
   Ed. Renato Fasano
   Ricordi

Concerto, flute, G major   13'
   cnt—str (without va)
   Authenticity doubtful.
   Boosey   *Sikorski*

Concerto, violin, B-flat major   18'
   0 2 0 1—2 0 0 0—str
   Ed. Adriano Lualdi.
   Carisch

Magnificat   13'
   chorus   solos SATB
   cnt—str
   Ed. Clayton Westermann.
   Kalmus

Stabat mater   41'
   soprano and alto solos
   cnt—str
   Although sometimes performed with treble chorus, the work
   is intended for soloists, not chorus.
   Kalmus   *Ricordi*   *Schott*

Perle, George   1915 -

Concerto, piano, no.2   19'
   *2 2 2 2—4 2 0 0—tmp+2—str | 8' 6' 5' |
   ECS

New fanfares   2'
   0 0 0 0—4 3 3 0
   Galaxy

Serenade no.2 for eleven players   15'
   1 1 1 1—tsx—0 1 0 0—1perc (incl tmp)—pf—vn, va, vc
   Presser

Six bagatelles   6'
   *3 *3 *3 *3—4 3 3 1—tmp+2—hp, cel—str
   Presser

Three movements for orchestra   16'
　*4 3 *3 2—4 3 3 1—tmp+3—hp, cel, pf—str
　Contents—Prelude; Contrasts; Ostinato.
　Merion

Persichetti, Vincent   1915 - 1987

Night dances, op.114   19'
　*3 *3 *3 2—4 3 3 1—tmp+3—str
　Elkan-Vogel

Symphony, op.61   18'
　str
　Elkan-Vogel

Peterson, Wayne   1927 -

The face of the night, the heart of the dark   19'
　=3 *3 *3 *3—4 3 3 1—tmp+3—hp, pf/cel—str
　Peters

Pfitzner, Hans   1869 - 1949

Das Christ-Elflein, op.20 (The Christmas elf): Overture   10'
　*2 2 2 2—2 0 0 0—tmp+1—hp—str
　Boosey   *Kalmus*   *Schott*

Kleine Sinfonie, op.44   16'
　2 2 2 2—0 1 0 0—1perc—hp—str   6' 2' 5' 3'
　This work may be out of print. The original publisher was
　Brockhaus.

Palestrina: Prelude, Act I   6'
　4 *3 *4 *4—4 2 4 1—tmp—hp—str
　Schott offers also a reduced version by Hans Zanotelli.
　Kalmus   *Schott*

Palestrina: Prelude, Act II   7'
　*4 *3 =4 *4—6 4 4 1—tmp+2—str
　Two of the flutists double on piccolo. Schott offers also a reduced
　version by Hans Zanotelli.
　Kalmus   *Schott*

Palestrina: Prelude, Act III   8'
　2 *3 *3 3—4 0 4 1—tmp+2—hp—str
　Schott also offers also a reduced version by Hans Zanotelli.
　Kalmus   *Schott*

Phillips, Burrill   1907 - 1988

Selections from McGuffey's reader   17'
　*3 2 2 2—4 3 3 1—tmp+3—hp, cel—str
　C. Fischer

Piccinni, Niccolò   1728 - 1800
Iphigenie en Tauride: Overture 8'
 2 2 0 2—0 2 0 0—tmp—str
Doblinger

Picker, Tobias   1954 -
Keys to the city (Piano concerto no.2) 18'
 *2 2 *2 *2—4 2 3 1—tmp+1—str
 The clarinets double on ssx & asx respectively.
Helicon

Old and Lost Rivers 6'
 *3 2 *3 3—6 2 0 1—tmp+2—hp, pf—str
 2 trombones may substitute for horns 5 & 6.
Helicon

Pierné, Gabriel   1863 - 1937
Marche des petits soldats de plomb, op.14, no.6 (March of the lead 4'
soldiers)
 1 0 1 0—0 1 0 0—1perc—pf—str
Kalmus   *Leduc*

Pinkham, Daniel   1923 -
Catacoustical measures 5'
 *4 *3 *4 *4—4 4 4 1—tmp+3—hp, cel, pf—str
Peters

Signs of the zodiac 21'
 optional speaker
 *3 *3 *3 2—4 3 3 1—tmp+2—hp, pf/cel—str
Peters

Symphony no.1 17'
 *3 *3 *3 *3—4 3 3 1—tmp+2—hp, cel/pf—str
Peters

Symphony no.2 16'
 *3 *3 *3 2—4 3 3 1—tmp+5—hp, pf—str
Peters

Piston, Walter   1894 - 1976
Concertino, piano & chamber orchestra 14'
 *2 2 2 2—2 0 0 0—str
AMP

Concerto for orchestra 14'
 3 *3 *3 *3—4 3 3 1—tmp+5—pf—str
AMP

Concerto, flute 19'
 2 *3 *3 2—4 2 0 0—tmp+2—hp—str
AMP

Concerto, viola   23'
   *3 *3 *3 *3—4 2 3 1—tmp+4—hp—str
   AMP

Divertimento for nine instruments   8'
   1 1 1 1—2vn, va, vc, db
   AMP

The incredible flutist: Suite   17'
   *3 *3 *3 *3—4 3 3 1—tmp+4—pf—str
   AMP

Lincoln Center festival overture   12'
   *3 *3 *3 *3—4 3 3 1—tmp+4—2hp—str
   AMP

Pine tree fantasy   10'
   *3 *3 *3 *3—4 2 3 1—tmp+4—str
   AMP

Serenata   12'
   2 2 2 2—4 2 0 0—tmp—hp—str   3' 6' 3'
   AMP

Sinfonietta   15'
   2 2 2 2—2 0 0 0—str   6' 5' 4'
   Boosey

Symphony no.1   27'
   *3 *3 *3 *3—4 3 3 1—tmp—str
   Schirmer, G.

Symphony no.2   25'
   *3 *3 *3 *3—4 3 3 1—tmp+4—str   10' 11' 4'
   AMP

Symphony no.3   34'
   *3 *3 *3 *3—4 3 3 1—tmp+4—2hp—str   10' 5' 13' 6'
   Boosey

Symphony no.4   23'
   *3 *3 *3 *3—4 3 3 1—tmp+5—2hp—str   6' 5' 8' 4'
   AMP

Symphony no.5   23'
   *3 *3 *3 *3—4 3 3 1—tmp+3—2hp—str
   AMP

Symphony no.6   28'
   *3 *3 *3 *3—4 3 3 1—tmp+4—2hp—str   8' 3' 13' 4'
   AMP

Symphony no.7   19'
   *3 *3 *3 *3—4 3 3 1—tmp+5—2hp—str   6' 9' 4'
   AMP

Symphony no.8   20'
  *3 *3 *3 *3—4 3 3 1—tmp+4—2hp—str
  AMP

Three New England sketches   17'
  *3 *3 *3 *3—4 3 3 1—tmp+4—2hp—str   8' 3' 6'
  AMP

Toccata   9'
  *3 *3 *3 *3—4 3 3 1—tmp+5—str
  Boosey

Plain, Gerald   1940 -

Clawhammer   12'
  2 2 2 2—2 1 1 0—2perc—hp, electronic keyboard—str 6.5.4.3.2
  Oxford

Pleyel, Ignaz   1757 - 1831

Symphony, op.3, no.1, D major   16'
  0 2 0 0—2 0 0 0—str   6' 3' 2' 5'
  Ed. Helmut Riessberger.
  Doblinger

Pokorny, Franz Xaver   1729 - 1794

Concerto, flute, D major
  see: Boccherini, Luigi
      Concerto, flute, G.489, D major

Ponce, Manuel   1882 - 1948

Concierto del sur   25'
  solo guitar   13' 6' 6'
  1 1 1 1—tmp+1—str
  Peer

Ponchielli, Amilcare   1834 - 1886

Elegia   12'
  2 *3 *4 2—4 2 4 0—tmp—hp—str
  Two of the clarinetists play bass clarinet. Ed. Pietro Spada.
  Suvini

La Gioconda: Dance of the hours   9'
  *3 2 2 2—4 4 3 1—tmp+3—2hp—str
  Kalmus   *Ricordi*

Popper, David   1843 - 1913

Hungarian rhapsody, op.68   8'
  solo violoncello
  2 2 2 2—4 2 3 0—tmp—str
  Hofmeister   *Kalmus*   *Luck*

Tarantelle, op.33   5'
   solo violoncello
   2 2 2 2—2 0 0 0—tmp+2—str
   Timpani optional. Orchestrated by Paul Gilson.
   Kalmus   *Luck*

Porter, Quincy   1897 - 1966
Symphony no.2   25'
   *3 *2 2 2—4 2 3 1—tmp+1—str
   Peters

Poulenc, Francis   1899 - 1963
Aubade, piano & 18 instruments   22'
   2 *2 2 2—2 1 0 0—tmp—2va, 2vc, 2db   3' 2' 3'
   Rouart   2' 2' 3'
                                     1' 6'

Les Biches: Suite   16'
   *3 *3 *3 *3—4 3 3 1—tmp+2—hp, cel—str   3' 3' 4'
   Contents—Rondeau; Adagietto; Rag-mazurka; Andantino; Final. 3' 3'
   Heugel

Concerto, organ, G minor   22'
   tmp—str   9' 6' 7'
   Salabert

Concerto, piano   20'
   *2 *2 2 2—4 2 3 1—tmp—str   10' 6' 4'
   Salabert

Concerto, 2 pianos, D minor   20'
   *2 *2 2 2—2 2 2 1—1perc—str 8.8.4.4.4   8' 5' 7'
   Rouart

Concerto champêtre, harpsichord (or piano)   25'
   *2 *2 2 2—4 2 1 1—tmp+2—str 8.8.4.4.4   11' 6' 8'
   Both flutists double on piccolo.
   Rouart

Deux Marches et un Intermède   6'
   1 1 1 1—0 1 0 0—str   2' 2' 2'
   Rouart

Gloria   28'
   chorus   solo soprano   3' 3' 5'
   *3 *3 *3 *3—4 3 3 1—tmp—hp—str   1' 8' 8'
   Salabert

Sécheresses   18'
   chorus
   *2 *2 2 2—4 2 3 1—tmp+1—hp, cel—str
   Durand

Sinfonietta 29'
2 2 2 2—2 2 0 0—tmp—hp—str 8' 6' 8' 7'
Chester *MMB*

Stabat mater 35'
chorus   solo soprano
*3 *3 *3 3—4 2 3 1—tmp—2hp—str
Salabert

The story of Babar, the little elephant 22'
narrator
*2 *2 *2 *2—2 2 1 1—tmp—hp—str
Chester

Suite française 13'
0 2 0 2—0 2 3 0—hpsd—1perc 2' 3' 1'
After Claude Gervaise (16th century). 1' 2' 2'
Durand 2'

Powell, Mel   1923 -

Modules; an intermezzo for chamber orchestra 14'
1 1 1 1—2 1 1 0—2perc—hp, cel—vn, va, vc, db
Schirmer, G.

Previn, André   1929 -

Overture to a comedy 9'
*3 2 *3 2—4 3 3 1—tmp+3—hp—str
MCA

Prokofiev, Serge   1891 - 1953

Ala and Lolly
see his: Scythian Suite

Alexander Nevsky, op.78 36'
chorus   solo mezzo-soprano 3' 3' 6'
*3 *3 *3 *3—tsx—4 3 3 1—tmp+7—hp (doubled if possible)—str 2' 12' 6'
Kalmus *Russian* 4'

Andante 9'
str
Arr. from String quartet no.1, op.50, 3rd movement.
Boosey

Chout, op.21 (Buffoon): Symphonic suite 35'
*3 *3 *3 3—4 3 3 1—tmp+6—2hp, pf—str
Boosey

Cinderella: Suite no.1, op.107 29'
*3 *3 *3 *3—4 3 3 1—tmp+6—hp, pf—str 3' 4' 3'
Contents—Introduction; Pas de chat; Quarrel; Fairy Godmother 5' 6' 3'
& Fairy Winter; Mazurka; Cinderella goes to the ball; 3' 2'
Cinderella's Waltz; Midnight.
Kalmus *Russian*

Cinderella: Suite no.2, op.108　　　　　　　　　　　　　　　20'
　　*3 *3 *3 *3—4 3 3 1—tmp+4—hp, pf/cel—str
　　Contents—Cinderella's dream; Dancing lesson and gavotte; Fairy
　　of Spring & Fairy of Summer; Bourrée; Cinderella in the castle;
　　Galop.
　　Kalmus

Cinderella: Suite no.3, op.109　　　　　　　　　　　　　　　26'
　　*3 *3 *3 *3—4 3 3 1—tmp+4—hp, pf—str　　　　　　4' 5' 1'
　　Contents—Pavana; Cinderella and the prince; The three oranges;　4' 2' 2'
　　Southern borders (Temptation); Orientalia; The prince has found　4' 4'
　　Cinderella; Waltz melody; Amoroso.
　　Kalmus　　　　　　*Russian*

Classical symphony, op.25 (Symphony no.1)　　　　　　　　　15'
　　2 2 2 2—2 2 0 0—tmp—str　　　　　　　　　　　　5' 4' 2' 4'
　　Boosey　　　　　*Kalmus*　　　　　　*Russian*

Concerto, piano, no.1, op.10, D-flat major　　　　　　　　　16'
　　*3 2 2 *3—4 2 3 1—tmp+1—str　　　　　　　　　　7' 5' 4'
　　Kalmus　　　　　*Russian*

Concerto, piano, no.2, op.16, G minor　　　　　　　　　　　31'
　　2 2 2 2—4 2 3 1—tmp+2—str　　　　　　　　　　11' 3' 7'
　　Boosey　　　　　*Kalmus*　　　　　　　　　　　　　10'

Concerto, piano, no.3, op.26, C major　　　　　　　　　　　27'
　　*2 2 2 2—4 2 3 0—tmp+1—str　　　　　　　　　　9' 9' 9'
　　Boosey　　　　　*Kalmus*　　　　　　*Russian*

Concerto, piano (left hand), no.4, op.53　　　　　　　　　　25'
　　2 2 2 2—2 1 1 0—1perc—str　　　　　　　　　　4' 11' 8'
　　Kalmus　　　　　*Russian*　　　　　　　　　　　　　2'

Concerto, piano, no.5, op.55　　　　　　　　　　　　　　　23'
　　*2 2 2 2—2 2 2 1—tmp+2—str　　　　　　　　　　5' 4' 2'
　　Boosey　　　　　*Kalmus*　　　　　　　　　　　　7' 5'

Concerto, violin, no.1, op.19, D major　　　　　　　　　　　22'
　　*2 2 2 2—4 2 0 1—tmp+2—hp—str　　　　　　　10' 4' 8'
　　Boosey　　　　　*Kalmus*　　　　　　*Russian*

Concerto, violin, no.2, op.63, G minor　　　　　　　　　　　26'
　　2 2 2 2—2 2 0 0—1perc—str　　　　　　　　　　10' 9' 7'
　　Boosey　　　　　*Kalmus*　　　　　　*Russian*

Ivan the terrible, op.116　　　　　　　　　　　　　　　　　74'
　　narrator　　　solos ABar　　chorus　　optional children's chorus
　　*3 *3 =5 *4—asx, tsx—4 5 3 2—tmp+5—2hp, pf—str
　　Two of the flutists double on piccolo.
　　Film music arranged in the form of an oratorio by Abram
　　Stasevich.
　　Kalmus

Lieutenant Kijé, op.60: Suite   **20'**
    *3 2 2 2—tsx—4 2 3 1—opt cornet—3perc—hp, pf/cel—str
    Optional baritone voice; saxophone is optional if voice is used.
    Contents—The birth of Kijé; Romance; Kijé's wedding; Troika;
    The burial of Kijé.
    Boosey   *Kalmus*

> 4' 5' 3'
> 2' 6'

The love for three oranges: Symphonic suite   **15'**
    *3 *3 *3 *3—4 3 3 1—tmp+5—2hp—str
    Kalmus edition by Clinton F. Nieweg & Nancy Bradburd.
    Contents—Les Ridicules; Le Magicien Tchelio et Fata Morgana
    jouent aux cartes; Marche; Scherzo; Le Prince et la Princesse; Le
    Fuite.
    Boosey   *Kalmus*

> 3' 3' 2'
> 2' 3' 2'

The love for three oranges: March & Scherzo   **4'**
    *3 *3 *3 *3—4 3 3 1—tmp+5—2hp—str
    Boosey   *Kalmus*

> 2' 2'

Overture, op.42 (American)   **8'**
    1 1 2 1—0 2 1 0—tmp—2hp, cel, 2pf—1vc, 2db
    Boosey

Le Pas d'acier, op.41 (The steel step (The age of steel))   **35'**
    *3 *3 =4 *3—4 4 3 1—tmp+4—pf—str
    Boosey

Le pas d'acier (The steel step): Suite, op.41b   **13'**
    *3 *3 =4 *3—4 4 3 1—tmp+4—pf—str
    Boosey

> 2' 5' 3' 3'

Peter and the wolf, op.67   **25'**
    narrator
    1 1 1 1—3 1 1 0—tmp+1—str
    Boosey   *Kalmus*   *Russian*

Romeo and Juliet: Suite no.1   **27'**
    *3 *3 *3 *3—tsx—4 3 3 1—tmp+5—hp, pf—str
    Contents—Folk dance; Scene; Madrigal; Minuet; Masks; Romeo
    and Juliet; The death of Tybalt.
    Kalmus   *Russian*

> 4' 2' 4'
> 3' 2' 8'
> 4'

Romeo and Juliet: Suite no.2   **30'**
    *3 *3 *3 *3—tsx—4 3 3 1—tmp+2—hp, pf/cel—opt viola
    d'amore—str
    Contents—The Montagues and the Capulets; Juliet—the young
    girl; Friar Laurence; Dance; Romeo and Juliet before parting;
    Dance of the maids from the Antilles; Romeo at Juliet's grave.
    Kalmus   *Russian*

> 5' 4' 3'
> 2' 8' 2'
> 6'

Romeo and Juliet: Suite no.3   **18'**
    *3 *3 *3 *3—4 3 3 1—tmp+2—hp, cel, pf—str
    Contents—Romeo at the fountain; Morning dance; Juliet; Nurse;
    Morning serenade; Juliet's death.
    Kalmus   *Russian*

> 2' 2' 5'
> 2' 2' 5'

Scythian suite, op.20 (Ala and Lolly)   20'
  =4 *4 =4 *4—8 5 4 1—tmp+9—2hp, cel, pf—str   7' 3' 5' 5'
  5th tp is optional.
  Contents—Adoration of Vélèss and Ala; The hostile god & Dance
  of the dark spirits; Night; Glorious departure of Lolli & Cortège
  of the sun.
  Boosey

Sinfonia concertante, op.125   37'
  solo violoncello   11' 16'
  *2 2 2 2—4 3 3 1—tmp+2—cel—str   10'
  3rd tp is optional.
  Boosey

Sinfonietta, op.5/48   20'
  2 2 2 2—4 2 0 0—str   5' 4' 3'
  Boosey   *Kalmus*   4' 4'

A summer day, op.65 (Children's suite for small orchestra)   13'
  2 2 2 2—2 2 0 0—tmp+2—str   2' 1' 2'
  Contents—Morning; Tip and run; Waltz; Repentance; March;   3' 1' 2'
  Evening; The moon is over the meadows.   2'
  Boosey   *Kalmus*   *Russian*

Symphony no.1
  see his: Classical symphony, op.25

Symphony no.2, op.40   36'
  *3 *3 *3 *3—4 3 3 1—tmp+2—pf—str   12' 24'
  Boosey   *Kalmus*

Symphony no.3, op.44   34'
  *3 *3 *3 *3—4 3 3 1—tmp+2—2hp—str   14' 7' 7'
  Boosey   *Kalmus*   6'

Symphony no.4, op.47/112   34'
  *3 *3 =4 *3—4 3 3 1—tmp+3—hp, pf—str   12' 7' 6'
  Boosey   *Kalmus*   *Russian*   9'

Symphony no.5, op.100   46'
  *3 *3 =4 *3—4 3 3 1—tmp+4—hp, pf—str   14' 9'
  Kalmus   *Russian*   13' 10'

Symphony no.6, op.111   43'
  *3 *3 =4 *3—4 3 3 1—tmp+4—hp, cel, pf—str   15' 16'
  Kalmus   *Russian*   12'

Symphony no.7, op.131   31'
  *3 *3 *3 2—4 3 3 1—tmp+3—hp, pf—str   9' 8' 5' 9'
  Kalmus   *Russian*

War and peace: Overture   8'
  *3 *3 *3 *3—4 3 3 1—tmp+1—hp—str
  Kalmus

Proto, Frank   1941 -

Casey at the bat   13'
  narrator
  *3 *3 *3 *3—4 3 3 1—tmp+4—hp, pf, elec bass
  —electronic tape (crowd noises etc.)—str
  Liben

Doodles   8'-30'
  *2 2 *3 2—4 2 3 1—tmp+2—hp, pf, elec bass—str
  Playable with: 2 2 2 2—2 2 0 0—1perc—pf, elec bass—str.
  Variations on *Yankee doodle,* each variation featuring a different
  instrument. Alternative variations for certain instruments. (It is
  not intended that all variations be performed.) Finale (the theme
  played twice) may be used as an audience sing-along.
  Liben

Fantasy on the Saints   8'-12'
  *3 *3 *3 *3—4 3 3 1—tmp+4—hp, pf/cel, elec bass—str
  Optional jazz section that can be stretched out into a Dixieland
  jam session.
  Liben

Ptaszyńska, Marta   1943 -

Holocaust memorial cantata   40'
  solos STBar   chorus
  2 2 2 2—2 2 2 1—2perc—str
  Presser

Puccini, Giacomo   1858 - 1924

Capriccio sinfonico   16'
  *3 2 2 2—4 2 3 1—tmp+2—hp—str
  Elkan-Vogel

I crisantemi (The chrysanthemums)   6'
  str
  Originally for string quartet.
  Kalmus   *Luck*   *Ricordi*

Edgar: Preludio   8'
  *3 *3 *3 2—4 4 3 1—tmp+2—hp—str
  Elkan-Vogel

Manon Lescaut: Intermezzo from Act III   5'
  *3 *3 *3 2—4 3 3 1—tmp+1—hp—str
  Kalmus

Preludio sinfonico   12'
  *3 *2 2 2—4 2 3 1—tmp+2—hp—str
  Ed. Pietro Spada.
  Elkan-Vogel

Purcell, Henry 1659 - 1695

Abdelazar: Suite 13'
cnt—str
Ed. Edvard Fendler.
Mercury

Canon on a ground bass 4'
str
Arr. Wallingford Riegger.
AMP

Chacony in G minor 7'
opt hpsd—str
Ed. Benjamin Britten.
Boosey

Dido and Aeneas: Suite 11'
cnt—str
Ed. E.J.Dent.
Contents—Overture; The triumphing dance; Echo dance of furies;
Second act tune; Third act tune; Sailors' dance; Dance of witches
and sailors.
Perhaps out of print, but orchestral materials are in the Fleisher
Collection.
Oxford

The double dealer: Suite 8'
cnt—str
Ed. Paul Stassevitch.
Mercury

The fairy queen: Suite no.1 6'
str
Ed. William Reed.
Contents—Prelude; Rondeau; Jig; Hornpipe; Dance of the fairies.
Eulenburg

The fairy queen: Suite no.2 9'
str
Contents—Air; Monkey dance; Dance for the followers of the
night; Chaconne.
Eulenburg

The Gordian knot untied: Suite no.1 11'
2 2 2 1—2 2 0 0—tmp—str
Winds and timpani, added by Gustav Holst, are optional.
Contents—Overture; Air; Rondeau minuet; Air; Jig.
Novello

The Gordian knot untied: Suite no.2 7'
2 2 2 1—2 2 0 0—tmp—str
Winds and timpani, added by Gustav Holst, are optional.
Contents—Chaconne; Air; Minuet.
Novello

Indian queen: Trumpet overture   3'
   0 0 0 0—0 1 0 0—tmp—str
   Arr. Lionel Salter.
   Oxford

The married beau: Suite   12'
   2 2 2 1—2 2 0 0—tmp—str
   Arr. Gustav Holst.
   Novello

New pieces for small string orchestra
   str
   Ed. Hilmar Höckner.
   8 pieces from *Distressed innocence*; 8 pieces from *Amphitryon*.
   Hansen

Ode for St. Cecilia's day (1683), Z.329 (Laudate Ceciliam)   13'
   solos ATB
   cnt—str (without va)
   Ed. Bruce Wood.
   Novello

Ode for St. Cecilia's day (1683), Z.339 (Welcome to all the   15'
pleasures)   4' 4' 3' 4'
   chorus   solos SSATB
   cnt—str
   Ed. Walter Bergmann.
   Schott

Ode for St. Cecilia's day (ca.1685), Z.334 (Raise, raise the voice)   14'
   chorus (STB)   solos SB
   cnt—str (without va)
   Ed. Bruce Wood.
   Novello

Ode for St. Cecilia's day (1692), Z.328 (ed. Tippett & Bergmann)   57'
(Hail, bright Cecilia)
   chorus   solos SAATBB
   2 2 0 0—0 2 0 0—tmp—cnt—str
   Ed. Tippett and Bergmann.
   Schott

Ode for St. Cecilia's day (1692), Z.328 (ed. Dennison) (Hail, bright   40'
Cecilia)
   chorus   solos SAATBB
   2rec 2 0 0—bass rec—0 2 0 0—tmp—cnt—str
   Ed. Peter Dennison.
   Novello

The rival sisters: Overture   7'
   cnt—str
   Ed. Paul Stassevitch.
   Mercury

Sonata for trumpet & strings 6'
   str
   Ed. Alan Lumsden.
   Musica Rara

Te deum and Jubilate 19'
   chorus   solos SSAATB
   0 0 0 0—0 2 0 0—cnt—str
   Ed. Denis Arnold
   Eulenburg

Trumpet prelude (Trumpet voluntary) 3'
   *3 2 2 2—4 3 3 1—tmp+1—hp—str
   Orchestrated by Arthur Luck. Neither the title of this work nor
   its attribution to Purcell is correct. Actually it is *The Prince of
   Denmark's march*, by Jeremiah Clarke, *q.v.*
   Luck

The virtuous wife: Suite 10'
   2 2 2 1—2 2 0 0—tmp—str
   Arr. Gustav Holst.
   Contents—Overture; Slow air; Hornpipe; Minuet I; Minuet II;
   Allegro.
   Novello

Q

Quantz, Johann Joachim   1697 - 1773

Concerto, flute, C major 14'
   cnt—str
   Ed. Hanns-Dieter Sonntag.
   Peters

Concerto, flute, C minor
   cnt—str
   Ed. Dieter Sonntag.
   Pegasus

Concerto, flute, D major 15'
   cnt—str
   Ed. Hanns-Dieter Sonntag.
   Möseler

Concerto, flute, D major (Pour Potsdam) 16'
   cnt—str
   Bärenreiter   *Kalmus*

Concerto, flute, G major   16'
   cnt—str   5' 6' 5'
   Ed. Felix Schroeder.
   Eulenburg

R

Rabaud, Henri   1873 - 1949

La Procession nocturne, op.6   16'
   3 2 2 2—4 2 3 1—tmp—hp—str
   Durand   *Kalmus*

Rachmaninoff, Sergei   1873 - 1943

The bells, op.35   35'
   chorus   solos STB   6' 10' 8'
   *4 *4 *4 *4—6 3 3 1—tmp+5—hp, cel, pianino, opt org—str   11'
   Boosey   *Kalmus*

Capriccio bohémien, op.12   20'
   *3 2 2 2—4 2 3 1—tmp+5—hp—str
   Boosey   *Kalmus*

Cinq Études-tableaux   25'
   *3 *3 *3 *3—4 3 3 1—tmp+4—hp—str
   Originally for piano; orchestrated by Ottorino Respighi.
   Contents—La Mer et les Mouettes (The sea and the seagulls); La
   Foire (The fair); Marche funèbre (Funeral march); Le Chaperon
   Rouge et le Loup (Little Red Riding Hood and the wolf); Marche
   (March).
   Boosey

Concerto, piano, no.1, op.1, F-sharp minor   27'
   2 2 2 2—4 2 3 0—tmp—str   13' 6' 8'
   1891, rev.1917 & 1919.
   Boosey   *Foley*   *Kalmus*

Concerto, piano, no.2, op.18, C minor   33'
   2 2 2 2—4 2 3 1—tmp+2—str   11' 11'
   Boosey   *Foley*   *Kalmus*   11'

Concerto, piano, no.3, op.30, D minor   39'
   2 2 2 2—4 2 3 1—tmp+2—str   15' 10'
   Boosey   *Foley*   *Kalmus*   14'

Concerto, piano, no.4, op.40, G minor   24'
  *3 *3 2 2—4 2 3 1—tmp+5—str   9' 6' 9'
  1926, rev.1942.
  Foley   *Kalmus*

Isle of the dead
  see his: Toteninsel, op.29

Rhapsody on a theme of Paganini, op.43   22'
  solo piano
  *3 *3 2 2—4 2 3 1—tmp+4—hp—str
  Foley   *Kalmus*

The rock; fantasy, op.7   18'
  *3 2 2 2—4 2 3 1—tmp+2—hp—str
  Foley   *Forberg*   *Kalmus*   *Russian*

Symphonic dances, op.45   35'
  *3 *3 *3 *3—asx—4 3 3 1—tmp+5—hp, pf—str   11' 10'
  Foley   *Kalmus*   14'

Symphony, D minor (1891) (Youth symphony)   13'
  2 2 2 2—4 2 3 1—tmp—str
  Ed. Paul Lamm.
  Kalmus

Symphony no.1, op.13, D minor   42'
  *3 2 2 2—4 3 3 1—tmp+5—str   13' 9' 8'
  Breitkopf   *Kalmus*   *Russian*   12'

Symphony no.2, op.27, E minor   60'
  *3 *3 *3 2—4 3 3 1—tmp+3—str   20' 11'
  Fleisher Collection has a version employing cuts authorized (and   14' 15'
  used at least once) by the composer.
  Boosey   *Foley*   *Kalmus*

Symphony no.3, op.44, A minor   39'
  *3 *3 *3 *3—4 3 3 1—tmp+5—hp, cel—str   13' 12'
  Foley   *Kalmus*   14'

Three Russian songs, op.41   12'
  chorus of altos and basses   3' 5' 4'
  *3 *3 *3 *3—4 3 3 1—tmp+4—hp, pf—str
  Foley

Die Toteninsel, op.29 (Isle of the dead)   20'
  *3 *3 *3 *3—6 3 3 1—tmp+2—hp—str
  Boosey   *Foley*   *Kalmus*

Vocalise   6'
  2 *3 2 2—2 0 0 0—str
  16-20 violins playing solo line, accompanied by the remainder of
  the orchestra. Arr. by the composer for orchestra. Kalmus ed.
  Clinton Nieweg.
  Boosey   *Foley*   *Kalmus*   *Luck*

Vocalise (arr. Daniel Braden)   6'
  solo soprano
  str
  Kalmus

Raksin, David   1912 -

Toy concertino   6'
  *2 1 2 1—2 2 0 0—tmp+1—str
  concertino (8 players): tin fife; piccolo trumpet; 2 ocarinas; toy
  glockenspiel; bird warble alternating ratchets & duck squawk;
  toy snare drum alternating triangle and pop-gun; cuckoo call
  alternating toy accordion or toy concertina or harmonica.
  Broude Bros.

Rameau, Jean Philippe   1683 - 1764

Ballet suite   12'
  *2 *2 2 2—2 2 0 0—tmp+2—str
  Arr. Felix Mottl.
  Contents—Menuett (from *Platée*); Musette (from *Fêtes d'Hébé*);
  Tambourin (from *Fêtes d'Hébé*).
  Kalmus   *Peters*

Dardanus: Suite   11'
  2 2 0 2—str
  Ed. Paul Henry Lang.
  Mercury

Les Fêtes d'Hébé: Divertissement   20'
  *2 2 0 1—2 1 0 0—tmp—str
  Arr. Fernand Oubradous.
  EMT

Les Paladins: Suite no.2
  *2 2 0 2—2 0 0 0—cnt—str
  Ed. Roger Desormière.
  Oiseau Lyre

Platée: Suite des danses   8'
  *2 2 0 1—str
  Arr. Fernand Oubradous.
  EMT

Suite for string orchestra   15'
  str
  Arranged by R. Temple-Savage from six harpsichord pieces.
  Boosey

Ran, Shulamit   1949 -

Chicago skyline   5'
  0 0 0 0—6 4 3 2—tmp+3
  Presser

Concerto for orchestra 25'
=2 *2 =3 *3—4 3 3 1—tmp+3—pf—str
Presser

Legends
=3 *2 =3 *3—4 3 3 2—tmp+5—hp, cel, pf—str 16.14.12.12.9
Two of the clarinets double on bass clarinet.
Presser

Symphony 34'
*2 *2 =3 *3—6 4 3 1—tmp+4—str
Presser

Rands, Bernard   1935 -

Agenda, for young players 13'
2 2 2 2—2 2 2 0—2perc—str 6.6.4.4.2
2-6 percussion players who need have no knowledge of
conventional music notation may be added. Wind and string
forces may be increased. Graphic notation.
Universal

Canti del sole 28'
solo tenor
=1 0 =1 0—0 1 1 0—2perc—pf—vn, va, vc, db
Universal

Canti lunatici 29'
solo soprano
=2 2 =2 2—2 2 2 0—2perc—2hp, cel, pf—str (min 8.8.6.4.2)
Universal

Fanfare for a festival 2'
2 2 2 2—2 2 2 0—tmp—str
Universal

Hiraeth 30'
solo violoncello
=3 *3 *4 *3—4 3 3 1—tmp+4—2hp, cel, pf, elec org—str
Two of the flutists double on alto flute.
Universal

Madrigali (after Monteverdi/Berio) 22'
1 1 0 0—1 1 0 0—2perc—str 6.6.4.2.1
Universal

Ránki, György   1907 -

Sinfonia 1 19'
*2 *2 *2 *2—4 2 3 1—tmp+3—hp, pf/cel—str
EMB

Ravel, Maurice   1875 - 1937

Alborada del gracioso   9'
     *3 *3 2 *3—4 2 3 1—tmp+6—2hp—str
Kalmus ed. Nieweg & Bradburd.
Eschig   *Kalmus*

Bolero   13'
     *3 *3 =3 *3—ssx, tsx—4 4 3 1—tmp+4—hp, cel—str
One oboist doubles on oboe d'amore. Score actually calls for
sopranino saxophone also, but the passage in question is
normally played on soprano saxophone.
Durand

Concerto, piano, G major   23'
     *2 *2 +2 2—2 1 1 0—tmp+3—hp—str | 9' 9' 5' |
Durand

Concerto, piano (left hand), D major   19'
     *3 *3 =4 *3—4 3 3 1—tmp+4—hp—str
Durand

Daphnis et Chloé   50'
     chorus
     =4 *3 =4 *4—4 4 3 1—tmp+8—2hp, cel—str
The chorus may be dispensed with by playing the cues in the
orchestral parts; these cues are not indicated in the score.
Kalmus edition by Clinton F. Nieweg.
Durand   *Kalmus*

Daphnis et Chloé: Suite no.1   12'
     optional chorus | 5' 3' 4' |
     =4 *3 =4 *4—4 4 3 1—tmp+6—2hp, cel—str
Kalmus edition by Clark McAlister.
Contents—Nocturne; Interlude; Danse guerrière.
Durand   *Kalmus*

Daphnis et Chloé: Suite no.2   18'
     optional chorus | 6' 7' 5' |
     =4 *3 =4 *4—4 4 3 1—tmp+8—2hp, cel—str
Kalmus edition by Clinton F. Nieweg.
Contents—Lever Du Jour; Pantomime; Danse générale.
Durand   *Kalmus*

Don Quichotte à Dulcinée   6'
     solo baritone
     2 *2 2 2—2 1 0 0—1perc—hp—str
Contents—Chanson romanesque; Chanson épique; Chanson à
boire.
Durand

Gaspard de la nuit   **22'**
=3 *3 =4 *3—4 3 3 1—tmp+5—2hp, cel—str   7' 6' 9'
One trumpet doubles on flugelhorn. Orchestrated by Marius
Constant.
Contents—Ondine; Le Gibet; Scarbo.
Durand

Introduction & Allegro   **11'**
solo harp
1 1 0 0—str quartet
Kalmus

Ma Mère l'Oye (Mother Goose)   **29'**
*2 *2 2 *2—2 0 0 0—tmp+3—hp, cel—str   3' 4' 2'
Kalmus edition by Nancy Bradburd & Clinton F. Nieweg. 5' 4' 5'
The following two entries include between them nearly all the 6'
music of the complete ballet; only some connecting transitions are
eliminated and the order of movements is changed slightly.
Durand   *Kalmus*

Ma Mère l'Oye: Prélude et Danse du rouet   **7'**
*2 *2 2 2—2 0 0 0—tmp+2—hp, cel—str   3' 4'
Kalmus version ed. Clinton F. Nieweg.
Durand   *Kalmus*

Ma Mère l'Oye (Mother Goose): 5 pièces enfantines **16'**
*2 *2 2 *2—2 0 0 0—tmp+3—hp, cel—str   2' 3' 3'
Kalmus edition by Nancy Bradburd.   4' 4'
Contents—Pavane de la Belle au bois dormant (Pavane of the
Sleeping Beauty); Petit Poucet (Tom Thumb); Laideronnette,
impératrice des pagodes (Laideronnette, empress of the pagodas);
Les Entretiens de la Belle et de la Bête (Conversations of Beauty
and the beast); Le Jardin féerique (The enchanted garden).
Durand   *Kalmus*

Menuet antique   **9'**
*3 *3 *3 *3—4 3 3 1—tmp—hp—str
Enoch

Pavane pour une infante défunte (Pavane for a dead princess) **6'**
2 1 2 2—2 0 0 0—hp—str
Eschig   *Kalmus*

Rapsodie espagnole   **15'**
*4 *3 *3 *4—4 3 3 1—tmp+6—2hp, cel—str 4' 2' 3' 6'
Kalmus edition by Nancy Bradburd.
Contents—Prélude à la nuit; Malagueña; Habanera; Feria.
Durand   *C. Fischer*   *Kalmus*

Shéhérazade 17'
  soprano solo 10' 3' 4'
  *3 *3 2 2—4 2 3 1—tmp+3—2hp, cel—str
  Kalmus edition by Clinton F. Nieweg.
  Contents—Asie (Asia); La Flûte enchantée (The enchanted flute);
  L'Indifférént (The indifferent one).
  Durand   *C. Fischer*   *Kalmus*

Shéhérazade; ouverture de féerie 14'
  *3 *3 2 3—contrabass sarrusophone—4 4 3 1—tmp+5—2hp,
  cel—str
  Salabert

Le Tombeau de Couperin 17'
  *2 *2 2 2—2 1 0 0—hp—str 3' 6' 5' 3'
  Kalmus ed. Nieweg & Bradburd.
  Contents—Prélude; Forlane; Menuet; Rigaudon.
  Durand   *Kalmus*

Trois Poèmes de Stéphane Mallarmé 11'
  solo voice (mezzo -soprano or baritone)
  *2 0 *2 0—pf—str quartet
  Contents—Soupir; Placet futile; Surgi De La Croupe et du bond.
  Durand   *Kalmus*

Tzigane, violin & orchestra 10'
  *2 2 2 2—2 1 0 0—1perc—hp, cel—str
  Durand   *C. Fischer*

La Valse 12'
  *3 *3 *3 *3—4 3 3 1—tmp+6—2hp—str
  Durand

Valses nobles et sentimentales 16'
  2 *3 2 2—4 2 3 1—tmp+6—2hp, cel—str 1' 2' 2'
  Kalmus edition by Clinton F. Nieweg. 2' 1' 1'
  Durand   *Kalmus* 4' 3'

Read, Gardner   1913 -

First overture 8'
  *3 *3 *3 *3—4 3 3 1—tmp+3—hp, pf—str
  Optional: Eh, bcl, cbn, hp, pf. Original publisher was Composers
  Press. This work may be out of print, but materials are in the
  Fleisher Collection.

Night flight, op.44 7'
  *4 *3 *3 *3—4 3 3 1—tmp+3—hp—str
  Peters

Pennsylvania suite, op.67 16'
  *4 *3 *3 *3—4 3 3 1—tmp+2—hp, pf—str
  May be performed with: *3 *2 2 2—4 3 3 1—tmp+2—str.
  Based on folk songs of western Pennsylvania.
  Contents—Dunlap's Creek; I'm a beggar; John Riley.
  Belwin

Symphony no.3, op.75   25'
    *3 *3 *3 *3—4 3 3 1—tmp+3—pf—str
    Belwin

Reed, H. Owen   1910 -

La fiesta mexicana   23'
    *3 *3 *4 *3—4 4 4 2—tmp+4—hp—str | 9' 7' 7' |
    Eh & cbn are optional. Brief off-stage band can be covered by the
    above aggregate. Contents—Prelude & Aztec dance; Mass;
    Carnival.
    Belwin

Reger, Max   1873 - 1916

Serenade, B-flat major   8'
    2 2 2 2—4 0 0 0
    Completed by Martien van Woerkum & Kees Verheijen.
    Compusic

Symphonic prolog to a tragedy   35'
    *3 *3 *3 *3—6 3 3 1—tmp+2—str
    Peters

Variations and fugue on a merry theme of Joh. Adam Hiller, op.100   39'
    2 2 2 *3—4 2 3 1—tmp—hp—str
    Bote & Bock   *Kalmus*

Variations and fugue on a theme of Mozart, op.132   35'
    3 2 2 2—4 2 0 0—tmp—hp—str
    Kalmus   *Peters*

Vier Tondichtungen nach A. Böcklin, op.128 (Four tone-poems after   24'
A. Böcklin) | 8' 4' 8' 4' |
    *3 *2 2 *3—4 3 3 1—tmp+3—str
    Contents—Der geigende Eremit (The hermit fiddler); Im Spiel der
    Wellen (Play of the waves); Die Toteninsel (Isle of the dead);
    Bacchanal (Bacchanale).
    Kalmus

Reich, Steve   1936 -

The desert music   46'
    amplified chorus of 27 voices
    *4 *4 *4 *4—4 4 3 1—2tmp+7—2pf (4 players)—str 12.12.9.9.6
    3 of the fl dbl on pic; 3ob dbl on Eh; 3cl dbl on bcl; 3 of the
    pianists dbl on synth. Woodwinds are amplified, and 2va use
    contact microphones.
    An alternative version is for 10 singers (amplified) and reduced
    orchestra.
    Boosey

The four sections   25'
    *4 4 *4 *4—4 4 4 1—tmp+4—2pf (dbl 2 synth)—str 18.16.12.8.6 | 11' 2' 6' |
    Boosey | 6' |

Three movements 15'
    *4 *3 3 *4—4 3 3 1—5perc—2pf (8-hands)—str 14.14.8.8.8
    Two of the flutists double on piccolo; 2 of the bassoonists double
    on contrabassoon.
    Boosey

7'	4'	4'

Variations 21'
    3 3 0 0—0 3 3 1—2pf, 3 elec org (synth)—str
    For performance in "ensemble form," strings may play parts singly
    (min 2.2.2.2.1).
    Boosey

Reinecke, Carl   1824 - 1910

Symphony no.1, op.79, A major 26'
    2 2 2 2—4 2 3 0—tmp—str
    Kalmus

Symphony no.2, op.134, C minor (Hakon Jarl) 38'
    2 2 2 2—4 2 3 0—tmp—str
    Contents—Hakon Jarl; Thora; In Odin's Hain; Oluf's Sieg.
    Kalmus

Symphony no.3, op.227, G minor 33'
    2 2 2 2—4 2 3 0—tmp—str
    Kalmus

Respighi, Ottorino   1879 - 1936

Adagio con variazioni, violoncello & orchestra 8'
    *3 *3 2 2—2 0 0 0—hp—str
    This work may be out of print, but orchestral materials are in the
    Fleisher Collection.
    Bongiovani

Antiche danze ed arie (Ancient airs and dances): Set I 16'
    2 *3 0 2—2 1 0 0—hp, hpsd—str
    Based on lute music of the 16th century.
    Kalmus   *Ricordi*

3'	4'	5'	4'

Antiche danze ed arie (Ancient airs and dances): Set II 19'
    *3 *3 2 2—3 2 3 0—tmp—hp, hpsd 4-hands—str
    One hpsd player doubles on celeste.
    Based on lute music of the 16th century.
    Ricordi

4'	4'	5'	6'

Antiche danze ed arie (Ancient airs and dances): Set III 19'
    str
    Based on lute music of the 16th century.
    Ricordi

4'	8'	3'	4'

La Boutique fantasque (after Rossini): Suite 21'
    *3 *3 2 2—4 3 3 1—tmp+5—hp, cel—str
    Contents—Overture; Tarantella; Mazurka; Danse cosaque;
    Can-can; Valse lente; Nocturne; Galop.
    Chester   *Kalmus*

2'	2'	3'
2'	2'	4'
4'	2'	

Cinq Études-tableaux
see under: Rachmaninoff, Sergei

Fantasia slava 13'
solo piano
*3 *2 2 2—4 2 0 0—tmp+1—str
Ricordi

Feste romane (Roman festivals) 24'
*3 *3 =4 *3—4 4 3 1—3 buccine or extra trumpets—tmp+9 | 5' 7' 7' 5' |
—pf 4-hands, org, mand—str
Contents—Circenses (Circus games); Il giubileo (The jubilee);
L'ottobrata (Harvest festivals in October); La Befana
(Epiphany).
Ricordi

Fontane di Roma (Fountains of Rome) 15'
*3 *3 *3 2—4 3 3 1—tmp+2—2hp, cel, pf, opt org—str | 4' 3' 3' 5' |
Kalmus ed. Clinton F. Nieweg & Nancy M. Bradburd.
Contents—La fontana di Valle Giulia all'alba (The fountain of
Valle Giulia at dawn); La Fontana del Tritone al mattino (The
Triton fountain at morn); La Fontana de Trevi al meriggio (The
fountain of Trevi at midday); La fontana di Villa Medici al
tramonto (The Villa Medici fountain at sunset).
Kalmus   Ricordi

Impressioni brasiliane (Brazilian impressions) 20'
*3 *3 *3 2—4 3 2 1—tmp+3—hp, cel, pf—str | 10' 5' 5' |
Contents—Notte tropicale (Tropical night); Butantan (In a
snake-garden near São Paulo); Canzone e danza (Song and
dance).
Ricordi

Lauda per la nativitá del Signore 25'
chorus   solos SSA (or SAT)
*2 *2 0 2—1perc—pf 4-hands
Ricordi

Pini di Roma (Pines of Rome) 23'
*3 *3 *3 *3—4 3 4 0—6 buccine (2 soprano, 2 tenor, 2 bass) | 3' 7' 7' 6' |
—tmp+5—hp, cel, pf, org—str
Buccine may be substituted for by cues in the brass plus an
additional 5th & 6th hn and a 4th tp. 4th tbn part often played on
tuba.
Contents—I pini di Villa Borghese (The pines of the Villa
Borghese); Pini presso una catacomba (Pines near a catacomb); I
pini del Gianicolo (The pines of the Janiculum); I pini della Via
Appia (The pines of the Appian Way).
Ricordi

Rossiniana 25'
*3 *3 2 2—4 3 3 1—tmp+5—hp, cel—str
Freely transcribed from Rossini's *Les Riens*.
Simrock

Il tramonto 16'
  mezzo-soprano solo
  str orch (or str quartet)
  Ricordi

Trittico Botticelliano 18'
  1 1 1 1—1 1 0 0—1perc—hp, cel, pf—str 6' 7' 5'
  Contents—La primavera (Spring); L'adorazione dei Magi
  (Adoration of the Magi); La nascita di Venere (The birth of
  Venus).
  Ricordi

Gli uccelli (The birds) 19'
  *2 1 2 2—2 2 0 0—hp, cel—str 3' 5' 3'
  The movements are based on works of 17th- and 18th-century 4' 4'
  composers.
  Contents—Preludio (Prelude); La colomba (The dove); La gallina
  (The hen); L'usignolo (The nightingale); Il cuccù (The cuckoo).
  Ricordi

Vetrate di chiesa (Church windows) 27'
  *3 *3 *3 *3—4 3 3 1—tmp+4—hp, cel, pf, org—str 6' 6' 5'
  Contents—La fuga in Egitto (Flight into Egypt); San Michele 10'
  arcangelo (St. Michael, archangel); Il mattutino di Santa Chiara
  (The matins of Santa Chiara); San Gregorio Magno (St. Gregory
  the Great).
  Ricordi

Revueltas, Silvestre   1899 - 1940

Homenaje a Federico Garcia Lorca 13'
  *1 0 +1 0—0 2 1 1—1perc—pf—2vn, db
  Southern

Janitzio 15'
  *3 2 +2 2—4 2 2 1—3perc—str
  Peer

Reynolds, Roger   1934 -

Fiery wind 15'
  *3 *2 =2 *2—3 3 3 1—4perc—pf—str
  Two of the flutists double on piccolo.
  Peters

Graffiti 9'
  *3 *3 *3 *3—4 3 3 1—tmp+7—2hp, pf—str
  Peters

Quick are the mouths of earth 18'
  3 1 0 0—0 1 2 0—2perc—pf—3vc
  Peters

Wedge 8'
  *2 0 0 0—0 2 2 1—3perc—pf/cel—db
  Peters

Rezniček, Emil Nikolaus von   1860 - 1945

Donna Diana: Overture   5'
*3 2 2 2—4 2 0 0—tmp+1—opt hp—str
Kalmus   *Universal*

Rheinberger, Joseph   1839 - 1901

Concerto, organ, no.1, op.137, F major   24'
0 0 0 0—3 0 0 0—str   8' 8' 8'
Forberg   *Kalmus*

Concerto, organ, no.2, op.177, G minor   25'
0 0 0 0—2 2 0 0—tmp—str   10' 8' 7'
Forberg

Riegger, Wallingford   1885 - 1961

Dance rhythms, op.58   8'
2 2 2 2—2 2 2 0—tmp+4—hp—str
AMP

Music for orchestra, op.50   7'
*3 *3 2 *3—4 3 3 1—tmp+3—str
AMP

Rimsky-Korsakov, Nikolai   1844 - 1908

Capriccio espagnol, op.34   15'
*3 *2 2 2—4 2 3 1—tmp+5—hp—str   1' 5' 1'
Contents—Alborada; Variazioni; Alborada; Scena e canto   5' 3'
gitano; Fandango asturiano.
Belaieff   *Kalmus*

Christmas eve: Suite   23'
optional chorus
*3 2 +3 2—4 3 3 1—tmp+4—hp, cel—str
Contents—Introduction; Tableaux 6 & 7; Polonaise; Tableau
(movements are continuous).
Belaieff   *Kalmus*

Christmas eve: Polonaise   6'
*3 2 +3 2—4 3 3 1—tmp+4—hp—str
Belaieff   *Kalmus*

Concerto, piano, op.30, C-sharp minor   13'
2 2 2 2—2 2 3 0—tmp—str
In one movement.
Belaieff   *Kalmus*

Concerto, trombone & band   11'
*3 2 =5 2—2asx, tsx, bsx, alto clarinet—4 4 3 1—baritone   3' 3' 5'
horn—3perc
Adapted for American band by Walter Nallin.
MCA

Conte féerique
see his: Skazka, op.29 (Russian fairy tale)

Le Coq d'or (The golden cockerel): Suite — 25'
*3 *3 *3 *3—4 3 3 1—tmp+4—2hp, cel—str
| 9' 4' 6' 6' |

Contents—King Dodon at his palace; King Dodon on the
battlefield; King Dodon with the Queen of Chamakka; Nuptials
and the deplorable end of Dodon.
Kalmus   Russian

Le Coq d'or (The golden cockerel): Introduction & Wedding march — 9'
*3 *3 *3 *3—4 3 3 1—tmp+4—2hp, cel—str
| 5' 4' |
Forberg   Kalmus

Dubinushka, op.62 — 4'
optional chorus
*3 2 3 2—4 3 3 1—tmp+4—str
3rd trumpet is optional.
Belaieff   Kalmus   Russian

Fantaisie de concert sur les thèmes russes, op.33 — 12'
solo violin
2 2 2 2—2 2 0 0—tmp+1—str
Belaieff   Kalmus

The Maid of Pskov (Pskovityanka): Overture — 8'
*3 *3 *3 *3—4 3 3 1—tmp—str
This is the overture to the opera proper (3rd version), and not the
same work as the overture listed below. This work may be out of
print; materials are available in the Fleisher Collection.
Breitkopf

The Maid of Pskov (Pskovityanka): Overture & Three entr'actes — 27'
*3 2 2 2—4 2 3 1—tmp+2—str
Although published under this title, the overture is actually that
of *Boyarina Vera Sheloga,* op.54, which was a prologue to the
second version of *The maid of Pskov.* This is a different overture
from the one listed above.
Breitkopf   ´Kalmus

May night: Overture — 8'
2 2 2 2—4 2 3 0—tmp—str
Belaieff   Kalmus

Mlada: Suite — 15'
optional chorus
=4 *3 *4 *3—6 3 3 1—tmp+5—3hp—str
| 2' 4' 2' |
| 2' 5' |

Contents—Introduction; Rédowa; Danse lithuanienne; Danse
indienne; Cortège.
Belaieff   Kalmus

Overture on Russian themes, op.28 — 12'
*2 2 2 2—4 2 3 0—tmp+1—opt hp—str
Belaieff   Kalmus

Russian Easter overture, op.36 (Grand Paque russe)   14'
  *3 2 2 2—4 2 3 1—tmp+4—hp—str
  Belaieff   *Kalmus*

Sadko: Tableau musical, op.5   12'
  *3 2 2 2—4 2 3 1—tmp+3—hp—str
  Rev. 1891. Also known as *Sadko: Orchestral fantasy, 2nd
  version.*
  Kalmus

Scheherazade, op.35   42'
  *3 *2 2 2—4 2 3 1—tmp+5—hp—str | 10' 11' |
  Contents [traditional movement titles, not given in score]—1. The | 10' 11' |
  sea and Sindbad's ship; 2. The tale of Prince Kalendar; 3. The
  young prince and the princess; 4. The festival at Bagdad, The sea,
  The ship goes to pieces on a rock.
  Belaieff   *Kalmus*

Sinfonietta on Russian themes, op.31   20'
  2 2 2 2—4 2 3 0—tmp—str
  Belaieff   *Kalmus*

Skazka, op.29 (Russian fairy tale)   13'
  *3 2 2 2—4 2 3 1—tmp+3—hp—str
  Sometimes referred to as *Conte féerique.*
  Belaieff   *Kalmus*

Snegourotchka (The snow maiden): Suite   13'
  *3 *2 2 2—4 2 3 1—tmp+4—str | 4' 3' 2' 4' |
  Contents—Introduction; Dance of the birds; Cortège; Dance of the
  buffoons.
  Breitkopf   *Kalmus*   *Universal*

Snegourotchka: Dance of the buffoons   4'
  *3 2 2 2—4 2 3 1—tmp+4—str
  Kalmus

Symphony no.1, op.1, E-flat minor   27'
  2 2 2 2—4 2 3 0—tmp—str | 8' 8' 5' 6' |
  Breitkopf   *Kalmus*   *Russian*

Symphony no.2, op.9 (Antar)   29'
  *3 *2 2 2—4 2 3 1—tmp+4—hp—str | 11' 5' 5' |
  Breitkopf   *Kalmus*   *Russian* | 8' |

Symphony no.3, op.32, C major   35'
  *3 2 2 2—4 2 3 1—tmp—str | 14' 6' 9' |
  Belaieff   *Kalmus* | 6' |

Tsar Saltan: Suite, op.57   17'
  *3 *3 3 *3—4 2 3 1—tmp+4—hp, cel—str | 4' 6' 7' |
  Contrabassoon is optional. Contents—Allegretto alla marcia;
  Introduction to Act II; The three wonders.
  Breitkopf   *Kalmus*

Tsar Saltan: Flight of the bumblebee 3'
 2 2 2 2—2 0 0 0—str
 Breitkopf   *Kalmus*   *Russian*

The tsar's bride: Overture 7'
 *3 2 2 2—4 2 3 1—tmp—hp—str
 Belaieff   *Kalmus*

Rochberg, George 1918 -

Black sounds 12'
 *2 1 =2 0—2 2 2 1—tmp+3—pf/cel
 Presser

Cheltenham concerto 15'
 1 1 1 1—1 1 1 0—str
 Presser

Night music 12'
 *3 *3 *3 *3—4 3 3 1—tmp+1—hp—str
 Presser

Time-span (II) 10'
 3 *3 *3 2—4 3 3 1—2perc—cel, pf—str
 MCA

Rodgers, Richard 1902 - 1979

Carousel: The carousel waltz 9'
 *3 *3 *3 *3—4 3 3 1—tmp+4—hp—str
 Three of the flutists double on piccolo.
 R&H

Slaughter on Tenth Avenue 10'
 *2 *2 *3 2—4 3 3 1—tmp+3—hp, pf/cel—str
 Arr. Robert Russell Bennett.
 Chappell

Rodrigo, Joaqųn 1901 -

A la busca del más allá (In search of the beyond) 17'
 *3 *3 2 2—4 3 3 1—tmp+1—hp, cel—str
 Schott

Concierto andaluz 24'
 4 solo guitars 8' 10' 6'
 *2 2 2 2—4 2 0 0—str
 Salabert *Schott*

Concierto de Aranjuez 21'
 solo guitar 6' 10' 5'
 *2 *2 2 2—2 2 0 0—str
 A version by Nicanor Zabaleta for solo harp with orchestra is
 available from Schott.
 Schott *UME*

Concierto madrigal   30'
  2 solo guitars
  *2 1 1 1—1 1 0 0—str

2'	3'	2'
2'	1'	2'
2'	6'	5'
		5'

  Schott

Concierto serenata   24'
  solo harp

8'	10'	6'

  *2 2 2 2—2 2 0 0—str
  UME

Cuatro madrigales amatorios   9'
  solo soprano

3'	3'	1' 2'

  *2 2 1 0—1 1 0 0—1perc—str
  Arrangements of 16th-century songs. Contents—¿Con qué la
  lavaré?; Vos me matásteis; ¿De dónde venis, amore?; De los
  álamos vengo, madre.
  Chester

Fantasía para un gentilhombre   22'
  solo guitar
  *2 1 0 1—0 1 0 0—str
  Contents—Villano y Ricercare; Españoleta y Fanfare de la
  caballeria de Nápoles; Danza de las hachas; Canario.
  Schott

Zarabanda lejana y villancico   8'
  str
  Eschig

Rodríguez, Robert Xavier   1946 -

Scrooge   20'
  solo bass-baritone   chorus
  *2 *2 =2 *2—2 2 2 0—tmp+3—hp, pf/cel/hpsd—str
  Hns may be doubled; cel & hpsd may be synthesized. Concert
  scenes from Dickens' *A Christmas Carol.*
  Schirmer, G.

Rogers, Bernard   1893 - 1968

The musicians of Bremen   22'
  narrator
  *1 1 1 1—1 1 0 0—tmp+1—pf—str (without va)
  May be performed with one string player on a part.
  Presser

Once upon a time; five fairy tales for small orchestra   12'
  *2 2 2 2—2 2 1 0—tmp+3—hp, "clavi-cembalo (adapted
  piano)"—str
  Kalmus

Soliloquy for flute and strings   6'
  str
  C. Fischer

Three Japanese dances   12'
    optional mezzo-soprano
    =3 *3 *3 *3—4 2 3 1—tmp+4—hp, cel, pf—str
    One flutist also doubles on bass flute in C, but both bass and alto
    flutes are optional.
    Presser

Rorem, Ned   1923 -

Air music; ten variations for orchestra   20'
    *3 *3 =3 *3—4 3 3 1—4perc—hp, cel, pf—str
    All three of the flutists double on piccolo.
    Boosey

Concerto, organ   25'
    0 0 0 0—2 1 1 0—tmp—str
    Boosey

Concerto, piano (1969)   23'
    *3 *3 +3 *3—4 3 3 1—tmp+7—hp, cel—str
    3rd clarinet doubles on E-flat clarinet and alto saxophone.
    Boosey

Concerto, piano (left hand)   25'
    *2 2 2 2—2 2 2 0—tmp+3—hp, cel—str
    Boosey

Concerto, violin   22'
    *1 1 2 1—0 1 0 0—tmp—str
    Boosey

Design   18'
    *2 2 2 2—4 2 2 0—tmp+5—hp, cel, pf—str
    Boosey

Eagles   8'
    *3 *3 =4 *3—4 3 3 1—tmp+7—hp, cel, pf—str
    Boosey

Ideas for easy orchestra   12'
    1 1 1 1—2 1 1 0—tmp+2—hp, pf—str
    Eight movements, any of which may be performed separately, and
    each of which uses a different combination of instruments.
    Boosey

Lions (a dream)   14'
    combo: asx, drum set, pf, db
    *3 *3 +3 2—4 3 3 1—tmp+6—hp, cel—str
    Boosey

A Quaker reader   20'
    *2 *2 2 2—2 1 1 0—str
    Originally for organ.
    Boosey

Sinfonia 9'
  *3 *3 =4 *3—2 0 0 0—tmp+5—pf/cel
  Tmp, perc, & pf/cel are all optional.
  Peters

String symphony 23'
  str
  Contents—Waltz; Berceuse; Scherzo; Nocturne; Rondo.
  Boosey

  | 5' 2' 2' |
  | 8' 6' |

Symphony no.1 27'
  *2 2 2 2—4 2 2 0—tmp+5—hp—str
  Southern

Symphony no.2 18'
  *2 *2 2 2—2 1 1 0—tmp+2—hp, pf—str
  Boosey

Symphony no.3 24'
  *3 *3 *3 *3—4 3 3 1—tmp+6—hp, cel, pf—str
  Boosey

Water music 17'
  solo clarinet & violin
  *1 *1 0 1—1 0 0 0—2perc—hp, pf/cel—str
  Boosey

Rossini, Gioacchino   1792 - 1868

*Rossini editions in general have been poor and untrustworthy.
There are many competing versions, and the scores frequently
conflict with the parts. Critical editions of the Fondazione Rossini
Pesaro, published by Ricordi, are a great improvement as they
become available.*

L'assedio di Corinto (The siege of Corinth): Overture 10'
  *3 2 2 2—4 2 4 0—tmp+2—str
  4th tbn part often played on tuba.
  Carisch   *Heugel*   *Kalmus*   *Ricordi*

Il barbiere di Siviglia (The barber of Seville): Overture (critical 8'
edition)
  2 2 2 2—2 2 0 0—tmp+2—str
  This overture originally written for his *Aureliano in Palmira*
  (1813). Ricordi critical edition by Alberto Zedda, 1969. Kalmus
  also offers what it terms the "original Italian edition," the
  instrumentation of which resembles the above, but with the
  addition of a trombone.
  Ricordi

Il barbiere di Siviglia (The barber of Seville): Overture 8'
  *2 2 2 2—2 2 3 0—tmp+1—str
  This overture originally written for his *Aureliano in Palmira*
  (1813). Kalmus identifies this version with 3tbn as the "German
  edition."
  Breitkopf   *Kalmus*   *Luck*

La boutique fantasque
see under: Respighi, Ottorino, 1879-1936

La Cenerentola (Cinderella): Overture   8'
*2 2 2 2—2 2 1 0—tmp+1—str
Kalmus identifies this as the "original Italian edition." Luck's
Music Library offers a version with the following
instrumentation:
*2 2 2 1—2 2 0 0—tmp—str.
Kalmus   *Ricordi*

La gazza ladra (The thieving magpie): Overture   10'
*2 2 2 2—4 2 1 0—tmp+4—str
Ricordi critical edition by Alberto Zedda, 1979.
Kalmus version is identified as the "original Italian edition."
Kalmus   *Ricordi*

La gazza ladra (The thieving magpie): Overture (arr. Kogel)   10'
*2 2 2 2—4 2 3 1—tmp+3—str
Ed. & arr. Gustav Kogel. Kalmus identifies this as the "German
edition."
Breitkopf   *Kalmus*   *Luck*

Guillaume Tell (William Tell): Overture   12'
*2 *2 2 2—4 2 3 0—tmp+3—str
Breitkopf   *Kalmus*   *Ricordi*

Guillaume Tell: Pas de six   6'
*2 2 2 2—2 2 0 0—str
Kalmus

L'Italiana in Algeri: Overture (critical edition)   9'
*1 2 2 1—2 2 0 0—2perc—str
Critical ed. by Azio Corghi, 1981.
Ricordi

L'Italiana in Algeri: Overture   9'
1 2 2 2—2 2 0 0—tmp—str
Kalmus identifies this as the "German edition." Kalmus also offers
an "original Italian edition" with the following instrumentation:
2 2 2 2—2 2 1 0—tmp+2—str.
Breitkopf   *Kalmus*   *Luck*

The journey to Rheims
see his: Il viaggio a Reims

Matinées musicales
see under: Britten, Benjamin

Les Riens
see: Respighi, Ottorino, 1879-1936
     Rossiniana

Robert Bruce: Overture   7'
*2 2 2 2—4 4 3 1—tmp+3—str
Kalmus

La scala di seta (The silken staircase): Overture   7'
*1 2 2 1—2 0 0 0—str
Kalmus   *Ricordi*

Semiramide: Overture   12'
*2 2 2 2—4 2 3 0—tmp+1—str
Breitkopf   *Kalmus*   *Ricordi*

Serenata per piccolo complesso   8'
1 *2 0 0—str quartet
Kalmus

The siege of Corinth
see his: L'assedio di Corinto

Il signor Bruschino: Overture   5'
1 2 2 1—2 0 0 0—str
Carisch ed. E. De Guarnieri; Ricordi critical ed. by Arrigo
Gazzaniga, 1986.
Carisch   *Kalmus*   *Ricordi*

Soirées musicales
see under: Britten, Benjamin

Sonata no.1, G major   13'
2vn, vc, db   7' 4' 2'
Frequently performed by string orchestra.
Kalmus

Sonata no.2, A major   12'
2vn, vc, db   7' 3' 2'
Frequently performed by string orchestra.
Kalmus

Sonata no.3, C major   12'
2vn, vc, db   5' 4' 3'
Frequently performed by string orchestra.
Kalmus

Sonata no.4, B-flat major   14'
2vn, vc, db   7' 4' 3'
Frequently performed by string orchestra.
Kalmus

Sonata no.5, E-flat major   20'
2vn, vc, db   12' 4' 4'
Frequently performed by string orchestra.
Kalmus

Sonata no.6, D major   17'
2vn, vc, db   8' 3' 6'
Frequently performed by string orchestra.
Kalmus

Stabat mater · 61'
  chorus   solos SSTB
  2 2 2 2—4 2 3 0—tmp—str
  Kalmus   *Ricordi*   *Schirmer, G.*   *Schott*

7' 6' 7'
6' 5' 10'
5' 5' 5'
5'

Tancredi: Overture · 6'
  2 2 2 2—2 2 0 0—tmp+1—str
  This overture originally written for his *La pietra del paragone.*
  Ricordi critical ed. by Philip Gossett, 1984. Kalmus edition
  includes tmp but no perc.
  Kalmus   *Ricordi*

The thieving magpie
  see his: La gazza ladra

Il Turco in Italia: Overture · 9'
  2 2 2 2—2 2 1 0—tmp+2—str
  Ricordi critical ed. by Margaret Bent, 1988.
  Kalmus   *Ricordi*

Variations for clarinet and small orchestra · 9'
  1 0 2 1—2 0 0 0—str
  Other editions, from EMT, Sikorski, and Zanibon, list 2 oboes
  rather than 2 clarinets in the accompaniment.
  Kalmus

Il viaggio a Reims (The journey to Rheims): Overture · 8'
  *2 2 2 2—2 2 3 0—tmp+2—str
  Ricordi edition calls for an extra flute and an extra trombone.
  Carisch   *Kalmus*   *Ricordi*

William Tell
  see his: Guillaume Tell

Rouse, Christopher   1949 -

Bump · 8'
  3 3 =4 *3—4 3 3 1—5perc—hp, pf/cel—str
  Bass clarinet doubles on baritone saxophone. This is the 3rd
  movement of the composer's *Phantasmata.*
  Boosey   *Helicon*

Concerto, flute · 28'
  3 2 2 *2—4 2 3 1—tmp+3—hp—str
  Boosey

Concerto, trombone · 27'
  0 0 0 *3—4 3 3 1—tmp+4—hp—str
  Boosey

Concerto, violin · 22'
  *2 *2 *2 *2—4 2 3 1—tmp+3—hp, cel—str
  Boosey

Concerto, violoncello 27'
   *2 *2 *2 2—4 3 3 1—tmp+4—hp—str
   Boosey

The infernal machine 5'
   *3 3 =4 *3—4 3 3 1—5perc—hp, cel—str
   All 3 flutists double on piccolo; flutes & oboes all play crystal
   goblets (optional). This work later incorporated as 2nd
   movement of *Phantasmata*.
   Helicon

Iscariot 12'
   *1 *2 1 2—3 1 0 0—2perc—cel—str
   Boosey

Karolju 23'
   chorus
   *2 2 2 2—4 3 3 1—tmp+4—hp—str
   Original carols in Latin, Swedish, French, Spanish, Russian,
   Czech, German, & Italian.
   Boosey

Phantasmata 18'
   *3 3 =4 *3—4 3 3 1—5perc—hp, cel/pf—str 5' 5' 8'
   All 3 flutists double on piccolo; bass clarinet doubles baritone
   saxophone; all flutes & oboes play also crystal goblets
   (optional).
   Contents—The evestrum of Juan de la Cruz in the Sagrada
   Familia, 3 A.M.; The infernal machine; Bump
   Boosey

Symphony no.1 24'
   *2 *2 *2 *2—4 3 3 1—tmp+3—str
   2nd oboe doubles on English horn & oboe d'amore; horns double
   on Wagner tubas (euphoniums may be substituted).
   Boosey

Symphony no.2 21'
   *3 *3 *3 3—4 3 3 1—2tmp+3—hp—str
   Boosey

Roussel, Albert   1869 - 1937
Bacchus et Ariane, op.43: Suite no.1 17'
   *3 *3 *3 *3—4 4 3 1—tmp+4—2hp, cel—str
   Act I of the ballet.
   Durand

Bacchus et Ariane, op.43: Suite no.2 20'
   *3 *3 *3 *3—4 4 3 1—tmp+4—2hp, cel—str
   Contents—Ariadne's awakening; Ariadne and Bacchus; Bacchus'
   dance; The kiss; Bacchus' cortege; Ariadne's dance; Ariadne and
   Bacchus; Bacchanale and the coronation of Ariadne.
   Durand

Concerto for small orchestra, op.34 (Concert pour petit orchestre)   12'
   *2 2 2 2—2 1 0 0—tmp—str   3' 6' 3'
   Durand

Concerto, piano, op.36   17'
   *2 *2 2 2—2 2 0 0—tmp+3—str
   Durand

Évocations, op.15, no.1: Les Dieux dans l'ombre des cavernes   13'
   *3 *3 *3 *3—4 3 3 1—tmp+4—2hp—str
   Durand

Évocations, op.15, no.3: Aux Bords du fleuve sacré   23'
   chorus   solo ATBar
   *3 *3 *3 *3—4 3 3 1—tmp+2—2hp—str
   Durand

Fanfare pour un sacre païen (Fanfare for a pagan rite)   2'
   0 0 0 0—4 4 3 0—tmp
   Durand

Le Festin de l'araignée, op.17 (The spider's feast): Symphonic   16'
fragments
   *2 *2 2 2—2 2 0 0—tmp+2—hp, cel—str
   Durand   *Kalmus*

Le Marchand de sable qui passe... (incidental music)   19'
   1 0 1 0—1 0 0 0—hp—str   4' 4' 4' 7'
   Contents—Prelude; Scene; Interlude and scene; Scene finale.
   Eschig   *Kalmus*

Petite Suite, op.39   11'
   *2 2 2 2—2 2 0 0—tmp+3—str
   Contents—Aubade; Pastorale; Mascarade.
   Durand

Pour Un Fête de printemps, op.22   12'
   *3 *3 2 3—4 2 3 1—tmp+2—hp—str
   Durand

Rapsodie flamande, op.56   9'
   *3 *3 *3 *3—4 3 3 1—tmp+3—hp—str
   Durand

Sinfonietta, op.52   8'
   str   3' 2' 3'
   Durand

Suite in F, op.33   15'
   *3 *3 *3 3—4 4 3 1—tmp+3—hp, cel—str   4' 6' 5'
   Durand

Symphony no.2, op.23, B-flat   40'
   *3 *3 *3 *4—4 4 3 1—tmp+3—2hp, cel—str
   Durand

Symphony no.3, op.42, G minor ... 23'
*3 *3 *3 *3—4 4 3 1—tmp+5—2hp, cel—str ... 6' 8' 3' 6'
Durand

Symphony no.4, op.53, A major ... 20'
*3 *3 *3 *3—4 4 3 1—tmp+3—hp—str ... 6' 7' 3' 4'
Durand

Rózsa, Miklós   1907 - 1995

Concerto, violoncello, op.32 ... 30'
*2 *2 +2 2—4 3 3 1—tmp+3—hp, cel—str
Breitkopf

Rubbra, Edmund   1901 - 1986

Festival overture, op.62 ... 8'
2 2 2 2—4 2 3 1—tmp+1—str
Lengnick

Improvisation for violin & orchestra, op.89 ... 12'
2 *2 2 2—2 2 0 0—tmp+1—hp, cel—str
Lengnick

Rubinstein, Anton   1829 - 1894

Concerto, piano, no.3, op.45, G major ... 31'
2 2 2 2—2 2 0 0—tmp—str ... 11' 7'
C. Fischer   *Kalmus* ... 13'

Concerto, piano, no.4, op.70, D minor ... 29'
*3 2 2 2—2 2 0 0—tmp—str ... 11' 9' 9'
Kalmus   *Simrock*

Concerto, violoncello, no.2, op.96, D minor ... 18'
2 2 2 2—2 2 0 0—tmp—str
Kalmus

Melody in F, op.3, no.1 ... 5'
solo violoncello
2 2 2 2—2 0 0 0—tmp—str
Arr. Vincent d'Indy.
Kalmus

Ruggles, Carl   1876 - 1968

Angels ... 3'
0 0 0 0—0 4 3 0
Although scored for muted brass, this composition may be played
by any seven instruments of equal timbre.
AME

Men and mountains (original 1924 version) ... 15'
*2 *2 1 1—2 2 1 0—1perc—pf—2vn, 2va, 2vc, db
AME

Men and mountains (1936 version for large orchestra) 15'
　*3 *3 *3 *3—4 3 3 1—tmp+3—pf—str
　AME

Organum 8'
　*3 *3 =4 *3—4 3 3 1—tmp+1—pf—str
　AME

Portals 6'
　str
　AME

Sun-treader 15'
　*5 *5 =5 *4—6 5 5 1—tenor tuba
　(=euphonium)—tmp+1—2hp—str
　AME

Russo, William   1928 -

Street music; a blues concerto 30'
　solo harmonica & piano (may be played by one performer)
　*3 3 3 3—4 4 3 1—tmp+3—str
　Harmonica and piano soloist(s) have improvised solos as well as
　written-out passages. 9 members of the orchestra constitute a
　"small ensemble."
　Southern

Symphony no.2, op.32 (Titans) 20'
　*4 *4 *4 *4—4 5 4 1—tmp+2—hp, pf—str
　One of the trumpets (marked "solo trumpet") very high and jazzy.
　Southern

Rutter, John   1945 -

Suite antique 16'
　solo flute
　hpsd—str
　Contents—Prelude; Ostinato; Aria; Waltz; Chanson; Rondeau.
　Oxford

S

Saint-Georges, Joseph Boulogne,   1739 - 1799

Concerto, violin, no.1, G major 16'
　0 2 0 0—2 0 0 0—str
　Ed. Dominique-René de Lerma.
　Peer

Symphonie concertante, op.6, no.1, C major
  solos: 2 violins; or 1 violin & 1 violoncello
  0 2 0 0—2 0 0 0—str

Symphonie concertante, op.10, no.2, A major
  solos: 2 violins & viola
  0 2 0 0—2 0 0 0—str

Symphonie concertante, op.13, G major
  2 solo violins
  str
  Ed. J.F. Paillard.
  Costallat

Symphony no.1, op.11, no.1, G major   16'
  0 2 0 0—2 0 0 0—str
  Ed. Dominique-René de Lerma.
  Peer

Saint-Saëns, Camille   1835 - 1921

Africa, op.89   11'
  solo piano
  2 2 2 2—2 2 3 0—tmp+1—str
  Durand   *Kalmus*

Allegro appassionato, piano & orchestra, op.70   7'
  2 2 2 2—2 2 0 0—str
  Durand   *C. Fischer*   *Kalmus*

Allegro appassionato, violoncello & orchestra, op.43   4'
  2 2 2 2—2 0 0 0—str
  Durand   *Kalmus*

Le Carnaval des animaux (Carnival of the animals)   23'
  2 solo pianos
  *1 0 1 0—2perc—2vn, va, vc, db
  Often performed with full string sections. Occasionally a
  narrator is used, reading humorous verses by Ogden Nash.
  Durand   *Luck*

Christmas oratorio
  see his: Oratorio de Noël, op.12

Concerto, piano, no.1, op.17, D major   27'
  2 2 2 2—4 2 0 0—tmp—str   12' 8' 7'
  Durand   *C. Fischer*

Concerto, piano, no.2, op.22, G minor   24'
  2 2 2 2—2 2 0 0—tmp—str   11' 6' 7'
  3 optional cymbal notes in last movement would require an extra
  percussionist.
  Durand   *Kalmus*

Concerto, piano, no.3, op.29, E-flat major   29'
    2 2 2 2—2 2 3 0—tmp—str   14' 15'
    Durand   *Kalmus*

Concerto, piano, no.4, op.44, C minor   25'
    2 2 2 2—2 2 3 0—tmp—str   12' 13'
    Durand   *Kalmus*

Concerto, piano, no.5, op.103, F major   29'
    *3 2 2 2—4 2 3 0—tmp—str   11' 12'
    Durand   *Kalmus*   6'

Concerto, violin, no.1, op.20, A major   10'
    2 2 2 2—2 2 0 0—tmp—str
    Kalmus

Concerto, violin, no.2, op.58, C major   14'
    2 2 2 2—2 2 3 0—tmp—hp—str
    Durand   *Kalmus*

Concerto, violin, no.3, op.61, B minor   29'
    *2 2 2 2—2 2 3 0—tmp—str   9' 9' 11'
    Durand   *Kalmus*

Concerto, violoncello, no.1, op.33, A minor   19'
    2 2 2 2—2 2 0 0—tmp—str   5' 5' 9'
    Durand   *Kalmus*

Concerto, violoncello, no.2, op.119, D minor   17'
    2 2 2 2—4 2 0 0—tmp—str   11' 6'
    Durand   *Kalmus*

Coronation march
    see his: Marche du couronnement, op.117

Danse macabre, op.40   8'
    *3 2 2 2—4 2 3 1—tmp+3—opt hp—str
    Concertmaster solo with scordatura throughout.
    Kalmus ed. Nieweg.
    Durand   *Kalmus*

Le Déluge, op.45 (The flood)   45'
    chorus   solos SATB
    *3 2 2 2—4 4 5 3—2tmp+3—2hp—str
    2 of the trombones must be valve-trombones.
    Durand

La Foi, op.130: Trois Tableaux symphoniques   28'
    *3 *2 2 2—4 3 3 0—tmp+3—2hp (doubling a single real part),   11' 7'
    harm—str   10'
    Durand

Havanaise, op.83   11'
    solo violin
    2 2 2 2—2 2 0 0—tmp—str
    C. Fischer   *Kalmus*

Introduction and Rondo capriccioso, op.28   10'
  solo violin
  2 2 2 2—2 2 0 0—tmp—str
  C. Fischer   *Kalmus*

La Jeunesse d'Hercule   16'
  *3 2 2 2—4 5 3 1—tmp+3—2hp (doubling one real part)—str
  Durand   *Kalmus*

Marche du couronnement, op.117   8'
  *3 2 2 *3—4 4 3 1—tmp+3—hp—str
  Kalmus

Marche héroïque, op.34   7'
  *3 2 2 2—4 2 3 1—tmp+3—hp—str
  C. Fischer   *Kalmus*

Morceau de concert, harp & orchestra, op.154   16'
  2 2 2 2—2 2 0 0—tmp—str
  Durand   *Kalmus*

Morceau de concert, horn & orchestra, op.94   9'
  2 2 2 2—0 0 3 0—tmp—str
  Durand   *Kalmus*

La Nuit, op.114   10'
  female chorus   solo soprano
  2 2 2 2—4 0 0 0—hp—str
  Durand

Odelette, op.162   14'
  solo flute
  0 2 0 2—str
  Durand   *Kalmus*

Oratorio de Noël, op.12 (Christmas oratorio)   32'
  chorus   solos SAATB
  hp, org—str
  Durand   *Kalmus*   *Schirmer, G.*

3'	5'	3'
3'	3'	3'
4'	2'	6'

Orient et Occident, op.25   6'
  *3 *3 *3 *3—4 3 3 1—tmp+4—str
  Durand   *Kalmus*

Phaéton, op.39   9'
  *3 2 2 *3—4 2 3 1—3tmp+3—2hp—str
  Contrabassoon is optional.
  Durand   *Kalmus*

La Princesse jaune, op.30: Overture   6'
  2 *2 2 2—4 2 3 0—tmp+1—hp—str
  Durand   *Kalmus*

Requiem, op.54   40'
    chorus   solos SATB
    4 *4 0 4—4 0 4 0—4hp (doubling 2 real parts), org—str
    Durand   *Kalmus*

5'	3'	6'
4'	4'	3'
2'	2'	2'
		9'

Rhapsodie d'Auvergne, op.73   10'
    solo piano
    *3 2 2 2—4 2 3 0—tmp+1—str
    Durand   *Kalmus*

Romance, op.36   5'
    solo horn (or violoncello)
    2 1 2 1—str
    Durand   *Kalmus*

Romance, op.37   6'
    solo flute (or violin)
    0 2 2 2—4 2 0 0—tmp—str
    Durand   *Kalmus*

Le Rouet d'Omphale, op.31   9'
    *3 2 2 2—4 2 3 0—tmp+2—hp—str
    Durand   *Kalmus*

Samson et Dalila: Bacchanale   8'
    *3 *3 *3 *3—4 4 3 1—tmp+4—hp—str
    Score lists "harpes," though there is only a single part.
    Durand   *Kalmus*

Septet, op.65   15'
    tp—pf—2vn, va, vc, db
    Durand   *Luck*

Suite algérienne, op.60   19'
    *3 2 2 2—4 4 3 1—tmp+3—str

4'	6'	5'	4'

    Contents—Prélude (En Vue d'Alger); Rhapsodie mauresque;
    Rêverie du soir; Marche militaire française.
    Durand   *Kalmus*

Symphony no.1, op.2, E-flat major   29'
    *3 *2 *3 2—4 4 3 0—bass & contrabass saxhorns (=euphonium &

9'	4'	10'
		6'

    tuba)—2tmp+1—4hp (doubling a single real part)—str
    Durand   *Kalmus*

Symphony no.2, op.55, A minor   23'
    *3 *2 2 2—2 2 0 0—tmp—str

7'	4'	5'	7'

    Durand   *Kalmus*

Symphony no.3, op.78, C minor (Organ symphony)   36'
    *3 *3 *3 *3—4 3 3 1—tmp+2—org, pf 4-hands—str

11'	10'
7'	8'

    Durand   *Kalmus*

Tarantelle, op.6   7'
   solo flute   solo clarinet
   *1 2 0 2—2 2 2 0—tmp—str
   Durand   *Kalmus*

Salieri, Antonio   1750 - 1825

Sinfonia, D major (Giorno onomastico)   20'
   2 2 0 2—2 2 0 0—tmp—str   5' 5' 3' 7'
   2nd bn is optional. Boccaccini ed. by Pietro Spada; Ricordi ed. by
   Renzo Sabatini.
   Boccaccini   *Ricordi*

Sinfonia, D major (Veneziana)   10'
   0 2 0 0—2 0 0 0—str   4' 3' 3'
   Boccaccini ed. by Pietro Spada; Ricordi ed. by Renzo Sabatini.
   Boccaccini   *Ricordi*

Sallinen, Aulis   1935 -

Chamber music I, op.38   13'
   str (min 5.3.2.2.1)
   Novello

Chamber music II   14'
   solo alto flute
   s t r
   Novello

Concerto for chamber orchestra   22'
   *1 1 *2 1—1 0 0 0—str
   Novello

Shadows, op.52   11'
   *3 3 *3 *3—4 3 3 0—tmp+4—hp, pf—str
   Novello

Symphony no.1, op.24   16'
   *3 3 *3 *3—4 3 3 0—tmp+4—hp—str
   Novello

Symphony no.3   27'
   *4 3 *4 *3—4 3 3 1—tmp+3—hp, cel, pf—str
   Two of the flutists double on piccolo.
   Novello

Symphony no.5, op.57 (Washington mosaics)   39'
   *4 4 =4 *4—6 4 4 1—tmp+4—hp, cel, pf—str   14' 5' 5'
   Two of the flutists double on piccolo.   7' 8'
   Novello

Variations for orchestra (14 juventas variaatiota), op.8   12'
   *2 2 2 2—2 2 2 0—marimba—str
   Novello

Sammartini, Giovanni Battista   1701 - 1775

Concertino, G major   8'
  cnt—str
  Ed. Newell Jenkins.
  Peters   *Kalmus*

Concerto in E-flat   7'
  solo string quartet
  str orch
  Arr. and ed. Adam Carse.
  Augener

Concerto, violin (or violoncello piccolo), C major   12'
  cnt—str
  Ed. Newell Jenkins.
  Eulenburg

Magnificat   20'
  chorus   solos SATB
  0 2 0 0—0 2 0 0—cnt—str
  Eulenburg   *Schirmer, G.*

Sinfonia, J.-C.2, C major   15'
  0 2 0 1—2 0 0 0—tmp—str
  Ed. Fausto Torrefranca.
  Carisch

Sinfonia, J.-C.4, C major   7'
  0 0 0 0—2 0 0 0—str
  Ed. Ettore Bonelli.
  Zanibon   *Kalmus*

Sinfonia, J.-C.32, F major   12'
  cnt—str
  Ed. Newell Jenkins.
  Peters   *Kalmus*

Sinfonia, J.-C.39, G major   7'
  cnt—str
  Ed. Newell Jenkins.
  Peters

Sinfonia, J.-C.47, G major   9'
  2 2 0 0—2 0 0 0—cnt—str
  Flutes and oboes are optional. Ed. Fausto Torrefranca.
  Carisch

Sammartini, Giuseppe   1695 - 1750

Concerto grosso, op.5, no.6 (Christmas concerto)   15'
  2 solo violins
  cnt—str
  Ed. Karlheinz Schultz-Hauser.
  Vieweg

Samuel, Gerhard   1924 -

Requiem for survivors   18'
  *4 4 *4 *4—0 4 3 1—tmp+4—hp—str
  All 4 flutists double on piccolo; 1 clarinet doubles on tenor
  saxophone.
  Belwin

Sapieyevski, Jerzy   1945 -

Summer overture   10'
  *3 3 *3 3—5 3 3 1—tmp+2—hp—str
  Mercury

Surtsey   15'
  str
  Mercury

Sarasate, Pablo de   1844 - 1908

Carmen fantasie on themes of Bizet, op.25   12'
  solo violin
  *2 2 2 2—4 2 3 0—tmp+1—hp—str
  Kalmus

Introduction and tarantella, op.43   7'
  solo violin
  2 2 2 2—2 2 0 0—tmp+1—str
  C. Fischer   *Kalmus*

Zigeunerweisen, op.20 (Gypsy airs)   10'
  solo violin
  2 2 2 2—2 2 0 0—tmp +1—str
  1 percussionist optional.
  C. Fischer   *Kalmus*

Satie, Erik   1866 - 1925

Les Aventures de Mercure   20'
  *2 1 2 1—2 2 1 1—3perc—str
  Contents—Overture; La Nuit; Danse de tendresse; Signes du
  zodiaque; Entré et danse de Mercure; Danse des Graces; Bain des
  Graces; Fuite de Mercure; Colére de Cerbére; Polka des lettres;
  Nouvelle danse; Le Chaos; Final.
  Universal

Cinq Grimaces pour Un Songe d'une nuit d'été   3'
  *3 *3 2 *3—2 3 3 1—tmp+3—str
  Universal

Deux Préludes posthumes et une gnossienne   9'
  2 *2 2 2—2 2 2 0—hp—str
  Orchestrated by Francis Poulenc.
  Salabert

Gymnopédies nos.1 & 3   7'
2 1 0 0—4 0 0 0—1perc—2hp—str   4' 3'
Orchestrated by Claude Debussy.
Kalmus   *Salabert*

Gymnopédie no.2   4'
2 1 1 0—4 1 0 0—2perc—2hp, cel—str
Orchestrated by Roland-Manuel.
Salabert

Jack in the box   7'
*2 2 2 2—2 2 2 0—tmp+3—str   3' 2' 2'
Orchestrated by Darius Milhaud.
Universal

Parade   14'
*3 *3 +3 2—2 3 3 1—tmp+4—hp—str
Bizarre percussion requirements include siren, lottery wheel, typewriter, revolver, splashes of water, fog horn, "bouteillophone" (often played on xylophone), and "claquers" (players clap hands).
Salabert

Trois Petites Pièces montées   5'
1 1 1 1—1 2 1 0—2perc—str
This work may be out of print, but orchestral materials are in the Fleisher Collection.
Eschig

Scarlatti, Alessandro   1660 - 1725

Christmas cantata   15'
solo soprano
cnt—str
Ed. Edward Dent.
Oxford

Concerto, G minor
str
Ed. Paul Glass.
AMP

Concerto grosso no.1, F minor; no.2, C minor   16'
cnt—str   9' 7'
Ed. Walter Upmeyer.
Vieweg

Concerto grosso no.3, F major   8'
2 solo violins, solo violoncello
cnt—str
Vieweg   *Zanibon*

Concerto grosso no.6, E major   9'
  2 solo violins, solo violoncello
  cnt—str
  Ed. Renato Fasano.
  Ricordi

Piccola suite   10'
  str
  Assembled from various works by Franco Michele Napolitano.
  Kalmus   *Zanibon*

Sinfonia no.1, F major   8'
  2rec—cnt—str
  Bärenreiter   *Kalmus*   *Schott*

Sinfonia no.2, D major   7'
  1 0 0 0—0 1 0 0—cnt—str
  Ed. Raymond Meylan.
  Bärenreiter   *Kalmus*

Sinfonia no.4, E minor   14'
  1 1 0 0—cnt—str
  Ed. Raymond Meylan.
  Bärenreiter   *Kalmus*

Sinfonia no.5, D minor   9'
  2 0 0 0—cnt—str
  Ed. Raymond Meylan.
  Bärenreiter   *Kalmus*

Sinfonia no.6, A minor   12'
  rec—cnt—str
  Ed. Rolf-Julius Koch.
  Peters

Sinfonia no.8, G major   12'
  rec—cnt—str
  Ed. Rolf-Julius Koch.
  Peters

Sinfonia no.10, A minor   12'
  rec—cnt—str
  Ed. Rolf-Julius Koch.
  Peters

Scarlatti, Domenico   1685 - 1757

Five sonatas in form of a suite   10'
  str
  "Freely elaborated" from harpsichord sonatas by Ettore Bonelli.
  Kalmus   *Zanibon*

The good-humored ladies: Suite   14'
  2 2 2 2—4 2 0 0—tmp+1—hpsd—str
  Five harpsichord sonatas arr. by Vincenzo Tommasini.
  Chester   *Kalmus*

Serenata (Contest of the seasons)   50'
     chorus   solos SATB
     1 0 0 0—2 2 0 0—cnt—str
     Ed. Renato Fasano.
     Ricordi

Schafer, R. Murray   1933 -

Adieu Robert Schumann   19'
     mezzo-soprano solo
     2 2 2 2—2 2 2 0—tmp+1—pf, pre-recorded piano—str
     Universal

The garden of the heart   24'
     medium voice
     *3 2 *2 2—4 2 1 1—2perc—str
     Bcl part may be taken by bn.
     Arcana

Schein, Johann Hermann   1586 - 1630

Banchetto musicale: Suite no.1   9'
     str
     Ed. Arnold Schering.
     Kahnt

Schickele, Peter   1935 -

Celebration with bells   7'
     2 2 *3 2—opt asx & tsx—4 3 3 1—tmp+3—str
     Possible with winds: 2 1 *3 1—2 3 2 1.
     Elkan-Vogel

The chenoo who stayed to dinner   22'
     narrator
     *2 2 2 2—3 2 2 1—2perc—str (min 6.5.3.3.2)
     May be performed without narrator under the title *Legend*.
     Elkan-Vogel

Elegy   7'
     str
     Elkan-Vogel

Fanfare for the common cold   2'
     0 0 0 0—2 2 1 0
     Attributed to P.D.Q. Bach, 1807-1742 ?
     Presser

A zoo called Earth   15'
     taped narration (the composer's voice, altered to sound like that
     of an extraterrestrial visitor)
     *2 2 2 2—4 3 3 1—tmp+3—cel—str
     Presser

Schmidt, Franz   1874 - 1939

Das Buch mit sieben Siegeln (The book with seven seals)   110'
  solos SATTB   chorus
  *3 *3 =3 *3—4 3 3 1—tmp+3—org—str
  Universal

Symphony no.2, E-flat   47'
  *4 *3 =5 *3—8 4 3 1—tmp+4—str
  Kalmus   *Universal*

15' 19'
13'

Symphony no.4   46'
  *2 *3 +3 *3—4 3 3 1—tmp+3—2hp—str
  Universal

Schmitt, Florent   1870 - 1958

Étude, op.49 (Palais hanté (Haunted palace))   15'
  *3 *3 *3 2—opt sarrusophone—4 2 3 1—tmp+2—hp—str
  Kalmus

Feuillets de voyage, op.26   17'
  *3 *2 2 *3—4 2 3 1—tmp+2—hp—str
  Contents—Sérénade; Le Retour à l'endroit familier; Danse
  brittanique; Berceuse; Marche burlesque.
  Kalmus

Musiques de plein air, op.44   19'
  *3 *3 2 2—opt sarrusophone—4 2 3 1—tmp+2—2hp—str
  May be performed with: *2 *2 2 2—4 2 3 1—tmp+2—hp—str.
  Contents—La Procession dans la montagne; Danse désuète;
  Accalmie.
  Kalmus

Psalm 47   35'
  chorus   solo soprano
  *3 *3 *3 *4—4 3 3 1—tmp+5—2hp, cel, org—str
  Horns may be doubled.
  Salabert

Rapsodie viennoise, op.53, no.3   8'
  *3 2 2 2—sarrusophone—4 2 3 1—tmp+3—hp—str
  Kalmus

Reflets d'Allemagne   14'
  *3 2 2 2—4 2 3 1—tmp+2—hp—str
  Contents—Nuremberg; Dresde; Werder; Munich.
  Kalmus

Ronde burlesque, op.78   7'
  *3 2 2 *3—4 2 3 1—tmp+6—1 or 2hp, cel—str
  Heugel

La Tragédie de Salomé, op.50   28'
  3-6 female voices backstage (optional)
  *3 *3 *3 2—sarrusophone—4 3 3 1—tmp+4—2hp—str
  Contents—Prélude; Danse des perles; Les Enchantements sur la
  mer; Danse les éclairs; Danse de l'effroi.
  Kalmus

Schnittke, Alfred   1934 -

Concerto, oboe, harp & string orchestra   13'
  str
  Universal

Concerto, piano & strings   26'
  str 12.12.8.8.4
  Russian   *Sikorski*

Concerto, violin, no.4   33'
  +3 *3 *3 *3—asx—4 4 4 1—tmp+6—hp, cel, hpsd, prepared | 5' 7' 9' |
  pf—str | 12' |
  Universal

Concerto, violoncello   40'
  *3 *3 *3 *3—4 4 4 1—tmp+5—hp, pf, cel/hpsd—str
  All 3 flutists double on piccolo.
  Sikorski

Concerto grosso no.3   22'
  2 solo violins | 3' 4' 6' |
  1perc—hpsd/pf/cel—str 4.4.3.2.1 | 6' 3' |
  Sikorski

In memoriam...   27'
  =3 *3 *3 *3—4 4 4 1—tmp+4—hp, cel, 2pf, hpsd, org, elec gtr | 6' 5' 7' |
  —str (min 7.6.5.4.3) | 5' 4' |
  Originally for piano quintet.
  Peters

Moz-Art à la Haydn   12'
  2 solo violins
  str 3.3.2.2.1
  A humorous "deconstruction" involving dueling violinists,
  lighting effects, and an ending reminiscent of the Haydn *Farewell
  symphony.*
  Russian   *Sikorski*

Quasi una sonata (Sonata no.2)   20'
  solo violin
  *2 2 2 2—2 0 0 0—pf/hpsd—str 5.4.3.3.1
  Universal

Requiem   35'
  solos SSSAT   chorus
  0 0 0 0—0 1 1 0—tmp+3—org, pf, cel—elec gtr, bass gtr
  Peters

Symphony no.4   42'
  chorus or vocal quartet
  +1 1 1 1—1 1 1 0—4perc—cel, pf, hpsd—str (or str quintet)
  Chant   *Russian*

9' 5' 5'
12' 1' 5'
5'

Schoenberg, Arnold   1874 - 1951

Begleitungsmusik zu einer Lichtspielscene (Accompaniment to a   8'
cinematographic scene)
  *1 1 2 1—2 2 1 0—tmp+4—pf—str
  Peters

Chamber symphony no.1, op.9   22'
  1 *2 =3 *2—2 0 0 0—2vn, va, vc, db
  Kalmus   *Universal*

Chamber symphony no.1, op.9b (orchestral version)   22'
  *3 *3 =3 *3—4 2 3 0—str
  Orchestrated by the composer.
  Schirmer, G.   *Universal*

Chamber symphony no.2, op.38   22'
  *2 *2 2 2—2 2 0 0—str
  Schirmer, G.

9' 13'

Concerto, piano, op.42   21'
  *2 2 2 2—4 2 3 1—tmp+3—str
  Belmont   *Schirmer, G.*

5' 3' 7' 6'

Concerto, violin, op.36   32'
  *3 3 =3 3—4 3 3 1—tmp+4—str
  Schirmer, G.

12' 8'
12'

Concerto, violoncello   16'
  *2 2 2 2—2 2 1 0—tmp+3—hp, cel—str
  After a harpsichord concerto by G. M. Monn (1746).
  Schirmer, G.

6' 5' 5'

Five pieces for orchestra, op.16 (original version, 1909)   16'
  *4 *4 =5 *4—6 3 4 1—tmp+3—hp, cel—str
  One clarinetist also doubles on contrabass clarinet in A.
  Kalmus   *Peters*

2' 5' 3'
2' 4'

Five pieces for orchestra, op.16 (new version, 1949)   16'
  *4 *3 =4 *3—4 3 3 1—tmp+3—hp, cel—str
  A 1973 edition by Richard Hoffmann makes many corrections in
  this 1949 version.
  Peters

2' 5' 3'
2' 4'

Five pieces for orchestra, op.16 (chamber orchestra version)   16'
  *1 1 1 1—1 0 0 0—pf, harm—2vn, va, vc, db
  Arr. Felix Greissle.
  Peters

2' 5' 3'
2' 4'

Gurre-Lieder   99'
  chorus   solos SATTB   speaker   55' 4'
  *8 *5 =7 *5—10 6 7 1—bass tp—tmp+6—4hp, cel—str   40'
  Horns 7-10 double on Wagner tubas. Among the aggregate
  woodwind numbers above, the following numbers of secondary
  instruments are required: 4pic, 2Eh, 2scl, 2bcl, 2cbn.
  Publisher offers a version reduced by Erwin Stein for
  normal-size orchestra.
  Universal

Gurre-Lieder: Lied der Waldtaube (chamber version)   13'
  solo soprano
  *1 *2 =3 *2—2 0 0 0—pf, harm—2vn, va, vc, db
  Arr. for chamber orchestra by the composer. Versions for the
  huge *Gurre-Lieder* orchestra, and for a normally large orchestra
  are also available.
  Universal

Kol nidre   18'
  chorus   speaker
  *2 1 =3 1—2 2 2 1—tmp+3—str
  Boelke

Ode to Napoleon Bonaparte, op.41   16'
  reciter
  pf—str
  Belmont   *Schirmer, G.*

Pelléas und Mélisande, op.5   41'
  *4 *4 =5 *4—8 4 5 1—tmp+4—2hp—str
  Version for reduced orchestra is also available.
  Kalmus   *Universal*

Pierrot Lunaire, op.21   34'
  Sprechstimme   12' 11'
  *1 0 *1 0—pf—vn/va, vc   11'
  Kalmus   *Universal*

Prelude, op.44 (Genesis suite)   6'
  wordless chorus
  *3 *3 *3 *3—4 3 3 1—tmp+3—hp—str
  Belmont

Serenade, op.24   30'
  bass-baritone voice
  0 0 *2 0—gtr, mand—vn, va, vc
  Hansen

Six songs, op.8   23'
  soprano solo   4' 3' 2'
  *3 *3 *3 *3—4 3 3 1—tmp+3—hp—str   4' 5' 5'
  Universal

Suite for string orchestra   20'
   str
   Schirmer, G.

A survivor from Warsaw, op.46   9'
   male narrator   unison male chorus
   *2 2 2 2—4 3 3 1—tmp+5—hp—str 10.10.6.6.6
   Revised score by Jacques-Louis Monod (1979) is not as good an
   edition as that which comes with the rental parts; the latter is
   identical with the Schoenberg collected edition (ed. Josef Rufer &
   Christian Martin Schmidt).
   Boelke

Theme and variations, op.43b   14'
   *3 *3 *3 *3—4 3 3 1—tmp+3—str
   Originally for concert band.
   Belmont   *Schirmer, G.*

Variations for orchestra, op.31   23'
   *4 *4 =5 *4—4 3 4 1—tmp+5—hp, cel, mand—str
   Universal

Verklärte Nacht, op.4 (1917 version) (Transfigured night)   26'
   str
   Originally for string sextet. Arr. by the composer for string
   orchestra, 1917. Ed. Clinton F. Nieweg & Mark Laycock.
   Kalmus

Verklärte Nacht, op.4 (1943 version) (Transfigured night)   26'
   str
   Originally for string sextet. Revised by the composer, 1943.
   Broude Bros.

Schreiner, Adolph
The worried drummer   8'
   solo percussionist
   *2 2 2 2—2 2 1 0—str
   Belwin version ed. Saul Goodman. Luck and Kalmus version
   calls for 3 tbn.
   Belwin   *Kalmus*   *Luck*

Schreker, Franz   1878 - 1934
Intermezzo, op.8   5'
   str
   Kalmus   *Luck*

Kammersymphonie   25'
   1 1 1 1—1 1 1 0—tmp+1—hp, cel, pf, harm—str 2.2.2.3.2
   Strings may be augmented to 6.6.4.6.3.
   Kalmus

Schubert, Franz   1797 - 1828

Alfonso und Estrella, D.732: Overture   7'
  2 2 2 2—2 2 3 0—tmp—str
  Used as the overture to the *Rosamunde* incidental music.
  Breitkopf   *Kalmus*

Claudine von Villa Bella, D.239: Overture   8'
  2 2 2 2—2 2 0 0—tmp—str
  Breitkopf

Des Teufels Lustschloss, D.84: Overture   9'
  2 2 2 2—2 2 3 0—tmp—str
  Breitkopf   *Kalmus*

Fierrabras, D.796: Overture   9'
  2 2 2 2—4 2 3 0—tmp—str
  Breitkopf   *Kalmus*

Die Freunde von Salamanka, D.326: Overture   7'
  2 2 2 2—2 2 0 0—tmp—str
  Breitkopf

Grande Marche héroïque   4'
  *3 2 2 2—4 2 3 1—tmp+1—str
  Orchestrated by Franz Liszt from a work for piano 4-hands,
  D.819 no.3.
  Kalmus

Der häusliche Krieg, D.787: Overture   7'
  2 2 2 2—2 2 0 0—tmp—str
  Completed by Fritz Racek.
  Doblinger

Konzertstück, D.345, D major   8'
  solo violin
  0 2 0 0—0 2 0 0—tmp—str
  Breitkopf   *Kalmus*

Magnificat, D.486
  chorus   solos SATB
  0 2 0 2—0 2 0 0—tmp—org—str
  Kalmus   *Schirmer, G.*

Marche militaire, D.733 (op.51), no.1   5'
  *3 2 2 2—4 3 3 1—tmp+5—str
  Arr. Leopold Damrosch, from a work for piano 4-hands.
  Luck   *Schirmer, G.*

Mass no.1, D.105, F major   43'
  chorus   solos SSATTB
  0 2 2 2—2 2 3 0—tmp—org—str
  Breitkopf   *Gray*   *G.Schirmer*

Mass no.2, D.167, G major   22'
    chorus   solos STB

| 3' 3' 5' |
| 2' 4' 5' |

    0 2 0 2—0 2 0 0—tmp—org—str
Winds and timpani were added by Ferdinand Schubert, and are optional.
Breitkopf   *Gray*   *Kalmus*

Mass no.3, D.324, B-flat major   30'
    chorus   solos SATB
    0 2 0 2—0 2 0 0—tmp—org—str
Breitkopf   *Gray*   *Kalmus*

Mass no.4, D.452, C major   26'
    chorus   solos SATB

| 3' 4' 6' |
| 2' 3' 4' |
| 4' |

    0 2 0 0—0 2 0 0—tmp—org—str
Clarinets may substitute for oboes, or all winds & timpani may be omitted.
Breitkopf   *Kalmus*   *Schirmer, G.*

Mass no.5, D.678, A-flat major   45'
    chorus   solos SATB

| 5' 13' |
| 10' 3' 8' |
| 6' |

    1 2 2 2—2 2 3 0—tmp—org—str
Breitkopf   *Gray*   *Kalmus*

Mass no.6, D.950, E-flat major   58'
    chorus   solos SATTB

| 7' 14' |
| 17' 4' 6' |
| 10' |

    0 2 2 2—2 2 3 0—tmp—str
Breitkopf   *Gray*   *Kalmus*   *Peters*

Mirjams Siegesgesang, D.942 (Miriam's song of triumph)   16'
    soprano solo   chorus
    2 2 2 *3—4 3 3 1—tmp+2—hp—str
Orchestrated by Felix Mottl.
Breitkopf   *Kalmus*

Octet, D.803, F major   63'
    0 0 1 1—1 0 0 0—2vn, va, vc, db

| 15' 13' |
| 6' 11' 7' |
| 11' |

    Luck   *Peters*

Offertorium, D.963 (Intende voci)   15'
    tenor solo   chorus
    0 1 2 2—2 0 3 0—str
Breitkopf

Overture, D.8, C minor (arr. Hess)   6'
    str
Ed. Ernst Hess. Originally for string quintet (2vn, 2va, vc); later arranged by Schubert for string quartet (identified as D.8A). The latter version (D.8A) has been arranged by Hess for string orchestra.
Peters

Overture, D.8, C minor (arr. Hofmann)   6'
  1 0 2 1—2 0 0 0—str
  Orchestrated by Wolfgang Hofmann.
  Peters

Overture, D.12, D major   9'
  2 2 2 2—2 2 3 0—tmp—str
  Breitkopf   *Kalmus*

Overture, D.26, D major   9'
  2 2 2 2—2 2 3 0—tmp—str
  Breitkopf   *Kalmus*

Overture, D.470, B-flat major   7'
  0 2 0 2—2 2 0 0—tmp—str
  Breitkopf

Overture, D.556, D major   7'
  2 2 2 2—2 0 0 0—tmp—str
  Breitkopf

Overture, D.590, D major (In the Italian Style)   8'
  2 2 2 2—2 2 0 0—tmp—str
  Breitkopf   *Kalmus*

Overture, D.591, C major (In the Italian Style)   7'
  2 2 2 2—2 2 0 0—tmp—str
  Breitkopf   *Kalmus*

Overture, D.648, E minor   8'
  2 2 2 2—4 2 3 0—tmp—str
  Breitkopf

Quartet, strings, D.810, D minor (Der Tod und das Mädchen; Death   40'
and the maiden)
  str
  Arr. for string orchestra by Gustav Mahler.
  Ed. David Matthews & Donald Mitchell.
  Weinberger

Rondo, violin & strings, D.438, A major   14'
  str
  Breitkopf   *Kalmus*

Rosamunde, D.797
  see also his: Alfonso und Estrella: Overture

Rosamunde, D.797   55'
  alto solo   chorus

11'	9'	4'
4'	4'	8'
2'	4'	2'
		7'

  2 2 2 2—4 2 3 0—tmp—str
  Contents—1. Entr'acte I; 2. Ballet music I; 3a. Entr'acte II; 3b.
  Romance [alto aria]; 4. Spirits' chorus [male chorus]; 5. Entr'acte
  III; 6. Pastoral music [no strings]; 7. Shepherds' chorus [mixed
  chorus]; 8. Huntsmen's chorus [mixed chorus]; 9. Ballet music II.
  Breitkopf

Rosamunde: Overture, D.644　　　　　　　　　　　　　　　10'
　2 2 2 2—4 2 3 0—tmp—str
　Actually the overture to *Die Zauberharfe*, and published by
　Breitkopf under that title, though commonly known as
　Rosamunde.
　Breitkopf　　　　*Kalmus*

Rosamunde: Ballet music　　　　　　　　　　　　　　　　16'
　2 2 2 2—2 2 3 0—tmp—str　　　　　　　　　　　　　9' 7'
　Contents—Nos.2 and 9 of the incidental music.
　Breitkopf　　　　*Kalmus*

Rosamunde: Entr'actes　　　　　　　　　　　　　　　　　23'
　2 2 2 2—2 2 3 0—tmp—str　　　　　　　　　　　11' 4' 8'
　Contents—Nos.1, 3a, and 5 of the incidental music.
　Breitkopf　　　　*Kalmus*

Salve Regina, D.106, B-flat major　　　　　　　　　　　　8'
　tenor solo
　0 2 0 2—2 0 0 0—org—str
　Breitkopf

Salve Regina, D.223, op.47, F major　　　　　　　　　　　6'
　soprano solo
　0 0 2 2—2 0 0 0—org—str
　Kalmus

Salve Regina, D.676, op.153, A major　　　　　　　　　　13'
　soprano solo
　str
　Breitkopf　　　　*Kalmus*

Der Spiegelritter, D.11: Overture　　　　　　　　　　　　10'
　2 2 2 2—2 2 0 0—tmp—str
　Breitkopf

Stabat mater, D.175, G minor (The little)　　　　　　　　　6'
　chorus
　0 2 2 2—0 0 3 0—org—str
　Kalmus

Stabat mater, D.383, F minor　　　　　　　　　　　　　37'
　chorus　　　　solos STB
　2 2 0 *3—2 0 3 0—str
　Breitkopf　　　　*Kalmus*

Symphony no.1, D.82, D major　　　　　　　　　　　　　29'
　1 2 2 2—2 2 0 0—tmp—str　　　　　　　　　　　11' 7' 5'
　Breitkopf　　　　*Kalmus*　　　　　　　　　　　　　6'

Symphony no.2, D.125, B-flat major　　　　　　　　　　　29'
　2 2 2 2—2 2 0 0—tmp—str　　　　　　　　　　　10' 9' 4'
　Breitkopf　　　　*Kalmus*　　　　　　　　　　　　　6'

Symphony no.3, D.200, D major
  2 2 2 2—2 2 0 0—tmp—str
  Breitkopf   *Kalmus*

26'

| 10' 5' 4' |
| 7' |

Symphony no.4, D.417, C minor (Tragic)
  2 2 2 2—4 2 0 0—tmp—str
  Breitkopf   *Kalmus*

31'

| 7' 10' 6' |
| 8' |

Symphony no.5, D.485, B-flat major
  1 2 0 2—2 0 0 0—str
  Breitkopf   *Kalmus*   *Peters*

27'

| 5' 11' 5' |
| 6' |

Symphony no.6, D.589, C major (Little)
  2 2 2 2—2 2 0 0—tmp—str
  Breitkopf   *Kalmus*

27'

| 7' 5' 6' 9' |

Symphony no.7, D.729, E major (Newbould)
  2 2 2 2—4 2 3 0—tmp—str
  Realization by Brian Newbould from Schubert's sketches.
  Bois

39'

| 12' 8' 6' |
| 13' |

Symphony [no.7], D.729, E major (Weingartner)
  2 2 2 2—4 2 3 0—tmp—str
  Completed from Schubert's sketches by Felix Weingartner.
  Universal

33'

Symphony no.8, D.759, B minor (Unfinished)
  2 2 2 2—2 2 3 0—tmp—str
  A critical edition of the score with historical and analytical
  essays is available from Norton.
  Breitkopf catalog lists this work as *Symphony no.7*.
  Breitkopf   *Kalmus*   *Peters*

25'

| 12' 13' |

Symphony, D.812, op.140, C major (Grand duo)
  *3 2 2 2—4 2 3 0—tmp—str
  Orchestrated by Joseph Joachim from Schubert's *Grand duo*,
  op.140, for piano 4-hands.
  Kalmus

42'

| 13' 11' |
| 5' 13' |

Symphony no.9, D.944, C major (The great)
  2 2 2 2—2 2 3 0—tmp—str
  Often listed as *Symphony No.7*. Breitkopf catalog lists this work
  as *Symphony no.8*.
  Breitkopf   *Kalmus*

48'

| 14' 12' |
| 10' 12' |

Symphony no.10, D.936a
  see under: Berio, Luciano
               Rendering

Tantum ergo, D.962
  chorus   solos SATB
  0 2 2 2—2 2 3 0—tmp—str
  Peters   *Schirmer, G.*

6'

Der Teufel als Hydraulicus, D.4: Overture   5'
   2 0 2 2—2 0 0 0—str
   Breitkopf   *Carisch*

Teufels Lustschloss
   see his: Des Teufels Lustschloss

Trauermarsch, D.859, op.55, C minor
   2 2 2 2—4 2 3 1—tmp+1—str
   Transcribed by Wilhelm Kienzl. Originally *Grande Marche*
   funèbre for piano duet.
   Luck

Die vierjährige Posten, D.190: Overture   8'
   2 2 2 2—2 2 0 0—tmp—str
   Breitkopf   *Heugel*

Wanderer fantasy, D.760, op.15   21'
   solo piano
   2 2 2 2—2 2 3 0—tmp—str
   Arr. by Franz Liszt, from a work for piano.
   Kalmus

Die Zauberharfe
   see his: Rosamunde: Overture, D.644

Die Zwillingsbrüder, D.647: Overture   5'
   2 2 2 2—2 2 0 0—tmp—str
   Breitkopf   *Kalmus*

Schuetz, Heinrich   1585 - 1672
   see: Schütz, Heinrich, 1585-1672

Schuller, Gunther   1925 -

American triptych   14'
   *3 *3 *3 *3—4 3 3 1—tmp+3—hp—str
   AMP

Concertino for jazz quartet and orchestra   19'
   solo jazz quartet: vibraphone, piano, percussion, string bass
   *2 2 2 2—2 3 2 0—1perc—str
   MJQ

Concerto no.2 for orchestra   22'
   =4 *4 =5 *4—4 4 4 1—tmp+5—hp, cel, pf, opt org—str
   All 4 flutists double on pic; among the 5 clarinetists, 1 doubles
   E-flat & bcl, 1 plays cl only, 1 doubles cl & bcl, 1 doubles cl &
   asx, and 1 doubles bcl and contrabass cl.
   AMP

Contours   23'
   *1 1 =2 1—1 1 1 0—3perc—hp—str
   AMP   *Schott*

Five bagatelles   15'
   *3 *3 *2 *3—4 3 3 1—tmp+2—hp, pf—str
   AMP

Five etudes for orchestra   14'
   *3 3 2 2—4 3 3 1—tmp+3—hp, pf—str
   AMP

Journey into jazz   16'
   jazz ensemble: asx, tsx, tp, db, drums   narrator
   1 1 1 1—1 1 0 0—1perc—hp—str
   AMP

Of reminiscences and reflections   15'
   =4 *4 =4 *4—6 4 4 1—tmp+5—hp, pf/cel—str
   2 of the flutists double on pic, 2 on afl; 2 of the clarinetists double
   on bcl.
   Schirmer, G.

Seven studies on themes of Paul Klee   23'
   *3 *3 *3 *3—4 3 3 1—tmp+5—hp, pf—str
   Universal

Spectra   23'
   =4 *4 =4 *4—4 4 3 1—tmp+4—hp—str
   AMP   *Schott*

Schuman, William   1910 - 1992

American festival overture   9'
   *3 *3 *3 *3—4 3 3 1—tmp+3—str
   Cbn is optional.
   Schirmer, G.

Credendum (An article of faith)   18'
   *4 *4 =5 *4—6 4 3 2—tmp+4—pf—str
   Merion

Judith   24'
   *3 *3 *3 *3—4 2 3 1—tmp+2—pf—str
   May be performed with woodwinds *2 *2 2 2.
   Schirmer, G.

New England triptych   16'
   *3 *3 =4 2—4 3 3 1—tmp+3—str   6' 7' 3'
   Contents—Be glad then America; When Jesus wept; Chester.
   Merion

Newsreel   8'
   *3 *3 =5 *4—2asx, tsx —4 3 3 1—tmp+4—pf—str
   Possible with reduced instrumentation:
   *2 1 2 1—2 3 3 1—tmp+4—str.
   If piano/conductor is used, possible with:
   0 0 2 0—0 1 1 0—1perc—4vn, 2va.
   Schirmer, G.

On freedom's ground; an American cantata   40'
    baritone solo   chorus
    *3 *3 *3 2—4 3 3 1—tmp+4—pf/cel—str
    All three flutists double on piccolo. Contents—Back then; Our
    risen states; Like a great statue; Come dance; Immigrants still.
    Merion

The orchestra song   4'
    *2 1 *2 1—4 3 3 1—tmp+3 (or 6)—str
    Bcl is optional.
    Merion

A song of Orpheus   20'
    violoncello solo
    *3 *3 *3 2—4 0 0 0—hp—str
    Merion

Symphony no.3   28'
    *3 *3 =4 2—4 4 4 1—tmp+3—pf—str | 13' 15' |
    Optional additional instruments: fl, ob, cl, bn, cbn, 4hn.
    Schirmer, G.

Symphony no.4   25'
    *3 *4 =5 *3—4 3 3 1—tmp+3—str
    Schirmer, G.

Symphony no.5 (Symphony for strings)   17'
    str | 4' 8' 5' |
    Schirmer, G.

Symphony no.6   27'
    *3 *3 *3 *3—4 3 3 1—tmp+2—str
    Schirmer, G.

Symphony no.7   29'
    *3 *3 *3 *3—4 3 3 1—tmp+3—pf—str | 11' 3' 9' |
    Optional additional instruments increase the size | 6' |
    of the wind sections to: *4 *4 =5 *4—6 4 3 2.
    Merion

Symphony no.8   31'
    *4 *3 *3 *3—6 4 4 1—tmp+5—2hp, pf—str
    Optional additional instruments: ob, cl, bn.
    Merion

Symphony no.9 (Le Fosse ardeatine)   28'
    *3 *3 *3 *3—4 4 3 1—tmp+5—pf—str
    Merion

Symphony no.10 (American muse)   30'
    *4 *4 =5 *4—6 4 4 1—tmp+4—hp, cel, pf—str
    Two of the flutists double on piccolo.
    Merion

Undertow   25'
    *3 *3 3 3—4 2 3 1—tmp+2—pf—str
    Schirmer, G.

Schumann, Clara Wieck   1819 - 1896

Concerto, piano, op.7, A minor   21'
    2 2 2 2—2 2 1 0—tmp—str   6' 5' 10'
    Ed. Janina Klassen.
    Breitkopf

Schumann, Georg   1866 - 1952

Liebesfrühling, Ouvertüre, op.28   15'
    *3 2 2 *3—4 3 3 1—tmp+2—str
    This work may be out of print, but orchestral materials are in the
    Fleisher Collection.
    Breitkopf

Schumann, Robert   1810 - 1856

Adagio and allegro, op.70   12'
    solo horn (or violoncello)
    2 1 2 2—2 0 0 0—tmp—str
    Orchestrated by Blair Fairchild.
    Schott

Adventlied, op.71
    chorus   solos SATB
    2 2 2 2—4 2 3 0—tmp—str
    Breitkopf   *Kalmus*

Braut von Messina: Overture   9'
    *3 2 2 2—2 2 3 0—tmp—str
    Breitkopf   *Kalmus*

Concert-allegro with introduction, op.134   13'
    solo piano
    2 2 2 2—2 2 1 0—tmp—str
    Breitkopf   *Kalmus*

Concerto, piano, op.54, A minor   31'
    2 2 2 2—2 2 0 0—tmp—str   15' 5'
    Breitkopf   *Kalmus*   11'

Concerto, violin, D minor   31'
    2 2 2 2—2 2 0 0—tmp—str   14' 17'
    Schott

Concerto, violoncello, op.129, A minor   25'
    2 2 2 2—2 2 0 0—tmp—str   12' 5' 8'
    Breitkopf   *Kalmus*

Concertstück, op.86, F major   21'
  4 solo horns
  *3 2 2 2—2 2 3 0—tmp—str
  Orchestral horns are optional.
  Breitkopf   *Kalmus*   *KaWe*

Fantasia, op.131   14'
  solo violin
  2 2 2 2—2 2 0 0—tmp—str
  Breitkopf   *Kalmus*

Faust: Overture   6'
  2 2 2 2—4 2 3 0—tmp—str
  This work is out of print, but orchestral materials are in the
  Fleisher Collection.

Genoveva, op.81: Overture   10'
  2 2 2 2—4 2 3 0—tmp—str
  Breitkopf   *Kalmus*

Hermann und Dorothea, op.136: Overture   8'
  *3 2 2 2—2 2 0 0—1perc—str
  Breitkopf   *Kalmus*

Introduction & Allegro appassionato, op.92   15'
  solo piano
  2 2 2 2—2 2 0 0—tmp—str
  Breitkopf   *Kalmus*

Julius Caesar, op.128: Overture   9'
  *2 2 2 2—4 2 3 1—tmp—str
  Breitkopf   *Kalmus*

Manfred, op.115   61'
  chorus   solos SATB   12' 16'
  *3 *2 2 2—4 3 3 1—tmp+2—hp—str   23' 10'
  Breitkopf   *C. Fischer*   *Kalmus*

Manfred: Overture   11'
  2 2 2 2—4 3 3 0—tmp—str
  Breitkopf   *Kalmus*

Manfred: Suite   8'
  2 *2 2 2—2 1 0 0—hp—str
  This work may be out of print, but orchestral materials are in the
  Fleisher Collection.
  Contents—Entr'acte; Ranz des vaches [unaccompanied English
  horn solo]; Apparition de la fée des Alpes.
  Durand

Manfred: Zwischenaktmusik   4'
  2 2 2 2—2 0 0 0—str
  No.5 of the complete music.
  Kalmus

Mass, op.147, C minor   42'
  chorus   solos STB
  2 2 2 2—2 2 3 0—tmp—opt org—str | 5' 9' 6' |
  Breitkopf   *Kalmus* | 3' 12' 7' |

Overture, scherzo, & finale   17'
  2 2 2 2—2 2 3 0—tmp—str
  Trombones are optional. | 7' 4' 6' |
  Breitkopf   *Kalmus*

Requiem, op.148, D-flat major   43'
  chorus   solos SATB
  2 2 2 2—2 2 3 0—tmp—str
  Breitkopf   *Kalmus*

Requiem für Mignon, op.98b   15'
  chorus   solos SSAAB
  2 2 2 2—2 2 3 0—tmp—opt hp—str
  Breitkopf   *Kalmus*

Symphony no.1, op.38, B-flat major (Spring)   30'
  2 2 2 2—4 2 3 0—tmp+1—str | 12' 6' 5' |
  Breitkopf   *Kalmus* | 7' |

Symphony no.2, op.61, C major   38'
  2 2 2 2—2 2 3 0—tmp—str | 13' 8' 9' |
  Breitkopf   *Kalmus* | 8' |

Symphony no.3, op.97, E-flat major (Rhenish)   32'
  2 2 2 2—4 2 3 0—tmp—str | 9' 7' 4' |
  Breitkopf   *Kalmus* | 6' 6' |

Symphony no.4, op.120, D minor   28'
  2 2 2 2—4 2 3 0—tmp—str | 10' 3' 5' |
  Breitkopf   *Kalmus* | 10' |

Träumerei   3'
  str
  Arr. Arthur Luck, from *Kinderscenen*, op.15, no.7.
  Luck

Schurmann, Gerard   1928 -

Concerto, piano   29'
  *2 *2 2 2—4 2 3 1—tmp+3—str
  Novello

Six studies of Francis Bacon   30'
  *3 *3 =3 *3—4 4 3 1—tmp+4—hp, pf/cel—str
  All 3 flutists double on piccolo.
  Contents—Introduction; Figures in a landscape; Popes; Isabel;
  Crucifixion; George and the bicycle; Self-portrait.
  Novello

Variants   18'
  *1 *2 0 2—2 0 0 0—str
Novello

Schütz, Heinrich   1585 - 1672

Historia der Auferstehung Jesu Christi (Easter oratorio)   35'
  chorus   solos SSAATTBB
  hpsd, org—str
  Bärenreiter ed. Walter Simon Huber.
Bärenreiter   *Kalmus*

Historia der Geburt Jesu Christi (Christmas oratorio)   50'
  chorus   solos STB
  2rec 0 0 1—0 2 2 0—cnt—2 violettas (=treble viols)—str
  This listing follows the Bärenreiter version, which is based on
  the Schütz collected edition. Other editions from Breitkopf,
  Kalmus, and G. Schirmer differ somewhat in instrumentation.
Bärenreiter

Schwantner, Joseph   1943 -

Aftertones of infinity   14'
  *2 *2 2 2—4 2 3 1—tmp+2—hp, pf/cel—str
  Oboists each play 2 crystal glasses. Orchestral players sing.
Peters

Concerto, piano   29'
  *2 *2 *2 2—2 2 2 1—2perc—cel—str
  "The piano should be discreetly amplified to slightly enhance its
  presence."
Helicon

Freeflight; fanfares & fantasy for orchestra   6'
  *3 3 *3 *3—4 3 3 1—tmp+3—hp, pf—str
Helicon

From a dark millennium   12'
  *3 *3 =3 3—4 3 4 1—tmp+4—amplified pf, amplified cel—2db
  Two of the flutists double on piccolo; 2 of the clarinetists double
  on bass clarinet. Players must sing and whistle in specified
  passages.
Helicon

From afar; fantasy for guitar & orchestra   16'
  *3 *3 *3 *3—4 3 3 1—tmp+3—hp, pf/cel—str
Helicon

New morning for the world (Daybreak of freedom)   27'
  narrator
  *4 *3 *3 3—4 3 4 1—tmp+4—hp, cel, pf—str
  Words of Martin Luther King Jr.
Helicon

A sudden rainbow 15'
    *3 *3 *3 *3—4 3 3 1—tmp+3—hp, pf/cel (amplified)—str
    Helicon

Toward light 20'
    *3 *3 *3 *3—4 3 3 1—tmp+3—hp, 2pf—str
    One of the pianists doubles on celesta.
    Contents—Someday memories; Toward light; Shadowed images.
    Helicon

Schwartz, Elliott   1936 -

Island 12'
    *3 2 *3 *2—4 2 3 1—tmp+2—pf—str
    Contents—Coney Island; England; Monhegan Island (Maine).
    C. Fischer

Texture 8'
    1 1 1 1—1 1 1 0—str (or str quintet)
    Broude, A.

Schwertsik, Kurt   1935 -

Concerto, violin, op.31 20'
    *2 1 =2 2—2 1 0 1—tmp+1—hp—str
    Contents—Phantasie I; Albumblatt; Vogellied; Aubade; Phantasie
    II.
    Boosey

Der irdischen Klänge, 2.Teil (Fünf Naturstücke, op.45) 16'
    *3 2 *3 *3—3 3 3 1—tmp+5—hp—str
    Contents—Wind; Donner; Regen; Wasser; Vogel.
    Boosey

Scriabin, Alexander   1872 - 1915

Concerto, piano, op.20, F-sharp minor 28'
    *3 2 2 2—4 2 3 0—tmp—str   8' 9' 11'
    Belaieff   *Kalmus*

Le Divin Poème, op.43 (The divine poem; Symphony no.3) 50'
    *4 *4 *4 *4—8 5 3 1—tmp+2—2hp—str 16.16.12.12.8   25' 15'
    Belaieff   *Kalmus*   10'

Le Poème de l'extase, op.54 (The poem of ecstasy; Symphony no.4) 22'
    *4 *4 *4 *4—8 5 3 1—tmp+5—2hp, cel, org (or harm)—str
    Belaieff   *Kalmus*

Prométhée, le poème du feu, op.60 (Prometheus, poem of fire; Sym. 24'
no.5)
    solo piano   *clavier à lumières*   chorus
    *4 *4 *4 *4—8 5 3 1—tmp+6—2hp, cel, org—str
    Boosey   *Kalmus*

Symphony no.1, op.26, E major   51'
  chorus   solo tenor & mezzo-soprano   8' 9' 10'
  *3 2 3 2—4 3 3 1—tmp—hp—str   3' 8' 13'
  Belaieff   *Kalmus*

Symphony no.2, op.29, C minor   41'
  *3 2 3 2—4 3 3 1—tmp+1—str   6' 9' 12'
  Belaieff   *Kalmus*   6' 8'

Sculthorpe, Peter   1929 -

Kakadu   15'
  2 *3 2 *3—4 4 3 1—tmp+3—str
  Faber

Mangrove   13'
  0 0 0 0—4 2 3 1—3perc—str
  Faber

Serocki, Kazimierz   1922 - 1981

Segmenti   7'
  *1 1 =2 1—asx—1 1 1 1—cornetto piccolo (or E-flat tp), tenor
  saxhorn (or another tbn)—tmp+3—hp, pf, hpsd/cel—elec gtr, elec
  mand
  Graphic notation.
  Moeck

Sessions, Roger   1896 - 1985

The black maskers: Suite   22'
  =3 *3 =4 *3—4 4 3 1—tmp+4—pf, opt org—str
  Marks

Concertino for chamber orchestra   17'
  =1 *1 =1 *1—2 1 1 0—2perc—pf—str 2.2.2.2.1
  Marks

Concerto for orchestra   15'
  *3 *3 =4 *3—4 3 3 1—tmp+4—hp—str
  Two of the flutists double on piccolo.
  Merion

Concerto, violin   29'
  +3 *3 =3 *3—basset horn (or alto cl)—4 2 2 0—tmp+1—   9' 6' 4'
  str (without vn)   10'
  Marks

Concerto, violin & violoncello   20'
  *3 *2 *3 *2—3 1 2 0—tmp+5—pf—str
  Merion

Idyll of Theocritus   42'
  soprano solo
  2 *2 *2 2—4 2 3 1—tmp+2—hp, cel—str (max 8.8.6.5.4)
  Marks

Symphony [No.1]   23'
    *3 *3 =4 *3—4 4 3 1—tmp+5—pf—str
    Marks

Symphony no.2   28'
    *3 *3 *3 2—4 3 3 1—tmp+3—pf—str
    Schirmer, G.   10' 2' 9'
                                                                    7'

Symphony no.3   32'
    *3 *3 =4 *3—4 2 3 1—tmp+4—hp, cel—str
    Marks

Symphony no.4   24'
    *3 *3 =4 *3—4 3 3 1—tmp+4—hp, pf/cel—str
    Marks

Shapey, Ralph   1921 -

Concerto fantastique   54'
    *3 *3 =3 *3—4 4 5 1—2tmp+11—str
    All of the flutists double on piccolo; 2 clarinetists double on
    E-flat clarinet.
    Presser

Rituals   13'
    *3 *3 *3 *3—asx, tsx, bsx —3 2 2 1—tmp+8—pf—str
    Presser

Symphonie concertante   29'
    11 soloists: fl/pic—ob/Eh—cl/scl/bcl—bn/cbn—hn—tp—tbn   11' 5'
    —vn—va—vc—db   13'
    *3 *3 =3 *3—3 3 4 1—2tmp+8—cel, pf—str
    In the orchestra: all flutes double on piccolo; 2 clarinets double
    on E-flat clarinet.
    Presser

Shchedrin, Rodion   1932 -

Anna Karenina   27'
    optional female narrator
    =4 *3 +3 *3—4 3 3 1—tmp+4—2hp, cel/pf—str 16.14.12.10.8
    Russian

The chimes (Bells ringing)   10'
    *4 2 *4 2—4 4 4 0—tmp+4—cel/pf—str 16.14.12.10.8
    Two of the flutists double on piccolo; 2 clarinetists double on
    bass clarinet.
    Kalmus   *Russian*   *Sikorski*

Geometrie des Tones   15'
    1 1 1 1—1 1 1 0—2perc—hp, cel, hpsd, synth—2vn, va, vc, db
    Ensemble divided into 2 groups: one on stage and one backstage
    or in a balcony.
    Universal

The little humpbacked horse: Suite [no.1]   25'
  *3 *3 *3 *3—4 3 3 1—tmp+4—2hp, pf/cel—str
  Contents—Introduction; Grief; Elder brothers and Ivan; The little
  humpbacked horse; Revival of the Tzar Maiden; Tzar—the pea;
  Silver Mountain; Gypsy dance; Adagio and finale.
  Kalmus   *Russian*

Music for strings, oboes, horns & celesta   22'
  0 2 0 0—2 0 0 0—cel—str
  Sikorski

The seagull: Suite   20'
  =3 *3 *3 2—4 3 3 1—tmp+3—hp, cel, hpsd—str
  Schirmer, G.

Selbstportrait (Self-portrait)   19'
  =3 *3 3 *3—4 3 3 1—tmp+4—hp, pf/cel—str 16.14.12.10.8
  Russian   *Universal*

Stikhira for the millenary of Christianization of Russia   23'
  =4 *3 +3 *3—4 3 3 1—tmp+4—hp, cel/pf—str 16.14.12.10.8
  Two of the flutists double on alto flute; 2 oboists play English
  horn.
  Sikorski

Symphonic fanfares (Festive overture)   5'
  *3 2 2 2—4 3 3 1—tmp+4—str
  Kalmus   *Russian*

Sheng, Bright   1955 -

Fanfare I: Arrows to the page   5'
  *3 *3 +3 *3—4 3 3 1—4perc—hp, pf/cel—str
  Two of the flutists double on piccolo.
  Schirmer, G.

H'un (Lacerations): In memoriam 1966-1976   22'
  =2 *2 *2 *2—3 2 2 0—2perc—hp, pf—str
  Both flutists double on piccolo; both clarinetists double on bass
  clarinet.
  Schirmer, G.

Shostakovich, Dmitri   1906 - 1975

The age of gold, op.22: Suite   15'
  *2 *2 =3 *2—ssx—4 3 3 1—baritone horn—tmp+4—harm—str   `3' 9' 1' 2'`
  Contents—Introduction; Adagio; Polka; Danse.
  Kalmus   *Russian*   *Universal*

The age of gold, op.22: Polka   2'
  *2 *2 =3 *2—ssx—4 3 3 1—tmp+2—str
  Kalmus

Ballet Suite no.1   14'
   *2 1 2 1—3 2 2 1—tmp+3—pf/cel—str
   Contents—Valse lyrique; Dance; Romance; Polka; Valse
   badinage; Galop.
   Kalmus   *Russian*

> 2' 2' 3'
> 2' 3' 2'

Concerto, piano, no.1, op.35   21'
   solo trumpet as well as solo piano
   str
   Kalmus   *Russian*

> 6' 8' 1' 6'

Concerto, piano, no.2, op.102   20'
   *3 2 2 2—4 0 0 0—1perc (tmp+sd)—str
   MCA

> 7' 7' 6'

Concerto, violin, op.99   39'
   *3 *3 *3 *3—4 0 0 1—tmp+2—2hp, cel—str
   The 2hp double a single brief part. Originally op.77; revised by
   the composer as op.99. The original version is available from
   Kalmus.
   MCA

> 12' 6'
> 16' 5'

Concerto, violoncello, no.1, op.107   28'
   *2 2 2 *2—1 0 0 0—tmp—cel—str
   Kalmus   *MCA*

> 6' 12'
> 10'

Concerto, violoncello, no.2, op.126   33'
   *2 2 2 *3—2 0 0 0—tmp+3—hp—str
   Russian   *Sikorski*

> 14' 4'
> 15'

Festive overture, op.96   7'
   *3 3 3 *3—4 3 3 1—tmp+4—str
   Optional extra brass: 4 3 3 0.
   Kalmus   *Russian*

The gadfly: Suite, op.97a   44'
   *3 3 3 *3—4 3 3 1—tmp+4—hp, cel/pf—str
   The clarinetists double on 3 alto saxophones.
   Kalmus   *Russian*

The golden age
   see his: The age of gold

Hamlet: Film suite (1964), op.116   35'
   *3 2 2 2—4 3 3 1—tmp+5—hp, pf/hpsd—str
   Contents—Introduction; Ball at the palace; The ghost; In the
   garden; Scene of the poisoning; The arrival and scene of the
   players; Ophelia; The duel and death of Hamlet.
   Kalmus   *Russian*

Hamlet: Incidental music (1932), op.32   19'
   1 1 1 1—2 2 1 1—tmp+3—str
   Kalmus

Memorable year 1919, op.89 (Nezabivayemiy 1919-y)
*3 3 3 *3—4 6 6 1—tmp+4—hp, cel, pf—str
Sometimes referred to as *The unforgettable year 1919*. This work
may be out of print.
MCA

Song of the forests, op.81   37'
chorus, boys' chorus   tenor & bass solos   6' 3' 6'
*3 *3 3 2—4 9 9 1—tmp+4—2hp—str   2' 4' 7'
Six of the trumpets and six of the trombones appear only in the   9'
last movement, as a separate brass choir.
Russian

Symphony no.1, op.10, F minor   28'
*3 2 2 2—4 3 3 1—tmp+4—pf—str   8' 4' 8' 8'
Kalmus

Symphony no.2, op.14, B major (To the October Revolution)   20'
chorus
*3 2 2 2—4 3 3 1—tmp+4—str
Kalmus   *Russian*

Symphony no.3, op.20, E-flat major (May Day)   29'
optional chorus
*3 2 2 2—4 2 3 1—tmp+3—str
Kalmus   *Russian*

Symphony no.4, op.43, C minor   60'
*6 *4 =6 *4—8 4 3 2—2tmp+7—2hp, cel—str   25' 9'
Kalmus   *Russian*   26'

Symphony no.5, op.47, D minor   44'
*3 2 +3 *3—4 3 3 1—tmp+4—2hp (playing a single real part),   15' 5'
pf/cel—str   14' 10'
Kalmus   *Russian*

Symphony no.6, op.54, B minor   30'
*3 *3 =4 *3—4 3 3 1—tmp+5—hp, cel—str   15' 7' 8'
Kalmus   *Russian*

Symphony no.7, op.60, C major (Leningrad)   69'
*3 *3 =4 *3—8 6 6 1—tmp+4—2hp, pf—str   26' 11'
Kalmus   *Russian*   17' 15'

Symphony no.8, op.65, C minor   61'
*4 *3 =4 *3—4 3 3 1—tmp+5—str   23' 6' 7'
Breitkopf   *Kalmus*   *Russian*   10' 15'

Symphony no.9, op.70, E-flat major   27'
*3 2 2 2—4 2 3 1—tmp+2—str   5' 8' 3'
Breitkopf   *Kalmus*   *Russian*   5' 6'

Symphony no.10, op.93, E minor   45'
*3 *3 +3 *3—4 3 3 1—tmp+3—str   20' 4' 9'
Kalmus   *Russian*   12'

Symphony no.11, op.103, G minor (The year 1905)   55'
    *3 *3 *3 *3—4 3 3 1—tmp+5—2-4hp, cel—str
    Luck   Russian

14'	17'
10'	14'

Symphony no.12, op.112, D minor ("The year 1917" or "Lenin")   38'
    *3 3 3 *3—4 3 3 1—tmp+5—str
    Breitkopf   Kalmus   Russian

12'	11'
5'	10'

Symphony no.13, op.113 (Babi Yar)   59'
    bass solo   male chorus
    *3 *3 =3 *3—4 3 3 1—tmp+4—2-4hp, cel, pf—str
    MCA

16'	8'
11'	12'
	12'

Symphony no.14, op.135   55'
    soprano & bass solos
    2perc—cel—str 5.5.4.3.2
    MCA

Symphony no.15, op.141, A major   42'
    *3 2 2 2—4 2 3 1—tmp+6—cel—str (min 16.14.12.12.10)
    MCA

8'	16'	4'
		14'

Shulman, Alan   1915 - 1993
Threnody   6'
    str
    Broude, A.

Sibelius, Jean   1865 - 1957
The bard, op.64   6'
    2 2 *3 2—4 2 3 0—tmp+1—hp—str
    Breitkopf

Canzonetta, op.62a   4'
    str
    Breitkopf   Kalmus

Concerto, violin, op.47, D minor   31'
    2 2 2 2—4 2 3 0—tmp—str
    Kalmus   Lienau

16'	8'	7'

Finlandia, op.26   8'
    2 2 2 2—4 3 3 1—tmp+1—str
    Breitkopf   Kalmus

Humoresque I, op.87, no.1, D minor   4'
    solo violin
    2 2 2 2—2 0 0 0—tmp—str
    Hansen

Humoresque II, op.87, no.2, D major   3'
    solo violin
    0 0 0 0—2 0 0 0—tmp—str
    Hansen

Karelia overture, op.10 9'
*3 2 2 2—4 3 3 1—tmp+3—str
Breitkopf   *Kalmus*

Karelia suite, op.11 14'
*3 2 2 2—4 3 3 1—tmp+3—str 4' 6' 4'
Optional English horn. Contents—Intermezzo; Ballade; March.
Breitkopf   *Kalmus*

Kuolema: Valse triste 6'
1 0 1 0—2 0 0 0—tmp—str
Breitkopf   *Kalmus*

Legends, op.22 (Lemminkäinen suite (Lemminkais-sarja))

1. Lemminkäinen and the maidens of Saari 16'
*2 2 2 2—4 3 3 0—tmp+2—str
Both flutists double on piccolo.
Breitkopf

2. The swan of Tuonela (Tuonelan joutsen) 10'
solo English horn
0 1 *1 2—4 0 3 0—tmp+1—hp—str
Originally no.3 of the four Legends.
Breitkopf   *Kalmus*

3. Lemminkäinen in Tuonela 17'
2 *2 *2 2—4 3 3 0—2perc—str
Originally no.2 of the four Legends.
Breitkopf

4. Lemminkäinen's return (Lemminkaisen paluu) 7'
*2 2 2 2—4 3 3 1—tmp+3—str
Breitkopf   *Kalmus*

Luonnotar (Kalevala), op.70 10'
soprano solo
2 2 *3 2—4 2 3 0—2tmp—2hp—str
Breitkopf

Night ride and sunrise, op.55 16'
*3 2 *3 *3—4 2 3 1—tmp+3—str
Kalmus   *Lienau*

The Oceanides, op.73 17'
*3 *3 *3 *3—4 3 3 0—2tmp—2hp—str
Breitkopf   *Kalmus*

Pan and Echo, op.53a (Dance intermezzo no.3) 5'
2 2 2 2—4 2 3 0—tmp+2—str
Kalmus   *Lienau*

Pelléas and Mélisande, op.46 25'
*1 *1 2 2—2 0 0 0—tmp—str 3' 5' 2'
Kalmus   *Lienau* 2' 2' 2'
  3' 6'

Pohjola's daughter, op.49
*3 *3 *3 *3—4 4 3 1—tmp—hp—str   17'
Kalmus   Lienau

Rakastava, op.14   11'
tmp/triangle—str   4' 2' 5'
Contents—The lover; The lovers' path; Good evening—farewell!
Breitkopf   Kalmus

Romance, op.42, C major   5'
str
Breitkopf   Kalmus

En saga, op.9 (A saga)   20'
*2 2 2 2—4 3 3 1—2perc—str
Breitkopf   Kalmus

The swan of Tuonela
see his: Legends, op.22, no.2

Symphony no.1, op.39, E minor   38'
*2 2 2 2—4 3 3 1—tmp+2—hp—str   11' 9' 5'
Both flutists double on piccolo in 4th movement.   13'
Breitkopf   Kalmus

Symphony no.2, op.43, D major   43'
2 2 2 2—4 3 3 1—tmp—str   10' 14'
Breitkopf   Kalmus   7' 12'

Symphony no.3, op.52, C major   29'
2 2 2 2—4 2 3 0—tmp—str   10' 8'
Kalmus   Lienau   11'

Symphony no.4, op.63, A minor   36'
2 2 2 2—4 2 3 0—tmp+1—str   10' 5'
Breitkopf   Kalmus   11' 10'

Symphony no.5, op.82, E-flat major   30'
2 2 2 2—4 3 3 0—tmp—str   13' 9' 8'
Hansen

Symphony no.6, op.104, D minor   28'
2 2 *3 2—4 3 3 0—tmp—hp—str   8' 6' 4'
Hansen   Kalmus   10'

Symphony no.7, op.105, C major   21'
*2 2 2 2—4 3 3 0—tmp—str
Both flutists double on piccolo.
Hansen

Tapiola, op.112   18'
*3 *3 *3 *3—4 3 3 0—tmp—str
Breitkopf

The tempest: Prelude   5'
*3 2 =3 2—4 3 3 1—tmp+3—str
Hansen

The tempest: Suite no.1 20'
*3 2 =3 2—4 3 3 1—tmp+4—hp—str
Hansen

The tempest: Suite no.2 12'
2 2 *2 2—4 0 0 0—tmp+1—hp—str
Hansen

Valse triste
see his: Kuolema: Valse triste

Siegmeister, Elie 1909 - 1991

Five fantasies of the theater 12'
*2 *2 =3 *3—4 3 3 1—tmp+4—hp, pf—str
Contents—Beckett; Ionesco; Brecht; Pirandello; O'Casey.
C. Fischer

Lonesome hollow 7'
*2 *2 +2 2—4 2 2 0—tmp+1—hp or pf—str
C. Fischer

Sunday in Brooklyn 16'
*3 *2 =3 2—asx—4 3 3 1—tmp+4—hp, cel, pf—str | 4' 3' 4'
Two of the flutists double on piccolo. Contents—Prospect Park; | 1' 4'
Sunday driver; Family at home; Children's story; Coney Island.
C. Fischer

Theater set 15'
*2 *2 *3 *2—4 3 3 1—tmp+3—hp, pf—str
Contrabassoon optional.
Contents—Intrada; Blues and pursuit; Revelation; Triple attack.
C. Fischer

Western suite 20'
*2 *2 =3 2—4 3 3 1—tmp+4—str | 6' 3' 4'
Contents—Prairie morning; Round-up; Night-herding; Buckaroo; | 3' 4'
Riding home.
C. Fischer

Singleton, Alvin 1940 -

Shadows 20'
=3 *3 =3 *3—4 3 3 1—2tmp+2—hp—str
EAM

Skalkottas, Nikos 1904 - 1949

Five Greek dances 9'
str
Ed. Walter Goehr.
Universal

Ten sketches for strings 19'
str
Universal

Skoryk, Myroslav   1938 -

Hutsul triptych; suite from "Shadows of forgotten ancestors"   15'
*3 *3 *3 *3—4 3 3 1—tmp+2—hp, pf—str   4' 5' 6'
Schirmer, G.

Skrowaczewski, Stanisław   1923 -

Ricercari notturni   27'
solo saxophone, doubling on soprano, alto and baritone
*3 0 0 2—2 2 3 1—tmp+3—amplified hpsd—str 8.8.6.6.4
Alternative soloist: B-flat clarinet doubling on bass clarinet.
EAM

Skryabin, Alexander   1872 - 1915

see: Scriabin, Alexander, 1872-1915

Slonimsky, Nicolas   1894 - 1995

My toy balloon; variations on a Brazilian tune   6'
*3 2 2 2—2 2 3 1—tmp+6—pf (doubling on opt cel), opt hp—str
Includes popping of balloons at end.
Shawnee

Smetana, Bedrich   1824 - 1884

The bartered bride: Overture   7'
*3 2 2 2—4 2 3 0—tmp—str
Breitkopf   *Kalmus*

The bartered bride: Three dances   11'
*3 2 2 2—4 2 3 0—tmp+3—str   4' 2' 5'
Arr. Hugo Riesenfeld.
Contents—Polka; Furiant; Dance of the comedians.
Kalmus

Hakon Jarl   10'
*3 2 *3 2—4 2 3 1—tmp+3—hp—str
Kalmus   *Lengnick*   *Simrock*   *Supraphon*

Má vlast (My fatherland)   72'

    1. Vysehrad (The high castle)   12'
*3 2 2 2—4 2 3 1—tmp+2—2hp—str
Breitkopf   *Kalmus*   *Supraphon*

    2. Vltava (The Moldau)   12'
*3 2 2 2—4 2 3 1—tmp+3—hp—str
Breitkopf   *Kalmus*   *Supraphon*

    3. Sárka   9'
*3 2 2 2—4 2 3 1—tmp+2—str
Kalmus   *Supraphon*

4. Z ceskych luhuv a hájuv (From Bohemia's meadows and forests)   12'
*3 2 2 2—4 2 3 1—tmp+2—str
Breitkopf   *Kalmus*   *Supraphon*

5. Tábor   13'
*3 2 2 2—4 2 3 1—tmp+1—str
Kalmus   *Supraphon*

6. Blaník   14'
*3 2 2 2—4 2 3 1—tmp+2—str
Kalmus   *Supraphon*

Richard III   11'
*3 2 2 2—4 2 3 1—tmp+3—hp—str
Kalmus   *Lengnick*   *Supraphon*

Valdstynuv tabor (Wallenstein's camp)   14'
*3 2 2 2—4 4 3 1—tmp+4—str
Kalmus   *Simrock*   *Supraphon*

Wallenstein's camp
see his: Valdstynuv tabor

Smith, Gregory   1957 -

Mr. Smith's composition   19'
narrator
*3 *3 *3 *3—4 3 3 1—tmp+2—hp—str
Eh, bcl & cbn are optional.
Stanton

Smith, Hale   1925 -

Contours   9'
*2 2 *2 2—4 4 3 1—tmp+5—hp, pf/cel—str
Peters

Ritual and incantations   16'
*2 *2 *2 2—4 3 3 1—tmp+3—hp, pf—str
Peters

Smith, Julia   1911 -

Folkways symphony   13'
*2 2 2 2—asx—2 2 1 0—tmp+2—hp, pf 4-hands—str
Harp, bassoons, & saxophone are optional.
Contents—Day's a-breakin'; Night herding song; Cowboy's waltz; Stomping leather.
C. Fischer

Smith Brindle, Reginald   1917 -

Concerto, guitar   15'
1 1 1 1—3perc—pf, elec org—str 5.4.3.2.1
Schott

Sowerby, Leo   1895 - 1968

Comes autumn time   5'
*3 2 *3 2—4 3 3 1—tmp+3—hp, cel—str
Boston   *Kalmus*

From the northland; impressions of the Lake Superior country   20'
*3 *3 =4 *3—4 3 3 1—tmp+3—hp, cel, pf—str
Contents—Forest voices; Cascades; Burnt Rock Pool; The Shining
Big-Sea Water.
Schirmer, G.

Medieval poem   16'
solo organ   off-stage voice (woman or boy)
1 *1 *2 1—2 1 0 0—tmp+1—str
C. Fischer

Prairie; a poem for orchestra   17'
*3 *3 *3 *3—4 3 3 1—tmp+4—cel—str
C. Fischer

Spohr, Ludwig   1784 - 1859

Concerto, clarinet, op.26, C minor   20'
2 2 0 2—2 2 0 0—tmp—str
Bärenreiter   *Kalmus*   *Musica Rara*   *Peters* | 11' 3' 6' |

Concerto, violin, no.8, op.47, A minor (Gesangsszene)   19'
1 0 2 1—2 0 0 0—tmp—str
In one movement.
Breitkopf   *Kalmus*   *Peters*

Concerto, violin, no.9, op.55, D minor   27'
2 2 2 2—2 2 3 0—tmp—str
Breitkopf   *Kalmus* | 10' 8' 9' |

Nonet, op.31, F major   32'
1 1 1 1—1 0 0 0—vn, va, vc, db
Peters | 11' 6' 7' 8' |

Octet, op.32, E major   29'
0 0 1 0—2 0 0 0—vn, 2va, vc, db
Bärenreiter | 9' 6' 8' 6' |

Stamitz, Anton   1754 - ca.1809

Concerto, viola, no.4, D major
str
Ed. Walter Lebermann.
Breitkopf   *Luck*

Stamitz, Johann Wenzel Anton   1717 - 1757

Concerto, flute, C major   25'
cnt—str
Ed. Herbert Koelbel.
Peters

Concerto, flute, D major   15'
  str (without va)
  Eulenburg   *Kalmus*

Concerto, oboe, C major   14'
  cnt—str
  Ed. H. Töttcher & H.F. Hartig.
  Sikorski

Concerto, viola, G major   15'
  cnt—str
  Ed. Rudolf Laugg.
  Peters

Sinfonia pastorale, op.4, no.2, D major   15'
  0 2 0 0—2 0 0 0—cnt—str
  Vieweg

Symphony, op.3, no.3, G major   12'
  2hn (opt)—str
  Ed. Adam Carse.
  Augener

Three Mannheim symphonies
  str
  Ed. Adolf Hoffmann.
  Kalmus   *Möseler*

  No.1, G major   11'
                                                       5' 3' 3'

  No.2, A major   15'
                                                       6' 6' 3'

  No.3, B-flat major   12'
                                                       4' 5' 3'

Stamitz, Karl   1745 - 1801

Concerto, bassoon, F major   15'
  0 2 0 0—2 0 0 0—str
  Ed. Johannes Wojciechowski.
  Sikorski

Concerto, clarinet, E-flat major   17'
  2 0 0 0—2 0 0 0—str   8' 5' 4'
  Hofmeister   *Sikorski*

Concerto, clarinet, F major   17'
  0 2 0 0—2 0 0 0—str   8' 4' 5'
  EMB   *Eulenburg*

Concerto, clarinet, no.3, B-flat major   14'
  0 2 0 0—2 0 0 0—str   8' 3' 3'
  Ed. Johannes Wojciechowski.
  Peters

Concerto, clarinet & bassoon, B-flat major   20'
    0 0 0 0—2 0 0 0—str
    Ed. Johannes Wojciechowski.
    Sikorski

Concerto, clarinet & violin (or 2 clarinets)   18'
    0 2 0 0—2 0 0 0—str
    8' 6' 4'
    Oboes & horns are optional. Published under the title *Concerto
    no.4.*
    Boosey   *EMB*

Concerto, flute, G major
    str   16'
    Ed. Ingo Gronefeld.
    Leuckart

Concerto, viola, op.1, D major   22'
    0 0 2 0—2 0 0 0—str
    Kalmus   *Peters*

Concerto, violoncello, no.1, G major   20'
    2 0 0 0—2 0 0 0—str
    10' 4' 6'
    Ed. Walter Upmeyer.
    Bärenreiter   *Kalmus*

Concerto, violoncello, no.2, A major   19'
    2 0 0 0—2 0 0 0—str
    9' 5' 5'
    Ed. Walter Upmeyer.
    Bärenreiter   *Kalmus*

Concerto, violoncello, no.3, C major   18'
    0 2 0 0—2 0 0 0—str
    9' 5' 4'
    Ed. Walter Upmeyer.
    Bärenreiter   *Kalmus*

Sinfonia concertante, D major   20'
    solo violin & viola
    0 0 0 0—2 0 0 0—str
    Kalmus   *Kneusslin*

Stanford, Charles Villiers   1852 - 1924
Irish rhapsody no.1, op.78   12'
    *2 *2 *3 *3—4 3 3 1—tmp+3—hp—str
    Bcl is optional.
    Kalmus

Starer, Robert   1924 -
Elegy for strings   3'
    str
    MCA

Samson agonistes   13'
    *3 *3 *3 *3—4 3 3 1—tmp+4—pf/cel—str
    MCA

Stevens, Halsey   1908 - 1989

Sinfonia breve   15'
  *2 2 2 2—4 2 3 1—tmp+1—hp, pf/cel—str
  CFE

> 5' 6' 4'

Symphonic dances   15'
  =3 *3 *3 *3—4 3 3 1—tmp+3—2hp, pf/cel—str
  Peters

Still, William Grant   1895 - 1978

Afro-American symphony   23'
  *3 *3 *4 2—4 3 3 1—tmp+3—hp, cel, tenor banjo—str
  Novello

> 7' 5' 4' 7'

Bells   7'
  *3 *3 *3 *2—4 3 3 1—tmp+1—hp, cel, pf—str
  Contents—Phantom chapel; Fairy knoll.
  MCA

Darker America   13'
  2 *2 2 2—1 1 1 0—1perc—pf—str
  C. Fischer

Festive overture   10'
  *3 *3 *3 2—4 3 3 1—tmp+4—hp, cel—str
  WGS

In memoriam: The colored soldiers who died for democracy   6'
  *3 *3 *3 2—4 3 3 1—tmp+3—hp—str
  MCA

Poem   14'
  *3 *3 *3 *2—4 3 3 1—tmp+3—hp, cel—str
  MCA

Wood notes   20'
  *2 *2 2 2—2 3 2 0—tmp—hp, cel—str
  Southern

Stillman-Kelley, Edgar   1857 - 1944

see: Kelley, Edgar Stillman, 1857-1944

Stockhausen, Karlheinz   1928 -

Gruppen, for three orchestras   25'
  =5 *5 =5 3—bsx—8 6 6 1—contrabass tbn—12perc
  —2hp, 2cel, pf, elec gtr—str 14.12.10.8.6
  One clarinetist also doubles on alto saxophone; one celesta must
  have 5 octaves. Three conductors are required.
  Universal

Kontra-Punkte no.1   12'
1 0 *2 1—0 1 1 0—hp, pf—vn, vc
A "farewell symphony" in which various instruments fade out
until just the piano is left.
Universal

Punkte   21'
=3 *3 =3 *3—3 3 2 1—tmp+2—2hp, 2pf (one dbl cel)—str 8.8.8.6.4
One oboist also doubles on oboe d'amore.
Universal

Strauss, Johann, Jr.   1825 - 1899

An der schönen blauen Donau, op.314 (On the beautiful blue   9'
Danube)
*2 2 2 2—4 2 1 1—tmp+2—hp—str
(optional male chorus)
Breitkopf   *Doblinger*   *Kalmus*   *Luck*

Egyptian march, op.335   4'
*2 2 2 2—4 2 3 1—5perc—str
Doblinger   *Kalmus*   *Luck*

Emperor waltzes
see his: Kaiser-Walzer

Fledermaus: Overture   9'
*2 2 2 2—4 2 3 0—tmp+2—str
Breitkopf   *Doblinger*   *Kalmus*   *Luck*

Die Fledermaus: Suite
*2 2 2 2—4 2 3 0—tmp+4—hp—str
Arr. Hans Schwieger.
Boosey

Fledermaus: Du und du, op.367   5'
*2 2 2 2—4 2 3 0—tmp+2—str
Breitkopf   *Kalmus*   *Luck*

Frühlingsstimmen, op.410 (Voices of spring)   6'
*2 2 2 2—4 2 3 0—tmp+1—hp—str
Breitkopf   *Doblinger*   *Kalmus*   *Luck*

Geschichten aus dem Wienerwald, op.325 (Tales from the Vienna   11'
Woods)
*2 2 2 2—4 3 3 1—tmp+2—hp, opt zither—str
Breitkopf   *Doblinger*   *Kalmus*   *Luck*

Graduation ball (arr. Antal Dorati)   48'
2 2 2 2—4 2 3 0—tmp+4—hp—str
Belwin

Gypsy baron
see his: Zigeunerbaron

Kaiser-Walzer, op.437 (Emperor waltzes)   10'
  2 2 2 2—4 2 3 0—tmp+1—hp—str
Breitkopf   *Doblinger*   *Kalmus*   *Luck*

Künstler Quadrille, op.201   6'
  *2 2 2 2—4 2 1 1—tmp+1—str
Quotes amusingly from Mendelssohn (*Wedding March*), Weber
(*Oberon* & *Freischütz*), Paganini (*Campanella*), Schubert
(*Wandering*) and Berlioz (*Rakoczy March*).
Doblinger   *Kalmus*   *Luck*

Morgenblätter, op.279 (Morning papers)   10'
  *2 2 2 2—4 2 1 1—tmp+2—str
Doblinger   *Kalmus*   *Luck*

On the beautiful blue Danube
  see his: An der schönen blauen Donau

Perpetuum mobile, op.257   3'
  *2 2 +2 2—4 2 1 0—tmp+1—hp—str
Doblinger   *C. Fischer*   *Kalmus*   *Luck*

Pizzicato polka (composed with Josef Strauss)   3'
  *2 2 2 2—4 3 3 1—tmp+2—str
Frequently performed with just strings and 2perc.
Doblinger   *Luck*

Rosen aus dem Süden, op.388 (Roses from the south)   7'
  *2 2 2 2—4 2 3 0—tmp+3—hp—str
Breitkopf   *Doblinger*   *Kalmus*   *Luck*

Tales from the Vienna Woods
  see his: Geschichten aus dem Wienerwald

Thunder and lightning polka
  see his: Unter Donner und Blitz

Unter Donner und Blitz, op.324 (Thunder and lightning polka)   3'
  *2 2 2 2—4 3 3 1—tmp+3—str
Doblinger   *Kalmus*   *Luck*

Voices of spring
  see his: Frühlingsstimmen

Wein, Weib, und Gesang, op.333 (Wine, women and song)   7'
  *2 2 2 2—4 2 3 0—tmp+2—hp—str
Breitkopf   *Doblinger*   *Kalmus*   *Luck*

Wiener Blut, op.354 (Vienna blood)   7'
  *2 2 2 2—4 2 3 0—tmp+2—str
Breitkopf   *Kalmus*   *Luck*

Zigeunerbaron (Gypsy Baron): Overture   8'
  *2 2 2 2—4 2 3 0—tmp+3—hp—str
Doblinger   *Kalmus*   *Luck*

Strauss, Johann, Sr.   1804 - 1849

Radetzky march, op.228   3'
   *3 2 2 2—4 2 3 1—2perc—str
   Kalmus   *Luck*

Strauss, Josef   1827 - 1870

Dorfschwalben aus Österreich, op.164 (Village swallows)   8'
   *2 2 +2 2—4 2 1 0—tmp+3—hp—str
   Kalmus   *Luck*

Mein Lebenslauf ist Lieb' und Lust, op.263   7'
   *2 2 2 2—4 4 3 1—tmp+1—hp—str
   Kalmus   *Luck*

Pizzicato polka
   see under: Strauss, Johann, Jr.

Sphärenklänge, op.235 (Music of the spheres)   9'
   2 2 +2 2—4 4 3 1—tmp+2—hp—str
   Kalmus   *Luck*

Strauss, Richard   1864 - 1949

Eine Alpensinfonie, op.64 (Alpine symphony)   47'
   *4 *3 =4 *4—heckelphone—20 6 6 2—2tmp+3—2hp, cel, org—str
   Horns 5-8 double on Wagner tubas; two of the flutists double on
   piccolo. Possible with brass 8 4 5 2.
   Kalmus   *Leuckart*

Also sprach Zarathustra, op.30 (Thus spake Zarathustra)   33'
   *4 *4 =4 *4—6 4 3 2—tmp+3—2hp, org—str

2'	4'	2'
2'	2'	4'
5'	8'	4'

   Kalmus   *Peters*

Aus Italien, op.16   47'
   *3 *2 2 *3—4 2 3 0—tmp+4—hp—str

13'	11'
15'	8'

   Kalmus   *Peters*

Le Bourgeois Gentilhomme (Der Bürger als Edelmann): Suite   36'
   *2 *2 2 *2—2 1 1 0—tmp+5—hp, pf—str 6.0.4.4.2

4'	2'	2'
5'	2'	3'
5'	3'	10'

   Kalmus   *Leuckart*

Brentano Lieder
   see his: Sechs Lieder, op.68

Burleske   17'
   solo piano
   *3 2 2 2—4 2 0 0—tmp—str
   Kalmus

Cäcilie, op.27, no.2   2'
   high voice
   2 2 2 2—4 2 3 1—tmp—hp—str 10.10.6.6.4
   Kalmus   *Luck*   *Universal*

Concerto, horn, no.1, op.11, E-flat major   16'
  2 2 2 2—2 2 0 0—tmp—str   11' 5'
  Kalmus   *Universal*

Concerto, horn, no.2, E-flat major   20'
  2 2 2 2—2 2 0 0—tmp—str   15' 5'
  Boosey

Concerto, oboe, D major   28'
  2 *1 2 2—2 0 0 0—str   9' 10' 9'
  Boosey

Dance of the seven veils
  see his: Salome, op.54: Salome's dance

Death and transfiguration
  see his: Tod und Verklärung

Don Juan, op.20   17'
  *3 *3 2 *3—4 3 3 1—tmp+3—hp—str
  Kalmus critical edition by Clinton F. Nieweg & Nancy Bradburd.
  Kalmus   *Peters*

Don Quixote, op.35   38'
  solo violoncello
  *3 *3 =3 *4—6 3 3 1—tenor tuba (euphonium) —tmp+2—hp—str
  Kalmus   *Peters*

Duet-concertino   18'
  solo clarinet & bassoon   6' 3' 9'
  hp—str
  Boosey

Four last songs
  see his: Vier letzte Lieder

Ein Heldenleben, op.40   40'
  *4 *4 =4 *4—8 5 3 1—tenor tuba (euphonium)—tmp+4—2hp—str
  Kalmus   *Leuckart*

Macbeth, op.23   18'
  *3 *3 *3 *3—4 3 3 1—tmp+2—btp—str
  Kalmus   *Peters*

Metamorphosen   26'
  23 solo strings (5.5.5.5.3)
  Boosey

Morgen, op.27, no.4   2'
  medium or high voice   solo violin
  0 0 0 0—3 0 0 0—hp—str
  Kalmus   *Luck*   *Universal*

Romanze   12'
  violoncello solo
  2 2 2 2—2 0 0 0—str
  Schott

Der Rosenkavalier: Suite   22'
   *3 *3 =4 *3—4 3 3 1—tmp+5—1 or 2hp, cel—str
   May be performed with 3cl, including bcl.
   Boosey

Der Rosenkavalier: Waltzes, first sequence   13'
   3 3 +3 3—basset horn—4 3 3 1—tmp+5—2hp (doubling a single
   part)—str
   Boosey

Salome, op.54: Salome's dance   12'
   *4 *3 =6 *4—heckelphone—6 4 4 1—2tmp+6—2hp, cel—str
   Boosey   *Kalmus*

Sechs Lieder, op.68 (Six songs)   24'
   high voice
   *3 *3 *3 *3—4 3 3 1—tmp+2—2hp—str

3'	4'	4'
3'	3'	7'

   Contents—An die Nacht; Ich wollt ein Sträusslein binden; Säusle,
   liebe Myrte; Als mir dein Lied erklang; Amor; Lied der Frauen.
   (Poems by Clemens von Brentano)
   Boosey   *Fuerstner*

Serenade, op.7, E-flat major   10'
   2 2 2 *3—4hn
   Tuba or double bass may be substituted for contrabassoon.
   Kalmus   *Universal*

Suite, op.4, B-flat major   25'
   2 2 2 *3—4hn
   Tuba may be substituted for contrabassoon.
   Kalmus   *Leuckart*

Symphonia domestica, op.53   44'
   *4 *3 =5 *5—ob d'amore—8 4 3 1—tmp+2—2hp—str

5'	7'	6'
12'	14'	

   4 opt sx (soprano, alto, baritone, bass).
   Bote & Bock   *Kalmus*

Symphony, op.12, F minor   45'
   2 2 2 2—4 2 3 1—tmp—str

16'	7'
10'	12'

   Kalmus   *Universal*

Symphony for winds, op.posth., E-flat major   36'
   2 2 *4 *3—basset horn—4 0 0 0
   Boosey

Three hymns, op.71   29'
   high voice
   *3 *3 *4 *3—4 3 3 1—tmp—2hp, cel—str

10'	10'
9'	

   Contents—Hymne an die Liebe; Rückkehr in die Heimat; Die
   Liebe.
   Boosey

Thus spake Zarathustra
   see his: Also sprach Zarathustra

Tod und Verklärung, op.24 (Death and transfiguration)   23'
3 *3 *3 *3—4 3 3 1—tmp+1—2hp—str
Kalmus   *Peters*

Till Eulenspiegels lustige Streiche, op.28   15'
*4 *4 =4 *4—4 3 3 1—tmp+2—str
Opt extra brass: 4hn, 3tp.
Kalmus   *Peters*

Vier letzte Lieder (Four last songs)   24'
solo soprano   5' 5' 6' 8'
*4 *3 *3 *3—4 3 3 1—tmp—hp, cel—str
Contents—Frühling; September; Beim Schlafengehen; Im
Abendroth.
Boosey

Wanderers Sturmlied, op.14   16'
chorus
*3 2 2 *3—4 2 3 0—tmp—str
Kalmus   *Universal*

Stravinsky, Igor   1882 - 1971

Abraham and Isaac   12'
baritone solo
+3 *2 *2 2—1 2 2 1—str
Boosey

Agon   20'
*3 *3 *3 *3—4 4 3 0—tmp+1—hp, pf, mand—str
Boosey

Apollon Musagéte (original version)   29'
str   8' 21'
Ed. Nancy Bradburd.
Kalmus

Apollon Musagéte (1947 version)   29'
str   8' 21'
Boosey

Babel   7'
male chorus   male narrator
*3 2 *3 *3—4 3 3 0—tmp—hp—str
Schott

Le Baiser de la fée (The fairy's kiss)   45'
*3 *3 *3 2—4 3 3 1—tmp+1—hp—str
Revised 1950.
Boosey

Le Baiser de la fée (The fairy's kiss): Divertimento   22'
*3 *3 *3 2—4 3 3 1—tmp+1—hp—str   5' 6' 4' 7'
Revised 1950.
Contents—Sinfonia; Danses suisses; Scherzo; Pas de deux.
Boosey

Canon, for concert introduction or encore   1'
*3 *3 *3 *3—4 3 3 1—tmp+1—hp, pf—str
On a Russian popular tune (same tune as used in the 7/4 passage from *L'Oiseau de feu*).
Boosey

Canticum sacrum   17'
solo tenor & baritone   chorus
1 *3 0 *3—0 3 3 0—btp, contrabass tbn—hp, org—str (without vn or vc)
Boosey

Capriccio for piano & orchestra   17'
concertino: solo vn, va, vc, db | 6' 6' 5' |
*3 *3 =3 2—4 2 3 1—tmp—str
Kalmus offers original 1929 version; Boosey the 1949 revision.
Boosey   *Kalmus*

Le Chant du rossignol (Song of the nightingale)   19'
*2 *2 +2 2—4 3 3 1—tmp+4—2hp, cel, pf—str | 5' 3' 11' |
Boosey

Chorale-variations on "Vom Himmel hoch da komm' ich her"   18'
chorus
2 *3 0 *3—0 3 3 0—hp—str (without vn or vc)
A "recomposition" of J.S.Bach's *Canonic variations* for organ.
Boosey

Circus polka   4'
*2 2 2 2—4 2 3 1—tmp+3—str
Schott

Concerto for piano & wind instruments   19'
*3 *3 2 *2—4 4 3 1—tmp—double basses | 7' 7' 5' |
Revised 1950.
Boosey

Concerto, violin, D major   22'
*3 *3 +3 *3—4 3 3 1—tmp—str | 6' 5' 5' 6' |
Brief bass drum part may be covered by timpanist.
A new critical edition is in preparation by the publisher.
Schott

Concerto in D   12'
str | 6' 3' 3' |
Boosey

Concerto in E-flat (Dumbarton Oaks)   12'
1 0 1 1—2 0 0 0—3vn, 3va, 2vc, 2db
Schott

Danses concertantes   20'
1 1 1 1—2 1 1 0—tmp—str
Schott

Ebony concerto   10'
  solo clarinet with jazz orchestra   `3' 3' 4'`
  0 0 0 0—2asx, 2tsx, bsx—1 5 3 0—1perc—pf, hp, gtr—db
  The 2asx players double on cl; 2nd tsx doubles on cl & bcl.
  Boosey

Eight instrumental miniatures   6'
  2 2 2 2—1 0 0 0—2vn, 2va, 2vc
  Chester

The fairy's kiss
  see his: Le Baiser de la fée

Le Faune et la Bergère   9'
  mezzo-soprano solo
  *3 2 2 2—4 2 3 1—tmp+2—str
  Belaieff   *C. Fischer*

Feu d'artifice, op.4 (Fireworks)   5'
  *3 *2 *3 2—6 3 3 1—tmp+4—2hp, cel—str
  A critical edition is in preparation by Schott.
  Kalmus   *Schott*

Firebird
  see his: L'Oiseau de feu

Four etudes for orchestra   12'
  *3 *3 =4 2—4 3 2 1—tmp—hp, pf—str
  Boosey

Four Norwegian moods   8'
  *2 *2 2 2—4 2 2 1—tmp—str   `2' 3' 1' 2'`
  Schott

L'Histoire du soldat (The soldier's tale): Suite   26'
  0 0 1 1—0 1 1 0—1perc—vn, db   `2' 3' 3'`
  1987 ed. by John Carewe (Chester) resolves many textual   `3' 3' 6'`
  problems.   `1' 3' 2'`
  Chester   *Kalmus*

In memoriam Dylan Thomas   6'
  tenor solo
  4tbn—str quartet
  Boosey

Jeu de cartes   23'
  *2 *2 2 2—4 2 3 1—tmp+1—str   `5' 10' 8'`
  Schott

Mass (1948)   18'
  chorus   solos SATTB   `3' 4' 4'`
  0 *3 0 2—0 2 3 0   `4' 3'`
  Boosey

Monumentum pro Gesualdo di Venosa ad CD annum   7'
  0 2 0 2—4 2 3 0—str (without db)   `2' 2' 3'`
  Boosey

Movements for piano and orchestra   10'
*2 *2 *2 1—0 2 3 0—hp, cel—str
Boosey

Les Noces   23'
chorus   solos SATB
tmp+6—4pf
Chester   *Kalmus*

Octet   14'
1 0 1 2—0 2 2 0
Revised 1952.   4' 7' 3'
Boosey

Ode (Triptychon for orchestra)   11'
*3 2 2 2—4 2 0 0—tmp—str
Contents—Eulogy; Eclogue; Epitaph.
Schott

Oedipus rex   51'
male chorus   solos ATTBB   speaker
*3 *3 +3 *3—4 4 3 1—tmp+1—hp, pf—str   24' 27'
Revised 1948.
Boosey

L'Oiseau de feu (Firebird)   47'
*4 *4 =4 *4—4 3 3 1—backstage: 3tp, 4 Wagner
tubas—tmp+4—3hp, cel, pf—str
Of the woodwinds listed above, 2pic, 2bcl, and 2cbn are
required.
Schott version is new edition by Herbert Schneider.
Kalmus   *Schott*

L'Oiseau de feu (Firebird): Suite (1911 version)   30'
*4 *4 =4 *4—4 3 3 1—tmp+4—3hp, cel, pf—str
Of the woodwinds listed above, 2pic, 2bcl, and 2cbn are
required. This work is sometimes identified as *First suite from
Firebird*.
    Contents—Introduction and Kastcheï's enchanted garden;
Supplications of the firebird; The princesses play with the golden
apples; Round dance of the princesses; Infernal dance of all the
subjects of Kastcheï.
Chester   *Kalmus*   *Schott*

L'Oiseau de feu (Firebird): Suite (1919 version)   22'
*2 *2 2 2—4 2 3 1—tmp+3—hp, pf (dbl on opt cel)—str   3' 2' 6'
(Only one bar of Eh; remainder is for 2ob.) Reorchestrated by the   5' 6'
composer in 1919; sometimes identified as *Second suite from
Firebird*.
    Contents—Introduction; L'Oiseau de feu et sa danse &
Variation de l'oiseau de feu; Ronde des princesses; Danse
infernale du roi Kastcheï; Berceuse et Final.
Chester   *Kalmus*   *Schott*

L'Oiseau de feu (Firebird): Suite (1945 version)   30'
  *2 2 2 2—4 2 3 1—tmp+3—hp, pf—str
  A reorchestration of the 1919 suite, with the insertion of five
  new sections (*Pantomime I* through *Pantomime III*, inclusive).
  Sometimes identified as *Third suite from Firebird.*
    Contents—Introduction (3'); Prelude, Dance of the firebird, &
  Variations (2'); Pantomime I (1'); Pas de deux (3'); Pantomime II
  (1'); Scherzo (Dance of the Princesses) (3'); Pantomime III (1');
  Rondo (5'); Infernal dance (5'); Lullaby (Berceuse) (3'); Final
  hymn (3').
  Chester   *Schott*

L'Oiseau de feu (Firebird): Berceuse & Finale   6'
  *2 2 2 2—4 2 3 1—tmp+3—hp, cel—str | 3' 3' |
  (Celeste has only 8 notes.)
  Kalmus   *Luck*

Orpheus   30'
  *3 *2 2 2—4 2 2 0—tmp—hp—str
  Boosey

Pas de deux   6'
  from Tchaikovsky's *Sleeping Beauty*
  1 1 2 1—1 2 2 0—tmp—pf—str
  Recommended minimum strings: 5vn, 4va, 3vc, 2db.
  Arr. for small orchestra by Stravinsky for the ballet *Bluebird*
  (*L'Oiseau bleu*). Unaccountably published under the name of the
  arranger, rather than that of the composer.
  Schott

Persephone   48'
  chorus, children's chorus   solo tenor   female narrator
  *3 *3 *3 *3—4 3 3 1—tmp+1—2hp, pf—str
  Revised 1948.
  Boosey

Petrouchka (original version, 1911)   34'
  *4 *4 *4 *4—4 4 3 1—tmp+4—2hp, cel 4-hands, pf—str | 10' 4' 7' |
  Two of the flutists double on piccolo. A critical edition of this | 13' |
  version with historical and analytical essays is available from
  Norton.
  Contents—The Shrove-tide Fair; Petrouchka's cell; The Moor's
  cell; The Shrove-tide Fair.
  Boosey   *Kalmus*

Petrouchka (1947 version)   34'
  *3 *3 *3 *3—4 3 3 1—tmp+3—hp, cel, pf—str | 10' 4' 7' |
  Alternative concert-ending reduces duration by about 3 minutes. | 13' |
  Contents—The Shrove-tide Fair; Petrouchka's cell; The Moor's
  cell; The Shrove-tide Fair.
  Boosey

Pribaoutki (Chansons plaisantes) 6'
   medium voice
   1 *1 1 1—vn, va, vc, db
   Contents—L'Oncle Armand; Le Four; Le Colonel; Le Vieux et le
   Lièvre.
   Chester   *Kalmus*

Pulcinella: Suite 21'
   solo string quintet (2vn, va, vc, db)

2'	3'	4'
2'	1'	4'
	1'	4'

   2 2 0 2—2 1 1 0—str
   Revised 1949.
   Boosey

Rag-time 4'
   1 0 1 0—1 1 1 0—1perc—cimbalom—2vn, va, db
   Chester   *Kalmus*

Requiem canticles 15'
   chorus   alto & bass solos
   =4 0 0 2—4 2 3 0—2tmp+2—hp, cel, pf—str
   Boosey

Le Sacre du printemps (The rite of spring) 33'
   =5 *5 =5 *5—8 5 3 2—2tmp+4—str
   Horns 7-8 double on Wagner tubas; one trumpet also doubles on
   bass trumpet. Among the woodwinds, 2pic, 2Eh, 2bcl, and 2cbn
   are required.
   Revised 1947 & 1965. (Kalmus edition is the original 1913
   version.)
   Boosey   *Kalmus*

Le Sacre du printemps (The rite of spring; McPhee reduction) 33'
   =3 *3 =3 *3—4 3 3 1—tmp+2—str (min 10.8.6.6.4)
   One trombone doubles on bass trumpet. Reduced orchestration by
   Jonathan McPhee.
   Boosey

Le Sacre du printemps (The rite of spring; Rudolf reduction) 33'
   =3 *3 *3 *3—4 3 3 1—tmp+3—str
   Orchestra reduction by Robert Rudolf, allegedly with the
   sanction of the composer. However, certain changes in metrical
   notation are introduced, intended to simplify performance, but
   with the possible effect of distorting the composer's intentions.
   Belwin

Le Sacre du printemps: Danse sacrale 9'
   =5 *5 =5 *5—8 4 3 2—tmp+1—btp—str
   This 1943 revision of the final portion of the ballet, originally
   published by *AMP*, was intended to be more readily playable
   than the original because of rescoring, rebarring, enharmonic
   spelling, and larger metric units. However, in his 1947 and 1965
   revisions, the composer did not make use of the 1943 version. It
   may be assumed that this publication, interesting as it is, is *not*
   Stravinsky's final word on the subject.
   Boosey

Scènes de ballet   16'
    *2 2 2 1—2 3 3 1—tmp—pf—str
    AMP

Scherzo à la russe (symphonic version)   5'
    *3 2 2 2—4 3 3 1—tmp+4—hp, pf—str
    Critical edition in preparation by Schott. Also available in a
    version for jazz orchestra.
    Boosey

Scherzo fantastique   16'
    =4 *3 =4 *3—4 3 0 0—1perc—2hp, cel—str
    Kalmus   *Schott*

Septet   11'
    0 0 1 1—1 0 0 0—pf—vn, va, vc
    Boosey

A sermon, a narrative, and a prayer   17'
    chorus   alto & tenor solos   speaker
    +2 2 *2 2—4 3 3 1—2perc—hp, pf—str
    Boosey

Song of the nightingale
    see his: Le Chant du rossignol

Suite no.1 for small orchestra   6'
    *2 1 2 2—1 1 1 1—1perc—str   2' 2' 1' 1'
    Contents—Andante; Napolitana; Española; Balalaika.
    Chester   *Kalmus*

Suite no.2 for small orchestra   7'
    *2 1 2 2—1 2 1 1—3perc—pf—str   1' 2' 2' 2'
    Contents—Marche; Valse; Polka; Galop.
    Chester   *Kalmus*

Symphonies of wind instruments   12'
    3 *3 3 *3—4 3 3 1
    Revised 1947. Kalmus offers the original 1920 version only.
    Boosey   *Kalmus*

Symphony no.1, E-flat major   34'
    *3 2 3 2—4 3 3 1—tmp+3—str   10' 6'
    Forberg   *Kalmus*   10' 8'

Symphony in C   28'
    *3 2 2 2—4 2 3 1—tmp—str   10' 6' 5'
    Schott   7'

Symphony in three movements (1945)   22'
    *3 2 *3 *3—4 3 3 1—tmp+1—hp, pf—str   10' 6' 6'
    Schott

Symphony of Psalms   21'
    chorus   3' 6' 12'
    *5 *5 0 *4—4 5 3 1—tmp+1—hp, 2pf—str (without vn or va)
    Revised 1948.
    Boosey

Threni: id est Lamentationes Jeremiae Prophetae   35'
    chorus   solos SATTBB
    2 *3 *3 0—sarrusophone—4 0 3 1—contralto bugle
    (=flugelhorn)—tmp—hp, cel, pf—str
    One clarinet doubles on alto clarinet. Revised 1962.
    Boosey

Two songs by Paul Verlaine   5'
    solo baritone
    2 0 2 0—2 0 0 0—str
    Contents—La Bonne Chanson; Sagesse.
    Boosey

Variations (Aldous Huxley in memoriam)   6'
    +3 *3 *3 2—4 3 3 0—hp, pf—str
    Boosey

Stuart-Coolidge, Peggy   1913 - 1982
    see: Coolidge, Peggy Stuart, 1913-1982

Stucky, Steven   1949 -
Concerto for orchestra   28'
    =3 *3 *3 *3—4 4 3 1—tmp+3—hp, pf/cel—str
    Two of the flutists double on piccolo.
    Merion

Dreamwaltzes   15'
    *3 *3 *3 *3—4 4 3 1—tmp+3—hp, pf/cel—str
    Two of the flutists double on piccolo.
    Merion

Impromptus   18'
    *3 *3 *4 *3—4 4 3 1—tmp+3—hp, pf—str
    Merion

Subotnick, Morton   1933 -
Play no.2   12'
    2 2 *3 2—3 2 2 0—tmp+1—2-track electronic tape—str
    Graph notation.
    MCA

Suk, Josef   1874 - 1935
Meditace na starocesky chorál "Svaty Václave," op.35 (Meditation   7'
on the old Bohemian chorale "Saint Wenceslas")
    str (or str quartet)
    Kalmus

Pohádka, op.16 (Ein Märchen; Fairy tale)   31'
  *3 *3 *3 2—4 2 3 1—tmp+3—hp—str
  Contents—1. Liebe und Leid der Königskinder; 2. Intermezzo,
  Volkstanz; 3. Intermezzo, Trauermusik; 4. Königin Runa's Fluch,
  Sieg der Liebe.
  Kalmus   *Simrock*

Serenade, op.6, E-flat   30'
  str | 6' 6' 10' |
  Kalmus   *Simrock* | 8' |

Symphony no.1, op.14, E major   40'
  *3 2 2 2—4 2 3 1—tmp—str
  Kalmus

Symphony no.2, op.27 (Asrael)   58'
  *3 *3 *3 *3—4 3 3 1—tmp+2—hp—str | 15' 7' |
  Breitkopf   *Kalmus* | 12' 10' |
                                                           | 14' |

Sullivan, Arthur   1842 - 1900

Concerto, violoncello   17'
  2 2 2 2—2 2 0 0—tmp—str | 3' 7' 7' |
  Score and parts lost; reconstructed from surviving solo parts by
  David Mackie & Charles Mackerras.
  Weinberger

Overture di ballo   11'
  *2 2 2 2—4 2 3 1—tmp+4—str
  Optional extra tuba or cbn (originally serpente).
  Novello ed. Roger Harris.
  Kalmus   *Novello*

Overture in C (In memoriam)   13'
  2 2 2 2—4 2 3 1—tmp+2—org—str
  Kalmus   *Novello*

The tempest: Three dances   11'
  2 2 2 2—2 2 3 0—tmp+2—str | 2' 2' 7' |
  Contents—Masque; Banquet dance; Dance of nymphs and
  reapers.
  Kalmus   *Novello*

Suolahti, Heikki   1920 - 1936

Sinfonia piccola   25'
  *2 *2 2 2—4 3 3 1—tmp+2—hp—str
  Boosey

Suppé, Franz von   1819 - 1895

Banditenstreiche (Jolly robbers): Overture   8'
  *2 2 2 2—4 2 3 0—tmp+2—gtr—str
  Alkor   *Kalmus*

Boccaccio: Overture   7'
   *2 2 2 2—4 2 3 0—tmp+3—str
   Kalmus

Dichter und Bauer (Poet and peasant): Overture   10'
   *2 2 2 2—4 2 3 1—tmp+2—hp—str
   Kalmus

Die leichte Kavallerie (Light Cavalry): Overture   8'
   *2 2 2 2—4 2 3 0—3perc—str
   Version available from Luck's includes a timpani part added by
   an unknown arranger.
   Kalmus   *Luck*

Ein Morgen, ein Mittag und ein Abend in Wien (Morning, noon and   8'
night in Vienna): Overture
   *2 2 2 2—4 2 3 0—tmp+2—str
   Kalmus

Pique Dame: Overture   8'
   2 2 2 2—4 2 3 1—tmp+4—str
   Kalmus

Die schöne Galathea (The beautiful Galathea): Overture   7'
   *2 2 2 2—4 2 3 0—tmp+2—str
   Kalmus   *Luck*

Surinach, Carlos   1915 -
Drama jondo   8'
   *3 *3 *3 2—4 3 3 1—tmp+3—hp—str
   AMP

Fandango   8'
   *3 *3 *3 2—4 3 3 1—tmp+2—hp—str
   AMP

Feria magica   6'
   *2 2 2 2—4 2 3 1—tmp+2—hp—str
   AMP

Ritmo jondo   20'
   *1 *1 1 1—1 1 1 0—tmp+4—str (min 2.2.2.2.1; max 5.4.4.3.2)
   AMP

Svendsen, Johan   1840 - 1911
Rapsodie norvégienne no.3, op.21 (Norwegian rhapsody)   9'
   2 2 2 2—4 2 3 0—tmp—str
   Hansen

Svoboda, Tomáš   1939 -
Child's dream, op.66   11'
   children's choir
   *3 2 2 2—4 3 3 0—tmp+3—cel, pf—str
   Stangland

Concerto for chamber orchestra, op.125   23'
  1 1 1 1—1perc—hp—solo soprano (textless)—str
  Stangland

Concerto, marimba, op.148   26'
  *3 2 *3 2—4 3 3 1—tmp+1—hp, cel, pf—str
  Stangland

Concerto, piano, no.1, op.71   18'
  1 1 1 1—1 1 0 0—tmp—str
  Stangland

Concerto, piano, no.2, op.134   45'
  *3 2 *3 2—4 3 3 1—tmp+4—str
  Stangland

Concerto, violin, op.77   19'
  2 2 2 2—2 2 3 0—tmp—str
  Stangland

Dance suite, op.128   23'
  *3 2 2 2—4 2 3 1—tmp+2—str
  Stangland

Ex libris, op.113   8'
  *3 2 *3 *3—4 3 4 1—tmp+4—str
  Stangland

Festive overture, op.103   9'
  *3 2 *3 2—4 4 4 1—tmp+5—str
  Stangland

Journey, op.127   24'
  solo mezzo-soprano & baritone   chorus
  2 2 2 2—2asx—4 3 3 1—tmp+6—str
  Stangland

Meditation, op.143   6'
  solo oboe
  str (or str quintet)
  Stangland

Nocturne, op.100 (Cosmic sunset)   20'
  2 2 2 2—2 2 3 0—tmp+2—hp, pf, gtr—str
  Trombones and guitar are optional. Horns may be doubled.
  Stangland

Overture of the season, op.89   8'
  *3 2 2 2—4 3 3 1—tmp+2—str
  Stangland

Serenade, op.115   7'
  *3 2 2 2—4 3 3 1—tmp+1—str
  Stangland

Sinfoniette (à la renaissance), op.60   20'
  *3 2 2 2—4 3 3 1—tmp+3—str
  Stangland

Swing dance, op.135a 6'
　*3 2 2 2—asx—4 3 3 1—tmp+2—str
　Stangland

Symphony no.1, op.20 (Of Nature) 36'
　*3 2 *3 2—4 3 4 1—tmp+3—pf—str
　Revised 1985.
　Stangland

Symphony no.2, op.41 28'
　=3 2 *3 2—4 3 4 1—tmp+3—pf—str
　Stangland

Symphony no.3, op.43, for organ and orchestra 28'
　solo organ; solo string quintet: 2vn, 2va, vc
　*3 2 =4 2—contrabass cl, asx—4 3 4 1—tmp+7—pf—str
　18.16.14.12.8
　Stangland

Symphony no.4, op.69 (Apocalyptic) 27'
　*3 2 *3 2—contrabass cl, asx —4 3 4 1—tmp+7—hp, cel—str
　Stangland

Symphony no.5, op.92 (In unison) 33'
　=4 *3 =4 2—4 3 3 1—tmp+5—hp, pf—str
　Stangland

Symphony no.6, op.137 38'
　solo clarinet
　*3 2 1 2—4 3 3 1—tmp+2—str
　Stangland

Three cadenzas for piano & orchestra, op.135 31'
　*3 2 2 2—asx—4 2 3 0—tmp+3—str
　Stangland

Three pieces for orchestra, op.45 10'
　*3 2 2 2—4 2 3 1—tmp+3—str
　Stangland

Swanson, Howard　　　1907 - 1978

Concerto for orchestra 20'
　2 2 2 2—2 2 3 1—tmp+2—str
　Weintraub

Fantasy piece 19'
　solo soprano saxophone or clarinet
　str
　Weintraub

Music for strings 10'
　str
　Weintraub

Night music   9'
  1 1 1 1—1 0 0 0—str
  Perhaps intended for individual string players rather than
  sections.
  Weintraub

Short symphony   12'
  2 2 2 2—2 2 1 0—tmp—str
  Weintraub

Symphony no.1   25'
  *2 2 2 2—4 2 3 1—tmp+2—str
  Schirmer, G.

Symphony no.3   25'
  *3 *3 *3 *2—4 3 3 1—tmp+4—cel—str   12' 6' 7'
  Schirmer, G.

Szöllösy, András   1921 -

Sonorità   13'
  4 0 *4 0—4 0 0 0—str 12.12.8.6.4
  EMB

Szymanowski, Karol   1882 - 1937

Concerto, violin, no.1, op.35   26'
  *3 *3 =4 *3—4 3 3 1—tmp+4—2hp, cel, pf—str   6' 6' 3'
  PWM   *Universal*   11'

Konzert-Ouverture, op.12   16'
  *3 *3 =4 *3—6 3 3 1—tmp+3—hp—str
  Composed 1905. A revised version for larger orchestra, 1913, is
  available from *PWM*.
  Universal

Stabat mater, op.53   20'
  solos SABar   chorus
  2 *2 2 *2—4 2 0 0—tmp+4—hp, opt org—str 8.8.6.6.4
  PWM

Symphony no.3, op.27, B-flat major (Song of the night; Piesn o nocy)   25'
  solo tenor   chorus   8' 8' 9'
  *4 *4 =5 *4—6 4 3 1—contrabass tbn—tmp+5
  —2hp, cel, pf, org—str 16.14.12.10.8
  Universal

T

Takemitsu, Tōru   1930 - 1996

Dream/window   -15'
=3 *3 *3 *3—4 3 3 0—4perc—2hp, cel, gtr (amplified)—str
13.13.13.9.8
Two of the flutists double on piccolo. Special seating plan splits
the main string body into two separated groups.
Schott

Music of tree   17'
=3 *3 =4 *3—ssx—4 4 3 1—3perc—hp, cel, pf, gtr—str
16.14.12.10.8
Peters

Rain coming   13'
+1 1 1 1—1 1 1 0—1perc—pf/cel—str
Schott

Riverrun   14'
solo piano
=3 *3 +3 *3—contrabass cl—4 3 3 0—4perc—2hp, cel—str
14.12.10.8.6
Schott

A string around autumn   17'
solo viola
=3 *3 =3 *3—contrabass cl—4 3 3 0—4perc
—2hp, pf/cel—str 14.12.10.8.6
One of the oboists doubles on oboe d'amore.
Schott

Tree line   14'
+1 1 *2 *1—2 1 1 0—2perc—hp, pf/cel—str
Schott

Twill by twilight   12'
=4 *3 =4 *3—4 4 3 1—5perc—2hp, cel, pf—str 16.14.12.10.8
Schott

Visions   13'
=4 *3 =3 *3—contrabass cl—4 3 3 0—btp—4perc—2hp, cel, pf | 6' 7' |
—str 16.14.12.10.8
2nd fl doubles on pic; 3rd fl dbl on pic & afl; 4th fl dbl on bfl; 2nd
ob dbl on ob d'amore; 3rd ob dbl on Eh.
Contents—Mystère; Les Yeux clos.
Schott

Tan Dun   1957 -

Death and fire; dialogue with Paul Klee   27'
=3 2 2 *3—4 3 3 1—4perc—hp—str
Schirmer, G.

3'	3'	2'
3'	7'	1'
1'	3'	2'
		2'

Intercourse of fire and water (Yi¹)   25'
solo violoncello
*2 2 *2 *2—2 2 2 0—tmp+3—hp, pf—str
Strings: min 6.6.4.4.2; max 12.10.8.8.5. Both flutists double on
piccolo.
Schirmer, G.

On Taoism   15'
solos: voice, bass clarinet, contrabassoon
*3 1 1 1—2 1 2 0—6perc—hp, pf—str 14.12.10.8.6
Voice may be of any kind: soprano, mezzo, tenor, bass, or
actor/actress. Certain wind & string players also play Chinese
bells.
Schirmer, G.

Orchestral theatre I: Xun   20'
solo xun (optional)
*3 2 *3 *3—4 3 3 1—4perc—hp—str
All players also vocalize. 10 of the woodwind players double on
xuns (the xun is an ancient Chinese ceramic wind instrument,
resembling an ocarina). The work may be played in an
orchestra-only version, omitting solo and orchestral xuns
entirely.
Schirmer, G.

Orchestral theatre II: Re   22'
bass voice
*3 *3 *3 2—4 3 3 1—tmp+3—hp, pf—str
2 conductors. All 3 flutists play piccolo. Orchestra is divided;
woodwinds surround audience. All orchestra members (including
conductors) vocalize at certain points, as does the audience.
Schirmer, G.

Tann, Hilary   1947 -

Adirondack light   19'
narrator
*2 2 2 2—2 2 0 0—tmp+1—str
Oxford

The open field; in memoriam Tiananmen Square (June 1989)   11'
*3 2 2 2—4 3 3 1—tmp+3—str
Special seating for the 3tp.
Oxford

Through the echoing timber 4'
*3 2 2 2—4 3 3 1—tmp+2—str
Oxford

Water's edge 9'
str
| 3' 3' 3' |
Contents—Dawn light; From the riverbed; Toward dusk.
Oxford

With the heather and small birds 10'
*2 2 2 2—2 2 0 0—tmp+1—str
Both flutists double on piccolo.
Oxford

Tansman, Alexandre   1897 - 1986

Sinfonietta 15'
1 1 1 1—1 1 2 0—tmp+2—pf/cel—str
Universal

Toccata 8'
*3 *3 *3 *3—4 4 3 1—tmp+5—hp, cel, pf—str
Eschig

Triptych 16'
str
Eschig

Variations on a theme by Girolamo Frescobaldi 14'
str
Eschig

Tartini, Giuseppe   1692 - 1770

Concerto no.58, F major 12'
0 2 0 0—2 0 0 0—str
Ed. Ettore Bonelli.
Kalmus   *Zanibon*

Concerto, violin, no.57, D major 20'
0 0 0 0—2 2 0 0—tmp—str
Ed. Ettore Bonelli.
Kalmus   *Zanibon*

Concerto, violoncello, A major 12'
opt org—str
Originally for viola da gamba. Ed. Oreste Ravanello.
Kalmus   *Zanibon*

Sinfonia, D major 13'
str
Ed. Hans Erdmann.
Schott

Sinfonia pastorale, D major 11'
  solo violin
  cnt—str
  Kahnt

Tavener, John   1944 -

Akhmatova requiem 50'
  solos SB
  0 0 0 0—3 3 3 0—tmp+5—cel—str
  Chester

Celtic requiem 23'
  solos SAATTBB   children's choir
  0 0 1 0—optional aeolian bagpipes—0 1 1 0—tmp+7
  —pf, org, elec gtr/bass gtr—str
  Chester   *Hansen*

The whale; a Biblical fantasy 35'
  chorus   solo mezzo & baritone   speaker
  =2 2 *2 *2—4 3 3 1—tmp+8—hp, pf, org, Hammond org
  —pre-recorded tape—str (without vn)
  Chester

Taverner, John   ca.1490 - 1545

In nomine
  see: Maxwell Davies, Peter
       First fantasia on an "In nomine" of John Taverner
       Second fantasia on John Taverner's "In nomine"

Taylor, Deems   1885 - 1966

Through the looking glass, op.12 32'
  *3 *3 *3 *3—4 3 3 1—tmp+3—pf—str
  Colombo

Tchaikovsky, Piotr Ilyich   1840 - 1893

Capriccio italien, op.45 15'
  *3 *3 2 2—4 4 3 1—tmp+4—hp—str
  Breitkopf   *Kalmus*   *Russian*   *Universal*

Casse-noisette
  see his: Nutcracker

Concerto, piano, no.1, op.23, B-flat minor 32'
  2 2 2 2—4 2 3 0—tmp—str   17' 8' 7'
  Breitkopf   *Kalmus*   *Universal*

Concerto, piano, no.2, op.44, G major 37'
  2 2 2 2—4 2 0 0—tmp—str   21' 8' 8'
  Alkor

Concerto, piano, no.2, op.44, G major (Siloti version)   30'
   2 2 2 2—4 2 0 0—tmp—str   16' 7' 7'
   Revised and abridged by Alexander Siloti, allegedly according to
   the composer's suggestions.
   Kalmus   *Simrock*

Concerto, piano, no.3, op.75, E-flat major   16'
   *3 2 2 2—4 2 3 1—tmp—str
   Kalmus   *Russian*   *Universal*

Concerto, violin, op.35, D major   33'
   2 2 2 2—4 2 0 0—tmp—str   19' 7' 7'
   Breitkopf   *Kalmus*   *Universal*

Eugen Onegin: Polonaise   4'
   2 2 2 2—4 2 3 0—tmp—str
   Kalmus   *Simrock*

Eugen Onegin: Waltz   7'
   *3 2 2 2—4 2 3 0—tmp—str
   Breitkopf   *Kalmus*

Fantasie de concert, op.56, G major (Concert fantasy)   34'
   solo piano   20' 7' 7'
   3 2 2 2—4 2 3 0—tmp+1—str
   The composer provides a special ending in case the first movement
   (of two) is to be used separately.
   Kalmus   *Universal*

Fatum, op.77   10'
   *3 *3 2 2—4 3 3 1—tmp+4—hp—str
   Belaieff   *Kalmus*

Francesca da Rimini, op.32   22'
   *3 *3 2 2—4 4 3 1—tmp+3—hp—str
   Kalmus   *Universal*

Hamlet, op.67   18'
   *3 *3 2 2—4 4 3 1—tmp+3—str
   Alkor   *Kalmus*   *Russian*   *Universal*

Marche solenelle du couronnement (Coronation march)   5'
   *3 *3 2 2—4 4 3 1—tmp+3—str
   Kalmus

Manfred, op.58   57'
   *3 *3 *3 3—4 4 3 1—tmp+5—2hp—str   16' 10'
   Kalmus   *Russian*   *Simrock*   12' 19'

Marche slave, op.31   10'
   *4 2 2 2—4 4 3 1—tmp+3—str
   Kalmus   *Simrock*

Mazeppa: Danse cosaque (Cossack dance)   5'
   *3 *3 2 2—4 4 3 1—tmp+3—str
   Kalmus

Mozartiana
  see his: Suite no.4, op.61, G major

Nutcracker, op.71 (Shchelkunchik; Casse-noisette)   85'
  backstage children's chorus   45' 40'
  *3 *3 *3 2—4 2 3 1—tmp+2—2hp, cel—str
  Orchestral reduction by W. McDermott available from
  Mapleson:
  2 2 2 2—2 2 2 0—tmp, perc—hp, cel—str
  Kalmus

Nutcracker (Shchelkunchik; Casse-noisette): Suite no.1, op.71A   24'
  *3 *3 *3 2—4 2 3 1—tmp+1—hp, cel (or pf)—str   4' 3' 2'
  Contents—Overture miniature; Marche; Danse de la fée-dragée;   1' 2' 1'
  Danse russe trepak; Danse arabe; Danse chinoise; Danse des   4' 7'
  mirlitons; Valse des fleurs.
  Breitkopf   Kalmus   Russian

Nutcracker (Shchelkunchik; Casse-noisette): Suite no.2, op.71b   15'
  *3 *3 *3 2—4 2 3 1—tmp+1—2hp, cel (or pf)—str
  Contents—Scenes & divertissement from Act II; Pas de deux;
  Decorating and lighting of the Christmas tree; Little galop of the
  children and entrance of the parents; "Tempo di Grossvater."
  Kalmus

Overture 1812, op.49 (Ouverture solennelle)   16'
  *3 *3 2 2—4 4 3 1—tmp+5—str
  Extra brass ("banda") ad libitum.
  Breitkopf   Kalmus

Pezzo capriccioso, op.62   7'
  violoncello solo
  2 2 2 2—4 0 0 0—tmp—str
  Luck   Simrock   Universal

Romeo and Juliet (original version 1869)   23'
  *3 *3 2 2—4 2 3 1—tmp+2—hp—str
  Kalmus

Romeo and Juliet overture-fantasy (final version 1880)   19'
  *3 *3 2 2—4 2 3 1—tmp+2—hp—str
  Composed 1869; revised 1870 and 1880.
  Bote & Bock   Kalmus

Romeo and Juliet (duet), op.posth.   12'
  solo soprano and tenor
  2 *3 2 2—4 2 0 0—tmp—hp—str
  Completed & orchestrated by Sergei Taneyev.
  Billaudot

Serenade, op.48   28'
  str   9' 4' 8' 7'
  Breitkopf   Kalmus   Peters   Russian

Sérénade mélancolique, op.26   7'
  solo violin
  2 2 2 2—4 0 0 0—str
  C. Fischer   *Kalmus*   *Simrock*

Sleeping Beauty (Spyashchaya krasavitsa; Belle au bois dormant):   23'
Suite, op.66a
  *3 *3 2 2—4 4 3 1—tmp+2—hp—str   5' 6' 2'
  Contents—Introduction: La Fée des lilas; Adagio: Pas d'action;   4' 6'
  Pas de caractère (Le Chat botté et la chatte blanche); Panorama;
  Valse.
  Kalmus   *Russian*

Sleeping Beauty: Pas de deux (arr. Stravinsky)
  see under: Stravinsky, Igor
              Pas de deux

Souvenir d'un lieu cher, op.42   20'
  Originally for violin & piano; arr. by Glazunov for solo violin &
  orchestra.

  1. Méditation   11'
  solo violin
  2 2 2 2—2 0 0 0—hp—str
  Originally planned as the slow movement for the violin concerto.
  C. Fischer   *Kalmus*   *Universal*

  2. Scherzo   5'
  solo violin
  2 2 2 2—2 0 0 0—hp—str
  C. Fischer   *Kalmus*   *Universal*

  3. Mélodie   4'
  solo violin
  2 2 2 2—2 0 0 0—str
  C. Fischer   *Kalmus*   *Universal*

Suite no.1, op.43, D minor   41'
  *3 2 2 2—4 2 0 0—tmp—str   11' 6' 9'
  Originally for piano 4-hands.   2' 8' 5'
  Contents—Introduzione e fuga; Divertimento; Intermezzo;
  Marche miniature; Scherzo; Gavotte.
  Kalmus   *Simrock*

Suite no.1, op.43: Marche miniature   2'
  *3 2 2 0—2perc—vn I & II, each divisi
  Kalmus

Suite no.2, op.53, C major   35'
  *3 *3 2 2—4 2 3 1—tmp+3—hp, 4 (opt) accordions—str   11' 6' 5'
  Contents—Playing with sounds; Waltz; Burlesque scherzo;   9' 4'
  Dreams of childhood; Baroque dance.
  Kalmus   *Simrock*

Suite no.3, op.55, G major   **41'**
   *3 *3 2 2—4 2 3 1—tmp+3—str
   Contents—Elegy; Melancholic waltz; Scherzo; Theme and
   variations.
   Kalmus   *Simrock*

      11' 6' 5'
      19'

Suite no.4, op.61, G major (Mozartiana)   **25'**
   2 2 2 2—4 2 0 0—tmp+1—hp—str
   Contents—Gigue; Minuet; Prayer, after a transcription by Liszt;
   Theme and variations.
   Kalmus   *Universal*

      2' 3' 5'
      15'

Swan lake, op.20 (Lebedinoye ozero; Le Lac des cygnes)   **130'**
   *3 2 2 2—4 4 3 1—tmp+4—hp—str
   Kalmus

Swan lake (Lebedinoye ozero; Le Lac des cygnes): Suite, op.20a   **24'**
(Jurgenson)
   *3 2 2 2—4 4 3 1—tmp+3—hp—str
   Contents—1. Scène; 2. Valse; 3. Danses des cygnes; 4. Scène; 5.
   Danse hongroise (Czardas); 6. Scène.
   Originally published by Jurgenson. The following version has
   additional movements.
   Russian

      3' 7' 2'
      6' 3' 3'

Swan lake (Lebedinoye ozero; Le Lac des cygnes): Suite, op.20a   **31'**
(Kalmus)
   *3 2 2 2—4 4 3 1—tmp+3—hp—str
   Contents: 1. Scène; 2. Valse; 3. Danse des cygnes; 4. Scène; 5.
   Danse hongroise (Czardas); 6. Danse éspagnole; 7. Danse
   napolitaine; 8. Mazurka.
   Kalmus

      3' 7' 2'
      6' 3' 3'
      2' 5'

Symphony no.1, op.13, G minor (Winter dreams)   **44'**
   *3 2 2 2—4 2 3 1—tmp+2—str
   Kalmus   *Universal*

      11' 12'
      8' 13'

Symphony no.2, op.17, C minor (Little Russian)   **32'**
   *3 2 2 2—4 2 3 1—tmp+2—str
   Kalmus   *Russian*

      11' 6' 5'
      10'

Symphony no.3, op.29, D major (Polish)   **45'**
   *3 2 2 2—4 2 3 1—tmp—str
   Breitkopf   *Kalmus*   *Russian*

      14' 6'
      10' 6' 9'

Symphony no.4, op.36, F minor   **44'**
   *3 2 2 2—4 2 3 1—tmp+3—str
   Breitkopf   *Kalmus*   *Russian*

      18' 10'
      6' 10'

Symphony no.5, op.64, E minor   **50'**
   *3 2 2 2—4 2 3 1—tmp—str
   Breitkopf   *Kalmus*   *Russian*

      16' 14'
      6' 14'

Symphony no.6, op.74, B minor (Pathétique)   46'
   *3 2 2 2—4 2 3 1—tmp+2—str
   Breitkopf   *Kalmus*   *Russian*

18' 8' 9'
11'

Symphony no.7, E-flat major   40'
   *3 2 2 2—4 2 3 1—tmp+3—hp—str
   Reconstructed by S. Bogatyryev.
   Kalmus   *Russian*

13' 11'
7' 9'

The tempest (fantasy-overture), op.18   18'
   *3 2 2 2—4 2 3 1—tmp+2—str
   Symphonic fantasia after Shakespeare's play. This work is not to
   be confused with the composer's *L'Orage (The tempest)*, op.76,
   which was inspired by a play of Ostrovsky.
   Kalmus

Valse-scherzo, op.34   12'
   solo violin
   2 2 2 2—2 0 0 0—str
   Kalmus   *Universal*

Variations on a rococo theme, op.33   18'
   solo violoncello
   2 2 2 2—2 0 0 0—str
   Kalmus   *Simrock*

Le Voyévode, op.3: Overture   7'
   3 *3 2 2—4 2 3 1—tmp+3—str
   Overture to the opera composed 1867-68.
   Kalmus   *Universal*

Le Voyévode, op.78 (symphonic ballad)   10'
   3 *3 *3 2—4 2 3 1—tmp+1—hp, cel (or pf)—str
   Composed in 1890-91 after Pushkin's translation of
   Mickiewicz's ballad.
   Belaieff   *C. Fischer*   *Kalmus*

Tcherepnin, Alexander   1899 - 1977

Georgiana suite, op.92   17'
   2 2 2 2—4 2 3 1—tmp+5—str
   Eulenburg

Serenade, op.97   16'
   str
   Eulenburg

Symphony no.2, op.77, E-flat major   25'
   *3 *3 *3 *3—4 3 3 1—tmp+6—hp, cel, pf—str
   AMP

Telemann, Georg Philipp   1681 - 1767

Concert suite, F major   19'
    solo recorder
    cnt—str
    Ed. Adolf Hoffmann.
    Kalmus   *Nagel*

Concerto, flute, D major   17'
    cnt—str   4' 4' 5' 4'
    Ed. Felix Schroeder
    Eulenburg

Concerto, flute, E minor   12'
    cnt—str
    Kalmus

Concerto, 2 flutes, A minor   10'
    cnt—str
    Ed. Fritz Stein.
    Kalmus   *Nagel*

Concerto, horn, D major   12'
    0 1 0 0—cnt—str
    Peters

Concerto, 2 horns, E-flat major   16'
    cnt—str
    Ed. Max Seiffert.
    Breitkopf

Concerto, oboe, D minor   14'
    cnt—str
    Ed. Hermann Töttcher.
    Sikorski

Concerto, oboe, E minor   12'
    cnt—str   3' 3' 4' 2'
    Ed. Hermann Töttcher.
    Sikorski

Concerto, oboe, F minor   10'
    cnt—str
    Ed. Felix Schroeder.
    Eulenburg

Concerto, recorder, F major   13'
    cnt—str   3' 4' 3' 3'
    Ed. Manfred Ruetz.
    Bärenreiter

Concerto, recorder & flute, E minor   14'
    cnt—str
    Ed. Herbert Kölbel.
    Bärenreiter   *Kalmus*

Concerto, trumpet, D major   15'
0 2 0 0—cnt—str
Sikorski   *Simrock*

Concerto, viola, G major   12'
cnt—str   4' 3' 3' 2'
Ed. Hellmuth Christian Wolff.
Bärenreiter

Concerto, violin, A minor   10'
cnt—str
Ed. Hellmuth Christian Wolff.
Bärenreiter

Concerto, 2 violins, C major   11'
cnt—str
Ed. Adolf Hoffmann.
Kalmus   *Möseler*

Das ist je gewisslich wahr
see: Bach, Johann Sebastian
    Cantata no.141

Don Quichotte   16'
cnt—str
Ed. Gustav Lenzewski.
Kalmus   *Vieweg*

Ich weiss, dass mein Erlöser lebt
see: Bach, Johann Sebastian
    Cantata no.160

Overture in C major   13'
str (without cnt)
Ed. Helmut Mönkemeyer.
Peters

Overture in D major   10'
0 2 0 1—2 0 0 0—cnt—str
Ed. Friedrich Noack.
Bärenreiter   *Kalmus*

Overture (suite), G major
cnt—str
Ed. Gustav Lenzewski.
Vieweg

So du mit deinem Munde
Published as the second movement of Cantata no.145 by Johann
Sebastian Bach.

Suite, A minor   30'
solo recorder   10' 3' 6'
cnt—str   4' 2' 2'
Ed. Horst Buettner.   3'
Eulenburg   *Kalmus*

Suite, F major   17'
    0 0 0 0—2 0 0 0—cnt—str (without va)
    Ed. Horst Buettner.
    Eulenburg   *Kalmus*

Thomas, Ambroise   1811 - 1896

Mignon: Overture   8'
    *2 2 2 2—4 2 3 0—tmp+3—hp—str
    Breitkopf   *Heugel*   *Kalmus*

Raymond: Overture   7'
    *2 2 2 2—4 2 3 0—tmp+4—str
    Heugel   *Kalmus*

Thompson, Randall   1899 - 1984

Symphony no.1   31'
    *3 *3 *3 *3—4 2 3 1—tmp+3—hp, org—str | 11' 7' |
    C. Fischer   13' |

Symphony no.2 (1932)   28'
    *3 *3 3 3—4 3 3 1—tmp—str | 8' 4' 6' |
    C. Fischer   10' |

Thomson, Virgil   1896 - 1989

Bugles and birds—a portrait of Pablo Picasso   2'
    2 2 2 2—4 2 3 0—str
    Schirmer, G.

Dance in praise   9'
    chorus
    2 2 2 2—2 2 0 0—3perc—pf—str
    Text is *Gaudeamus igitur* (English or Latin).
    Boosey

Fugue and chorale on "Yankee Doodle"   5'
    1 1 *3 1—2 3 2 0—tmp+1—str
    Schirmer, G.

Louisiana story: Acadian songs and dances   15'
    *2 *2 2 2—2 2 2 0—2perc—hp or pf, accordion or pf—str
    Schirmer, G.

Louisiana story: Boy fights alligator (fugue)   4'
    2 2 2 2—4 2 3 1—tmp+3—str
    Schirmer, G.

Louisiana story: Suite   18'
    *2 *2 *2 *2—4 2 3 1—tmp+2—hp—str
    Schirmer, G.

Parson Weems and the cherry tree   25'
    *1 0 *1 0—0 1 1 0—1perc—vn, db
    Trumpet doubles on flugelhorn.
    Boosey

Pilgrims and pioneers   10'
  1 *1 *2 1—4 2 0 0—2perc—str
  Schirmer, G.

The plow that broke the plains: Suite   14'
  fl, ob (dbl opt Eh), cl, 2nd cl (dbl opt asx), (opt bcl/tsx), bn

1'	1'	3'
3'	1'	5'

  —brass 2 2 2 0—tmp+2—banjo/gtr (or pf or hp)—str
  If bcl & tsx are both lacking, a 2nd bn must be added.
  Schirmer, G.

The river: Suite   23'
  *1 *2 *2 1—2 2 2 0—tmp+2—banjo—str

9'	4'	6'	4'

  Southern

Sea piece with birds   5'
  *3 3 3 3—4 3 3 0—2perc—opt hp—str
  Schirmer, G.

The Seine at night   8'
  *3 *3 *3 *3—4 3 3 1—1perc—2hp, cel—str
  Schirmer, G.

A solemn music, and a joyful fugue   12'
  *3 *3 *3 3—4 3 3 1—tmp+4—str
  Schirmer, G.

Symphony on a hymn tune   19'
  *2 2 2 *3—4 2 3 1—tmp+3 (or 6)—str
  3rd bn (cbn) has only 22 notes near end of 4th movement.
  Southern

Wheat field at noon   6'
  *3 *3 *3 *3—4 3 3 0—3perc—hp—str
  Schirmer, G.

Thorne, Francis   1922 -

Elegy for orchestra   14'
  *2 *2 *2 2—4 2 3 1—tmp+2—hp—str
  Presser

Tippett, Michael   1905 -

Byzantium   25'
  solo soprano
  *3 *3 =3 *3—4 2 3 1—7perc—2hp, cel, synth—str
  All three flutists double on piccolo.
  Schott

A child of our time   66'
  chorus   solos SATB

24'	24'
	18'

  2 *3 2 *3—4 3 3 0—tmp—str
  Schott

Concerto for double string orchestra   23'
  str

6'	9'	8'

  Schott

Concerto for orchestra   32'
    2 *2 *2 *2—3 2 2 1—tmp+3—hp, pf—str
    Optimum strings: 6-8vn, 4va, 5vc, 4db.
    Schott

| 10' 12' |
| 10' |

Concerto, piano   32'
    2 2 2 2—4 2 3 0—tmp—cel—str
    Schott

Concerto, violin, viola & violoncello (Triple concerto)   32'
    =1 *2 *4 *3—4 2 2 0—tmp+6—hp, cel—str (min 8.8.6.4.4)
    English horn doubles on bass oboe; 2 of the clarinets play bass
    clarinet (though one is optional).
    Schott

Divertimento for chamber orchestra (Sellinger's round)   16'
    1 1 1 1—1 1 0 0—str
    Schott

Fantasia concertante on a theme of Corelli   16'
    concertino: 2 violins, violoncello
    2 string orchestras, one of which acts as continuo.
    Schott

Fantasia on a theme of Handel   16'
    solo piano
    *2 2 2 2—4 2 3 0—tmp+1—str
    Both flutists double on piccolo.
    Schott

Little music   8'
    str
    Contents—Prelude; Fugue; Air; Finale.
    Schott

The midsummer marriage: Ritual dances   28'
    optional chorus
    *2 2 2 2—4 2 3 0—tmp+1—hp, cel—str
    Both flutists double on piccolo.
    Schott

New year suite   30'
    *3 *3 *3 *3—asx, tsx, bsx/ssx—4 2 3 1—5perc—hp, elec gtr, bass
    gtr— taped effects—str (min 4.4.4.4.2)
    All 3 flutists double on piccolo.
    Schott

Songs for Dov   25'
    solo tenor
    *2 *2 *2 *2—3 1 1 0—tmp+5—hp, pf, elec gtr—str 2.2.2.3.2
    Strings may be increased to 6.6.4.6.4. Electric harpsichord may
    substitute for electric guitar; both flutists double on piccolo.
    Schott

Symphony no.1   35'
  *3 2 2 *3—4 3 3 1—tmp+1—str
  All 3 flutists double on piccolo.
  Schott

Symphony no.2   37'
  *2 2 2 2—4 2 3 1—tmp+1—hp, pf, opt cel—str
  Schott

10'	12'
6'	9'

Symphony no.3   57'
  solo soprano
  *3 *3 =3 *3—4 2 3 1—tmp+7—hp, cel, pf—str
  Two of the flutists double on piccolo; 1 trumpet doubles on
  flugelhorn.
  Schott

12'	16'
6'	4' 2'
5'	12'

Symphony no.4 (1976/77)   32'
  *2 *3 *3 *3—6 3 3 2—tmp+4—hp—str
  Both of the flutists double on piccolo.
  Schott

The vision of Saint Augustine   35'
  solo baritone   chorus
  *2 *2 *2 *2—4 2 3 1—tmp+5—hp, cel, pf—str
  Both flutists double on piccolo.
  Schott

Toch, Ernst   1887 - 1964

Circus, an overture   6'
  *3 2 2 2—3 3 3 1—3perc—pf—str
  Kalmus   *Mills*

Concerto, violoncello, op.35   25'
  *1 1 1 1—1 0 0 0—tmp+1—2vn, va, vc, db
  Schott

Pinocchio, a merry overture   6'
  *3 2 2 2—2 2 3 0—tmp+2—str
  AMP

Symphony no.3, op.75   28'
  *3 *3 +3 *3—4 4 3 1—tmp+5—org—str
  Percussion includes glass harmonica and glass balls (struck with
  mallets); these may be replaced by vibraphone 4-hands.
  Belwin

Symphony no.6, op.93   23'
  *2 2 2 2—3 3 3 0—tmp+4—str
  Belwin

Tomasi, Henri Frédien   1901 - 1971

Concerto, trumpet   16'
  *3 *3 2 2—4 0 3 1—tmp+3—hp, cel—str
  Leduc

7'	5' 4'

Torelli, Giuseppe   1658 - 1709

Concerto, op.6, no.1, G major   7'
   cnt—str
   Ed. Walter Kolneder.
   Schott

Concerto, trumpet, D major
   cnt—str
   Ed. Edward Tarr. A different work from the following.
   Musica Rara

Concerto, trumpet, D major   10'
   cnt—str
   Ed. Heinz Zickler. A different work from the preceding.
   Schott

Concerto, violin, op.8, no.8, C minor   6'
   cnt—str
   Ed. Ernst Praetorius.
   Eulenburg

Concerto, violin, op.8, no.9, E minor   14'
   cnt—str
   Peters   *Ricordi*   *Suvini*

Concerto, 2 violins, op.6, no.10, D minor   5'
   cnt—str
   Ed. Hans Engel.
   Kalmus   *Nagel*

Concerto, 2 violins, op.8, no.1, C major   11'
   cnt—str
   Ricordi   *Suvini*

Concerto, 2 violins, op.8, no.3, E major   7'
   cnt—str
   Ed. Piero Santi.
   Suvini

Concerto, 2 violins, op.8, no.7, D minor   9'
   cnt—str
   Ed. Piero Santi.
   Suvini

Concerto grosso, 2 violins, op.8, no.2, A minor   8'
   cnt—str
   Ed. Bernhard Paumgartner.
   Schott

Concerto grosso, 2 violins, op.8, no.5, G major   10'
   cnt—str
   Ed. Alfredo Casella.
   Ricordi

Concerto grosso, 2 violins, op.8, no.6, G minor (Christmas concerto)   7'
   cnt—str
   Peters   *Vieweg*

Sinfonia, op.6, no.6, E minor   7'
   cnt—str
   Ed. Arnold Schering.
   Kahnt

Sinfonia con tromba, D major   5'
   solo trumpet
   cnt—str
   King

Torke, Michael   1961 -

Adjustable wrench   11'
   0 1 2 1—1 2 1 0—marimba—pf, synthesizer—vn, va, vc, db
   Boosey

Ash   16'
   1 2 1 2—3 1 0 0—tmp—synth—str
   Boosey

December   12'
   str
   Boosey

Ecstatic orange   12'
   *3 2 2 2—4 3 3 1—tmp+3—pf—str
   Boosey

Javelin   9'
   *3 *3 =4 2—4 3 3 1—tmp+3—hp—str
   Boosey

Tower, Joan   1938 -

Concerto for orchestra   30'
   *3 *3 =3 *3—4 3 3 1—tmp+3—hp, pf—str
   AMP

Fanfare for the uncommon woman   3'
   0 0 0 0—4 3 3 1—tmp+4
   AMP

Fanfare for the uncommon woman for orchestra   5'
   *2 2 2 2—4 3 3 1—tmp+3—str
   A different work from the previous one.
   AMP

Second fanfare for the uncommon woman   5'
   0 0 0 0—4 3 3 1—tmp+3
   AMP

Third fanfare for the uncommon woman   4'
   2 brass quintets, each with 2tp, hn, tbn, tuba
   AMP

Sequoia   16'
*2 2 2 2—4 2 3 1—tmp+4—hp, pf/cel—str
Two of the flutists double on piccolo.
AMP

Silver ladders   23'
*3 *3 *3 *3—4 3 3 1—tmp+4—hp, pf/cel—str
AMP

Tredici, David Del   1937 -
see: Del Tredici, David, 1937-

Trimble, Lester   1923 - 1986
Duo concertante   18'
2 solo violins
*2 *2 *2 2—4 2 3 0—tmp+4—hp, cel—str
Celesta intended to be covered by one of the percussionists.
Peters

Tsontakis, George   1951 -
Perpetual Angelus   15'
*2 2 2 2—4 2 1 0—tmp+2—hp—str
Merion

Winter lightning   15'
*3 *3 *3 *3—4 3 3 1—tmp+3—hp, pf—str
Merion

Turina, Joaquín   1882 - 1949
Canto a Sevilla   40'
solo soprano
*3 2 2 2—4 3 3 1—tmp+2—hp, cel—str
UME

Danzas fantásticas   17'
*3 *3 *3 *3—4 3 3 1—tmp+3—hp—str | 5' 7' 5' |
UME

La procesion del rocio   9'
*3 *3 *3 *3—4 3 3 1—tmp+4—hp—str
Kalmus

Rapsodia sinfónica   9'
solo piano
str
UME

Sinfonia sevillana   22'
*3 *3 *3 *3—4 3 3 1—tmp+2—hp, cel—str | 8' 7' 7' |
UME

Turok, Paul   1929 -

A Joplin overture   7'
  *3 *3 *3 2—4 3 3 1—tmp+3—hp—str
  Schirmer, G.

U

Ussachevsky, Vladimir   1911 - 1990
Rhapsodic variations
  see under: Luening, Otto

V

Vanhal, Joh. Baptist (Jan Křtitel)   1739 - 1813
  also spelled: Wanhal, Johann Baptist

Concerto, double bass, E-flat major   18'
  0 2 0 0—2 0 0 0—str
  Score and parts to the same work are also available in D major
  (in case the traditional scordatura for double bass soloists is not
  used).
  Doblinger

Sinfonia, G minor   14'
  0 2 0 1—4 0 0 0—str
  Peters edition calls for 2hn rather than 4, and uses the German
  spelling of the composer's name (Wanhal).
  Doblinger   Peters

Varèse, Edgard   1883 - 1965
Amériques (original version)   26'
  =8 *5 =6 *6—heckelphone, contrabass cl—8 10 8 3—2tmp+13
  —2hp, (cel played by percussionist)—str
  Three of the flutists play piccolo; 2 of the bassoonists play
  contrabassoon. 4 of the trumpets and 3 of the trombones
  constitute a "Fernorchester."
  Revised and edited by Klaus Angermann, 1991.
  Ricordi

Amériques (1927 version)   23'
    =5 *4 =5 *5—heckelphone—8 6 4 2—contrabass tbn—2tmp+9
    —2hp, (cel played by percussionist)—str
    Two of the flutists play piccolo; 2 of the bassoonists play
    contrabassoon.
    Revised and edited by Chou Wen-chung, 1973.
    Ricordi

Arcana   16'
    *5 *4 =5 *5—heckelphone—8 5 3 2—contrabass tbn—tmp+6—str
    Three of the flutists double on piccolo; 2 clarinetists play E-flat
    cl; 2 bassoonists play cbn. Rev. 1960.
    Ricordi

Déserts   24'
    *2 0 =2 0—2 3 3 2—tmp+4—pf
    2-channel magnetic tapes interpolated between instrumental
    sections. May be performed without electronic interpolations, in
    which case the duration is 14'.
    Ricordi

Ecuatorial   11'
    several bass voices or male chorus
    0 0 0 0—0 4 4 0—tmp+5—pf, org, 2 ondes martenots
    Originally for bass voices (1934); revised in 1961 for male
    chorus.
    Ricordi

Hyperprism   5'
    *1 0 +1 0—3 2 2 0—9perc
    Ed. R. Sacks, 1986.
    Ricordi

Intégrales   12'
    *2 1 +2 0—1 2 2 0—contrabass tbn—4perc
    Both flutists play piccolo. Rev. ed. by Chou Wen-chung, 1980.
    Ricordi

Ionisation   8'
    12perc—pf (also covers some percussion)
    Ricordi

Nocturnal   7'
    solo soprano   chorus of bass voices
    *2 1 +2 1—1 2 2 0—contrabass tbn—tmp+5—pf—str
    Posthumous work, completed and edited by Chou Wen-chung,
    1969.
    Ricordi

Octandre   7'
    *1 1 +1 1—1 1 1 0—db
    Rev. ed. by Chou Wen-chung, 1980.
    Ricordi

Offrandes   **8'**
   solo soprano
   *2 1 1 1—1 1 1 0—8perc—hp—2vn, va, vc, db   **4' 4'**
   Reinforcement of the string parts authorized to the extent of
   6.4.4.2.2 total strings.
   Contents—Chanson de Là-haut; La Croix du sud.
   Ricordi

Vaughan Williams, Ralph   1872 - 1958

Concerto, oboe (1944)   **19'**
   str   **7' 3' 9'**
   Oxford

Concerto, 1 piano or 2 pianos   **25'**
   *2 2 2 2—4 2 3 1—tmp+2—opt org—str
   Oxford

Concerto, tuba   **12'**
   *2 1 2 1—2 2 2 0—tmp+2—str   **4' 5' 3'**
   Oxford

Concerto, violin, D minor (Concerto accademico)   **16'**
   str
   Oxford

English folk song suite   **10'**
   *2 1 2 1—2 2 2 0—tmp+3—str   **3' 4' 3'**
   Originally for band; arr. for orchestra by Gordon Jacob.
   Boosey

Fantasia on a theme by Thomas Tallis   **15'**
   solo string quartet—string orchestra
   Curwen

Fantasia on "Greensleeves"   **4'**
   1 (or 2) 0 0 0—hp (or pf)—str
   Arr. by Ralph Greaves from the score of the opera *Sir John in
   love.*
   Oxford

Five variants of "Dives and Lazarus"   **11'**
   hp (preferably doubled)—str
   Oxford

Flos campi   **18'**
   solo viola   textless chorus
   *1 1 1 1—1 1 0 0—2perc—hp, cel—str
   Oxford

Hodie (This day)   **54'**
   chorus   solos STB
   *3 *3 2 *3—4 3 3 1—tmp+4—hp, cel, pf, org—str
   Possible with: *2 *2 2 2—2 2 3 1—tmp+4—cel, pf—str.
   Oxford

In the fen country   14'
3 *3 *3 2—4 2 3 1—tmp—str
Rev. 1935.
Oxford

Job; a masque for dancing   43'
=3 *3 *3 *3—asx—4 3 3 1—tmp+3—2hp, org—str
Possible with: *2 *2 2 2—4 2 3 1—tmp+1—hp—str.
Oxford

The lark ascending   13'
solo violin
2 1 2 2—2 0 0 0—1perc—str
Also possible with only one of each wind instrument.
Oxford

Magnificat   12'
contralto solo   female chorus
2 0 0 0—hp, opt cel—str
A version with accompaniment for full orchestra is also
available.
Oxford

Prelude (49th parallel)   2'
2 *2 2 2—4 2 3 1—tmp+1—hp—str
Cued so that it may be played by strings and any other available
parts.
Oxford

Serenade to music   14'
16 solo voices (4S, 4A, 4T, 4B)
*2 *2 2 2—4 2 3 1—tmp+1—hp—str
May be performed by chorus instead of 16 solo voices,
or by some combination of chorus and 4 or more solo voices.
Oxford

Symphony no.1 (A sea symphony)   63'
soprano & baritone solos   chorus | 18' 10' |
*3 *3 =4 *3—4 3 3 1—tmp+4—2hp, org—str | 7' 28' |
Playable with: *2 *2 2 2—4 3 3 1—tmp+4—hp—str (by means of
cues and special parts for 2nd fl, Eh, and 2nd bn).
Galaxy   *Kalmus*

Symphony no.2, G major (London)   44'
*3 *3 *3 *3—4 4 3 1—tmp+4—hp—str | 13' 10' |
Revised version, 1920. Playable with winds *2 *2 2 2—4 2 3 1. | 7' 14' |
Galaxy   *Kalmus*

Symphony no.3 (Pastoral)   34'
solo soprano (or tenor) | 10' 8' 6' |
*3 *3 *3 2—4 3 3 1—tmp+2—hp, cel—str | 10' |
Possible without the voice, and with:
*2 *2 2 2—4 2 3 1—tmp+2—hp—str.
Curwen

Symphony no.4, F minor   30'
*3 *3 *3 *3—4 2 3 1—tmp+2—str
Possible with woodwinds *2 *2 2 2.
Oxford

8' 9' 5' 8'

Symphony no.5, D major   39'
2 *2 2 2—2 2 3 0—tmp—str
Oxford

12' 5'
12' 10'

Symphony no.6, E minor   31'
*3 *3 *3 *3—4 3 3 1—tmp+3—hp—str
Bass clarinetist doubles on tenor saxophone. Revised 1950.
Oxford

7' 8' 5'
11'

Symphony no.7 (Antarctica)   41'
brief female chorus & solo soprano
*3 *3 *3 *3—4 3 3 1—tmp+4—hp, cel, pf, org—str
Oxford

9' 5' 17'
10'

Symphony no.8, D minor   27'
*2 2 2 3—2 2 3 0—tmp+5—2hp, cel—str
2nd hp, 3rd bn, & 5th perc are optional.
2nd movement is for winds; 3rd is for strings.
Oxford

10' 4' 8'
5'

Symphony no.9, E minor   33'
*3 *3 *3 *3—2asx, tsx—4 2 3 1—flugelhorn—tmp+3—2hp,
cel—str
2 of the saxophones are optional; 3rd tp may substitute for
flugelhorn.
Oxford

8' 8' 5'
12'

Toward the unknown region   14'
chorus
3 *3 *3 2—4 3 3 1—tmp—2hp, org—str
Cued to permit performance with: 2 1 2 2—2 2 0 0—tmp—hp (or
pf)—str.
Kalmus   *Stainer*

Two hymn-tune preludes   8'
1 1 1 1—1 0 0 0—str
Contents—Eventide; Dominus regit me.
Oxford

5' 3'

The wasps: Overture   9'
*2 2 2 2—4 2 0 0—tmp+3—hp—str
Possible with winds: *2 1 2 1—2 1 0 0.
Curwen   *Kalmus*

The wasps: March past of the kitchen utensils   4'
*2 2 2 2—2 1 0 0—tmp+2—str
2nd ob & 2nd bn are optional.
Curwen

The wasps: Suite   26'
   *2 2 2 2—4 2 3 0—tmp+4—hp—str

| | 10' 3' 3' |
| 4' 6' |

   Contents—Overture; Entr'acte; March past of the kitchen
utensils; Entr'acte; Ballet and final tableau.
   Curwen also offers a version for reduced orchestra.
   Curwen   *Kalmus*

Veracini, Francesco Maria   1690 - ca.1750

Aria schiavona   4'
   opt cnt—str
   Ed. Franco Margola.
   Kalmus   *Zanibon*

Concerto, violin, D major   6'
   cnt—str
   Ed. Bernhard Paumgartner.
   Bärenreiter

Concerto grande da chiesa; or della incoronazione   12'
   solo violin
   0 2 0 0—0 2 0 0—tmp—cnt—str
   Zanibon

Menuet et gavotte   4'
   solo violoncello
   s t r
   Kalmus   *Salabert*

Quatro pezzi (from Sonate accademiche)   16'
   s t r
   Originally for violin and continuo; "Elaborated and freely
interpreted" by Ettore Bonelli.
   Contents—Largo; Allegro assai; Giga; Aria rustica.
   Kalmus   *Zanibon*

Verdi, Giuseppe   1813 - 1901

Aïda: Prelude   6'
   *3 2 2 2—4 2 3 1—tmp—str
   Kalmus   *Leduc*   *Ricordi*

Aïda: Triumphal march & ballet   11'
   *3 2 2 2—4 4 3 1—tmp+3—str

| | 7' 4' |

   Kalmus also offers an "original version" (which includes
13 *banda* parts), as well as a "concert version" for:
   *2 2 2 2—4 2 3 1—tmp, perc—str.
   Luck

La forza del destino: Overture   8'
   *2 2 2 2—4 2 3 1—tmp+1—2hp—str
   Kalmus   *Ricordi*

Messa da requiem   84'
   chorus   solos SATB
   *3 2 2 4—4 8 3 1—tmp+1—str
   Kalmus   *Peters*   *Ricordi*   *Schirmer, G.*

| 9' 37' |
| 10' 3' 5' |
| 6' 14' |

Nabucco: Overture   8'
   *2 2 2 2—4 2 3 1—tmp+2—str
   Kalmus   *Luck*   *Ricordi*

Requiem
   see his: Messa da requiem

Stabat mater   12'
   chorus
   3 2 2 4—4 3 4 0—tmp+1—hp—str
   Kalmus   *Peters*   *Ricordi*

Te deum   15'
   double chorus   soprano solo
   3 *3 *3 4—4 3 4 0—tmp—str
   Kalmus   *Peters*   *Ricordi*

La traviata: Prelude to Act I   4'
   1 1 1 2—4 0 0 0—str
   Bärenreiter   *Kalmus*   *Ricordi*

La traviata: Prelude to Act III   4'
   1 1 2 2—1 0 0 0—str
   Kalmus   *Luck*   *Ricordi*

I vespri siciliani: Overture   9'
   *2 2 2 2—4 4 3 1—tmp+2—str
   Kalmus   *Ricordi*

Vieuxtemps, Henri   1820 - 1881

Concerto, violin, no.4, op.31, D minor   27'
   2 2 2 2—4 2 3 0—tmp—hp—str
   C. Fischer   *Kalmus*

Concerto, violin, no.5, op.37, A minor   18'
   1 2 2 2—2 2 0 0—tmp—str
   Bote & Bock   *C. Fischer*   *Kalmus*

Villa-Lobos, Heitor   1887 - 1959

Bachianas brasileiras no.1   20'
   8vc
   AMP

| 7' 9' 4' |

Bachianas brasileiras no.2   21'
  *1 1 1 *1—tsx/bsx —2 0 1 0—tmp+5—cel, pf—str   7' 5' 5' 4'
  Contents—1. Preludio: O canto do capadocio (The song of the
  countryman); 2. Aria: O canto da nossa terra (The song of our
  country); 3. Dansa: Lembrança do sertão (Memory of the desert);
  4. Toccata: O tremzinho do caipira (The little train of the
  Brazilian countryman).
  Ricordi

Bachianas brasileiras no.3   25'
  solo piano
  *3 *3 *3 *3—4 2 4 1—tmp+2—str
  Colombo

Bachianas brasileiras no.4   22'
  *3 *3 *3 *3—4 3 2 1—tmp+3—cel—str   8' 4' 6' 4'
  Colombo

Bachianas brasileiras no.5   10'
  soprano solo—8vc   6' 4'
  AMP

Bachianas brasileiras no.5: Aria (full orchestra)   7'
  *2 *2 *2 2—2 2 2 0—tmp+7—cel, opt gtr, opt hp—str
  Arr. John Krance.
  AMP

Bachianas brasileiras no.5: Aria (strings)   7'
  optional gtr—str
  Arr. John Krance.
  AMP

Bachianas brasileiras no.8   27'
  *3 *3 *3 *3—4 4 4 1—tmp+3—str   7' 8' 6' 6'
  Eschig

Bachianas brasileiras no.9   11'
  str   8' 3'
  For orchestra of strings or of human voices.
  Eschig

Chôros no.8   20'
  2 solo pianos
  *3 *3 *5 *3—asx—4 2 4 1—tmp+4—2hp, cel—str
  Eschig

Chôros no.10 (Rasga o coração)   20'
  chorus
  2 2 2 *3—asx—3 2 2 0—tmp+3—hp, pf—str
  Eschig

Ciranda das sete notas   10'
  solo bassoon
  str
  Southern

Concerto, guitar & small orchestra 22'
1 1 1 1—1 0 1 0—str
6' 11' 5'
Eschig

Danses africaines 20'
*3 *3 *3 *3—4 4 3 1—tmp+5—2hp, cel, pf—str
Eschig

Fantasia 14'
solo B-flat saxophone (soprano or tenor)
0 0 0 0—3 0 0 0—str
Southern

Mômoprecóce; fantaisie pour piano et orchestre 28'
solo piano
*1 *2 1 *2—asx—3 1 1 0—tmp+2—cel—str
An elaboration for piano and orchestra of an earlier series of
short piano pieces.
Eschig

Sinfonietta no.1, B-flat major (A memoria de Mozart) 18'
2 2 2 2—2 2 2 0—tmp—str
Southern

Sinfonietta no.2, C major 17'
*1 *1 *1 1—asx—3 2 2 1—tmp+1—hp, cel—str
Southern

Suite for strings 8'
str
Contents—Timida (Timid music); Misteriosa (Mysterious music);
Inquieta (Restless music).
Eschig

Uirapurú (The magic bird) 18'
*3 *3 *3 *3—ssx—4 3 3 1—tmp+2—2hp, cel,
pf—violinophone—str
AMP

Viotti, Giovanni Battista   1755 - 1824

Concerto, piano, G minor 41'
2 2 2 2—2 2 0 0—tmp—str
Ed. R. Giazotto.
Ricordi

Concerto, violin, no.19, G minor 31'
2 2 2 0—2 0 0 0—str
15' 6'
Ricordi
10'

Concerto, violin, no.22, A minor 27'
1 2 2 2—2 2 0 0—tmp—str
11' 8' 8'
Breitkopf   *Kalmus*

Vitali, Tomaso Antonio   1663 - 1745

Ciaccona (arr. Guido Guerrini)   18'
  solo violin
  opt cnt—str
  Sometimes attributed to Giovanni Battista Vitali (1632-1692),
  father of Tomaso. Probably it is by neither of the Vitalis, but
  rather by an unknown composer of the period.
  Zanibon

Vivaldi, Antonio   1678 - 1741

Concerto, bassoon, RV 477 (P.46), C major   11'
  cnt—str
  Ed. Gian Francesco Malipiero.
  Ricordi

Concerto, bassoon, RV 484 (P.137), E minor   10'
  cnt—str
  Ricordi

Concerto, bassoon, RV 485 (P.318), F major   10'
  cnt—str
  Ed. Walter Kolneder.
  Peters

Concerto, bassoon, RV 498 (P.70), A minor   10'
  cnt—str
  Ricordi

Concerto, flute, RV 428 (P.155) op.10, no.3, D major (Il cardellino)   11'
  0 1 0 1—cnt—vn
  Also variously known as *Del gardellino, The goldfinch,* and *The
  bullfinch.*
  AMP   *Kalmus*   *Peters*   *Ricordi*

Concerto, flute or recorder, RV 439 (P.342) op.10, no.2, G minor (La   12'
notte)
  0 0 0 1—cnt—str
  AMP   *Ricordi*

Concerto, flute, oboe & bassoon, RV 570 (P.261), op.44, no.16, F   7'
major (La tempesta di mare) | 3' 2' 2' |
  cnt—str
  Ed. Felix Schroeder. Flute part possibly intended for recorder.
  Eulenburg

Concerto, guitar, RV 93 (P.209), D major   9'
  cnt—str | 3' 4' 2' |
  Ed. Dick Visser. Originally for lute.
  Peters

Concerto, 2 horns, RV 538 (P.320), F major   7'
  cnt—str
  Ricordi

Concerto, 2 horns, RV 539 (P.321), F major   9'
   cnt—str
   Ricordi

Concerto, mandolin, RV 425 (P.134), C major   7'
   cnt—str
   Ed. Gian Francesco Malipiero.
   Ricordi

Concerto, oboe, RV 447 (P.41), C major   15'
   cnt—str
   Ricordi

Concerto, oboe, RV 454 (P.259), op.8, no.9, D minor   7'
   cnt—str   3' 2' 2'
   Ricordi

Concerto, oboe, RV 455 (P.306), F major   10'
   cnt—str
   Ricordi

Concerto, oboe & bassoon, RV 545 (P.129), op.42, no.3, G major   11'
   cnt—str
   Ed. Felix Schroeder.
   Eulenburg

Concerto, oboe & violin, RV 548 (P.406), B-flat major   9'
   cnt—str
   Ricordi

Concerto for orchestra, RV 151 (P.143), G major (Alla rustica)   4'
   cnt—str
   Peters   *Ricordi*

Concerto for orchestra, RV 155 (P.407), G minor   12'
   cnt—str
   Ricordi

Concertos, piccolo
   *It is not known what instrument Vivaldi had in mind for these
   concertos. The term he used was* flautino, *which could have been
   sopranino recorder or flageolet. The modern transverse piccolo
   flute did not yet exist.*

Concerto, piccolo, RV 443 (P.79), C major   11'
   cnt—str
   Eulenburg   *Ricordi*

Concerto, piccolo, RV 445 (P.83), A minor   10'
   cnt—str
   Ed. Gian Francesco Malipiero.
   Ricordi

Concerto, recorder, RV 441 (P.440), op.44, no.19, C minor   13'
   cnt—str
   Ed. Felix Schroeder.
   Eulenburg

Concerto, 2 trumpets, RV 537 (P.75), C major 7'
    cnt—str   3' 1' 3'
    Ricordi

Concertos, violin, op.8, no.1-4
    see his: Le quattro staggioni (The four seasons)

Concerto, violin, op.8, no.5, RV 253 (P.415), E-flat major (La 8'
tempesta di mare)
    cnt—str
    Ricordi

Concerto, violin, op.8, no.6, RV 122 (P.7), C major (Il piacere) 8'
    cnt—str
    Ricordi

Concerto, violin, op.8, no.7, RV 242 (P.258), D minor 7'
    cnt—str
    Ricordi

Concerto, violin, op.8, no.8, RV 332 (P.337), G minor 9'
    cnt—str
    Ricordi

Concerto, violin, op.8, no.10, RV 362 (P.338), B-flat major (La 8'
caccia)
    cnt—str
    Ricordi

Concerto, violin, op.8, no.11, RV 210 (P.153), D major 13'
    cnt—str
    Ricordi

Concerto, violin, op.8, no.12, RV 178 (P.8), C major 9'
    cnt—str
    Ricordi

Concerto, 2 violins, op.3, no.8, RV 522 (P.2), A minor 11'
    cnt—str
    Peters

Concerto, violin & violoncello, RV 547 (P.388), B-flat major 11'
    cnt—str
    Ricordi

Concerto, violoncello, RV 401 (P.434), C minor 11'
    cnt—str
    Ricordi

Concerto, violoncello, RV 406 (P.282), op.26, no.9, D minor 12'
    cnt—str
    Ed. Felix Schroeder.
    Eulenburg

Concerto, violoncello, RV 418 (P.35), op.26, no.17, A minor 10'
    cnt—str
    Ed. Walter Kolneder.
    Peters

Concerto, violoncello, RV 422 (P.24), A minor   10'
  cnt—str
  Luck   *Ricordi*

Concerto, 2 violoncellos, RV 531 (P.411), G minor   10'
  cnt—str
  Eulenburg   *Ricordi*

The four seasons
see his: Le quattro staggioni

Gloria, RV 589   27'
  chorus   solos SSA
  0 1 0 0—0 1 0 0—cnt—str
  Kalmus edition by Clayton Westermann; Ricordi edition by Gian
  Francesco Malipiero; Walton edition by Mason Martens. Peters
  edition lists solos SA only.
  Kalmus   *Peters*   *Ricordi*   *Walton*

Gloria, RV 589 (arr. Alfredo Casella)   31'
  chorus   solos SSA
  0 2 0 0—0 2 0 0—org—str
  Altered and romanticized. Vocal and orchestral parts for this
  version are not compatible with those of other editions.
  Ricordi

Introduction & Gloria, RV 639 & 588   35'
  chorus   solos SSAT
  0 2 0 0—0 1 0 0—cnt—str
  Ed. Clayton Westermann.
  Kalmus

Magnificat
  *Two versions of this work are readily available. RV 610 (about
  15' in duration) is the original version. RV 611 (about 22' long) is
  identical, except that 5 new virtuoso arias (written for particular
  singers) are substituted for 3 of the movements of RV 610. Several
  of the editions listed below include all these alternatives, so as to
  permit performance of either of the two versions. Details vary
  from one edition to another.*
    *The composer also prepared two other versions: RV 610a (some
  movements adapted for double chorus) and RV 610b (single-
  chorus version, but without oboes, and with 2 trumpets added in
  several movements).*

Magnificat, RV 610 (ed. H.C. Robbins Landon)   15'
  chorus   solos SSATB
  0 2 0 2—0 0 3 0—cornetto—cnt—str
  Winds are optional.
  Universal

Magnificat, RV 610 or 611 (ed. Günter Graulich)   15' or
  chorus   solos SSAT   22'
  0 2 0 0—cnt—str
  Carus

Magnificat, RV 610 or 611 (ed. G. F. Malipiero) 15' or
  chorus   solos SSAT 22'
  0 2 0 0—cnt—str
  If the RV 611 version is performed, the 2 oboes are not required.
  Ricordi

Magnificat, RV 610 or 611 (ed. Clayton Westermann) 15' or
  chorus   solos SSATB 22'
  0 2 0 0—cnt—str
  Kalmus

Le quattro staggioni, op.8, nos.1-4 (The four seasons) 43'

  1. La primavera, RV 269 (P.241), E major (Spring) 11'
  solo violin 3' 3' 5'
  cnt—str
  Carisch   *Eulenburg*   *Kalmus*   *Ricordi*

  2. L'estate, RV 315 (P.336), G minor (Summer) 10'
  solo violin 5' 2' 3'
  cnt—str
  Carisch   *Eulenburg*   *Kalmus*   *Ricordi*

  3. L'autunno, RV 293 (P.257), F major (Autumn) 9'
  solo violin 4' 2' 3'
  cnt—str
  Carisch   *Eulenburg*   *Kalmus*   *Ricordi*

  4. L'inverno, RV 297 (P.442), F minor (Winter) 7'
  solo violin 3' 2' 2'
  cnt—str
  Carisch   *Eulenburg*   *Kalmus*   *Ricordi*

Sinfonia nos. 1 & 2, RV 719 & 146 12'
  cnt—str 6' 6'
  Ed. Ludwig Landshoff.
  Kalmus   *Peters*

Sinfonia no.3, RV 149, G major 6'
  cnt—str
  Ed. Ludwig Landshoff.
  Kalmus   *Peters*

Sinfonia, RV 169 (P.Sinf.21), B minor (Al santo sepolcro) 6'
  str (without cnt)
  Ricordi

Stabat mater 20'
  contralto solo
  org or hpsd—str
  Ed. Renato Fasano.
  Universal

W

Wagenseil, Georg Christoph   1715 - 1777

Concerto, harpsichord, D major   16'
str (without va)
Breitkopf

Concerto, trombone, E-flat major   13'
2 0 0 1—2 0 0 0—cnt—str
Ed. Paul R. Bryan. Editor suggests use of an alto trombone,
though the solo part is readily playable on a tenor trombone.
Universal

Concerto, violoncello, A major   10'
cnt—str
Ed. Enrico Mainardi & Fritz Racek.
Doblinger

Concerto, violoncello, C major   22'
0 2 0 0—2 2 0 0—cnt (opt)—str
Trumpets are optional. Ed. Fritz Racek.
Doblinger

Sinfonia, G minor   15'
0 2 0 1—cnt—str
Ed. Alison Copland.
Universal

Wagner, Richard   1813 - 1883

Adagio, clarinet & strings, D-flat major   4'
str
This work was actually composed by Heinrich Joseph Baermann,
1784-1847, and is published under that composer's name by
Breitkopf.
Kalmus

Christoph Columbus: Overture   8'
*3 2 2 2—4 6 3 1—tmp—str
Breitkopf   *Kalmus*

Eine Faust-Ouvertüre (A Faust overture)   12'
*3 2 2 3—4 2 3 1—tmp—str
Rev. 1855.
Breitkopf   *Kalmus*

Der fliegende Holländer (The flying Dutchman): Overture   11'
*3 *2 2 2—4 2 3 1—tmp—hp—str
Breitkopf   *Kalmus*

Götterdämmerung: Gesang der Rheintöchter (Song of the   10'
Rhinemaidens)
2 2 2 2—4 2 3 0—tmp+2—hp—str
Arr. H. Zumpe.
Kalmus   *Schott*

Götterdämmerung: Immolation scene   18'
soprano solo
*4 *4 *4 3—8 3 4 1—btp—2tmp+3—6hp (doubling 2 real
parts)—str
Horns 5-8 double on Wagner tubas.
Kalmus   *Schott*

Götterdämmerung: Siegfried's funeral music (Trauermarsch;   8'
Siegfried's Tod)
*4 *4 *4 3—4 3 4 1—btp, 4 Wagner tubas—2tmp+3—6hp
(doubling 2 real parts)—str
Breitkopf   *Kalmus*   *Schott*

Götterdämmerung: Siegfried's death & funeral music (Stasny)   12'
*2 2 2 2—4 2 3 1—tmp+3—hp—str
Arr. L.Stasny.
Kalmus   *Luck*

Götterdämmerung: Siegfried's Rhine journey (Rheinfahrt)   10'
*3 2 2 2—4 3 3 1—tmp+2—hp—str
Optional instruments: 1 fl, 1 tp, glockenspiel. Arr. Humperdinck.
An insert (available on rental from Luck) restores 45 bars
omitted by Humperdinck; it includes additional parts (not
essential) for Eh, bcl, and 3rd bn. Duration with insert: 13'
Kalmus   *Luck*   *Schott*

Grosser Festmarsch (American centennial march)   12'
*4 3 3 *4—4 3 3 1—btp—tmp+4—str
Kalmus   *Luck*   *Schott*

Huldigungsmarsch   7'
*3 2 *3 2—4 3 3 1—tmp+4—str
Kalmus   *Schott*

Kaisermarsch   9'
*3 3 3 3—4 3 3 1—tmp+4—str
Kalmus   *Luck*

Lohengrin: Prelude, Act I   8'
3 *3 *3 3—4 3 3 1—tmp+1—str
Breitkopf   *Kalmus*

Lohengrin: Prelude, Act III   3'
3 3 3 3—4 3 3 1—tmp+3—str
Breitkopf   *Kalmus*

Lohengrin: Elsa's procession to the cathedral (Feierlicher Zug zum Münster)   4'

    opt double male chorus & chorus of women & boys
    3 *3 *3 3—4 3 3 1—tmp—str
    Breitkopf   *Kalmus*

Die Meistersinger: Prelude   9'
    *3 2 2 2—4 3 3 1—tmp+2—hp—str
    Breitkopf   *Kalmus*   *Schott*

Die Meistersinger: Three excerpts from Act III   23'
    *3 2 2 2—4 3 3 1—tmp+2—hp—str   7' 3' 13'
    Arr. W. Hutschenruyter.
    Contents—Einleitung zum 3. Akt (Introduction to Act III); Tanz der Lehrbuben (Dance of the apprentices); Aufzug der Meistersinger (Procession of the Meistersingers).
    Breitkopf   *Kalmus*

Parsifal: Prelude   13'
    3 *4 3 *4—4 3 3 1—tmp—str
    Breitkopf   *Kalmus*

Parsifal: Good Friday spell (Charfreitagszauber)   11'
    3 *4 *4 *4—4 3 3 1—tmp—str
    Hutschenruyter version (Breitkopf) playable with:
    3 *3 2 2—4 2 3 1—tmp—str.
    Breitkopf   *Kalmus*   *Schott*

Das Rheingold: Entry of the Gods into Valhalla (Einzug der Götter)   9'
    2 2 2 2—4 3 3 1—tmp+1—hp—str
    Arr. H. Zumpe.
    Kalmus   *Schott*

Rienzi: Overture   12'
    *3 2 2 *3—4 4 3 1—tmp+4—str
    Breitkopf   *Kalmus*

Rule Britannia!   10'
    *4 2 +3 *3—4 4 3 1—tmp+4—str
    Ed. Felix Mottl. Two of the flutists double on piccolo.
    Kalmus

Siegfried: Forest murmurs (Waldweben)   9'
    *2 2 2 2—4 2 3 0—tmp+1—str
    Schott version requires tuba also. Breitkopf publishes a version ed. by W. Hutschenruyter, for larger orchestra.
    Kalmus   *Schott*

Siegfried idyll   18'
    1 1 2 1—2 1 0 0—str
    In the first performance of this work Wagner used only one string player to a part (including however 2 violas, the second player doubling on trumpet). Thereafter he used orchestral strings.
    Breitkopf   *Kalmus*

Symphony, C major   26'
  2 2 2 *3—4 2 3 0—tmp—str
  Kalmus   *Luck*

Tannhäuser: Overture (Dresden version)   14'
  *3 2 2 2—4 3 3 1—tmp+3—str
  There appears to be no textual difference between the advertised
  "original version" and the "concert version ed. by F. Hoffmann."
  Breitkopf   *Kalmus*

Tannhäuser: Overture & Venusberg music (Paris version)   21'
  *3 2 2 2—4 3 3 1—2tmp+4—hp—str
  Kalmus

Tannhäuser: Venusberg music (Bacchanale)   12'
  *3 2 2 2—4 3 3 1—2tmp+4—hp—str
  Kalmus

Tannhäuser: Arrival of the guests at the Wartburg (Einzug der   8'
Gäste)
  3 2 2 2—4 3 3 1—tmp+3—str
  Breitkopf   *Kalmus*

Tannhäuser: Prelude, Act III   8'
  *3 2 2 2—4 3 3 1—tmp—str
  Breitkopf   *Kalmus*

Tristan und Isolde: Prelude and Liebestod   17'
  optional soprano solo
  *3 *3 *3 3—4 3 3 1—tmp—hp—str
  A critical edition of the score with historical and analytical
  essays is available from Norton.
  Breitkopf   *Kalmus*

Tristan und Isolde: Nachtgesang   10'
  2 *3 *3 3—4 1 3 1—tmp—hp—str
  Eh, bcl, 3rd bn are optional. Arr. Arthur Seidel.
  Breitkopf   *C. Fischer*   *Kalmus*

Tristan und Isolde: Prelude, Act III   8'
  0 *2 2 2—4 0 0 0—tmp—str
  Playable with 1 ob/Eh. Arr. Arthur Seidel.
  Breitkopf   *Kalmus*

Die Walküre: Ride of the Valkyries (Walkürenritt)   5'
  *4 *4 *4 3—8 3 4 1—tmp+3—str
  Two of the flutists double on piccolo.
  Kalmus   *Luck*   *Schott*

Die Walküre: Ride of the Valkyries (Walkürenritt) arr.   5'
Hutschenruyter
  *3 *3 *4 *3—6 3 3 1—tmp+3—str
  Arr. Wouter Hutschenruyter.
  Can be played with winds: *3 *3 3 2—4 3 3 1.
  Breitkopf   *C. Fischer*   *Luck*

Die Walküre: Ride of the Valkyries (Walkürenritt) arr. Sheffer   5'
   *3 2 2 2—4 3 3 1—tmp+2—str
   Reduced instrumentation by Jonathan Sheffer.
   FMD

Die Walküre: Wotan's farewell & Magic fire music (Wotans   18'
Abschied und Feuerzauber)
   optional bass-baritone solo
   *2 2 2 2—4 2 3 1—tmp+2—hp—str
   Kalmus   *Schott*

Wesendonck Lieder
   Originally for soprano & piano.

   1. Der Engel   3'
   soprano solo
   2 2 2 2—2 0 0 0—str
   Orchestrated by Felix Mottl.
   Kalmus

   2. Stehe still   4'
   soprano solo
   2 2 2 2—4 1 0 0—tmp—str
   Orchestrated by Felix Mottl.
   Kalmus

   3. Im Treibhaus   6'
   soprano solo
   2 2 2 2—3 0 0 0—str
   Orchestrated by Felix Mottl.
   Kalmus

   4. Schmerzen   3'
   soprano solo
   2 2 2 2—4 1 0 0—str
   Orchestrated by Felix Mottl.
   Kalmus

   5. Träume   5'
   soprano solo (or solo violin; Wagner's specification)
   0 0 2 2—2 0 0 0—str
   Orchestrated by the composer.
   Kalmus

Waldteufel, Emil   1837 - 1915

Les Patineurs, op.183 (The skaters' waltz)   8'
   *2 2 2 2—4 2 3 1—tmp+2—str
   Kalmus   *Luck*

Walker, George   1922 -

Address for orchestra   19'
*4 *4 *4 *4—4 2 2 1—tmp+3—hp—str
1959; rev.1991.
MMB

Lyric for strings   6'
str
1947; rev. 1990.
Based on the 2nd movement of the composer's *String quartet no.1*.
MMB

Overture in praise of folly   8'
*3 *3 *3 *3—4 4 3 1—tmp+5—hp, pf/cel—str
MMB

Walker, Gwyneth   1947 -

The light of three mornings   17'
1 1 1 0—1 1 1 0—1perc—str (min 4.2.1.1.1)   5' 7' 5'
3rd movement, *Hints and tappings*, may be performed separately.
MMB

Open the door   4'
2 2 2 2—4 2 3 1—tmp+2—str
MMB

Walton, William   1902 - 1983

As you like it; a poem for orchestra after Shakespeare   13'
solo soprano   3' 3' 2'
*3 *2 2 2—4 2 2 0—tmp+3—2hp, hpsd—str   3' 2'
Arr. by Christopher Palmer from the film score.
Contents—Prelude; Moonlight; Under the greenwood tree; The
fountain; Wedding procession.
Oxford

Belshazzar's feast   34'
chorus   baritone solo   5' 5' 4'
*3 2 =3 *3—asx (or Eh)—4 9 9 3—tmp+4—2hp, opt pf, org—str   5' 3' 2'
6tp, 6tbn, and 2 of the tubas are optional.   5' 1' 4'
Oxford

Capriccio burlesco   7'
*3 *3 =4 *3—4 3 3 1—tmp+3—hp—str
Oxford

Concerto, viola   27'
*2 *2 *2 2—4 2 3 0—tmp—hp—str   9' 5' 13'
Revised 1962.
Oxford

Concerto, violin   31'
*2 *2 2 2—4 2 3 0—tmp+2—hp—str   11' 7'
Oxford   13'

Concerto, violoncello   30'
  *2 *2 *2 *2—4 2 3 1—tmp+3—hp, cel—str
  Oxford   9' 7' 14'

Crown imperial (Coronation march)   7'
  *3 *3 *3 *3—4 3 3 1—tmp+3—hp, opt org—str
  Playable with winds reduced to: 2 2 2 2—4 2 3 0.
  Oxford

Façade   43'
  reciter
  *1 0 *1 0—asx—0 1 0 0—1perc—1 or 2vc
  Oxford

Façade 2   11'
  reciter   1' 4' 1'
  *1 0 1 0—asx—0 1 0 0—1perc—vc   1' 1' 1'
  8 more songs to go with the original *Façade*.   1' 1'
  Oxford

Façade: Suite no.1   9'
  *2 *2 2 2—4 2 1 1—tmp+3—str   1' 3' 2'
  3rd & 4th hn are optional. Contents—Polka; Valse; Swiss   2' 1'
  jodelling song; Tango-Pasodoblé; Tarantella, Sevillana.
  Oxford

Façade: Suite no.2   10'
  *2 *3 2 2—asx—2 2 1 0—1perc—str   1' 1' 2'
  Either the asx or the Eh may be omitted.   2' 2' 2'
  Contents—Fanfare; Scotch rhapsody; Country dance; Noche
  espagnole; Popular song; Old Sir Faulk.
  Oxford

Hamlet and Ophelia   14'
  *2 *2 2 2—4 2 3 0—tmp+2—hp, cel—str
  Oxford

Improvisations on an impromptu of Benjamin Britten   16'
  *3 *3 *3 *3—4 3 3 1—tmp+3—hp—str   5' 3' 4' 4'
  Oxford

Johannesburg festival overture   7'
  *3 *3 3 *3—4 3 3 1—tmp+3—hp—str
  Reduced version by Vilem Tausky available, for:
  2 *2 2 2—4 2 3 (opt tuba)—tmp+1 (or 2)—hp—str.
  Oxford

Portsmouth Point   6'
  *3 *3 *3 *3—4 3 3 1—tmp+4—str
  Reduced version by Constant Lambert available, for:
  *2 1 2 1—2 2 1 0—1 or 2perc—str.
  Oxford

Prologo e fantasia   6'
  *3 *3 *3 *3—4 3 3 1—tmp+4—hp, pf—str
  Oxford

Symphony no.1   43'
   *2 2 2 2—4 3 3 1—2tmp+2—str
   Rev. 1968.
   Oxford

13'	7'
10'	13'

Symphony no.2   28'
   *3 *3 =3 *3—4 3 3 1—tmp+4—2hp, cel, pf—str
   Oxford

9'	10'	9'

Variations on a theme by Hindemith   23'
   *3 *3 *3 *3—4 3 3 1—tmp+3—hp—str
   Oxford

Wanhal, Johann Baptist   1739 - 1813

   see: Vanhal, Joh. Baptist (Jan Křtitel), 1739-1813

Wański, Jan   1762 - ca.1830

Symphony in D major   22'
   2 0 0 0—1 0 0 0—str

7'	3'	4'	8'

   On themes from the overture to the opera *Pasterz nad Wisla* (The
   shepherd by the Vistula).
   PWM

Symphony in G major   19'
   2 0 0 0—1 0 0 0—str

5'	5'	4'	5'

   On themes from the overture to the opera *Kmiotek* (The peasant).
   PWM

Ward, Robert   1917 -

Adagio and allegro   12'
   *2 *2 2 2—4 3 3 1—tmp+1—str
   Peer

Euphony for orchestra   10'
   *2 *2 2 2—4 2 3 1—tmp+1—str
   Highgate

Jubilation—an overture   7'
   *3 *3 *3 *3—4 3 3 1—tmp—pf—str
   Highgate

Sonic structure   11'
   *3 *3 *3 *3—4 3 3 1—tmp+2—hp—str
   Highgate

Symphony no.3   21'
   *2 *2 *2 2—2 1 0 0—pf—str
   Highgate

Warlock, Peter   1894 - 1930
Capriol suite   11'
  *2 2 2 2—2 2 3 1—1perc—str
Also available in a version for string orchestra.
Curwen

2' 3' 1'
2' 2' 1'

Warshauer, Meira Maxine   1949 -
Ahavah (Love)   19'
  mezzo-soprano solo   chorus
  *3 *3 *3 *3—4 3 3 1—tmp+3—hp—str
Two of the flutists double on piccolo.
Kol Meira

9' 4' 6'

As the waters cover the sea; a tribute to Mozart   12'
  *3 *2 2 2—4 3 3 1—tmp+2—pf/cel—str
All three flutists double on piccolo.
Kol Meira

Revelation   8'
  *3 *3 *3 *3—4 3 3 1—tmp+3—pf/cel—str
Two of the flutists double on piccolo.
Kol Meira

Shacharit   35'
  chorus   solo soprano, tenor/narrator
  *3 2 2 2—4 2 3 1—tmp+4—hp—str
Transcontinental

Weber, Ben   1916 - 1979
Dolmen   9'
  0 2 0 1—2 0 0 0—str
Marks

Symphony on poems of William Blake, op.33   32'
  baritone solo
  *1 1 *2 1—1 0 1 0—1perc—hp, cel—vc
CFE

Weber, Carl Maria von   1786 - 1826
Abu Hassan: Overture   4'
  *2 2 2 2—2 2 1 0—tmp+3—str
Breitkopf   *Kalmus*

Andante & Rondo ongarese, op.35   9'
  solo bassoon or viola
  2 2 0 2—2 2 0 0—tmp—str
C. Fischer   *Kalmus*   *Luck*   *Peters*

Aufforderung zum Tanz, op.65 (Invitation to the dance)   9'
  *2 2 2 4—4 4 3 0—tmp—2hp—str
Orchestrated by Berlioz.
Breitkopf   *Kalmus*

Beherrscher der Geister (Ruler of the spirits)   7'
    *2 2 2 2—4 2 3 0—tmp—str
    A concert overture, being a revision, 1811, of the overture to the
    incomplete opera *Rübezahl* of 1805.
    Breitkopf   *Kalmus*

Concertino, clarinet & orchestra, op.26, E-flat major   10'
    1 2 0 2—2 2 0 0—tmp—str
    Breitkopf   *Kalmus*

Concertino, horn & orchestra, op.45, E major   12'
    1 0 2 2—2 2 0 0—tmp—str
    Kalmus   *KaWe*

Concerto, bassoon, op.75, F major   17'
    2 2 0 2—2 2 0 0—tmp—str   8' 5' 4'
    Breitkopf   *Kalmus*

Concerto, clarinet, no.1, op.73, F minor   18'
    2 2 0 2—3 2 0 0—tmp—str   7' 4' 7'
    3rd hn in 2nd mvt only.
    Breitkopf   *Kalmus*

Concerto, clarinet, no.2, op.74, E-flat major   19'
    2 2 0 2—2 2 0 0—tmp—str   8' 7' 4'
    Breitkopf   *Kalmus*

Concerto, piano, no.1, op.11, C major   20'
    2 2 0 2—2 2 0 0—tmp—str   9' 4' 7'
    Kalmus

Concerto, piano, no.2, op.32, E-flat major   21'
    2 0 2 2—2 2 0 0—tmp—str
    Kalmus

Euryanthe: Overture   8'
    2 2 2 2—4 2 3 0—tmp—str
    Breitkopf   *Kalmus*

Der Freischütz: Overture   10'
    2 2 2 2—4 2 3 0—tmp—str
    Breitkopf   *Kalmus*

Invitation to the dance
    see his: Aufforderung zum Tanz

Jubel overture, op.59   8'
    *4 2 2 2—4 2 3 0—tmp+3—str
    Two of the flutists double on piccolo.
    Breitkopf   *Kalmus*

Konzertstück, piano & orchestra, op.79, F minor   17'
    2 2 2 2—2 2 1 0—tmp—str
    Breitkopf   *Kalmus*

Oberon: Overture   9'
    2 2 2 2—4 2 3 0—tmp—str
    Breitkopf   *Kalmus*

Peter Schmoll: Overture   8'
   2 2 0 2—2 2 0 0—tmp—str
   Breitkopf   *Kalmus*

Polonaise brillante, piano & orchestra, op.72   8'
   2 2 2 2—2 2 3 0—tmp+2—str
   Orchestrated by Franz Liszt.
   C. Fischer   *Kalmus*   *Luck*

Preziosa: Overture   9'
   2 2 2 2—2 2 0 0—tmp+4—str
   Breitkopf   *Kalmus*

Ruler of the spirits
   see his: Beherrscher der Geister

Silvana: Overture   5'
   2 2 2 2—2 2 1 0—tmp—str
   Kalmus

Symphony no.1, op.19, C major   25'
   1 2 0 2—2 2 0 0—tmp—str   7' 7' 4' 7'
   Alkor   *Kalmus*

Symphony no.2, C major   18'
   1 2 0 2—2 2 0 0—tmp—str   10' 5' 1'
   Alkor   *Kalmus*   2'

Turandot: Overture & march   6'
   *2 2 2 2—2 2 1 0—tmp+4—str
   Kalmus

Webern, Anton   1883 - 1945

Das Augenlicht, op.26   7'
   chorus
   1 1 1 0—asx—1 1 1 0—tmp+2—hp, cel, mand—str (without db)
   Universal

Cantata no.1, op.29   8'
   chorus   soprano solo
   1 1 *2 0—1 1 1 0—tmp+2—hp, cel, mand—str
   Universal

Cantata no.2, op.31   13'
   chorus   solos SB
   *2 *2 *2 1—asx—1 1 1 1—1perc—hp, cel—str
   Universal

Concerto, op.24   8'
   1 1 1 0—1 1 1 0—pf—vn, va
   Universal

Fünf Sätze, op.5 (Five movements)   11'
   str
   Arr. by the composer from a work for string quartet.
   Universal

Fünf Stücke, op.10 (Five pieces for orchestra)　　　　　　6'
　　*1 1 =2 0—1 1 1 0—4perc—hp, cel, gtr, harm, mand—vn, va, vc, db
　　Universal

1'	1'	2'
1'	1'	

Geistliche Lieder, op.15　　　　　　　　　　　　　　　6'
　　high voice
　　1 0 *1 0—0 1 0 0—hp—vn/va
　　Universal

1'	1'	1'
1'	2'	

Im Sommerwind　　　　　　　　　　　　　　　　　　12'
　　3 *3 *5 2—6 2 0 0—tmp+2—2hp—str
　　C. Fischer

Lieder, op.8　　　　　　　　　　　　　　　　　　　　3'
　　medium voice
　　0 0 *1 0—1 1 0 0—hp, cel—vn, va, vc
　　Universal

Lieder, op.13　　　　　　　　　　　　　　　　　　　6'
　　solo soprano
　　*1 0 *2 0—1 1 1 0—1perc—hp, cel—vn, va, vc, db
　　Universal

Lieder, op.14　　　　　　　　　　　　　　　　　　　8'
　　high voice
　　0 0 *2 0—vn, vc
　　Universal

Lieder, op.19　　　　　　　　　　　　　　　　　　　2'
　　chorus

1'	1'

　　0 0 *2 0—cel, gtr—vn
　　Universal

Passacaglia, op.1　　　　　　　　　　　　　　　　　11'
　　*3 *3 *3 *3—4 3 3 1—tmp+2—hp—str
　　Universal

Sechs Stücke, op.6 (Six pieces for orchestra)　　　　　13'
　　*2 2 *3 *2—4 4 4 1—tmp+5—hp, cel—str
　　Revised version,1928.

1'	2'	1'
4'	3'	2'

　　Universal

Symphony, op.21　　　　　　　　　　　　　　　　　10'
　　0 0 *2 0—2 0 0 0—hp—str (without db)

7'	3'

　　Universal

Variations for orchestra op.30　　　　　　　　　　　8'
　　1 1 *2 0—1 1 1 1—tmp—hp, cel—str
　　Universal

Weill, Kurt   1900 - 1950

Aufstieg und Fall der Stadt Mahagonny: Suite   25'
*2 1 1 2—asx, tsx/ssx—2 2 2 1—tmp+2—pf, bass gtr, banjo—str
Tuba doubles on 3rd tbn; both flutists double on piccolo. Arr.
Wilhelm Brückner-Rüggeberg.
EAM   *Universal*

Das Berliner Requiem   25'
solo tenor & baritone   male chorus
0 0 2 2—2asx (2nd dbl on tsx)—2 2 2 0—tmp+2—gtr, banjo, org
or harm
Optional tuba. If no chorus is available, the work may be done
with solo voices T, Bar, B.
Ed. David Drew
Contents—Grosser Dankchoral; Vom ertrunkene Mädchen; Hier
ruht die Jungfrau; Erster Bericht über den unbekannten Soldaten;
Zweiter Bericht über den unbekannten Soldaten; Grosser
Dankchoral.
Universal

Concerto, violin   33'
*2 1 2 2—2 1 0 0—tmp+1—double basses
Universal

Kleine Dreigroschenmusik (suite from "Threepenny opera")   20'
*2 0 2 2—asx, tsx (dbl opt ssx)—0 2 1 1—tmp+1   2' 2' 2'
—pf, banjo (dbl gtr & bandoneon ad lib), opt hp   3' 2' 3'
Contents—Overture; Die Moritat von Mackie Messer;   2' 4'
Anstatt-dass Song; Die Ballade von angenehmen Leben; Pollys
Lied; Tango-Ballade; Kanonen-Song; Dreigroschen-Finale.
EAM   *Universal*

Symphony no.1 (1921) (Berliner Sinfonie)   22'
*2 1 *2 2—2 1 1 0—tmp+4—str
Horns may be doubled.
EAM   *Schott*

Symphony no.2 (1933)   28'
*2 2 2 2—2 2 2 0—tmp—str
EAM   *Heugel*   *Presser*

Weinberger, Jaromir   1896 - 1967

Svanda dudák (Shvanda the bagpiper): Polka & fugue   8'
*3 2 2 2—4 3 3 1—tmp+4—hp, opt org—str   2' 6'
4 additional tp backstage playing in unison.
AMP   *Luck*

Under the spreading chestnut tree (Variations & fugue on an old   16'
English tune)
*3 2 2 2—4 3 3 1—tmp+3—hp, pf—str
Two of the flutists double on piccolo.
AMP

Weiner, Leó   1885 - 1960

Divertimento no.5, op.39 (Impressioni ungheresi)   11'
  *2 2 2 2—4 2 3 0—tmp—hp—str
  EMB

Preludio, Notturno e Scherzo diabolico, op.31
  *2 2 2 2—4 2 3 0—tmp—hp—str
  EMB

Weinzweig, John   1913 -

Concerto, harp   18'
  1 1 1 1—1 0 0 0—str quintet or str orchestra
  Leeds Canada

Weiss, Adolph   1891 - 1971

American life (Scherzo jazzoso)   6'
  *3 *3 *3 *3—ssx, asx, tsx—4 3 3 1—tmp+4—str
  This work may be out of print, but orchestral materials are in the
  Fleisher Collection.

I segreti   12'
  *3 *3 *3 *3—4 4 3 1—tmp+3—hp, cel—str
  This work may be out of print, but orchestral materials are in the
  Fleisher Collection.

Welcher, Dan   1948 -

Haleakala (How Maui snared the sun)   21'
  narrator
  *3 *3 *3 *3—4 3 3 1—tmp+4—hp, pf/cel—str
  Two of the flutists double on piccolo; 1 horn plays conch shell.
  Elkan-Vogel

Night watchers (Symphony no.2)   29'
  *3 *3 =3 *3—4 3 3 1—tmp+4—hp, pf/cel—str
  Contents—Putting up the stars (Fantasia); Music of the spheres
  (Romanza); The delight of God (Scherzo); Twilight of the dawn
  (Finale).
  Presser

Wellesz, Egon   1885 - 1974

Suite, violin & chamber orchestra, op.38   18'
  violin solo
  1 *1 1 1—va, vc
  Universal

Wernick, Richard   1934 -

Visions of terror and wonder   28'
  solo mezzo-soprano
  =4 *4 =4 *4—4 3 3 1—2tmp+5—hp, cel—str
  The above woodwinds include 2 piccolos, 2 alto flutes, and 2
  E-flat clarinets.
  Presser

White, Paul   1895 - 1973

Five miniatures for orchestra   6'
  *1 *1 1 1—2 2 3 0—2perc—hp—str
  Contents—By the lake; Caravan song; Waltz for Teenie's doll;
  Hippo dance; Mosquito dance.
  Elkan-Vogel

Wieniawski, Henri   1835 - 1880

Concerto, violin, no.1, op.14, F-sharp minor   25'
  2 2 2 2—2 2 3 0—tmp—str   13' 5' 7'
  C. Fischer   *Kalmus*   *PWM*

Concerto, violin, no.2, op.22, D minor   22'
  2 2 2 2—2 2 3 0—tmp—str   11' 5' 6'
  Kalmus   *PWM*   *Schott*

Legend, violin & orchestra, op.17   9'
  2 2 2 2—2 0 0 0—tmp—str
  C. Fischer   *Kalmus*   *PWM*

Polonaise brillante no.1, op.4, D major (Polonaise de concert)   6'
  solo violin
  2 2 2 2—2 2 2 0—tmp—str
  C. Fischer   *Luck*   *PWM*

Polonaise brillante no.2, op.21, A major   7'
  solo violin
  2 2 2 2—2 2 3 0—tmp—str
  Ed. Robert M. Wrobel.
  C. Fischer   *Kalmus*   *PWM*

Scherzo-tarantelle, op.16   6'
  solo violin
  2 2 2 2—2 2 0 0—tmp+2—str
  Trumpets are optional. Orchestrated by Paul Gilson.
  Kalmus   *Sikorski*

Wilder, Alec   1907 - 1980

Carl Sandburg suite   16'
  *2 *2 2 2—2 2 2 0—tmp+1—hp—str
  AMP

Concerto, oboe 24'
    tmp+2—str
    (Perhaps intended for tmp+1, using a drum set.)
    AMP

Williams, John   1932 -

Star wars: Suite 30'
    *3 2 *3 2—4 3 3 1—tmp+2—hp, pf/cel—str
    Schirmer, G.

Wilson, Olly   1937 -

Expansions III 15'
    *3 *3 2 2—4 3 3 1—tmp+2—hp, pf—str
    Gunmar

Houston fanfare 3'
    2 2 2 2—4 3 3 1—3perc—hp, pf—str
    Gunmar

Witt, Friedrich   1770 - 1837

Jena symphony 23'
    1 2 0 2—2 2 0 0—tmp—str
    Ed. Fritz Stein. Formerly attributed to Beethoven.
    Breitkopf   *Kalmus*

Symphony in A 29'
    1 2 0 2—2 0 0 0—str
    Breitkopf   *Kalmus*

Wolf, Hugo   1860 - 1903

Der Corregidor: Prelude & interlude 8'
    *3 *3 2 2—4 3 3 1—tmp+1—str   5' 3'
    Bote & Bock

Der Corregidor: Suite 16'
    *3 *2 2 2—4 2 3 1—tmp+3—str
    Arr. Hans Gál.
    Contents—Prelude; Fandango & march; Spanish intermezzo;
    Notturno & entr'acte.
    Boosey

Italian serenade 8'
    solo viola
    2 2 2 2—2 0 0 0—str
    Originally for string quartet (1887). 1892 version for orchestra
    was to be the first movement of a larger work which was never
    finished. The fragment was edited by Max Reger and published
    posthumously. Wolf had at first alternated solo English horn
    with solo viola; later changed his mind and gave it all to the
    viola.
    Bote & Bock   *Breitkopf*   *Kalmus*   *MWV*

Penthesilea — 27'
*3 *3 2 3—4 4 3 1—tmp+4—hp—str — 6' 5' 16'
Contents—1. Aufbruch der Amazonen nach Troja (March of the
Amazons on Troy); 2. Der Traum Penthesileas vom Rosenfest
(Penthesilea's dream of the Rose-Festival); 3. Kämpfe,
Leidenshaften, Wahnsinn, Vernichtung (Strife, fury, frenzy,
destruction).
Alkor   Breitkopf   Kalmus   MWV

Scherzo & finale — 15'
*3 2 2 2—4 3 3 1—tmp+2—str — 8' 7'
Alkor   Breitkopf   Kalmus

Spanisches Liederbuch: Two sacred songs — 5'
mezzo-soprano solo
0 0 3 0—2 0 0 0—2vn, va, vc, db
Instrumentation by Igor Stravinsky.
Contents—Herr, was trägt der Boden hier; Wunden trägst du.
Boosey

Wolff, Christian   1934 -
Burdocks — var
For one or more orchestras; any number of players; any
instruments or sound sources (but there are places which require
specific pitches to be played). In ten sections, not necessarily to be
played consecutively.
Peters

Wolf-Ferrari, Ermanno   1876 - 1948
Concertino, English horn, op.34 — 25'
0 0 0 0—2 0 0 0—str — 7' 5' 8' 5'
Leuckart

L'amore medico (Doctor Cupid): Intermezzo — 3'
2 *3 *3 2—4 1 0 0—tmp—hp—str
Kalmus

The jewels of the Madonna: Intermezzo no.1 — 4'
1 1 2 1—2 0 0 0—pf—str
Additional parts for 2 cornets and one trombone consist of
nothing but cues; may be used if other instruments are missing.
Luck   Weinberger

The jewels of the Madonna: Intermezzo no.2 (small orchestra) — 3'
1 1 2 1—2 2 1 0—pf—str
Luck   Weinberger

The jewels of the Madonna: Intermezzo no.2 (large orchestra) — 3'
*3 *3 *3 3—4 3 3 1—tmp+1—hp—str
Kalmus

Il segreto di Susanna (The secret of Suzanne): Overture — 4'
*3 2 2 2—4 2 3 0—tmp—hp—str
Kalmus   Weinberger

Wuorinen, Charles   1938 -

Chamber concerto, violoncello & 10 players   17'
   1 1 1 1—2perc—pf—vn, va, db
   Peters

Concerto, piano, no.3   27'
   *3 2 *3 2—4 2 3 1—tmp+3—hp—str
   Peters

Contrafactum   20'
   *3 *3 *3 *3—4 3 3 2—2tmp+5—2pf—str
   Peters

Crossfire   11'
   *3 2 =3 2—4 3 3 1—tmp+2—pf—str
   Peters

Grand bamboula   6'
   str (min 6.5.4.4.2)
   Peters

Machault mon chou   11'
   2 *2 *3 *3—4 2 3 1—tmp+1—hp—str
   Material is drawn from the *Messe de Nostre Dame* by Guillaume
   de Machaut.
   Peters

The magic art   75'
   *1 *2 *1 2—2 2 1 0—tmp—hp, pf—str (min 6.4.3.3.1)

| 6' 7' 6' |
| 7' 6' 6' |
| 17' 15' |
| 5' |

   An instrumental masque drawn from the works of Henry Purcell.
   Suites of various lengths may be constructed from the individual
   movements.
   Peters

Movers and shakers   27'
   *3 *3 =3 *3—4 3 3 1—tmp+5—hp, pf—str
   Peters

A reliquary for Igor Stravinsky   17'
   *4 2 *2 *3—4 2 3 1—tmp+4—hp, pf—str
   Incorporates fragments from an unfinished orchestra piece by
   Stravinsky.
   Peters

X

Xenakis, Yannis   1922 -

Akrata   12'
*1 1 =2 *3—contrabass cl—2 3 2 1
Two of the bassoonists play contrabassoon.
Boosey

Anaktoria   11'
0 0 1 *1—1 0 0 0—2vn, va, vc, db
Contrabassoon is optional.
Salabert

Analogique A   6'
3vn, 3vc, 3db
Salabert

Atrees   15'
1 0 *2 0—1 1 1 0—3perc—vn, vc
Salabert

Metastaseis B   8'
*2 2 *1 0—3 2 2 0—tmp+4—str 12.12.8.8.6
Boosey

ST / 48—1,240162   11'
*2 2 *2 *2—2 2 2 0—tmp+3—str 8.8.6.6.4
Boosey

Syrmos   15'
str 6.6.0.4.2
Boosey

Y

Yardumian, Richard   1917 - 1985

Armenian suite   16'
*4 *4 =4 *4—6 4 4 1—tmp+5—hp—str
Elkan-Vogel

Cantus animae et cordis   15'
   str
   Elkan-Vogel

Ysaÿe, Eugene   1858 - 1931
Chant d'hiver, op.15   12'
   solo violin
   2 2 2 2—2 0 0 0—tmp—str
   Enoch

Z

Zachau (Zachow), Friedrich Wilhelm   1663 - 1712
Tantum ergo
   see under: Mozart, Wolfgang Amadeus, 1756-1791

Zemlinsky, Alexander   1871 - 1942
Lyrische Symphonie, op.18   48'
   solo soprano & baritone
   *4 *3 *4 *3—4 3 3 1—tmp+3—hp, cel, harm—str

11'	7'	7'
8'	2'	5'
		8'

   Two of the flutists double on piccolo.
   Universal

Psalm 23, op.14   10'
   chorus
   *4 *3 *3 3—4 3 3 1—tmp+3—2hp, cel—str
   Universal

Six songs, op.13   16'
   solo voice (medium)
   *4 *3 *3 2—2 3 3 0—tmp+2—hp, cel/pf, harm—str

3'	2'	2'
2'	3'	4'

   Two of the flutists double on piccolo. Contents—Die drei
   Schwestern; Die Mädchen mit den verbundenen Augen; Lied der
   Jungfrau; Als ihr Geliebter schied; Und kehrt er einst Heim; Sie
   kam zum Schloss gegangen.
   Universal

Zimmermann, Bernd Alois   1918 - 1970
Stillness and return; two sketches for orchestra   9'
   4 *4 *4 *1—asx—4 2 1 0—contrabass tbn—5perc
   —hp, accordion—vn, va, 3vc, 3db
   Schott

Zwilich, Ellen Taaffe   1939 -

Celebration for orchestra 10'
  *4 *3 *3 *3—4 3 3 1—tmp+3—hp, pf/cel—str
  Merion

Concerto grosso 1985 14'
  1 *2 0 1—2 0 0 0—hpsd—str
  Jerona

3'	2'	5'
1'	3'	

Concerto, bass trombone 20'
  tmp+1—str (max 12.12.12.12.8)
  Merion

7'	7'	6'

Concerto, violin & violoncello 18'
  2 *2 2 2—2 2 0 0—tmp—str
  Merion

Prologue & variations 14'
  str
  Merion

Symphony no.1 (Three movements for orchestra) 18'
  *2 *2 *2 *2—4 2 3 1—tmp+3—hp, pf—str
  Margun

7'	7'	4'

Symphony no.2 ('Cello symphony) 25'
  *3 *3 =3 *3—4 3 3 1—tmp+3—pf—str
  Merion

9'	10'	6'

Symphony no.3 19'
  *3 *3 *3 *3—4 3 3 1—tmp+3—str
  Merion

9'	4'	6'

APPENDICES

APPENDIX A: CHORUS

Double chorus

Mixed chorus
    Large orchestra
    Medium orchestra
    Small orchestra
    String orchestra
    Without strings

Female chorus

Male Chorus

Children's chorus

Works within the larger categories are subdivided by duration. If solo voices are also required, these are given in parentheses. Works that fit more than one category are repeated as appropriate.

Within each category or subdivision, works are listed in chronological order according to the composer's birth date.

For complete information on any of these works, refer back to the main alphabetical listing by composer.

DOUBLE CHORUS

Monteverdi—Vespro della beata vergine (SSATTBB)
Hofer—Te deum
Bach—Cantatas nos.50, 215 (SATB); Matthäuspassion (SATBB)
Handel—Israel in Egypt (SSATBB); Occasional oratorio (SSATB)
Mozart—Venite populi, K.260 (248a)
Berlioz—Te deum (T)
Mendelssohn—Psalm 98, op.91
Verdi—Te deum (S)
Wagner—Lohengrin: Elsa's procession to the cathedral
Mahler—Symphony no.8 (SSSAATBB)
Bartók—Cantata profana (TBar)
Ligeti—Requiem (SMz)
Jones—Symphony no.2

MIXED CHORUS

Large orchestra

20' or less

Verdi—Stabat mater
Rimsky-Korsakov—Mlada: Suite
Zemlinsky—Psalm 23
Rachmaninoff—Three Russian songs
Schoenberg—Prelude, Genesis suite
Ravel—Daphnis et Chloé: Suites 1-2
Kabalevsky—Symphony no.3
Barber—Prayers of Kierkegaard (ST); Vanessa: Under the willow tree
Pärt—Credo
Warshauer—Ahavah (Mz)

21'-30'

Dvořák—Te deum (SB)

[MIXED CHORUS, *Large orchestra*]
Mahler—Waldmärchen (SATBar)
Delius—Sea drift (Bar)
Roussel—Évocations: Aux Bords du
  fleuve sacré (ATBar)
Scriabin—Prométhée, le poème du feu
Stravinsky—Symphony of Psalms
Szymanowski—Symphony no.3 (T)
Poulenc—Gloria (S)
Dallapiccola—Canti di liberazione
Husa—Apotheosis of this earth
Nono—Il canto sospeso (SAT)
Martino—Paradiso choruses (3S 4Mz
  3T 2Bar)

31'-45'

Berlioz—Symphonie funèbre et tri-
  omphale, op.15
Gounod—Messe solennelle (STB)
Saint-Saëns—Le Déluge (SATB); Req-
  uiem (SATB)
Janáček—Glagolitic mass (SATB)
Mahler—Das klagende Lied (SAT)
Delius—Appalachia
Schmitt—Psalm 47 (S)
Rachmaninoff—The bells (STB)
Ives—Symphony no.4
Prokofiev—Alexander Nevsky (Mz)
Milhaud—Les Choëphores (SSA);
  Symphony no.3
Orff—Trionfo di Afrodite (SSTTB)
Poulenc—Stabat mater (S)
Duruflé—Requiem (MzBar)
Walton—Belshazzar's feast (Bar)
Shostakovich—Song of the forests
  (TB)
Schuman, Wm.—On freedom's
  ground (Bar)
Britten—Spring symphony (SAT)
Bernstein—Symphony no.3 (S, speak-
  er)
Górecki—Beatus vir (Bar)
Adams, John—Harmonium

46'-60'

Berlioz—Lelio (TTB, speaker)
Vaughan Williams—Hodie (STB)
Holst—First choral symphony (S)
Ravel—Daphnis et Chloé
Bloch, E.—Sacred service (Bar)
Stravinsky—Persephone (T, female
  narrator)
Orff—Carmina burana (STB)
Reich—The desert music

Over 60'

Haydn—Die Schöpfung (STB or
SSTBB)
Berlioz—La Damnation de Faust (Mz
  T Bar B)
Berlioz—Requiem (T); Roméo et Ju-
  liette (ATB)
Liszt—Christus (SATB)
Verdi—Messa da requiem (SATB)
Dvorák—Requiem (SATB)
Elgar—The apostles (SATBBB); The
  dream of Gerontius (ATB); The king-
  dom (SATB)
Mahler—Symphony no.2 (SA)
Debussy—Le Martyre de Saint Sébas-
  tien (SAA, narrator)
Vaughan Williams—Symphony no.1
  (SBar)
Schmidt—Das Buch mit sieben Sie-
  geln (SATTB)
Schoenberg—Gurre-Lieder (SATTB,
  speaker)
Prokofiev—Ivan the terrible (ABar,
  narrator)
Honegger—Jeanne d'Arc au bûcher
  (SSSATB & 4 spoken roles)
Britten—War requiem (STB)
Penderecki—Passio et mors domini
  nostri Iesu Christi secundum Lucam
  (SBB)

Medium orchestra

10' or less

Mozart—Kyrie, K.341
Beethoven—Meeresstille und glück-
  liche Fahrt; Die Ruinen von Athen:
  March and chorus
Schubert—Tantum ergo (SATB)
Mendelssohn—Tu es Petrus
Franck—Psalm 150
Bruckner—Psalm 150
Buck—Festival overture on the Ameri-
  can national air
Rimsky-Korsakov—Dubinushka
Holst—Christmas day (SATB)
Ives—Lincoln the great commoner
Boulez—Le Soleil des eaux (STB)

20' or less

Haydn—Te deum
Beethoven—Fantasia, piano, chorus
  & orchestra (SSATTB)
Schubert—Mirjams Siegesgesang (S);
  Offertorium (T)
Mendelssohn—Psalm 114
Schumann—Requiem für Mignon
  (SSAAB)
Brahms—Nänie; Schicksalslied
Strauss, R.—Wanderers Sturmlied

[MIXED CHORUS, *Medium orchestra*]
Vaughan Williams—Serenade to music (4S 4A 4T 4B); Toward the unknown region
Ives—Holidays symphony: Thanksgiving and/or Forefathers' Day
Stravinsky—Canticum sacrum (TBar); Chorale-variations; Requiem canticles (AB); A sermon, a narrative, and a prayer (AT, speaker)
Szymanowski—Stabat mater (SABar)
Villa-Lobos—Chôros no. 10
Hanson—Cherubic hymn; Lament for Beowulf
Copland—Canticle of freedom
Shostakovich—Symphony no. 2
Rodríguez—Scrooge (B)

21'-30'

Mendelssohn—Christus (STBB); Lauda Sion (SATB); Psalm 42 (STTBB); Psalm 95 (SST); Symphony no. 2 (SST)
Bruckner—Te Deum (SATB)
Rimsky-Korsakov—Christmas eve: Suite
Kodály—Psalmus hungaricus; Te deum (SATB)
Tippett—The midsummer marriage: Ritual dances
Shostakovich—Symphony no. 3
Britten—Cantata academica, carmen basiliense (SATB)
Maxwell Davies—The shepherd's calendar (Treble or S)
Jones—Symphony no. 2
Del Tredici—Pop-pourri (SMzCt)
Svoboda—Journey (MzBar)
Rouse—Karolju
Danielpour—Journey without distance (S)

31'-45'

Haydn—Mass, Hob.XXII:11 [3rd inst] (SATB)
Mozart—Litaniae de venerabili altaris sacramento, K.243 (SATB)
Beethoven—Cantata on the death of Emperor Joseph II (SSATB); Christus am Ölberg (STB); Mass, op.86, C major (SATB)
Schubert—Mass no.1 (SSATTB); Mass no.5 (SATB); Stabat mater (STB)
Mendelssohn—Die erste Walpurgisnacht (ATBB)
Schumann—Mass (STB); Requiem (SATB)
Bruckner—Mass no.1 (SATB); Missa solemnis (SATB)

Fauré—Requiem (full orchestra version) (SBar)
Parry—Ode on St. Cecilia's Day (SBar)
Coleridge-Taylor—Song of Hiawatha: Hiawatha's wedding feast (T), The death of Minnehaha (SB), Hiawatha's departure (STB)
Kodály—Missa brevis
Stravinsky—Threni (SATTBB)
Walton—Belshazzar's feast (Bar)
Tippett—The vision of Saint Augustine (Bar)
Ptaszynska—Holocaust memorial cantata (STBar)
Tavener—The whale (MzBar)
Warshauer—Sacharit (S, T/narrator)

46'-60'

Schütz—Historia der Geburt Jesu Christi (STB)
Haydn—Die sieben letzten Worte (SATB)
Mozart—Davidde penitente (SST); Mass, K.427 (SSTB or SSATB)
Cherubini—Messa solenne, G major; Requiem, C minor
Schubert—Mass no.6 (SATTB); Rosamunde (A)
Bruckner—Mass no.3, F minor (SATB)
Dubois—Les Sept Paroles du Christ (STB)
Scriabin—Symphony no.1 (MzT)
Vaughan Williams—Hodie (STB)
Holst—First choral symphony (S)

Over 60'

Handel—Messiah (orch by Mozart or Prout) (SATB)
Haydn—Die Jahreszeiten (STB or SSTBB); Die Schöpfung (STB or SSTBB)
Mozart—Mass, K.427 (Schmitt) (SMzTB)
Beethoven—Missa solemnis (SATB); Symphony no.9 (SATB)
Rossini—Stabat mater (SSTB)
Berlioz—L'Enfance du Christ (STT Bar BBB); Messe solennelle (STB)
Mendelssohn—Elijah (SSATB); Lobgesang (SST); St. Paul (SATBB)
Schumann—Manfred (SATB)
Franck—Rédemption (S)
Brahms—Ein deutsches Requiem (SBar)
Dvořák—Stabat mater (SATB)
Parker—Hora novissima (SATB)
Vaughan Williams—Symphony no.1 (SBar)

[MIXED CHORUS, *Medium orchestra*]
Honegger—Le Roi David (large orchestra version) (SAT, speaker)
Tippett—A child of our time (SATB)
Jones—The temptation of Jesus (B)

Duration uncertain

Schumann—Adventlied (SATB)

Small orchestra

10' or less

Bach—Cantatas nos.118 [2nd setting]; 141 (ATB); 145 (STB); Jesu, joy of man's desiring
Handel—Passion nach Barthold Heinrich Brockes (6S 4A 3T 5B); Zadok the priest (SSAATBB)
Gossec—Christmas suite
Mozart—Alma dei creatoris, K.277 (SAT) ; Benedictus sit deus, K.117 (S); Gloria from the Twelfth mass; Regina coeli, K.276 (SATB); Scande coeli limina, K.34 (S); Tantum ergo, K.142 (S); Tantum ergo, K.197; Veni sancte spiritus, K.47 (SATB)
Schubert—Stabat mater, D.175
Hensel—Hiob (SATB)
Mendelssohn—Hymne, op.69 (A); Verleih' uns Frieden
Fauré—Pavane
Ives—General William Booth enters into heaven; Three harvest home chorales
Webern—Das Augenlicht; Cantata no.1 (S); Lieder, op.19
Milhaud—Symphonies for small orchestra: no.6 (SATB)
Thomson, V.—Dance in praise

11'-20'

Buxtehude—Magnificat
Purcell—Ode for St. Cecilia's day (1683), Z.339 (SSATB); Ode for St. Cecilia's day (ca.1685), Z.334 (SB); Te deum and Jubilate (SSAATB)
Vivaldi—Magnificat, RV 610 (SSATB or SSAT)
Bach—Cantatas nos.4, 8, 15, 24, 26, 27, 28, 71, 77, 85, 86, 91, 96, 98, 99, 106, 112, 116, 121, 122, 124, 130, 132, 133, 137, 138, 139, 149, 150, 151, 155, 162, 163, 164, 165, 167, 168, 172 [1731 version], 173, 181, 183, 185, 188 (all with soloists SATB); nos.14, 25, 61, 73, 143, 179 (STB); nos.72, 79, 89, 129, 176 (SAB); nos.23, 144 (SAT); nos.2, 22, 33, 40, 46, 60, 67, 81, 83, 90, 108, 135, 136, 142, 153, 154, 156, 159, 166, 175, 190 (ATB); no.193 (SA); nos.59, 68, 192 (SB); no.191 (ST); nos.48, 103, 148 (AT); no.65 (TB); nos.52, 84 (S); no.55 (T); nos.56, 158 (B)
Handel—Jubilate for the Peace of Utrecht (AAB); Psalm 96 (ST)
Sammartini, Giov. Battista—Magnificat (SATB)
Pergolesi—Magnificat (SATB)
Haydn—Masses, Hob.XXII:1 (SS); Hob.XXII:7 (S)
Mozart—Dixit et Magnificat, K.193 (STB); Mass, K.258 (SATB); Missae brevis, K.49, K.65, K.140, K.220, K.259, K.275 (all with soloists SATB); Regina coeli, K.108 (S); Regina coeli, K.127 (S); Te deum laudamus, K.141
Hensel—Lobgesang (SA)
Mendelssohn—Psalm 115 (STBar)
Vaughan Williams—Flos campi; Toward the unknown region
Schoenberg—Kol nidre (speaker)
Webern—Cantata no.2 (SB)
Copland—Old American songs: First set or Second set
Finzi—In terra pax (SBar)
Lambert—Rio Grande (A)
Britten—Cantata misericordium (TB)
Bernstein—Chichester psalms (ST)
Hollingsworth—Stabat mater
Maxwell Davies—Veni sancte spiritus (SAB)

21'-30'

Charpentier—Te deum (SSATB)
Vivaldi—Gloria, RV 589 (SSA); Magnificat, RV 611 (SSATB or SSAT)
Bach—Cantatas nos.5, 6, 9, 10, 11, 13, 17, 29, 36, 37, 38, 42, 43, 44, 62, 63, 69, 70, 74, 78, 80, 88, 93, 94, 100, 101, 105, 110, 111, 113, 114, 115, 119, 120, 147, 171, 172 [1724 version], 180, 188, 214 (all with soloists SATB); nos.177, 184 (SAT); nos.39, 64, 187 (SAB); nos.1, 18, 19, 31, 95, 107, 127, 140, 211 (STB); nos.7, 12, 16, 34, 45, 87, 102, 117, 123, 125, 126, 128, 174, 178, 182 (ATB); nos.32, 47, 57, 195 (SB); nos.109, 134, 161 (AT); nos.104, 131, 157 (TB); no.169 (A); Magnificat (SSATB); Mass, BWV 233, F major (SAB)
Handel—Psalm 89 (STB)
Haydn—Mass, Hob.XXII:6 (SATB)

[MIXED CHORUS, *Small orchestra*]
Mozart—Litaniae lauretanae, K.195
(SATB); Masses, K.257, 262, 317,
337 (all with soloists SATB); Vesper-
ae solennes de confessor (SATB);
Masses nos.3 (SATB), 4 (SATB)
Stravinsky—Les Noces (SATB)
Mennin—The Christmas story (ST)
Martino—The white island

31'-45'

Purcell—Ode for St. Cecilia's day
(1692), Z.328 (SAATBB)
Schütz—Historia der Auferstehung
Jesu Christi (SSAATTBB)
Vivaldi—Gloria, RV 589 (Casella)
(SSA)
Vivaldi—Introduction & Gloria, RV
639 & 588 (SSAT)
Bach—Cantatas nos.3, 21, 30, 41,
75, 76, 92, 97, 146, 186, 198, 205,
206, 207, 207a, 213 (all with solo-
ists SATB); no.208 (SSTB); no.197
(SAB); no.194 (STB); nos.20, 66
(ATB); Masses, BWV 234 (SAB), BWV
235, (ATB), BWV 236 (SATB)
Handel—Dettingen Te deum (B)
Bach, C.P.E.—Magnificat
Haydn—Mass, Hob.XXII:4, 8, 9, 11,
12 (all with soloists SATB); Mass,
Hob.XXII:10 (SATB or SSATBB)
Haydn, M.—Missa pro defunctis
(SATB); Missa Sancti Hieronymi
Mozart—Litaniae de venerabili altaris
sacramento, K.125 (SATB); Masses,
K.139, K.167; Requiem, K.626
(Maunder) (SATB); Vesperae de dom-
inica, K.321 (SATB)
Nunés-Garcia—Requiem
Bruckner—Requiem (SATB)
Dvorák—Mass, op.86 (SATB)
Fauré—Requiem (SBar)
Duruflé—Requiem (MzBar)
Hovhaness—Magnificat, op.157 (STB)
Schnittke—Symphony no.4 (chorus *or*
solos SATB)

46'-60'

Purcell—Ode for St. Cecilia's day
(1692), Z.328 (SAATBB)
Bach—Cantata no.201 (SATTBB);
Easter oratorio (SATB)
Handel—The choice of Hercules
(SSAT); Ode for St. Cecilia's Day (ST)
Scarlatti, D.—Serenata (SATB)
Haydn—Mass, Hob.XXII:13, 14 (each
SATB or SSATTB)
Kraus—Der Tod Jesu (SAB)
Mozart—Requiem, K.626 (Süssmayr

or Beyer) (SATB)
Britten—Saint Nicolas, op.42 (T)

Over 60'

Monteverdi—Vespro della beata ver-
gine (SSATTBB)
Bach—Johannespassion (SATBB);
Mass, BWV 232, B minor (SSATB);
Weihnachtsoratorium (SATB)
Handel—Alexander's feast (STB); L'Al-
legro, il penseroso ed il moderato
(SATB); Belshazzar (SAATTBB);
Joshua (SSATB); Judas Maccabaeus
(SSATBB); Messiah (SATB); Samson
(SATBB); Saul (2S A 5T 4B); Solo-
mon (SSSSATB)
Haydn—Mass, Hob.XXII:5 (SATB);
Stabat mater, Hob.XXbis (SATB)
Honegger—Le Roi David (original ver-
sion) (SAT, speaker)

Duration uncertain

Bach, W.F.—Ehre sei Gott in der
Höhe (SATB)
Haydn, M.—Veni, sancte spiritus
Cherubini—Mass no.4 (SSSSTTBB)
Schubert—Magnificat, D.486 (SATB)
Bruckner—Mass, C major (1841)

String orchestra

15' or less

Buxtehude—Magnificat
Purcell—Ode for St. Cecilia's day
(1683), Z.339 (SSATB); Ode for St.
Cecilia's day (ca.1685), Z.334 (SB)
Monteverdi—Laudate dominum
(Psalm 117) (SSTTB)
Vivaldi—Magnificat (Robbins Landon)
(SSATB)
Pergolesi—Magnificat (SATB)
Haydn—Masses, Hob.XXII:1 (SS),
Hob.XXII:3, Hob.XXII:7 (S)
Mozart—Ave verum corpus; Inter na-
tos mulierum, K.72; Litaniae laure-
tanae, K.109; Misericordias domini,
K.222; Missa brevis, K.140 (SATB);
Sancta Maria, K.273
Donizetti—Ave Maria (S)
Finzi—In terra pax (SBar)

16'-30'

Vivaldi—Magnificat (Malipiero) (SSAT)
Bach—Cantatas nos.4 (SATB), 153
(ATB), 196 (STB)

[MIXED CHORUS, *String orchestra*]
Mozart—Missae brevis, K.49, K.192,
K.194, K.275 (all with soloists SATB)
Schubert—Masses nos.2 (STB), 4
(SATB)

Over 30'

Schütz—Historia der Auferstehung
Jesu Christi (SSAATTBB)
Handel—Dixit dominus (SSATB)
Saint-Saëns—Oratorio de Noël
(SAATB)

Duration uncertain

Buxtehude—Das neugebor'ne Kindelein

Without strings

Bach—Cantata no.118 [1st setting]
Bruckner—Mass no.2, E minor
Respighi—Lauda per la natività del
Signore (SSAT)
Stravinsky—Mass (SATTB); Les Noces
(SATB)
Varèse—Ecuatorial
Dallapiccola—Canti di prigionia
Bernstein—Chichester psalms
(reduced version) (ST)
Schnittke—Requiem (SSSAT)

FEMALE CHORUS

Mendelssohn—Midsummernight's
dream (SS)
Liszt—Dante symphony
Cornelius—Mass, D minor (CWV 91)
(SSA)
Saint-Saëns—La Nuit (S)
Elgar—The apostles (SATBBB)
Mahler—Symphony no.3 (A)
Debussy—La Damoiselle élue (Mz);
Nocturnes
Busoni—Turandot: Suite
Vaughan Williams—Magnificat (A);
Symphony no.7 (S)
Holst—The planets
Bartók—Three village scenes
Messiaen—Trois Petites Liturgies de
la présence divine
Maxwell Davies—Caroline Mathilde:
Suite from Act II (SA)
Chin—Die Troerinnen (SSM)

MALE CHORUS

Mozart—Laut verkünde unsre Freude,
K.623 (TTB); Die Maurerfreude,
K.471 (T)
Cherubini—Requiem, D minor
Liszt—A Faust symphony (T)
Wagner—Lohengrin: Elsa's procession
to the cathedral
Bruckner—Helgoland
Strauss, Joh., Jr.—An der schönen
blauen Donau
Brahms—Alto rhapsody (A); Rinaldo
(T)
Grieg—Landsighting (Bar)
Busoni—Concerto, piano, op.39
Schoenberg—Survivor from Warsaw
(male narrator)
Stravinsky—Babel (male narrator);
Oedipus rex (ATBB, speaker)
Varèse—Ecuatorial; Nocturnal (S)
Weill—Das Berliner Requiem (TBar)
Danielpour—Journey without dis-
tance (S)

CHILDREN'S CHORUS

Bach—Matthäuspassion (SATBB)
Berlioz—La Damnation de Faust (Mz
T Bar B); Te deum (T)
Liszt—Dante symphony
Wagner—Lohengrin: Elsa's procession
to the cathedral
Tchaikovsky—Nutcracker
Elgar—The apostles (SATBBB)
Mahler—Symphony no.3 (A); Sympho-
ny no.8 (SSSAATBB)
Ingelbrecht—Rapsodie de printemps
Kodály—Psalmus hungaricus
Stravinsky—Persephone (T, female
narrator)
Prokofiev—Ivan the terrible (ABar)
Honegger—Jeanne d'Arc au bûcher
(SSSATB & 4 spoken roles)
Orff—Carmina burana (STB)
Shostakovich—Song of the forests
(TB)
Britten—Spring symphony (SAT); War
requiem, op.6 (STB)
Bernstein—Symphony no.3 (Kaddish)
(S)
Martino—Paradiso choruses (3S 4Mz
3T 2Bar)
Penderecki—Passio et mors domini
nostri Iesu Christi secundum Lucam
(SBB)
Maxwell Davies—The turn of the tide
Jones—The temptation of Jesus
Svoboda—Child's dream
Tavener—Celtic requiem (SAATTBB)

APPENDIX B: SOLO VOICES

Soprano

Alto or Mezzo-soprano

Tenor

Baritone or Bass

Several solo voices
    2 solo voices
    3 solo voices
    4 solo voices (SATB)
    4 or more solo voices (not SATB)

Speaker (Narrator)

Works within the larger categories are subdivided by duration. Within each category or subdivision, works are listed in chronological order according to the composer's birth date.

For complete information on any of these works, refer back to the main alphabetical listing by composer.

SOPRANO

10' or less

Mozart—A questo seno—Or che il cielo; Ah se in ciel, benigne stelle; Alcandro, lo confesso—Non so d'onde viene; Alma grande e nobil core; Basta, vincesti—Ah non lasciarmi; Bella mia fiamma—Resta, oh cara; Ch'io mi scordi di te—Non temer; Chi sà, chi sà, qual sia; Ergo interest—Quaere superna; Kommet her, ihr frechen Sünder ; Ma che vi fece—Sperai vicino il lido; Mia speranza—Ah, non sai; Misera, dove son—Ah, non son io che parlo; Nehmt meinen Dank; No, no, che non sei capace; Vado, ma dove, o dei; Voi avete un cor fedele; Vorrei spiegarvi, oh Dio
Schubert—Salve regina, D.223
Wagner—Wesendonck Lieder (each individual song less than 10')

Strauss, R.—Cäcilie; Morgen
Sibelius—Luonnotar (Kalevala)
Rachmaninoff—Vocalise (arr. Braden)
Varèse—Offrandes
Webern—Geistliche Lieder, op.15; Lieder, op.13; Lieder, op.14
Villa-Lobos—Bachianas brasileiras no.5
Rodrigo—Cuatro madrigales amatorios

11'-20'

Scarlatti, A.—Christmas cantata
Bach—Cantata nos.51, 52, 84
Mozart—Ah, lo previdi—Ah, t'invola—Deh, non varcar; Ch'io mi scordi di te—Non temer; Exsultate jubilate; Popoli di Tessagua—Io non chiedo, eterni dei
Beethoven—Ah, perfido
Schubert—Mirjams Siegesgesang; Salve Regina, D.676
Wagner—Götterdämmerung: Immo-

[SOPRANO; *11'-20'*]
lation scene; Tristan und Isolde:
Prelude and Liebestod
Glière—Concerto, coloratura soprano
Ravel—Shéhérazade
Berg—Altenberg Lieder; Sieben frühe
Lieder; Der Wein; Wozzeck: Three
excerpts
Gerhard—Cancionero de Pedrell
Carter—A mirror on which to dwell
Barber—Andromache's farewell;
Knoxville: summer of 1915
La Montaine—Songs of the rose of
Sharon
Del Tredici—An Alice symphony:
Illustrated Alice, The lobster
quadrille
Albert—Flower of the mountain
Knussen—Where the wild things are:
Songs and a Sea-interlude
Tan—On Taoism

21'-30'

Bach—Cantatas nos.199; 202; 204;
209
Berlioz—Cléopâtre
Wagner—Wesendonck Lieder
(complete)
Chausson—Poème de l'amour et de la
mer
Mahler—Sieben Lieder aus letzten
Zeit
Strauss, R.—Sechs Lieder, op.68;
Three hymns, op.71; Vier letzte
Lieder
Schoenberg—Six songs, op.8
Finzi—Dies natalis
Tippett—Byzantium
Britten—Les Illuminations
Foss—Time cycle
Druckman—Lamia
Baker—Le Chat qui pêche
Rands—Canti lunatici
Moore, Carman—Gospel fuse
Del Tredici—An Alice symphony: In
Wonderland; Pop-pourri; Syzygy;
Vintage Alice
Andriessen—Dances
Svoboda—Concerto for chamber
orchestra
Pasatieri—Sieben Lehmannlieder

Over 30'

Bach—Cantata no.210
Beethoven—Egmont
Mahler—Lieder aus "Des Knaben
Wunderhorn"; Symphony no.4
Vaughan Williams—Symphony no.3

Turina—Canto a Sevilla
Berg—Lulu: Suite
Sessions—Idyll of Theocritus
Foss—Song of songs
Del Tredici—An Alice symphony;
Child Alice: In memory of a summer
day; Final Alice

ALTO OR MEZZO-SOPRANO

10' or less

Bach—Cantatas nos.53, 200
Mozart—Ombra felice—Io ti lascio
Mendelssohn—Hymne, op.96
Wolf—Spanisches Liederbuch: Two
sacred songs
Strauss, R.—Morgen
Ives—Charlie Rutlage; General
William Booth enters into heaven
Stravinsky—Le Faune et la Bergère;
Pribaoutki
Webern—Lieder, op.8

11'-20'

Vivaldi—Stabat mater
Bach—Cantata no.54
Brahms—Alto rhapsody
Mussorgsky—Songs and dances of
death
Mahler—Lieder eines fahrenden
Gesellen
Debussy—La Damoiselle élue
Granados—Dante
Ravel—Trois Poèmes de Mallarmé
Respighi—Il tramonto
Rogers—Three Japanese dances
Copland—Old American songs: 1st or
2nd set
Britten—Phaedra
Argento—Casa Guidi
Adams, Leslie—Three Dunbar songs
Schafer—Adieu Robert Schumann
Maxwell Davies—Stone litany
Tan—On Taoism

21'-30'

Bach—Cantatas nos.35, 169, 170
Chausson—Poème de l'amour et de la
mer
Elgar—Sea pictures
Mahler—Kindertotenlieder; Sieben
Lieder aus letzten Zeit
Falla—El amor brujo: Ballet suite
Gruenberg—The creation
Copland—Eight poems of Emily
Dickinson

[ALTO OR MEZZO-SOPRANO; *21'-30'*]
Fortner—The creation
Bernstein—Symphony no.1
Adler—Symphony no.5
Druckman—Dark upon the harp
Schafer—The garden of the heart
Wernick—Visions of terror and
   wonder
Larsen—Mary Cassatt; seven songs

Over 30'

Berlioz—Les Nuits d'été
Mahler—Lieder aus Des Knaben
   Wunderhorn
Foss—Song of songs
Boulez—Le Marteau sans maître

TENOR

10' or less

Mozart—Clarice cara mia sposa; Con
   ossequio, con rispetto; Die Maurer-
   freude; Misero, o sogno—Aura, che
   intorno spiri; Per pietà, non ricer-
   cate; Se al labbro mio non credi; Si
   mostra la sorte
Schubert—Salve Regina, D.106
Borodin—La mer
Strauss, R.—Cäcilie; Morgen
Stravinsky—In memoriam Dylan
   Thomas
Webern—Geistliche Lieder, op.15;
   Lieder, op.14
Britten—Now sleeps the crimson petal

11'-20'

Bach—Cantatas nos.55, 160, 189
Mozart—Se al labbro mio non credi
Fauré—Shylock
Busoni—Rondo arlecchinesco
Berg—Sieben frühe Lieder
Gerhard—Cancionero de Pedrell
Tan—On Taoism

21'-30'

Chausson—Poème de l'amour et de la
   mer
Mahler—Sieben Lieder aus letzten
   Zeit
Strauss, R.—Sechs Lieder, op.68;
   Three hymns, op.71
Finzi—Dies natalis
Tippett—Songs for Dov
Britten—Gloriana: Symphonic suite;

Les Illuminations; Nocturne;
   Serenade for tenor, horn & strings
London—Peter Quince at the clavier
Rands—Canti del sole

Over 30'

Berlioz—Les Nuits d'été
Brahms—Rinaldo
Mahler—Lieder aus Des Knaben
   Wunderhorn
Vaughan Williams—Symphony no.3
Britten—Saint Nicolas, op.42
Maxwell Davies—Into the labyrinth

BARITONE OR BASS

10' or less

Mozart—Alcandro, lo confesso—Non
   so d'onde viene; Un bacio di mano;
   Così dunque—Aspri rimorsi atroci;
   Io ti lascio; Mentre ti lascio, o figlia;
   Per questa bella mano; Rivolgete a
   lui lo sguardo
Strauss, R.—Morgen
Ives—Charlie Rutlage; General
   William Booth enters into heaven
Ravel—Don Quichotte à Dulcinée
Stravinsky—Pribaoutki; Two songs by
   Paul Verlaine
Webern—Lieder, op.8

11'-20'

Bach—Cantatas nos.56, 158, 203
Wagner—Walküre: Wotan's farewell &
   Magic fire music
Mussorgsky—Songs and dances of
   death
Mahler—Lieder eines fahrenden
   Gesellen
Ravel—Trois Poèmes de Mallarmé
Stravinsky—Abraham and Isaac
Prokofiev—Lieutenant Kijé: Suite
Copland—Old American songs: 1st or
   2nd set
Foss—Song of anguish
Adams, Leslie—Three Dunbar songs
Rodríguez—Scrooge
Adams, John—The wound-dresser
Tan—On Taoism

21'-30'

Bach—Cantata no.82
Cimarosa—Il maestro di cappella
Chausson—Poème de l'amour et de la
   mer

[BARITONE OR BASS; *21'-30'*]
Mahler—Kindertotenlieder; Sieben
  Lieder aus letzten Zeit
Schoenberg—Serenade, op.24
Gruenberg—The creation
Copland—Eight poems of Emily
  Dickinson
Fortner—The creation
Schafer—The garden of the heart
Gruber—Frankenstein!!
Tan—Orchestral theatre II: Re

Over 30'

Berlioz—Les Nuits d'été
Mahler—Lieder aus Des Knaben
  Wunderhorn
Weber, Ben—Symphony on poems of
  William Blake

SEVERAL SOLO VOICES

2 solo voices

Bach—Cantatas nos.32, 49, 57, 58,
  59, 152, 212 (all with soloists SB);
  Cantata no.157 (TB)
Pergolesi—Stabat mater (SA)
Mozart—Nun liebes Weibchen, ziehst
  mit mir (SB)
Tchaikovsky—Romeo and Juliet
  (duet), op.posth. (ST)
Mahler—Das Lied von der Erde (AT,
  or TBar)
Nielsen—Symphony no.3 (SBar)
Zemlinsky—Lyrische Symphonie
  (SBar); Six songs, op.13 (MzBar)
Shostakovich—Symphony no.14 (SB)
Bernstein—Arias and barcaroles
  (MzBar)
Nono—Canti di vita e d'amore (ST)
Maxwell Davies—Black Pentecost
  (MzBar); Caroline Mathilde: Suite
  from Act II
Del Tredici—Pop-pourri (SMz, or S &
  countertenor)
Andriessen—Mausoleum (2Bar)
Tavener—Akhmatova requiem (SB)

3 solo voices

Monteverdi—Combattimento di
  Tancredi e Clorinda (SAT)
Purcell—Ode for St. Cecilia's day
  (1683), Z.329 (ATB)
Bach—Cantatas nos. 60, 81, 83, 87,
  90, 153, 154, 156, 159, 166, 174,
  175 (all with ATB); 89 (SAB); 211
  (STB)

Mozart—Mandina amabile, (STB)
Berlioz—Nuits d'été (MzTBar)
Debussy—L'Enfant prodigue (STBar)
Varèse—Ecuatorial (3 or more basses)

4 solo voices (SATB)

Bach—Cantatas nos.15, 42, 85, 86,
  88, 132, 151, 155, 162, 163, 164,
  165, 167, 168, 183, 185, 188
Milhaud—Symphonies for small
  orchestra: no.6
Schnittke—Symphony no.4

4 or more solo voices (not SATB)

Mozart—Dite almeno in che mancai
  (STBB)
Vaughan Williams—Serenade to
  music (4S 4A 4T 4B)
Martin—Le Vin herbé (3S 3A 3T 3B)
Bernstein—Songfest (SMzATBarB)
Berio—Sinfonia (SSAATTBB)
Moore, Carman—Gospel fuse (SSAA)
Andriessen—De staat (4 female
  voices)

SPEAKER (NARRATOR)

15' or less

Schoenberg—A survivor from
  Warsaw, op.46
Stravinsky—Babel
Copland—Lincoln portrait
Walton—Façade 2
Kleinsinger—Tubby the tuba
Kubik—Gerald McBoing Boing
Kirk—An orchestra primer
Foss—Elegy for Anne Frank
Hollingsworth—Three ladies beside
  the sea
Schickele—A zoo called Earth (taped
  narration)
Kolb—Chromatic fantasy
Proto—Casey at the bat
Bamert—Circus parade
Peck—Playing with style
Peck—The thrill of the orchestra
Tan—On Taoism

16'-30'

Saint-Saëns—Le Carnaval des
  animaux
Schoenberg—Kol nidre; Ode to
  Napoleon Bonaparte
Stravinsky—A sermon, a narrative,

[SPEAKER OR NARRATOR; *16'-30'*]
and a prayer
Prokofiev—Peter and the wolf
Rogers—The musicians of Bremen
Harsányi—L'Histoire du petite tailleur
Poulenc—The story of Babar, the little elephant
Britten—Young person's guide to the orchestra
Gould—The jogger and the dinosaur (rapper)
Pinkham—Signs of the zodiac
Laderman—Magic prison (2 narrators: 1 female, 1 male)
Lees—The trumpet of the swan
Schuller—Journey into jazz
Lombardo—Drakestail
Schickele—The chenoo who stayed to dinner
Armer—The great instrument of the Geggerets
Schwantner—New morning for the world

Kechley—Alexander and the wind-up mouse
Tann—Adirondack light
Smith, G.—Mr. Smith's composition

Over 30'

Berlioz—Lelio
Debussy—Le Martyre de Saint Sébastien
Schoenberg—Gurre-Lieder; Pierrot Lunaire
Stravinsky—Oedipus rex; Persephone
Prokofiev—Ivan the terrible
Honegger—Jeanne d'Arc au bûcher (4 spoken roles: 1 female, 3 male); Le Roi David
Walton—Façade
Bernstein—Symphony no.3 (Kaddish)
Bach, Jan—The happy prince
Bamert—Once upon an orchestra
Warshauer—Shacharit

APPENDIX C: SOLO INSTRUMENTS

Piano
Piano (left hand)
2 or more pianos
Harpsichord
2 or more harpsichords
Organ
Multiple diverse keyboards

Violin
2 or more violins
Viola
Violoncello
Double bass
Multiple diverse strings
  2 solo strings
  2 violins & violoncello
  Solo string quartet
  Other combinations

Flute
2 flutes
Recorder
Piccolo
Alto flute
Oboe

English horn
Clarinet
Bassoon
Saxophone

Horn
2 or more horns
Trumpet
2 trumpets
Trombone
Tuba

Percussion
Harp
Guitar
2 or more guitars
Mandolin
Several diverse instruments
  2 soloists
  3 soloists
  4 soloists
  5 soloists
  6 or more soloists

Jazz soloists

Works within the larger categories are subdivided by duration. Within each category or subdivision, works are listed in chronological order according to the composer's birth date.

For complete information on any of these works, refer back to the main alphabetical listing by composer.

PIANO

10' or less

Mozart—Concertos, piano, K.107
  (21b) nos.2 & 3; Concert-rondo,
  K.382
Weber, C.M.—Polonaise brillante
Mendelssohn—Rondo brillant
Chopin—Grande Polonaise, op.22
Gottschalk—Grande Tarantelle
Saint-Saëns—Allegro appassionato,
  op.70; Rhapsodie d'Auvergne
Stravinsky—Movements
Turina—Rapsodia sinfónica

Gershwin—"I got rhythm" variations
Ellington—New world a-comin'
Addinsell—Warsaw concerto
Françaix—Concertino, piano
Foss—Elegy for Anne Frank

11'-20'

Haydn—Concerto, harpsichord (or
  piano), Hob.XVIII:5
Mozart—Concertos, piano, nos.1-4,
  6, 8
Weber, C.M.—Concerto, piano, no.1;
  Konzertstück, op.79

[PIANO; *11'-20'*]

Mendelssohn—Capriccio brillant
Chopin—Concert-allegro, op.46; Fantasy on Polish airs; Krakowiak, op.14; Variations on "La ci darem la mano"
Schumann—Concert-allegro with introduction, op.134; Introduction & Allegro appassionato, op.92
Liszt—Concerto, piano, no.1; Concerto pathétique; Hungarian fantasy; Malédiction; Rhapsodie espagnole; Totentanz
Franck—Les Djinns; Symphonic variations
Saint-Saëns—Africa, op.89
Tchaikovsky—Concerto, piano, no.3
Rimsky-Korsakov—Concerto, piano, op.30, C-sharp minor
Fauré—Ballade; Fantasy
Albéniz—Rapsodia española
Strauss, R.—Burleske
Roussel—Concerto, piano, op.36
Respighi—Fantasia slava
Bartók—Rhapsody, piano and orchestra, op.1
Stravinsky—Capriccio; Concerto for piano & wind instruments
Becker—Concerto arabesque
Martinu—Fantasia concertante
Prokofiev—Concerto, piano, no.1
Honegger—Concertino
Milhaud—Le Carnaval d'Aix; Concertos, piano, nos.1, 3; Suite concertante
Benjamin—Concertino
Piston—Concertino
Hindemith—Concerto, piano, op.36, no.1 (Kammermusik no.2)
Gershwin—Rhapsody in blue; Second rhapsody
Poulenc—Concerto, piano
Copland—Concerto, piano
Kabalevsky—Concerto, piano, no.3
Lambert—Rio Grande
Tippett—Fantasia on a theme of Handel
Shostakovich—Concerto, piano, no.2
Messiaen—Couleurs de la Cité céleste; Oiseaux exotiques
Gould—Interplay
Panufnik—Concerto, piano
Perle—Concerto, piano, no.2
Babbitt—Concerto, piano
La Montaine—Birds of paradise
Chou—Pien
Hollingsworth—Concerto, piano
Takemitsu—Riverrun
Pärt—Credo
Bolcom—Orphée-sérénade
Svoboda—Concerto, piano, no.1

21'-30'

Mozart—Concertos, piano, nos.5, 11-21, 23, 25-26
Beethoven—Concerto, piano, no.2
Kuhlau—Concerto, piano, op.7
Weber, C.M.—Concerto, piano, no.2
Schubert—Wanderer fantasy, D.760
Mendelssohn—Concertos, piano, nos.1, 2
Liszt—Concerto, piano, no.2
Schumann, Clara—Concerto, piano, op.7, A minor
Lalo—Concerto, piano, F minor
Rubinstein—Concerto, piano, no.4
Saint-Saëns—Concertos, piano, nos.1-5
Tchaikovsky—Concerto, piano, no.2 (Siloti version)
Massenet—Concerto, piano
Grieg—Concerto, piano, op.16
Indy—Symphonie sur un chant montagnard français, op.25
Albéniz—Concerto, piano, no.1
MacDowell—Concertos, piano, nos.1, 2
Debussy—Fantasie
Delius—Concerto, piano, C minor
Busoni—Indianische Fantasie
Scriabin—Concerto, piano, op.20; Prométhée, le poème du feu
Vaughan Williams—Concerto, 1 piano or 2 pianos
Rachmaninoff—Concertos, piano, nos.1, 4; Rhapsody on a theme of Paganini
Schoenberg—Concerto, piano, op.42
Hahn—Concerto, piano, E major
Ravel—Concerto, piano, G major
Falla—Noches en los jardines de España
Dohnányi—Variations on a nursery song, op.25
Bloch, E.—Concerto grosso no.1
Bartók—Concertos, piano, nos.1-3; Scherzo, op.2
Villa-Lobos—Bachianas brasileiras no.3; Mômoprecóce
Prokofiev—Concertos, piano, nos.3, 5
Hindemith—Theme and variations ("The four temperaments")
Gerhard—Concerto, piano
Poulenc—Aubade; Concerto champêtre (harpsichord or piano)
Badings—Concerto, piano (1940)
Carter—Concerto, piano
Barber—Concerto, piano, op.38
Britten—Diversions on a theme, op.21
Ginastera—Concerto, piano, no.1
La Montaine—Concerto, piano, op.9
Lees—Concerto, piano, no.2

[PIANO; *21'-30'*]

Russo—Street music; a blues concerto (piano & harmonica; may be same player)
Schurmann—Concerto, piano
Martino—Concerto, piano
Schnittke—Concerto, piano & strings
Wuorinen—Concerto, piano, no.3
Kolb—Voyants
Schwantner—Concerto, piano
Höller—Pensées
Davis—Wayang no.5
Danielpour—Metamorphosis
Horne—Concerto, piano

Over 30'

Viotti—Concerto, piano, G minor
Mozart—Concertos, piano, nos.9, 22, 24, 27
Beethoven—Concertos, piano, nos.1, 3-6
Chopin—Concertos, piano, nos.1, 2
Schumann—Concerto, piano, op.54
Litolff—Concerto symphonique, no.4
Rubinstein—Concerto, piano, no.3
Brahms—Concertos, piano, nos.1, 2
Tchaikovsky—Concertos, piano, nos.1, 2 (original version); Fantasie de concert
Dvořák—Concerto, piano, op.33
Paderewski—Concerto, piano, op.17
Busoni—Concerto, piano, op.39
Rachmaninoff—Concertos, piano, nos.2, 3
Dohnányi—Concerto, piano, no.1
Prokofiev—Concerto, piano, no.2
Gershwin—Concerto, piano, F major
Chávez—Concerto, piano
Khachaturian—Concerto, piano
Tippett—Concerto, piano
Menotti—Concerto, piano
Britten—Concerto, piano, no.1, op.13
Bernstein—Symphony no.2
Henze—Concerto, piano, no.2; Requiem (neun geistliche Konzerte)
Svoboda—Concerto, piano, no.2; Three cadenzas for piano & orchestra, op.135

PIANO (LEFT HAND)

Ravel—Concerto, piano (left hand), D major
Prokofiev—Concerto, piano, no.4 (left hand)
Rorem—Concerto, piano (1969); Concerto, piano (left hand)

2 OR MORE PIANOS

Mozart—Concerto, 3 pianos, no.7, K.242 (a version for 2 pianos also exists); Concerto, 2 pianos, no.10, K.365
Mendelssohn—Concertos, 2 pianos, A-flat major & E major
Saint-Saëns—Le Carnaval des animaux (2 pianos)
Vaughan Williams—Concerto, 1 piano or 2 pianos
Bartók—Concerto, 2 pianos & percussion
Villa-Lobos—Chôros no.8 (2 pianos)
Poulenc—Concerto, 2 pianos, D minor
Bowles—Concerto, 2 pianos (versions for percussion & winds, and for full orchestra)
Britten—Scottish ballade (2 pianos)
Berio—Concerto, 2 pianos

HARPSICHORD

15' or less

Bach—Concertos, harpsichord, nos.4, 5, 7
Galuppi—Concerto, harpsichord, F major
Haydn—Concertino, harpsichord, Hob.XIV:11; Concertos, harpsichord, Hob.XVIII:5; Hob.XVIII:7; Hob.XVIII:F1
Bach, J.C.—Concerto, harpsichord, op.13, no.2
Dittersdorf—Concerto, harpsichord, B-flat major
Falla—Concerto, harpsichord, D major

Over 15'

Bach—Concertos, harpsichord, nos.1, 2, 3, 6
Bach, C.P.E.—Concerto, harpsichord, H.427 (W.23), D minor
Wagenseil—Concerto, harpsichord, D major
Haydn—Concertos, harpsichord, Hob.XVIII:4, Hob.XVIII:11
Bach, J.C.—Concertos, harpsichord, op.7, no.5; op.13, no.4; Concerto, harpsichord, E-flat major
Poulenc—Concerto champêtre, harpsichord (or piano)

2 OR MORE HARPSICHORDS

Bach—Concertos, 2 harpsichords, nos.1-3; Concertos, 3 harpsichords, nos.1-2; Concerto, 4 harpsichords, BWV 1065

ORGAN

15' or less

Handel—Concertos, organ, op.4, nos.2, 3, 5, 6; op.7, nos.1, 5, 6
Haydn—Concerto, organ, no.2; Concerto, organ, F major
Mozart—Sonatas, organ & orchestra, nos.1-17
Barber—Toccata festiva, op.36

Over 15'

Handel—Concertos, organ, op.4, nos.1, 4; op.7, nos.2-4
Haydn—Concerto, organ, Hob.XVIII:1, C major
Saint-Saëns—Symphony no.3
Rheinberger—Concertos, organ, nos.1-2
Hindemith—Concerto, organ, op.46, no.2 (Kammermusik no.7); Concerto, organ (1962)
Sowerby—Medieval poem
Poulenc—Concerto, organ, G minor
Copland—Symphony for organ and orchestra
Rorem—Concerto, organ
Svoboda—Symphony no.3, organ & orchestra

MULTIPLE DIVERSE KEYBOARDS

Carter—Double concerto, harpsichord & piano
Messiaen—Trois Petites Liturgies; Turangalîla-symphonie (both with-piano & ondes martenot)

VIOLIN

10' or less

Torelli—Concerto, violin, op.8, no.8
Vivaldi—Concerto, violin, op.8, nos.5-8, 10, 12; Le quattro staggioni (Four seasons), nos.2 (Summer), 3 (Autumn), 4 (Winter)

Telemann—Concerto, violin, A minor
Veracini—Concerto, violin, D major
Mozart—Adagio, K.261; Rondos, K.269, K.373
Beethoven—Romances nos.1, 2
Paganini—Moto perpetuo, op.11
Schubert—Konzertstück, D.345
Chopin—Romanze
Wagner—Wesendonck Lieder: no.5, Träume
Borodin—Nocturne (arr. Rimsky-Korsakov)
Saint-Saëns—Concerto, violin, no.1; Introduction and Rondo capriccioso; Romance, op.37
Wieniawski—Legend, op.17; Polonaise brillante nos.1-2; Scherzo-tarantelle
Bruch—Adagio appassionato, op.57
Tchaikovsky—Sérénade mélancolique, op.26; Souvenir d'un lieu cher, nos.2-3
Dvořák—Romance, op.11
Massenet—Thaïs: Méditation
Sarasate—Introduction and tarantella; Zigeunerweisen, op.20
Strauss, R.—Morgen, op.27, no.4
Sibelius—Humoresques I & II
Ravel—Tzigane
Bartók—Rhapsody no.1, violin & orchestra
Milhaud—Concertino de printemps
Hindemith—Trauermusik
Cowell—Fiddler's jig
Finzi—Introit, op.6
Daugherty—Metropolis symphony: no.1, Lex

11'-20'

Torelli—Concerto, violin, op.8, no.9
Vitali—Ciaccona
Albinoni—Concerto, op.9, no.10
Vivaldi—Concerto, violin, op.8, no.11, RV 210; Le quattro staggioni: no.1 (Spring)
Bach—Concertos, violin, nos.1-2
Veracini—Concerto grande da chiesa
Tartini—Concerto, violin, no.57; Sinfonia pastorale
Leclair—Concertos, violin, op.7, nos.4-5
Sammartini, Giov. Battista—Concerto, violin (or violoncello piccolo)
Pergolesi—Concerto, violin, B-flat major
Haydn—Concerto, violin, Hob.VIIa:1
Saint-Georges—Concerto, violin, no.1
Paganini—Concerto, violin, no.1, op.6 (arr. Wilhelmj)
Spohr—Concerto, violin, no.8, op.47
Schubert—Rondo, D.438
Berlioz—Rêverie et Caprice, op.8

[VIOLIN; *11'-20'*]

Schumann, R.—Fantasia, op.131
Vieuxtemps—Concerto, violin, no.5
Saint-Saëns—Concerto, violin, no.2;
  Havanaise, op.83
Tchaikovsky—Souvenir d'un lieu
  cher, no.1 (11'); complete (20'); Val-
  se-scherzo, op.34
Rimsky-Korsakov—Fantaisie de con-
  cert sur les thèmes russes
Sarasate—Carmen fantasie
Chausson—Poème, op.25
Ysaÿe—Chant d'hiver, op.15
Vaughan Williams—Concerto, violin,
  D minor; The lark ascending
Bloch, E.—Baal Shem; Suite hé-
  braïque
Bartók—Deux portraits, op.5; Rhap-
  sody no.2, violin & orchestra
Wellesz—Suite, op.38
Rubbra—Improvisation, op.89
Kabalevsky—Concerto, violin, op.48
Khrennikov—Concerto, violin, op.14
Hollingsworth—Concerto, violin
Maxwell Davies—A spell for green
  corn
Schnittke—Quasi una sonata
Schwertsik—Concerto, violin, op.31
Bolcom—Concerto-serenade
Svoboda—Concerto, violin, op.77

21'-30'

Haydn—Concertos, violin, Hob.VIIa:4,
  Hob.VIIa:B2
Haydn, M.—Concerto, violin, A major
Boccherini—Concerto, violin, G.486
Viotti—Concerto, violin, no.22
Mozart—Concertos, violin, nos.1-4,
  6-7
Spohr—Concerto, violin, no.9
Mendelssohn—Concerto, violin,
  op.64; Concerto, violin (posth.)
Vieuxtemps—Concerto, violin, no.4
Lalo—Concerto, violin, op.20
Saint-Saëns—Concerto, violin, no.3
Wieniawski—Concertos, violin, no.1-2
Bruch—Concertos, violin, nos.1-2;
  Scottish fantasy
Delius—Concerto, violin
Glazunov—Concerto, violin, op.82
Bartók—Concerto, violin, no.1
Stravinsky—Concerto, violin, D major
Szymanowski—Concerto, violin, no.1
Berg—Concerto, violin
Martinu—Concerto, violin
Prokofiev—Concertos, violin, nos.1-2
Milhaud—Concerto, violin, no.2
Hindemith—Concerto, violin, op.36,
  no.3 (Kammermusik no.4); Concerto,
  violin (1939)
Sessions—Concerto, violin

Korngold—Concerto, violin, op.35
Goldschmidt—Concerto, violin
Khachaturian—Concerto-rhapsody
Carter—Concerto, violin
Barber—Concerto, violin, op.14
Menotti—Concerto, violin
Diamond—Concerto, violin, no.3
Rorem—Concerto, violin
Lees—Concerto, violin
Henze—Concerto, violin, no.2
Maxwell Davies—Concerto, violin
Bennett, Richard R.—Concerto, violin
Bolcom—Concerto, violin
Rouse—Concerto, violin

Over 30'

Vivaldi—Le quattro staggioni (Four
  seasons, complete)
Viotti—Concerto, violin, no.19
Mozart—Concerto, violin, no.5; Sere-
  nade no.4, K.203
Beethoven—Concerto, violin, op.61
Paganini—Concertos, violin, nos.1-2
Schumann, R.—Concerto, violin,
  D minor
Lalo—Symphonie espagnole
Goldmark—Concerto, violin, op.28
Joachim—Concerto, violin, op.11
Brahms—Concerto, violin, op.77
Bruch—Concerto, violin, no.3; Sere-
  nade, op.75
Tchaikovsky—Concerto, violin, op.35
Dvořák—Concerto, violin, op.53
Elgar—Concerto, violin, op.61
Nielsen—Concerto, violin, op.33
Sibelius—Concerto, violin, op.47
Schoenberg—Concerto, violin, op.36
Bloch, E.—Concerto, violin
Bartók—Concerto, violin, no.2
Gruenberg—Concerto, violin, op.47
Weill—Concerto, violin
Walton—Concerto, violin
Khachaturian—Concerto, violin
Shostakovich—Concerto, violin, op.99
Britten—Concerto, violin, no.1
Bernstein—Serenade
Imbrie—Concerto, violin
Penderecki—Concerto, violin
Schnittke—Concerto, violin, no.4
Adams, John—Concerto, violin

2 OR MORE VIOLINS

Torelli—Concertos, 2 violins,
  op.6, no.10; op.8, nos.1, 3, 7;
  Concerti grossi, 2 violins, op.8,
  nos.2, 5, 6
Vivaldi—Concerto, 2 violins,
  op.3, no.8, RV 522

[2 OR MORE VIOLINS]

Telemann—Concerto, 2 violins, C major
Manfredini—Concerti grossi, op.3, nos.10 & 12 (2 violins)
Bach—Concerto, 2 violins, BWV 1043
Sammartini, Giuseppe—Concerto grosso, op.5, no.6 (2 violins)
Locatelli—Concerto grosso, op.7, no.12 (4 violins)
Bach, J.C.—Sinfonia concertante, E-flat major (2 violins)
Saint-Georges—Symphonie concertante, op.6, no.1 (2 violins)
Saint-Georges—Symphonie concertante, op.13 (2 violins)
Mozart—Concertone, 2 violins & orchestra, K.190
Holst—Concerto, 2 violins, op.49
Arnold—Concerto, 2 violins & string orchestra, op.77
Trimble—Duo concertante (2 violins)
Schnittke—Concerto grosso no.3 (2 violins)

VIOLA

Telemann—Concerto, viola, G major
Handel—Concerto, viola, B minor
Stamitz, Joh.—Concerto, viola, G major
Stamitz, Karl—Concerto, viola, op.1
Stamitz, Anton—Concerto, viola, no.4, D major
Weber, C.M.—Andante & Rondo ongarese, op.35
Berlioz—Harold in Italy
Wolf—Italian serenade
Loeffler—La Mort de Tintagiles (solo viola d'amore)
Vaughan Williams—Flos campi
Holst—Lyric movement
Bartók—Concerto, viola, op. posth.
Martinu—Rhapsody-concerto
Piston—Concerto, viola
Hindemith—Concert music for viola & large chamber orchestra, op.48; Concerto, viola, op.36, no.4 (Kammermusik no.5); Concerto, viola d'amore, op.46, no.1; Der Schwanendreher; Trauermusik
Hanson—Lux aeterna, op.24
Walton—Concerto, viola
Partos—Yiskor
Dello Joio—Lyric fantasies
Henze—Compases para preguntas ensimismadas
Musgrave—Concerto, viola
Takemitsu—A string around autumn
Penderecki—Concerto, viola

Holloway—Concerto, viola, op.56
León—Para viola y orquesta

VIOLONCELLO

15' or less

Vivaldi—Concertos, violoncello, RV 401, 406, 418, 422
Veracini—Menuet et gavotte
Tartini—Concerto, violoncello, A major
Leo—Concerto, violoncello, D major
Wagenseil—Concerto, violoncello, A major
Boccherini—Concerto, violoncello, G.477
Schumann, R.—Adagio and allegro, op.70
Rubinstein—Melody in F, op.3, no.1
Saint-Saëns—Allegro appassionato, op.43; Romance, op.36
Bruch—Ave Maria; Kol Nidrei
Tchaikovsky—Pezzo capriccioso, op.62
Popper—Hungarian rhapsody, op.68; Tarantelle, op.33
Fauré—Elegy, op.24
Boëllmann—Symphonic variations
Strauss, R.—Romanze
Glazunov—Chant du ménestrel
Respighi—Adagio con variazioni
Malipiero—Concerto, violoncello
Milhaud—Concerto, violoncello, no.1
Hindemith—Trauermusik
Penderecki—Sonata, violoncello & orchestra

16'-30'

Wagenseil—Concerto, violoncello, C major
Haydn—Concertos, violoncello, Hob.VIIb:2 (original & Gevaert arrangement); Hob.VIIb:5
Boccherini—Concertos, violoncello, G.474; G.482 (original and Grützmacher version)
Stamitz, Karl—Concertos, violoncello, nos.1-3
Schumann, R.—Concerto, violoncello, op.129, A minor
Lalo—Concerto, violoncello, D minor
Rubinstein—Concerto, violoncello, no.2, op.96, D minor
Saint-Saëns—Concertos, violoncello, nos.1-2
Tchaikovsky—Variations on a rococo theme
Dvořák—Concerto, violoncello (no.2) .

[VIOLONCELLO; *16'-30'*]

Sullivan—Concerto, violoncello
Elgar—Concerto, violoncello, op.85
Herbert—Concerto, violoncello, no.2, op.30, E minor
Delius—Concerto, violoncello
Schoenberg—Concerto, violoncello
Bloch, E.—Schelomo; Voice in the wilderness
Toch—Concerto, violoncello, op.35
Milhaud—Concerto, violoncello, no.2
Hindemith—Concerto, violoncello, op.36, no.2 (Kammermusik no.3)
Walton—Concerto, violoncello
Goldschmidt—Concerto, violoncello
Khachaturian—Concerto-rhapsody, violoncello & orchestra
Kabalevsky—Concerto, violoncello, no.1
Shostakovich—Concerto, violoncello, no.1
Rózsa—Concerto, violoncello, op.32
Barber—Concerto, violoncello, op.22
Schuman, Wm.—A song of Orpheus
Bernstein—Mass: Three meditations
Babadjanyan—Concerto, violoncello
Foss—Cello concert
Henze—Ode an den Westwind
Baker—Concerto, violoncello
Martino—Concerto, violoncello
Rands—Hiraeth
Wuorinen—Chamber concerto, violoncello & 10 players
Gruber—Concerto, violoncello
Rouse—Concerto, violoncello
Tan—Intercourse of fire and water (Yi1)

Over 30'

Dvořák—Concerto, violoncello, op.104
Strauss, R.—Don Quixote
Prokofiev—Sinfonia concertante, op.125
Shostakovich—Concerto, violoncello, no.2
Britten—Symphony for violoncello & orchestra
Maxwell Davies—Strathclyde concerto no.2
Schnittke—Concerto, violoncello
Danielpour—Concerto, violoncello

Duration uncertain

Boismortier—Concerto, D major (solo violoncello, viola da gamba, or bassoon)

DOUBLE BASS

Dittersdorf—Concertos, double bass, E major & E-flat major
Vanhal—Concerto, double bass, E-flat major
Mozart—Per questa bella mano
Dragonetti—Grande allegro; Pezzo di concerto
Bottesini—Concerto, double bass, no.2
Koussevitzky—Concerto, double bass, op.3 (original and Meyer-Tormin orchestration)
Miari—Concerto, double bass
Maxwell Davies—Strathclyde concerto no.7

MULTIPLE DIVERSE STRINGS

2 solo strings

Vivaldi—Concerto, violin & violoncello, RV 547
Vivaldi—Concerto, 2 violoncellos, RV 531
Graun—Concerto, violin & viola
Bach, J.C.—Sinfonia concertante, A major (violin & violoncello)
Dittersdorf—Sinfonia concertante, double bass & viola
Saint-Georges—Symphonie concertante, op.6, no.1 (violin & violoncello)
Stamitz, Karl—Sinfonia concertante, D major (violin & viola)
Mozart—Sinfonia concertante, K.364 (violin & viola)
Brahms—Concerto, violin & violoncello, op.102, A minor
Delius—Concerto, violin & violoncello
Sessions—Concerto, violin & violoncello
Maxwell Davies—Strathclyde concerto no.5 (violin & viola)
Zwilich—Concerto, violin & violoncello

2 violins & violoncello

Corelli—Concerti grossi, op.6, nos.1-12
Scarlatti, A.—Concerti grossi nos.3, 6
Manfredini—Concerto grosso, op.3, no.9
Handel—Concerto grosso, no.7; Concerto grosso, op.3, no.2; Concerti grossi, op.6, nos.1-12
Marcello, B.—Concerti grossi, op.1, nos.1, 6-10

[2 VIOLINS & VIOLONCELLO]

Geminiani—Concerto grosso, C major (after Corelli, op.5, no.3)
Locatelli—Concerto grosso, op.1, no.9
Boyce—Concerto grosso, B minor
Tippett—Fantasia concertante on a theme of Corelli

Solo string quartet

Marcello, B.—Concerti grossi, op.1, nos.2-5
Geminiani—Concerto grosso no.5; Concerto grosso no.12 (after Corelli); Concerti grossi, op.3, nos.1-6; op.7, no.1
Locatelli—Concerto grosso, op.7, no.6
Sammartini, Giov. Battista—Concerto in E-flat
Mozart—Serenade no.6, K.239
Elgar—Introduction and allegro, op.47
Vaughan Williams—Fantasia on a theme by Thomas Tallis
Bloch, E.—Concerto grosso no.2
Blacher—Orchesterfantasie
Canning—Fantasy on a hymn by Justin Morgan (2 solo string quartets)
Britten—Cantata misericordium (with chorus & vocal soloists)
Britten—Young Apollo (also solo piano)
Lees—Concerto, string quartet & orchestra

Other combinations of solo strings

Bach—Brandenburg concerto no.3 (3vn, 3va, 3vc, plus db & cnt)
Bach—Brandenburg concerto no.6 (2va, 2va da gamba, plus vc, db & cnt)
Locatelli—Concerto grosso, op.1, no.8, (2vn, 2va, vc)
Saint-Georges—Symphonie concertante, op.10, no.2 (2vn, va)
Stravinsky—Pulcinella: Suite (2vn, va, vc, db)
Tippett—Concerto, violin, viola & violoncello
Canning—Fantasy on a hymn by Justin Morgan (4vn, 2va, 2vc)

FLUTE

15' or less

Vivaldi—Concertos, flute, RV 428, RV 439

Telemann—Concerto, flute, E minor
Quantz—Concertos, flute, C major & D major
Galuppi—Concerto, flute, D major
Pergolesi—Concerto, flute, G major
Frederick II—Concertos, flute, nos.3-4
Gluck—Concerto, flute, G major
Stamitz, Joh.—Concerto, flute, D major
Grétry—Concerto, flute, C major
Mozart—Andante, K.315
Donizetti—Concertino, flute, C major
Saint-Saëns—Odelette; Romance, op.37
Fauré—Fantasy, flute & chamber orchestra
Chaminade—Concertino, flute, op.107
Busoni—Divertimento, flute & chamber orchestra, op.52
Bloch, E.—Suite modale
Griffes—Poem for flute and orchestra
Rogers—Soliloquy for flute and strings
Hanson—Serenade, op.35
Kennan—Night soliloquy

Over 15'

Telemann—Concerto, flute, D major
Bach—Suite (Overture) no.2
Quantz—Concertos, flute, D major & G major
Stamitz, Joh.—Concerto, flute, C major
Haydn—Concerto, flute, Hob.VIIf:D1
Boccherini—Concerto, flute, G.489
Stamitz, Karl—Concerto, flute, G major
Mozart—Concertos, flute, nos.1-2
Nielsen—Concerto, flute (1926)
Ibert—Concerto, flute
Piston—Concerto, flute
Brant—Angels and devils
Bernstein—Halil
Maxwell Davies—Strathclyde concerto no.6
Harbison—Concerto, flute
Rutter—Suite antique
Rouse—Concerto, flute

Duration uncertain

Quantz—Concerto, flute, C minor
Galuppi—Concerto, flute, G major

2 FLUTES

Telemann—Concerto, 2 flutes,
  A minor
Galuppi—Concerto, 2 flutes, E minor
Haydn—Concerto, 2 flutes,
  Hob.VIIh:1
Cimarosa—Concerto (concertante), 2
  flutes, G major
Daugherty—Metropolis symphony:
  no.3, MXYZPTLK (2nd flute doubles
  on piccolo)

RECORDER

Vivaldi—Concerto, flute or recorder,
  RV 439; Concerto, recorder, RV 441
Telemann—Concert suite, F major;
  Concerto, recorder, F major; Suite, A
  minor

PICCOLO

Vivaldi—Concertos, piccolo, RV 443,
  RV 445

ALTO FLUTE

Sallinen—Chamber music II

OBOE

Albinoni—Concertos, op.7, no.3; op.9,
  no.2
Vivaldi—Concertos, oboe, RV 447,
  RV 454, RV 455
Telemann—Concertos, oboe, D minor,
  E minor, F minor, F major
Graupner—Concerto, oboe, F major
Handel—Concertos, oboe, nos.1-3;
  Concerto, oboe, E-flat major
Marcello, B.—Concerto, oboe, C minor
Stamitz, Joh.—Concerto, oboe,
  C major
Haydn—Concerto, oboe, Hob.VIIg:C
Cimarosa—Concerto, oboe, C minor
Mozart—Concerto, oboe, K.314
Donizetti—Concertino, oboe, F major
Bellini—Concerto, oboe, E-flat major
Strauss, R.—Concerto, oboe, D major
Vaughan Williams—Concerto, oboe
Martinu—Concerto, oboe
Goosens—Concerto in one movement,
  op.45
Wilder—Concerto, oboe
Carter—Concerto, oboe
Barlow—Rhapsody for oboe

Maxwell Davies—Strathclyde concerto
  no.1
Bennett, Richard R.—Concerto, oboe
Corigliano—Aria
Svoboda—Meditation, op.143

ENGLISH HORN

Donizetti—Concertino, English horn,
  G major
Sibelius—Legends: No.2, The swan of
  Tuonela
Wolf-Ferrari—Concertino, English
  horn, op.34
Alwyn—Autumn legend

CLARINET

Stamitz, Karl—Concertos, clarinet,
  E-flat major & F major; Concerto,
  clarinet, no.3, B-flat major
Mozart—Concerto, clarinet, K.622
Baermann—Adagio
Spohr—Concerto, clarinet, op.26
Weber, C.M.—Concertino, op.26;
  Concertos, clarinet, nos.1-2
Rossini—Variations for clarinet and
  small orchestra
Donizetti—Concertino, clarinet,
  B-flat major
Wagner [attr.]—Adagio
Debussy—Rhapsody, clarinet &
  orchestra
Nielsen—Concerto, clarinet, op.57
Busoni—Concertino, op.48
Stravinsky—Ebony concerto
Milhaud—Scaramouche
Gershwin—Promenade (Walking the
  Dog)
Copland—Concerto, clarinet
Finzi—Concerto, clarinet, op.31
Swanson—Fantasy piece
Lutoslawski—Preludia taneczne
Arnold—Concerto, clarinet, no.2
Skrowaczewski—Ricercari notturni
  (clarinet doubling on bass clarinet)
Maxwell Davies—Strathclyde concerto
  no.4
Corigliano—Concerto, clarinet
Svoboda—Symphony no.6

BASSOON

Vivaldi—Concertos, bassoon, RV 477,
  RV 484, RV 485, RV 498
Graupner—Concerto, bassoon,
  G major
Boismortier—Concerto, D major

[BASSOON]
Stamitz, Karl—Concerto, bassoon
Mozart—Concerto, bassoon, K.191
Mozart [attr.]—Concerto, bassoon, no.2
Weber, C.M.—Andante & Rondo ongarese; Concerto, bassoon, op.75
Fucik—Der alte Brummbär
Villa-Lobos—Ciranda das sete notas
Panufnik—Concerto, bassoon
Maxwell Davies—Strathclyde concerto no.8
Daugherty—Dead Elvis

SAXOPHONE

Debussy—Rhapsody, alto saxophone
Glazunov—Concerto, alto saxophone, op.109
Villa-Lobos—Fantasia (soprano or tenor)
Ibert—Concertino da camera (alto)
Martin—Ballade (alto)
Milhaud—Scaramouche (alto)
Swanson—Fantasy piece (soprano)
Maurice—Tableaux de Provence (alto)
Skrowaczewski—Ricercari notturni (soloist doubles on soprano, alto, & baritone saxophones)
Dubois, P.—Concerto, alto saxophone
Martino—Concerto, alto saxophone
Bond—Urban Bird (alto)

HORN

Telemann—Concerto, horn, D major
Haydn—Concertos, horn, nos.1-2
Haydn, M.—Concertino, horn, D major
Mozart—Concertos, horn, nos.1-4; Concert-rondo, horn & orchestra, K.371
Weber, C.M.—Concertino, horn & orchestra, op.45
Schumann, R.—Adagio and allegro, op.70
Saint-Saëns—Morceau de concert, horn & orchestra, op.94; Romance, op.36
Strauss, R.—Concertos, horn, nos.1-2
Glière—Concerto, horn, op.91
Hindemith—Concerto, horn (1949)
Larsson—Concertino, horn, op.45, no.5
Hovhaness—Artik
Britten—Now sleeps the crimson petal (solo horn & solo tenor)
Britten—Serenade for tenor, horn & strings, op.31
Hamilton—Voyage

Hoddinott—Concerto, horn, op.65

2 OR MORE HORNS

Vivaldi—Concertos, 2 horns, RV 538, 539
Telemann—Concerto, 2 horns, E-flat major
Kuhlau—Concertino, 2 horns, F minor
Schumann, R.—Concertstück, op.86 (4 horns)
Chávez—Concerto, 4 horns

TRUMPET

Purcell—Sonata for trumpet & strings
Clarke—Suite, D major
Torelli—Concerto, trumpet, D major (2 works by this title); Sinfonia con tromba
Telemann—Concerto, trumpet, D major
Fasch—Concerto, trumpet, D major
Mozart, Leopold—Concertos, trumpet, D major & G major
Haydn—Concerto, trumpet, Hob.VIIe:1
Haydn, M.—Concerto, trumpet, no.2
Hummel—Concerto, trumpet, E major or E-flat major
Goedicke—Concert etude, op.49
Bloch, E.—Proclamation
Tomasi—Concerto, trumpet
Panufnik—Concerto in modo antico
Husa—Concerto, trumpet & wind orchestra
Chou—Soliloquy of a bhiksuni
Maxwell Davies—Concerto, trumpet
MacMillan—Epiclesis

2 TRUMPETS

Vivaldi—Concerto, 2 trumpets, RV 537
Hamilton—Circus
Adams, John—Tromba lontana

TROMBONE

Wagenseil—Concerto, trombone, E-flat major
David—Concertino no.4
Rimsky-Korsakov—Concerto, trombone & band
Bloch, E.—Symphony for trombone & orchestra

[TROMBONE]
Milhaud—Concertino d'hiver
Hovhaness—Overture, op.76, no.1
Bassett—Concerto lirico
Zwilich—Concerto, bass trombone
Rouse—Concerto, trombone
Larsen—Mary Cassatt (trombone &
solo mezzo-soprano)

TUBA

Vaughan Williams—Concerto, tuba
Kleinsinger—Tubby the tuba

PERCUSSION

Bartók—Concerto, 2 pianos and percussion (2 or 3 percussionists)
Milhaud—Concerto, marimba & vi-
braphone, op.278 (1 percussionist);
Concerto, percussion & small
orchestra (1 percussionist)
Schreiner—The worried drummer
(1 percussionist)
Kubik—Gerald McBoing Boing
(1 percussionist)
Panufnik—Concertino for timpani,
percussion & strings (2 percussion-
ists)
Foss—Concerto, percussion
(3 percussionists)
Kraft—Configurations; concerto for
4 percussionists & jazz orchestra;
Three miniatures (4 percussionists)
Erb—Concerto for solo percussionist
Mayuzumi—Concertino, xylophone
Colgrass—Déjà vu (4 percussionists);
Rhapsodic fantasy (1 percussionist)
Svoboda—Concerto, marimba
Peck—The glory and the grandeur
(3 percussionists)
Daugherty—Flamingo (2 tambourine
soloists)
MacMillan—Veni, veni, Emmanuel
(1 percussionist)

HARP

Handel—Concerto, harp, op.4, no.6
Dittersdorf—Concerto, harp, A major
Boieldieu—Concerto, harp, C major
Saint-Saëns—Morceau de concert,
harp & orchestra, op.154
Debussy—Danses sacrée et profane
Glière—Concerto, harp, op.74
Ravel—Introduction & Allegro
Grandjany—Aria in classic style
Berezowsky—Concerto, harp, op.31

Rodrigo—Concierto de Aranjuez
(originally for guitar); Concierto sere-
nata
Alwyn—Lyra angelica
Badings—Concerto, harp
Weinzweig—Concerto, harp
Ginastera—Concerto, harp, op.25

GUITAR

Vivaldi—Concerto, guitar, RV 93
Ponce—Concierto del sur
Villa-Lobos—Concerto, guitar & small
orchestra
Castelnuovo-Tedesco—Concerto, gui-
tar, op.99
Rodrigo—Concierto de Aranjuez; Fan-
tasia para un gentilhombre
Berkeley—Concerto, guitar, op.88
Smith Brindle—Concerto, guitar
Bennett, Richard R.—Concerto, guitar
& chamber ensemble
Brouwer—Concerto de Toronto; Con-
certo elegiaco; Retrats catalans
Schwantner—From afar
Mackey—Deal (solo electric guitar,
with optional solo drum set)

2 OR MORE GUITARS

Rodrigo—Concierto andaluz (4
guitars); Concierto madrigal
(2 guitars)

MANDOLIN

Vivaldi—Concerto, mandolin, RV 425

BAGPIPES

Maxwell Davies—Cross Lane Fair
Maxwell Davies—An Orkney wedding

XUN

Tan: Orchestral theatre I: Xun

SEVERAL DIVERSE
SOLO INSTRUMENTS

2 soloists

Vivaldi—Concerto, oboe & bassoon,
RV 545

[2 DIVERSE SOLOISTS]

Vivaldi—Concerto, oboe & violin, RV 548

Telemann—Concerto, recorder & flute, E minor

Bach—Concerto, violin & oboe, BWV 1060

Handel—Concerto grosso, op.3, no.3 (vn & fl, or vn & ob)

Haydn—Concertos, flute & oboe, Hob.VIIh:2-5; Concerto, violin & piano (or harpsichord), Hob.XVIII:6

Stamitz, Karl—Concerto, clarinet & bassoon, B-flat major; Concerto, clarinet & violin (or 2 clarinets)

Mozart—Ch'io mi scordi di te—Non temer, K.505 (soprano & pf); Concerto, flute & harp, K.299; Per questa bella mano, K.612 (bass voice & db)

Saint-Saëns—Tarantelle (fl & cl)

Strauss, R.—Duet-concertino (cl & bn)

Bloch, E.—Concertino (fl & va, or fl & cl)

Berg—Chamber concerto, op.8 (vn & pf)

Honegger—Concerto da camera (fl & Eh)

Copland—Quiet city (tp & Eh, or tp & ob)

Shostakovich—Concerto, piano, no.1 (solo tp as well as pf)

Rorem—Water music (cl & vn)

Berio—Concertino, clarinet & violin

Henze—Double concerto (ob & hp)

Russo—Street music; a blues concerto (pf & harmonica)

Maxwell Davies—Cross Lane Fair (Northumbrian pipes & bodhran)

Maxwell Davies—Strathclyde concerto no.3 (hn & tp)

Schnittke—Concerto, oboe, harp & string orchestra

Bolcom—Fives (vn & pf)

Adolphe—Three pieces for kids & chamber orchestra: no.1, Concertino (fl & ob)

Mackey—Deal (elec gtr & drum set)

3 soloists

Vivaldi—Concerto, flute, oboe & bsn, RV 570 (fl, ob, bn)

Bach—Brandenburg concerto no.4 (vn, 2rec); Brandenburg concerto no.5 (hpsd, fl, vn); Concerto, flute, violin & harpsichord, BWV 1044

Handel—Concerto, organ, op.4, no.3 (org, vn, vc)

Beethoven—Concerto, violin, violoncello & piano, op.56

Barber—Capricorn concerto (fl, ob, tp)

Kubik—Symphony concertante (tp, va, pf)

Tan—On Taoism (voice, bcl, cbn)

4 soloists

Bach—Brandenburg concerto no.2 (vn, rec, ob, tp)

Haydn—Sinfonia concertante, op.84, Hob.I:105 (ob, bn, vn, vc)

Mozart—Sinfonia concertante, K.297b (ob, cl, bn, hn); Sinfonia concertante, K.297b [Levin reconstruction] (fl, ob, hn, bn)

Bartók—Concerto, 2 pianos and percussion (2pf, 2perc)

Berio—Tempi concertati (fl, vn, 2pf)

Birtwistle—Nomos (fl, cl, hn, bn)

Del Tredici—Syzygy (sop, hn, 2 perc)

5 soloists

Hindemith—Concerto for woodwinds, harp & orchestra (fl, ob, cl, bn, hp)

Britten—Young Apollo (pf, str 4t)

Foss—Night music for John Lennon (2tp, hn, tbn, tuba [or 2nd tbn])

Del Tredici—An Alice symphony: The lobster quadrille (2ssx, mand, ten banjo, accordion)

6 or more soloists

Bach—Brandenburg concerto no.1 (vn, 3ob, 2hn)

Martin—Concerto, 7 winds (fl, ob, cl, bn, hn, tp, tbn)

Raksin—Toy concertino (8 players on toy insts)

Lutoslawski—Preludes & fugue for 13 solo strings (7vn, 3va, 2vc, 1db)

Shapey—Symphonie concertante (fl/pic, ob/Eh, cl/scl/bcl, bn/cbn, hn, tp, tbn, vn, va, vc, db)

Amram—Triple concerto (3 solo quintets: woodwind [fl, ob, cl, bn, hn], brass [2tp, hn, tbn, tuba], and jazz [asx, bsx, pf, db, drums])

Maxwell Davies—Strathclyde concerto no.9 (pic, afl, Eh, scl, bcl, cbn)

Svoboda—Symphony no.3 (org, str quintet)

JAZZ SOLOISTS

Ellington—Grand slam jam (varied soloists)

Ellington—New world a-comin' (pf)

[JAZZ SOLOISTS]
Brubeck, H.—Dialogues for jazz combo & orchestra (varied soloists)
Lewis—The golden striker (pf, bass, drums)
Lewis—Jazz ostinato (vib, pf, bass, drums)
Rorem—Lions (asx, pf, bass, drums)
Schuller—Concertino for jazz quartet & orchestra (pf, vib, bass, drums); Journey into jazz (asx, tsx, tp, bass, drums)

Russo—Street music; a blues concerto (harmonica, piano)
Amram—Triple concerto (3 solo quintets: woodwind [fl, ob, cl, bn, hn], brass [2tp, hn, tbn, tuba], and jazz [asx, bsx, pf, bass, drums])
Baker—Le Chat qui pêche (sop, asx/tsx, pf, bass, drums)
Hartway—Cityscapes (asx, pf, bass, drums); Country suite (fl, pf, bass, drums)
Bond—Urban Bird (asx)

APPENDIX D: ORCHESTRAL WORKS
LISTED BY INSTRUMENTATION

This appendix is good for browsing. It is intended to help those who are looking for certain combinations of instruments, or who may not exceed certain limits of instrumentation. It treats orchestral works only—not accompaniments.

The categories used progress generally from smaller combinations to larger. Any category may include works requiring slightly less in the way of instrumentation; conversely, if more instruments are called for than are in the heading, they are listed in square brackets.

Works using optional instruments are often listed in more than one category.

Works in the larger categories are subdivided according to duration. Within each category or subdivision, works are arranged chronologically according to the composer's birth date.

For complete information on any work, refer to the main alphabetical listing by composer.

STRINGS	WOODWINDS	BRASS	PERC	OTHER	PAGE
		brass and/or percussion			487
works without strings	any	any	any	any	487
str orch					487
str orch				cnt	489
str orch			perc	hp, cel, pf, hpsd	490
individual str players	any	any	any	any	490
str	single winds & percussion			hp, cel, pf	491
str	2fl or 2rec				493
str		2-8 hn			493
str	0202	2000		cnt	493
str	2202	2000		cnt	494
str	2202	2200	tmp	cnt	494
str	2222	2200	tmp		495
str	2222	2200	3	hp, cel, pf	496
str	2222	2231	1		497
str	2222	2331	4	hp, cel, pf	497
str	2222	4200	3	hp, cel, pf	499
str	2222	4330	tmp		499
str	2222	4230	4		500
str	2222	4431	5		500
str	2222	4431	5	hp, cel, pf	502
str	8 woodwinds	4300	tmp	cnt	503
str	3222	4331	4		503
str	3222	4431	5	hp, cel, pf	505
str	3322	4431	6	2hp, cel, pf	506
str	9/10 woodwinds	4331	4		507
str	9/10 woodwinds	4431	6	hp, cel, pf	508
str	3332	4331	5	hp, cel, pf	509
str	11 woodwinds	4431	5	hp, cel, pf	510
str	3333	4331	5		510
str	3333	4431	6	2hp, cel, pf	511
str	3333	larger than previous categories			514
str	13 woodwinds	4431	7	2hp, cel, pf	514
str	4454	6641	8	3hp, cel, pf	515
str	larger than all previous categories				517
	instrumentation indeterminate				517
	multiple orchestras				517

BRASS AND/OR PERCUSSION

Brass only

Gabrieli—Canzona noni toni, a 12, for three brass choirs; Sonata pian' e forte
Dukas—La Pèri: Fanfare
Ruggles—Angels
Copland—Ceremonial fanfare
Perle—New fanfares
Schickele—Fanfare for the common cold
Tower—Third fanfare for the uncommon woman

Percussion only

Varèse—Ionisation
Chávez—Toccata for percussion

Brass and percussion

Janácek—Sokal fanfare
Debussy—Le Martyre de Saint Sébastien: Two fanfares
Roussel—Fanfare pour un sacre païen
Copland—Fanfare for the common man
Druckman—Dark upon the harp
Tower—Fanfare for the uncommon woman; Second fanfare for the uncommon woman
Ran—Chicago skyline

WORKS WITHOUT STRINGS

15' or less

Mozart—Divertimentos, K.166, K.186, K.188; Die Entführung aus dem Serail: Marsch der Janitscharen
Beethoven—Zapfenstreich march
Donizetti—Sinfonia for winds
Mendelssohn—Overture for winds
Strauss, R.—Serenade, op.7
Joplin—The entertainer
Reger—Serenade, B-flat major
Grainger—The immovable do
Stravinsky—Octet; Symphonies of wind instruments
Varèse—Hyperprism; Intégrales
Milhaud—Symphonies for small orch: No.5, Dixtuor d'instruments à vent
Chávez—Xochipilli
Poulenc—Suite française
Copland—Inaugural fanfare
Brant—Galaxy 2; Verticals ascending
Britten—The sword in the stone

Rochberg—Black sounds
Serocki—Segmenti
Xenakis—Akrata
Chou—Beijing in the mist; Pien; Soliloquy of a bhiksuni
Rorem—Sinfonia
Harbison—Music for 18 winds
Kolb—Chromatic fantasy
Schwantner—From a dark millennium

Over 15'

Handel—Royal fireworks music
Mozart—Serenades nos.10-12
Berlioz—Symphonie funèbre et triomphale
Gounod—Petite Symphonie
Strauss, R.—Suite, op.4; Symphony for winds, op.posth., E-flat major
Varèse—Déserts
Berg—Chamber concerto, op.8 [solo vn, solo pf]
Antheil—Ballet mécanique
Weill—Kleine Dreigroschenmusik
Brant—Angels and devils
Kurka—The good soldier Schweik: Suite
Birtwistle—Verses for ensembles
Adams, John—Grand pianola music

Duration uncertain

Boudreau—Versus

STRING ORCHESTRA

5' or less

Pachelbel—Canon
Purcell—Canon on a ground bass
Veracini—Aria schiavona
Haydn, M.—Symphony, P.8
Chopin—Mazurka no.7
Schumann, R.—Träumerei
Grieg—Erotik
Fauré—Shylock: Nocturne
Foote—Irish folk song
Elgar—Elegy, op.58
Sibelius—Canzonetta; Romance
Kalinnikov—Chanson triste
Vaughan Williams—Prelude (49th parallel)
Ives—Hymn (Largo cantabile)
Schreker—Intermezzo, op.8
Grainger—The immovable do; Irish tune from County Derry; Molly on the shore
Cowell—Ballad
Copland—Rodeo: Hoe down (str orch)

[String orchestra; 5' or less]]
Finzi—Prelude
Carter—Elegy
Dello Joio—Arietta
Lutoslawski—Overture for strings
Starer—Elegy for strings
Jones—Elegy
Pärt—Silouans song

6'-10'

Gabrieli—Canzona [double string
orchestra]
Monteverdi—Orfeo: Sinfonie e ritor-
nelli
Schein—Banchetto musicale: Suite
no.1
Corelli—Suite for string orchestra
Purcell—Chacony in G minor; The
fairy queen: Suites nos.1-2; The
Gordian knot untied: Suite no.2
Scarlatti, A.—Piccola suite
Vivaldi—Sinfonia, RV 169
Scarlatti, D.—Five sonatas
Marcello, B.—Introduction, aria &
presto, A minor
Geminiani—Concerto grosso, op.2,
no.2
Leclair—Sonata, D major (str orch)
Pergolesi—Concertino, E-flat major
Abel—Symphonies, op.1, nos.5-6
Boccherini—Sinfonia concertante,
strings, G.268; Symphony A, G.500
Mozart—Adagio & fugue, K.546; Di-
vertimento, K.137
Donizetti—Allegro in C major
Schubert—Overture, D.8 (arr. Hess)
Mendelssohn—Sinfonias nos.1-5
Borodin—Nocturne (arr. Sargent)
Dvořák—Notturno, op.40
Grieg—Two elegiac melodies, op.34;
Two melodies, op.53
Puccini—I crisantemi
Roussel—Sinfonietta, op.52
Holst—Brook Green suite
Suk—Meditace na starocesky chorál
"Svaty Václave"
Ruggles—Portals
Bartók—Rumanian folk dances
Cadman—American suite
Villa-Lobos—Bachianas brasileiras
no.5: Aria [gtr]; Suite for strings
Prokofiev—Andante
Hindemith—Suite of French dances
Cowell—Hymn and fuguing tune no.2
Finzi—Romance, op.11
Rodrigo—Zarabanda lejana y villanci-
co
Skalkottas—Five Greek dances
Tippett—Little music
Swanson—Music for strings
Barber—Adagio for strings

Fine—Serious song
Panufnik—Jagiellonian triptych
Shulman—Threnody
Walker, George—Lyric for strings
Ligeti—Ramifications
Adler—Elegy for string orchestra
Amram—Autobiography for strings
Górecki—Three pieces in old style
Penderecki—Emanations (2 string
orchs); To the victims of Hiroshima
Pärt—Festina Lente
Schickele—Elegy
Glass—Arioso no.2
Corigliano—Voyage
Wuorinen—Grand bamboula
Tann—Water's edge

11'-15'

Purcell—The Gordian knot untied:
Suite no.1
Fux—Overture, C major
Telemann—Overture in C major
Rameau—Suite for string orchestra
Tartini—Sinfonia, D major
Stamitz, Joh.—Symphony, op.3, no.3;
Three Mannheim symphonies:
Nos.1, 2, 3
Rossini—Sonatas nos.1-4
Mozart—Divertimenti, K.136, K.138
Mendelssohn—Sinfonias nos.6, 10
Grieg—Two Norwegian airs, op.63
Foote—Suite, op.63
Elgar—Serenade, op.20
Arensky—Variations on a theme by
Tchaikovsky
Vaughan Williams—Fantasia on a
theme by Thomas Tallis
Holst—St. Paul's suite
Stravinsky—Concerto in D
Webern—Fünf Sätze, op.5
Berg—Lyric suite: Three pieces
Becker—Soundpiece no.2b
Villa-Lobos—Bachianas brasileiras
no.9
Martin—Passacaille
Warlock—Capriol suite
Tansman—Variations on a theme by
Frescobaldi
Barbirolli—An Elizabethan suite [4hn
in last mvt only]
Copland—Two pieces
Krenek—Sinfonietta; Symphonic
elegy
Hovhaness—Psalm and fugue, op.40a
Dahl—Variations on a theme by
C.P.E. Bach
Françaix—Sei Preludi
Coolidge—Pioneer dances
Panufnik—Divertimento; Old Polish
suite
Diamond—Rounds for string orch

[String orchestra; *11'-15'*]
Kay, U.—Suite for strings
Yardumian—Cantus animae et cordis
Xenakis—Syrmos
Sallinen—Chamber music I, op.38
Harbison—Merchant of Venice
Zwilich—Prologue & variations
Peck—Signs of life
Sapieyevski—Surtsey
Kernis—Musica celestis
Torke—December

16'-20'

Lully—Le Triomphe de l'amour: Ballet
  suite
Veracini—Quatro pezzi
Gossec—Symphony op.6, no.6
Mozart—Eine kleine Nachtmusik
Beethoven—Grosse Fuge, op.133
Rossini—Sonatas nos.5-6
Mendelssohn—Sinfonia no.12
Foote—Serenade, op.25
Nielsen—Little suite, op.1
Schoenberg—Suite for string orch
Respighi—Antiche danze ed arie: Set
  III
Martin—Etudes for string orchestra
Tansman—Triptych
Tcherepnin—Serenade, op.97
Copland—Nonet for strings
Skalkottas—Ten sketches for strings
Schuman, Wm.—Symphony no.5
Britten—Simple symphony
Persichetti—Symphony, op.61
Babbitt—Transfigured notes
Kay, U.—Six dances for string orch

21'-25'

Mendelssohn—Sinfonia no.7
Brahms—Liebeslieder waltzes
Grieg—Holberg suite
Parry—An English suite; Suite in F
Herbert—Serenade, op.12
Bartók—Divertimento
Honegger—Symphony no.2 [opt tp]
Chávez—Symphony no.5
Tippett—Concerto for double str orch
Gutche—Symphony no.5
Britten—Variations on a theme of-
  Frank Bridge
Dello Joio—Meditations on Eccle-
  siastes
Ginastera—Concerto for strings
Overton—Symphony for strings
Arnold—Symphony for strings
Rorem—String symphony

26'-30'

Tchaikovsky—Serenade, op.48
Dvořák—Serenade, op.22
Janácek—Idyla
Strauss, R.—Metamorphosen
Schoenberg—Verklärte Nacht
Suk—Serenade, op.6
Miaskovsky—Sinfonietta, op.32, no.2
Stravinsky—Apollon Musagéte
Alwyn—Sinfonietta
Gould—Stringmusic
Adams, John—Shaker loops

Over 30'

Schubert—Quartet, strings, D.810
Mendelssohn—Octet, strings, op.20;
  Sinfonias nos.8 (string version) & 9
Korngold—Symphonic serenade

Duration uncertain

Purcell—New pieces for small string
  orchestra
Lully—Ballet music
Scarlatti, A.—Concerto, G minor

STRING ORCHESTRA
WITH CONTINUO

10' or less

Biber—Battalia
Pachelbel—Canon
Torelli—Concerto, op.6, no.1; Sinfo-
  nia, op.6, no.6
Purcell—The double dealer: Suite; The
  rival sisters: Overture
Scarlatti, A.—Concerti grossi nos.1, 2
Albinoni—Concertos, op.5, nos.4 & 7
Vivaldi—Concerto for orch, RV 151;
  Sinfonias nos.1, 2, 3 (RV 719, 146,
  149)
Handel—Alcina: Overture
Veracini—Aria schiavona
Sammartini, Giov. Battista— Concer-
  tino, G major; Sinfonia, J.-C.39
Galuppi—Concerti a quattro, nos.1, 2
Frederick II—Symphonies nos.1, 2
Bach, C.P.E.—Symphonies, H.661,
  H.662
Gluck—Overture, D major; Sinfonia,
  G major
Abel—Symphonies, op.1, nos.5, 6

[String orchestra with continuo]

Over 10'

Monteverdi—Combattimento di Tancredi e Clorinda
Purcell—Abdelazar: Suite; Dido and Aeneas: Suite
Fux—Overture, C major
Vivaldi—Concerto for orch, RV 155
Telemann—Don Quichotte
Locatelli—Concerto grosso, op.1, no.6; Trauer-Symphonie
Sammartini, Giov. Battista—Sinfonia, J.-C.32
Bach, W.F.—Sinfonia, F major
Bach, C.P.E.—Symphonies, H.657, H.658, H.659, H.660

Duration uncertain

Telemann—Overture (suite), G major
Manfredini—Christmas symphony, op.2, no.12
Geminiani—Concerto grosso, op.2, no.3

STRING ORCHESTRA WITH HARP, PIANO, CELESTA, HARPSICHORD, AND/OR PERCUSSION

Purcell—Chacony in G minor
Mendelssohn—Sinfonia no.11
Strauss, Joh., Jr.—Pizzicato polka
Grieg—Erotik
Mahler—Symphony no.5: Adagietto
Delius—Hassan: Intermezzo & Serenade
Sibelius—Rakastava
Vaughan Williams—Fantasia on "Greensleeves" [fl]; Five variants of "Dives and Lazarus"
Schoenberg—Ode to Napoleon Bonaparte
Coleridge-Taylor—Novellettes, op.52, nos.1-4
Bartók—Music for strings, percussion and celesta
Becker—Soundpiece no.1b
Martin—Petite Symphonie concertante
Panufnik—Lullaby [2hp]
Górecki—Symphony no.1
Penderecki—Anaklasis
Pärt—Festina Lente; Fratres

WORKS USING INDIVIDUAL STRING PLAYERS RATHER THAN SECTIONS

Small ensemble (10 instruments or less)

Beethoven—Septet, op.20
Spohr—Nonet, op.31; Octet, op.32
Rossini—Serenata per piccolo complesso; Sonatas nos.1-6
Schubert—Octet, D.803
Mendelssohn—Octet, strings, op.20
Saint-Saëns—Septet, op.65
Ives—The unanswered question
Schoenberg—Pierrot Lunaire
Ruggles—Angels
Grainger—The immovable do
Stravinsky—L'Histoire du soldat: Suite; Septet
Varèse—Octandre
Webern—Concerto, op.24
Villa-Lobos—Bachianas brasileiras no.1
Milhaud—Symphonies for small orchestra, nos.1-4
Piston—Divertimento for nine insts.
Thomson, V.—Parson Weems and the cherry tree
Harsányi—L'Histoire du petite tailleur
Crawford—Music for small orchestra
Walton—Façade; Façade 2
Dallapiccola—Piccola musica notturna
Swanson—Night music
Pentland—Symphony for ten parts
Britten—Sinfonietta
Kubik—Gerald McBoing Boing
Xenakis—Anaktoria; Analogique A
Chou—Yü ko
Feldman—Atlantis
Musgrave—Chamber concerto no.1
Stockhausen—Kontra-Punkte no.1
Reich—Variations
Harbison—Merchant of Venice
Adams, John—Shaker loops
Daugherty—Dead Elvis

Medium ensemble (11-15 players)

Mozart—Serenade no.10, K.361
Wagner—Siegfried idyll
Saint-Saëns—Le Carnaval des animaux
Dvořák—Serenade, op.44
Debussy—Prélude à "L'Après-midi d'un faune" (arr.)
Strauss, R.—Serenade, op.7
Joplin—The entertainer; Maple leaf rag; Ragtime dance
Schoenberg—Chamber symphony no.1; Five pieces for orchestra, op.16 (chamber orch)

[Individual string players; *Medium ensemble*]
Stravinsky—Concerto in E-flat; Eight
  instrumental miniatures; Rag-time
Rogers—The musicians of Bremen
Hindemith—Kammermusik no.1;
  Suite of French dances
Cowell—Sinfonietta
Revueltas—Homenaje a Federico Gar-
  cia Lorca
Copland—Appalachian spring: Suite
  (orig inst)
Finney—Landscapes remembered
Bacewicz—Contradizione
Schuman, Wm.—Newsreel
Lutoslawski—Preludes & fugue for 13
  solo strings
Kubik—Divertimento I for 13 players
Perle—Serenade no.2
Babbitt—Composition for 12 instru-
  ments
Weber, Ben—Symphony on poems of
  William Blake
Maderna—Serenata no.2
Xenakis—Atrees
Ligeti—Ramifications
Davidovsky—Inflexions
Maxwell Davies—Carolisima serenade
Reynolds—Quick are the mouths of
  earth; Wedge
Sallinen—Chamber music I, op.38
Schwartz—Texture
Bolcom—Orphée-sérénade
Kolb—Soundings
Adams, John—Chamber symphony
Torke—Adjustable wrench

Large ensemble (over 15 players)

Strauss, R.—Le Bourgeois Gentil-
  homme: Suite; Metamorphosen
Ives—Chromâtimelôdtune
Ruggles—Men and mountains (orig)
Bartók—Three village scenes
Webern—Fünf Stücke, op.10
Ibert—Divertissement
Prokofiev—Overture, op.42
Milhaud—La Création du monde
Sessions—Concertino for chamber
  orchestra
Copland—Music for the theatre
Lutoslawski—Venetian games
Blomdahl—Game for eight
Zimmermann—Stillness and return
Powell—Modules
Brown—Available forms 1
Feldman—Atlantis
Shchedrin—Geometrie des Tones
Bach, Jan—The happy prince
Bolcom—A summer divertimento
Kolb—Soundings

STRINGS
SINGLE WINDS & PERCUSSION
HARP, CELESTA, PIANO

10' or less

Purcell—Indian queen: Trumpet over-
  ture
Scarlatti, A.—Sinfonia no.2
Haydn—Kindersymphonie, Hob.II:47
Mozart—Contradances, K.609
Rossini—Serenata per piccolo com-
  plesso
Franck—Eight short pieces
Grieg—Lyric pieces, op.68, nos.4 & 5
Debussy—Prélude à "L'Après-midi
  d'un faune' (arr.)
Pierné—Marche des petits soldats de
  plomb
Satie—Trois Petites Pièces montées
  [2tp, 2perc]
Joplin—The entertainer; Maple leaf
  rag; Ragtime dance
Vaughan Williams—Prelude (49th
  parallel); Two hymn-tune preludes
Holst—Brook Green suite
Ives—Charlie Rutlage; Chromâtime-
  lôdtune; Holidays symphony:
  Washington's Birthday [3 Jew's
  harps]; Symphony no.4: Fugue; Tone
  roads nos.1, 3
Stravinsky—Rag-time [cimbalom]
Varèse—Octandre
Webern—Concerto, op.24; Fünf
  Stücke, op.10 [2cl, 4perc]
Honegger—Pastorale d'été
Milhaud—Symphonies for small
  orchestra, nos.1 [2fl], 2, 3
Piston—Divertimento for nine instru-
  ments
Hindemith—Suite of French dances
  [lute]
Cowell—Polyphonica
Poulenc—Deux Marches et un Inter-
  mède
Copland—Symphony no.1: Prelude
  (arr. for chamber orch)
Luening—Prelude to a hymn tune by
  William Billings
Finzi—A Severn rhapsody
Dallapiccola—Piccola musica nottur-
  na
Swanson—Night music
Glanville-Hicks—Gymnopédie no.1
Pentland—Symphony for ten parts
  [2perc]
Britten—The sword in the stone
Kubik—Gerald McBoing Boing
Babbitt—Composition for 12 instru-
  ments
La Montaine—A summer's day
Benson—Chants and graces [4perc]

[Single winds & perc-hp, cel, pf-str; *10' or less*]

Feldman—Atlantis [2perc]
Musgrave—Chamber concerto no.1
London—The imaginary invalid: Overture
Pärt—Wenn Bach Bienen gezüchtet hätte...
Schwartz—Texture
Daugherty—Dead Elvis

11'-15'

Scarlatti, A.—Sinfonias nos.4, 6, 8, 10
Saint-Saëns—Septet, op.65
Ives—Ragtime dances [2perc]
Bartók—Three village scenes [2cl]
Stravinsky—Concerto in E-flat [2hn]; Septet
Becker—When the willow nods [2perc]
Ibert—Divertissement; Symphonie marine [2perc]
Hindemith—Kammermusik no.1
Cowell—Sinfonietta
Tansman—Sinfonietta [2tbn, 3perc]
Revueltas—Homenaje a Federico Garcia Lorca [2tp]
Copland—Three Latin-American sketches
Walton—Façade 2
Finney—Landscapes remembered
Britten—Sinfonietta
Perle—Serenade no.2
Rochberg—Cheltenham concerto
Kirchner—Toccata [4perc]
Xenakis—Anaktoria
Chou—Beijing in the mist [2perc]
Ligeti—Melodien [2hn]
Powell—Modules [2hn, 2perc]
Hollingsworth—Three ladies beside the sea [narrator, 2fl]
Anderson, T. J.—Chamber symphony [2perc]
Stockhausen—Kontra-Punkte no.1 [2cl]
Takemitsu—Rain coming
Shchedrin—Geometrie des Tones [2perc]
Birtwistle—Carmen arcadiae mechanicae perpetuum
Kolb—Chromatic fantasy
McCabe—The lion, the witch and the wardrobe: Suite [2cl, 2tp, 3perc]
Torke—Adjustable wrench [2cl, 2tp]

16'-20'

Roussel—Le Marchand de sable qui passe... (incidental music)
Schoenberg—Five pieces for orchestra, op.16 (chamber orch)
Respighi—Trittico Botticelliano

Stravinsky—Danses concertantes [2hn]
Hindemith—Tuttifäntchen: Suite [2perc]
Sessions—Concertino for chamber orchestra [2hn, 2perc]
Copland—Music for movies [2tp]
Tippett—Divertimento for chamber orchestra
Bacewicz—Contradizione
Kubik—Divertimento I for 13 players
Surinach—Ritmo jondo [4perc]
Kay, U.—Scherzi musicali
Maderna—Serenata no.2 [2cl]
Birtwistle—Endless parade
Maxwell Davies—Carolísima serenade; Sinfonia for chamber orch
Bolcom—Orphée-sérénade
Kolb—Soundings [pre-recorded tape]
Walker, Gwyneth—The light of three mornings
Caltabiano—Concertini [2hn]

Over 20'

Beethoven—Septet, op.20
Spohr—Nonet, op.31
Schubert—Octet, D.803
Saint-Saëns—Le Carnaval des animaux
Schoenberg—Pierrot Lunaire
Schreker—Kammersymphonie [harm]
Stravinsky—L'Histoire du soldat: Suite
Villa-Lobos—Bachianas brasileiras no.2 [2hn, 6perc]
Prokofiev—Peter and the wolf [3hn]
Honegger—Le Dit des jeux du monde; Symphony no.2
Milhaud—Le Carnaval de Londres [2perc]
Rogers—The musicians of Bremen
Thomson, V.—Parson Weems and the cherry tree
Harsányi—L'Histoire du petite tailleur
Copland—Appalachian spring: Suite (orig inst)
Walton—Façade
Weber, Ben—Symphony on poems of William Blake [2cl]
Maxwell Davies—Sinfonia concertante
Rands—Madrigali [2perc]
Sallinen—Concerto for chamber orch
Svoboda—Concerto for chamber orch

Duration variable or uncertain

Crawford—Music for small orchestra
Brown—Available forms 1 [3cl]

STRINGS
2 FLUTES or 2 RECORDERS

Lully—Roland: Chaconne
Charpentier, M.-A.—Noëls pour les instruments [bn]
Scarlatti, A.—Sinfonias nos.1, 5 [cnt]
Bach, W.F.—Sinfonia, D minor
Abel—Symphonies, op.1, nos.5 & 6
Bach, J.C.—Symphony, op.9, no.2 [cnt]
Foote—Air & gavotte
Vaughan Williams—Fantasia on "Greensleeves" [hp]

STRINGS
2 (OR MORE) HORNS

Telemann—Suite, F major [cnt]
Sammartini, Giov. Battista— Sinfonias, J.-C.4; J.-C.47 [cnt]
Galuppi—Sinfonias, D major, F major
Gluck—Sinfonias, D major, F major
Stamitz, Joh.—Symphony, op.3, no.3
Haydn—Divertimento no.9, Hob.II:21
Boccherini—Symphony "A", G.500
Mozart—Divertimentos no.7, K.205 [bn]; no.10, K.247; no.15, K.287; no.17, K.334; Ein musikalischer Spass; Serenade no.8, K.286
Grainger—Irish tune from County Derry
Barbirolli—An Elizabethan suite [4hn in last mvt only]

STRINGS
WINDS 0202-2000
CONTINUO

10' or less

Telemann—Overture in D major
Handel—Concerti grossi, op.3, nos.5-6
Handel—Overtures to Alcina, Alexander's feast, Judas Maccabaeus, Samson; Solomon: Entrance of the Queen of Sheba
Leo—Santa Elena al Calvario: Sinfonia
Arne—Symphonies nos.1-2
Boyce—Overtures: Ode for his majesty's birthday (1769), Ode for the new year (1772), Peleus and Thetis; Symphonies nos.2, 3, 4, 6
Gluck—Orfeo ed Euridice: Dance of the furies
Abel—Symphonies, op.1, no.5-6
Haydn—Symphony no.2
Gossec—Christmas suite

Bach, J.C.—Symphonies, op.3, no.1; op.3, no.2; op.6, no.1; op.21, no.3
Haydn, M.—Symphony, P.26
Paisiello—Sinfonia, D major; Sinfonia in tre tempi, D major
Boccherini—Overture, op.43, G.521; Symphonies nos.1 & 12
Cimarosa—I traci amanti: Overture
Salieri—Sinfonia, D major (Veneziana)
Mozart—Contradance, K.534; Overtures to Apollo et Hyacinthus, Bastien und Bastienne, La finta giardiniera; Symphonies nos.4, 5, 10, 11; Symphony, K.196/121
Weber, Ben—Dolmen

11'-20'

Albinoni—Concerto, op.9, no.9
Handel—Concerto grosso, op.3, no.4; Overtures to Rodrigo, Saul [incl solo org], Solomon, Theodora
Tartini—Concerto no.58
Wagenseil—Sinfonia, G minor
Stamitz, Joh.—Sinfonia pastorale, op.4, no.2
Abel—Symphony, op.14, no.2
Haydn—Symphonies A & B; Symphonies nos.1, 3-5, 10-12, 14-19, 21-23, 25-29, 34-37, 40, 46, 58-59, 65, 67
Bach, J.C.—Symphonies, op.3, no.4; op.6, no.6; op.9, no.2; op.21, no.1
Haydn, M.—Symphony, P.33, P.42
Golabek—Symphony in D maj (I & II)
Saint-Georges—Symphony no.1, op.11, no.1
Vanhal—Sinfonia, G minor
Boccherini—Symphony no.13-20, 26
Mozart—Cassation no.2, K.99; Symphonies nos.1-2, 6, 12-13, 15-17, 33, Symphony, K.Anh.223
Pleyel—Symphony, op.3, no.1

Over 20'

Bach—Suite (Overture) no.1
Handel—Water music: Suite no.1
Haydn—Symphonies nos.42-45, 47, 49, 51-52, 55, 64, 66, 68
Boccherini—Symphonies nos.6 & 11
Mozart—Cassation no.1; Divertimento no.11; Symphony no.29
Amram—Shakespearian concerto
Shchedrin—Music for strings, oboes, horns & celesta

[0202-2000-cnt-str]

Duration uncertain

Lalande—Christmas symphony
Handel—Orlando: Overture

STRINGS
WINDS 2202-2000
CONTINUO

10' or less

Rameau—Platée: Suite des danses
Handel—Concerto grosso, op.3, no.1
[2cnt]
Sammartini, Giov. Battista—Sinfonia,
J.-C.47
Graun—Sinfonia, F major, M.95
Boyce—Symphonies nos.1 & 7
Bach, C.P.E.—Symphony, H.665
Gluck—Orfeo ed Euridice: Dance of
the blessed spirits
Haydn, M.—Symphony, P.29
Boccherini—Overture, op.43, G.521
Cimarosa—Sinfonia, D major
Mozart—Contradances, K.267, K.610;
Overtures to La finta semplice, Mi-
tridate; Serenade no.2; Symphony
no.24
Hindemith—Spielmusik, op.43, no.1

11'-20'

Rameau—Dardanus: Suite
Bach—Suite (Overture) no.2
Handel—Water music: Suite no.3
Arne—Symphony no.4
Boyce—Symphony no.8
Bach, C.P.E.—Symphony, H.663
Haydn—Symphonies nos.9, 24, 30,
62-63, 77-78, 85
Bach, J.C.—Symphonies, op.18,
nos.1, 3, 5, 6
Haydn, M.—Symphonies, P.16, P.21
Golabek—Symphony in C major
Boccherini—Symphonies nos.5, 9-10,
18, 21, 23, 27
Mozart—Symphonies nos.14, 21, 27,
37
Wanski—Symphony in G major
Berkeley—Windsor variations
Musgrave—Night music
Schurmann—Variants
Zwilich—Concerto grosso 1985

Over 20'

Haydn—Symphonies nos.6-8, 71, 74,
76, 79-81, 83-84, 87, 89, 91

Boccherini—Symphonies nos.3, 8, 25
Wanski—Symphony in D major
Witt—Symphony in A
Schubert—Symphony no.5

Duration uncertain

Lully—Roland: Chaconne
Lalande—Christmas symphony
Rameau—Les Paladins: Suite no.2
Boccherini—Symphony no.7

STRINGS
WINDS 2202-2200
TIMPANI
CONTINUO

10' or less

Lully—Roland: Suite
Handel—Alceste: Instrumental pieces
Handel—Occasional oratorio: Over-
ture [3tp]
Arne—Symphony no.3
Boyce—Overture (Ode for the new
year [1758])
Boyce—Symphony no.5
Gluck—Overtures to Iphigenie in Au-
lis, Orfeo ed Euridice
Piccinni—Iphigenie en Tauride: Over-
ture
Haydn, M.—Andromeda ed Perseo:
Overture
Paisiello—La scuffiara: Overture
Cimarosa—Il maestro di cappella:
Overture
Mozart—Contradances, K.587, 603;
German dances, K.605; Overtures to
Lucio Silla, Il re pastore; Marches,
K.62, K.189, K.214, K.215, K.237,
K.249, K.335; Symphony,
K.111/120; Symphony, K.141a;
Symphonies nos.22, 23, 26
Weber, C.M.—Peter Schmoll: Overture
Schubert—Overture, D.470
Hindemith—Suite of French dances
[lute]
Maxwell Davies—Threnody on a
plainsong

11'-20'

Rameau—Les Fêtes d'Hébé: Diver-
tissement
Handel—Water music: Suite no.2
Sammartini, Giov. Battista—Sinfonia,
J.-C.2
Bach, C.P.E.—Symphony, H.663
Haydn—Symphonies nos.20, 32-33,
37-38, 41, 50, 69-70, 75, 96

[2202-2200-tmp-cnt-str; *11'-20'*]
Bach, J.C.—Symphony, op.18, no.4
Dittersdorf—Sinfonia, C major
Salieri—Sinfonia, D major (Giorno onomastico)
Mozart—German dances, K.536 [2fl & pic]; Idomeneo: Ballet music; Marches, K.408; Symphonies nos.7-9, 20, 30; Symphony, K.320; Thamos, König in Ägypten: Zwischenaktmusiken
Weber, C.M.—Symphony no.2

21'-30'

Handel—Royal fireworks music (ed. Baines & MacKerras) [3ob]
Gluck—Don Juan: Four movements [tbn]
Haydn—Symphonies nos.48, 53-54, 56-57, 60-61, 73, 82, 86, 88, 90, 92-95, 97-98, 102
Mozart—Symphonies nos.28, 34, 36, 38, 41, Symphony, K.204
Witt—Jena symphony
Weber, C.M.—Symphony no.1

Over 30'

Bach—Musikalisches Opfer [3ob]
Handel—Water music
Mozart—Serenades nos.3-5, 7, 9; Symphony, K.250

STRINGS
WINDS 2222-2200
TIMPANI

10' or less

Purcell—The Gordian knot untied: Suite no.2; The virtuous wife: Suite
Haydn—March for the Royal Society of Musicians
Paisiello—Nina: Overture; Sinfonia funebre
Cimarosa—Il matrimonio segreto: Overture
Mozart—Contradance, K.535; German dances, K.602; Mauerische Trauermusik [basset hn]; Overture, K.311a; Overtures to La clemenza di Tito, Così fan tutte, Don Giovanni, Idomeneo, Le nozze di Figaro, Der Schauspieldirektor
Beethoven—Coriolan overture; Prometheus: Overture
Weber, C.M.—Preziosa: Overture [5perc]
Rossini—Overtures to La Cenerentola, L'Italiana in Algeri, La scala di seta,

Il signor Bruschino, Tancredi; Guillaume Tell: Pas de six
Schubert—Overtures to Claudine von Villa Bella, Die Freunde von Salamanka, Der häusliche Krieg, Der Spiegelritter, Der Teufel als Hydraulicus, Die vierjährige Posten, Die Zwillingsbrüder; Overtures D.8 (arr. Hofmann), D.556, D.590, D 591
Arriaga—Los esclavos felices: Overture
Mendelssohn—The Hebrides; Heimkehr aus der Fremde; Märchen von der schönen Melusine; Midsummernight's dream: Intermezzo, Nocturne, Scherzo
Schumann, R.—Manfred: Zwischenaktmusik
Verdi—La traviata: Prelude to Act III
Rimsky-Korsakov—Tsar Saltan: Flight of the bumblebee
Fauré—Pavane
Elgar—Salut d'amour
Delius—Two pieces for small orch
Mascagni—Cavalleria rusticana: Intermezzo
Sibelius—Kuolema: Valse triste
Ives—The unanswered question
Bartók—Rumanian folk dances
Etler—Elegy for small orchestra
Maxwell Davies—Ojai Festival overture
Adolphe—Three pieces for kids & chamber orch: Rainbow

11'-20'

Purcell—The Gordian knot untied: Suite no.1; The married beau: Suite
Abel—Symphony, op.7, no.6
Bach, J.C.—Symphony, op.18, no.2
Mozart—Divertimento [no.1] K.113; German dances, K.567 & K.600; Symphonies nos.3, 31, 35
Beethoven—Contradances; Musik zu einem Ritterballet
Schumann, R.—Overture, scherzo, & finale
Wagner—Siegfried idyll
Delibes—Le Roi s'amuse: Airs de danse
Koechlin—Partita, op.205
Roussel—Concerto for small orch
Kodály—Summer evening
Prokofiev—Classical symphony
Piston—Sinfonietta
Berkeley—Sinfonietta
Britten—Sinfonietta
Effinger—Little symphony no.1
Panufnik—Harmony
Peck—The thrill of the orchestra

[2222-2200-tmp-str]

21'-30'

Haydn—Symphonies nos.99, 101, 103-104
Mozart—Les Petits Riens, K.Anh.10; Symphony no.39
Cherubini—Symphony, D major
Beethoven—Symphonies nos.1, 8
Schubert—Symphonies nos.1-3, 6
Arriaga—Symphony, D major
Mendelssohn—Symphony no.4
Gounod—Symphony no.1
Sibelius—Pelléas and Mélisande
Schoenberg—Chamber symphony no.2

Over 30'

Mozart—Serenade no.1, K.100; Symphony no.40
Beethoven—Prometheus [basset horn]; Symphonies nos.2, 4, 7
Mendelssohn—Sinfonia no.8 (version with winds); Symphony no.1
Maxwell Davies—Sinfonietta accademica; Symphony no.4
Bolcom—Symphony no.3

Duration uncertain

Adolphe—Three pieces for kids & chamber orch: TDT

STRINGS
WINDS 2222-2200
3 PERCUSSION
HARP, CELESTA, PIANO

10' or less

Bach, J.C.—Symphony, D major [3cl]
Mozart—Die Entführung aus dem Serail: Overture [4perc]
Beethoven—Die Ruinen von Athen, op.113: Turkish march [3bn]
Boieldieu—Le Calife de Bagdad: Overture
Rossini—Overtures to Il barbiere di Siviglia, L'Italiana in Algeri, Tancredi
Schumann, R.—Manfred: Suite
Chabrier—Habanera
Humperdinck—Hänsel und Gretel: Knusperwalzer (Crackle-waltz)
Debussy—Danse [4perc]; Sarabande
Delius—Hassan: Intermezzo & Serenade; Irmelin: Prelude [3cl]
Mascagni—Cavalleria rusticana: Intermezzo

Järnefelt—Praeludium
Pfitzner—Das Christ-Elflein: Overture
Vaughan Williams—The wasps: Overture [3perc], March past of the kitchen utensils
Ravel—Ma Mère l'Oye: Prélude et Danse du rouet; Pavane pour une infante défunte
Falla—El amor brujo: Ritual fire dance
Wolf-Ferrari—The jewels of the Madonna: Intermezzo no.1
Webern—Symphony, op.21
Becker—Two pieces for orchestra: Among the reeds and rushes
Ibert—Hommage á Mozart
Benjamin—Two Jamaican pieces [asx]
Cowell—Carol for orchestra
Dallapiccola—Piccola musica notturna
Raksin—Toy concertino
Martino—Divertisements for youth orchestra
Maxwell Davies—Chat Moss
Bolcom—Commedia for (almost) 18th-century orchestra
Tann—With the heather and small birds

11'-20'

Rameau—Ballet suite
Grétry—Zémire et Azor: Ballet suite
Mozart—German dances, K.571
Fauré—Masques et Bergamasques
Debussy—Petite Suite [4perc]
Pfitzner—Kleine Sinfonie, op.44
Roussel—Le Festin de l'araignée: Symphonic fragments
Ravel—Le Tombeau de Couperin
Falla—El sombrero de tres picos: Suite no.1
Respighi—Gli uccelli
Prokofiev—A summer day
Britten—Suite on English folk tunes
Maderna—Serenata no.2
Lees—Concerto for chamber orch
Henze—Aria de la Folía española [mandolin]; Symphony no.1
Druckman—Nor spell nor charm
Harbison—The most often used chords
Tann—Adirondack light

Over 20'

Haydn—Symphony no.100
Falla—El amor brujo: Ballet suite
Martinu—Toccata e due canzoni
Honegger—Symphony no.4
Poulenc—Sinfonietta

[2222-2200-3perc-hp, cel, pf-str; *Over 20*]
Ward—Symphony no.3
Bolcom—A summer divertimento
Proto—Doodles [elec bass]

**STRINGS
WINDS 2222-2231
1 PERCUSSION**

10' or less

Gluck—Alceste: Overture
Mozart—Don Giovanni: Overture (arr.
Busoni); Die Zauberflöte: Overture
Cherubini—Overtures to Démophoon,
Faniska, L'Hôtellerie portugaise
Boieldieu—La Dame blanche: Overture
Paganini—Moto perpetuo (arr. Molinari)
Weber, C.M.—Silvana: Overture
Schubert—Overtures, D.12 & D.26;
Overtures to Alfonso und Estrella,
Des Teufels Lustschloss
Bellini—Symphonies, C min & D maj
Adam—Si J'Étais Roi: Overture
Glinka—Kamarinskaya
Mendelssohn—Athalia: Kriegsmarsch
der Priester; Trumpet overture
Bruckner—March in D minor; Three
pieces for orchestra
Balakirev—Overture on three Russian
folk songs
Mussorgsky—Scherzo, B-flat major
Janácek—Adagio
Stravinsky—Suite no.1 for small orch
Copland—Down a country lane
Walton—Façade: Suite no.2 [asx]
Benson—Five brief encounters
Maxwell Davies—Jimmack the postie
Jones—In retrospect
Rands—Fanfare for a festival
Peck—Playing with style

11'-20'

Schubert—Rosamunde: Ballet music
Mendelssohn—Midsummernight's
dream: Overture
Schumann, R.—Overture, scherzo, &
finale
Bruckner—Overture, G minor
Holst—Egdon Heath; Hammersmith
Ives—Symphony no.3
Stravinsky—Danses concertantes
Villa-Lobos—Sinfonietta no.1
Warlock—Capriol suite
Finney—Landscapes remembered
Swanson—Short symphony
Rorem—A Quaker reader
Berio—Variazioni per orchestra da

camera
Maxwell Davies—First fantasia on an
In nomine of John Taverner
Sallinen—Variations for orchestra

Over 20'

Clementi—Symphonies nos.1-4
Schubert—Rosamunde: Entr'actes;
Symphonies nos.8, 9
Mendelssohn—Symphony no.5
Schumann, R.—Symphony no.2
Grieg—Symphony, C minor
Vaughan Williams—Symphony no.5
Milhaud—Saudades do Brazil
Weill—Symphony no.2
Carter—Symphony no.1

**STRINGS
WINDS 2222-2331
4 PERCUSSION
HARP, CELESTA, PIANO**

10' or less

Monteverdi—Orfeo: Overture [2hp]
Bach—Musikalisches Opfer: Ricercare
Haydn, M.—Pastorello, P.91
Weber, C.M.—Abu Hassan: Overture;
Turandot: Overture & march [5perc]
Rossini—Overtures to Il barbiere di
Siviglia, La Cenerentola, L'Italiana in
Algeri, Il Turco in Italia, Il viaggio a
Reims
Lanner—Die Werber Walzer
Lortzing—Zar und Zimmermann:
Overture
Glinka—Valse fantaisie
Mendelssohn—Overtures to Athalia,
St. Paul; Midsummernight's dream:
Wedding march
Gounod—Marche funèbre d'une marionette
Delibes—Coppelia: Entr'acte & Waltz
Balakirev—Overture on three Russian
folk songs
Chabrier—Le Roi malgré lui: Danse
slav & Fête polonaise
Charpentier, G.—Louise: Prelude to
Act III & Air de Louise [2hp]
German—Henry VIII: Three dances
Glazunov—The seasons: Three movements [6perc]
Satie—Deux Préludes posthumes et
une gnossienne; Jack in the box;
Trois Petites Pièces montées [2tp,
2perc]
Vaughan Williams—English folk song
suite
Holst—Capriccio
Ives—Country band march [asx]; The

[2222-2331-4perc-hp, cel, pf-str; *10' or less*]
gong on the hook and ladder; Overture and march 1776
Coleridge-Taylor—Christmas overture
Falla—La vida breve: Spanish dance no.1
Wolf-Ferrari—The jewels of the Madonna: Intermezzo no.2 (small orch)
Bartók—Dances of Transylvania; Hungarian peasant songs
Stravinsky—Pas de deux; Suite no.2
Webern—Variations for orch, op.30
Griffes—The white peacock [2hp]
Riegger—Dance rhythms [5perc]
Villa-Lobos—Bachianas brasileiras no.5: Aria (full orch) [8perc]
Martinu—Comedy on the bridge: Little suite
Hindemith—Cupid and Psyche: Overture
Jacob—The barber of Seville goes to the devil
White—Five miniatures for orchestra
Gerhard—Albada, interludi i dansa
Cowell—Hymn and fuguing tunes nos.3 & 16
Korngold—Theme and variations, op.42
Copland—Billy the Kid: Prairie night & Celebration dance, Waltz; John Henry; Rodeo: Corral nocturne, Saturday night waltz; Variations on a Shaker melody
Luening—Synthesis [tape]
Walton—Façade: Suite no.1; Portsmouth Point
Kabalevsky—The comedians: Galop
Barber—Die natali: Silent night
Schuman, Wm.—Newsreel [5perc]
Britten—Paul Bunyan: Overture [3cl]; Soirées musicales
Foss—Salomon Rossi suite
Chou—All in the spring wind; Landscapes
Frackenpohl—Short overture
Cunningham—Lullabye for a jazz baby [3cl]
Martino—Divertisements for youth orchestra
Davidovsky—Inflexions
Corigliano—Elegy for orchestra
León—Batá
Davis—Notes from the underground [5perc]

11'-20'

Bach—Suites nos.3, 4 [3ob]
Gluck—Ballet suite no.2
Sullivan—The tempest: Three dances
Satie—Les Aventures de Mercure
Roussel—Petite Suite, op.39

Ives—Three places in New England (chamber orch)
Ravel—Ma Mère l'Oye: 5 pièces enfantines
Bartók—Hungarian sketches
Stravinsky—Scènes de ballet
Milhaud—Aubade; Le Boeuf sur le toit; Cortège funèbre; La Création du monde [asx]; Suite française
Rogers—Once upon a time
Still—Darker America
Gerhard—Alegrías: Suite; Don Quixote: Dances
Thomson, V.—Louisiana story: Acadian songs and dances; The plow that broke the plains: Suite
Auric—La Chambre
Shostakovich—Hamlet: Incidental music (1932), op.32
Swanson—Concerto for orchestra
Wilder—Carl Sandburg suite
Smith, J.—Folkways symphony [asx]
Britten—Matinées musicales
Coolidge—Pioneer dances
Diamond—Music for Shakespeare's Romeo and Juliet
Babbitt—Ars combinatoria
Husa—Fantasies for orchestra
Xenakis—ST/48—1,240162
Rorem—Ideas for easy orchestra; Symphony no.2
Stockhausen—Kontra-Punkte no.1
Takemitsu—Tree line
Colgrass—Letter from Mozart
Maxwell Davies—An Orkney wedding, with sunrise [Highland bagpipes]
Rands—Agenda, for young players
Bennett, Richard R.—Serenade
Armer—The great instrument of the Geggerets
McCabe—The lion, the witch and the wardrobe: Suite
Svoboda—Nocturne, op.100 [gtr]
Plain—Clawhammer
Peck—The thrill of the orchestra
Kechley—Alexander and the wind-up mouse
Danielpour—First light
Liebermann, Lowell—The domain of Arnheim

Over 20'

Mozart, Leopold—Musikalische Schlittenfahrt [4tp]
Chabrier—Suite pastorale
Strauss, R.—Le Bourgeois Gentilhomme: Suite [6perc]
Vaughan Williams—Symphony no.8 [6perc]
Ravel—Ma Mère l'Oye
Honegger—Le Dit des jeux du monde

[2222-2331-4perc-hp, cel, pf-str; *Over 20*]
Thomson, V.—The river: Suite [banjo]
Poulenc—The story of Babar, the little elephant
Copland—Appalachian spring: Suite (full orch); Music for the theatre
Weill—Aufstieg und Fall der Stadt Mahagonny: Suite [2sx, bass gtr, banjo]; Symphony no.1 [5perc]
Tippett—Concerto for orchestra [3hn]
Menotti—Sebastian: Suite
Gould—The jogger and the dinosaur
Ginastera—Variaciones concertantes
Berio—Rendering
Schuller—Contours
London—In Heinrich's shoes
Maxwell Davies—Caroline Mathilde: Suites from Acts I & II
Bennett, Richard R.—Sonnets to Orpheus [2hp]
Bach, Jan—The happy prince
Wuorinen—The magic art
Adams, John—Chamber symphony

STRINGS
WINDS 2222-4200
3 PERCUSSION
HARP, CELESTA, PIANO

10' or less

Mozart—Betulia liberata: Overture; German dances, K.605; Symphony no.32
Cherubini—Medea: Overture
Beethoven—Overtures: Egmont, Leonore, Namensfeier, Die Ruinen von Athen
Verdi—La traviata: Prelude to Act I
Wagner—Tristan und Isolde: Prelude, Act III
Bizet—Les Pecheurs de perles: Overture
Mussorgsky—Khovantchina: Introduction
Dvořák—Legends, op.59, nos.1-10
Elgar—Dream-children
Mahler—Symphony no.1: Blumine
Debussy—Clair de lune
Satie—Gymnopédies nos.1-3 [2hp]
Vaughan Williams—The wasps: Overture [4perc]
Kodály—Háry János: Intermezzo
Martinu—Overture
Thomson, V.—Pilgrims and pioneers

11'-20'

Lully—Ballet suite
Handel—Water music suite (arr. Harty)

Scarlatti, D.—The good-humored ladies: Suite
Haydn—Symphony no.39
Vanhal—Sinfonia, G minor
Mozart—Symphonies nos.18-19
Chopin—Les Sylphides (arr. Glazunov) [4perc]
Franck—Les Éolides
Bizet—Jeux d'enfants: Petite Suite [4perc]
Fauré—Pelléas et Mélisande: Suite; Shylock
Debussy—Le Coin des enfants
Sibelius—The tempest: Suite no.2
Kodály—Galanta dances
Prokofiev—Sinfonietta, op.5/48
Piston—Serenata
Ginastera—Estancia: Ballet suite [8perc]
Bolcom—Symphony no.1 [tbn]
Rouse—Iscariot
Torke—Ash

Over 20'

Handel—Il pastor fido: Suite
Haydn—Die sieben letzten Worte (orch version)
Haydn—Symphonies nos.13, 31, 72
Kraus—Symphony, C minor (1783)
Mozart—Divertimento [no.2] K.131; Symphony no.25
Beethoven—Symphony no.3
Schubert—Symphony no.4
Mendelssohn—Symphonies nos.2-3
Brahms—Serenade no.1
Bizet—Symphony no.1
Tchaikovsky—Suites nos.1 [3fl] & 4
Parry—Symphony no.3
Bartók—Suite no.2 [2hp]
Kernis—Symphony in waves

STRINGS
WINDS 2222-4330
TIMPANI

15' or less

Gluck—Iphigenie in Aulis: Overture
Cherubini—Overtures to Abenceragen, Anacreon, Les Deux Journées
Beethoven—Overtures: Fidelio, Leonore nos.2-3, Die Weihe des Hauses
Weber, C.M.—Overtures to Beherrscher der Geister, Euryanthe, Der Freischütz, Oberon
Berwald—Estrella de Soria: Overture
Schubert—Fierrabras: Overture; Overture, D.648, E minor; Rosamunde: Overture, D.644
Berlioz—Béatrice et Bénédict: Over

[2222-4330-tmp-str; *15' or less*]
ture

Glinka—A life for the Tsar: Overture
Mendelssohn—Die Hochzeit des Camacho, Ruy Blas
Schumann, R.—Overtures to Faust, Genoveva, Manfred
Gade—Efterklange af Ossian
Borodin—In the steppes of central Asia
Brahms—Hungarian dances nos.5, 6 (arr. Parlow)
Paine—Oedipus tyrannus: Prelude
Svendsen—Rapsodie norvégienne no.3
Tchaikovsky—Eugen Onegin: Polonaise
Massenet—Manon: Minuet & Gavotte
Rimsky-Korsakov—May night: Overture
Stravinsky—Monumentum pro Gesualdo di Venosa ad CD annum
Thomson, V.—Bugles and birds

Over 15'

Berwald—Symphonies in C major, D major, E-flat major, G minor
Schubert—Rosamunde; Symphony no.7, D.729 (2 versions)
Schumann, R.—Symphonies nos.1, 3, 4
Bruckner—Studiensymphonie; Nullte Symphony; Symphonies nos.2, 3, 4
Reinecke—Symphonies nos.1-3
Borodin—Symphonies nos.1, 3
Bruch—Symphony no.1
Paine—Symphonies nos.1-2
Dvořák—Symphonic variations; Symphony no.7
Rimsky-Korsakov—Sinfonietta on Russian themes; Symphony no.1
Parry—Symphony no.3
Chadwick—Symphony no.2
Sibelius—Symphonies nos.3, 5, 7
Einem—Meditations

STRINGS
WINDS 2222-4230
4 PERCUSSION

10' or less

Auber—Overtures to Le Domino noir, Fra Diavolo [5perc], Lestocq, Marco Spada
Donizetti—Overtures to Don Pasquale, La Fille du régiment
Lortzing—Zar und Zimmermann: Overture
Glinka—Summer night in Madrid

[6perc]
Nicolai—The merry wives of Windsor: Overture
Flotow—Alessandro Stradella: Overture
Wagner—Siegfried: Forest murmurs
Litolff—Robespierre: Overture
Offenbach—La Vie parisienne: Overture [3sx]
Suppé—Overtures to Banditenstreiche [gtr], Boccaccio, Die leichte Kavallerie, Ein Morgen, ein Mittag und ein Abend in Wien, Die schöne Galathea
Strauss, Joh., Jr.—Fledermaus: Overture, Du und du; Wiener Blut
Brahms—Hungarian dances nos.2, 7 (arr. Hallén); nos.17-21 (arr. Dvořák)
Bruch—Swedish dances, op.63, nos.1-7
Dvořák—Slavonic dances, op.46, nos.1-8; op.72, nos.1-8
Grieg—Wedding day at Troldhaugen
Humperdinck—Hänsel und Gretel: Knusperwalzer
Sibelius—Pan and Echo
Milhaud—Ouverture méditerranéene

Over 10'

Kuhlau—William Shakespeare: Overture
Rossini—Overtures to Guillaume Tell, Semiramide
Berlioz—Le Roi Lear: Overture
Goldmark—Ländliche Hochzeit
Rimsky-Korsakov—Overture on Russian themes
Sibelius—Symphony no.4
Busoni—Rondo arlecchinesco
Kodály—Marosszek dances
Prokofiev—Peter and the wolf [3hn]
Luening—Rhapsodic variations [tape]
Weill—Symphony no.1 [5perc]

STRINGS
WINDS 2222-4431
5 PERCUSSION

10' or less

Bach—Jesu, joy of man's desiring
Haydn, M.—Pastorello, P.91 [cnt]
Mozart—German dances, K.605
Cherubini—Ali Baba: Overture
Weber, C.M.—Preziosa: Overture
Hérold—Zampa: Overture
Meyerbeer—Fackeltanz no.1
Rossini—Overtures to La gazza ladra, Robert Bruce
Bellini—Overtures to Norma, Il pirata

[2222-4431-5perc-str; *10' or less*]
Berlioz—Carnaval romain; Le Cor saire; Les Troyens: Overture
Schumann, R.—Julius Caesar: Overture
Thomas—Raymond: Overture
Flotow—Martha: Overture
Verdi—Overtures to Nabucco, I vespri siciliani
Moniuszko—The countess: Overture;Halka: Mazur
Suppé—Pique Dame: Overture
Strauss, Joh., Jr.—Egyptian march; Künstler Quadrille; Morgenblätter; Pizzicato polka; Unter Donner und Blitz
Delibes—Coppelia: Valse de la poupée & Czardas
Waldteufel—Les Patineurs
Bruch—Swedish dances, op.63, nos.8-15
Mussorgsky—Intermezzo in the classic style
Dvořák—Fest-Marsch
Grieg—Wedding day at Troldhaugen
Sibelius—Finlandia; Legends: Lemminkäinen's return
Holst—A Somerset rhapsody
Stravinsky—Circus polka; Four Norwegian moods
Honegger—Prélude pour "La Tempête" de Shakespeare
Milhaud—Murder of a great chief of state
Jacob—Fantasia on the Alleluia hymn
Thomson, V.—Louisiana story: Boy fights alligator
Cowell—Hymn and fuguing tunes nos.3 & 16
Rubbra—Festival overture, op.62
Walton—Façade: Suite no.1
Schuman, Wm.—The orchestra song
McBride—Pumpkin-eater's little fugue
Britten—Gloriana: Courtly dances
Ward—Euphony for orchestra
Xenakis—Metastaseis B
Birtwistle—Machaut à ma manière
Corigliano—To music
Tower—Fanfare for the uncommon woman for orchestra
Peck—Playing with style
Walker, Gwyneth—Open the door

11'-20'

Buxtehude—Four chorale preludes
Handel—Royal fireworks music (arr. Harty)
Liszt—Festklänge; Hungarian rhapsody no.2 (arr. Müller-Berghaus)
Gade—Efterklange af Ossian
Franck—Rédemption: Morceau symphonique
Lalo—Le Roi d'Ys: Overture
Bruckner—Symphony no.4: Finale 1878 (Volksfest)
Bizet—Ouverture
Massenet—Scènes pittoresques
Sullivan—Overture di ballo; Overture in C [org]
Elgar—Three Bavarian dances
Sibelius—Legends: Lemminkäinen and the maidens of Saari, Lemminkäinen in Tuonela; En saga
Rachmaninoff—Symphony, D minor
Hindemith—Concert music for strings & brass [without woodwinds]
Thomson, V.—Symphony on a hymn tune
Tcherepnin—Georgiana suite [6perc]
Khachaturian—Masquerade: Suite
Lutoslawski—Little suite
Kay, U.—Fantasy variations; Serenade for orchestra
Ward—Adagio and allegro
Kirk—An orchestra primer
Bergsma—Documentary one
Lees—The trumpet of the swan
Sculthorpe—Mangrove
Maxwell Davies—An Orkney wedding, with sunrise [Highland bagpipes]
Peck—The thrill of the orchestra
Picker—Keys to the city
MacMillan—The confession of Isobel Gowdie

Over 20'

Liszt—Die Ideale
Bruckner—Symphonies nos.4, 5, 6
Goldmark—Symphony no.2
Brahms—Symphony no.2
Bruch—Symphony no.3
Dvořák—A hero's song; Symphonies nos.6, 8
Massenet—Scènes alsaciennes
Strauss, R.—Symphony, op.12
Nielsen—Aladdin: 7 pieces; Symphony no.6
Sibelius—Symphony no.2
Vaughan Williams—Symphony no.4
Stravinsky—Jeu de cartes
Toch—Symphony no.6
Hindemith—Mathis der Maler: Symphony; Nobilissima visione; Symphonic dances
Walton—Symphony no.1
Swanson—Symphony no.1
Dello Joio—The triumph of Saint Joan
Schickele—The chenoo who stayed to dinner
Monroe—The amazing symphony orchestra

[2222-4431-5perc-str; *Over 20*]
Rouse—Symphony no. 1

Duration uncertain

Schubert—Trauermarsch, D.859

STRINGS
WINDS 2222-4431
5 PERCUSSION
HARP, CELESTA, PIANO

10' or less

Handel—Xerxes: Largo
Adam—Si J'Étais Roi: Overture
Glinka—Jota aragonesa
Liszt—Hungarian rhapsody no.5
Thomas—Mignon: Overture
Verdi—La forza del destino: Overture
Wagner—Götterdämmerung: Gesang
der Rheintöchter, Siegfried's Rhine
journey; Das Rheingold: Entry of the
Gods into Valhalla; Tristan und
Isolde: Nachtgesang
Offenbach—Overtures to La Belle Hél-
ène, Orpheus in the underworld; Les
Contes d'Hoffmann: Intermezzo &
Barcarolle
Suppé—Dichter und Bauer: Overture
Strauss, Joh., Jr.—An der schönen
blauen Donau; Frühlingsstimmen;
Kaiser-Walzer; Perpetuum mobile;
Rosen aus dem Süden; Wein, Weib,
und Gesang; Zigeunerbaron: Over-
ture
Strauss, Jos.—Dorfschwalben aus
Österreich; Mein Lebenslauf ist Lieb'
und Lust; Sphärenklänge
Saint-Saëns—La Princesse jaune:
Overture
Delibes—Coppelia: Prelude & Ma-
zurka
Bruch—Loreley: Prelude
Dvorák—Fest-Marsch
Massenet—Hérodiade: Prelude, Act III
Grieg—Bell ringing; Wedding day at
Troldhaugen
Humperdinck—Eine Trauung in der
Bastille
Delius—The walk to the Paradise Gar-
den
Vaughan Williams—Prelude
Schoenberg—Begleitungsmusik zu
einer Lichtspielscene
Grainger—Shepherd's hey [8perc]
Stravinsky—L'Oiseau de feu: Ber-
ceuse & Finale
Bacon—The muffin man
Finzi—Nocturne
Walton—Crown imperial; Johannes-
burg festival overture
Siegmeister—Lonesome hollow
Barber—Essay no. 1
Britten—Soirées musicales
Gould—Symphonette no.2
Fine—Diversions for orchestra
Surinach—Feria magica
Ginastera—Oberatura para el
"Fausto" Criollo [6perc]
Bernstein—West side story: Overture
Bergsma—A carol on Twelfth Night
Foss—American fanfare
Smith, H.—Contours
Floyd—In celebration
Hoag—An after-intermission overture
for youth orchestra
Maxwell Davies—Five Klee pictures
Wilson—Houston fanfare
Daugherty—Metropolis symphony: Oh
Lois!

11'-20'

Berlioz—Rob Roy
Wagner—Götterdämmerung: Sieg-
fried's death & funeral music
(Stasny); Die Walküre: Wotan's fare-
well & Magic fire music
Strauss, Joh., Jr.—Geschichten aus
dem Wienerwald
Delibes—Sylvia: Suite
Bizet—Carmen: Suites nos.1-2; Jolie
Fille de Perth: Scènes bohémiennes;
Patrie
Dvorák—Slavonic rhapsodies, op.45,
nos.2-3
Massenet—Le Cid: Ballet music [2hp]
Grieg—Sigurd Jorsalfar: Three
orchestral pieces
Rimsky-Korsakov—Overture on Rus-
sian themes
Fauré—Dolly
Foote—Four character pieces after the
Rubáiyát of Omar Khayyám
Humperdinck—Dornröschen: Suite
Janácek—Lachian dances
Debussy—Printemps
Schmitt—Musiques de plein air [2hp]
Ives—Holidays symphony: Thanksgiv-
ing and/or Forefathers' Day; Three
places in New England (chamber
orch)
Coleridge-Taylor—Hiawatha: Suite
Carpenter—Sea drift
Bartók—Dance suite
Stravinsky—Le Chant du rossignol
[2hp]
Weiner—Divertimento no.5, op.39
Villa-Lobos—Sinfonietta no.2 [asx]
Ibert—Louisville concerto
Martinu—Estampes
Bliss—Things to come: Concert suite

[2222-4431-5perc-hp, cel, pf-str; *11'-20'*]
Hindemith—Sinfonietta in E
Still—Wood notes
Thomson, V.—Louisiana story: Suite
Poulenc—Secheresses
Copland—Lincoln portrait; Orchestral variations; Prairie journal
Krenek—Eleven transparencies for orchestra
Walton—Hamlet and Ophelia
Dallapiccola—Variations for orchestra
Kabalevsky—The comedians
Creston—Invocation and dance
Shostakovich—Ballet Suite no.1
Ránki—Sinfonia 1
Stevens—Sinfonia breve
Barber—Souvenirs
Hovhaness—Exile symphony; Symphony no.15
Britten—Canadian carnival; The prince of the pagodas: Pas de six
Kay, U.—Umbrian scene
Foss—Exeunt [elec gtr]
Thorne—Elegy for orchestra
Rorem—Design [6perc]
Benson—A Delphic serenade
Hollingsworth—Divertimento
Smith, H.—Ritual and incantations
Musgrave—Peripeteia; Rainbow
Adams, Leslie—Ode to life
Schickele—A zoo called Earth [taped narration]
Tower—Sequoia
Zwilich—Symphony no.1
Bamert—Circus parade
Schwantner—Aftertones of infinity
Adams, John—The Chairman dances
Tsontakis—Perpetual Angelus
Danielpour—First light

21'-30'

Delibes—Coppelia: Suite no.1
Mussorgsky—Pictures at an exhibition (arr. Goehr)
Vaughan Williams—The wasps: Suite
Stravinsky—L'Oiseau de feu: Suite (1919 & 1945 versions)
Krenek—Symphony
Egk—Variationen über ein karibisches Thema
Tippett—The midsummer marriage: Ritual dances
Carter—The minotaur: Ballet suite; Variations for orchestra
Barber—Medea
Schuman, Wm.—Judith
Gould—Fall River legend: Ballet suite
Bernstein—Facsimile; Fancy free: Suite
Kay, H.—Cakewalk: Concert suite
Suolahti—Sinfonia piccola

Bassett—Variations for orchestra
Rorem—Symphony no.1 [6perc]
Lees—Symphony no.2
Henze—Symphony no.8
Sheng—H'un (Lacerations)

Over 30'

Adam—Giselle
Strauss, Joh., Jr.—Graduation ball
Bizet—Roma
Dvořák—Symphony no.4
Albéniz—Iberia (arr. Surinach)
Sibelius—Symphony no.1
Vaughan Williams—Job; Symphonies nos.2-3
Gerhard—Symphony no.1
Tippett—Symphony no.2
Maxwell Davies—Second fantasia on John Taverner's "In nomine" [2 tubas]

Duration uncertain

Strauss, Joh., Jr.—Die Fledermaus: Suite
Weiner—Preludio, Notturno e Scherzo diabolico

STRINGS
8 WOODWINDS
BRASS 4300
TIMPANI
CONTINUO

Handel—Concerti a due cori, nos.1-3; Royal fireworks music
Mozart—Divertimento [no.1] K.113
Szöllösy—Sonorità

STRINGS
WINDS 3222-4331
4 PERCUSSION

10' or less

Bach—Sheep may safely graze
Mozart—Turkish march, K.331
Rossini—L'assedio di Corinto: Overture
Donizetti—Linda di Chamounix: Prelude; Roberto Devereux: Overture
Schubert—Grande Marche héroïque
Berlioz—Les Troyens: Royal hunt and storm
Strauss, Joh., Sr.—Radetzky march
Chopin—Polonaise, op.40, no.1
Schumann, R.—Overtures to Braut

[3222-4331-4perc-str; *10' or less*]
von Messina, Hermann und Dorothea
Liszt—Hamlet, Huldigungs-Marsch, Rákóczi march
Verdi—Aïda: Prelude
Wagner—Christoph Columbus: Overture [6tp]; Tannhäuser: Arrival of the guests, Prelude Act III; Die Walküre: Ride of the Valkyries (arr. Sheffer)
Cornelius—Der Barbier von Bagdad: Overture (B minor)
Smetana—The bartered bride: Overture; Má vlast: Sárka
Goldmark—Im Frühling
Borodin—Petite Suite: Scherzo & Nocturne; Prince Igor: Overture
Brahms—Hungarian dances nos.1, 3, 10 (arr. Brahms); nos.5, 6, 7 (arr. Schmeling)
Saint-Saëns—Danse macabre
Buck—Festival overture on the American national air
Mussorgsky—The fair at Sorochinsk: Gopak; Khovantchina: Entr'acte
Paine—As you like it: Overture
Tchaikovsky—Eugen Onegin: Waltz; Suite no.1: Marche miniature
Dvořák—Slavonic rhapsody, op.45, no.1
Grieg—In autumn
Chadwick—Rip van Winkle: Overture
Humperdinck—Hänsel und Gretel: Prelude
Reznicek—Donna Diana: Overture
MacDowell—The Saracens: Two fragments after the Song of Roland
Mascagni—Cavalleria rusticana: Prelude & Siciliana
Nielsen—Maskarade: Overture, Hanedans; Saul and David: Prelude Act II
Sibelius—Karelia overture, op.10
Busoni—Lustspiel overture
Ives—Variations on America
Coleridge-Taylor—The bamboula; Danse nègre
Becker—Two pieces for orchestra: The mountains
Toch—Pinocchio
Dahl—Quodlibet on American folk tunes & folk dances
Einem—Capriccio, op.2
Arnold—Tam O'Shanter overture
Shchedrin—Symphonic fanfares
Svoboda—Overture of the season; Serenade, op.115; Three pieces for orchestra, op.45
Tann—Through the echoing timber

11'-20'

Gluck—Ballet suite no.1

Mozart—German dances, K.509, K.536
Beethoven—German dances; Wellingtons Sieg [6tp]
Liszt—Battle of the Huns; Funeral triumph of Tasso; Von der Wiege bis zum Grabe
Wagner—Tannhäuser: Overture (Dresden version)
Smetana—The bartered bride: Three dances; Má vlast: Z ceskych luhuv a hájuv (From Bohemia's meadows and forests), Tábor, Blaník
Gottschalk—Symphony no.2
Brahms—Tragische Ouvertüre
Tchaikovsky—The tempest
Dvořák—Husitská
Grieg—Peer Gynt: Suite no.1
Chadwick—Melpomene
Wolf—Der Corregidor: Suite; Scherzo & finale
MacDowell—Hamlet & Ophelia; Lamia; Lancelot and Elaine; Suite no.1
Glazunov—Chopiniana
Nielsen—Helios overture
Sibelius—Karelia suite, op.11
Coleridge-Taylor—Petite Suite de concert
Stravinsky—Ode
Revueltas—Janitzio
Read—Pennsylvania suite
Einem—Ballade
Svoboda—Sinfoniette (à la renaissance)
Tann—The open field

21'-30'

Mozart—German dances, K.586
Borodin—Petite Suite
Brahms—Serenade no.2
Saint-Saëns—Symphony no.2
Rimsky-Korsakov—The Maid of Pskov: Overture & Three entr'actes
MacDowell—Suite no.2 [4tbn]
Nielsen—Symphony no.1
Kodály—Symphony
Stravinsky—Symphony in C
Hanson—Symphony no.4
Porter—Symphony no.2
Giannini—Symphony no.2
Shostakovich—Symphonies nos.3, 9
Arnold—Symphony no.6
Svoboda—Dance suite

Over 30'

Beethoven—Symphony no.6
Schubert—Symphony, D.812, op.140 (Grand duo)

[3222-4331-4perc-str; *Over 30*]
Gade—Symphony no.1
Bruckner—Symphony no.1
Tchaikovsky—Suite no.1; Symphonies nos.1-6
Dvořák—Symphony no.2
Rimsky-Korsakov—Symphony no.3
Dukas—Symphony in C major
Nielsen—Symphony no.2
Hadley—Symphony no.2
Suk—Symphony no.1
Glière—Symphony no.1
Einem—Wiener Symphonie
Arnold—Symphony no.3

STRINGS
WINDS 3222-4431
5 PERCUSSION
HARP, CELESTA, PIANO

10' or less

Purcell—Trumpet prelude
Auber—Masaniello: Overture
Berlioz—La Damnation de Faust: Rakoczy march
Liszt—Hungarian rhapsodies nos.3 [cimb] & 6
Wagner—Götterdämmerung: Siegfried's Rhine journey; Die Meistersinger: Prelude
Lalo—Rapsodie norvégienne
Cornelius—Der Barbier von Bagdad: Overture (D major; arr. Mottl)
Borodin—Prince Igor: Polovtsian march
Saint-Saëns—Danse macabre; Marche héroïque; Le Rouet d'Omphale
Mussorgsky—Khovantchina: Dance of the Persian maidens; Solemn march
Massenet—Phèdre: Overture
Grieg—Peer Gynt: Prelude
Rimsky-Korsakov—Snegourotchka: Dance of the buffoons; The tsar's bride: Overture
Chadwick—Euterpe
Humperdinck—Hänsel und Gretel: Hexenritt
Delius—Sleigh ride
Mascagni—L'amico Fritz: Intermezzo; Cavalleria rusticana: Prelude & Siciliana
Glazunov—The seasons: Winter; Valse de concert, no.2
Wolf-Ferrari—Il segreto di Susanna: Overture
Cadman—Oriental rhapsody from Omar Khayyam
Grainger—The immovable do; Molly on the shore
Kodály—Háry János: Intermezzo

Stravinsky—Scherzo à la russe
Toch—Circus, an overture
Slonimsky—My toy balloon [7perc]
Weinberger—Svanda dudák: Polka & fugue [4tp backstage]
Copland—An outdoor overture; Rodeo: Hoe-down (full orch)
Alwyn—Festival march
Arnold—Four Cornish dances
Corigliano—Promenade overture
Larsen—Overture for the end of a century

11'-20'

Halévy—La Juive: Overture
Berlioz—Les Troyens: Ballet
Liszt—Hungarian rhapsody no.4; Mephisto waltzes nos.1-2; Nocturnal procession; Les Préludes; Von der Wiege bis zum Grabe
Verdi—Aïda: Triumphal march & ballet
Wagner—Der fliegende Holländer: Overture
Smetana—Má vlast: Vltava; Richard III; Valdstynuv tabor (Wallenstein's camp)
Brahms—Hungarian dances nos.11-16 (arr. Parlow)
Saint-Saëns—Suite algérienne
Mussorgsky—Night on bald mountain
Dvořák—Husitská
Grieg—Lyric suite, op.54; Norwegian dances; Peer Gynt: Suite no.2
Rimsky-Korsakov—Russian Easter overture; Sadko: Tableau musical; Skazka, op.29 (Russian fairy tale); Snegourotchka: Suite
Noskowski—The steppe
Chadwick—Sinfonietta, D major
Humperdinck—Hänsel und Gretel: Three excerpts
Puccini—Capriccio sinfonico; Preludio sinfonico
Glazunov—Stenka Razine
Schmitt—Reflets d'Allemagne
Rabaud—La Procession nocturne
Rachmaninoff—The rock
Holst—The perfect fool: Ballet music
Respighi—Antiche danze ed arie: Set I
Bartók—Mikrokosmos suite
Kodály—Theater overture
Gerhard—Pedrelliana
Hanson—Symphony no.5
Weinberger—Under the spreading chestnut tree
Copland—The tender land: Suite
Creston—Two choric dances
Phillips—Selections from McGuffey's reader
Anderson, Leroy—Irish suite

[3222-4431-5perc-hp, cel, pf-str; *11'-20'*]
Carter—Pocahontas: Suite
Coolidge—Pioneer dances
Khrennikov—Symphony no.1
Ginastera—Pampeana no.3
Overton—Symphony no.2
Reynolds—Fiery wind
Warshauer—As the waters cover the
  sea
Torke—Ecstatic orange
Smith, G.—Mr. Smith's composition

21'-30'

Wagner—Die Meistersinger: Three ex-
  cerpts from Act III
Borodin—Symphony no.2
Paine—Shakespeare's Tempest
Tchaikovsky—Swan lake: Suite
  (Jurgenson)
Grieg—Old Norwegian melody with
  variations; Symphonic dances
Rimsky-Korsakov—Symphony no.2
Kodály—Concerto for orchestra; Var-
  iations on a Hungarian folksong
Stravinsky—Orpheus
Copland—Billy the Kid: Suite
Shostakovich—Symphony no.1
Reich—The four sections [2pf]
Holloway—Scenes from Schumann

Over 30'

Liszt—A Faust symphony
Tchaikovsky—Swan lake (complete);
  Swan lake: Suite (Kalmus); Sympho-
  ny no.7
Nielsen—Symphony no.5
Kalinnikov—Symphony no.2
Reger—Variations and fugue on a
  theme of Mozart
Shostakovich—Symphony no.15
  [7perc]

STRINGS
WINDS 3322-4431
6 PERCUSSION
2 HARPS, CELESTA, PIANO

10' or less

Weber, C.M.—Aufforderung zum Tanz
  [4bn]
Meyerbeer—Les Huguenots: Overture
Schubert—Marche militaire, D.733
  (op.51), no.1
Berlioz—La Damnation de Faust:
  Dance of the sylphs; Les Troyens:
  Trojan march
Ponchielli—La Gioconda: Dance of the
  hours
Mussorgsky—The fair at Sorochinsk:
  Introduction
Paine—Poseidon and Amphitrite
Tchaikovsky—Fatum; Marche sole-
  nelle du couronnement; Mazeppa:
  Danse cosaque; Le Voyévode: Over-
  ture
Dvořák—Carnival overture
Wolf—Der Corregidor: Prelude & in-
  terlude
Debussy—Marche écossaise sur un
  thème populaire; Prélude à "L'Après-
  midi d'un faune"
Delius—Dance rhapsody no.2
Rachmaninoff—Vocalise
Schoenberg—A survivor from Warsaw
Grainger—Shepherd's hey [8perc]
Barber—Essay no.2

11'-20'

Liszt—Héroïde funèbre; Légendes;
  Nocturnal procession; Orpheus; Pro-
  metheus
Wagner—Tannhäuser: Venusberg
  music
Smetana—Má vlast: Vysehrad
Goldmark—Sakuntala: Overture
Borodin—Prince Igor: Polovtsian
  dances
Saint-Saëns—La Jeunesse d'Hercule
  ["petite bugle"]
Balakirev—Russia
Tchaikovsky—Capriccio italien; Ham-
  let; Overture 1812; Romeo and Ju-
  liet overture-fantasy (final version
  1880)
Dvořák—Othello overture; Rhapsody,
  op.14; Watersprite
Rimsky-Korsakov—Capriccio espag-
  nol
Luigini—Ballet égyptien
Liadov—Eight Russian folk songs
Ippolitov-Ivanov—Turkish fragments
Albéniz—Rapsodia española
Glazunov—The seasons: Autumn
Schmitt—Musiques de plein air
Rachmaninoff—Capriccio bohémien
Holst—Beni mora
Ravel—Valses nobles et sentimentales
  [7perc]
Falla—El sombrero de tres picos:
  Suite no.2
Respighi—Antiche danze ed arie: Set
  II
Bloch, E.—Evocations
Bartók—Deux Portraits
Enesco—Rumanian rhapsodies 1-2
Malipiero—Sinfonia per Antigenida
Martinu—Sinfonia concertante for 2
  orchestras

[3322-4431-6perc-2hp, cel, pf-str; *11'-20*]
Milhaud—Suite provençale
Rodrigo—A la busca del más allá
Walton—As you like it
Dallapiccola—Due pezzi per orchestra
Alwyn—Symphony no.5
Hovhaness—And God created great
   whales [tape]; Floating world [8perc];
   Variations and fugue
Britten—Young person's guide to the
   orchestra
Schuller—Five etudes for orchestra
Wilson—Expansions III

21'-30'

Liszt—Hungaria
Wagner—Tannhäuser: Overture & Ve-
   nusberg music
Saint-Saëns—La Foi: Trois Tableaux
   symphoniques
Tchaikovsky—Francesca da Rimini;
   Romeo and Juliet (orig version
   1869); Sleeping Beauty: Suite
Dvořák—Czech suite
Massenet—Suite no.1
Ippolitov-Ivanov—Caucasian sketches
Falla—El sombrero de tres picos
Respighi—La Boutique fantasque
   (after Rossini): Suite; Rossiniana
Alwyn—Symphony no.2
Reich—Variations [2pf, 3 elec org]

Over 30'

Balakirev—Symphony no.1 [3cl]
Tchaikovsky—Suites nos.2-3
Dvořák—Symphonies nos.1, 3, 9
Rimsky-Korsakov—Scheherazade
Debussy—La Boîte à joujoux
Kalinnikov—Symphony no.1
Rachmaninoff—Symphony no.1
Alwyn—Symphony no.1
Shostakovich—Hamlet: Film suite
   (1964), op.116

**STRINGS
9/10 WOODWINDS
BRASS 4331
4 PERCUSSION**

10' or less

Handel—Overture, D major
Gluck—Alceste: Overture
Beethoven—König Stephan: Overture
Weber, C.M.—Jubel overture
Berlioz—Waverley
Glinka—Russlan and Ludmilla: Over-
   ture

Brahms—Akademische Festouvertüre
Fauré—Pénélope: Prelude
Humperdinck—Königskinder: Pre-
   lude, Introduction to Act II
Sibelius—The tempest: Prelude
Thomson, V.—Fugue and chorale on
   "Yankee Doodle"
Copland—Our town
Shostakovich—The age of gold: Polka
Dahl—Quodlibet on American folk
   tunes & folk dances
Britten—Paul Bunyan: Overture
Dello Joio—Five images for orchestra
Mecham—The jayhawk
Mamlok—Grasshopper
Schickele—Celebration with bells
Svoboda—Swing dance

11'-20'

Berlioz—Les Franc-Juges [2 tubas];
   Roméo et Juliette: Love scene
Mendelssohn—Meeresstille und
   glückliche Fahrt
Liszt—Hungarian rhapsody no.2
Wagner—Eine Faust-Ouvertüre
Brahms—Variations on a theme of
   Haydn
Dvořák—In nature's realm; Midday
   witch; Suite, op.98b
Schumann, G.—Liebesfrühling
Holst—Egdon Heath
Casella—Paganiniana
Thomson, V.—Symphony on a hymn
   tune
Kay, U.—Southern harmony
Subotnick—Play no.2

Over 20'

Beethoven—Symphony no.5
Mendelssohn—Symphony no.5
Wagner—Symphony, C major
Brahms—Symphonies nos.1, 3, 4
Elgar—Enigma variations
Glazunov—Symphony no.4
Beach—Symphony no.2
Scriabin—Symphony no.2
Reger—Vier Tondichtungen, op.128
Ives—Symphonies nos.1-2
Stravinsky—Symphony no.1
Hindemith—Lustige Sinfonietta
Tippett—Symphony no.1

STRINGS
9/10 WOODWINDS
BRASS 4431
6 PERCUSSION
HARP, CELESTA, PIANO

10' or less

Monteverdi—Orfeo: Toccata & ritor-
nelli
Bach, J.C.—Symphony, D major
Weber, C.M.—Aufforderung zum Tanz
[2hp]
Wagner—Huldigungsmarsch
Smetana—Hakon Jarl
Borodin—Nocturne (arr. Tcherepnin)
Saint-Saëns—Marche du couronne-
ment, op.117
Delibes—Coppelia: Ballade & Thème
slave varié
Gomes—Il Guarany: Overture
Tchaikovsky—Marche slave
Rimsky-Korsakov—Christmas eve: Po-
lonaise; Dubinushka
Janácek—Jealousy
Liadov—The enchanted lake
Delius—Irmelin: Prelude
Glazunov—Cortéges solennel [no.1],
op.50; no.2, op.91
Sibelius—The bard
Granados—Goyescas: Intermezzo
[2hp]
Schmitt—Rapsodie viennoise; Ronde
burlesque [7perc]
Ives—Holidays symphony: The Fourth
of July [7perc]
Wolf-Ferrari—L'amore medico: Inter-
mezzo
Stravinsky—Feu d'artifice [6hn]
Milhaud—Ouverture philharmonique
Sowerby—Comes autumn time
Gershwin—Promenade
Harris—Ode to consonance [baritone
horn]
Copland—Rodeo: Saturday night
waltz
Rodgers—Slaughter on Tenth Avenue
Walton—Façade: Suite no.2
Barber—Die natali: Silent night
Dahl—Quodlibet on American folk
tunes & folk dances
Gillis—Short overture to an unwritten
opera
Moncayo—Huapango
Brant—Verticals ascending
Britten—Peter Grimes: Passacaglia
Chou—And the fallen petals
Cunningham—Lullabye for a jazz
baby
Previn—Overture to a comedy
Svoboda—Festive overture [4tbn]
Hailstork—Celebration
Adams, John—Tromba lontana

11'-20'

Berlioz—Benvenuto Cellini: Overture
[6tp]
Liszt—Hungarian rhapsody no.1; Tas-
so, lament and triumph
Wagner—Rienzi: Overture
Gounod—Faust: Ballet music
Lalo—Le Roi d'Ys: Overture
Bizet—L'Arlésienne: Suites nos.1-2
Dvorák—Wood dove
Stanford—Irish rhapsody no.1
Janácek—Lachian dances
Elgar—Cockaigne
Glazunov—Valse de concert, no.1
Sibelius—The tempest: Suite no.1
Granados—Tres danzas españolas
Schmitt—Feuillets de voyage
Ives—Holidays symphony: Thanksgiv-
ing and/or Forefathers' Day; Three
places in New England (large orch)
Grainger—In a nutshell [8-12perc]
Webern—Sechs Stücke, op.6 [4tbn]
Butterworth—A Shropshire lad
Coates—London suite
Prokofiev—Lieutenant Kijé: Suite
Milhaud—Symphony no.12
Bennett, Robt. R.—Suite of old Ameri-
can dances
Hindemith—Concerto for orchestra
Copland—Prairie journal; El salón
México
Shostakovich—The age of gold: Suite
[baritone horn]
Siegmeister—Five fantasies of the the-
ater; Theater set; Western suite
Britten—Peter Grimes: Four sea inter-
ludes
Gould—Spirituals for orchestra
Panufnik—Autumn music
Bernstein—On the town: Three dance
episodes
Bergsma—Chameleon variations
Foss—Quintets for orchestra
Berio—Requies
Henze—Antifone [7perc]
Crumb—Echoes of time and the river
Hoddinott—Sinfonietta 3
Sculthorpe—Kakadu
Martino—Ritorno
Schwartz—Island
Wuorinen—Crossfire; Machault mon
chou

21'-30'

Dvorák—Golden spinning wheel
Rimsky-Korsakov—Christmas eve:
Suite
Chadwick—Symphonic sketches
Glazunov—Scènes de ballet, op.52

[9/10ww-4431-6perc-hp, cel, pf-str; *21'-30'*]
Sibelius—Symphony no.6
Vaughan Williams—Symphony no.8
Hanson—Symphony no.1
Gershwin—Catfish Row
Copland—The red pony
Foss—Geod
Laderman—Magic prison [org]
Williams—Star wars: Suite
Jones—Symphony no.2
Svoboda—Symphony no.2 [4tbn]
Adams, John—Fearful symmetries
Ran—Concerto for orchestra
Tan—Death and fire

Over 30'

Berlioz—Symphonie fantastique [2hp, 2 tubas]
Liszt—Ce Qu'on Entend Sur La Montagne
Franck—Symphony in D minor
Delibes—Coppelia
Balakirev—King Lear: Incidental music; Symphony no.2
Strauss, R.—Aus Italien
Reger—Variations and fugue on a theme of Hiller
Hindemith—Die Harmonie der Welt: Symphony
Svoboda—Symphony no.1 [4tbn]
Proto—Doodles [elec bass]
Ran—Symphony [6hn]

STRINGS
WINDS 3332-4331
5 PERCUSSION
HARP, CELESTA, PIANO

10' or less

Couperin—La Sultane: Overture and allegro
Handel—Prelude & fugue, D minor
Tchaikovsky—Le Voyévode, op.78 (symphonic ballad)
Liadov—Kikimora
Puccini—Manon Lescaut: Intermezzo from Act III
Stravinsky—Variations
Still—Festive overture; In memoriam
Copland—Our town; Rodeo: Buckaroo holiday, Hoe-down (full orch)
Khachaturian—Gayane: Sabre dance [asx], Three pieces [asx]
Barber—Fadograph of a yestern scene; Night flight; Overture to The school for scandal; Vanessa: Intermezzo, Under the willow tree
Schuman, Wm.—American festival overture

Surinach—Drama jondo; Fandango
Rochberg—Time-span (II)
Mennin—Canto
Feldman—Structures for orchestra
Turok—A Joplin overture
Lavista—Clepsidra

11'-20'

Dvořák—Scherzo capriccioso
Rimsky-Korsakov—Tsar Saltan: Suite
Satie—Parade
Schmitt—Étude, op.49
Vaughan Williams—In the fen country
Karlowicz—Lithuanian rhapsody
Respighi—Impressioni brasiliane
Stravinsky—Four etudes [4cl]
Still—Poem
Gershwin—American in Paris
Harris—Symphony no.3 [2 tubas]
Copland—Inscape
Barber—Andromache's farewell; Die natali
Diamond—The world of Paul Klee
Persichetti—Night dances
Kay, U.—Theater set for orchestra
Mennin—Concertato
Druckman—Aureole
Lombardo—Drakestail
Shchedrin—The seagull: Suite
Maxwell Davies—Prolation [4tbn]

21'-30'

Tchaikovsky—Nutcracker: Suite no.1
Carpenter—Adventures in a perambulator
Stravinsky—Le Baiser de la fée: Divertimento
Martinu—Symphonies nos.2-3
Sessions—Symphony no.2
Khachaturian—Gayane: Suites nos.2, 3 [asx]; Spartacus: Suite no.2
Swanson—Symphony no.3
Mennin—Symphony no.6
Pinkham—Signs of the zodiac
Druckman—Brangle
Tan—Orchestral theatre II: Re

Over 30'

Khachaturian—Gayane: Suite no.1 [asx]
Prokofiev—Symphony no.7
Rachmaninoff—Symphony no.2
Stravinsky—Le Baiser de la fée
Vaughan Williams—Symphony no.3
Tchaikovsky—Nutcracker [2hp]
Suk—Pohádka

[3332-4331-5perc -hp, cel, pf-str]

Duration uncertain

Grofé—American biographies: Henry Ford

STRINGS
11 WOODWINDS
BRASS 4431
5 PERCUSSION
HARP, CELESTA, PIANO

15' or less

Meyerbeer—Le Prophète: Coronation march
Wagner—Tristan und Isolde: Nachtgesang; Die Walküre: Ride of the Valkyries (arr. Hutschenruyter)
Franck—Le Chasseur maudit
Ponchielli—Elegia [4tbn]
Chabrier—Joyeuse Marche
Chaminade—Callirhoe suite
Puccini—Edgar: Preludio
Satie—Cinq Grimaces pour Un Songe d'une nuit d'été
Roussel—Pour Un Fête de printemps
Riegger—Music for orchestra
Honegger—Mouvement symphonique no.3 [asx]
Milhaud—Les Funérailles de Phocion
Hindemith—Neues vom Tage: Overture
Harris—Elegy for orchestra
Copland—Lincoln portrait
Finzi—The fall of the leaf; Nocturne
Berkeley—Symphony no.3
Panufnik—Heroic overture
Nelhybel—Music for orchestra
Berio—Nones [6perc, elec gtr]
Schuller—Five bagatelles
Maxwell Davies—Sir Charles—his pavan
Svoboda—Ex libris [4tbn]
Picker—Old and Lost Rivers

Over 15'

Handel—Royal fireworks music (ed. Baines & MacKerras) [5tp]
Meyerbeer—Le Prophète: Ballet music
Janácek—Taras Bulba [org]
Wolf—Penthesilea
Strauss, R.—Don Juan
Sibelius—Night ride and sunrise
Gilbert—Dance in the Place Congo
Bloch, E.—Trois Poèmes juifs
Stravinsky—Symphony in three movements (1945)
Hindemith—Pittsburgh symphony

Hanson—Symphony no.2
Korngold—Schauspiel-Ouvertüre; Sinfonietta, op.5
Chávez—Symphony no.4
Ellington—Black, brown and beige: Suite [asx]; Night creature
Shostakovich—Symphony no.5
Siegmeister—Sunday in Brooklyn
Gould—Latin-American symphonette
Panufnik—Nocturne
Husa—Two sonnets by Michelangelo [asx]
Erb—Symphony of overtures
Maxwell Davies—Symphony no.2
Bennett, Richard R.—Concerto for orchestra
Wuorinen—A reliquary for Igor Stravinsky
Tan—Orchestral theatre I: Xun

Duration uncertain

Ran—Legends

STRINGS
WINDS 3333-4331
5 PERCUSSION

15' or less

Bach—Passacaglia, BWV 582
Wagner—Kaisermarsch; Lohengrin: Prelude Act I, Prelude Act III, Elsa's procession to the cathedral
Saint-Saëns—Orient et Occident
Rimsky-Korsakov—The Maid of Pskov: Overture
Liadov—Baba-Yaga
Elgar— Pomp and circumstance, no.5
Holst—Hammersmith
Schoenberg—Theme and variations, op.43b
Weiss—American life [3sx]
Honegger—Pacific 231; Rugby
Piston—Pine tree fantasy
Thomson, V.—Sea piece with birds; A solemn music, and a joyful fugue
Cowell—Synchrony
Harris—When Johnny comes marching home [euphonium]
Chávez—Resonancias
Walton—Portsmouth Point
Blacher—Orchester-Ornament
Farkas—Prelude & fugue
Shostakovich—Festive overture
Gutche—Holofernes overture
Messiaen—Hymne; Les Offrandes oubliées
Schuman, Wm.—American festival overture

[3333-4331-5perc-str; *15' or less*]
Henze—Quattro poemi
Penderecki—Als Jakob erwachte...
[5hn]
Peck—The thrill of the orchestra
Chen—Duo ye no.2

Over 15'

Liszt—Mazeppa
Wagner—Tristan und Isolde: Prelude & Liebestod
Bruckner—Symphony no.9: Finale (2 versions)
Strauss, R.—Macbeth [btp]
Nielsen—Symphonies nos.3-4
Sibelius—Tapiola
Vaughan Williams—Symphony no.4
Schoenberg—Chamber symphony no.1, op.9b (orch version)
Karlowicz—Odwieczne piesni
Miaskovsky—Symphonies nos.21-22
Stravinsky—Le Sacre du printemps (reduced versions)
Honegger—Symphonies nos.1, 5
Piston—Symphonies nos.1-2
Hindemith—Philharmonic concerto; Symphonic metamorphosis of themes by Weber; Symphony in E-flat
Hanson—Symphony no.3
Thompson, R.—Symphony no.2
Copland—Statements
Blacher—Orchestra-variations on a theme of Paganini
Kabalevsky—Symphonies nos.1-2
Shostakovich—Symphony no.10
Messiaen—L'Ascension
Schuman, Wm.—Symphony no.6
Dello Joio—Variations, chaconne & finale
Diamond—Symphony no.2
Kay, U.—Markings; Southern harmony
Mennin—Symphony no.7
Maxwell Davies—Symphony no.3
Zwilich—Symphony no.3

**STRINGS
WINDS 3333-4431
6 PERCUSSION
2 HARPS, CELESTA, PIANO**

10' or less

Bach—Sheep may safely graze
Berlioz—Roméo et Juliette: Queen Mab scherzo
Wagner—Götterdämmerung: Siegfried's Rhine journey
Saint-Saëns—Phaéton; Samson et

Dalila: Bacchanale
Balakirev—Islamey (arr. Liapounow) [4fl]
Mussorgsky—Boris Godunov: Polonaise
Chabrier—España; Gwendolyn: Overture
Lysenko—Taras Bulba: Overture
Rimsky-Korsakov—Le Coq d'or: Introduction & Wedding march
Humperdinck—Königskinder: Introduction to Act III
Elgar— Pomp and circumstance, nos.1, 2, 4
Leoncavallo—I pagliacci: Intermezzo
Albéniz—Catalonia; Navarra
Roussel—Rapsodie flamande
Lehár—The merry widow: Overture
Holst—The lure
Ives—Holidays symphony: Decoration Day
Glière—The red poppy: Russian sailors' dance
Ravel—Menuet antique
Brian—Symphony no.22 [8perc]
Falla—La vida breve: Interlude & dance
Wolf-Ferrari—The jewels of the Madonna: Intermezzo no.2 (large orch)
Stravinsky—Canon
Turina—La procesion del rocio
Griffes—Clouds
Ibert—Bostoniana
Prokofiev—The love for three oranges: March & Scherzo; War and peace: Overture
Honegger—Chant de joie
Piston—Toccata
Still—Bells
Thomson, V.—The Seine at night; Wheat field at noon
Tansman—Toccata
Copland—Danzón cubano; Jubilee variation on a theme by Goosens; Preamble for a solemn occasion
Mosolov—Iron foundry
Rodgers—Carousel: The carousel waltz
Walton—Crown imperial; Johannesburg festival overture; Prologo e fantasia
Kabalevsky—Colas Breugnon: Overture; Overture pathétique
Alwyn—Festival march
Finney—Hymn, fuguing tune & holiday
Carter—Holiday overture
Barber—Music for a scene from Shelley
Lutoslawski—Postludium
Read—First overture
Perle—Six bagatelles
Kay, U.—Of new horizons

[3333-4431-6perc-2hp, cel, pf-str; *10' or less*]
Ward—Jubilation—an overture
Foss—Ode for orchestra
Walker, George—Overture in praise of folly
Berio—Ritirata notturna di Madrid
Martirano—Contrasto
Jones—Fanfare and celebration
Bolcom—Ragomania!
Harbison—Remembering Gatsby
Proto—Fantasy on the Saints [elec bass]
Schwantner—Freeflight
Hartway—Freedom festival
Warshauer—Revelation
Daugherty—Metropolis symphony: Krypton
Sheng—Fanfare I: Arrows to the page

11'-20'

Liszt—Hungarian rhapsody no.1
Lalo—Namouna: Ballet suite no.2 [4bn]
Balakirev—Thamar
Mussorgsky—Pictures at an exhibition (arr. Tushmalov)
Tchaikovsky—Nutcracker: Suite no.2
Rimsky-Korsakov—Tsar Saltan: Suite
Indy—Istar
Chadwick—Aphrodite
Elgar—In the south
Kelley—The pit and the pendulum
Debussy—Six Épigraphes antiques
Strauss, R.—Der Rosenkavalier: Waltzes, first sequence [basset horn]
Dukas—La Pèri [7perc]
Sibelius—The Oceanides; Pohjola's daughter
Roussel—Bacchus et Ariane: Suites nos.1-2; Évocations, op.15, no.1; Suite in F, op.33; Symphony no.4
Schmitt—Musiques de plein air
Converse—The mystic trumpeter
Alfvén—Midsommarvaka
Mason—Chanticleer
Holst—The perfect fool: Ballet music
Ravel—Sheherazade; ouverture de féerie
Ruggles—Men and mountains (large orch)
Respighi—Fontane di Roma
Bartók—Two pictures; The miraculous mandarin: Suite [org]
Stravinsky—Agon [mandolin]
Turina—Danzas fantásticas
Webern—Passacaglia, op.1
Griffes—The pleasure dome of Kubla Khan
Villa-Lobos—Danses africaines; Uirapurú [ssx, violinophone]
Martin—Les Quatre Éléments [asx]

Bliss—Introduction and allegro
Prokofiev—Cinderella: Suite no.2; The love for three oranges: Symphonic suite; Romeo and Juliet: Suite no.3
Weiss—I segreti
Milhaud—Symphony no.11
Moore, Douglas—Pageant of P.T. Barnum [7perc]
Rogers—Three Japanese dances
Piston—Concerto for orchestra; The incredible flutist; Lincoln Center festival overture; Symphonies nos.7-8; Three New England sketches
Sowerby—Prairie
Auric—Phèdre
Chávez—Initium
Ellington—Les Trois Rois noirs
Poulenc—Les Biches: Suite
Copland—Symphony no.2
Walton—Improvisations on an impromptu of Benjamin Britten
Khachaturian—Spartacus: Suite no.3
Kabalevsky—Colas Breugnon: Suite
Carter—Adagio tenebroso; Concerto for orchestra; Partita
Stevens—Symphonic dances
Barber—Symphony no.1
Hovhaness—Floating world [8perc]; Fra Angelico; Meditation on Orpheus
Britten—The prince of the pagodas: Pas de six
Gould—Soundings
Lutoslawski—Three postludes for orchestra
Blomdahl—Sisyphos [6perc]
Ginastera—Iubilum [4tbn]
Kay, U.—Chariots; Suite for orchestra
Ward—Sonic structure
Rochberg—Night music
Kirchner—Music for orchestra
Husa—Symphonic suite
Imbrie—Legend; Symphony no.3
Bassett—Echoes from an invisible world; From a source evolving
Pinkham—Symphonies nos.1-2
Rorem—Air music
Starer—Samson agonistes
Schuller—American triptych
Henze—Los caprichos
Peterson—The face of the night, the heart of the dark
Musgrave—Concerto for orchestra
Bloch, A.—Enfiando per orchestra
Takemitsu—Dream/window [gtr]
Baker—Kosbro
Colgrass—As quiet as...
Shchedrin—Selbstportrait
Sallinen—Shadows; Symphony no.1
Schwertsik—Der irdischen Klänge, 2.Teil
Bennett, Richard R.—Zodiac
Corigliano—Fantasia on an ostinato; Three hallucinations; Tournaments

[3333-4431-6perc-2hp, cel, pf-str; *11'-20'*]
Skoryk—Hutsul triptych
Singleton—Shadows
Proto—Casey at the bat [elec bass];
Fantasy on the Saints [elec bass]
Bamert—Snapshots
Schwantner—A sudden rainbow; Toward light
Peck—Peace overture
Paulus—Concertante
Stucky—Dreamwaltzes
Tsontakis—Winter lightning
Chen—Symphony no.2
Beaser—Double chorus for orchestra
Daugherty—Metropolis symphony:
Red cape tango
Mackey—TILT
Smith, G.—Mr. Smith's composition

21'-30'

Lalo—Namouna: Ballet suite no.1
[4bn]
Mussorgsky—Pictures at an exhibition (arr. Ravel) [asx]
Rimsky-Korsakov—Le Coq d'or: Suite
Chausson—Symphony, op.20
Elgar—Falstaff
Mahler—Symphony no.10: mvts I and III (Krenek); 1st mvt (Ratz)
Debussy—Nocturnes
Strauss, R.—Der Rosenkavalier:
Suite; Tod und Verklärung
Roussel—Symphony no.3
Schmitt—La Tragédie de Salomé
Hadley—Salome
Vaughan Williams—Symphony no.8
[6perc]
Rachmaninoff—Cinq Études-tableaux
Dohnányi—Ruralia hungarica
Respighi—Vetrate di chiesa [org]
Turina—Sinfonia sevillana
Toch—Symphony no.3
Villa-Lobos—Bachianas brasileiras nos.4 & 8 [4tbn]
Prokofiev—Cinderella: Suite no.1
[7perc], Suite no.3
Honegger—Symphony no.3
Milhaud—Symphonies nos.1, 2, 10
Piston—Symphonies nos.4, 5, 6
Hindemith—Symphonia serena
Gerhard—Concerto for orchestra
Tcherepnin—Symphony no.2 [7perc]
Antheil—Symphonies nos.4, 5, 6
Copland—Music for a great city
Walton—Symphony no.2; Variations on a theme by Hindemith
Khachaturian—Spartacus: Suite no.1
Jolivet—Symphony no.1
Schuman, Wm.—Judith; Undertow;
Symphonies nos.7, 9
Britten—Gloriana: Symphonic suite;

Sinfonia da requiem
Gould—Symphony of spirituals
Lutoslawski—Symphony no.2
Read—Symphony no.3, op.75
Fine—Symphony (1962)
Blomdahl—Symphony no.3
Dutilleux—Symphony no.2 [hpsd]
Ginastera—Popol vuh [4tbn]
Husa—Music for Prague 1968; Symphony no.1
Rorem—Symphony no.3 [7perc]
Laderman—Concerto for orchestra
Lees—Symphony no.5
Schuller—Seven studies on themes of Paul Klee
Henze—Symphonies nos.2, 3 [tsx], 4
Argento—In praise of music
Druckman—Windows
Schurmann—Six studies of Francis Bacon
Stockhausen—Punkte
Hoddinott—Symphony no.5
Shchedrin—The little humpbacked horse: Suite [no.1]
Blackwood—Symphony no.2
Maxwell Davies—Symphony no.5
Jones—Symphony no.3
Bolcom—Seattle Slew (dance suite)
Harbison—Symphony no.1
Tower—Concerto for orchestra; Silver ladders
Wuorinen—Movers and shakers
Zwilich—Symphony no.2
Monroe—The amazing symphony orchestra
Welcher—Haleakala; Night watchers
Paulus—Concerto for orchestra
Rouse—Symphony no.2
Stucky—Concerto for orchestra
Asia—Symphony no.1

31'-40'

Saint-Saëns—Symphony no.3
Busoni—Turandot: Suite
Vaughan Williams—Symphonies nos.6, 9 [1-3sx]
Rachmaninoff—Symphony no.3
Bartók—Concerto for orchestra
Stravinsky—Petrouchka (1947 version)
Taylor—Through the looking glass
Martinu—Symphonies nos.1, 5
Prokofiev—Chout: Symphonic suite [7perc]; Symphonies nos.2-3
Grofé—Grand Canyon suite
Piston—Symphony no.3
Thompson, R.—Symphony no.1
Shostakovich—Symphony no.12
Bernstein—Symphony no.2
Husa—Concerto for orchestra [5hn]
Imbrie—Symphony no.1

[3333-4431-6perc-2hp, cel, pf-str; *31'-40'*]
Holloway—Second concerto for
orchestra

Over 40'

Liszt—Dante symphony [harm]
Tchaikovsky—Manfred
Parry—Symphonic fantasy
Elgar—Symphony no.1
Vaughan Williams—Job; Symphonies
nos.2, 7 [org]
Holst—The planets
Schmidt—Symphony no.4
Suk—Symphony no.2
Bloch, E.—America
Shostakovich—The gadfly: Suite;
Symphony no.11
Maxwell Davies—Symphony [no.1]
Bamert—Once upon an orchestra
Daugherty—Metropolis symphony

STRINGS
WOODWINDS 3333
OTHERWISE LARGER THAN
PREVIOUS CATEGORIES

20' or less

Bach—Komm süsser Tod
Wagner—Christoph Columbus: Over-
ture
Dvořák—Watersprite
Elgar—Cockaigne
Pfitzner—Palestrina: Prelude, Act III
Rachmaninoff—Die Toteninsel
Ravel—Alborada del gracioso; Bolero;
La Valse
Grainger—In a nutshell
Ibert—Escales
Hanson—Merry Mount: Suite
Weinberger—Svanda dudák: Polka &
fugue
Gershwin—American in Paris
Harris—Horn of plenty
Ellington—Les Trois Rois noirs
Halffter—La muerte de Carmen: Ha-
banera
Shostakovich—Festive overture
Gutche—Holofernes overture
Carter—A symphony of 3 orchestras
Hovhaness—Mysterious mountain
Ginastera—Ollantay
Foss—Folksong for orchestra
Ligeti—Apparitions
Feldman—...Out of "Last pieces"
Henze—Barcarola
Penderecki—De natura sonoris no.2
Reynolds—Graffiti
Wuorinen—Contrafactum
Schwantner—From a dark millenni-

um
Sapieyevski—Summer overture
Chin—santika Ekatala

21'-30'

Saint-Saëns—Symphony no.1
Loeffler—A pagan poem
MacDowell—Suite no.2 [4tbn]
Glière—The red poppy: Suite
Carpenter—Skyscrapers
Respighi—Pini di Roma
Harris—Symphony no.5
Copland—Symphony no.1
Hartmann—Symphony no.6
Britten—Sinfonia da requiem
Lutoslawski—Concerto for orchestra
Foss—Baroque variations
Górecki—Old Polish music
Schnittke—In memoriam...
Ishii—Kyō-Sō

Over 30'

Bruckner—Symphonies nos.7, 8, 9
Paderewski—Symphony
Reger—Symphonic prolog to a tragedy
Ives—Symphony no.4 (1965 edition)
Tippett—Symphony no.4
Messiaen—Turangalila-symphonie
Shapey—Concerto fantastique
Penderecki—Symphony no.2

Duration uncertain

Shostakovich—Memorable year 1919

STRINGS
13 WOODWINDS
BRASS 4431
7 PERCUSSION
2 HARPS, CELESTA, PIANO

10' or less

Bach—Toccata & fugue, BWV 565
Berlioz—La Damnation de Faust:
Will-o-the-wisps
Wagner—Rule Britannia!
Franck—Psyché: individual move-
ments
Chabrier—Bourée fantasque
Elgar—Pomp and circumstance, no.3
Debussy—Images: Rondes de prin-
temps; L'Isle joyeuse
Ruggles—Organum
Ingelbrecht—Rapsodie de printemps
Grainger—The immovable do

[13ww-4431-7perc-2hp, cel, pf-str; *10' or less*]
Bax—Overture to a picaresque comedy
Griffes—Bacchanale
Ibert—Bacchanale
Gershwin—Cuban overture
Walton—Capriccio burlesco
Barber—Commando march; Night flight
Galindo—Sones de mariachi
Read—Night flight, op.44
Bernstein—Candide: Overture; Slava! [elect gtr, tape]
Zimmermann—Stillness and return [asx, accordion]
Zwilich—Celebration for orchestra
Adams, John—Short ride in a fast machine
Rouse—Bump; The infernal machine
Torke—Javelin

11'-20'

Gottschalk—La Nuit des tropiques [baritone horn]
Chadwick—Tam O'Shanter
Dukas—L'Apprenti Sorcier
Bax—In the faery hills
Becker—Symphony no.3
Martinu—The frescos of Piero della Francesca
Prokofiev—Le Pas d'acier: Suite
Sowerby—From the northland
Sessions—Concerto for orchestra
Copland—El salón México
McPhee—Tabuh-Tabuhan [2pf]
Creston—Dance overture; Invocation and dance
Barber—Essay no.3; Medea's meditation and dance of vengeance
Schuman, Wm.—New England triptych
Read—Pennsylvania suite, op.67
Diamond—Symphony no.5
Perle—Three movements for orchestra
Bernstein—Divertimento for orchestra
Rorem—Lions (a dream)
Aschaffenburg—Three dances for orch
Takemitsu—Music of tree [ssx, gtr]
Jones—Let us now praise famous men
Höller—Aura
Rouse—Phantasmata
Stucky—Impromptus
Beaser—Chorale variations

21'-30'

Albéniz—Iberia (arr. Arbós) [tsx]
Strauss, R.—Der Rosenkavalier: Suite
Ravel—Gaspard de la nuit

Martinu—Symphony no.6
Prokofiev—Romeo and Juliet: Suites nos.1-2
Milhaud—Suite symphonique no.2
Still—Afro-American symphony [tenor banjo]
Sessions—The black maskers: Suite; Symphonies nos.1, 4
Chávez—La hija de Colquide; Symphony no.3
Creston—Symphonies nos.2, 3
Shostakovich—Symphony no.6
Barber—Symphony no.2
Bernstein—On the waterfront: Symphonic suite; West side story: Symphonic dances [asx]
Lewis, R.H.—Three movements on scenes of Hieronymous Bosch [cimb, mand]
Crumb—Variazioni for large orchestra [mand]
Shchedrin—Anna Karenina; Stikhira for the millenary of Christianization of Russia
Del Tredici—Child Alice: Happy voices
Harbison—Symphony no.2
Albert, Stephen—Symphony no.2
Lloyd—Symphony no.2
Mackey—Eating greens

Over 30'

Elgar—Symphony no.2
Charpentier, G.—Impressions d'Italie [asx]
Mahler—Symphony no.4
Roussel—Symphony no.2
Rachmaninoff—Symphonic dances
Bax—Symphony no.7
Berg—Lulu: Suite [asx]
Martinu—Symphony no.4
Prokofiev—Le Pas d'acier; Symphonies nos.4, 5, 6
Sessions—Symphony no.3
Dawson—Negro folk symphony
Copland—Symphony no.3
Khachaturian—Symphony no.2
Maxwell Davies—Worldes blis
Svoboda—Symphony no.5
Albert, Stephen—River run [asx]
Melby—Symphony no.1

STRINGS
WINDS 4454-6641
8 PERCUSSION
3 HARPS, CELESTA, PIANO

10' or less

Bach—Toccata & fugue, BWV 565
Wagner—Die Walküre: Ride of the

[4454-6641-8perc-3hp, cel, pf-str; *10' or less*]
Valkyries (arr. Hutschenruyter)
Balakirev—Islamey (arr. Casella)
Debussy—Images: Gigues; Le Martyre de Saint Sébastien: La Chambre magique
Pfitzner—Palestrina: Preludes, Acts I & II
Ligeti—Atmosphères
Pinkham—Catacoustical measures
Rorem—Eagles
Shchedrin—The chimes
Jones—Fanfare and celebration
Corigliano—Campane di Ravello
Picker—Old and Lost Rivers

11'-20'

Berlioz—Roméo et Juliette: Romeo alone; Festivities at Capulet's
Wagner—Grosser Festmarsch; Parsifal: Prelude; Good Friday spell
Rimsky-Korsakov—Mlada: Suite
Debussy—Images: Ibéria; Jeux
Delius—Brigg Fair; Dance rhapsody no.1
Strauss, R.—Till Eulenspiegels lustige Streiche
Schoenberg—Five pieces for orchestra, op.16 (2 versions)
Ravel—Daphnis et Chloé: Suite no.1; Rapsodie espagnole
Stravinsky—Scherzo fantastique
Szymanowski—Konzert-Ouverture, op.12
Bax—November woods
Casella—Italia
Webern—Im Sommerwind
Berg—Three pieces for orchestra, op.6; Wozzeck: Three excerpts [soprano solo]
Gerhard—Epithalamion
Harris—Symphony no.7
Chávez—Symphony no.2
Copland—Connotations; Dance symphony; Symphonic ode
Hovhaness—Floating world
Ginastera—Panambi: Suite
Yardumian—Armenian suite
Walker, George—Address for orchestra
Ligeti—Lontano
Lees—Symphony no.3
Samuel—Requiem for survivors
Schuller—Of reminiscences and reflections
Adler—Concerto for orchestra
Russo—Symphony no.2
London—A hero of our time
Takemitsu—Twill by twilight; Visions
Martino—Mosaic for grand orch [elec gtr]

Rands—Agenda, for young players
Reich—Three movements
Kolb—Grisaille
Davis—ESU variations

21'-30'

Debussy—Le Martyre de Saint Sébastien: Fragments symphoniques; La Mer
Schoenberg—Variations for orchestra, op.31 [mand]
Karlowicz—Stanislaw i Anna Oswiecimowie
Bartók—Four orchestral pieces, op.12
Kodály—Háry János: Suite [cimb]
Stravinsky—L'Oiseau de feu: Suite (1911 version)
Harris—Symphony no.5
Messiaen—Chronochromie
Schuman, Wm.—Symphonies nos.3, 4, 10
Panufnik—Symphony no.10
Orbón—Tres versiones sinfónicas
Schuller—Concerto no.2 for orchestra; Spectra
Lazarof—Concerto for orchestra
Penderecki—Symphony no.1 [harm]
Maxwell Davies—St. Thomas Wake
Sallinen—Symphony no.3
Svoboda—Symphonies nos.3, 4
Schwantner—New morning for the world

Over 30'

Berlioz—Symphonie funèbre et triomphale [2 tubas]
Mahler—Symphonies nos.5, 10 (Cooke & Wheeler versions)
Delius—Appalachia
Strauss, R.—Also sprach Zarathustra
Holst—The planets
Ives—Universe symphony [24perc]
Bartók—Suite no.1
Stravinsky—Petrouchka (orig version, 1911)
Shostakovich—Symphony no.8
Schuman, Wm.—Symphony no.8
Blackwood—Symphony no.1
Górecki—Symphony no.3
Penderecki—Adagio
Sallinen—Symphony no.5
Corigliano—Symphony no.1 [2 tubas]
Adams, John—Harmonielehre

Duration variable

Brown—Available forms 2

INSTRUMENTATION LARGER THAN ALL PREVIOUS CATEGORIES

20' or less

Bach—Komm, Gott, Schöpfer, heiliger Geist, BWV 631; Passacaglia, BWV 582; Prelude & fugue, BWV 552; Schmücke dich, o liebe Seele
Wagner—Götterdämmerung: Siegfried's funeral music; Die Walküre: Ride of the Valkyries
Strauss, R.—Salome: Salome's dance
Granados—Dante
Koechlin—Les Bandar-log
Ravel—Daphnis et Chloé: Suite no.2
Ruggles—Sun-treader
Stravinsky—Le Sacre du printemps: Danse sacrale
Varèse—Arcana
Prokofiev—Scythian suite
Chávez—Symphony no.1
Ellington—Harlem
Copland—Symphonic ode
Schuman, Wm.—Credendum; Newsreel
Blomdahl—Forma ferritonans
Maderna—Aura
Shapey—Rituals
Kraft—Contextures: Riots
Berio—Allelujah; Still
Henze—Symphony no.5
Penderecki—De natura sonoris [no.1]; Flourescences
Jones—Let us now praise famous men
Knussen—Choral

21'-40'

Balakirev—King Lear: Incidental music
Janácek—Sinfonietta
Strauss, R.—Ein Heldenleben
Koechlin—La Course de printemps
Scriabin—Le Poème de l'extase; Prométhée, le poème du feu
Ives—Symphony no.4 (critical edition)
Respighi—Feste romane
Bartók—Kossuth; The wooden prince: Suite
Stravinsky—Le Sacre du printemps
Varèse—Amériques (2 versions)
Ibert—Le Chevalier errant
Gershwin—Porgy and Bess: Symphonic picture
Harris—Symphony no.9
Tippett—New year suite
Reed—La fiesta mexicana
Schuman, Wm.—Symphony no.7
Foss—Geod
Stockhausen—Gruppen

Over 40'

Mahler—Symphonies nos.1, 2, 3, 6, 7, 9, 10 (Carpenter or Mazzetti versions)
Strauss, R.—Eine Alpensinfonie; Symphonia domestica
Scriabin—Le Divin Poème
Schmidt—Symphony no.2
Schoenberg—Pelléas und Mélisande
Glière—Symphony no.3
Ravel—Daphnis et Chloé
Stravinsky—L'Oiseau de feu
Shostakovich—Symphonies nos.4, 7

INSTRUMENTATION INDETERMINATE

Ruggles—Angels
Cage—Atlas eclipticalis
Feldman—Intersection no.1 for orchestra; Marginal intersection
Wolff—Burdocks

MULTIPLE ORCHESTRAS

Gabrieli—Canzona
Handel—Concerti a due cori, nos.1-3
Bach, J.C.—Symphonies, op.18, nos.1, 5
Mozart—Serenade no.8, K.286
Ives—Universe symphony
Bartók—Music for strings, percussion and celesta
Martin—Petite Symphonie concertante
Martinu—Sinfonia concertante for 2 orchestras
Tippett—Concerto for double string orch
Carter—A symphony of three orchestras
Brant—Verticals ascending
Dutilleux—Symphony no.2
Brown—Available forms 2
Henze—Symphony no.6
Stockhausen—Gruppen
Shchedrin—Geometrie des Tones
Penderecki—Emanations
Maxwell Davies—St. Thomas Wake;The turn of the tide
Schnittke—Moz-Art à la Haydn
Wolff—Burdocks
Bolcom—Fives
Kolb—Soundings
Tan—Orchestral theatre II: Re

APPENDIX E: ORCHESTRAL WORKS
LISTED BY DURATION

This appendix is intended for browers who are looking for a particular sort of piece to fill out a program—a French baroque work, let us say, of about 8 minutes in duration. Here is how it works:

Orchestral pieces (not accompaniments) are grouped by duration. Within each group, they are subdivided according to the composer's nationality, and within each subdivision are listed chronologically by composer's birthdate. Thus the French baroque piece mentioned above would appear in the 6'-10' group, the French & Belgian subdivision, near the beginning of the list: Lully, Couperin, Rameau and LeClair are possibilities.

The composer's nationality is normally taken to be the country of origin, though there are exceptions (Lully, though Italian by birth, is inextricably bound with the history of French music). See also Appendix F, in which composers are listed under more than one nationality where appropriate.

For complete information on any work, refer to the main alphabetical listing by composer.

5' OR LESS

American

Foote—Irish folk song
Joplin—The entertainer; Maple leaf rag; Ragtime dance
Ives—Charlie Rutlage; Country band march; The gong on the hook and ladder; Hymn; Overture and march 1776
Ruggles—Angels
Griffes—Bacchanale; Clouds
Becker—Two pieces for orchestra (each piece)
Sowerby—Comes autumn time
Thomson, V.—Bugles and birds; Fugue and chorale on "Yankee Doodle"; Louisiana story: Boy fights alligator; Sea piece with birds
Cowell—Ballad; Polyphonica
Bacon—The muffin man
Gershwin—Promenade
Copland—Billy the Kid: Prairie night & Celebration dance, Waltz; Cere-

monial fanfare; Down a country lane; Fanfare for the common man; Inaugural fanfare; John Henry; Jubilee variation; Rodeo (individual mvts); Symphony no.1: Prelude; Variations on a Shaker melody
Carter—Elegy
Barber—Die natali: Silent night; Vanessa: Intermezzo, Under the willow tree
Schuman, Wm.—The orchestra song
McBride—Pumpkin-eater's little fugue
Dahl—Quodlibet on American folk tunes & folk dances
Gillis—Short overture to an unwritten opera
Brant—Galaxy 2
Dello Joio—Arietta
Etler—Elegy for small orchestra
Perle—New fanfares
Bernstein—Candide: Overture; Slava!; West side story: Overture
La Montaine—A summer's day
Foss—American fanfare
Chou—Soliloquy of a bhiksuni; Yü ko

[5' OR LESS; American]

Pinkham—Catacoustical measures
Frackenpohl—Short overture
Starer—Elegy for strings
Hoag—An after-intermission overture for youth orchestra
Jones—Elegy; Fanfare and celebration
Rands—Fanfare for a festival
Schickele—Fanfare for the common cold
Wilson—Houston fanfare
Corigliano—Campane di Ravello; To music
Tower—various "Fanfares for the uncommon woman"
Hailstork—Celebration
Adams, John—Short ride in a fast machine; Tromba lontana
Walker, Gwyneth—Open the door
Rouse—The infernal machine
Adolphe—Three pieces for kids & chamber orch: Rainbow

Eastern European

Chopin—Mazurka no.7; Polonaise, op.40, no.1
Moniuszko—Halka: Mazur
Dvořák—Fest-Marsch; Legends, op.59 (each); Slavonic dances (each dance)
Lysenko—Taras Bulba: Overture
Janácek—Sokal fanfare
Bartók—Dances of Transylvania
Kodály—Háry János: Intermezzo
Lutosławski—Overture for strings; Postludium
Pärt—Silouans song

French & Belgian

Meyerbeer—Le Prophète: Coronation march
Berlioz—La Damnation de Faust: Dance of the sylphs, Rakoczy march, Will-o-the-wisps; Les Troyens: Trojan march
Offenbach—La Vie parisienne: Overture
Franck—Eight short pieces (individually); Psyché: Psyché enlevée par les Zéphirs, Les Jardins d'Eros
Delibes—Coppelia: Entr'acte & Waltz, Valse de la poupée & Czardas
Bizet—Les Pecheurs de perles: Overture
Chabrier—Bourée fantasque; Habanera; Joyeuse Marche; Le Roi malgré lui: Danse slav
Massenet—Hérodiade: Prelude to Act III; Manon: Minuet & Gavotte

Fauré—Shylock: Nocturne
Debussy—Clair de lune; Le Martyre de Saint Sébastien: La Chambre magique, Two fanfares
Pierné—Marche des petits soldats de plomb
Dukas—La Pèri: Fanfare
Satie—Cinq Grimaces; Gymnopédie no.2; Trois Petites Pièces montées
Roussel—Fanfare pour un sacre païen
Varèse—Hyperprism
Ibert—Hommage á Mozart
Milhaud—Murder of a great chief of state; Ouverture méditerranéene; Symphonies for small orch: Le Printemps, Pastorale, Sérénade

German & Austrian

Pachelbel—Canon
Bach—Jesu, joy of man's desiring; Komm, Gott, Schöpfer, heiliger Geist; Komm süsser Tod; Schmücke dich, o liebe Seele; Sheep may safely graze
Handel—Overtures to Alcina, Alexander's feast; Solomon: Entrance of the Queen of Sheba; Xerxes: Largo
Gluck—Orfeo ed Euridice: Dance of the furies, Overture; Overture, D major; Sinfonia, D major
Haydn—March for the Royal Society of Musicians
Haydn, M.—Andromeda ed Perseo, P.25: Overture; Symphony, P.8
Mozart—Overtures to Apollo et Hyacinthus, Bastien und Bastienne, Betulia liberata, La clemenza di Tito, Così fan tutte, La finta giardiniera, Idomeneo, Mitridate, Le nozze di Figaro, Il re pastore, Der Schauspieldirektor; Contradances, K.534, K.535, K.587, K.603, K.610; Die Entführung aus dem Serail: Marsch der Janitscharen; Marches, K.62,, K.189, K.214, K.215, K.237, K.249; Turkish march
Beethoven—Prometheus: Overture; Die Ruinen von Athen: Turkish march; Zapfenstreich march
Weber, C.M.—Overtures to Abu Hassan, Silvana
Schubert—Grande Marche héroïque; Marche militaire; Overtures to Der Teufel als Hydraulicus, Die Zwillingsbrüder
Strauss, Joh., Sr.—Radetzky march
Mendelssohn—Athalia: Kriegsmarsch der Priester; Midsummernight's dream: Intermezzo, Scherzo, Wedding march
Schumann, R.—Manfred: Zwischenaktmusik; Träumerei

[5' OR LESS; German & Austrian]

Wagner—Lohengrin: Prelude Act III, Elsa's procession; Die Walküre: Ride of the Valkyries

Bruckner—March in D minor

Strauss, Joh., Jr.—Egyptian march; Fledermaus: Du und du; Perpetuum mobile; Pizzicato polka; Unter Donner und Blitz

Brahms—Hungarian dances

Bruch—Swedish dances

Humperdinck—Hänsel und Gretel: Hexenritt, Knusperwalzer; Königskinder: Introduction to Act II

Reznicek—Donna Diana: Overture

Schreker—Intermezzo, op.8

Italian

Monteverdi—Orfeo: Overture, Toccata & ritornelli

Albinoni—Concerto, op.5, no.4

Vivaldi—Concerto for orchestra, RV 151

Veracini—Aria schiavona

Leo—Santa Elena al Calvario: Sinfonia

Galuppi—Concerto a quattro, no.2

Paisiello—Nina: Overture

Boccherini—Overture, op.43, G.521

Cimarosa—Il maestro di cappella: Overture

Paganini—Moto perpetuo, op.11 (arr. Molinari)

Rossini—Il signor Bruschino: Overture

Donizetti—Sinfonia for winds

Verdi—La traviata: Preludes to Acts I & III

Leoncavallo—I pagliacci: Intermezzo

Puccini—Manon Lescaut: Intermezzo

Mascagni—Intermezzi from L'amico Fritz, Cavalleria rusticana

Wolf-Ferrari—Intermezzi from L'amore medico, The jewels of the Madonna; Il segreto di Susanna: Overture

Russian

Glinka—Russlan and Ludmilla: Overture

Borodin—Prince Igor: Polovtsian march

Mussorgsky—The fair at Sorochinsk: Introduction, Gopak; Khovantchina: Introduction, Entr'acte; Scherzo, B-flat major

Tchaikovsky—Eugen Onegin: Polonaise; Marche solenelle du couronnement; Mazeppa: Danse cosaque; Suite no.1: Marche miniature

Rimsky-Korsakov—Dubinushka; Snegourotchka: Dance of the buffoons; Tsar Saltan: Flight of the bumblebee

Liadov—Baba-Yaga

Glazunov—Cortége solennel no.2; The seasons: Three movements

Kalinnikov—Chanson triste

Stravinsky—Canon; Circus polka; Feu d'artifice; Rag-time; Scherzo à la russe

Prokofiev—The love for three oranges: March & Scherzo

Mosolov—Iron foundry

Khachaturian—Gayane: Sabre dance

Kabalevsky—Colas Breugnon: Overture; The comedians: Galop; Overture pathétique

Shostakovich—The age of gold: Polka

Shchedrin—Symphonic fanfares

Spanish & Latin American

Albéniz—Navarra

Granados—Goyescas: Intermezzo

Falla—El amor brujo: Ritual fire dance; La vida breve: Spanish dance no.1

United Kingdom

Purcell—Canon on a ground bass; Indian queen: Trumpet overture; Trumpet prelude

Boyce—Overture (Ode for the new year 1758); Overture (Ode for the new year 1772); Symphony no.2

Elgar—Elegy; Pomp and circumstance, nos.1-5; Salut d'amour

Delius—Hassan: Intermezzo & Serenade; Irmelin: Prelude; Sleigh ride; Two pieces for small orchestra (each mvt)

Vaughan Williams—Fantasia on "Greensleeves"; Prelude (49th parallel); The wasps: March past of the kitchen utensils

Coleridge-Taylor—Christmas overture; Novellettes, op.52, nos.1, 3, 4

Grainger—The immovable do; Irish tune from County Derry; Molly on the shore; Shepherd's hey

Benjamin—Two Jamaican pieces

Jacob—The barber of Seville goes to the devil

Finzi—Prelude

Glanville-Hicks—Gymnopédie no.1

Britten—Paul Bunyan: Overture

Maxwell Davies—Sir Charles—his pavan; Threnody on a plainsong

Tann—Through the echoing timber

[5' OR LESS]

Other nationalities

Grieg—Bell ringing; Erotik
Nielsen—Maskarade: Overture, Hanedans
Sibelius—Canzonetta; Pan and Echo; Romance; The tempest: Prelude
Järnefelt—Praeludium
Ran—Chicago skyline
Sheng—Fanfare I: Arrows to the page

6' TO 10'

American (United States)

Buck—Festival overture on the American national air
Paine—As you like it: Overture; Oedipus tyrannus: Prelude; Poseidon and Amphitrite
Chadwick—Euterpe; Rip van Winkle: Overture
MacDowell—The Saracens: Two fragments after the Song of Roland
Ives—Chromâtimelôdtune; Holidays symphony: Decoration Day, The Fourth of July; Symphony no.4: Fugue; Tone roads nos.1 & 3; The unanswered question; Variations on America
Ruggles—Organum; Portals
Cadman—American suite; Oriental rhapsody from Omar Khayyam
Griffes—The white peacock
Riegger—Dance rhythms; Music for orchestra
Weiss—American life
Piston—Divertimento for nine instruments; Pine tree fantasy; Toccata
Slonimsky—My toy balloon
Still—Bells; Festive overture; In memoriam
White—Five miniatures for orchestra
Thomson, V.—Pilgrims and pioneers; The Seine at night; Wheat field at noon
Cowell—Carol for orchestra; Hymn and fuguing tunes nos.2, 3, 16
Gershwin—Cuban overture
Harris—Elegy for orchestra; Horn of plenty; Ode to consonance; When Johnny comes marching home
Copland—Danzón cubano; Our town; An outdoor overture; Preamble for a solemn occasion; Rodeo: Buckaroo holiday
Luening—Prelude to a hymn tune by William Billings; Synthesis
Rodgers—Carousel: The carousel waltz; Slaughter on Tenth Avenue

Finney—Hymn, fuguing tune & holiday
Gutche—Holofernes overture
Swanson—Music for strings; Night music
Carter—Holiday overture
Siegmeister—Lonesome hollow
Barber—Adagio for strings; Commando march; Essays nos.1, 2; Fadograph of a yestern scene; Music for a scene from Shelley; Night flight; Overture to The school for scandal
Schuman, Wm.—American festival overture; Newsreel
Brant—Verticals ascending
Dello Joio—Five images for orchestra
Gould—Symphonette no.2
Read—First overture; Night flight
Fine—Diversions for orchestra; Serious song
Kubik—Gerald McBoing Boing
Perle—Six bagatelles
Shulman—Threnody
Surinach—Drama jondo; Fandango; Feria magica
Babbitt—Composition for twelve instruments
Weber, Ben—Dolmen
Kay, U.—Of new horizons
Ward—Euphony for orchestra; Jubilation
Rochberg—Time-span (II)
Bergsma—A carol on Twelfth Night
Foss—Ode for orchestra; Salomon Rossi suite
Walker, George—Lyric for strings; Overture in praise of folly
Chou—All in the spring wind; And the fallen petals; Landscapes
Mennin—Canto
Rorem—Eagles; Sinfonia
Benson—Chants and graces; Five brief encounters
Mecham—The jayhawk
Smith, H.—Contours
Feldman—Atlantis; Marginal intersection; ...Out of "Last pieces"; Structures for orchestra
Floyd—In celebration
Martirano—Contrasto
Adler—Elegy for string orchestra
Cunningham—Lullabye for a jazz baby
Previn—Overture to a comedy
Turok—A Joplin overture
Amram—Autobiography for strings
Martino—Divertisements for youth orchestra
Reynolds—Graffiti; Wedge
Jones—In retrospect
Schickele—Celebration with bells; Elegy
Schwartz—Texture

[6'-10'; American]

Glass—Arioso no.2

Bolcom—Commedia for (almost) 18th-century orchestra; Ragomania!

Corigliano—Elegy for orchestra; Promenade overture; Voyage

Harbison—Remembering Gatsby

Wuorinen—Grand bamboula

Zwilich—Celebration for orchestra

Proto—Doodles; Fantasy on the Saints

León—Batá

Schwantner—Freeflight

Hartway—Freedom festival

Peck—Playing with style

Rouse—Bump

Warshauer—Revelation

Larsen—Overture for the end of a century

Davis—Notes from the underground

Daugherty—Dead Elvis; Metropolis symphony: Krypton, Oh Lois!

Picker—Old and Lost Rivers

Torke—Javelin

Eastern European

Liszt—Hamlet; Huldigungs-Marsch; Hungarian rhapsodies nos.3, 5, 6; Rákóczi march

Moniuszko—The countess: Overture

Smetana—The bartered bride: Overture; Hakon Jarl; Má vlast: Sárka

Dvorák—Carnival overture; Notturno; Slavonic rhapsody, op.45, no.1

Janácek—Adagio; Jealousy

Lehár—The merry widow: Overture

Suk—Meditace na starocesky chorál "Svaty Václave"

Bartók—Hungarian peasant songs; Rumanian folk dances

Martinu—Comedy on the bridge: Little suite; Overture

Weinberger—Svanda dudák: Polka & fugue

Tansman—Toccata

Farkas—Prelude & fugue

Panufnik—Heroic overture; Jagiellonian triptych; Lullaby

Nelhybel—Music for orchestra

Serocki—Segmenti

Ligeti—Apparitions; Atmosphères; Ramifications

Górecki—Three pieces in old style

Penderecki—Als Jakob erwachte...; Anaklasis; De natura sonoris nos.1, 2; Emanations; To the victims of Hiroshima

Pärt—Festina Lente; Wenn Bach Bienen gezüchtet hätte...

Svoboda—Ex libris; Festive overture; Overture of the season; Serenade; Swing dance; Three pieces for orchestra, op.45

Sapieyevski—Summer overture

French & Belgian

Lully—Roland: Suite

Couperin—La Sultane: Overture and allegro

Rameau—Platée: Suite des danses

Leclair—Sonata, D major (str orch)

Gossec—Christmas suite

Boieldieu—Overtures to Le Calife de Bagdad, La Dame blanche

Auber—Overtures to Le Domino noir, Fra Diavolo, Lestocq, Marco Spada; Masaniello

Hérold—Zampa: Overture

Meyerbeer—Fackeltanz no.1; Les Huguenots: Overture

Adam—Si J'Étais Roi: Overture

Berlioz—Béatrice et Bénédict: Overture; Carnaval romain; Le Corsaire; Roméo et Juliette: Queen Mab scherzo; Les Troyens: Overture, Royal hunt and storm; Waverley

Thomas—Overtures to Mignon, Raymond

Gounod—Marche funèbre d'une marionette

Offenbach—Overtures to La Belle Hélène, Orpheus in the underworld; Les Contes d'Hoffmann: Intermezzo & Barcarolle

Franck—Psyché: Sommeil de Psyché, Psyché et Éros

Lalo—Rapsodie norvégienne

Saint-Saëns—Danse macabre; Marche du couronnement; Marche héroïque; Orient et Occident; Phaéton; La Princesse jaune: Overture; Le Rouet d'Omphale; Samson et Dalila: Bacchanale

Delibes—Coppelia: Prelude & Mazurka, Ballade & Thème slave varié

Waldteufel—Les Patineurs

Chabrier—España; Gwendolyn: Overture; Le Roi malgré lui: Fête polonaise

Massenet—Phèdre: Overture

Fauré—Pavane; Pénélope: Prelude

Charpentier, G.—Louise: Prelude to Act III & Air de Louise

Debussy—Danse; Images: Gigues, Rondes de printemps; L'Isle joyeuse; Marche écossais; Prélude à "L'Après-midi d'un faune"; Sarabande

Satie—Deux Préludes posthumes et une gnossienne; Gymnopédies nos.1 & 3; Jack in the box

Roussel—Rapsodie flamande; Sinfonietta, op.52

[6'-10'; French & Belgian]

Schmitt—Rapsodie viennoise; Ronde burlesque

Ravel—Alborada del gracioso; Ma Mère l'Oye: Prélude et Danse du rouet; Menuet antique; Pavane pour une infante défunte

Ingelbrecht—Rapsodie de printemps

Varèse—Ionisation; Octandre

Ibert—Bacchanale; Bostoniana

Honegger—Chant de joie; Mouvement symphonique no.3; Pacific 231; Pastorale d'été; Prélude pour "La Tempête" de Shakespeare; Rugby

Milhaud—Les Funérailles de Phocion; Ouverture philharmonique; Symphonies for small orch: Dixtuor à cordes, Dixtuor d'instruments à vent

Poulenc—Deux Marches et un Intermède

German & Austrian

Schein—Banchetto musicale: Suite no.1

Biber—Battalia

Telemann—Overture in D major

Bach—Musikalisches Opfer: Ricercare (arr. Webern); Toccata & fugue, BWV 565

Handel—Alceste: Instrumental pieces; Concerti grossi, op.3, nos.1, 5-6; Overtures to Judas Maccabaeus, Occasional oratorio, Samson; Overture, D major; Prelude & fugue, D minor

Graun—Sinfonia, F major, M.95

Bach, W.F.—Sinfonia, D minor

Frederick II—Symphonies nos.1-2

Bach, C.P.E.—Symphonies, H.661, H.662, H.665

Gluck—Overtures to Alceste, Iphigenie in Aulis; Orfeo ed Euridice: Dance of the blessed spirits; Sinfonia, G major

Abel—Symphonies, op.1, nos.5-6

Haydn—Kindersymphonie; Symphony no.2

Bach, J.C.—Symphonies, op.3, nos.1-2; op.6, no.1; op.21, no.3; Symphony, D major

Haydn, M.—Pastorello, P.91; Symphonies, P.26, P.29

Mozart—Adagio & fugue; Contradances, K.267, K.609; Divertimento, K.188; Overtures to Don Giovanni, Die Entführung aus dem Serail, La finta semplice, Lucio Silla, Die Zauberflöte; German dances, K.602, K.605; Marches, K.335; Serenade no.2; Symphonies nos.4-5, 10-11, 22-24, 26, 32; Symphony, K.111/

K.120; Symphony, K.196/121

Beethoven—Overtures to Coriolan, Egmont, Fidelio, König Stephan, Leonore No.1, Namensfeier, Die Ruinen von Athen

Weber, C.M.—Aufforderung zum Tanz; Overtures to Beherrscher der Geister, Euryanthe, Der Freischütz, Jubel, Oberon, Peter Schmoll, Preziosa; Turandot: Overture & march

Schubert—Overtures to Alfonso und Estrella, Claudine von Villa Bell, Des Teufels Lustschloss, Fierrabras, Die Freunde von Salamanka, Der häusliche Krieg, Rosamunde, Der Spiegelritter, Die vierjährige Posten; Overtures, D.8, D.12, D.26, D.470, D.556, D.590, D.591, D.648

Lanner—Die Werber Walzer

Lortzing—Zar und Zimmermann: Overture

Mendelssohn—Overtures to Athalia, Heimkehr aus der Fremde, Die Hochzeit des Camacho, Ruy Blas, St. Paul; The Hebrides; Märchen von der schönen Melusine; Midsummernight's dream: Nocturne; Overture for winds; Sinfonias nos.1-5; Trumpet overture

Nicolai—The merry wives of Windsor: Overture

Schumann, R.—Overtures to Braut von Messina, Faust, Genoveva, Hermann und Dorothea, Julius Caesar; Manfred: Suite

Flotow—Overtures to Alessandro Stradella, Martha

Wagner—Christoph Columbus: Overture; Götterdämmerung: Gesang der Rheintöchter, Siegfried's funeral music, Siegfried's Rhine journey; Huldigungsmarsch; Kaisermarsch; Lohengrin: Prelude Act I; Die Meistersinger: Prelude; Das Rheingold: Entry of the Gods into Valhalla; Rule Britannia; Siegfried: Forest murmurs; Tannhäuser: Arrival of the guests, Prelude Act III; Tristan und Isolde: Nachtgesang, Prelude Act III

Suppé—Overtures to Banditenstreiche, Boccaccio, Dichter und Bauer, Die leichte Kavallerie, Ein Morgen, ein Mittag und ein Abend in Wien, Die schöne Galathea

Bruckner—Three pieces for orchestra

Cornelius—Der Barbier von Bagdad: Overture (2 different versions)

Strauss, Joh., Jr.—An der schönen blauen Donau; Overtures to Fledermaus, Zigeunerbaron; Frühlingsstimmen; Kaiser-Walzer; Künstler Quadrille; Morgenblätter; Rosen aus dem Süden; Wein, Weib und Gesang;

[6'-10'; German & Austrian]

Wiener Blut

Strauss, Jos.—Dorfschwalben aus Österreich; Mein Lebenslauf ist Lieb' und Lust; Sphärenklänge

Goldmark—Im Frühling

Brahms—Akademische Festouvertüre

Bruch—Loreley: Prelude

Humperdinck—Hänsel und Gretel: Prelude; Königskinder: Prelude, Introduction to Act III; Eine Trauung in der Bastille

Mahler—Symphony no.1: Blumine; Symphony no.5: Adagietto

Wolf—Der Corregidor: Prelude & interlude

Strauss, R.—Serenade, op.7

Pfitzner—Das Christ-Elflein: Overture; Palestrina: Preludes, Acts I, II, III

Reger—Serenade, B-flat major

Schoenberg—Begleitungsmusik zu einer Lichtspielscene; A survivor from Warsaw

Webern—Concerto, op.24; Fünf Stücke, op.10; Symphony, op.21; Variations for orchestra op.30

Toch—Circus; Pinocchio

Hindemith—Overtures to Cupid and Psyche, Neues vom Tage; Spielmusik, op.43, no.1; Suite of French dances

Korngold—Theme and variations

Einem—Capriccio, op.2

Zimmermann—Stillness and return

Henze—Quattro poemi

Italian

Gabrieli—Canzonas; Sonata pian' e forte

Monteverdi—Orfeo: Sinfonie e ritornelli

Corelli—Suite for string orchestra

Torelli—Concerto, op.6, no.1; Sinfonia, op.6, no.6

Scarlatti, A.—Piccola suite; Sinfonias nos.1, 2, 5

Albinoni—Concerto, op.5, no.7

Vivaldi—Sinfonia no.3, RV 149; Sinfonia, RV 169

Scarlatti, D.—Five sonatas in form of a suite

Marcello, B.—Introduction, aria & presto, A minor

Geminiani—Concerto grosso, op.2, no.2

Sammartini, Giov. Battista—Concertino, G major; Sinfonias, J.-C.4, J.C.39, J.-C.47

Galuppi—Concerto a quattro, no.1; Sinfonias, D major, F major

Pergolesi—Concertino, E-flat major

Piccinni—Iphigenie en Tauride: Overture

Paisiello—La scuffiara: Overture; Sinfonia, D major; Sinfonia funebre; Sinfonia in tre temp

Boccherini—Sinfonia concertante, G.268; Symphonies nos.1, 12, "A"

Cimarosa—Overtures to Il matrimonio segreto, I traci amanti; Sinfonia, D major

Salieri—Sinfonia, D major (Veneziana)

Cherubini—Overtures to Abenceragen, Ali Baba, Anacreon, Démophoon, Les Deux Journées, Faniska, L'Hôtellerie portugaise, Medea

Rossini—Overtures to L'assedio di Corinto, Il barbiere di Siviglia, La Cenerentola, La gazza ladra, L'Italiana in Algeri, Robert Bruce, La scala di seta, Tancredi, Il Turco in Italia, Il viaggio a Reims; Guillaume Tell: Pas de six; Serenata per piccolo complesso

Donizetti—Allegro in C major; Overtures to Don Pasquale, La Fille du régiment, Linda di Chamounix, Roberto Devereux

Bellini—Overtures to Norma, Il pirata; Symphonies in C minor, D major

Verdi—Aïda: Prelude; Overtures to La forza del destino, Nabucco, I vespri siciliani

Ponchielli—La Gioconda: Dance of the hours

Puccini—I crisantemi; Edgar: Preludio

Mascagni—Cavalleria rusticana: Prelude & Siciliana

Busoni—Lustspiel overture

Dallapiccola—Piccola musica notturna

Berio—Allelujah; Nones; Ritirata notturna di Madrid

Russian

Glinka—Jota aragonesa; Kamarinskaya; A life for the Tsar: Overture; Summer night in Madrid; Valse fantaisie

Borodin—In the steppes of central Asia; Nocturne; Petite Suite: Scherzo & Nocturne; Prince Igor: Overture

Balakirev—Islamey; Overture on three Russian folk songs

Mussorgsky—Boris Godunov: Polonaise; Intermezzo in the classic style; Khovantchina: Dance of the Persian maidens; Solemn march

Tchaikovsky—Eugen Onegin: Waltz; Fatum; Marche slave; Le Voyévode: Overture; Le Voyévode (symphonic

[6'-10'; Russian] ballad)

Rimsky-Korsakov—Christmas eve: Polonaise; Le Coq d'or: Introduction & Wedding march; Overtures to The Maid of Pskov, May night, The tsar's bride

Liadov—The enchanted lake; Kikimora

Glazunov—Cortége solennel no. 1; The seasons: Winter; Valse de concert, no. 2

Rachmaninoff—Vocalise

Glière—The red poppy: Russian sailors' dance

Stravinsky—Eight instrumental miniatures; Four Norwegian moods; Monumentum pro Gesualdo; L'Oiseau de feu: Berceuse & Finale; Pas de deux; Le Sacre du printemps: Danse sacrale; Suites nos. 1 & 2; Variations

Prokofiev—Andante; Overture, op.42; War and peace: Overture

Khachaturian—Gayane: Three pieces

Shostakovich—Festive overture

Shchedrin—The chimes

Spanish & Latin American

Arriaga—Los esclavos felices: Overture

Gomes—Il Guarany: Overture

Albéniz—Catalonia

Falla—La vida breve: Interlude & dance

Turina—La procesion del rocio

Villa-Lobos—Bachianas brasileiras no.5; Suite for strings

Gerhard—Albada

Chávez—Xochipilli

Rodrigo—Zarabanda lejana y villancico

Halffter—La muerte de Carmen: Habanera

Galindo—Sones de mariachi

Moncayo—Huapango

Ginastera—Oberatura para el "Fausto" Criollo

Davidovsky—Inflexions

Lavista—Clepsidra

United Kingdom

Purcell—Chacony in G minor; The double dealer: Suite; The fairy queen: Suites nos. 1-2; The Gordian knot untied: Suite no.2; The rival sisters: Overture; The virtuous wife: Suite

Arne—Symphonies nos. 1-3

Boyce—Overture (Ode for his majesty's birthday 1769); Overture (Peleus and Thetis); Symphonies nos. 1, 3-7

Litolff—Robespierre: Overture

Elgar—Dream-children

Delius—Dance rhapsody no.2; The walk to the Paradise Garden

German—Henry VIII: Three dances

Vaughan Williams—English folk song suite; Two hymn-tune preludes; The wasps: Overture

Holst—Brook Green suite; Capriccio; The lure; A Somerset rhapsody

Coleridge-Taylor—The bamboula; Danse nègre; Novellette, op.52, no.2

Brian—Symphony no.22

Bax—Overture to a picaresque comedy

Jacob—Fantasia on the Alleluia hymn

Finzi—The fall of the leaf; Nocturne; Romance; A Severn rhapsody

Rubbra—Festival overture, op.62

Walton—Capriccio burlesco; Crown imperial; Façade: Suites nos. 1-2; Johannesburg festival overture; Portsmouth Point; Prologo e fantasia

Alwyn—Festival march

Tippett—Little music

Pentland—Symphony for ten parts

Britten—Gloriana: Courtly dances; Peter Grimes: Passacaglia; Soirées musicales; The sword in the stone

Arnold—Four Cornish dances; Tam O'Shanter overture

Musgrave—Chamber concerto no. 1

Birtwistle—Machaut à ma manière

Maxwell Davies—Chat Moss; Five Klee pictures; Jimmack the postie; Ojai Festival overture

Tann—Water's edge; With the heather and small birds

Knussen—Choral

Other nationalities

Berwald—Estrella de Soria: Overture

Svendsen—Rapsodie norvégienne no.3

Grieg—In autumn; Lyric pieces, op.68, nos.4 & 5; Peer Gynt: Prelude; Two elegiac melodies, op.34; Two melodies, op.53; Wedding day at Troldhaugen

Nielsen—Saul and David: Prelude to Act II

Sibelius—The bard; Finlandia; Karelia overture; Kuolema: Valse triste; Legends: Lemminkäinen's return

Skalkottas—Five Greek dances

Xenakis—Analogique A; Metastaseis B

Chen—Duo ye no.2

11' TO 15'

American (United States)

Foote—Suite, op.63
Chadwick—Melpomene
Mason—Chanticleer
Ives—Holidays symphony: Thanksgiving and/or Forefathers' Day; Ragtime dances
Carpenter—Skyscrapers
Ruggles—Men and mountains; Suntreader
Griffes—The pleasure dome of Kubla Khan
Becker—Soundpiece nos.1b, 2b; When the willow nods
Weiss—I segreti
Rogers—Once upon a time; Three Japanese dances
Piston—Concerto for orchestra; Lincoln Center festival overture; Serenata; Sinfonietta
Still—Darker America; Poem
Hanson—Merry Mount: Suite; Symphony no.5
Sessions—Concerto for orchestra
Thomson, V.—Louisiana story: Acadian songs and dances; The plow that broke the plains: Suite; A solemn music, and a joyful fugue
Cowell—Sinfonietta; Synchrony
Ellington—Les Trois Rois noirs
Copland—Inscape; Lincoln portrait; Orchestral variations; Prairie journal; El salón México; Symphony no.2; Three Latin-American sketches; Two pieces
Krenek—Sinfonietta; Symphonic elegy
Creston—Dance overture; Invocation and dance; Two choric dances
Finney—Landscapes remembered
Swanson—Short symphony
Stevens—Sinfonia breve; Symphonic dances
Siegmeister—Five fantasies of the theater; Theater set
Barber—Andromache's farewell; Essay no.3; Medea's meditation and dance of vengeance
Hovhaness—And God created great whales; Floating world; Meditation on Orpheus; Psalm and fugue; Variations and fugue
Smith, J.—Folkways symphony
Dahl—Variations on a theme by C.P.E. Bach
Coolidge—Pioneer dances
Gould—Dinosaurian dances
Effinger—Little symphony no.1
Diamond—Rounds for string orchestra; The world of Paul Klee
Perle—Serenade no.2

Kay, U.—Chariots; Fantasy variations; Suite for strings; Theater set for orchestra; Umbrian scene
Ward—Adagio and allegro; Sonic structure
Yardumian—Cantus animae et cordis
Bernstein—Divertimento for orchestra; On the town: Three dance episodes
Rochberg—Black sounds; Cheltenham concerto; Night music
Kirchner—Music for orchestra; Toccata
Kirk—An orchestra primer
Overton—Symphony no.2
Bergsma—Chameleon variations
Imbrie—Legend
Shapey—Rituals
Foss—Folksong for orchestra; Quintets for orchestra
Thorne—Elegy for orchestra
Bassett—From a source evolving
Chou—Beijing in the mist; Pien
Mennin—Concertato
Powell—Modules
Rorem—Ideas for easy orchestra; Lions (a dream)
Benson—A Delphic serenade
Hollingsworth—Divertimento; Three ladies beside the sea
Starer—Samson agonistes
Schuller—American triptych; Five bagatelles; Five etudes for orchestra; Of reminiscences and reflections
Feldman—Intersection no.1 for orchestra
Aschaffenburg—Three dances for orchestra
Anderson, T. J.—Chamber symphony
Druckman—Aureole; Nor spell nor charm
Baker—Kosbro
Martino—Ritorno
Adams, Leslie—Ode to life
Colgrass—As quiet as...
Subotnick—Play no.2
Reynolds—Fiery wind
Rands—Agenda, for young players
Schickele—A zoo called Earth
Reich—Three movements
Schwartz—Island
Wilson—Expansions III
Corigliano—Fantasia on an ostinato; Three hallucinations; Tournaments
Harbison—Merchant of Venice; Music for 18 winds
Wuorinen—Crossfire; Machault mon chou
Kolb—Chromatic fantasy; Grisaille
Zwilich—Concerto grosso 1985; Prologue & variations
Proto—Casey at the bat; Doodles
Schwantner—Aftertones of infinity;

[11'-15'; American]
From a dark millennium; A sudden
rainbow
Peck—Peace overture; Signs of life;
The thrill of the orchestra
Adams, John—The Chairman dances
Paulus—Concertante
Rouse—Iscariot
Stucky—Dreamwaltzes
Warshauer—As the waters cover the
sea
Davis—ESU variations
Tsontakis—Perpetual Angelus; Winter
lightning
Daugherty—Metropolis symphony:
Red cape tango
Danielpour—First light
Mackey—TILT
Kernis—Musica celestis
Torke—Adjustable wrench; December;
Ecstatic orange

Eastern European

Stamitz, Joh.—Sinfonia pastorale,
op.4, no.2; Symphony, op.3, no.3;
Three Mannheim symphonies (each
symphony)
Golabek—Symphonies in C major, D
major (I)
Vanhal—Sinfonia, G minor
Liszt—Funeral triumph of Tasso;
Hungarian rhapsodies nos.1, 2, 4;
Mephisto waltzes nos.1-2; Nocturnal
procession; Orpheus; Prometheus;
Von der Wiege bis zum Grabe
Smetana—The bartered bride: Three
dances; Má vlast: nos.1, 2, 4, 5, 6;
Richard III; Wallenstein's camp
Dvořák—Husitská; In nature's realm;
Midday witch; Othello overture;
Scherzo capriccioso; Slavonic rhap-
sodies, op.45, nos.2-3
Bartók—Deux Portraits; Hungarian
sketches; Three village scenes
Enesco—Rumanian rhapsodies
nos.1-2
Kodály—Galanta dances; Marosszek
dances; Theater overture
Weiner—Divertimento no.5
Tansman—Sinfonietta; Variations on
a theme by Frescobaldi
Lutoslawski—Little suite; Venetian
games
Panufnik—Divertimento; Old Polish
suite
Szöllösy—Sonorità
Ligeti—Lontano; Melodien
Bloch, A.—Enfiando per orchestra
Penderecki—Flourescences
Pärt—Fratres
Skoryk—Hutsul triptych

Sapieyevski—Surtsey

French & Belgian

Lully—Ballet suite
Rameau—Ballet suite; Dardanus:
Suite; Suite for string orchestra
Grétry—Zémire et Azor: Ballet suite
Halévy—La Juive: Overture
Berlioz—Benvenuto Cellini: Overture;
Les Franc-Juges; Rob Roy; Roméo et
Juliette: Romeo alone & Festivities at
Capulet's; Les Troyens: Ballet
Gounod—Faust: Ballet music
Franck—Le Chasseur maudit; Les
Éolides; Rédemption: Morceau sym-
phonique
Lalo—Namouna: Ballet suite no.2; Le
Roi d'Ys: Overture
Saint-Saëns—Septet
Delibes—Le Roi s'amuse: Airs de
danse dans le style ancien
Bizet—Carmen: Suite no.1; Jeux
d'enfants: Petite Suite; Jolie Fille de
Perth: Scènes bohémiennes; Ouver-
ture; Patrie
Fauré—Masques et Bergamasques
Chaminade—Callirhoe suite
Debussy—Petite Suite; Printemps; Six
Épigraphes antiques
Dukas—L'Apprenti Sorcier
Satie—Parade
Koechlin—Les Bandar-log
Roussel—Concerto for small orches-
tra; Évocations: Les Dieux dans
l'ombre des cavernes; Petite Suite;
Pour Un Fête de printemps; Suite
in F
Schmitt—Étude; Reflets d'Allemagne
Ravel—Bolero; Daphnis et Chloé:
Suite no.1; Rapsodie espagnole; She-
herazade (ouverture); La Valse
Varèse—Integrales
Ibert—Divertissement; Escales; Louis-
ville concerto; Symphonie marine
Milhaud—Le Boeuf sur le toit; Cortège
funèbre; Suite française
Poulenc—Suite française
Messiaen—Hymne; Les Offrandes ou-
bliées
Françaix—Sei Preludi

German & Austrian

Fux—Overture, C major
Telemann—Overture in C major
Bach—Passacaglia, BWV 582
Handel—Concerti a due cori, nos.1, 3;
Concerto grosso, op.3, no.4; Over-
tures to Rodrigo, Saul, Solomon,
Theodora; Royal fireworks music;

[11'-15'; German & Austrian]
Water music: Suites nos.2-3
Bach, W.F.—Sinfonia, F major
Bach, C.P.E.—Symphonies, H.657, H.658, H.659, H.660, H.663
Gluck—Ballet suite no.2; Sinfonia, F major
Wagenseil—Sinfonia, G minor
Abel—Symphonies, op.7, no.6; op.14, no.2
Haydn—Symphonies A, B, nos.1, 4, 9-10, 14, 16-17, 19-21, 24-25, 27, 30, 34, 37-38
Bach, J.C.—Symphonies, op.3, no.4; op.6, no.6; op.9, no.2; op.18, nos.1-4, 6; op.21, no.1
Haydn, M.—Symphonies, P.16, P.33
Dittersdorf—Sinfonia, C major
Mozart—Divertimenti K.113, K.166, K.186; German dances, K.536, K.567, K.600; Idomeneo: Ballet music; Marches, K.408; Symphonies nos.1-3, 7-9, 16, 37, K.Anh.223, K.320
Beethoven—Contradances; Leonore overtures nos.2-3; Musik zu einem Ritterballet; Die Weihe des Hauses
Kuhlau—William Shakespeare: Overture
Mendelssohn—Meeresstille und glückliche Fahrt; Midsummernight's dream: Overture; Sinfonias nos.6, 10
Schumann, R.—Manfred: Overture
Wagner—Eine Faust-Ouvertüre; Der fliegende Holländer; Götterdämmerung: Siegfried's death & funeral music; Grosser Festmarsch; Parsifal: Prelude, Good Friday spell; Rienzi: Overture; Tannhäuser: Overture, Venusberg music
Bruckner—Overture, G minor
Strauss, Joh., Jr.—Geschichten aus dem Wienerwald
Brahms—Tragische Ouvertüre
Humperdinck—Hänsel und Gretel: Three excerpts
Wolf—Scherzo & finale
Strauss, R.—Der Rosenkavalier: Waltzes, first sequence; Salome: Salome's dance; Till Eulenspiegels lustige Streiche
Schumann, G.—Liebesfrühling
Schoenberg—Theme and variations, op.43b
Webern—Fünf Sätze, op.5; Im Sommerwind; Passacaglia, op.1; Sechs Stücke, op.6
Berg—Lyric suite: Three pieces
Hindemith—Concerto for orchestra, op.38; Kammermusik no.1
Blacher—Orchester-Ornament
Einem—Ballade
Stockhausen—Kontra-Punkte no.1

Italian

Scarlatti, A.—Sinfonias nos.4, 6, 8, 10
Albinoni—Concerto, op.9, no.9
Vivaldi—Concerto for orchestra, RV 155; Sinfonias nos. 1 & 2, RV 719 & 146
Scarlatti, D.—The good-humored ladies: Suite
Tartini—Concerto no.58; Sinfonia, D major
Locatelli—Concerto grosso, op.1, no.6; Trauer-Symphonie
Sammartini, Giov. Battista—Sinfonias, J.-C.2, J.-C.32
Boccherini—Symphonies nos.9, 14-16, 18-19
Rossini—Overtures to Guillaume Tell, Semiramide; Sonatas nos.1-4
Verdi—Aïda: Triumphal march & ballet
Ponchielli—Elegia
Puccini—Preludio sinfonico
Busoni—Rondo arlecchinesco
Respighi—Fontane di Roma
Dallapiccola—Due pezzi per orchestra; Variations for orchestra
Berio—Requies; Still; Variazioni per orchestra da camera

Russian

Borodin—Prince Igor: Polovtsian dances
Balakirev—Russia
Mussorgsky—Night on bald mountain
Tchaikovsky—Capriccio italien; Nutcracker: Suite no.2
Rimsky-Korsakov—Capriccio espagnol; Mlada: Suite; Overture on Russian themes; Russian Easter overture; Sadko: Tableau musical; Skazka; Snegourotchka: Suite
Liadov—Eight Russian folk songs
Ippolitov-Ivanov—Turkish fragments
Arensky—Variations on a theme by Tchaikovsky
Glazunov—Chopiniana; The seasons: Autumn; Valse de concert, no.1
Rachmaninoff—Symphony, D minor (1891)
Stravinsky—Concerto in D; Concerto in E-flat; Four etudes; Octet; Ode; Septet; Symphonies of wind instruments
Prokofiev—Classical symphony; Suites from The love for three oranges, Le Pas d'acier; A summer day
Kabalevsky—The comedians
Shostakovich—Ballet Suite no.1
Shchedrin—Geometrie des Tones

[11'-15'; Russian]
Schnittke—Moz-Art à la Haydn

Spanish & Latin American

Albéniz—Rapsodia española
Granados—Dante; Tres danzas españolas
Falla—El sombrero de tres picos: Suites nos.1-2
Villa-Lobos—Bachianas brasileiras no.9
Gerhard—Alegrías: Suite; Pedrelliana
Chávez—Resonancias; Symphonies nos.1-2; Toccata for percussion
Revueltas—Homenaje a Federico Garcia Lorca; Janitzio
Ginastera—Estancia: Ballet suite; Iubilum; Ollantay; Panambí: Suite

United Kingdom

Purcell—Suites from Abdelazar, Dido and Aeneas, The Gordian knot untied (no.1), The married beau
Arne—Symphony no.4
Boyce—Symphony no.8
Sullivan—Overture di ballo; Overture in C; The tempest: Three dances
Stanford—Irish rhapsody no.1
Elgar—Cockaigne; Serenade, op.20; Three Bavarian dances
Delius—Dance rhapsody no.1
Vaughan Williams—Fantasia on a theme by Thomas Tallis; Five variants of "Dives and Lazarus"; In the fen country
Holst—Beni mora; Egdon Heath; Hammersmith; The perfect fool: Ballet music; St. Paul's suite
Grainger—In a nutshell
Bax—In the faery hills; November woods
Butterworth—A Shropshire lad
Coates—London suite
Bliss—Introduction and allegro; Things to come: Concert suite
Warlock—Capriol suite
Barbirolli—An Elizabethan suite
Walton—As you like it; Façade 2; Hamlet and Ophelia
Berkeley—Sinfonietta; Symphony no.3; Windsor variations
Britten—Canadian carnival; Matinées musicales; The prince of the pagodas: Pas de six; Sinfonietta; Suite on English folk tunes
Musgrave—Peripeteia; Rainbow
Hoddinott—Sinfonietta 3
Sculthorpe—Kakadu; Mangrove
Birtwistle—Carmen arcadiae mechan-

icae perpetuum
Maxwell Davies—First fantasia on an In nomine of John Taverner; An Orkney wedding, with sunrise
Bennett, Richard R.—Serenade
McCabe—The lion, the witch and the wardrobe: Suite
Tann—The open field

Other nationalities

Gade—Efterklange af Ossian
Grieg—Peer Gynt: Suites nos.1-2; Two Norwegian airs, op.63
Nielsen—Helios overture
Sibelius—Karelia suite; Rakastava; The tempest: Suite no.2
Alfvén—Midsommarvaka
Martin—Passacaille
Blomdahl—Forma ferritonans
Xenakis—Akrata; Anaktoria; Atrees; ST/48—1,240162; Syrmos
Takemitsu—Dream/window; Rain coming; Tree line; Twill by twilight; Visions
Sallinen—Chamber music I; Shadows; Variations for orchestra
Bamert—Circus parade; Snapshots
Chin—šàntika Ekatàla

16'-20'

American (United States)

Gottschalk—La Nuit des tropiques; Symphony no.2
Foote—Four character pieces after the Rubáiyát of Omar Khayyám; Serenade, op.25
Chadwick—Aphrodite; Sinfonietta, D major; Tam O'Shanter
Kelley—The pit and the pendulum
MacDowell—Hamlet & Ophelia; Lamia; Lancelot and Elaine; Suite no.1
Gilbert—Dance in the Place Congo
Converse—The mystic trumpeter
Ives—Symphony no.3; Three places in New England
Carpenter—Sea drift
Bloch, E.—Evocations
Becker—Symphony no.3
Moore, Douglas—Pageant of P.T. Barnum
Bennett, Robt. R.—Suite of old American dances
Piston—The incredible flutist: Suite; Symphonies nos.7-8; Three New England sketches
Sowerby—From the northland; Prairie
Still—Wood notes

[16'-20'; American]

Sessions—Concertino for chamber orchestra

Thomson, V.—Louisiana story: Suite; Symphony on a hymn tune

Gershwin—American in Paris

Harris—Symphonies nos.3, 7

Ellington—Black, brown and beige: Suite; Harlem; Night creature

Antheil—Ballet mécanique

Copland—Connotations; Dance symphony; Music for movies; Nonet for strings; Statements; Symphonic ode; The tender land: Suite

Krenek—Eleven transparencies for orchestra

Luening—Rhapsodic variations

McPhee—Tabuh-Tabuhan

Weill—Kleine Dreigroschenmusik

Phillips—Selections from McGuffey's reader

Swanson—Concerto for orchestra

Wilder—Carl Sandburg suite

Anderson, Leroy—Irish suite

Carter—Adagio tenebroso; Concerto for orchestra; Partita; Pocahontas: Suite; A symphony of three orchestras

Siegmeister—Sunday in Brooklyn; Western suite

Barber—Die natali; Souvenirs; Symphony no.1

Schuman, Wm.—Credendum; New England triptych; Symphony no.5

Hovhaness—Exile symphony; Fra Angelico; Mysterious mountain; Symphony no.15

Brant—Angels and devils

Gould—The jogger and the dinosaur: Suite; Latin-American symphonette; Soundings; Spirituals for orchestra

Read—Pennsylvania suite

Kubik—Divertimento I for thirteen players

Diamond—Music for Shakespeare's Romeo and Juliet; Symphony no.5

Perle—Three movements for orchestra

Persichetti—Night dances; Symphony, op.61

Surinach—Ritmo jondo

Babbitt—Ars combinatoria; Transfigured notes

Kay, U.—Markings; Scherzi musicali; Serenade for orchestra; Six dances for string orchestra; Southern harmony; Suite for orchestra

Yardumian—Armenian suite

Bergsma—Documentary one

Imbrie—Symphony no.3

Foss—Exeunt

Walker, George—Address for orchestra

Bassett—Echoes from an invisible world

Kraft—Contextures: Riots — decade '60

Pinkham—Symphonies nos.1-2

Rorem—Air music; Design; A Quaker reader; Symphony no.2

Lees—Concerto for chamber orchestra; Symphony no.3; The trumpet of the swan

Samuel—Requiem for survivors

Smith, H.—Ritual and incantations

Erb—Symphony of overtures

Peterson—The face of the night, the heart of the dark

Adler—Concerto for orchestra

Russo—Symphony no.2

Crumb—Echoes of time and the river

Lombardo—Drakestail

Martino—Mosaic for grand orchestra

Colgrass—Letter from Mozart

Reynolds—Quick are the mouths of earth

Jones—Let us now praise famous men

Bolcom—Fives; Orphée-sérénade; Symphony no.1

Harbison—The most often used chords

Tower—Sequoia

Wuorinen—Contrafactum; A reliquary for Igor Stravinsky

Kolb—Soundings

Zwilich—Symphonies nos.1, 3

Singleton—Shadows

Schwantner—Toward light

Walker, Gwyneth—The light of three mornings

Rouse—Phantasmata

Stucky—Impromptus

Picker—Keys to the city

Caltabiano—Concertini

Liebermann, Lowell—The domain of Arnheim

Torke—Ash

Eastern European

Golabek—Symphony in D major (II)

Wanski—Symphony in G major

Chopin—Les Sylphides (arr. Glazunov)

Liszt—Battle of the Huns; Festklänge; Héroïde funèbre; Légendes; Mazeppa; Les Préludes; Tasso, lament and triumph

Dvořák—Rhapsody, op.14; Suite, op.98b; Watersprite; Wood dove

Noskowski—The steppe

Janácek—Lachian dances

Karlowicz—Lithuanian rhapsody

Bartók—Dance suite; Two pictures; Mikrokosmos suite; The miraculous

[16'-20'; Eastern European]
mandarin: Suite
Kodály—Summer evening
Szymanowski—Konzert-Ouverture,
op.12
Martinu—Estampes; The frescos of
Piero della Francesca; Sinfonia con-
certante for 2 orchestras
Weinberger—Under the spreading
chestnut tree
Tansman—Triptych
Ránki—Sinfonia 1
Bacewicz—Contradizione
Lutoslawski—Three postludes for
orchestra
Panufnik—Autumn music; Harmony;
Nocturne
Husa—Fantasies for orchestra; Sym-
phonic suite; Two sonnets by Miche-
langelo
Górecki—Symphony no.1
Svoboda—Nocturne, op.100; Sinfo-
niette (à la renaissance)

French & Belgian

Lully—Le Triomphe de l'amour: Ballet
suite
Charpentier, M.-A.—Noëls pour les in-
struments
Rameau—Les Fêtes d'Hébé: Diver-
tissement
Gossec—Symphony op.6, no.6
Saint-Georges—Symphony no.1,
op.11, no.1
Meyerbeer—Le Prophète: Ballet music
Berlioz—Le Roi Lear: Overture; Roméo
et Juliette: Love scene
Saint-Saëns—La Jeunesse d'Hercule;
Suite algérienne
Delibes—Sylvia: Suite
Bizet—L'Arlésienne: Suites 1-2; Car-
men: Suite no.2
Massenet—Le Cid: Ballet music;
Scènes pittoresques
Fauré—Dolly; Pelléas et Mélisande:
Suite; Shylock
Luigini—Ballet égyptien
Indy—Istar
Debussy—Le Coin des enfants; Im-
ages: Ibéria; Jeux
Dukas—La Pèri
Satie—Les Aventures de Mercure
Koechlin—Partita, op.205
Roussel—Bacchus et Ariane: Suites
1-2; Le Festin de l'araignée: Sym-
phonic fragments; Le Marchand de
sable qui passe...; Symphony no.4
Schmitt—Feuillets de voyage; Mu-
siques de plein air
Rabaud—La Procession nocturne
Ravel—Daphnis et Chloé: Suite no.2;

Ma Mère l'Oye: 5 pièces enfantines;
Le Tombeau de Couperin; Valses no-
bles et sentimentales
Varèse—Arcana
Milhaud—Aubade; La Création du
monde; Suite provençale; Sym-
phonies nos.11-12
Auric—La Chambre; Phèdre
Poulenc—Les Biches: Suite; Sécher-
esses

German & Austrian

Buxtehude—Four chorale preludes
Telemann—Don Quichotte; Suite, F
major
Bach—Prelude & fugue, BWV 552;
Suites nos.2-4
Handel—Concerto a due cori, no.2;
Royal fireworks music; Water music
suite (arr. Harty)
Gluck—Ballet suite no.1
Haydn—Symphonies nos.3, 5, 11-12,
15, 18, 22-23, 26, 28-29, 32-33, 35-
36, 39-41, 46, 50, 58-59, 62-63, 65,
67, 69-70, 75, 77-78, 85, 96
Bach, J.C.—Symphony, op.18, no.5
Haydn, M.—Symphonies, P.21, P.42
Mozart—Cassation no.2; German
dances, K.509, K.571; Eine kleine
Nachtmusik; Ein musikalischer
Spass; Serenade no.8; Symphonies
nos.6, 12-15, 17-21, 27, 30-31, 33,
35; Thamos, König in Ägypten:
Zwischenaktmusiken
Pleyel—Symphony, op.3, no.1
Beethoven—German dances; Grosse
Fuge; Wellingtons Sieg
Weber, C.M.—Symphony no.2
Schubert—Rosamunde: Ballet music
Mendelssohn—Sinfonia no.12
Schumann, R.—Overture, scherzo, &
finale
Wagner—Siegfried idyll; Tristan und
Isolde: Prelude & Liebestod; Die Wal-
küre: Wotan's farewell & Magic fire
music
Bruckner—Symphony no.3: Adagio 2;
Symphony no.4: Finale 1878
(Volksfest)
Goldmark—Sakuntala: Overture
Brahms—Variations on a theme of
Haydn
Humperdinck—Dornröschen: Suite
Wolf—Der Corregidor: Suite
Strauss, R.—Don Juan; Macbeth
Pfitzner—Kleine Sinfonie, op.44
Schoenberg—Five pieces for orches-
tra, op.16; Ode to Napoleon Bona-
parte; Suite for string orchestra
Berg—Three pieces for orchestra,
op.6; Wozzeck: Three excerpts

[16'-20'; German & Austrian]

Hindemith—Concert music for strings & brass; Philharmonic concerto; Sinfonietta in E; Tuttifäntchen: Suite
Korngold—Schauspiel-Ouvertüre
Blacher—Orchestra-variations on a theme of Paganini
Kurka—The good soldier Schweik: Suite
Henze—Antifone; Aria de la Folía española; Barcarola; Los caprichos; Symphonies nos.1, 5
Schwertsik—Der irdischen Klänge, 2.Teil
Höller—Aura

Italian

Monteverdi—Combattimento di Tancredi e Clorinda
Scarlatti, A.—Concerti grossi nos.1-2
Veracini—Quatro pezzi
Boccherini—Symphonies nos.5, 10, 13, 17, 20-21, 23, 26-27
Salieri—Sinfonia, D major (Giorno onomastico)
Rossini—Sonatas nos.5-6
Puccini—Capriccio sinfonico
Respighi—Antiche danze ed arie (3 sets); Impressioni brasiliane; Trittico Botticelliano; Gli uccelli
Malipiero—Sinfonia per Antigenida
Casella—Italia; Paganiniana
Maderna—Aura; Serenata no.2

Russian

Borodin—Symphony no.3
Balakirev—Thamar
Mussorgsky—Pictures at an exhibition (arr. Tushmalov)
Tchaikovsky—Hamlet; Overture 1812; Romeo and Juliet (final version 1880); The tempest
Rimsky-Korsakov—Sinfonietta on Russian themes; Tsar Saltan: Suite
Glazunov—Stenka Razine
Rachmaninoff—Capriccio bohémien; The rock; Die Toteninsel
Miaskovsky—Symphony no.21
Stravinsky—Agon; Le Chant du rossignol; Danses concertantes; Scènes de ballet; Scherzo fantastique
Prokofiev—Cinderella: Suite no.2; Lieutenant Kijé: Suite; Romeo and Juliet: Suite no.3; Scythian suite; Sinfonietta
Tcherepnin—Georgiana suite; Serenade, op.97
Khachaturian—Masquerade: Suite; Spartacus: Suite no.3

Kabalevsky—Colas Breugnon: Suite
Shostakovich—Hamlet: Incidental music (1932), op.32
Khrennikov—Symphony no.1
Shchedrin—The seagull: Suite; Selbstportrait

Spanish & Latin American

Turina—Danzas fantásticas
Villa-Lobos—Bachianas brasileiras no.1; Danses africaines; Sinfoniettas nos.1-2; Uirapurú
Gerhard—Don Quixote: Dances; Epithalamion
Chávez—Initium
Rodrigo—A la busca del más allá
Ginastera—Pampeana no.3

United Kingdom

Elgar—In the south
Delius—Brigg Fair
Coleridge-Taylor—Hiawatha: Suite; Petite Suite de concert
Walton—Improvisations on an impromptu of Benjamin Britten
Alwyn—Symphony no.5
Tippett—Divertimento for chamber orch
Britten—Peter Grimes: Four sea interludes; Simple symphony; Young person's guide to the orchestra
Musgrave—Concerto for orchestra; Night music, for chamber orchestra
Birtwistle—Endless parade
Maxwell Davies—Carolisima serenade; Prolation; Sinfonia for chamber orchestra
Bennett, Richard R.—Zodiac
Tann—Adirondack light
MacMillan—The confession of Isobel Gowdie

Other nationalities

Grieg—Lyric suite, op.54; Norwegian dances; Sigurd Jorsalfar: Three orchestral pieces
Nielsen—Little suite, op.1
Sibelius—Legends: Lemminkäinen and the maidens of Saari, Lemminkäinen in Tuonela; Night ride and sunrise; The Oceanides; Pohjola's daughter; En saga; Tapiola; The tempest: Suite no.1
Martin—Etudes for string orchestra; Les Quatre Éléments
Skalkottas—Ten sketches for strings
Blomdahl—Sisyphos

[16'-20'; Other nationalities]
Schurmann—Variants
Takemitsu—Music of tree
Sallinen—Symphony no.1
Chen—Symphony no.2
Tan—Orchestral theatre I: Xun

21' TO 25'

American (United States)

Paine—Shakespeare's Tempest
Herbert—Serenade, op.12
Loeffler—A pagan poem
Hadley—Salome
Bloch, E.—Trois Poèmes juifs
Rogers—The musicians of Bremen
Piston—Symphonies nos.2, 4, 5
Still—Afro-American symphony
Sessions—The black maskers: Suite;
  Symphonies nos.1, 4
Thomson, V.—Parson Weems and the
  cherry tree; The river: Suite
Porter—Symphony no.2
Gershwin—Catfish Row; Porgy and
  Bess: Symphonic picture
Antheil—Symphonies nos.5-6
Copland—Appalachian spring; Billy
  the Kid: Suite; Music for a great city;
  Music for the theatre; The red pony;
  Symphony no.1
Krenek—Symphony
Weill—Aufstieg und Fall der Stadt
  Mahagonny: Suite; Symphony no.1
Giannini—Symphony no.2
Gutche—Symphony no.5
Swanson—Symphonies nos.1, 3
Carter—The minotaur: Ballet suite;
  Variations for orchestra
Reed—La fiesta mexicana
Schuman, Wm.—Judith; Symphony
  no.4; Undertow
Dello Joio—Meditations on Eccle-
  siastes; Variations, chaconne & fi-
  nale
Gould—Fall River legend: Ballet suite;
  The jogger and the dinosaur
Read—Symphony no.3, op.75
Fine—Symphony (1962)
Ward—Symphony no.3
Bernstein—Facsimile; Fancy free:
  Suite; On the waterfront: Symphonic
  suite; West side story: Symphonic
  dances
Kay, H.—Cakewalk: Concert suite
Overton—Symphony for strings
Foss—Baroque variations
Bassett—Variations for orchestra
Pinkham—Signs of the zodiac
Rorem—String symphony; Symphony
  no.3
Laderman—Concerto for orchestra;

Magic prison
Lees—Symphony no.2
Schuller—Concerto no.2 for orches-
  tra; Contours; Seven studies on
  themes of Paul Klee; Spectra
Lewis, R.H.—Three movements on
  scenes of Hieronymous Bosch
Druckman—Brangle; Dark upon the
  harp; Windows
Crumb—Variazioni for large orchestra
Amram—Shakespearian concerto
Blackwood—Symphony no.2
Jones—Symphonies nos.2-3
Rands—Madrigali
Schickele—The chenoo who stayed to
  dinner
Reich—The four sections; Variations
Del Tredici—Child Alice: Happy voices
Bolcom—Seattle Slew (dance suite); A
  summer divertimento
Harbison—Symphonies nos.1-2
Tower—Silver ladders
Zwilich—Symphony no.2
Albert, Stephen—Symphony no.2
Monroe—The amazing symphony
  orchestra
Adams, John—Chamber symphony
Welcher—Haleakala
Paulus—Concerto for orchestra
Rouse—Symphonies nos.1-2
Asia—Symphony no.1
Mackey—Eating greens

Eastern European

Wanski—Symphony in D major
Liszt—Hungaria
Dvořák—Czech suite; Golden spin-
  ning wheel; A hero's song; Serenade,
  op.44; Symphonic variations
Janácek—Sinfonietta; Taras Bulba
Karlowicz—Odwieczne piesni; Stanis-
  law i Anna Oswiecimowie
Dohnányi—Ruralia hungarica
Bartók—Divertimento; Four orches-
  tral pieces, op.12; Kossuth
Kodály—Concerto for orchestra; Háry
  János: Suite; Variations on a Hun-
  garian folksong
Martinu—Symphony no.2; Toccata e
  due canzoni
Panufnik—Symphony no.10
Husa—Music for Prague 1968
Lazarof—Concerto for orchestra
Svoboda—Concerto for chamber
  orchestra; Dance suite

French & Belgian

Gounod—Petite Symphonie

[21'-25'; French & Belgian]

Lalo—Namouna: Ballet suite no.1
Saint-Saëns—Le Carnaval des animaux; Symphony no.2
Delibes—Coppelia: Suite no.1
Chabrier—Suite pastorale
Massenet—Scènes alsaciennes; Suite no.1
Debussy—Le Martyre de Saint Sébastien: Fragments symphoniques; La Mer; Nocturnes
Roussel—Symphony no.3
Ravel—Gaspard de la nuit
Varèse—Amériques (1927 version); Déserts
Honegger—Symphonies nos.1, 2, 5
Milhaud—Suite symphonique no.2; Symphony no.10
Poulenc—The story of Babar, the little elephant
Jolivet—Symphony no.1

German & Austrian

Bach—Suite no.1
Handel—Il pastor fido: Suite; Royal fireworks music (ed. Baines & MacKerras)
Mozart, Leopold—Musikalische Schlittenfahrt
Haydn—Symphonies nos.6-8, 13, 31, 43-45, 47, 49, 51-53, 55-57, 60-61, 64, 66, 68, 71-74, 76, 79-80, 83-84, 87-91, 93-95, 97, 99-100, 102
Kraus—Symphony, C minor (1783)
Mozart—Cassation no.1; Divertimento no.7; Les Petits Riens; Serenades nos.11-12; Symphonies nos.25, 28, 34, 38 & K.204
Witt—Jena symphony
Weber, C.M.—Symphony no.1
Schubert—Rosamunde: Entr'actes; Symphony no.8
Mendelssohn—Sinfonia no.7
Wagner—Die Meistersinger: Three excerpts from Act III; Tannhäuser: Overture & Venusberg music
Bruckner—Symphony no.9: Finale (Carragan version)
Brahms—Liebeslieder waltzes
Mahler—Symphony no.10: mvts 1 & 3 (Krenek); 1st mvt (Ratz)
Strauss, R.—Der Rosenkavalier: Suite; Suite, op.4; Tod und Verklärung
Reger—Vier Tondichtungen, op.128
Schoenberg—Chamber symphonies no.1-2; Variations for orchestra, op.31
Schreker—Kammersymphonie
Toch—Symphony no.6

Hindemith—Lustige Sinfonietta; Mathis der Maler: Symphony; Nobilissima visione; Pittsburgh symphony; Symphonic metamorphosis
Hartmann—Symphony no.6
Einem—Meditations
Henze—Symphonies nos.2, 3, 8
Stockhausen—Gruppen; Punkte

Italian

Boccherini—Symphonies nos.3, 6, 8, 11, 25
Clementi—Symphony no.2
Cherubini—Symphony, D major
Respighi—La Boutique fantasque: Suite; Feste romane; Pini di Roma; Rossiniana
Menotti—Sebastian: Suite
Berio—Rendering

Russian

Borodin—Petite Suite
Mussorgsky—Pictures at an exhibition (arr. Goehr)
Tchaikovsky—Francesca da Rimini; Nutcracker: Suite no.1; Romeo and Juliet (orig version); Sleeping Beauty: Suite; Suite no.4; Swan lake: Suite (Jurgenson)
Rimsky-Korsakov—Christmas eve: Suite; Le Coq d'or: Suite
Ippolitov-Ivanov—Caucasian sketches
Scriabin—Le Poème de l'extase; Prométhée, le poème du feu
Rachmaninoff—Cinq Études-tableaux
Stravinsky—Le Baiser de la fée: Divertimento; Jeu de cartes; L'Oiseau de feu: Suite (1919 version); Symphony in three movements (1945)
Prokofiev—Peter and the wolf
Tcherepnin—Symphony no.2
Khachaturian—Gayane: Suite no.3; Spartacus: Suite no.2
Kabalevsky—Symphony no.1
Shchedrin—The little humpbacked horse: Suite [no.1]; Music for strings, oboes, horns & celesta; Stikhira for the millenary of Christianization of Russia

Spanish & Latin American

Arriaga—Symphony, D major
Falla—El amor brujo: Ballet suite
Turina—Sinfonia sevillana
Villa-Lobos—Bachianas brasileiras nos.2, 4
Gerhard—Concerto for orchestra

[21'-25'; Spanish & Latin American]
Chávez—La hija de Colquide; Symphonies nos.4-5
Ginastera—Concerto for strings, op.33; Popol vuh; Variaciones concertantes
Orbón—Tres versiones sinfónicas

United Kingdom

Parry—An English suite; Suite in F
Walton—Variations on a theme by Hindemith
Tippett—Concerto for double string orch
Britten—Sinfonia da requiem; Variations on a theme of Frank Bridge
Arnold—Symphony for strings
Hoddinott—Symphony no.5
Maxwell Davies—Caroline Mathilde: Suite from Act I; St. Thomas Wake
Bennett, Richard R.—Concerto for orchestra
Holloway—Scenes from Schumann
Lloyd—Symphony no.2

Other nationalities

Berwald—Symphony, D major
Grieg—Holberg suite; Old Norwegian melody with variations
Nielsen—Aladdin: 7 pieces
Sibelius—Pelléas and Mélisande; Symphony no.7
Martin—Petite Symphonie concertante
Blomdahl—Game for eight; Symphony no.3
Suolahti—Sinfonia piccola
Sallinen—Concerto for chamber orchestra
Ishii—Kyo-So
Ran—Concerto for orchestra
Sheng—H'un (Lacerations)
Tan—Orchestral theatre II: Re

26' TO 40'

American (United States)

Paine—Symphony no.1
Chadwick—Symphonic sketches; Symphony no.2
MacDowell—Suite no.2
Hadley—Symphony no.2
Ives—Symphonies nos.1, 2, 4; Universe symphony
Carpenter—Adventures in a perambulator; Skyscrapers
Taylor—Through the looking glass

Grofé—Grand Canyon suite
Piston—Symphonies nos.1, 3, 6
Hanson—Symphonies nos.1-4
Sessions—Symphonies nos.2-3
Dawson—Negro folk symphony
Harris—Symphonies nos.5, 9
Thompson, R.—Symphonies nos.1-2
Antheil—Symphony no.4
Weill—Symphony no.2
Creston—Symphonies nos.2-3
Carter—Symphony no.1
Barber—Medea; Symphony no.2
Schuman, Wm.—Symphonies nos.3, 6-10
Dello Joio—The triumph of Saint Joan
Gould—Stringmusic; Symphony of spirituals
Weber, Ben—Symphony on poems of William Blake
Bernstein—Symphony no.2
Imbrie—Symphony no.1
Foss—Geod
Mennin—Symphonies nos.6-7
Rorem—Symphony no.1
Lees—Symphony no.5
Argento—In praise of music
Blackwood—Symphony no.1
Bach, Jan—The happy prince
Bolcom—Symphony no.3
Tower—Concerto for orchestra
Wuorinen—Movers and shakers
Albert, Stephen—River run
Proto—Fantasy on the Saints
Schwantner—New morning for the world
Adams, John—Fearful symmetries; Grand pianola music; Harmonielehre; Shaker loops
Welcher—Night watchers
Stucky—Concerto for orchestra
Kernis—Symphony in waves

Eastern European

Liszt—Ce Qu'on Entend Sur La Montagne; Die Ideale
Dvořák—Serenade, op.22; Symphonies nos.1, 3-5, 7-9
Janácek—Idyla
Suk—Pohádka; Serenade, op.6; Symphony no.1
Bartók—Concerto for orchestra; Music for strings, percussion and celesta; Suites nos.1-2; The wooden prince: Suite
Kodály—Symphony
Martinu—Symphonies nos.1, 3-6
Harsányi—L'Histoire du petite tailleur
Lutoslawski—Concerto for orchestra; Preludes & fugue for 13 solo strings; Symphony no.2

[26'-40'; Eastern European]
Husa—Concerto for orchestra; Symphony no.1
Górecki—Old Polish music
Penderecki—Adagio; Symphonies nos.1-2
Svoboda—Concerto, marimba; Symphonies nos.1-5

French & Belgian

Berlioz—Symphonie funèbre et triomphale
Gounod—Symphony no.1
Franck—Symphony in D minor
Saint-Saëns—La Foi: Trois Tableaux; Symphonies nos.1, 3
Bizet—Roma; Symphony no.1
Chausson—Symphony, op.20
Charpentier, G.—Impressions d'Italie
Debussy—La Boîte à joujoux
Dukas—Symphony in C major
Koechlin—La Course de printemps
Roussel—Symphony no.2
Schmitt—La Tragédie de Salomé
Ravel—Ma Mère l'Oye
Varèse—Amériques (orig version)
Ibert—Le Chevalier errant
Honegger—Symphonies nos.3-4
Milhaud—Le Carnaval de Londres; Saudades do Brazil; Symphonies nos.1-2
Poulenc—Sinfonietta
Messiaen—L'Ascension; Chronochromie
Dutilleux—Symphony no.2

German & Austrian

Handel—Water music: Suite no.1
Gluck—Don Juan: Four movements
Haydn—Symphonies nos.42, 48, 54, 81-82, 86, 92, 98, 101, 103-104
Mozart—Divertimenti K.136, 137, 138; Divertimenti nos.2, 10-11, 15; German dances, K.586; Serenades nos.1, 3, 5, 9; Symphonies nos.29, 36, 39-41 & K.250
Beethoven—Septet, op.20; Symphonies nos.1-2, 4-8
Witt—Symphony in A
Spohr—Nonet, op.31; Octet, op.32
Schubert—Quartet, strings, D.810; Symphonies nos.1-7
Mendelssohn—Octet, strings, op.20; Sinfonias nos.8, 9, 11
Mendelssohn—Symphonies nos.1-5
Schumann, R.—Symphonies nos.1-4
Wagner—Symphony, C major
Bruckner—Symphony no.9: Finale

(Samale et. al.)
Reinecke—Symphonies nos.1-3
Goldmark—Symphony no.2
Brahms—Serenade no.2; Symphonies nos.2-4
Bruch—Symphonies nos.1, 3
Wolf—Penthesilea
Strauss, R.—Also sprach Zarathustra; Le Bourgeois Gentilhomme: Suite; Ein Heldenleben; Metamorphosen; Symphony for winds, op.posth.
Reger—Symphonic prolog to a tragedy; Variations and fugue on a theme of Hiller; Variations and fugue on a theme of Mozart
Schoenberg—Pierrot Lunaire; Verklärte Nacht
Berg—Lulu: Suite
Toch—Symphony no.3
Hindemith—Die Harmonie der Welt: Symphony; Symphonia serena; Symphonic dances; Symphony in E-flat
Korngold—Symphonic serenade, op.39
Egk—Variationen über ein karibisches Thema
Einem—Wiener Symphonie
Henze—Symphonies nos.4, 6

Italian

Clementi—Symphonies nos.1, 3-4
Busoni—Turandot: Suite
Respighi—Vetrate di chiesa

Russian

Borodin—Symphonies nos.1-2
Balakirev—King Lear: Incidental music; Symphony no.2
Mussorgsky—Pictures at an exhibition (arr. Ravel)
Tchaikovsky—Serenade, op.48; Suite no.2; Swan lake: Suite (Kalmus); Symphonies nos.2, 7
Rimsky-Korsakov—The Maid of Pskov: Overture & Three entr'actes; Symphonies nos.1-3
Rimsky-Korsakov—Symphonies nos.2-3
Glazunov—Scènes de ballet, op.52; Symphony no.4
Kalinnikov—Symphonies nos.1-2
Rachmaninoff—Symphonic dances; Symphony no.3
Glière—The red poppy: Suite; Symphony no.1
Miaskovsky—Sinfonietta; Symphony no.22
Stravinsky—Apollon Musagéte; L'Histoire du soldat: Suite; L'Oiseau de

[26'-40'; Russian]

feu: Suite (1911 & 1945); Orpheus; Petrouchka; Le Sacre du printemps; Symphony no.1; Symphony in C
Prokofiev—Chout: Symphonic suite; Cinderella: Suites nos.1, 3; Le Pas d'acier; Romeo and Juliet: Suites nos.1-2; Symphonies nos.2-4, 7
Khachaturian—Gayane: Suites nos.1-2; Spartacus: Suite no.1
Kabalevsky—Symphony no.2
Shostakovich—Hamlet: Film suite; Symphonies nos.1, 3, 6, 9, 12
Shchedrin—Anna Karenina
Schnittke—In memoriam...

Spanish & Latin American

Albéniz—Iberia (arr. Arbós)
Falla—El sombrero de tres picos
Villa-Lobos—Bachianas brasileiras no.8
Gerhard—Symphony no.1
Chávez—Symphony no.3

United Kingdom

Parry—Symphony no.3
Elgar—Enigma variations; Falstaff
Delius—Appalachia
Vaughan Williams—Symphonies nos.3-6, 8-9; The wasps: Suite
Walton—Symphony no.2
Alwyn—Sinfonietta; Symphony no.2
Tippett—Concerto for orchestra; The midsummer marriage: Ritual dances; New year suite; Symphonies nos.1-2, 4
Britten—Gloriana: Symphonic suite
Arnold—Symphonies nos.3, 6
Williams—Star wars: Suite
Birtwistle—Verses for ensembles
Maxwell Davies—Caroline Mathilde: Suite from Act II; Second fantasia on John Taverner's "In nomine"; Sinfonia concertante; Sinfonietta accademica; Symphony no.5; Worldes blis
Bennett, Richard R.—Sonnets to Orpheus
Holloway—Second concerto for orchestra, op.40

Other nationalities

Berwald—Symphonies in C major, E-flat major, G minor
Gade—Symphony no.1
Grieg—Symphonic dances; Symphony, C minor

Nielsen—Symphonies nos.1-6
Sibelius—Symphonies nos.1, 3-6
Schurmann—Six studies of Francis Bacon
Sallinen—Symphonies nos.3, 5
Ran—Symphony
Tan—Death and fire

41' TO 60'

American (United States)

Paine—Symphony no.2
Beach—Symphony no.2
Bloch, E.—America
Copland—Symphony no.3
Diamond—Symphony no.2
Shapey—Concerto fantastique
Corigliano—Symphony no.1
Melby—Symphony no.1
Daugherty—Metropolis symphony

Eastern European

Liszt—Dante symphony; Faust Symphony (with shortened ending)
Dvořák—Symphonies nos.2, 6
Paderewski—Symphony
Suk—Symphony no.2
Górecki—Symphony no.3

French & Belgian

Berlioz—Symphonie fantastique
Ravel—Daphnis et Chloé
Honegger—Le Dit des jeux du monde

German & Austrian

Bach—Musikalisches Opfer
Handel—Water music
Mozart—Divertimento no.17; Serenades nos.4, 7, 10
Beethoven—Prometheus; Symphony no.3
Schubert—Rosamunde; Symphony, D.812,(Grand duo); Symphony no.9, D.944 (The great)
Bruckner—Studiensymphonie; Nullte symphony; Symphonies nos.1-3, 6
Strauss, Joh., Jr.—Graduation ball (arr. Dorati)
Goldmark—Ländliche Hochzeit
Brahms—Serenade no.1; Symphony no.1
Mahler—Symphonies nos.1, 4
Strauss, R.—Eine Alpensinfonie; Aus Italien; Symphonia domestica; Symphony, op.12

[41'-60'; German & Austrian]

Schmidt—Symphonies nos.2, 4
Schoenberg—Pelléas und Mélisande
Berg—Chamber concerto, op.8
Korngold—Sinfonietta, op.5

Russian

Balakirev—Symphony no.1
Tchaikovsky—Manfred; Suites nos.1,
  3; Symphonies nos.1, 3-6
Rimsky-Korsakov—Scheherazade
Scriabin—Le Divin Poème; Symphony
  no.2
Rachmaninoff—Symphonies nos.1-2
Stravinsky—Le Baiser de la fée; L'Oi-
  seau de feu
Prokofiev—Symphonies nos.5-6
Khachaturian—Symphony no.2
Shostakovich—The gadfly: Suite;
  Symphonies nos.4-5, 10-11, 15

Spanish & Latin American

Albéniz—Iberia (arr. Surinach)

United Kingdom

Parry—Symphonic fantasy
Elgar—Symphonies nos.1-2
Vaughan Williams—Job; Symphonies
  nos.2, 7
Holst—The planets
Bax—Symphony no.7
Walton—Façade; Symphony no.1
Alwyn—Symphony no.1
Maxwell Davies—Symphonies nos.1-4

Other nationalities

Sibelius—Symphony no.2
Bamert—Once upon an orchestra

OVER 60'

American (United States)

Wuorinen—The magic art
Proto—Doodles; Fantasy on the
  Saints

Eastern European

Liszt—A Faust symphony

French & Belgian

Adam—Giselle
Delibes—Coppelia
Messiaen—Turangalila-symphonie

German & Austrian

Haydn—Die sieben letzten Worte
  [orchestral version]
Schubert—Octet, D.803
Bruckner—Symphonies nos.2-5, 7-9
Mahler—Symphonyies nos.2-3, 5-7,
  9-10

Russian

Tchaikovsky—Nutcracker; Swan lake
Glière—Symphony no.3
Shostakovich—Symphonies nos.7-8

VARIABLE DURATION

American (United States)

Cage—Atlas eclipticalis
Brown—Available forms 1
Brown—Available forms 2
Wolff—Burdocks
Proto—Doodles; Fantasy on the
  Saints

APPENDIX F
SIGNIFICANT ANNIVERSARIES
OF COMPOSERS

This appendix lists the significant anniversaries (multiples of 50 years) of the birth- and death-dates of the composers represented in this book.

1997
John Adams, 1947-
Heinrich Joseph Baermann, 1784-1847
Léon Boëllmann, 1862-1897
Walter Boudreau, 1947-
Johannes Brahms, 1833-1897
Alfredo Casella, 1883-1947
Henry Cowell, 1897-1965
Gaetano Donizetti, 1797-1848
Reynaldo Hahn, 1875-1947
Fanny Mendelssohn Hensel, 1805-1847
David Kechley, 1947-
Erich Wolfgang Korngold, 1897-1957
Jean Marie Leclair, 1697-1764
Felix Mendelssohn, 1809-1847
Quincy Porter, 1897-1966
Johann Joachim Quantz, 1697-1773
Franz Schubert, 1797-1828
Hilary Tann, 1947-
Alexandre Tansman, 1897-1986
Gwyneth Walker, 1947-

1998
Ernst Bacon, 1898-1990
William Dawson, 1898-1990
Gaetano Donizetti, 1797-1848
George Gershwin, 1898-1937
Roy Harris, 1898-1979
Tibor Harsányi, 1898-1954
Franz Lehár, 1870-1948
Jonathan Lloyd, 1948-
Hubert Parry, 1848-1918
Manuel Ponce, 1882-1948
Dan Welcher, 1948-
Ermanno Wolf-Ferrari, 1876-1948

1999
Georges Auric, 1899-1983
John Barbirolli, 1899-1970
Ernest Chausson, 1855-1899
Carlos Chávez, 1899-1978
Frédéric Chopin, 1810-1849
Domenico Cimarosa, 1749-1801
Karl Ditters von Dittersdorf, 1739-1799
Duke Ellington, 1899-1974
Jacques Halévy, 1799-1862
Otto Nicolai, 1810-1849
Stephen Paulus, 1949-
Hans Pfitzner, 1869-1949
Francis Poulenc, 1899-1963
Henri Rabaud, 1873-1949
Shulamit Ran, 1949-
Silvestre Revueltas, 1899-1940
Christopher Rouse, 1949-
Joseph Boulogne, Chevalier de Saint-Georges, 1739-1799
Nikos Skalkottas, 1904-1949
Johann Strauss, Jr., 1825-1899
Johann Strauss, Sr., 1804-1849
Richard Strauss, 1864-1949
Steven Stucky, 1949-
Alexander Tcherepnin, 1899-1977
Randall Thompson, 1899-1984
Joaquín Turina, 1882-1949
Meira Maxine Warshauer, 1949-

2000
Tomaso Albinoni, 1671-1750
George Antheil, 1900-1959
Johann Sebastian Bach, 1685-1750
Nicolai Berezowsky, 1900-1953
Aaron Copland, 1900-1990

Charles Koechlin, 1867-1950
Ernst Krenek, 1900-1991
Libby Larsen, 1950-
Otto Luening, 1900-
Alexandre Luigini, 1850-1906
Alessandro Marcello, ca.1684-ca.1750
Nikolai Miaskovsky, 1881-1950
Alexander Mosolov, 1900-1973
Sammartini, Giuseppe, 1695-1750
Arthur Sullivan, 1842-1900
Francesco Maria Veracini, 1690-
 ca.1750
Kurt Weill, 1900-1950
Colin McPhee, 1900-1964
Antonio Salieri, 1750-1825
Niccolò Piccinni, 1728-1800

2001
Vincenzo Bellini, 1801-1835
John Alden Carpenter, 1876-1951
Domenico Cimarosa, 1749-1801
Ruth Crawford (Seeger), 1901-1953
Anthony Davis, 1951-
Werner Egk, 1901-1983
Gerald Finzi, 1901-1956
Giovanni Gabrieli, 1551-1612
Vincent d'Indy, 1851-1931
Vassili Kalinnikov, 1866-1901
Serge Koussevitzky, 1874-1951
Constant Lambert, 1905-1951
Joseph Lanner, 1801-1843
Albert Lortzing, 1801-1851
Joseph Rheinberger, 1839-1901
Joaquín Rodrigo, 1901-
Edmund Rubbra, 1901-1986
Giovanni Battista Sammartini, 1701-
 1775
Arnold Schoenberg, 1874-1951
Ruth Crawford Seeger, 1901-1953
Karl Stamitz, 1745-1801
Henri Frédien Tomasi, 1901-1971
George Tsontakis, 1951-
Giuseppe Verdi, 1813-1901

2002
Muzio Clementi, 1752-1832
Maurice Duruflé, 1902-1986
Oliver Knussen, 1952-
Richard Rodgers, 1902-1979

Georg Schumann, 1866-1952
Charles Villiers Stanford, 1852-1924
William Walton, 1902-1983

2003
Adolph-Charles Adam, 1803-1856
Daniel Asia, 1953-
Arnold Bax, 1883-1953
Nicolai Berezowsky, 1900-1953
Lennox Berkeley, 1903-1989
Hector Berlioz, 1803-1869
Boris Blacher, 1903-1975
Arcangelo Corelli, 1653-1713
Ruth Crawford (Seeger), 1901-1953
Arthur Foote, 1853-1937
Vittorio Giannini, 1903-1966
Berthold Goldschmidt, 1903-
Johann Gottlieb Graun, 1703-1771
Aram Khachaturian, 1903-1978
Daniel Gregory Mason, 1873-1953
Johann Pachelbel, 1653-1706
Serge Prokofiev, 1891-1953
Hugo Wolf, 1860-1903
Chen Yi, 1953-

2004
Richard Addinsell, 1904-1977
Robert Beaser, 1954-
Heinrich von Biber, 1644-1704
George Whitefield Chadwick, 1854-
 1931
Marc-Antoine Charpentier, 1634-1704
Luigi Dallapiccola, 1904-1975
Michael Daugherty, 1954-
Antonín Dvořák, 1841-1904
Mikhail Glinka, 1804-1857
Tibor Harsányi, 1898-1954
Engelbert Humperdinck, 1854-1921
Charles Ives, 1874-1954
Leos Janáček, 1854-1928
Dmitri Kabalevsky, 1904-1987
Tobias Picker, 1954-
Nikos Skalkottas, 1904-1949
Anton Stamitz, 1754-ca.1809
Johann Strauss, Sr., 1804-1849

2005
Bruce Adolphe, 1955-
William Alwyn, 1905-1985

Luigi Boccherini, 1743-1805
Joseph Bodin de Boismortier, 1691-1755
Ernest Chausson, 1855-1899
Georges Enesco, 1881-1955
Ferenc Farkas, 1905-
Ernesto Halffter, 1905-1989
Karl Amadeus Hartmann, 1905-1963
Fanny Mendelssohn Hensel, 1805-1847
Arthur Honegger, 1892-1955
André Jolivet, 1905-1974
Constant Lambert, 1905-1951
Anatol Liadov, 1855-1914
Bright Sheng, 1955-
Michael Tippett, 1905-
Giovanni Battista Viotti, 1755-1824

2006

Adolph-Charles Adam, 1803-1856
Anton Arensky, 1861-1906
Juan Crisóstomo Arriaga, 1806-1826
Gustave Charpentier, 1860-1956
Paul Creston, 1906-1985
Richard Danielpour, 1956-
Ross Lee Finney, 1906-
Gerald Finzi, 1901-1956
Baldassare Galuppi, 1706-1785
Reinhold Glière, 1875-1956
Michael Haydn, 1737-1806
Joseph Martin Kraus, 1756-1792
Alexandre Luigini, 1850-1906
Steven Mackey, 1956-
Wolfgang Amadeus Mozart, 1756-1791
Johann Pachelbel, 1653-1706
John Knowles Paine, 1839-1906
Robert Schumann, 1810-1856
Dmitri Shostakovich, 1906-1975

2007

Henk Badings, 1907-1987
Dietrich Buxtehude, ca.1637-1707
Cécile Chaminade, 1857-1944
Jeremiah Clarke, ca.1674-1707
Eric Coates, 1886-1957
Edward Elgar, 1857-1934
Wolfgang Fortner, 1907-1987
Mikhail Glinka, 1804-1857
Alexander Goedicke, 1877-1957
Edvard Grieg, 1843-1907

Gene Gutche, 1907-
Joseph Joachim, 1831-1907
Edgar Stillman Kelley, 1857-1944
Erich Wolfgang Korngold, 1897-1957
Robert Kurka, 1921-1957
Michel-Richard de Lalande, 1657-1726
Ödön Partos, 1907-1977
Burrill Phillips, 1907- 1988
Ignaz Pleyel, 1757-1831
György Ránki, 1907-
Miklós Rózsa, 1907-1995
Domenico Scarlatti, 1685-1757
Jean Sibelius, 1865-1957
Johann Wenzel Anton Stamitz, 1717-1757
Howard Swanson, 1907-1978
Tan Dun , 1957-
Alec Wilder, 1907-1980

2008

Leroy Anderson, 1908-1975
Elliott Carter, 1908-
Johann Friedrich Fasch, 1688-1758
Armas Järnefelt, 1869-1958
Lars-Erik Larsson, 1908-1987
Ruggero Leoncavallo, 1858-1919
Edward MacDowell, 1861-1908
Olivier Messiaen, 1908-1992
José Pablo Moncayo (García), 1912-1958
Giacomo Puccini, 1858-1924
Nikolai Rimsky-Korsakov, 1844-1908
Pablo de Sarasate, 1844-1908
Florent Schmitt, 1870-1958
Halsey Stevens, 1908-1989
Giuseppe Torelli, 1658-1709
Ralph Vaughan Williams, 1872-1958
Eugene Ysaÿe, 1858-1931

2009

Isaac Albéniz, 1860-1909
George Antheil, 1900-1959
Grażyna Bacewicz,, 1909-1969
Ernest Bloch, 1880-1959
Dudley Buck, 1839-1909
Ronald Caltabiano, 1959-
George Frideric Handel, 1685-1759
Franz Joseph Haydn, 1732-1809
Victor Herbert, 1859-1924

Mikhail Ippolitov-Ivanov, 1859-1935
Mieczysław Karłowicz, 1876-1909
James MacMillan, 1959-
Bohuslav Martinu, 1890-1959
Felix Mendelssohn, 1809-1847
Sigismund Noskowski, 1846-1909
Henry Purcell, 1659-1695
Elie Siegmeister, 1909-1991
Ludwig Spohr, 1784-1859
Anton Stamitz, 1754-ca.1809
Giuseppe Torelli, 1658-1709
Heitor Villa-Lobos, 1887-1959

2010

Isaac Albéniz, 1860-1909
Hugo Alfvén, 1872-1960
Thomas Arne, 1710-1778
Wilhelm Friedemann Bach, 1710-1784
Mily Balakirev, 1837-1910
Samuel Barber, 1910-1981
Arthur Benjamin, 1893-1960
Paul Bowles, 1910-
Gustave Charpentier, 1860-1956
Luigi Cherubini, 1760-1842
Frédéric Chopin, , 1810-1849
Ferdinand David, 1810- 1873
Ernst von Dohnányi, 1877-1960
Johann Joseph Fux, 1660-1741
Blas Galindo, 1910-1993
Christoph Graupner, 1683-1760
Aaron Jay Kernis, 1960-
Gustav Mahler, 1860-1911
Paule Maurice, 1910-1967
Otto Nicolai, 1810-1849
Ignace Jan Paderewski, 1860-1941
Giovanni Battista Pergolesi, 1710-1736
H. Owen Reed, 1910-
Carl Reinecke, 1824-1910
Emil Nikolaus von Reznicek, 1860-
1945
Alessandro Scarlatti, 1660-1725
William Schuman, 1910-1992
Robert Schumann, 1810-1856
Leó Weiner, 1885-1960
Hugo Wolf, 1860-1903

2011

Anton Arensky, 1861-1906
John J. Becker, 1886-1961

William Boyce, 1711-1779
Thomas Canning, 1911-
Unsuk Chin, 1961-
Percy Grainger, 1882-1961
Alan Hovhaness, 1911-
Lowell Liebermann, 1961-
Franz Liszt, 1811-1886
Charles Martin Loeffler, 1861-1935
Edward MacDowell, 1861-1908
Gustav Mahler, 1860-1911
Robert McBride, 1911-
Gian Carlo Menotti, 1911-
Wallingford Riegger, 1885-1961
Julia Smith, 1911-
Johan Svendsen, 1840-1911
Ambroise Thomas, 1811-1896
Michael Torke, 1961-

2012

Wayne Barlow, 1912-
Léon Boëllmann, 1862-1897
John Cage, 1912-1992
Samuel Coleridge-Taylor, 1875-1912
Ingolf Dahl, 1912-1970
Claude Debussy, 1862-1918
Frederick Delius, 1862-1934
Irving Fine, 1914-1962
Friedrich von Flotow, 1812-1883
Jean Françaix, 1912-
Frederick II (The Great), 1712-1786
Giovanni Gabrieli, 1551-1612
Francesco Geminiani, 1687-1762
Edward German, 1862-1936
Don Gillis, 1912-1978
Peggy Glanville-Hicks, 1912-1990
Eugene Goosens, 1893-1962
Jacques Halévy, 1799-1862
Jacques Ibert, 1890-1962
Mykola Lysenko, 1842-1912
Francesco Manfredini, 1684-1762
Jules Massenet, 1842-1912
José Pablo Moncayo (García), 1912-
1958
Barbara Pentland, 1912-
David Raksin, 1912-
Jan Wański, 1762-ca.1830

2013

Henry Brant, 1913-

Benjamin Britten, 1913-1976
Peggy Stuart Coolidge, 1913- 1982
Arcangelo Corelli, 1653-1713
Norman Dello Joio, 1913-
Domenico Dragonetti, 1763-1846
Alvin Etler, 1913-1973
Morton Gould, 1913-1996
André Grétry, 1741-1813
Karl Amadeus Hartmann, 1905-1963
Paul Hindemith, 1895-1963
Kent Kennan, 1913-
Tikhon Khrennikov, 1913-
Witold Lutosławski, 1913-1994
Pietro Mascagni, 1863-1945
Horatio Parker, 1863-1919
Gabriel Pierné, 1863-1937
David Popper, 1843-1913
Francis Poulenc, 1899-1963
Gardner Read, 1913-
Johann Baptist (Jan Křtitel) Vanhal,
   1739-1813
Giuseppe Verdi, 1813-1901
Tomaso Antonio Vitali, 1663- 1745
Richard Wagner, 1813-1883
John Weinzweig, 1913-

2014

Carl Philipp Emanuel Bach, 1714-1788
Cecil Effinger, 1914-
Irving Fine, 1914-1962
Christoph Willibald Gluck, 1714-1787
Louis Gruenberg, 1884-1964
George Kleinsinger, 1914-1982
Gail Kubik, 1914-1984
Jean Marie Leclair, 1697-1764
Anatol Liadov, 1855-1914
Pietro Locatelli, 1695-1764
Colin McPhee, 1900-1964
Giacomo Meyerbeer, 1791-1864
Andrzej Panufnik, 1914-1991
Jean Philippe Rameau, 1683-1764
Richard Strauss, 1864-1949
Ernst Toch, 1887-1964

2015

Henry Cowell, 1897-1965
David Diamond, 1915-
Paul Dukas, 1865-1935
Alexander Glazunov, 1865-1936

Karl Goldmark, 1830-1915
Désiré-Émile Ingelbrecht, 1880-1965
Carl Nielsen, 1865-1931
George Perle, 1915-
Vincent Persichetti, 1915-1987
Alexander Scriabin, 1872-1915
Alan Shulman, 1915-1993
Jean Sibelius, 1865-1957
Carlos Surinach, 1915-
Edgard Varèse, 1883-1965
Georg Christoph Wagenseil, 1715-1777
Emil Waldteufel, 1837-1915

2016

Milton Babbitt, 1916-
Karl-Birger Blomdahl, 1916-1968
Howard Brubeck, 1916-
Ferruccio Busoni, 1866-1924
George Butterworth, 1885-1916
Henri Dutilleux, 1916-
Vittorio Giannini, 1903-1966
Alberto Ginastera, 1916-1983
Enrique Granados, 1867-1916
Vassili Kalinnikov, 1866-1901
Giovanni Paisiello, 1740-1816
Quincy Porter, 1897-1966
Max Reger, 1873-1916
Erik Satie, 1866-1925
Georg Schumann, 1866-1952
Deems Taylor, 1885-1966
Ben Weber, 1916-1979

2017

Amy Marcy Cheney Beach, 1867-1944
Niels Gade, 1817-1890
Enrique Granados, 1867-1916
Scott Joplin, 1868-1917
Ulysses Kay, 1917- 1995
Zoltán Kodály, 1882-1967
Charles Koechlin, 1867-1950
Paule Maurice, 1910-1967
Claudio Monteverdi, 1567-1643
José Mauricio Nunés-Garcia, 1767-1830
Reginald Smith Brindle, 1917-
Johann Wenzel Anton Stamitz, 1717-
   1757
Georg Philipp Telemann, 1681-1767
Robert Ward, 1917-
Jaromir Weinberger, 1896-1967

Richard Yardumian, 1917-1985

2018

Leonard Bernstein, 1918-1990
Franz Berwald, 1796-1868
Karl-Birger Blomdahl, 1916-1968
Mario Castelnuovo-Tedesco, 1895-1968
François Couperin, 1668-1733
Claude Debussy, 1862-1918
Gottfried von Einem, 1918-
Henry F. Gilbert, 1868-1928
Charles Gounod, 1818-1893
Scott Joplin, 1868-1917
Henry Charles Litolff, 1818-1891
Hubert Parry, 1848-1918
George Rochberg, 1918-
Bernard Rogers, 1893-1968
Gioacchino Rossini, 1792-1868
Carl Ruggles, 1876-1968
Leo Sowerby, 1895-1968
Bernd Alois Zimmermann, 1918-1970

2019

Grażyna Bacewicz, 1909-1969
Hector Berlioz, 1803-1869
Louis Moreau Gottschalk, 1829-1869
Armas Järnefelt, 1869-1958
Hershy Kay, 1919- 1981
Leon Kirchner, 1919-
Theron Kirk, 1919-
Ruggero Leoncavallo, 1858-1919
Stanisław Moniuszko, 1819-1872
Douglas Moore, 1893-1969
Leopold Mozart, 1719-1787
Vaclav Nelhybel, 1919-1996
Jacques Offenbach, 1819-1880
Horatio Parker, 1863-1919
Hans Pfitzner, 1869-1949
Albert Roussel, 1869-1937
Clara Wieck Schumann, 1819-1896
Franz von Suppé, 1819-1895

2020

John Barbirolli, 1899-1970
Ludwig van Beethoven, 1770-1827
Max Bruch, 1838-1920
Ingolf Dahl, 1912-1970
Roberto Gerhard, 1896-1970

Charles Tomlinson Griffes, 1884-1920
David Horne, 1970-
John La Montaine, 1920-
Franz Lehár, 1870-1948
John Lewis, 1920-
Bruno Maderna, 1920-1973
Hall Overton, 1920-1972
Florent Schmitt, 1870-1958
Josef Strauss, 1827-1870
Heikki Suolahti, 1920-1936
Giuseppe Tartini, 1692-1770
Henri Vieuxtemps, 1820-1881
Friedrich Witt, 1770-1837
Bernd Alois Zimmermann, 1918-1970

2021

Tomaso Albinoni, 1671-1750
Malcolm Arnold, 1921-
Daniel-François Auber, 1782-1871
Arno Babadjanyan, 1921-1983
William Bergsma, 1921-1994
Giovanni Bottesini, 1821-1889
Frederick Shepherd Converse, 1871-1940
Johann Gottlieb Graun, 1703-1771
Henry Hadley, 1871-1937
Engelbert Humperdinck, 1854-1921
Karel Husa, 1921-
Andrew Imbrie, 1921-
Robert Kurka, 1921-1957
Camille Saint-Saëns, 1835-1921
Ralph Shapey, 1921-
Igor Stravinsky, 1882-1971
András Szöllösy, 1921-
Henri Frédien Tomasi, 1901-1971
Adolph Weiss, 1891-1971
Alexander Zemlinsky, 1871-1942

2022

Hugo Alfvén, 1872-1960
Havergal Brian, 1876-1972
Lukas Foss, 1922-
César Franck,, 1822-1890
Ferde Grofé, 1892-1972
Iain Hamilton, 1922-
Stanisław Moniuszko, 1819-1872
Hall Overton, 1920-1972
Heinrich Schütz, 1585-1672
Alexander Scriabin, 1872-1915

Kazimierz Serocki, 1922-1981
Francis Thorne, 1922-
Ralph Vaughan Williams, 1872-1958
George Walker, 1922-
Yannis Xenakis, 1922-

2023
Karl Friedrich Abel, 1723-1787
Leslie Bassett, 1923-
Chou Wen-chung , 1923-
Ferdinand David, 1810- 1873
Alvin Etler, 1913-1973
William Kraft, 1923-
Edouard Lalo, 1823-1892
György Ligeti, 1923-
Bruno Maderna, 1920-1973
Gian Francesco Malipiero, 1882-1973
Daniel Gregory Mason, 1873-1953
Peter Mennin, 1923-1983
Alexander Mosolov, 1900-1973
Daniel Pinkham, 1923-
Mel Powell, 1923-
Johann Joachim Quantz, 1697-1773
Henri Rabaud, 1873-1949
Sergei Rachmaninoff, 1873-1943
Max Reger, 1873-1916
Ned Rorem, 1923-
Stanisław Skrowaczewski, 1923-
Lester Trimble, 1923-1986
Paul White, 1895-1973

2024
Warren Benson, 1924-
Anton Bruckner, 1824-1896
Ferruccio Busoni, 1866-1924
Jeremiah Clarke, ca.1674-1707
Peter Cornelius, 1824-1874
Théodore Dubois,, 1837-1924
Duke Ellington, 1899-1974
Gabriel Fauré, 1845-1924
Arthur Frackenpohl, 1924-
Victor Herbert, 1859-1924
Stanley Hollingsworth, 1924-
Gustav Holst, 1874-1934
Charles Ives, 1874-1954
André Jolivet, 1905-1974
Serge Koussevitzky, 1874-1951
Ezra Laderman, 1924-
Benjamin Lees, 1924-

Frank Martin, 1890-1974
Darius Milhaud, 1892-1974
Luigi Nono, 1924-1990
Giacomo Puccini, 1858-1924
Carl Reinecke, 1824-1910
Gerhard Samuel, 1924-
Franz Schmidt, 1874-1939
Arnold Schoenberg, 1874-1951
Bedrich Smetana, 1824-1884
Charles Villiers Stanford, 1852-1924
Robert Starer, 1924-
Josef Suk, 1874-1935
Giovanni Battista Viotti, 1755-1824
Egon Wellesz, 1885-1974

2025
Leroy Anderson, 1908-1975
Luciano Berio, 1925-
Georges Bizet, 1838-1875
Boris Blacher, 1903-1975
Arthur Bliss, 1891-1975
François Boieldieu,, 1775-1834
Pierre Boulez, 1925-
Samuel Coleridge-Taylor, 1875-1912
Luigi Dallapiccola, 1904-1975
Reinhold Glière, 1875-1956
Marcel Grandjany, 1891-1975
Reynaldo Hahn, 1875-1947
Kirke Mecham, 1925-
Julián Orbón,, 1925-1991
Maurice Ravel, 1875-1937
Antonio Salieri, 1750-1825
Giovanni Battista Sammartini, 1701-1775
Erik Satie, 1866-1925
Alessandro Scarlatti, 1660-1725
Gunther Schuller, 1925-
Dmitri Shostakovich, 1906-1975
Hale Smith, 1925-
Johann Strauss, Jr., 1825-1899

APPENDIX G: COMPOSER GROUPS
FOR THEMATIC PROGRAMING

American (United States)	Greek
Argentinian	Hungarian
Armenian	Irish
Australian	Israeli
Basque	Italian
Belgian	Japanese
Black composers	Jewish
Brazilian	Mexican
British	Norwegian
Bulgarian	Polish
Canadian	Rumanian
Chinese	Russian
Cuban	Scottish
Czech or Bohemian	Spanish
Danish	Swedish
Dutch	Swiss
Finnish	Ukrainian
French	Welsh
German & Austrian	Women composers

Occasionally it is necessary to create programs of music by particular groups of composers, such as Polish composers, black composers, women composers. This appendix is intended to help in that process.

Obviously, many composers appear in more than one of these groups. Meyerbeer, for example, was Jewish, born in Germany, and did much of his important work in France. Tania León is black, female, born in Cuba, and has lived in the United States for many years.

Within each category, composers are listed chronologically according to birth date.

AMERICAN (UNITED STATES)
Louis Moreau Gottschalk, 1829-1869
Dudley Buck, 1839-1909
John Knowles Paine, 1839-1906
Arthur Foote, 1853-1937
George Whitefield Chadwick, 1854-1931
Edgar Stillman Kelley, 1857-1944
Victor Herbert, 1859-1924
Charles Martin Loeffler, 1861-1935
Edward MacDowell, 1861-1908
Horatio Parker, 1863-1919
Amy Marcy Cheney Beach, 1867-1944
Henry F. Gilbert, 1868-1928
Scott Joplin, 1868-1917
Frederick Shepherd Converse, 1871-1940
Henry Hadley, 1871-1937
Daniel Gregory Mason, 1873-1953
Charles Ives, 1874-1954
John Alden Carpenter, 1876-1951
Carl Ruggles, 1876-1968
Ernest Bloch, 1880-1959
Charles Wakefield Cadman, 1881-1946
Percy Grainger, 1882-1961
Edgard Varèse, 1883-1965
Charles Tomlinson Griffes, 1884-1920
Louis Gruenberg, 1884-1964
Wallingford Riegger, 1885-1961
Deems Taylor, 1885-1966
John J. Becker, 1886-1961
Ernst Toch, 1887-1964
Adolph Weiss, 1891-1971
Ferde Grofé, 1892-1972
Douglas Moore, 1893-1969
Bernard Rogers, 1893-1968
Robert Russell Bennett, 1894-1981
Walter Piston, 1894-1976
Nicolas Slonimsky, 1894-1995
Paul Hindemith, 1895-1963
Leo Sowerby, 1895-1968
William Grant Still, 1895-1978
Paul White, 1895-1973
Howard Hanson, 1896-1981
Roger Sessions, 1896-1985
Virgil Thomson, 1896-1989
Henry Cowell, 1897-1965
Quincy Porter, 1897-1966
Ernst Bacon, 1898-1990
William Dawson, 1898-1990

George Gershwin, 1898-1937
Roy Harris, 1898-1979
Duke Ellington, 1899-1974
Randall Thompson, 1899-1984
George Antheil, 1900-1959
Nicolai Berezowsky, 1900-1953
Aaron Copland, 1900-1990
Ernst Krenek, 1900-1991
Otto Luening, 1900-
Colin McPhee, 1900-1964
Kurt Weill, 1900-1950
Ruth Crawford (Seeger), 1901-1953
Richard Rodgers, 1902-1979
Vittorio Giannini, 1903-1966
Paul Creston, 1906-1985
Ross Lee Finney, 1906-
Gene Gutche, 1907-
Burrill Phillips, 1907-1988
Miklós Rózsa, 1907-1995
Howard Swanson, 1907-1978
Alec Wilder, 1907-1980
Leroy Anderson, 1908-1975
Elliott Carter, 1908-
Halsey Stevens, 1908-1989
Elie Siegmeister, 1909-1991
Samuel Barber, 1910-1981
Paul Bowles, 1910-
H. Owen Reed, 1910-
William Schuman, 1910-1992
Thomas Canning, 1911-
Alan Hovhaness, 1911-
Robert McBride, 1911-
Gian Carlo Menotti, 1911-
Julia Smith, 1911-
Wayne Barlow, 1912-
John Cage, 1912-1992
Ingolf Dahl, 1912-1970
Don Gillis, 1912-1978
David Raksin, 1912-
Henry Brant, 1913-
Peggy Stuart Coolidge, 1913-1982
Norman Dello Joio, 1913-
Alvin Etler, 1913-1973
Morton Gould, 1913-1996
Kent Kennan, 1913-
Gardner Read, 1913-
Cecil Effinger, 1914-
Irving Fine, 1914-1962
George Kleinsinger, 1914-1982
Gail Kubik, 1914-1984

[AMERICAN (UNITED STATES)]
David Diamond, 1915-
George Perle, 1915-
Vincent Persichetti, 1915-1987
Alan Shulman, 1915-1993
Carlos Surinach, 1915-
Milton Babbitt, 1916-
Howard Brubeck, 1916-
Ben Weber, 1916-1979
Ulysses Kay, 1917-1995
Robert Ward, 1917-
Richard Yardumian, 1917-1985
Leonard Bernstein, 1918-1990
George Rochberg, 1918-
Hershy Kay, 1919-1981
Leon Kirchner, 1919-
Theron Kirk, 1919-
John La Montaine, 1920-
John Lewis, 1920-
Hall Overton, 1920-1972
William Bergsma, 1921-1994
Karel Husa, 1921-
Andrew Imbrie, 1921-
Ralph Shapey, 1921-
Lukas Foss, 1922-
Francis Thorne, 1922-
George Walker, 1922-
Leslie Bassett, 1923-
Chou Wen-chung, 1923-
William Kraft, 1923-
Peter Mennin, 1923-1983
Daniel Pinkham, 1923-
Mel Powell, 1923-
Ned Rorem, 1923-
Lester Trimble, 1923-1986
Warren Benson, 1924-
Arthur Frackenpohl, 1924-
Stanley Hollingsworth, 1924-
Ezra Laderman, 1924-
Benjamin Lees, 1924-
Gerhard Samuel, 1924-
Robert Starer, 1924-
Kirke Mecham, 1925-
Julián Orbón, 1925-1991
Gunther Schuller, 1925-
Hale Smith, 1925-
Earle Brown, 1926-
Morton Feldman, 1926-1987
Carlisle Floyd, 1926-
Robert Hall Lewis, 1926-

Dominick Argento, 1927-
Walter Aschaffenburg, 1927-
Donald Erb, 1927-
Salvatore Martirano, 1927-
Wayne Peterson, 1927-
Samuel Adler, 1928-
T. J. Anderson, 1928-
Arthur Cunningham, 1928-
Jacob Druckman, 1928-1996
Ursula Mamlok, 1928-
William Russo, 1928-
George Crumb, 1929-
Edwin London, 1929-
André Previn, 1929-
Paul Turok, 1929-
David Amram, 1930-
David Baker, 1931-
Charles Kelso Hoag, 1931-
Mario Lombardo, 1931-
Donald Martino, 1931-
Leslie Adams, 1932-
Michael Colgrass, 1932-
Henri Lazarof, 1932-
John Williams, 1932-
Easley Blackwood, 1933-
Morton Subotnick, 1933-
Roger Reynolds, 1934-
Richard Wernick, 1934-
Christian Wolff, 1934-
Samuel Jones, 1935-
Bernard Rands, 1935-
Peter Schickele, 1935-
Carman Moore, 1936-
Steve Reich, 1936-
Elliott Schwartz, 1936-
Jan Bach, 1937-
David Del Tredici, 1937-
Philip Glass, 1937-
Olly Wilson, 1937-
William Bolcom, 1938-
John Corigliano, 1938-
John Harbison, 1938-
Joan Tower, 1938-
Charles Wuorinen, 1938-
Elinor Armer, 1939-
Barbara Kolb, 1939-
Tomáš Svoboda, 1939-
Ellen Taaffe Zwilich, 1939-
Gerald Plain, 1940-
Alvin Singleton, 1940-

[AMERICAN (UNITED STATES)]
Stephen Albert, 1941-1992
Adolphus Hailstork, 1941-
John Melby, 1941-
Frank Proto, 1941-
Ervin Monroe, 1942-
Tania León, 1943-
Marta Ptaszyńska, 1943-
Joseph Schwantner, 1943-
James Hartway, 1944-
Victoria Bond, 1945-
Thomas Pasatieri, 1945-
Russell Peck, 1945-
Robert Xavier Rodríguez, 1946-
John Adams, 1947-
David Kechley, 1947-
Hilary Tann, 1947-
Gwyneth Walker, 1947-
Dan Welcher, 1948-
Stephen Paulus, 1949-
Shulamit Ran, 1949-
Christopher Rouse, 1949-
Steven Stucky, 1949-
Meira Maxine Warshauer, 1949-
Libby Larsen, 1950-
Anthony Davis, 1951-
George Tsontakis, 1951-
Daniel Asia, 1953-
Chen Yi, 1953-
Robert Beaser, 1954-
Michael Daugherty, 1954-
Tobias Picker, 1954-
Bruce Adolphe, 1955-
Bright Sheng, 1955-
Richard Danielpour, 1956-
Steven Mackey, 1956-
Gregory Smith, 1957-
Ronald Caltabiano, 1959-
Aaron Jay Kernis, 1960-
Lowell Liebermann, 1961-
Michael Torke, 1961-

ARGENTINIAN
Alberto Ginastera, 1916-1983
Mario Davidovsky, 1934-

ARMENIAN
Aram Khachaturian, 1903-1978
Alan Hovhaness, 1911-
Richard Yardumian, 1917-1985

Arno Babadjanyan, 1921-1983

AUSTRALIAN
Percy Grainger, 1882-1961
Arthur Benjamin, 1893-1960
Peggy Glanville-Hicks, 1912-1990
Peter Sculthorpe, 1929-

BASQUE
Juan Crisóstomo Arriaga, 1806-1826

BELGIAN
François Joseph Gossec, 1734-1829
André Grétry, 1741-1813
César Franck, 1822-1890
Eugene Ysaÿe, 1858-1931

BLACK
Joseph Boulogne, Chevalier de Saint-
   Georges, 1739-1799
José Mauricio Nunés-Garcia, 1767-1830
Antônio Carlos Gomes, 1836-1896
Scott Joplin, 1868-1917
Samuel Coleridge-Taylor, 1875-1912
William Grant Still, 1895-1978
William Dawson, 1898-1990
Duke Ellington, 1899-1974
Howard Swanson, 1907-1978
Ulysses Kay, 1917-1995
John Lewis, 1920-
George Walker, 1922-
Hale Smith, 1925-
T. J. Anderson, 1928-
Arthur Cunningham, 1928-
Leslie Adams, 1932-
Carman Moore, 1936-
Olly Wilson, 1937-
Alvin Singleton, 1940-
Adolphus Hailstork, 1941-
Tania León, 1943-
Anthony Davis, 1951-

BRAZILIAN
José Mauricio Nunés-Garcia, 1767-1830
Antônio Carlos Gomes, 1836-1896
Heitor Villa-Lobos, 1887-1959

BRITISH
Henry Purcell, 1659-1695

[BRITISH]
Jeremiah Clarke, ca.1674-1707
Thomas Arne, 1710-1778
William Boyce, 1711-1779
Muzio Clementi, 1752-1832
Henry Charles Litolff, 1818-1891
Arthur Sullivan, 1842-1900
Hubert Parry, 1848-1918
Edward Elgar, 1857-1934
Frederick Delius, 1862-1934
Edward German, 1862-1936
Ralph Vaughan Williams, 1872-1958
Gustav Holst, 1874-1934
Samuel Coleridge-Taylor, 1875-1912
Havergal Brian, 1876-1972
Arnold Bax, 1883-1953
George Butterworth, 1885-1916
Eric Coates, 1886-1957
Arthur Bliss, 1891-1975
Arthur Benjamin, 1893-1960
Eugene Goosens, 1893-1962
Peter Warlock, 1894-1930
Gordon Jacob, 1895-1984
Roberto Gerhard, 1896-1970
John Barbirolli, 1899-1970
Gerald Finzi, 1901-1956
Edmund Rubbra, 1901-1986
William Walton, 1902-1983
Lennox Berkeley, 1903-1989
Berthold Goldschmidt, 1903-
Richard Addinsell, 1904-1977
William Alwyn, 1905-1985
Constant Lambert, 1905-1951
Michael Tippett, 1905-
Benjamin Britten, 1913-1976
Andrzej Panufnik, 1914-1991
Reginald Smith Brindle, 1917-
Malcolm Arnold, 1921-
Iain Hamilton, 1922-
Gerard Schurmann, 1928-
Alun Hoddinott, 1929-
Henri Lazarof, 1932-
Harrison Birtwistle, 1934-
Peter Maxwell Davies, 1934-
Bernard Rands, 1935-
Richard Rodney Bennett, 1936-
John McCabe, 1939-
Robin Holloway, 1943-
John Tavener, 1944-
John Rutter, 1945-

Jonathan Lloyd, 1948-
Oliver Knussen, 1952-

BULGARIAN
Henri Lazarof, 1932-

CANADIAN
Colin McPhee, 1900-1964
Barbara Pentland, 1912-
Henry Brant, 1913-
John Weinzweig, 1913-
R. Murray Schafer, 1933-
Walter Boudreau, 1947-
Chen Yi, 1953-
Bright Sheng, 1955-
Tan Dun, 1957-

CHINESE
Chen Yi, 1953-
Bright Sheng, 1955-
Tan Dun, 1957-

CUBAN
Leo Brouwer, 1939-
Tania León, 1943-

CZECH or BOHEMIAN
Johann Wenzel Anton Stamitz, 1717-
 1757
Franz Xaver Pokorny, 1729-1794
Joh. Baptist (Jan Křtitel) Vanhal, 1739-
 1813
Karl Stamitz, 1745-1801
Anton Stamitz, 1754-ca.1809
Bedrich Smetana, 1824-1884
Antonín Dvořák, 1841-1904
David Popper, 1843-1913
Leos Janáček, 1854-1928
Josef Suk, 1874-1935
Bohuslav Martinu, 1890-1959
Jaromir Weinberger, 1896-1967
Vaclav Nelhybel, 1919-1996
Karel Husa, 1921-
Tomáš Svoboda, 1939-

DANISH
Niels Gade, 1817-1890
Carl Nielsen, 1865-1931

DUTCH
Henk Badings, 1907-1987
Gerard Schurmann, 1928-
Louis Andriessen, 1939-

FINNISH
Jean Sibelius, 1865-1957
Armas Järnefelt, 1869-1958
Heikki Suolahti, 1920-1936
Aulis Sallinen, 1935-

FRENCH
Jean Baptiste Lully, 1632-1687
Marc-Antoine Charpentier, 1634-1704
Michel-Richard de Lalande, 1657-1726
Franois Couperin, 1668-1733
Jean Philippe Rameau, 1683-1764
Joseph Bodin de Boismortier, 1691-
   1755
Jean Marie Leclair, 1697-1764
Joseph Boulogne, Chevalier de Saint-
   Georges, 1739-1799
François Boieldieu, 1775-1834
Daniel-François Auber, 1782-1871
Louis Joseph F. Hérold, 1791-1833
Giacomo Meyerbeer, 1791-1864
Jacques Halévy, 1799-1862
Adolph-Charles Adam, 1803-1856
Hector Berlioz, 1803-1869
Ambroise Thomas, 1811-1896
Charles Gounod, 1818-1893
Jacques Offenbach, 1819-1880
Henri Vieuxtemps, 1820-1881
Edouard Lalo, 1823-1892
Camille Saint-Saëns, 1835-1921
Léo Delibes, 1836-1891
Théodore Dubois, 1837-1924
Emil Waldteufel, 1837-1915
Georges Bizet, 1838-1875
Emmanuel Chabrier, 1841-1894
Jules Massenet, 1842-1912
Gabriel Fauré, 1845-1924
Alexandre Luigini, 1850-1906
Vincent d'Indy, 1851-1931
Ernest Chausson, 1855-1899
Cécile Chaminade, 1857-1944
Gustave Charpentier, 1860-1956
Léon Boëllmann, 1862-1897
Claude Debussy, 1862-1918
Gabriel Pierné, 1863-1937

Paul Dukas, 1865-1935
Erik Satie, 1866-1925
Charles Koechlin, 1867-1950
Albert Roussel, 1869-1937
Florent Schmitt, 1870-1958
Henri Rabaud, 1873-1949
Reynaldo Hahn, 1875-1947
Maurice Ravel, 1875-1937
Raoul Laparra, 1876-1943
Désiré-Émile Ingelbrecht, 1880-1965
Edgard Varèse, 1883-1965
Jacques Ibert, 1890-1962
Marcel Grandjany, 1891-1975
Arthur Honegger, 1892-1955
Darius Milhaud, 1892-1974
Georges Auric, 1899-1983
Francis Poulenc, 1899-1963
Henri Frédien Tomasi, 1901-1971
Maurice Duruflé, 1902-1986
André Jolivet, 1905-1974
Olivier Messiaen, 1908-1992
Paule Maurice, 1910-1967
Jean Françaix, 1912-
Henri Dutilleux, 1916-
Pierre Boulez, 1925-
Pierre Max Dubois, 1930-

GERMAN & AUSTRIAN
Heinrich Schütz, 1585-1672
Johann Hermann Schein, 1586-1630
Andreas Hofer, 1629-1684
Dietrich Buxtehude, ca.1637-1707
Heinrich von Biber, 1644-1704
Johann Pachelbel, 1653-1706
Johann Joseph Fux, 1660-1741
Johann Ludwig Bach, 1677-1741
Georg Philipp Telemann, 1681-1767
Christoph Graupner, 1683-1760
Johann Sebastian Bach, 1685-1750
George Frideric Handel, 1685-1759
Johann Friedrich Fasch, 1688-1758
Johann Joachim Quantz, 1697-1773
Johann Gottlieb Graun, 1703-1771
Wilhelm Friedemann Bach, 1710-1784
Frederick II (The Great), 1712-1786
Carl Philipp Emanuel Bach, 1714-1788
Christoph Willibald Gluck, 1714-1787
Georg Christoph Wagenseil, 1715-1777
Leopold Mozart, 1719-1787
Karl Friedrich Abel, 1723-1787

[GERMAN and AUSTRIAN]
Franz Joseph Haydn, 1732-1809
Johann Christian Bach, 1735-1782
Michael Haydn, 1737-1806
Karl Ditters von Dittersdorf, 1739-1799
Joseph Martin Kraus, 1756-1792
Wolfgang Amadeus Mozart, 1756-1791
Ignaz Pleyel, 1757-1831
Wenzel Müller, 1767-1835
Ludwig van Beethoven, 1770-1827
Friedrich Witt, 1770-1837
Johann Nepomuk Hummel, 1778-1837
Heinrich Joseph Baermann, 1784-1847
Ludwig Spohr, 1784-1859
Friedrich Kuhlau, 1786-1832
Carl Maria von Weber, 1786-1826
Giacomo Meyerbeer, 1791-1864
Franz Schubert, 1797-1828
Joseph Lanner, 1801-1843
Albert Lortzing, 1801-1851
Johann Strauss, Sr., 1804-1849
Fanny Mendelssohn Hensel, 1805-1847
Felix Mendelssohn, 1809-1847
Ferdinand David, 1810-1873
Otto Nicolai, 1810-1849
Robert Schumann, 1810-1856
Friedrich von Flotow, 1812-1883
Richard Wagner, 1813-1883
Clara Wieck Schumann, 1819-1896
Franz von Suppé, 1819-1895
Anton Bruckner, 1824-1896
Peter Cornelius, 1824-1874
Carl Reinecke, 1824-1910
Johann Strauss, Jr., 1825-1899
Josef Strauss, 1827-1870
Karl Goldmark, 1830-1915
Joseph Joachim, 1831-1907
Johannes Brahms, 1833-1897
Max Bruch, 1838-1920
Joseph Rheinberger, 1839-1901
Engelbert Humperdinck, 1854-1921
Gustav Mahler, 1860-1911
Emil Nikolaus von Reznicek, 1860-1945
Hugo Wolf, 1860-1903
Richard Strauss, 1864-1949
Georg Schumann, 1866-1952
Hans Pfitzner, 1869-1949
Franz Lehár, 1870-1948
Alexander Zemlinsky, 1871-1942

Max Reger, 1873-1916
Franz Schmidt, 1874-1939
Arnold Schoenberg, 1874-1951
Franz Schreker, 1878-1934
Anton Webern, 1883-1945
Alban Berg, 1885-1935
Egon Wellesz, 1885-1974
Ernst Toch, 1887-1964
Paul Hindemith, 1895-1963
Carl Orff, 1895-1982
Erich Wolfgang Korngold, 1897-1957
Ernst Krenek, 1900-1991
Kurt Weill, 1900-1950
Werner Egk, 1901-1983
Boris Blacher, 1903-1975
Berthold Goldschmidt, 1903-
Karl Amadeus Hartmann, 1905-1963
Wolfgang Fortner, 1907-1987
Gottfried von Einem, 1918-
Bernd Alois Zimmermann, 1918-1970
Robert Kurka, 1921-1957
Gerhard Samuel, 1924-
Hans Werner Henze, 1926-
Samuel Adler, 1928-
Ursula Mamlok, 1928-
Karlheinz Stockhausen, 1928-
Kurt Schwertsik, 1935-
H[einz] K[arl] Gruber, 1943-
York Höller, 1944-

GREEK
Nikos Skalkottas, 1904-1949
Yannis Xenakis, 1922-

HUNGARIAN
Franz Liszt, 1811-1886
Franz Lehár, 1870-1948
Ernst von Dohnányi, 1877-1960
Béla Bartók, 1881-1945
Zoltán Kodály, 1882-1967
Leó Weiner, 1885-1960
Tibor Harsányi, 1898-1954
Ferenc Farkas, 1905-
Ödön Partos, 1907-1977
György Ránki, 1907-
Miklós Rózsa, 1907-1995
András Szöllösy, 1921-
György Ligeti, 1923-
Sándor Balassa, 1935-

IRISH
Charles Villiers Stanford, 1852-1924
Victor Herbert, 1859-1924

ISRAELI
Ödön Partos, 1907-1977
Shulamit Ran, 1949-

ITALIAN
Giovanni Gabrieli, 1551-1612
Claudio Monteverdi, 1567-1643
Jean Baptiste Lully, 1632-1687
Arcangelo Corelli, 1653-1713
Giuseppe Torelli, 1658-1709
Alessandro Scarlatti, 1660-1725
Tomaso Antonio Vitali, 1663-1745
Tomaso Albinoni, 1671-1750
Antonio Vivaldi, 1678-1741
Francesco Manfredini, 1684-1762
Alessandro Marcello, ca.1684-ca.1750
Domenico Scarlatti, 1685-1757
Benedetto Marcello, 1686-1739
Francesco Geminiani, 1687-1762
Francesco Maria Veracini, 1690-ca.1750
Giuseppe Tartini, 1692-1770
Leonardo Leo, 1694-1744
Pietro Locatelli, 1695-1764
Giuseppe Sammartini, 1695-1750
Giovanni Battista Sammartini, 1701-1775
Baldassare Galuppi, 1706-1785
Giovanni Battista Pergolesi, 1710-1736
Niccolò Piccinni, 1728-1800
Giovanni Paisiello, 1740-1816
Luigi Boccherini, 1743-1805
Domenico Cimarosa, 1749-1801
Antonio Salieri, 1750-1825
Muzio Clementi, 1752-1832
Giovanni Battista Viotti, 1755-1824
Luigi Cherubini, 1760-1842
Domenico Dragonetti, 1763-1846
Niccolò Paganini, 1782-1840
Gioacchino Rossini, 1792-1868
Gaetano Donizetti, 1797-1848
Vincenzo Bellini, 1801-1835
Giuseppe Verdi, 1813-1901
Giovanni Bottesini, 1821-1889
Amilcare Ponchielli, 1834-1886
Ruggero Leoncavallo, 1858-1919
Giacomo Puccini, 1858-1924
Pietro Mascagni, 1863-1945
Ferruccio Busoni, 1866-1924
Ermanno Wolf-Ferrari, 1876-1948
Ottorino Respighi, 1879-1936
Gian Francesco Malipiero, 1882-1973
Alfredo Casella, 1883-1947
Mario Castelnuovo-Tedesco, 1895-1968
Luigi Dallapiccola, 1904-1975
Gian Carlo Menotti, 1911-
Bruno Maderna, 1920-1973
Luigi Nono, 1924-1990
Luciano Berio, 1925-
Giangiacomo Miari, 1929-

JAPANESE
Toshirō Mayuzumi, 1929-
Tōru Takemitsu, 1930-1996
Maki Ishii, 1936-

JEWISH[1]
Giacomo Meyerbeer, 1791-1864
Jacques Halévy, 1799-1862
Fanny Mendelssohn Hensel, 1805-1847
Felix Mendelssohn, 1809-1847
Ferdinand David, 1810-1873
Jacques Offenbach, 1819-1880
Louis Moreau Gottschalk, 1829-1869
Anton Rubinstein, 1829-1894
Karl Goldmark, 1830-1915
Joseph Joachim, 1831-1907
Camille Saint-Saëns, 1835-1921
Henri Wieniawski, 1835-1880
Emil Waldteufel, 1837-1915
Gustav Mahler, 1860-1911
Paul Dukas, 1865-1935
Ferruccio Busoni, 1866-1924
Alexander Zemlinsky, 1871-1942
Serge Koussevitzky, 1874-1951
Arnold Schoenberg, 1874-1951
Reinhold Glière, 1875-1956
Reynaldo Hahn, 1875-1947
Franz Schreker, 1878-1934
Ernest Bloch, 1880-1959
Louis Gruenberg, 1884-1964
Egon Wellesz, 1885-1974
Ernst Toch, 1887-1964

[1] Researched by Helen Rowin of the Detroit Public Library

[JEWISH]
Darius Milhaud, 1892-1974
Arthur Benjamin, 1893-1960
Bernard Rogers, 1893-1968
Nicolas Slonimsky, 1894-1995
Mario Castelnuovo-Tedesco, 1895-1968
Jaromir Weinberger, 1896-1967
Erich Wolfgang Korngold, 1897-1957
Alexandre Tansman, 1897-1986
George Gershwin, 1898-1937
George Antheil, 1900-1959
Aaron Copland, 1900-1990
Kurt Weill, 1900-1950
Richard Rodgers, 1902-1979
Ödön Partos, 1907-1977
Elie Siegmeister, 1909-1991
William Schuman, 1910-1992
Henry Brant, 1913-
Morton Gould, 1913-1996
John Weinzweig, 1913-
Irving Fine, 1914-1962
David Diamond, 1915-
Alan Shulman, 1915-1993
Ben Weber, 1916-1979
Leonard Bernstein, 1918-1990
Hershy Kay, 1919-1981
Leon Kirchner, 1919-
Lukas Foss, 1922-
Mel Powell, 1923-
Ezra Laderman, 1924-
Robert Starer, 1924-
Gunther Schuller, 1925-
Morton Feldman, 1926-1987
Samuel Adler, 1928-
Jacob Druckman, 1928-1996
André Previn, 1929-
David Amram, 1930-
Henri Lazarof, 1932-
Morton Subotnick, 1933-
Mario Davidovsky, 1934-
Richard Wernick, 1934-
Steve Reich, 1936-
Philip Glass, 1937-
Shulamit Ran, 1949-
Meira Maxine Warshauer, 1949-
Richard Danielpour, 1956-
Aaron Jay Kernis, 1960-

MEXICAN
Manuel Ponce, 1882-1948
Carlos Chávez, 1899-1978
Silvestre Revueltas, 1899-1940
Blas Galindo, 1910-1993
José Pablo Moncayo (García), 1912-1958
Mario Lavista, 1943-

NORWEGIAN
Johan Svendsen, 1840-1911
Edvard Grieg, 1843-1907

POLISH
Jakub Gołabek, 1739-1789
Jan Wański, 1762-ca.1830
Frédéric Chopin, 1810-1849
Stanisław Moniuszko, 1819-1872
Henri Wieniawski, 1835-1880
Sigismund Noskowski, 1846-1909
Ignace Jan Paderewski, 1860-1941
Mieczysław Karłowicz, 1876-1909
Karol Szymanowski, 1882-1937
Alexandre Tansman, 1897-1986
Grażyna Bacewicz, 1909-1969
Witold Lutosławski, 1913-1994
Andrzej Panufnik, 1914-1991
Kazimierz Serocki, 1922-1981
Stanisław Skrowaczewski, 1923-
Augustyn Bloch, 1929-
Henryk Górecki, 1933-
Krzysztof Penderecki, 1933-
Marta Ptaszyńska, 1943-
Jerzy Sapieyevski, 1945-

RUMANIAN
Georges Enesco, 1881-1955

RUSSIAN
Mikhail Glinka, 1804-1857
Anton Rubinstein, 1829-1894
Alexander Borodin, 1833-1887
Mily Balakirev, 1837-1910
Modest Mussorgsky, 1839-1881
Piotr Ilyich Tchaikovsky, 1840-1893
Nikolai Rimsky-Korsakov, 1844-1908
Anatol Liadov, 1855-1914
Mikhail Ippolitov-Ivanov, 1859-1935
Anton Arensky, 1861-1906
Alexander Glazunov, 1865-1936

[RUSSIAN]

Vassili Kalinnikov, 1866-1901
Alexander Scriabin, 1872-1915
Sergei Rachmaninoff, 1873-1943
Serge Koussevitzky, 1874-1951
Reinhold Glière, 1875-1956
Alexander Goedicke, 1877-1957
Nikolai Miaskovsky, 1881-1950
Igor Stravinsky, 1882-1971
Serge Prokofiev, 1891-1953
Nicolas Slonimsky, 1894-1995
Alexander Tcherepnin, 1899-1977
Nicolai Berezowsky, 1900-1953
Alexander Mosolov, 1900-1973
Aram Khachaturian, 1903-1978
Dmitri Kabalevsky, 1904-1987
Dmitri Shostakovich, 1906-1975
Tikhon Khrennikov, 1913-
Rodion Shchedrin, 1932-
Alfred Schnittke, 1934-

SCOTTISH

Thea Musgrave, 1928-
James MacMillan, 1959-
David Horne, 1970-

SPANISH

Juan Crisóstomo Arriaga, 1806-1826
Edouard Lalo, 1823-1892
Pablo de Sarasate, 1844-1908
Isaac Albéniz, 1860-1909
Enrique Granados, 1867-1916
Manuel de Falla, 1876-1946
Joaquín Turina, 1882-1949
Roberto Gerhard, 1896-1970
Joaquín Rodrigo, 1901-
Ernesto Halffter, 1905-1989
Carlos Surinach, 1915-
Julián Orbón, 1925-1991

SWEDISH

Joseph Martin Kraus, 1756-1792
Franz Berwald, 1796-1868
Hugo Alfvén, 1872-1960
Dag Wirén, 1905-1986
Lars-Erik Larsson, 1908-1987
Karl-Birger Blomdahl, 1916-1968

SWISS

Ernest Bloch, 1880-1959
Frank Martin, 1890-1974
Arthur Honegger, 1892-1955
Roberto Gerhard, 1896-1970
Matthias Bamert, 1942-

UKRAINIAN

Mykola Lysenko, 1842-1912
Reinhold Glière, 1875-1956
Alexander Mosolov, 1900-1973
Myroslav Skoryk, 1938-

WELSH

Alun Hoddinott, 1929-
Hilary Tann, 1947-

WOMEN

Fanny Mendelssohn Hensel, 1805-1847
Clara Wieck Schumann, 1819-1896
Cécile Chaminade, 1857-1944
Amy Marcy Cheney Beach, 1867-1944
Ruth Crawford (Seeger), 1901-1953
Grażyna Bacewicz, 1909-1969
Peggy Glanville-Hicks, 1912-1990
Peggy Stuart Coolidge, 1913-1982
Ursula Mamlok, 1928-
Thea Musgrave, 1928-
Joan Tower, 1938-
Elinor Armer, 1939-
Barbara Kolb, 1939-
Ellen Taaffe Zwilich, 1939-
Tania León, 1943-
Marta Ptaszyńska, 1943-
Victoria Bond, 1945-
Hilary Tann, 1947-
Gwyneth Walker, 1947-
Meira Maxine Warshauer, 1949-
Libby Larsen, 1950-
Chen Yi , 1953-

APPENDIX H

RESOURCES

OLIS (Orchestra Library Information Service)
Edwin A. Fleisher Collection
MOLA (Major Orchestra Librarians' Association)
Center for Black Music Research
Women composers
Keys of vocal accompaniments
National anthems
Conductors Guild
American Music Center
International Association of Music Information Centres

OLIS (Orchestra Library Information Service)

American Symphony Orchestra League   Tel: 202-776-0212
1156 Fifteenth Street NW, Suite 800   Fax: 202-776-0224
Washington DC 20005-1704   E-mail: league@symphony.org

Software that contains a database of information about orchestral music, and permits organizations or individual users to establish records of performance history, repertoire, guest artists and contracts. It is intended for use by the entire staff of an orchestra (artistic, library, marketing, operations, and administration). OLIS has been in existence since 1986.

The heart of the database is information on more than 4000 orchestral works, including instrumentation, durations, available editions, and special performance requirements. Individual movement titles are listed—a convenience in preparing the printed concert programs. In most cases durations are given for individual movements, and instrumentation variances from one movement to another are indicated. In many cases the style is briefly described, as well as the genre and even the key of the work.

For vocal works, the choral or solo requirements are specified, and the source of the text and its original language are given. Entries show the availability of piano-vocal scores and choral scores.

Historical information includes the dates and places of the composer's birth and death, the date of composition, and the composer's citizenship, country of primary residence, and gender.

Other helpful information includes an indication of works that have proved useful for youth concerts and a designation of the source of any errata lists that may exist for scores and/or parts.

The cost of the OLIS package (software and database) is presently in the $3000-4000 range. Some changes and improvements in the technology and marketing are under consideration, and the database may ultimately be available on-line.

EDWIN A. FLEISHER COLLECTION

Free Library of Philadelphia   Tel: 215-686-5313
1901 Vine Street   Fax: 215-563-3628
Philadelphia PA 19103-1116   Email: smithk@library.phila.gov

The Fleisher Collection was originally the library of a youth training orchestra founded and financed by Edwin A. Fleisher. In 1929 it was given to the Free Library of Philadelphia, where it still resides, and where it has grown into the largest lending library of orchestral scores and parts in the world.

Originally the Fleisher Collection had no music for orchestra plus voices (solo or choral). Since 1980, however, these works have gradually been added. (The Free Library, incidentally, is also the home of the Henry S. Drinker Choral Library, which has some sets of orchestral parts for choral works; phone 215-686-5364.)

Sets of material otherwise difficult or impossible to obtain are available on loan for a nominal fee. Music that is readily available commercially is loaned only to organizations within the state of Pennsylvania. Examination scores are loaned to conductors directly through their institutions (orchestras, universities, and the like).

The expert staff will also handle reference questions by phone, mail, or fax. An interesting and useful newsletter is published from time to time.

The Fleisher Collection will prepare scores and parts of new works under certain conditions.

MOLA (Major Orchestra Librarians' Association)

Tel: 215-893-1929   Fax: 215-875-7664

MOLA is a professional service organization whose members represent the libraries of over 80 orchestras, opera companies, and ballet companies, mostly in the United States, but also including Canada, Europe, Australia, Asia, and the Middle East. Although the officers change from year to year, the official clearinghouse is MOLA Central at the Philadelphia Orchestra Library. For additional information, contact Clinton F. Nieweg, Principal Librarian, at the above numbers.

The membership represents vast collective knowledge and experience, and seems to foster an ethic of eagerness to help solve any problem in the arcane world of editions, scores, and parts.

An information-packed newsletter, *Marcato*, is published quarterly, and is available by subscription for $10 US per year in North America, or $15 US per year elsewhere. Highly recommended.

CENTER FOR BLACK MUSIC RESEARCH

Columbia College Chicago
600 South Michigan Avenue
Chicago, Illinois 60605-1996

Tel: 312-663-1600 ext.5559
Fax: 312-663-9019
E-mail: cbmr@mail.colum.edu

The purpose of the Center for Black Music Research is to discover, disseminate, preserve, and promote black music in all its forms—from jazz, blues, gospel, and ragtime to opera and concert works. It houses a library with archival collections and database, and publishes the *Black Music Research Journal*, and the *CBMR Digest*, as well as various monographs. The Center also presents conferences and mounts performances by the Black Music Repertory Ensemble.

Orchestral materials relating to black music constitute just one small part of the Center's activities, but the staff can assist with research inquiries about concert music, and can provide repertoire suggestions as well as background information. For these, contact the CBMR Library and Archives at extension 5586.

WOMEN COMPOSERS

Women's Philharmonic
44 Page St, Suite 604D
San Francisco, California 94102

Tel: 415-437-0123
Fax: 415-437-0121
E-mail: womensphil@aol.com

The activities of the former National Women Composers Resource Center are now being conducted under the name of its parent organization, the Women's Philharmonic. Its mission is to reconstruct neglected music by women composers, to commission works by women composers, and to bring that music before new audiences. It houses a database of more than 200 composers from all over the world and all historical periods. It can assist with programming suggestions, and can provide information on instrumentation, publisher, special performance requirements, and duration for many works. It is possible to rent scores and parts for certain reconstructed repertoire from the Women's Philharmonic.

KEYS OF VOCAL ACCOMPANIMENTS

Educational Music Service
Tel: 914-469-5790
Fax: 914-469-5817

Luck's Music Library
Tel: 800-348-8749
Fax: 313-583-1114

The venerable firm of Mapleson had the most extensive list of vocal accompaniments in a variety of keys designed to accommodate the preferences of singers. Alas, Mapleson has gone out of business, but much of its list has been acquired by Educational Music Service, and can be had from them. Luck's Music Library also has arias in various keys, though not as broad and diverse a selection as that of the former Mapleson catalog. Both companies are listed among the publishers at the end of this book.

NATIONAL ANTHEMS

US Army Band
US Marine Band
US Navy School of Music
US Air Force Band

Tel: 703-696-3648
Tel: 202-433-4298; Fax: 202-433-4752
Tel: 202-433-6105
Tel: 202-767-4393

The United States Government has assigned the responsibility for keeping track of correct current national anthems for all nations to the US Army Band at Fort Myer, Virginia. Band arrangements, which can easily be adapted for orchestral use, may usually be obtained from this source or one of the other military bands.

Governments of other countries are likely to maintain similar arrangements through either their military or foreign affairs departments.

CONDUCTORS GUILD, INC.

103 South High Street, Room 6
West Chester PA 19382-3262

Tel: 610-430-6010
Fax: 610-430-6034
E-mail: conguild@aol.com

An organization of nearly 2000 conductors mostly from the United States, but including over 30 other nations. Publishes a quarterly newsletter and a semiannual *Journal*, both of which are full of useful information. The *Journal* regularly features lists of errata in scores and parts of various standard repertoire works.

The Guild holds an annual conference, and presents a series of conductor workshops. Other publications include an annual membership directory, and the monthly *Conductor Opportunities*, which lists professional vacancies, workshops, competitions, and other opportunities of interest to conductors.

AMERICAN MUSIC CENTER, INC.

30 W. 26th Street, Suite 1001   Tel: 212-366-5260
New York, New York 10010-2011   Fax: 212-366-5265
Web site: http://www.amc.net/amc   E-mail: center@amc.net

The American Music Center houses a library of more than 35,000 scores and 15,000 recordings, from which loans may be arranged. Information is available on career development, funders of new music, commissioning sources, publishers, performing ensembles, composer organizations, and the like. Grants to composers are available to help offset the costs of extracting and copying parts for premiere performances.

INTERNATIONAL ASSOCIATION OF MUSIC INFORMATION CENTRES

Contemporary Music Centre   Tel: +353-1-661-2105
95 Lower Baggot Street   Fax: +353-1-676-2639
Dublin 2 Ireland   E-mail: iamic@cmc.ie

A worldwide network of organizations promoting new music. Music information centers have large libraries of music and recordings, as well as up-to-date collections of biographical and research material. Many issue publications and recordings also. An English-speaking staff member is often available at these centers.

The following list, arranged by country, includes members of IAMIC plus a number of additional organizations which, while not members, may be useful contacts. These non-members are identified by an asterisk. (The "+" before the telephone number indicates that the initial cluster of one to three digits represents the country code.)

Albania
*Institute of Fine Arts
Biblioteka e Akademisë Arteve
Bld. Dëshmorët e Kombit
Tiranë
Albania
Fax: +355-42-23617

Australia
Australian Music Centre Ltd.
1st Floor, 18 Argyle St
The Rocks
NSW 2000
Australia
Tel: +61-2-247 4677
Fax: +61-2-241 2873
E-mail: info@amcoz.com.au
Internet: http://www.amcoz.com.au/amc

Austria
Musik Informations Zentrum Österreich
  (MICA)
Spengergasse 39
A-1051 Wien
Austria
Tel: +43-1-545 59 69
Fax: +43-1-545 59 69-9
Email: music.austria@mica.co.at

Belgium
Centre Belge de Documentation Musicale
  (CeBeDeM)
Rue d'Arlon 75-77
B-1040 Bruxelles
Belgium
Tel: +32-2-230 94 30 / +32-2-230 94 37
Fax: +32-2-231 18 00 / +32-2-230 94 37
E-mail: 101573.3644@compuserve.com
Internet: http://www.arcadis.be/cebedem/

Brazil
*CDMC-Brasil/UNICAMP
(Universidade Estadual de Campinas -
  Etat de São Paulo)
Cx. P. 6136
13083-970 CAMPINAS - SP
Brazil
Tel: +55-19-239 1503 p. 29
Fax: +55-19-239 5806
E-mail: cdmusica@turing.unicamp.br
Internet: http://obelix.unicamp.br/musica

Canada
Canadian Music Centre
Chalmers House, 20 St. Joseph Street
Toronto, Ontario M4Y 1J9
Canada
Tel: +1-416-961 6601
Fax: +1-416-961 7198
E-mail: cmc@interlog.com
Internet: http://www.ffa.ucalgary.ca/cmc

Colombia
Centro de Documentación Musical
Calle 24, No. 5-60, 4 Piso
Santafé de Bogotá 1
Colombia
Tel: +57-1-283 6903

Croatia
*Croatian Music Information Centre
Zagreb Concert Management
Kneza Mislava 18
HR-10 000 Zagreb
Croatia
Tel: +385-1-410 221
Fax: +385-1-443 022

Czech Republic
Hudební Informační Středisko
  (Czech Music Information Centre)
Besední 3
11800 Praha 1
Czech Republic
Tel: +42-2-24 51 00 75
Fax: +42-2-53 97 20
E-mail: czmic@login.cz

Denmark
Dansk Musik Informations Center
Gråbrødre Torv 16
DK-1154 København K
Denmark
Tel: +45-33 11 20 66
Fax: +45-33 32 20 16
E-mail: mic@mic.bibnet.dk
Internet: http://www.bibnet.dk/mic/

Estonia
*Eesti Muusika Infokeskus
  (Estonian Music Information Centre)
Lauteri 7

Tallinn EE0001, Estonia
Tel/Fax: +372-2-454395

Finland
Suomalaisen Musiikin Tiedotuskeskus
  (Finnish Music Information Centre)
Lauttasaarentie 1
FIN-00200 Helsinki
Finland
Tel: +358-0-68101 316
Fax: +358-0-682 0770

France
Centre de Documentation de la Musique
  Contemporaine
Cité de la Musique
16, place de la Fontaine aux Lions
75019 Paris
France
Tel: +33-1-47 15 49 81
Fax: +33-1-47 15 49 89

Centre Europeen de Documentation et
  d'Information des Maitrises d'Enfants
  (CEDIME)
30-34 boulevard Bambetta
06130 Grasse
France
Tel: +33-93 40 19 50
Fax: +33-93 36 55 84

Georgia
Georgian Music Information Centre
David Agmashenebeli Ave. 123
380064 Tbilisi
Republic of Georgia
Tel: +995-8832-95 48 61 /
  +995-8832-96 86 78

Germany
Internationales Musikinstitut Darmstadt
Nieder-Ramstädter Strasse 190
D-64285 Darmstadt
Germany
Tel: +49-6151-132 416/17
Fax: +49-6151-132 405

Great Britain
British Music Information Centre
10 Stratford Place
London W1N 9AE
Great Britain
Tel: +44-171-499 8567
Fax: +44-171-499 4795
E-mail: bmic@bmic.co.uk

Greece
*Greek Music Information Centre
Institute for Research on Music and
  Acoustics (IEMA)
Adrianou 105
Athens 105 58
Greece
Tel: +30-1-33 10 129
Fax: +30-1-32 24 192
E-mail: kmos@culture.gr

Hungary
Magyar Zenei Tanács Zenei Információs
  Központ (Hungarian Music Information
  Centre)
Hungarian Music Council
H-1364 Budapest, P.O. Box 47
Hungary
Tel: +36-1-117 9598
Fax: +36-1-117 8267

Iceland
Islensk Tónverkamidstöd (Iceland Music
  Information Centre)
Sídumúli 34
IS-108 Reykjavik
Iceland
Tel: +354-568 3122
Fax: +354-568 3124
E-mail: icemic@vortex.is
Internet: http://rvik.ismennt.is/-
  music/tvmstodx.html

Ireland
Contemporary Music Centre
95 Lower Baggot St
Dublin 2
Ireland
Tel: +353-1-661 2105
Fax: +353-1-676 2639
E-mail: info@cmc.ie

Israel
Israel Music Institute
144, Hayarkon St
63451 Tel Aviv
Israel
Tel: +972-3-544 0219 / +972-3-524 6475
Fax: +972-3-524 5276

Japan
*Japan Federation of Composers Inc.
307 5th Sky Blvd.
Tokyo
Japan 151
Tel: +81-03-5474-1853
Fax: +81-03-5474-1854

Nippon Kindai Ongakukan
  (Documentation Center of Modern Japanese Music)
8-14, Azabudai 1-chôme
Minato-ku, Tokyo

106 Japan
Tel: +81-3-3224 1584
Fax: +81-3-3224 1654

*Resource Center for Japanese Music
7 East 20th Street, Suite 6F
New York NY 10003
USA
Fax: +1-212-529-7855
E-mail: mfjrc@aol.com

*Sapporo International Communication
  Plaza Foundation
North 1, West 3, Chuo-ku
Sapporo
060 Japan
Tel: +81-11-211 3675
Fax: +81-11-232 3833

Latin America
*Latin American Music Center
Indiana University School of Music
Bloomington IN 47405
USA
Tel: +1-812-855-2991
Fax: +1-812-855-4936

Latvia
*International New Music Centre
25 Jelgavas Str.
Riga
LU-1004 Latvia
Tel/fax: +371-782 8538

Lithuania
*Lithuanian Composers' Union
Mickeviciaus 29
2600 Vilnius
Lithuania
Tel: +370-2-220939/223026
Fax: +370-2-223027

Mexico
Centro Nacional de Investigación, Docu-
  mentación e Información Musical
  (CENIDIM)
Centro Nacional de las Artes, Torre de In-
  vestigación 7 Piso
Cals. Tlalpan y Rio Churubusco
Col Country Club, 04220
Mexico D.F
Mexico
Tel: +52-2-420 44 15
Fax: +52-2-420 44 54

Netherlands
Donemus
Paulus Potterstraat 16
NL-1017 CZ Amsterdam
Netherlands
Tel: +31-20-676 4436
Fax: +31-20-673 3588
E-mail: donemus@pi.net

Internet: http://www.netcetera.nl/donemus

Gaudeamus Foundation
Swammerdamstraat 38
1091 RV Amsterdam
Netherlands
Tel: +31-20-694 7349
Fax: +31-20-694 7258
E-mail: gaud@xs4all.nl
Internet: http://www.xs4all.nl/-gaud

Stichting Repertoire Informatiecentrum
  Muziek (RIM)
Drift 23, 3512 BR Utrecht
Netherlands
Tel: Information +31-30-234 0000
Tel: Administration +31-30-232 2046
Fax: +31-30-231 2641

New Zealand
New Zealand Music Centre (SOUNZ)
PO Box 10-042
Wellington
New Zealand
Tel: +64-4-495 2520
Fax: +64-4-495 2522

Norway
Norsk Musikkinformasjon
Tollbugata 28
N-0157 Oslo
Norway
Tel: +47-22 42 90 90
Fax: +47-22 42 90 91
E-mail: nmic@notam.uio.no
Internet: http://www.notam.uio.no/nmi

Poland
Polskie Centrum Muzyczne
  (Polish Music Centre)
Fredry 8, Room 305
00-097 Warszawa
Poland
Tel: +48-2-635 2230

*Library of the Polish Composers' Union
27 Rynek Starego Miasta
00-272 Warsaw
Poland
Tel: +48-22-31 16 34
Fax: +48-22-31 06 07

*Muzeum Instrumentów Muzycznych
Stary Rynek 45/47
61-772 Poznan
Poland
Tel: +48-61-52 08 57 /
  +48-61-52 80 11 W. 278
Fax: +48-61-51 58 98
E-mail: japod@hum.amu.edu.pl

Portugal
Fundação Calouste Gulbenkian
Avenida de Berna 45
P-1093 Lisboa
Portugal
Tel: +351-1-793 5131
Fax: +351-1-793 7296

Russia
*St Petersburg Music Club
1 Duniskaya Str
St Petersburg 191011
Russia
Fax +7-812-151 8269

Scotland
Scottish Music Information Centre
1 Bowmont Gardens
Glasgow G12 9LR
Scotland
Tel: +44-141-334 6393
Fax: +44-141-337 1161
Internet:
  http://www.music/gla.ac.uk/HTMLFolder/
  Resources/SMIC/homepage.html

Slovak Republic
Hudobné Informacné Stredisko
  Hudobného Fondu (Music Information
  Centre of the Music Fund)
Medená 29
811 02 Bratislava
SK-Slovakia
Tel: +42-7-533 1380
Tel/fax: +42-7-533 3569
E-mail: his@his.sanet.sk
Internet: http://www.sarba.sk/logos/music.
  institution.mic.html

Spain
Centro de Documentación Musical
Torregalindo 10
E-28016 Madrid
Spain
Tel: +34-1-350 8600
Fax: +34-1-359 1579

Sweden
Svensk Music
P.O. Box 27327
S-102 54 Stockholm
Sweden
Tel: +46-8-783 8800
Fax: +46-8-783 9510
E-mail: swedmic@stim.se
Internet: http://www.mic.stim.se

Switzerland
Foundation Suisa pour la musique
Rue de l'Hôpital 22
CH-2001 Neuchâtel
Switzerland
Tel: +41-38-25 25 36
Fax: +41-38-24 04 72

Ukraine
Music Information Centre of the Ukraine
  Composers Union
ul. Sofiuska 16/16
252001 Kiev 1
Ukraine
Tel: +380-44-228 3304
Fax: +380-44-229 6940

United States of America
American Music Center
30 West 26th Street, Suite 1001
New York, NY 10010-2011
USA
Tel: +1-212-366 5260
Fax: +1-212-366 5265
E-mail: center@amc.net
Internet: http://www.amc.net/amc

*Moravian Music Foundation
20 Cascade Avenue
Winston-Salem NC 27127-2904
USA
Tel: +1-910-725-0651
Fax: +1-910-725-4514

Venezuela
*Centro de Investigación e Información de
  Musica Contemporanea (CIIMC)
Apartado Postal 17161
Caracas 1015-A
Venezuela
Tel/Fax: +582-752 91 58
E-mail: ciimc@club-internet.fr
Internet: http://www.club-
  internet.fr/perso/ciimc

Wales
Welsh Music Information Centre, c/o
  ASSL
University of Wales College of Cardiff
Cardiff CF1 1XL
Wales
Tel: +44-1222-874000 ext. 5126
Fax: +44-1222-371921

Yugoslavia
Yugoslav Music Information Centre
  (SOKOJ)
Union of Yugoslav Composers' Organisa-
tions
Mišarska St 12-14
JU-11000 Beograd
Yugoslavia
Tel/fax: +381-11-345 192
Fax: +381-11-336 168

---

* Not a member of the International Association of Music Information Centres.

APPENDIX I: BRUCKNER SYMPHONIES

The plethora of editions of Bruckner symphonies may be grouped into three categories:

1. Late 19th- and early 20th-century publications. These are said to be the unfortunate result of tampering by various Bruckner colleagues, and thus not trustworthy guides to the composer's intentions. However, they do contain much valuable information about performing practice in Bruckner's time, particularly with respect to tempos. Active research is now going on as to which ingredients of these early editions can be trusted and should be used. Some of the editions have been kept in print by Kalmus and Eulenburg.

2. Critical editions of the International Bruckner Society produced in the 1930's and 40's, mostly under the editorship of Robert Haas. Many of these have been reprinted by Kalmus. In several cases where Bruckner left more than one version of a given symphony, Haas attempted to amalgamate them into one ideal version. This procedure has been questioned by modern scholars. Furthermore, the distinguished Bruckner scholar William Carragan has pointed to "evidence of Haas's rapid and sometimes slipshod methods and tendentious interpretations."

3. A second series of critical editions of the International Bruckner Society beginning in the 1950's and continuing to the present, mostly under the leadership of the late Leopold Nowak. Rather than seeking an "ideal" version, Nowak undertook to publish separately each version of a particular symphony that can be said to stem from Bruckner himself. Even after the publication of these scores, Nowak would from time to time make further corrections, so that the most recently printed Nowak scores of any symphony may be the most accurate versions.

A useful guide to the present understanding of the Bruckner symphonies problem may be found in William Carragan's article "The Bruckner Versions, Once More" (*American Record Guide*, March/April 1995, pp.55-57).

Juan I. Cahis goes a step further in a recent article ("The Bruckner Symphonies Problem Reconsidered," *Journal of the Conductors Guild*, XV/2, pp.66-79). He argues that many of the versions of particular symphonies are individual enough to be considered independent (though related) works of art—analogous to Beethoven's three *Leonora* overtures. He suggests assigning a number in chronological order to each "symphonic essay" (i.e. each version that can be said to have a coherent identity and to represent the composer's thoughts at a particular point).

Below is an adaptation of Mr. Cahis' Table I, with durations added:

Year composed	Symphony/ version	Cahis no.	Bruckner Society publication Editor & publication date	Duration
1863	00	1	Nowak, 1973	48'
1866	1/I	2	Haas, 1935; Nowak, 1953	50'
1868	0	3	Nowak, 1968	46'
1872	2/I	4	Carragan (in prep.)	68'
1873	3/I	5	Nowak, 1977	65'
1874	4/I	6	Nowak 1975	70'
1876/8	5	7	Haas, 1935; Nowak, 1951	81'
1877	2/II	8	Haas, 1938; Nowak 1965	53'
1876/7	3/II	9	Oeser, 1950; Nowak, 1980/81	61'
1878	4/II	10	Haas, 1936; Nowak, 1953/81	64'
1878/80	4/III	11	Haas, 1936/44; Nowak, 1953	70'
1881	6	12	Haas, 1935; Nowak, 1952	54'
1883	7	13	Haas, 1944; Nowak, 1954	64'
1887	8/I	14	Nowak, 1972	76'
1888	4/IV'	Suppl.1/14+	[no critical edition]	65'
1889	3/III	15	Nowak 1959	57'
1890	8/II	16	Haas, 1935; Nowak, 1955	70'
1891	1/II	17	Haas, 1935; Nowak, 1980	48'
1894/6	9	18	Orel, 1934; Nowak, 1951	63' (without finale)

Adoption of the Cahis numbers—or some version of them that achieves wide-spread acceptance—will be a great help in clarifying this complex problem.

Mr. Cahis also proposes the following performance list "for the 1990s and beyond," showing his recommendations where more than one possibility exists:

Symphony no.00
Symphony no.0
Symphony no.1   Linz version, 1866 (Cahis 2)
Symphony no.2   1872 version (Cahis 4)
Symphony no.3   1873 version (Cahis 5)
Symphony no.4   Both the 1874 version (Cahis 6) *and*
                  the 1878/80 version (Cahis 11)

' Mr. Cahis gives this work a supplemental number because it was not recomposed by Bruckner alone. However, Bruckner did participate actively during its publication process, and is believed to have agreed with many of the changes. (The indication "14+" in the Cahis number signifies that the work comes after Cahis 14.)

Symphony no.5
Symphony no.6
Symphony no.7
Symphony no.8   1890 version (Cahis 16) for first three movements
and 1887 version (Cahis 14) for the finale

Symphony no.9

The finale of Symphony no.9 was left unfinished at Bruckner's death. Two separate completions or reconstructions of this finale are available, and are listed in the body of this book. Both have been recorded, but as this book goes to press, neither is available through regular publishing channels, but only from the editors:

Carragan version:

William Carragan
Starfields
277 Tamarac Road
Troy NY 12180-9638
518-279-1147
email: carrawil@office.hvcc.edu

Samale-Phillips-Mazzuca-Cohrs version:

Maestro Gunnar Cohrs
Schweidnitzer Strasse 20
D-28 237-Bremen
Germany

APPENDIX J: TITLE INDEX

Distinctive titles of compositions are followed by their composers. Subtitles, nicknames, title translations and distinctive titles of excerpts are followed by the composer and title of the work as it appears in the main list.

Generic titles (symphony, suite) are not listed unless they are modified so as to become distinctive titles themselves (Symphony of Psalms, Suite provençale).

A la busca del más allá; Rodrigo
A memoria de Mozart; Villa-Lobos— Sinfonietta no.1
A questo seno; Mozart
Abdelazar: Suite; Purcell
The abduction from the seraglio;
    Mozart—Die Entführung aus dem Serail
Abenceragen; Cherubini
Abraham and Isaac; Stravinsky
Abschieds-Symphonie; Haydn—Symphony no.45
Abu Hassan; Weber, C.M.
Academic festival overture;
    Brahms—Akademische Festouvertüre
Acadian songs and dances; Thomson, V.—
    Louisiana story: Acadian songs and dances
Accompaniment to a cinematographic scene;
    Schoenberg—Begleitungsmusik zu einer Lichtspielscene
The accursed huntsman; Franck—Le Chasseur maudit
Ach Gott, vom Himmel sieh darein;
    Bach—Cantata no.2
Ach Gott, wie manches Herzeleid;
    Bach—Cantatas nos.3 & 58
Ach Herr, mich armen Sünder;
    Bach—Cantata no.135
Ach, ich sehe, jetzt; Bach—Cantata no.162
Ach, lieben Christen, seid getrost;
    Bach—Cantata no.114
Ach wie flüchtig, ach wie nichtig;
    Bach—Cantata no.26
Actus tragicus; Bach—Cantata no.106
Adagio for strings; Barber
Adagio tenebroso; Carter
Address for orchestra; Walker, George
Adieu Robert Schumann; Schafer
Adirondack light; Tann
Adjustable wrench; Torke
Adventlied; Schumann, R.
Adventures in a perambulator; Carpenter
Africa; Saint-Saëns
Afro-American symphony; Still
After Delacroix; Antheil—Symphony no.6
An after-intermission overture for youth orchestra; Hoag

Afternoon of a faun; Debussy—Prélude à "L'Après-midi d'un faune"
Aftertones of infinity; Schwantner
The age of anxiety; Bernstein—Symphony no.2
The age of gold; Shostakovich
The age of steel; Prokofiev—Le Pas d'acier
Agenda, for young players; Rands
Agon; Stravinsky
Ah, lo previdi; Mozart
Ah non lasciarmi; Mozart—Basta, vincesti
Ah, non sai; Mozart—Mia speranza
Ah, non son io che parlo; Mozart—Misera, dove son
Ah, perfido, op.65; Beethoven
Ah se in ciel, benigne stelle; Mozart
Ah, t'invola; Mozart—Ah, lo previdi
Ahavah; Warshauer
Aïda; Verdi
Air music; Rorem
Akademische Festouvertüre; Brahms
Akhmatova requiem; Tavener
Akrata; Xenakis
Al santo sepolcro; Vivaldi—Sinfonia, RV 169
Ala and Lolly; Prokofiev—Scythian suite
Aladdin; Nielsen
Albada; Gerhard
Alborada del gracioso; Ravel
Alcandro, lo confesso; Mozart
Alceste: Instrumental pieces; Handel
Alceste; Gluck
Alcina; Handel
Aldous Huxley in memoriam;
    Stravinsky—Variations
Alegrías: Suite; Gerhard
Alessandro Stradella; Flotow
Alexander and the wind-up mouse; Kechley
Alexander Nevsky; Prokofiev
Alexander's feast; Handel
Alexanderfest; Handel—Concerto grosso, no.7
Alfonso und Estrella; Schubert
Ali Baba; Cherubini
An Alice symphony; Del Tredici
All in the golden afternoon; Del Tredici—

Dance preludes; Lutoslawski—Preludia taneczne

Dance rhapsody; Delius

Dance rhythms; Riegger

Dance suite; Bartók; *also* Svoboda

Dance symphony; Copland

Dances; Andriessen

Dances of Transylvania; Bartók

Danse; Debussy

Danse cosaque; Tchaikovsky—Mazeppa

Danse macabre; Saint-Saëns

Danse nègre; Coleridge-Taylor

Danse sacrale; Stravinsky—Le Sacre du printemps

Danse slav; Chabrier—Le Roi malgré lui

Danses africaines; Villa-Lobos

Danses concertantes; Stravinsky

Danses sacrée et profane; Debussy

Dante; Granados; *also* Liszt

Danzas fantásticas; Turina

Danzón cubano; Copland

Daphnis et Chloé; Ravel

Dardanus; Rameau

Dark upon the harp; Druckman

Darker America; Still

Das ist je gewisslich wahr; Bach—Cantata no.141

The daughter of Colchis; Chávez—La hija de Colquide

Daughter of the regiment; Donizetti—La Fille du régiment

Davidde penitente; Mozart

Dazu ist erschienen der Sohn Gottes; Bach—Cantata no.40

De natura sonoris; Penderecki

Dead Elvis; Daugherty

Deal; Mackey

Death and fire; Tan

Death and the maiden; Schubert—Quartet, strings, D.810

Death and transfiguration; Strauss, R.—Tod und Verklärung

The death of Carmen; Halffter—La muerte de Carmen

The death of Jesus; Kraus—Der Tod Jesu

The death of Minnehaha; Coleridge-Taylor—The song of Hiawatha

December; Torke

Decoration Day; Ives—Holidays symphony

Deh, non varcar; Mozart—Ah, lo previdi

Déjà vu; Colgrass

Del gardellino; Vivaldi—Concerto, flute, RV 428

Delacroix; Antheil—Symphony no.6

Deliciae Basilienses; Honegger—Symphony no.4

Della casa del diavolo; Boccherini—Symphony no.6

Della serenata; Galuppi—Sinfonia, F major

A Delphic serenade; Benson

Le Déluge; Saint-Saëns

Dem Gerechten muss das Licht; Bach—Cantata no.195

Démophoon; Cherubini

Denn du wirst meine Seele; Bach, J. L.; *also* Bach, J.S.—Cantata no.15

Des Knaben Wunderhorn; Mahler—Lieder aus Des Knaben Wunderhorn

Des Teufels Lustschloss; Schubert

The desert music; Reich

Déserts; Varèse

Design; Rorem

Dettingen Te deum; Handel

Ein deutsches Requiem; Brahms

Les Deux Journées; Cherubini

Deux Marches et un Intermède; Poulenc

Deux Portraits; Bartók

Di tre re; Honegger—Symphony no.5

Dialogues for jazz combo & orch; Brubeck, H.

Dichter und Bauer; Suppé

Dido and Aeneas; Purcell

Die natali; Barber

Dies natalis; Finzi

Les Dieux dans l'ombre des cavernes; Roussel—Évocations, op.15, no.1

Dinosaurian dances; Gould—The jogger and the dinosaur

Il distratto; Haydn—Symphony no.60

Le Dit des jeux du monde; Honegger

Dite almeno in che mancai; Mozart

Diversions; Fine *also* Britten

Divertisements for youth orchestra; Martino

Divertissement; Ibert

Dives and Lazarus; Vaughan Williams—Five variants of "Dives and Lazarus"

Le Divin Poème; Scriabin

The divine poem; Scriabin—Le Divin Poème

Dixit dominus; Handel

Dixit et Magnificat; Mozart

Les Djinns; Franck

Doctor Cupid; Wolf-Ferrari—L'amore medico

Documentary one; Bergsma

Dolly; Fauré

Dolmen; Weber, Ben

The domain of Arnheim; Liebermann, Lowell

Dominicus; Mozart—Mass, K.66

Le Domino noir; Auber

Don Giovanni; Mozart

Don Juan; Strauss, R.; *also* Gluck

Don Pasquale; Donizetti

Don Quichotte; Telemann

Don Quichotte à Dulcinée; Ravel

Don Quixote; Strauss, R.

Don Quixote: Dances; Gerhard

Dona nobis pacem; Mendelssohn—Verleih' uns Frieden

Donna Diana; Reznicek

Das Donnerwetter; Mozart—Contradance, K.534

Doodles; Proto

Dorfschwalben aus Österreich; Strauss, Jos.

Dornröschen: Suite; Humperdinck

Double chorus for orchestra; Beaser

Double concerto; Brahms—Concerto, violin

Orlando; Handel
Orphée-sérénade; Bolcom
Orpheus; Liszt
Orpheus; Stravinsky
Orpheus in the underworld; Offenbach
Oster-Oratorium; Bach—Easter oratorio
Othello overture; Dvorák
Our town; Copland
L'Ours; Haydn—Symphony no.82
Out of "Last pieces"; Feldman
An outdoor overture; Copland
Ouverture méditerranéene; Milhaud
Ouverture philharmonique; Milhaud
Ouverture solennelle;
 Tchaikovsky—Overture 1812
Overture 1812; Tchaikovsky
Overture di ballo; Sullivan
Overture for the end of a century; Larsen
Overture in praise of folly; Walker, George
Overture in the Italian Style;
 Schubert—Overtures, D.590 & D.591
Overture of the season; Svoboda
Overture on Russian themes; Rimsky-Korsa-
 kov
Overture on three Russian folk songs; Bala-
 kirev
Overture pathétique; Kabalevsky
Overture to a comedy; Previn
Overture to a picaresque comedy; Bax
Overture to the Creole "Faust"; Ginastera—
 Oberatura para el "Fausto" Criollo
Oxford symphony; Haydn—Symphony no.92
Pacific 231; Honegger
A pagan poem; Loeffler
Paganiniana; Casella
Pageant of P.T. Barnum; Moore, Douglas
I pagliacci; Leoncavallo
Les Paladins; Rameau
Palais hanté; Schmitt—Étude, op.49
Palestrina; Pfitzner
Pallas Athena; Krenek—Symphony
Palo Duro Canyon; Jones—Symphony no.3
Pampeana no.3; Ginastera
Pan and Echo; Sibelius
Panambí: Suite; Ginastera
Para viola y orquesta; León
Parade; Satie
Paradis; Mozart—Concerto, piano, no.18,
 K.456
Paradiso choruses; Martino
Paris; Mozart—Overture, K.311a
Paris symphony; Mozart—Symphony no.31
Parsifal; Wagner
Parson Weems and the cherry tree; Thomson
Le Pas d'acier; Prokofiev
Passio et mors domini nostri Iesu Christi se-
 cundum Lucam; Penderecki
Passion nach Barthold Heinrich Brockes;
 Handel
La passione; Haydn—Symphony no.49
Il pastor fido: Suite; Handel
Pastoral symphony; Vaughan Williams—
 Symphony no.3

Pastorale; Milhaud—Symphonies for small
 orchestra
Pastorale d'été; Honegger
Pastorale symphony; Beethoven—Symphony
 no.6
Pastorello; Haydn, M.
Pathétique symphony;
 Tchaikovsky—Symphony no.6
Les Patineurs; Waldteufel
Patrie; Bizet
Paukenmesse; Haydn—Mass, Hob.XXII:9
Paukenschlag; Haydn—Symphony no.94
Paukenwirbel; Haydn—Symphony no.103
Paul Bunyan; Britten
Paulus; Mendelssohn—St. Paul
Pavane; Fauré
Pavane for a dead princess; Ravel—Pavane
 pour une infante défunte
Pavane pour une infante défunte; Ravel
La pazza per amore; Paisiello—Nina: Over-
 ture
Peace overture; Peck
The peacock; Kodály—Variations on a Hun-
 garian folksong
Pearlfishers; Bizet—Les Pecheurs de perles
Peasant cantata; Bach—Cantata no.212
Les Pecheurs de perles; Bizet
Pedrelliana; Gerhard
Peer Gynt; Grieg
Peleus and Thetis; Boyce—Overture (Peleus
 and Thetis)
Pelléas & Mélisande; Fauré; also Schoen-
 berg; also Sibelius
Pénélope: Prelude; Fauré
Pennsylvania suite; Read
Pensées; Höller
Penthesilea; Wolf
Per pietà, non ricercate; Mozart
Per questa bella mano; Mozart
The perfect fool: Ballet music; Holst
La Pèri; Dukas
Peripeteia; Musgrave
Perpetual Angelus; Tsontakis
Perpetuum mobile; Strauss, Joh., Jr.
Persephone; Stravinsky
Persian dances; Mussorgsky—Khovantchina:
 Dance of the Persian maidens
Pesther Carneval; Liszt—Hungarian rhapsody
 no.6
Peter and the wolf; Prokofiev
Peter Grimes; Britten
Peter Quince at the clavier; London
Peter Schmoll; Weber, C.M.
Petite Suite; Borodin; also Debussy; also
 Roussel; also Bizet
Petite Suite de concert; Coleridge-Taylor
Petite Symphonie; Gounod
Petite Symphonie concertante; Martin
Les Petits Riens; Mozart
Petrouchka; Stravinsky
Pezzo capriccioso; Tchaikovsky
Phaedra; Britten
Phaéton; Saint-Saëns

Phantasmata; Rouse
Phèdre; Auric; *also* Massenet
Philharmonic concerto; Hindemith
The philosopher; Haydn—Symphony no.22
Il piacere; Vivaldi—Concerto, violin, op.8, no.6, RV 122
Il pianto d'Arianna; Locatelli—Concerto grosso, op.7, no.6
Piccola musica notturna; Dallapiccola
Piccola suite; Scarlatti, A.
Piccolomini mass; Mozart—Mass, K.258
Pictures at an exhibition; Mussorgsky
Pien; Chou
Pierrot Lunaire; Schoenberg
Piesn o nocy; Szymanowski—Symphony no.3
Pilgrims and pioneers; Thomson, V.
Pine tree fantasy; Piston
Pines of Rome; Respighi—Pini di Roma
Pini di Roma; Respighi
Pinocchio; Toch
Pioneer dances; Coolidge
Pique Dame; Suppé
Il pirata; Bellini
The pit and the pendulum; Kelley
Pittsburgh symphony; Hindemith
Pizzicato polka; Strauss, Joh., Jr.
The planets; Holst
Platée; Rameau
Play no.2; Subotnick
Playing with style; Peck
The pleasure dome of Kubla Khan; Griffes
The plow that broke the plains; Thomson, V.
Pocahontas: Suite; Carter
Poem; Griffes; *also* Still
The poem of ecstasy; Scriabin—Le Poème de l'extase
Poème; Chausson
Poème de l'amour et de la mer; Chausson
Le Poème de l'extase; Scriabin
Poet and peasant; Suppé—Dichter und Bauer
Pohádka; Suk
Pohjola's daughter; Sibelius
Polish symphony; Tchaikovsky—Symphony no.3
A political overture; Bernstein—Slava!
Polonaise brillante; Weber, C.M.; *also* Wieniawski
Polonaise de concert; Wieniawski
Polovtsian dances; Borodin—Prince Igor
Polovtsian march; Borodin—Prince Igor
Polyphonica; Cowell
Pomp and circumstance; Elgar
Pop-pourri; Del Tredici
Popol vuh; Ginastera
Popoli di Tessagua; Mozart
Porgy and Bess; Gershwin
Portals; Ruggles
Ports of call; Ibert—Escales
Portsmouth Point; Walton
The Portuguese inn; Cherubini—L'Hôtellerie portugaise
Poseidon and Amphitrite; Paine

Posthorn serenade; Mozart—Serenade no.9
Postludium; Lutoslawski
La Poule; Haydn—Symphony no.83
Pour Potsdam; Quantz—Concerto, flute, D major
Pour Un Fête de printemps; Roussel
Prague symphony; Mozart—Symphony no.38
Prairie; Sowerby
Prairie journal; Copland
Prairie night & Celebration dance; Copland—Billy the Kid
Prayers of Kierkegaard; Barber
Preamble for a solemn occasion; Copland
Preise dein Glücke, gesegnetes Sachsen; Bach—Cantata no.215
Preise, Jerusalem, den Herrn; Bach—Cantata no.119
Prélude à "L'Après-midi d'un faune"; Debussy
Prelude to a hymn tune by William Billings; Luening
Les Préludes; Liszt
Preludia taneczne; Lutoslawski
Preludio sinfonico; Puccini
Première Suite de noëls; Gossec—Christmas suite
Preziosa; Weber, C.M.
Pribaoutki; Stravinsky
La primavera; Vivaldi—Le quattro staggioni
Prince Igor; Borodin
The Prince of Denmark's march; Clarke
The prince of the pagodas; Britten
La Princesse jaune; Saint-Saëns
Printemps; Debussy
Le Printemps; Milhaud—Symphonies for small orch: Le Printemps
La procesion del rocio; Turina
La Procession nocturne; Rabaud
Proclamation; Bloch, E.
Prolation; Maxwell Davies
Prologue & variations; Zwilich
Promenade; Gershwin
Promenade overture; Corigliano
Prométhée; Scriabin
Prometheus; Beethoven; *also* Liszt; *also* Scriabin
Le Prophète; Meyerbeer
Protée; Milhaud—Suite symphonique no.2
Psalm 23; Zemlinsky
Psalm 42; Mendelssohn
Psalm 47; Schmitt
Psalm 89; Handel
Psalm 95; Mendelssohn
Psalm 96; Handel
Psalm 98; Mendelssohn
Psalm 109; Handel—Dixit dominus
Psalm 114; Mendelssohn
Psalm 115; Mendelssohn
Psalm 150; Bruckner; *also* Franck
Psalm and fugue; Hovhaness
Psalmus hungaricus; Kodály
Pskovityanka; Rimsky-Korsakov—The Maid of Pskov

APPENDIX K: PUBLISHERS

I have tried to make the following list of publishers' addresses, phone numbers, and US representatives as current and accurate as possible. At the rate these things change, however, it will already have become out-of-date by the time this book appears in print. Firms move, change their phone numbers, get new E-mail addresses, take on representation of new foreign publishers, are bought by other firms—the mutations never end.

Therefore I have left generous margins for individuals to make note of changes as they are discovered.

There are two sources for updated information about publishers. The first has an excellent web site that includes current information on publishers, as well as useful material on copyright and fair use provisions:

> Music Publishers' Association
> 711 3rd Avenue
> New York NY 10017
> Web site: http://host.mpa.org/mpa

A second is the annual publication *Musical America International Directory of the Performing Arts*. This hefty tome can be found in most of the larger public or university libraries, or may be purchased from:

> Musical America
> K-III Directory Corp
> 10 Lake Drive
> Hightstown NJ 08520

It is filled with detailed information on all sorts of performing arts activities and companies, with major focus on the United States and Canada, but including many pages of "international" listings. The section "Publishers of Music" is helpful for current information.

ACA American Composers Alliance
170 W. 74th st.
New York NY 10023
Tel: 212-362-8900
Fax: 212-362-8902
E-mail: 75534.2232@compuserve.com

Alkor Alkor-Edition
US agent: FMD

AME American Music Edition
US agent: Presser

AMP Associated Music Publishers
see: G. Schirmer

A-R Editions A-R Editions, Inc.
801 Deming Way
Madison WI 53717
Tel: 608-836-9000
Fax: 608-831-8200

Arcana Arcana Editions
Box 1510
Bancroft Ontario, Canada K0L 1C0

ASCAP American Society of Composers, Authors & Publishers
1 Lincoln Plaza
New York NY 10023
Tel: 212-621-6223
Fax: 212-595-3342
E-mail: http://www.ascap.com/ace/ACE.html

Augener Augener, Ltd.
US agent: ECS

Bärenreiter Bärenreiter-Verlag
US agent: MAA

Barry Barry Ed. Com e Ind. SrL
Lavalle 1145-4 "A"
1048 Buenos Aires, Argentina
US agent: Boosey

Belaieff M. P. Belaieff
US agent: Peters

Belmont Belmont Music Publishers
P.O. Box 231
Pacific Palisades CA 90272
Tel: 310-454-1867
Fax: 310-573-1925

Belwin C C P/Belwin Inc.
15800 NW 48 Ave
Miami FL 33014
Tel: 800-327-7643; 305-620-1500
Fax: 305-621-4869

Berandol Berandol Music Ltd.
2600 John St., Unit 220
Markham Ontario L3R 3W3
Canada

Billaudot Editions Billaudot
14 rue de l'Echiquier
F-75010 Paris, France
US agent: Presser

BMI Broadcast Music Inc.
320 W. 57 St.
New York NY 10019
Tel: 212-586-2000
Fax: 212-246-2163
E-mail: http://rep.edge.net/

Boccaccini Boccaccini & Spada Editori
Via Francesco Duodo 10
1-00136 Rome, Italy
US agent: Presser

Boelke Boelke-Bomart Publications
US agent: Jerona

Bois Bureau de Musique Mario Bois
19 rue de Rocroy
F-75010 Paris, France
US agent: Presser

Bongiovani Casa Musicale Francesco Bongiovani
US agent: Belwin

Boosey Boosey & Hawkes, Inc.
Rentals/Sales: 52 Cooper Square, 10th Floor
New York NY 10003-7102
Tel: 212-979-1090
Fax: 212-979-7056 (Sales); 212-979-7057 (Rentals)
E-mail: http://www.ny.boosey.com/
Serious Music/Copyright/Stage Licensing: 24 E. 21 St
New York NY 10010-7200
Tel: 212-228-3300
Fax: 212-473-5730

Boston Boston Music Company
172 Tremont St.
Boston MA 02111
Tel: 617-426-5100; 800-634-4682
Fax: 617-695-9142

Bote & Bock Bote & Bock
US agent: AMP; Hal Leonard

Brass Press The Brass Press
136 8th Avenue North
Nashville TN 37203
US agent: King

Breitkopf Breitkopf & Härtel
Walkmühlstrasse 52
D-651965 Wiesbaden, Germany
US agent: AMP

Broude, A. Alexander Broude, Inc.
US agent: Plymouth

Broude Bros. Broude Brothers Ltd.
141 White Oaks Rd.
Williamstown MA 01267
Tel: 800-225-3197
Fax: 413-458-8131

Carisch Carisch S.p.A.
US agent: Boosey

Carus Carus-Verlag GmbH
Wannenstr. 45
D-70199 Stuttgart, Germany
Tel: 711-60 20 92
Fax: 711-60 82 47
US agent: Foster

CFE Composers Facsimile Edition
US agent: ACA

Chant Le Chant du Monde
US agent: G. Schirmer

Chappell Chappell & Co., Inc.
US agent: Warner/Chappell

Chester J. & W. Chester, Ltd.
Chester Music Ltd., London
8/9 Frith St.
London W1V 5TZ, England
Tel: 171-434-0066
Fax: 171-287-6329
US agent: G. Schirmer

Choudens Choudens Editions, Paris
38 Rue Jean Mermoz
F-75008 Paris, France
US agent: Peters

CMC Centre de Musique Canadienne
Québec Région
430 rue St.-Pierre, bureau 300
Montréal Québec H2Y 2M5
Canada
Tel: 416-961-6601
Fax: 416-961-7198

Colombo Franco Colombo Publications
US agent: Belwin

Compusic Edition Compusic
Amsterdam, Netherlands

Costallat Editions Costallat
US agent: Presser

Curwen J. Curwen & Sons
US agent: G. Schirmer

Dania Edition Dania
US agent: Peters

Dantalian Dantalian, Inc.
11 Pembroke St.
Newton MA 02158
Tel: 617-244-7230

Derby Derby Music Service
11007 N. 56th St, Suite N
Temple Terrace FL 33617
Tel: 813-988-3065

Deutscher Deutscher Verlag für Musik
US agent: EAM

Doblinger Ludwig Doblinger Verlag
US agent: FMD

Donemus Donemus Publishing House, Amsterdam
Paulus Potterstr. 14
1071 CZ Amsterdam, Netherlands
Tel: 20-764436
US agent: Presser

Dover Dover Publications Inc.
31 E. Second St.
Mineola NY 11501
Tel: 516-294-7000
Fax: 516-742-6953

Durand Durand SA Editions Musicales, France
215 Rue du Faubourg S. Honore
F-75008 Paris, France
US agent: Presser

EAM European American Music Distributors Corp.
P.O. Box 850
Valley Forge PA 19482
Tel: 610-648-0506
Fax: 610-889-0242
E-mail: eamdc@eamdc.com; http://www.eamdc.com/eam

ECS ECS Publishing
138 Ipswich St.
Boston MA 02215-3534
Tel: 617-236-1935
Fax: 617-236-0261

EDY Les Éditions Doberman-Yppan
C.P. 2021
Saint-Nicolas Québec GOS 3L0
Canada

Elkan-Vogel Elkan-Vogel Inc.
US agent: Presser

EMB Editio Musica Budapest
Vörösmarty tér 1, POB 322
H-1370 Budapest, Hungary
Tel: (1) 118-4190
US agent: Boosey; Presser

EMM Ediciones Mexicanas de Musica SA
Avda. Juarez 18
Despacho 206, Mexico 06050
US agent: Peer

EMS Educational Music Service
13 Elkay Dr.
Chester NY 10918
Tel: 914-469-5790
Fax: 914-469-5817

EMT Editions Musicales Transatlantiques
US agent: Presser

Enoch Enoch & Cie., France
193 Blvd. Pereire
F-75017 Paris, France
US agent: AMP

Eschig Editions Max Eschig
48 Rue de Rome
F-75008 Paris, France
US agent: Presser

Eulenburg Edition Eulenburg
US agent: EAM

Faber Faber Music Ltd
3 Queen Square
London WC1N 3AU, England
US agent: sales, Leonard; rental, FMD

C. Fischer Carl Fischer, Inc.
62 Cooper Square
New York NY 10003
Tel: 212-777-0900
Fax: 212-477-4129

J. Fischer J. Fischer & Bro.
US agent: Belwin

FMD Foreign Music Distributors
13 Elkay Dr.
Chester NY 10918
Tel: 914-469-5790
Fax: 914-469-5817

Foley Charles Foley, Inc.
US agent: C. Fischer

Forberg Robert Forberg — P. Jurgenson
US agent: Peters

Foster Mark Foster Music Co.
P.O. Box 4012, 28 E. Springfield
Champaign IL 61824-4012
Tel: 217-398-2760
Fax: 217-398-2791
E-mail: chennes@prairienet.org

Fuerstner Adolf Fuerstner Ltd.
US agent: Boosey

Furore Furore Verlag
Johannesstrasse 3
3500 Kassel, Germany

Galaxy Galaxy Music Corporation
US agent: ECS

Gehrmans Carl Gehrmans Musikförlag
Box 6005
S-102 31 Stockholm, Sweden
Tel: 8-16 52 00
US agent: Boosey

Glocken Glocken Verlag
US agent: EAM

Gray H. W. Gray Co. Inc.
US agent: Belwin

Gunmar See Margun

Hamelle Hamelle & Cie., France
175 Rue St. Honore
F-75040 Paris, France
Tel: (1) 42.96.89.11
US agent: Presser, King

Hansen Edition Wilhelm Hansen
Bornholmsgade 1
DK-1266 Copenhagen K, Denmark
Tel: 33 11 78 88
Fax: 33 14 81 78
US agent: G. Schirmer

Helicon Helicon Music Corp.
US agent: EAM

Henle G. Henle USA
Box 1753
2446 Centerline Ind'l Dr.
Maryland Heights MO 63043
Tel: 314-991-0487
Fax: 314-991-3807

Heugel Heugel & Cie.
175 Rue St. Honore
F-75040 Paris, France
Tel: (1) 42.96.89.11
US agent: Presser, King

Highgate Highgate Press
US agent: ECS

Hinrichsen Hinrichsen Edition, Ltd.
US agent: Peters

Hinshaw Hinshaw Music Inc.
Box 470
Chapel Hill NC 27514-0470
Tel: 919-933-1691
Fax: 919-967-3399

Hofmeister Friedrich Hofmeister Verlag
US agent: Peters

Ione Ione Press
US agent: ECS

Israeli Israeli Music Publications, Ltd.
25 Keren Hayesod
Jerusalem 94188, Israel
US agent: Presser

Jerona Jerona Music Corp.
P. O. Box 5010
Hackensack NJ 07606-4210
Tel: 201-488-0550
Fax: 201-569-7023

Jobert Societé des Editions Jobert
76 Rue Quincampoix
F-75003 Paris, France
Tel: (1) 42.72.83.43
US agent: Presser

Kahnt C. F. Kahnt Musikverlag
US agent: Peters

Kalmus Edwin F. Kalmus & Co., Inc.
6403 W. Rogers Circle
Boca Raton FL 33487
Tel: 800-434-6340; 407-241-6340
Fax: 407-241-6347

KaWe Edition KaWe
US agent: King

Kerby E. C. Kerby Ltd.
US agent: Leonard; Boosey

King Robert King Music Co.
140 Main St.
North Easton MA 02356
Fax: 508-238-2571

Kneusslin Editions Kneusslin
US agent: Peters

Kol Meira Kol Meira Publications
3526 Broundbrook Lane
Columbia SC 29206
Tel: 803-787-4332

Kunzelmann Edition Kunzelmann
US agent: FMD

Leduc Alphonse Leduc Editions
175 Rue St. Honore
F-75040 Paris Cédex, France
Tel: (1) 42.96.89.11
Fax: (1) 42.86.02.83
US agent: Presser; King

Leeds Canada Leeds Canada
Gordon V. Thompson
85 Scarsdale Road
Don Mills Ontario M3B 2R2
Canada

Lemoine Henry Lemoine et Cie.
17 Rue Pigalle
F-75009 Paris, France
US agent: Presser

Lengnick Alfred Lengnick & Co., Ltd.
Purly Oaks Studio, 421A Brighton Road
South Croydon, Surrey, England CR2-6YR
Tel: 1-660-7646
US agent: Presser

Leonard Hal Leonard Publishing Corp.
Box 13819; 7777 W. Bluemound Rd.
Milwaukee WI 53213
Tel: 414-774-3630
Fax: 414-774-3259

Leuckart F. E. C. Leuckart
Rheingoldstr. 4
D-80639 Munich, Germany
Tel: (89) 17 39 8
Fax: (89) 17 60 54

Liben Liben Music Publishers
1191 Eversole Rd.
Cincinnati OH 45230
Tel: 513-232-6920
Fax: 513-232-1866

Lienau Robert Lienau Musikverlag
Lankwitzer Strasse 9
1 Berlin 45, Germany

Little Piper Little Piper
P.O. Box 14038
Detroit MI 48214
Tel: 810-540-7970
Fax: 810-645-5446
E-mail: Piperpress@aol.com

Luck Luck's Music Library
P.O. Box 71397
Madison Heights MI 48071
Tel: 800-348-8749; 810-583-1820
Fax: 810-583-1114

MAA Music Associates of America
224 King St.
Englewood NJ 07631
Tel: 201-569-2898
Fax: 201-569-7023

Malcolm Malcolm Music Ltd.
US agent: Shawnee

Mapleson Mapleson Music Rental Library
US agent: EMS

Margun Margun Music Inc./Gunmar Music Inc.
167 Dudley Rd
Newton Centre MA 02159
Tel: 617-332-6398
Fax: 617-969-1079

Marks Edward B. Marks Music Corp.
US agent: Presser, Leonard

MCA MCA Music
US agent: Presser, Leonard

Mercury Mercury Music Corp.
US agent: Presser

Merion Merion Music Inc.
US agent: Presser

Mills Mills Music, Inc.
US agent: Belwin

MJQ MJQ Music, Inc.
1697 Broadway
New York NY 10019
Tel: 212-582-6667
Fax: 212-582-0627

MMB MMB Music Inc.
Contemporary Arts Bldg, 3526 Washington Ave
St. Louis MO 63103-1019
Tel: 800-543-3771; 314-531-9635
Fax: 314-531-8384
E-mail: mmbmuse@aol.com

Moeck Moeck Verlag
US agent: EAM

Möseler Karl Heinrich Möseler Verlag
Hoffmann-von-Fallersleben-Strasse 8-10
Postfach 1661
D-3340 Wolfenbüttel, Germany
US agent: Derby

Music Sales Music Sales Corp.
Corp. *see:* G. Schirmer
E-mail: http://www.musicsales.co.uk/musicsales/
cgi-bin/printpage.pl?hirelib.html

Music Theatre Music Theatre International
545 Eighth Ave.
New York NY 10018
Tel: 212-868-6749
Fax: 212-643-8465

Musica Rara Musica Rara
Le Traversier
Chemin de la Buire
F-84170 Monteux, France
US agent: EAM

MWV Musikwissenschaftlicher Verlag
Vienna, Austria
Tel: 43-1-515-0343
Fax: 43-1-515-0351
US agent: FMD; Peters

Nagel Nagels Verlag
Kassel, Germany

Nordiska Nordiska Musikförlaget
St. Eriksgatan 58
S-112 34 Stockholm, Sweden
Tel: (8) 650 13 13
Fax: (8) 650 19 19
US agent: Hansen

Norton W. W. Norton
500 5th Avenue
New York NY 10003

Novello Novello & Co.
US agent: G. Schirmer

Oiseau Lyre Editions de L'Oiseau-Lyre
2 rue des Ramparts
Monte Carlo, Monaco

Oxford Oxford University Press
198 Madison Ave.
New York NY 10016-4314
Tel: 212-726-7044 to 7051
Fax: 212-726-6444

Paterson Paterson's Publications, Ltd.
8-10 Lower James Street
London W1R 3PL, England
US agent: Music Sales Corp.

Pecktacular Pecktacular Music
3605 Brandywine Dr.
Greensboro NC 27410
Tel: 910-288-7034

Peer Peermusic
810 Seventh Ave.
New York NY 10019
Tel: 212-265-3910
Fax: 212-489-2465
US agent: Presser

Pegasus Pegasus
US agent: Peters

Pembroke Pembroke Music Co. Inc.
US agent: C. Fischer

Peters C. F. Peters Corp.
373 Park Ave. S.
New York NY 10016
Tel: 212-686-4147
Fax: 212-689-9412

Pine Valley Pine Valley Press
P.O. Box 582
Williamstown MA 01267
Tel: 212-489-2465

Plymouth Plymouth Music Co. Inc.
170 NE 33 St.
P.O. Box 24330
Fort Lauderdale FL 33334
Tel: 305-563-1844
Fax: 305-563-9006

Presser Theodore Presser Co.
Presser Place
Bryn Mawr PA 19010
Tel: 610-525-3636
Fax: 610-527-7841
E-mail: presser@netaxs.com

PWM Polskie Wydawnictwo Muzyczne
ul. Krasinskiego 11A
31-111 Kraków, Poland

Ricordi G. Ricordi & Co.
US agent: Boosey; Leonard

Robbins Robbins Music Corp.
US agent: Belwin; Presser

R&H Rodgers & Hammerstein Concert Library
229 W. 18 St., 11th fl.
New York NY 10001
Tel: 212-268-9300
Fax: 212-268-1245

Rouart Rouart-Lerolle et Cie.
US agent: G. Schirmer; Leonard

Russian Russian Authors Society
6A Bolshaya Bronnaya St.
Moscow 103670, United Kingdom
Russia
US agent: G. Schirmer

Salabert Editions Salabert
22 Rue Chauchat
F-75009 Paris, France
Tel: (1) 48.24.55.60
Fax: (1) 42.47.17.56
US agent: G. Schirmer; Leonard

Samfundet Samfundet Til Udgivelse af Dansk Musik
US agent: Peters

E.C. Schirmer E.C. Schirmer Music Co.
see: ECS

G.Schirmer G. Schirmer, Inc.
257 Park Ave. S., 20th Floor
New York NY 10010
Tel: 212-254-2100
Fax: 212-254-2013
E-mail: 102336.1611@compuserve.com; http://www.schirmer.com
Distribution Center: P.O. Box 572; 445 Bellvale Rd.
Chester NY 10918
Tel: 914-469-2271
Fax: 914-469-7544

Schott B. Schott's Söhne, Mainz
Weihergarten 5, Postfach 3640
D-55116 Mainz, Germany
US agent: EAM

Shawnee Shawnee Press, inc.
49 Waring Dr.
Delaware Water Gap PA 18327
Tel: 717-476-0550
Fax: 717-476-5247

Sikorski Musikverlage Hans Sikorski
Johnsallee 23, Postfach 13-2001
D-20148 Hamburg, Germany
Tel: (40) 4141-0023
Fax: (40) 4141-0040
US agent: G. Schirmer; Leonard

Simrock N. Simrock
US agent: AMP

Southern Southern Music Publishing Co., Inc.
US agent: Presser

Stainer Stainer & Bell Ltd.
PO Box 110, Victoria House, 23 Gruneisen Rd.
London N3 1DZ, England
Tel: (181) 343-3303
US agent: ECS

Stangland Thomas C. Stangland Co.
P.O.Box 19263
Portland OR 97219
Tel: 503-244-0634
Fax: 503-244-8442

Stanton Stanton Management
45-05 Newtown Road
Astoria NY 11103-1622
Tel: 718-956-6092
Fax: 718-956-5385

Supraphon Supraphon
US agent: FMD

Suvini Edizioni Suvini-Zerboni
Via Quintiliano 40
1-20138 Milan, Italy
Tel: (2) 50841
US agent: Boosey

Templeton Templeton Publishing Inc.
US agent: Shawnee

Transcontinental Transcontinental Music Publications
838 Fifth Avenue
New York NY 10021-7064
Tel: 212-650-4101
Fax: 212-650-4109

UCCP University College—Cardiff Press
P.O. Box 78
Cardiff, Wales CF1 1XL
United Kingdom

UME Union Musical Española
US agent: AMP

Universal Universal-Edition
US agent: EAM

Vieweg C. F. Vieweg
US agent: Leuckart

Walton Walton Music Corp.
Plymouth Music Co. Inc.
170 NE 33 St.
Fort Lauderdale FL 33334
Tel: 305-563-1844
Fax: 305-563-9006

Warner Warner/Chappell Music Inc.
10585 Santa Monica Blvd.
Los Angeles CA 90025-4950
Tel: 310-441-8600

Weinberger Josef Weinberger Ltd.
12-14 Mortimer St.
London W1N 7RD, England
Tel: (171) 580-2827
US agent: Boosey

Weintraub Weintraub Music Co.
US agent: G. Schirmer

WGS William Grant Still Music
22 S. San Francisco St., Suite 422
Flagstaff AZ 86001-5737
Tel: 520-526-9355
Fax: 520-526-0321

Wimbledon Wimbledon Music
1888 Century Park E. Ste. 1900
Century City CA 90067-1702

Zanibon Edizioni G. Zanibon
US agent: Boosey

ABOUT THE AUTHOR

As a neophyte conductor in the 1960s, David Daniels needed a reference book on orchestral music. Finding none that satisfied his specifications, he set out to compile one himself, never suspecting that it would subsequently see worldwide use and go through three editions.

Mr. Daniels' education includes a preparatory diploma from the Eastman School of Music, the B.A. degree in music from Oberlin College, the M.A. (musicology) from Boston University, and the M.F.A. (organ) and Ph.D. (conducting) from the University of Iowa.

He has served for twenty-eight years on the music faculty of Oakland University, and is music director of the Pontiac-Oakland Symphony and the Warren Symphony, all in Michigan. His guest conducting includes the Detroit Symphony, Michigan Opera Theatre, and the Orquesta Sinfonia de Maracaibo (Venezuela)—as well as annual choral works with the Fort Street Chorale and Chamber Orchestra (Detroit) and operas with the Boston Academy of Music.